Introduction to Managerial Accounting

Second Canadian Edition

Peter C. Brewer
Miami University, Oxford, Ohio

Ray H. Garrison
Professor Emeritus, Brigham Young University

Eric W. Noreen
University of Washington and INSEAD

Suresh S. Kalagnanam
University of Saskatchewan

Ganesh Vaidyanathan
University of Saskatchewan

 McGraw-Hill Ryerson

Toronto Montréal Boston Burr Ridge, IL Dubuque, IA Madison, WI New York San Francisco St. Louis Bangkok Bogotá Caracas Kuala Lumpur Lisbon London Madrid Mexico City Milan New Delhi Santiago Seoul Singapore Sydney Taipei

Introduction to Managerial Accounting
Second Canadian Edition

 McGraw-Hill Ryerson

The McGraw-Hill Companies

Extracts from MA1 and MA2 published by the Certified General Accountants Association of Canada, © CGA-Canada, 2002-2006, reproduced with permission. The contents of these examinations may be out of date; therefore the currency of the contents is the sole responsibility of the user.

ISBN-13: 978-0-07-096477-8
ISBN-10: 0-07-096477-7

2 3 4 5 6 7 8 9 10 CCI 0 9

Printed and bound in the United States of America

Editorial Director: Joanna Cotton
Senior Sponsoring Editor: Rhondda McNabb
Senior Marketing Manager: Joy Armitage-Taylor
Senior Developmental Editor: Denise Foote
Senior Editorial Associate: Christine Lomas
Supervising Editor: Elizabeth Priest
Copy Editor: Hope Miller
Production Coordinator: Sheryl MacAdam
Cover & Interior Design: Greg Devitt
Cover Image: © BilderLounge/SuperStock
Page Layout: Michelle Losier
Printer: Courier Companies Inc.

Library and Archives Canada Cataloguing in Publication

Introduction to managerial accounting / Peter C. Brewer ... [et al.]. — 2nd Canadian ed.

Includes index. Canadian ed written by Ray H. Garrison ... [et al.].
ISBN 978-0-07-096477-8

 1. Managerial accounting—Textbooks. I. Brewer, Peter C.

HF5657.4.I696 2008   658.15'11   C2007-906585-6

Dedication

Suresh Kalagnanam *wishes to dedicate this book to his wife, Viji, and his children, Pallavi and Siddharth.*

Ganesh Vaidyanathan *wishes to dedicate this text to his wife, Prabha, in affectionate acknowledgement that "the large overhead cost" that she has cheerfully borne during the past 20 years is attributable to him.*

About the Authors

Peter C. Brewer is a professor in the Department of Accountancy at Miami University, Oxford, Ohio. He holds a BS degree in accounting from Penn State University, an MS degree in accounting from the University of Virginia, and a PhD from the University of Tennessee. He has published more than 25 articles in a variety of journals, including *Management Accounting Research*, *The Journal of Information Systems*, *Cost Management*, *Strategic Finance*, *The Journal of Accountancy*, *Issues in Accounting Education*, and *The Journal of Business Logistics*.

Ray H. Garrison is emeritus professor of accounting at Brigham Young University, Provo, Utah. He received his BS and MS degrees from Brigham Young University and his DBA degree from Indiana University.

As a certified public accountant, Professor Garrison has been involved in management consulting work with both national and regional accounting firms. He has published articles in *The Accounting Review*, *Management Accounting*, and other professional journals. Innovation in the classroom has earned Professor Garrison the Karl G. Maeser Distinguished Teaching Award from Brigham Young University.

Eric W. Noreen is a globe-trotting academic who has held appointments at institutions in the United States, Europe, and Asia. He is emeritus professor of accounting at the University of Washington.

Professor Noreen has served as associate editor of *The Accounting Review* and the *Journal of Accounting and Economics*. He has numerous articles in academic journals, including the *Journal of Accounting Research*, *The Accounting Review*, the *Journal of Accounting and Economics*, *Accounting Horizons*, *Accounting, Organizations and Society*, *Contemporary Accounting Research*, the *Journal of Management Accounting Research*, and the *Review of Accounting Studies*.

Suresh Kalagnanam is an Associate Professor of Accounting at the Edwards School of Business, University of Saskatchewan, where he currently teaches and researches managerial accounting. He is a graduate of the University of Madras in India where he obtained his Bachelor of Engineering. He subsequently obtained an MBA from Gujarat University in India, an MBA and a Master of Science in Accounting from the University of Saskatchewan, and a PhD from the University of Wisconsin-Madison in the United States. He is also a Canadian Certified Management Accountant (CMA) and a Certified General Accountant (CGA). His scholarly work has been published in *Accounting Organizations and Society, International Journal of Business and Economics, Journal of Accounting Case Research, Journal of Cost Management, Management Accounting, Qualitative Research in Accounting and Management,* and other scholarly publications. Dr. Kalagnanam is a member of the American Accounting Association, Canadian Academic Accounting Association, CMA Canada, CGA-Canada, and the Institute of Management Accountants, and serves on the Editorial and Advisory Review Board of *Accounting Horizons*. In his spare time, he is involved in cultural activities and community services.

Ganesh Vaidyanathan is an Associate Professor and Head of the Department of Accounting in the Edwards School of Business at the University of Saskatchewan. He has a BA from the University of Toronto, an MA in Economics from the University of Waterloo, and an MASc and PhD in Management Sciences from the University of Waterloo. He holds the CGA (Certified General Accountant) and CMA (Certified Management Accountant) designations.

Dr. Vaidyanathan has more than 20 years of university teaching experience. He has taught a wide range of courses in management accounting and control, accounting information systems, micro-economics, finance, strategy, statistics, and management science. Prior to his current appointment at the University of Saskatchewan, he was an Associate Professor and Chair of the Department of Business Administration at Brandon University, Brandon, Manitoba from 1991 to 2001. He has also taught at Wilfrid Laurier University, The Conestoga College of Applied Arts and Technology, and the University of Waterloo. Dr. Vaidyanathan is author of a text in business statistics co-written with his father, Raja. His research has been published in *The Wall Street Journal, Journal of Applied Corporate Finance, Issues in Accounting Education,* and other scholarly publications. He is a member of CGA-Saskatchewan, CMA-Saskatchewan, the Canadian Academic Accounting Association, and the American Accounting Association, and has previously served on the Saskatchewan Board of the Certified General Accountants Association of Canada.

Outside of his professional interests, Dr. Vaidyanathan is an avid fan of blues music and Bollywood movies. Recently he has taken up cycling for recreation and fitness. He commutes to work daily on his bike—a 16-kilometre round trip—year-round.

Brief Table of Contents

To view and download online material, go to
www.mcgrawhill.ca/olc/brewer.

Contents

Chapter Twelve
Relevant Costs for Decision Making 484

Chapter Thirteen
Capital Budgeting Decisions 528

PART IV: REPORTING

To view and download online material, go to www.mcgrawhill.ca/olc/brewer.

Empowering Students
to Rise to New Levels

"When will I ever use managerial accounting?"

Many students ask this and similar questions about the relevance of their managerial accounting course. *Introduction to Managerial Accounting*, 2nd Canadian edition, by Brewer et al not only teaches students managerial accounting skills, but also how they apply in the real world.

More importantly, students will learn the critical thinking skills crucial to success in business. This combination of conceptual understanding and the ability to apply this knowledge in the real world empowers students to make business decisions and ascend to new heights.

Concise Coverage

Students want a text that is concise, and that presents material in a clear and readable manner. *Introduction to Managerial Accounting* presents everything students should know, keeping the material accessible and avoiding advanced topics related to cost management. Similarly, their biggest concern is making sure they can solve the end-of-chapter problems after reading the chapter. Market research indicates that Brewer et al achieves—and helps students achieve—this better than any other concise managerial accounting text on the market.

Decision-Making Focus

Every student who passes through your class needs to know how accounting information is used to make business decisions, especially if they plan to be future managers. That's why Brewer et al make decision making a pivotal component of *Introduction to Managerial Accounting*. In every chapter, you'll find the following key features, each designed to teach your students how to use accounting information like a manager. **Decision Maker** and **You Decide** boxes challenge students to develop analytical and critical thinking skills in solving a managerial accounting problem, in both corporate and entrepreneurial settings. **Building Your Skills** cases give students' decision-making skills an added boost by presenting them with a more in-depth scenario to work through.

Spotlight on Service

To reflect Canada's growing service-based economy, this text is filled with examples from service-based businesses. These examples are much more relevant and meaningful to non-majors than the manufacturing examples typically used in managerial accounting texts. In keeping with the text's decision-making focus, every service example is presented to help students relate the concepts in this book to the decisions made by real-world working managers. A student reading *Introduction to Managerial Accounting* should never have to ask, "Why am I learning this?"

Powerful Pedagogy

Introduction to Managerial Accounting has a wealth of pedagogy designed to make studying productive and hassle-free. On the following pages, you'll see the kind of engaging, helpful pedagogical features that have made Brewer one of the best-selling managerial accounting texts on the market.

Opening Vignette

Each chapter opens with a Business Focus feature that provides a real-world example for students, allowing them to see how the chapter's information and insights apply to the world outside the classroom. **Chapter Competencies** alert students to what they should expect as they progress through the chapter.

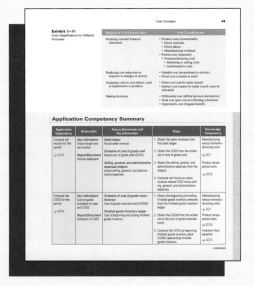

Application Competency Summary

The chapter opener features "Know" and "Apply" chapter competencies. A summary at the end of each chapter provides a snapshot of each action-oriented application competency by highlighting its key information, documents, steps, and concepts. These summaries enhance student learning by reinforcing essential tools of managerial accounting.

Powerful Pedagogy

Managerial Accounting in Action

These highly praised vignettes depict cross-functional teams working together in real-life settings on products and services that students recognize from their own lives. Students are shown step-by-step how managerial accounting concepts are implemented in organizations and how these concepts are applied to solve everyday business problems. First, "The Issue" is introduced through a dialogue. The student then works through the implementation process. Finally the "Wrap-Up" summarizes the big picture.

MANAGERIAL ACCOUNTING IN ACTION

The Wrap Up

Hampton Freeze, Inc.

After completing the master budget, Larry Giano took the documents to Tom Wills, chief executive officer of Hampton Freeze, for his review.

Larry: Here's the budget. Overall, the net income is excellent, and the net cash flow for the entire year is positive.
Tom: Yes, but I see on this cash budget that we have the same problem with negative cash flows in the first and second quarters that we had last year.
Larry: That's true. I don't see any way around that problem. However, there is no doubt in my mind that if you take this budget to the bank today, they'll approve an open line of credit that will allow you to borrow enough to make it through the first two quarters without any problem.
Tom: Are you sure? They didn't seem very happy to see me last year when I came in for an emergency loan.
Larry: Did you repay the loan on time?
Tom: Sure.
Larry: I don't see any problem. You won't be asking for an emergency loan this time. The bank will have plenty of warning. And, with this budget, you have a solid plan that shows when and how you are going to pay off the loan. Trust me, they'll go for it.
Tom: Fantastic! It would sure make life a lot easier this year.

In Business Today

These helpful boxed features offer a glimpse into how real companies use the managerial accounting concepts discussed within the chapter. Each chapter contains these current examples.

Budgeting for Success   IN BUSINESS TODAY

What would you do if you wanted to really impress your boss? How does being under budget on more than 500 projects in one year sound? Eugene Roman, the Chief Information Officer of Bell Canada, has created his own success through a unique combination of budgeting skills and being able to bounce from idea to idea. Information technology departments have a habit of running projects over budget, but Roman has been able to gain credibility by generating reliable financial forecasts. Roman attributes his success to superior management control, proper cost management, and the ability to view costs from a different angle. "My groups have always delivered to the numbers. We work to the goal of a budget being met, but not overstepped. It starts with good planning and execution, and considers trade-offs and risk analysis. If there are problems, we find out how to recover and make it work. That's part and parcel of the package."

Source: John Cooper, "When in Rome . . . Renaissance man Eugene Roman sets the standard for excellence at Bell Canada," *CMA Management*, April, 2002, pp. 37–39. Adapted with permission from CMA Canada.

The **Decision Maker** and **You Decide** features foster critical thinking and decision-making skills by providing real-world business scenarios that require the resolution of a business issue. The suggested solution is located at the end of the chapter.

DECISION MAKER   **Vice-President of Production**

You are faced with a make-or-buy decision. The company currently makes a component for one of its products but is considering whether it should instead purchase the component. If the offer from an outside supplier were accepted, the company would no longer need to rent the machinery that is currently being used to manufacture the component. You realize that the annual rental cost is a fixed cost, but recall some sort of warning about fixed costs. Is the annual rental cost relevant to this make-or-buy decision?

End-of-Chapter Material

Introduction to Managerial Accounting has earned a reputation for having the best end-of-chapter review and discussion material of any text in this market. Our problem and case material make a great starting point for class discussions and group projects. Other helpful features:

- Spreadsheets have become an increasingly common budgeting tool for managerial accountants; therefore, to assist students in understanding how budgets look in a spreadsheet, Microsoft® Excel® spreadsheet templates are available for use with select problems and cases.

- Ethics assignments serve as a reminder that good conduct is vital in business.

- Group projects can be assigned either as homework or as in-class discussion projects.

- The writing icon denotes problems that require students to use critical thinking, as well as writing skills, to explain their decision.

New to the 2nd Canadian edition

Your feedback helps us continue to improve.

In response to faculty suggestions:

- The authors have made structural changes in order to group the chapters under four central themes: product and service costing, planning and control, decision making, and reporting (online only). This approach allows students to clearly see how managerial accounting information can be used by managers for a variety of purposes.

- Chapter competencies have been updated and each one is now identified as "Know" or "Apply." End-of-chapter summaries of application competencies are included as snapshots of the tools in the managerial accounting toolkit and how to use them.

- Many new "In Business Today" boxes have been added. Drawn from recent events, these boxes provide interesting examples of how managerial accounting concepts are used by real businesses.

- End-of-chapter material has been expanded. The authors have also refreshed and updated end-of-chapter problems and exercises.

Other improvements include:

- New sections on strategy and corporate governance in Chapter 1.

- *Cost Behaviour* (now Chapter 3) has been moved earlier in the text to group it with the product and service costing chapters.

- Substantial revisions to *The Systems Design: Job-Order Costing* chapter (Chapter 4). To aid student comprehension, the chapter has been reorganized through the addition of two new sections.

- The addition of "Standard Costing and Variance Analysis in an Activity-Based Costing Environment" to Chapter 8: *Standard Costs*.

- Updates to responsibility for variances both for materials and labour in Chapter 8.

- Revision of section headings, flow of content, and exhibits in Chapter 9: *Flexible Budgets and Overhead Analysis* to improve clarity.

- Extensive revisions to Chapter 10: *Performance Measurement* and Chapter 11: *Cost-Volume-Profit Analysis*, including expansion of material on economic value added (EVA) in Chapter 10 and updates to sales mix and break-even analysis in Chapter 11.

- New material in the Cost Concepts for Decision Making section in Chapter 12: *Relevant Costs for Decision Making*.

Enriched Learning with Technology

LYRYX ASSESSMENT FOR MANAGERIAL ACCOUNTING

Lyryx Assessment for Managerial Accounting is a Web-based teaching and learning tool that has captured the attention of post-secondary institutions across the country. Developed specifically for Brewer—*Introduction to Managerial Accounting*, Second Canadian Edition, Lyryx Assessment is a leading-edge online assessment system that delivers significant benefits to both students and instructors.

After registering their course with us, instructors can create Labs of their choice by selecting problems from our test bank and setting deadlines. Instructors have access to all the students' marks and can view their best Labs. At any time, instructors can download the class grades for their own programs to analyze individual and class performance.

The assessment takes the form of a homework assignment called a Lab, which corresponds to the chapters in the Brewer text. The Labs are algorithmically generated and automatically graded, so students get instant scores and feedback—no need to wait until the next class to find out how well they did!

If students are doing their managerial accounting practice and homework, they will improve their performance in the course. Recent research regarding the use of Lyryx has shown when Labs are tied to assessment, even if worth only a small percentage of the total grade for the course, students *will* do their homework—*and more than once. The result is improved student success in managerial accounting!*

Please contact your *i*Learning Sales Specialist
for additional information on Lyryx Assessment for Managerial Accounting.

Student Supplements

*i*Study

 Available 24/7: providing instant feedback when students want, how they want, and where they want. This online *i*Study space was developed to help students master concepts and achieve better grades with all the learning tools they've come to expect, including chapter summaries, quiz questions, and additional problems. *i*Study offers the best, most convenient way to interact, learn, and succeed.

*i*Study can be purchased through the Online Learning Centre (www.mcgrawhill.ca/olc/brewer) or by purchasing a PIN code card through the campus bookstore. Instructors: Please contact your *i*Learning Sales Specialist for more information on how to make *i*Study part of your students' success.

Online Learning Centre (www.mcgrawhill.ca/olc/brewer)

The Student Centre of this Web site offers additional resources such as self-study multiple-choice quizzes, Microsoft® Excel® templates for select problems and cases in the text, and other bonus online content.

Instructor Supplements

Instructor's CD-ROM

This all-in-one resource incorporates the Instructor's Manual, Solutions Manual, Computerized Test Bank, Microsoft® PowerPoint® slides and Microsoft® Excel® templates plus solutions, each described below.

Instructor's Manual

The Instructor's Manual includes chapter overviews, lecture notes and tips, Application Competency Summary charts, and more.

Solutions Manual

This supplement contains completely worked-out solutions to all exercises, problems, and Building Your Skills assignments.

Computerized Test Bank

Nearly 2,000 questions are organized by chapter and include true/false, multiple-choice, and essay questions plus computational problems. Use it to make different versions of the same test, change the answer order, edit and add questions, and conduct online testing. Technical support for this software is available. The files are also available in RTF format for printing.

Microsoft® PowerPoint® Slides

These slides offer a great visual complement for your lectures. A complete set of slides covers each chapter.

Microsoft® Excel® Templates

These are the solutions to the Excel templates offered to students in the Online Learning Centre.

Online Learning Centre (www.mcgrawhill.ca/olc/brewer)

The Instructor Centre features downloadable supplements including the Instructor's Manual, Solutions Manual, Microsoft® PowerPoint® slides, and Microsoft® Excel® template solutions.

*i*Learning Sales Specialist

Your Integrated Learning Sales Specialist is a McGraw-Hill Ryerson representative who has the experience, product knowledge, training, and support to help you assess and integrate any of the following products, technology, and services into your course for optimum teaching and learning performance. Whether it's helping your students improve their grades, or putting your entire course online, your *i*Learning Sales Specialist is there to help you do it. Contact your local *i*Learning Sales Specialist today to learn how to maximize all of McGraw-Hill Ryerson's resources!

*i*Learning Services Program

McGraw-Hill Ryerson offers a unique iLearning Services package designed for Canadian faculty. Our mission is to equip providers of higher education with superior tools and resources required for excellence in teaching. For additional information visit http://www.mcgrawhill.ca/highereducation/iservices.

Teaching, Technology, and Learning Conference Series

The educational environment has changed tremendously in recent years, and McGraw-Hill Ryerson continues to be committed to helping you acquire the skills you need to succeed in this new milieu. Our innovative Teaching, Technology, and Learning Conference Series brings faculty together from across Canada with 3MTeaching Excellence award winners to share teaching and learning best practices in a collaborative and stimulating environment.

Primis Online

Primis Online gives you access to our resources in the best medium for your students: printed textbooks or electronic e-books. There are over 350,000 pages of content available from which you can create customized learning tools from our online database at www.mhhe.com/primis.

Reviewers

The efforts of many people are needed to develop and improve a text. Among these people are the reviewers and consultants who point out areas of concern, cite areas of strength, and make recommendations for change. In this regard, the following professors provided feedback that was enormously helpful in preparing *Introduction to Managerial Accounting:*

2nd Canadian edition reviewers:
Anthony Chan, *Ryerson University*
Andrea Chance, *George Brown College*
Roger Collins, *Thompson Rivers University*
Dennis Dober, *College of the North Atlantic*
Andrew Dykstra, *Georgian College*
Nauman Farooqi, *Mount Allison University*
Richard Farrar, *Conestoga College*
Irene Herremans, *University of Calgary*
Robert Holland, *Nova Scotia Community College*
Dave Kennedy, *Lethbridge College*
Brad MacDonald, *S.I.A.S.T. - Palliser*
Bonnie Martel, *Niagara College*
Bryan Parker, *British Columbia Institute of Technology*
Dolores Peterson, *Grant MacEwan College*
Rod Tilley, *Mount St. Vincent University*
Richard Wright, *Fanshawe College*

1st Canadian edition reviewers:
Karen Baker, *Loyalist College*
Bryan Bessner, *Ryerson University*
Donald Brown, *Brock University*
Andrew Dykstra, *Georgian College*
Graham Fane, *Capilano College*
Terry Fegarty, *Seneca College*
Terry Goldthorpe, *Centennial College*
Jane Kaake-Nemeth, *Durham College*
Barb Katz, *Kwantlen University College*
Peter Lubka, *University of Waterloo*
Gail Lynn Cook, *Brock University*
Ann MacGillivary, *Mount St. Vincent University*
Winston Marcellin, *George Brown College*
Claudia Parker, *Northern Alberta Institute of Technology (NAIT)*
Pina Salvaggio, *Dawson College*
Ken Smith, *College of the North Atlantic*
Bob Sproule, *University of Waterloo*
Nancy Tait, *Sir Sanford Fleming College*

CHAPTER

An Introduction to
Managerial Accounting

CHAPTER COMPETENCIES

After studying Chapter 1, you should be able to demonstrate the following competencies:

Competency		Know	Apply
CC1	Describe the work of management and the need for managerial accounting information.	○	
CC2	Differentiate between financial and managerial accounting.	○	
CC3	Describe the impact of globalization on business.	○	
CC4	Explain the lean business model and its corresponding management practices.	○	
CC5	Explain the importance of ethical responsibility, corporate governance, and codes of conduct.	○	

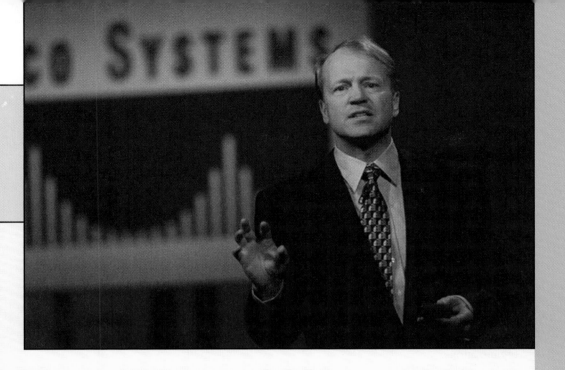

DECISION FEATURE
Making Fact-Based Decisions in Real Time

Cisco Systems and Alcoa are on the leading edge of their industries and real-time management accounting is one of the keys to their success. Managers at these companies can drill down into the company's management accounting system to find the latest data on revenues, margins, order backlogs, expenses, and other data, by region, by business unit, by distribution channel, by salesperson, and so on. The Chief Financial Officer of Cisco, Larry Carter, says that with this kind of live information "you can empower all your management team to improve decision making." Richard Kelson, the Chief Financial Officer of Alcoa, says: "The earlier you get information, the easier it is to fix a problem." For example, with up-to-date data, managers at Alcoa saw softness in aerospace markets early enough to shift production from hard alloys that are used in aircraft to other products. John Chambers, the CEO of Cisco, says: "At any time in the quarter, first-line managers can look at margins and products and know exactly what the effect of their decisions will be."

Source: Thomas A. Stewart, "Making Decisions in Real Time," *Fortune*, June 26, 2000, pp. 332–333.

A Look at This Chapter

After describing the three major activities of managers and the need for managerial accounting information, this chapter compares and contrasts financial and managerial accounting information. It then exposes you to the changes taking place in the business environment. The design of an appropriate managerial accounting system is critical for managers to be able to make solid decisions.

A Look Ahead

Chapter 2 focuses on the basics of a managerial accounting system by defining and explaining many terms that are used to classify costs in business. Because these terms will be used throughout the text, you should ensure that you are familiar with each of them.

Running a company like CIBC, Magna, Cisco, or Alcoa, is by no means an easy task. Senior managers must constantly study the business environment within which the company is operating: the economy, competition, technological developments, and government regulations. Public companies must also report their activities to investors (shareholders). Reporting to investors requires that companies record accounting transactions and prepare a balance sheet, an income statement, and a cash flow statement. Most of you are already familiar with these financial statements from your study of **financial accounting.**

A manager's duties do not end with reporting to investors. Managers must also ensure that the business is properly managed so that its objectives are achieved (this may include earning a certain level of profitability or maintaining a certain level of market share). In order to do this, managers must *plan* for the future, *direct* and *motivate* their employees, and *control* the operations—tasks that must be carried out *within* the organization. For this purpose, managers need information that focuses on internal activities. **Managerial accounting** provides managers with the essential information that they can use to run organizations.

This chapter introduces the main functions of management and then explains the need for managerial accounting information. Finally, it examines the changes taking place in the business environment and their impact on the design of managerial accounting systems.

The Work of Management and the Need for Managerial Accounting Information

⚪ **KNOW**

CC1: Describe the work of management and the need for managerial accounting information.

Every organization—large or small—has managers. Someone must be responsible for developing a strategy, making plans, organizing resources, directing personnel, and controlling operations. This is true of the Royal Bank of Canada, the Peace Corps, Simon Fraser University, the Catholic Church, and the Potash Corporation of Saskatchewan, as well as the local 7-Eleven convenience store.

In general, there are three types of business organizations: service, merchandising, and manufacturing. Service firms include such organizations as a doctor's clinic, an advertising agency, and a financial institution. Such firms do not sell any products but generate revenues by offering one or more types of services (e.g., legal counselling). Merchandising firms largely refer to retail and wholesale outlets that buy goods from suppliers and resell them to customers. Manufacturing firms engage in the production and sale of different types of products ranging from small consumer goods to large ships and aircrafts. Merchandising and manufacturing firms generate revenue by selling products (e.g., hockey sticks). More will be said later in this chapter about the treatment of costs incurred by these different types of businesses.

Strategy

In today's globally competitive environment, companies must have a viable strategy to succeed in the marketplace. Unfortunately, a single accepted definition of strategy does not exist. According to one definition, strategy consists of five elements providing answers to five different questions: (1) where will we be active? (2) how will we get there? (3) how will we win in the marketplace? (4) what will be our speed and sequence of moves? and (5) how will we obtain our returns? Another way of defining strategy is the ability to be different (from competitors)—choosing a different set of activities to deliver a unique mix of value. Regardless of a specific definition, most people agree that **strategy** pertains to the general direction in which an organization plans to move to achieve its goals and objectives.[1] An organization may use a combination of activities (that it calls its strategy) to achieve its goals.

We will use a particular organization—Good Vibrations, Inc.—to illustrate the work of management. What we have to say, however, is very general and can be applied to any organization. Good Vibrations runs a chain of retail outlets that sell a full range of music CDs. The chain's stores are concentrated in Pacific Rim cities such as Sydney, Singapore, Hong Kong, Beijing, Tokyo, and Vancouver. The company believes that a critical activity resulting from its strategy is to create an exciting shopping environment.

Therefore, it puts a great deal of effort into planning the layout and decor of its stores—which are often quite large and extend over several floors in key downtown locations. Management knows that different types of clientele are attracted to different kinds of music. The international rock section is generally decorated with bold, brightly coloured graphics, and the aisles are purposely narrow to create a crowded feeling much like you would experience at a popular nightclub on a Friday night. In contrast, the classical music section is wood-panelled and fully sound insulated, with the rich, spacious feeling of a country club meeting room. Managers at Good Vibrations, like managers everywhere, carry out three major activities—**planning, directing and motivating,** and **controlling.**

Planning

Planning involves selecting a course of action and specifying how the action will be implemented. The first step in planning is to identify alternatives and then to select the one that does the best job of furthering the organization's objectives. The basic objective of Good Vibrations is to earn profits for the owners of the company by attracting customers in as many markets as possible. To further this objective, every year, top management carefully considers a number of alternatives for expanding into new geographic markets. This year, management is considering opening new stores in Shanghai, Los Angeles, and Auckland.

When making this and other choices, management must balance the opportunities against the demands made on the company's resources. Management knows from bitter experience that opening a store in a major new market is a big step that cannot be taken lightly. It requires enormous amounts of time and energy from the company's most experienced, talented, and busy professionals. When the company attempted to open stores in both Beijing and Vancouver in the same year, resources were overextended. The result was that neither store opened on schedule, and operations in the rest of the company suffered. Therefore, entering new markets is planned very, very carefully.

Among other data, top management looks at the sales volumes, profit margins, and costs of the company's established stores in similar markets. These data, supplied by the management accountant, are combined with projected sales volume data at the proposed new locations to estimate the profits that would be generated by the new stores. In general, virtually all important alternatives considered by management in the planning process have some effect on revenues or costs, and management accounting data are essential in estimating those effects.

After considering all of the alternatives, top management of Good Vibrations decided to open a store in the burgeoning Shanghai market in the third quarter of the year, but to defer opening any other new stores to another year. As soon as this decision was made, detailed plans were drawn up for all parts of the company that would be involved in the Shanghai opening. For example, the Human Resources (HR) department's travel budget was increased, since it would be providing extensive on-site training to the new personnel hired in Shanghai.

---

[1] D.C. Hambrick and J.W. Fredrickson, "Are You Sure You Have a Strategy?" *Academy of Management Executive*, 2005, Vo. 19, No. 4, pp. 51–62; M.E. Porter, "What is Strategy?" *Harvard Business Review*, November–December 1996, pp. 61–78; and R. N. Anthony and V. Govindarajan, *Management Control Systems*, 12th Edition, (Toronto: McGraw-Hill Ryerson, 2007), p. 57.

As in the HR department example, the plans of management are often expressed formally in **budgets,** which are prepared annually and represent management's plans in specific, quantitative (often financial) terms, and the term *budgeting* is used to generally describe this part of the planning process. In addition to a travel budget, the HR department will be given goals in terms of new hires, courses taught, and detailed breakdowns of expected expenses. Similarly, the manager of each store will be given a target for sales volume, profit, expenses, pilferage losses, and employee training. These data will be collected, analyzed, and summarized for management use in the form of budgets prepared by management accountants.

Directing and Motivating

In addition to planning for the future, managers must oversee day-to-day activities to keep the organization functioning smoothly; this involves directing and motivating people. Managers assign tasks to employees, arbitrate disputes, answer questions, solve on-the-spot problems, and make many small decisions that affect customers and employees (which, in turn, will likely influence future financial performance). In effect, directing is the part of managers' work that deals with the routine and the here and now. Managerial accounting data, such as daily sales reports, are often used in this type of day-to-day decision making.

Controlling

In carrying out the **control** function, managers seek to ensure that the plan is being followed. **Feedback,** represented by the dashed lines in Exhibit 1–1, signals whether operations are on track and key to effective control. In sophisticated organizations, this feedback is provided by detailed reports of various types. One of these reports, which compares budgeted with actual results, is called a **performance report.** Performance reports suggest where operations are not proceeding as planned and where some parts of the organization may require additional attention. For example, before the opening of the new Shanghai store in the third quarter of the year, the store's manager will be given sales volume, profit, and expense targets for the fourth quarter of the year. As the fourth quarter progresses, periodic reports will be prepared in which the actual sales volume, profit, and expenses are compared with the targets. If the actual results fall below the targets, top management is alerted that the Shanghai store requires more attention. Experienced personnel can be flown in to help the new manager, or top management may come to the conclusion that plans will have to be revised. As we shall see in the following chapters, providing this kind of feedback to managers is one of the central purposes of managerial accounting.

The Results of Managers' Activities

As a customer enters one of the Good Vibrations stores, the results of management's planning, directing and motivating, and control activities will be evident in the many details that make the difference between a pleasant and an irritating shopping experience. The store will be clean, fashionably decorated, and logically laid out. Featured artists' videos will be played on TV monitors throughout the store, and the background rock music will be loud enough to send older patrons scurrying to the classical music section. Popular CDs will be in stock, and the latest hits will be available for private listening on earphones. Specific titles will be easy to find. Regional music, such as CantoPop in Hong Kong, will be prominently featured. Checkout clerks will be alert, friendly, and efficient. In short, what the customer experiences does not simply happen; it is the result of the efforts of managers who must visualize and fit together the processes that are needed to get the job done.

The Planning and Control Cycle

The work of management can be summarized in a model such as the one shown in Exhibit 1–1. The model, which depicts the **planning and control cycle,** illustrates the

Exhibit 1–1
The Planning and Control Cycle

Planning
budgeting
standard costing

Decision Making

Controlling
variance analysis
profit reports

Directing and Motivating

Feedback

smooth flow of management activities from planning through directing and motivating, controlling, and then back to planning again. All of these activities involve decision making, and so it is depicted as the hub around which the other activities revolve.

Comparison of Financial and Managerial Accounting

Financial accounting reports are prepared for the use of external parties, such as shareholders and creditors, whereas managerial accounting reports are prepared for managers inside the organization. This contrast in basic orientation results in a number of important differences between financial and managerial accounting, even though both financial and managerial accounting rely on the same underlying financial data. These differences are summarized in Exhibit 1–2.

As shown in Exhibit 1–2, in addition to having different audiences, financial and managerial accounting also differ in their emphasis between the past and the future, in the type of data provided to users, and in several other ways. These differences are discussed in the following paragraphs.

 KNOW

CC2: Differentiate between financial and managerial accounting.

Emphasis on the Future

Since planning is such an important part of the manager's job, managerial accounting has a strong future orientation. In contrast, financial accounting primarily provides summaries of past financial transactions. These summaries may be useful in planning, but only to a point. The difficulty with summaries of the past is that the future is not simply a reflection of what has happened in the past. Changes are constantly taking place in economic conditions, customer needs and desires, competitive conditions, and so on. All of these changes demand that the manager's planning be based, in large part, on estimates of what will happen, rather than on summaries of what has already happened.

Relevance and Flexibility of Data

Financial accounting data are expected to be objective and verifiable. However, for internal uses, the manager wants information that is relevant even if it is not completely objective or verifiable. By "relevant," we mean *appropriate for the decision at hand*. For example,

Exhibit 1–2

Comparison of Financial and Managerial Accounting

it is difficult to verify estimated sales volumes for a proposed new Good Vibrations store, but this is exactly the type of information that is most useful to managers in their decision making. In addition to monetary information, managers often need nonmonetary information to aid the decision-making process (e.g., impact on customer satisfaction). The managerial accounting information system should be flexible enough to provide whatever data are relevant for a particular decision.

Less Emphasis on Precision

Timeliness is often more important than precision to managers. If a decision must be made, a manager would much rather have a good estimate now than wait a week for a more precise answer. A decision involving tens of millions of dollars does not have to be based on estimates that are precise down to the penny, or even to the dollar. Estimates that are accurate to the nearest million dollars may be precise enough to make a good decision. Since precision is costly in terms of both time and resources, managerial accounting places less emphasis on precision than does financial accounting (the latter reports past activities for which precise data are usually available).

Segments of an Organization

Financial accounting is primarily concerned with reporting for the organization as a whole. By contrast, managerial accounting focuses much more on the parts, or **segments,** of an organization. These segments may be product lines, sales territories, divisions, departments, branch offices, or any other categorization of the company's activities that management finds useful. Financial accounting does require some breakdowns of revenues and costs by major segments in external reports, but this is a secondary emphasis. In managerial accounting, segment reporting is the primary emphasis.

Generally Accepted Accounting Principles (GAAP)

Financial accounting statements prepared for external users must be prepared in accordance with **generally accepted accounting principles (GAAP)**. External users must have some assurance that the reports have been prepared in accordance with a common set of ground rules. These common ground rules enhance comparability and help reduce fraud and misrepresentation, but they do not necessarily lead to the type of reports that would be most useful for internal decision making. For example, GAAP requires that land value be stated at its historical cost on financial reports. However, if management is considering moving a store to a new location and then selling the land the store currently sits on, management would like to know the current market value of the land—a vital piece of information that is ignored under GAAP.

Managerial accounting is not bound by GAAP. Managers set their own ground rules concerning the content and form of internal reports. The only constraint is that the expected benefits from using the information should outweigh the costs of collecting, analyzing, and summarizing the data. Nevertheless, as we shall see in subsequent chapters, it is undeniably true that financial reporting requirements have heavily influenced management accounting practice.

Managerial Accounting—Not Mandatory

Financial accounting is mandatory; that is, it must be done. Various outside parties, such as the Ontario Securities Commission (OSC) and the tax authorities, require periodic financial statements. Managerial accounting, on the other hand, is not mandatory. An organization is completely free to do as much or as little as it wishes. There are no regulatory bodies or other outside agencies that specify what is to be done or, for that matter, whether anything is to be done at all. Since managerial accounting is completely optional, the important question is always, "Is the information useful?" rather than, "Is the information required?"

As previously explained, the work of management focuses on (1) planning, which includes setting objectives and outlining how to attain these objectives; and (2) control, which includes the steps to take to ensure that objectives are realized. To carry out these planning and control responsibilities, managers need *information* about the organization. From an accounting point of view, this information often relates to the *costs* of the organization. In managerial accounting, the term *cost* is used in many different ways, as explained in Chapter 2.

Are Financial and Managerial Accounting Independent?

Our discussion of the differences between financial and managerial accounting may suggest that they are independent of each other, but this is not true. Usually, most organizations have a common database to capture the financial data that will be used for both financial and managerial accounting purposes. For example, accounting ledgers are an important primary source of data. Moreover, information from managerial accounting reports often feeds into financial accounting reports. Therefore, although there are important differences between financial and managerial accounting, they are not independent of each of other.

Increased Relevance of Managerial Accounting

Although managerial accounting information has always been useful to managers, its relevance and importance have greatly increased in the past two decades. This is because the last quarter century has been a period of tremendous change in the business environment. First, competitive boundaries have expanded due to globalization, which has been good for consumers because the increased competition has led to lower prices, higher quality, and more choices. However, this means that organizations must find new ways of doing business, which is the second aspect of change. The third issue is one of ethical responsibility and corporate governance among businesses and other organizations. More and more allegations are being made of management misconduct in many businesses, governments, and not-for-profit and charitable organizations. And, to add even more dynamism, the Internet has changed the face of business in several industries.

These changes are having a profound effect on managerial accounting practices, as we will see throughout this text. Managers require timely information not only on costs and profits, but also on key drivers of these outcomes. We now elaborate upon the changes in the business environment.

Globalization

 KNOW

CC3: Describe the impact of globalization on business.

Over the last three decades, several factors have led to an increase in worldwide competition in many industries. These include reductions in tariffs, quotas, and other barriers to free trade; improvements in global transportation systems; and increasing sophistication in international trade markets. These factors work together to reduce the costs of conducting international trade and make it possible for foreign companies to compete on a more equal footing with domestic firms. These changes have been most dramatic within the European Union (EU) and the North American Free Trade Agreement (NAFTA) free trade zones.

Very few organizations can now afford to be complacent. An organization that is successful in its local market can suddenly face competition from halfway around the globe. It is likely that this threat will become even more potent as business migrates more and more to the Internet. On the bright side, however, this means that businesses have greater opportunities (e.g., networking possibilities with new business partners and access to new markets). Similarly, more choices are available to customers: greater variety of goods and services, higher quality, and lower price.

What are the implications of globalization? One major implication is that organizations must find new ways of conducting business: new strategies, new management practices, more sophisticated management accounting systems. Another implication is that organizations must conduct their affairs in a responsible manner. We will now discuss each of these implications in greater detail.

The Lean Business Model

 KNOW

CC4: Explain the lean business model and its corresponding management practices.

International competition has forced companies to find new ways of doing business in order to offer better products/services, and to deliver them faster and at a cheaper price. Since the early 1980s, companies adopted different kinds of improvement programs; these fall under the umbrella of what experts now call the **lean business model.** The main idea underlying this model is the elimination of waste.

Consider a grocery store that sells fresh produce (fruits and vegetables) and bakery products among other things. The fresh produce damaged in transit, as well as the excess quantity ordered that sits on the shelves too long (and rots), are examples of waste. They cost the grocery store money; this cost cannot be recovered because the damaged and rotten produce cannot be sold to customers.

As another example, consider a beautician who decides to hire one additional employee just so that customers never have to wait. The idle time of this additional employee is also an example of waste (especially if the beautician cannot charge higher prices compared with the competition). Similarly, manufacturing companies that produce more than the required quantities in order to spread the cost of resources (equipment and labour) over a larger quantity of production also tend to create waste in the system in the form of excess inventory (or stock), which may remain unsold for a long time and become obsolete in the process. We now have a situation where the money has already been spent, but there is a certain amount of uncertainty about whether the goods produced can be sold.

In order to eliminate waste, companies must adopt and implement one or more management practices that focus on different aspects of the lean business model. Examples of these management practices include *just-in-time*, *total quality management*, *process re-engineering*, and *theory of constraints*. These management practices, or programs of continuous improvement, if properly implemented, can enhance quality, increase efficiencies, eliminate delays, and reduce costs, thereby adding to the profits. Unfortunately, they have not always been properly implemented; as a result, considerable controversy exists about their ultimate economic value. Although each of the previously mentioned programs is worthy of extended study, we will discuss them only briefly, leaving the details to operations management courses.

In addition to adopting these management practices, companies have also refined their management accounting systems. For example, many companies now use the concepts of *activity-based costing* (*ABC*) and *multi-dimensional performance measurement systems*—these concepts are discussed in later chapters.

The Power of Lean

IN BUSINESS TODAY

Lean thinking can benefit all types of businesses. For example, Dell Inc.'s lean production system can produce a customized personal computer within 36 hours. Even more impressive, Dell doesn't start ordering components and assembling computers until orders are booked. By ordering right before assembly, Dell's parts are on average 60 days newer than those of its competitors, which translates into a 6% profit advantage in components alone. No wonder Dell continues to be the envy of the computer industry!

In the service arena, Jefferson Pilot Financial (JPF) realized that "[l]ike an automobile on the assembly line, an insurance policy goes through a series of processes, from initial application to underwriting, or risk assessment, to policy issuance. With each step, value is added to the work in progress—just as a car gets doors or a coat of paint." Given this realization, JPF organized its work arrangements into a cellular layout and synchronized the rate of output to the pace of customer demand. JPF's lean thinking enabled it to reduce attending physician statement turnaround times by 70%, decrease labour costs by 26%, and reduce reissue errors by 40%.

Sources: Gary McWilliams, "Whirlwind on the Web," *BusinessWeek*, April 7, 1997, p. 134; Stephen Pritchard, "Inside Dell's Lean Machine," *Works Management*, December 2002, pp. 14–16; and Cynthia Karen Swank, "The Lean Service Machine," *Harvard Business Review*, October 2003, pp. 123–129.

Just-in-Time (JIT)

In a traditional manufacturing company, work is *pushed* through the system. Enough materials are released to workstations to keep everyone busy, and when a workstation completes its tasks, the partially completed goods are pushed forward to the next workstation, regardless of whether that workstation is ready to receive them. The result is that partially completed goods stack up, waiting for the next workstation to become available. They may not be completed for days, weeks, or even months. Additionally, when the units are finally completed, customers may not want them. If finished goods are produced faster than the market will absorb, the result is bloated finished goods inventories.

Companies typically maintained large amounts of inventory to shield themselves from any unanticipated disruptions, such as late shipments from suppliers, machine breakdowns, and unexpectedly large orders from customers.

While these inventories provide some insurance against unforeseen events, they have a cost. According to experts, in addition to tying up money, maintaining inventories encourages inefficient and sloppy work, results in too many defects, and dramatically increases the amount of time required to complete a product. Large inventories of partially completed goods create many other operating problems that are best discussed in more advanced courses. These problems are not obvious—if they were, companies would have long ago reduced their inventories. Managers at Toyota are credited with the insight that large inventories often create many more problems than they solve, so Toyota pioneered the *JIT approach*.

Lean Business Model in Practice

Cover-All Building Systems, a Saskatoon-based company, is a leading manufacturer of steel-framed, fabric-covered buildings with a North America–wide dealer network that is dedicated to being a customer-driven, principle-governed enterprise. From a Tommy Hilfiger retail outlet in Las Vegas to Spruce Meadows riding arenas in Calgary, Cover-All is providing innovative building solutions for an ever-expanding number of applications.

In the spirit of continuous improvement, the company decided in 1999 to adopt the lean business model. According to Nathan Stobbe, President, Cover-All has already experienced dramatic results that have led to a significant reduction in costs and increase in revenues. The measurement system put in place at the end of year 1 showed these cumulative results in the following two years: sales went up 30%, but manufacturing inventory went down 24%, and time from order to delivery on standard buildings went down 66%.

Since its inception, Cover-All Building Systems has been recognized locally and nationally for its achievements. Among the most recent honours garnered by the company are the provincial Achievement of Business Excellence (ABEX) in export and Business of the Year awards, and recognition as one of the 50 Best-Managed Private Companies in Canada for three consecutive years.

Source: http://www.coverall.ca/about_general.html and personal interview. Permission granted by Nathan Stobbe, President.

The JIT Approach

In contrast to the traditional approach, companies that use the **just-in-time (JIT) approach** purchase materials and produce units only as needed to meet actual customer demand. The theory is that simply producing goods does not do the company any good unless someone buys them. Moreover, excess inventories create a multitude of operating problems. In a JIT system, inventories are reduced to an absolute minimum. Under ideal conditions, a company operating a just-in-time system would purchase only enough materials each day to meet that day's needs. Moreover, the company would have no goods in process at the end of the day, and all goods completed during the day would have been shipped immediately to customers. As this sequence suggests, "just-in-time" means that raw materials are received just in time to go into production, manufactured parts are completed just in time to be assembled into products, and products are completed just in time to be shipped to customers. Although a manufacturing example is used here, the JIT approach can easily be extended to nonmanufacturing settings (e.g., the grocery store example).

Although few companies have been able to reach this ideal, many companies have been able to reduce inventories to only a fraction of their previous levels. The results have been a substantial reduction in ordering and warehousing costs, and much more effective operations.

The change from a traditional to a JIT approach is more profound than it may appear to be. Among other things, producing only in response to a customer order means that workers will be idle whenever demand falls below the company's production capacity. This can be an extremely difficult cultural change for an organization to make. It challenges the core beliefs of many managers and raises anxiety among workers who have become accustomed to being kept busy all of the time. It also requires fundamental changes in managerial accounting practices, as we will see in later chapters.

Zero Defects and JIT

Given that JIT requires smooth operations, the existence of quality problems can create havoc. If a completed order contains a defective unit, the company must ship the order with less than the promised quantity or it must restart the whole production process to make just one unit. At a minimum, this creates a delay in shipping the order and may generate a ripple effect that delays other orders. For this and other reasons, defects cannot be tolerated in a JIT system. Companies that are deeply involved in JIT tend to become zealously committed to a goal of **zero defects**. Even though it may be next to impossible to attain the zero defect goal, companies have found that they can come very close. For example, Motorola, Allied Signal, and many other companies now measure defects in terms of the number of defects per *million* units of product.

Benefits of a JIT System

The main benefits of JIT are as follows:

- Funds that have been tied up in inventories can be used elsewhere.
- Areas previously used to store inventories are made available for other, more productive uses.
- The time required to fill an order is reduced, resulting in quicker response to customers and consequentially greater potential sales.
- Defect rates are reduced, resulting in less waste and greater customer satisfaction.

As a result of benefits such as those cited, more companies are embracing JIT each year. However, the JIT approach is just one aspect of the lean business model.

Total Quality Management (TQM)

Another management practice that has become popular is known as *total quality management*. There are two major characteristics of **total quality management (TQM):** (1) a focus on serving customers, and (2) systematic problem solving using teams made up of front-line workers. A variety of specific tools is available to aid teams in their problem solving. One of these tools, **benchmarking,** involves studying organizations that are among the best in the world at performing a particular task. For example, when Xerox wanted to improve its procedures for filling customer orders, it studied how L. L. Bean, the mail-order company, processed its customer orders.

The Plan-Do-Check-Act Cycle

Perhaps the most important and pervasive TQM problem-solving tool is the *plan-do-check-act (PDCA) cycle*, which is also referred to as the *Deming Wheel*.[2] The **plan-do-check-act cycle** is a systematic, fact-based approach to continuous im-

---

[2] Dr. W. Edwards Deming, a pioneer in TQM, introduced many of the elements of TQM to Japanese industry after World War II. TQM was further refined and developed at Japanese companies, such as Toyota.

provement. The basic elements of the PDCA cycle are illustrated in Exhibit 1–3. The PDCA cycle applies a scientific method to problem solving. In the Plan phase, the problem-solving team analyzes data to identify possible causes for the problem and then proposes a solution. In the Do phase, an experiment is conducted. In the Check phase, the results of the experiment are analyzed. And, in the Act phase, if the results of the experiment are favourable, the plan is implemented. If the results of the experiment are not favourable, the team goes back to the original data and starts all over again.

Exhibit 1–3
The Plan-Do-Check-Act Cycle

- **Study the current process.**
- **Collect data.**
- **Analyze the data to identify possible causes.**
- **Develop a plan for improvement.**
- **Decide how to measure improvement.**

- **If successful, make the change permanent.**
- **If the results are not successful, try again.**

- **Implement the plan on a small scale, if possible.**
- **Collect data.**

Plan

Act   Do

Check

- **Evaluate the data collected during the Do phase.**
- **Did the expected improvement occur?**

An Example of TQM in Practice

Victor Manufacturing Plant (hereafter, VMP), a branch plant of Victor Corporation (which is the disguised name of a real company), provides a good example of TQM in practice.[3] VMP, based in southern Ontario, is a supplier to the large auto manufacturers (Daimler-Chrysler, Ford, General Motors, and Toyota). With quality becoming a very important consideration for the survival of all auto suppliers, VMP initiated a program of continuous improvement, called *Excellence in Manufacturing (EIM)*, by focusing on JIT and TQM programs. Very soon, quality pervaded everyone's thinking within the plant. Management at VMP soon realized the importance of establishing teams to identify and solve quality problems; these teams were known as *EIM groups*.

In identifying and solving the problem of high scrap on a particular production line, the team used the PDCA cycle. The EIM group proceeded as follows to identify the first-level source of the problem (as recorded in the minutes of the meeting):

> We decided to start at the trunnion grinders as our first objective at reducing scrap. As we investigated the problem, we found that over a period of one year, 4,000 pieces were

---

[3]Source: R. M. Lindsay, and S. S. Kalagnanam, *The Adoption of Just-In-Time Production Systems in Canada and Their Association with Management Control Practices*, (Hamilton: The Society of Management Accountants of Canada, 1993), pp. 69–78. Reprinted with permission from CMA Canada.

scrapped out at the grinders. We have 10 grinders, so when you break it down daily, it is less than two pieces a day per grinder. Then we looked at the Kingsbury drill scrap. It was 2,600 pieces for the year and we have only two machines.... Less than half our production goes through this operation, so we are double the percentage scrap off the Kingsbury drill. We will now work on reducing scrap at the Kingsbury.

After identifying the first-level source of the problem, the group ran experiments and collected more data to identify the potential causes of scrap at the Kingsbury drill, prepared charts documenting the causes, identified alternatives, implemented the chosen one, and ran more tests to ensure that scrap was eliminated. They then moved on to attack the next major problem causing scrap. Note how VMP followed the PDCA cycle to problem solving as a group.

To summarize, TQM provides tools and techniques for continuous improvement based on facts and analysis and, if properly implemented, avoids counterproductive organizational infighting.

Quality Management is Widely Used — IN BUSINESS TODAY

Many Canadian organizations have successfully implemented quality management principles and have received recognition from the National Quality Institute (NQI) whose mission is to inspire excellence in Canada. Recent recipients of the Canada Awards for Excellence include such organizations as Calian Technologies Ltd., Government of Alberta, Hill & Knowlton Canada, Ricoh Canada Inc., 3M Canada, NuComm International, Telus, Purolator Courier Ltd., and the Real Estate Board of Greater Vancouver.

Source: National Quality Institute Web site (www.nqi.ca). Copyright© 2007. Reprinted with permission.

Process Re-engineering

Process re-engineering is a radical approach to improvement that managers can use to remove waste from business processes. **Process re-engineering** diagrams a *business process* in detail, questions it, and then completely redesigns it in order to eliminate unnecessary steps, reduce opportunities for errors, and reduce costs. This is in direct contrast to approaches where an existing process is continuously tweaked to generate small incremental improvements. A **business process** is any series of steps that are followed in order to carry out a task in a business. For example, the steps followed to make a large pineapple and Canadian bacon pizza at Godfather's Pizza, or those followed by your bank when you deposit a cheque, represent a business process.

Process re-engineering focuses on *simplification* and *elimination of wasted effort*. A central idea of process re-engineering is that all activities that do not add value to a product or service should be eliminated. Activities that do not add value to a product or service that customers are willing to pay for are known as **non-value-added activities.** For example, moving large batches of partially completed goods from one workstation to another is a non-value-added activity that can be eliminated by redesigning the factory layout to bring the workstations closer together.[4]

---

[4]Activity-based costing and activity-based management, both of which are discussed in a later chapter, can be helpful in identifying areas in the company that could benefit from process re-engineering.

IN BUSINESS TODAY
Process Re-engineering Works

Processing travel claims can often be a nightmare. Necho Systems Corp., supplier of travel and entertainment (T&E) software, allowed various companies to process travel claims more efficiently for business trips. This particular software lets employees enter expenses quickly and easily using their personal digital assistants (PDAs), such as Palm Pilots, without having to go to the office and manually fill out claims. Most importantly, the forms can be filled during their free time (e.g., while waiting at a hotel or airport), since access is readily available. As for the employers, processing claims becomes straightforward because they are all in one place, which avoids the need for sorting through each claim manually, thereby reducing the amount of handling. An additional benefit is that security is enhanced when employers automate claims processing. It normally costs about $25 to $35 to manually process the claim, but the new software would reduce the cost by more than 50%, asserts Necho. As well, firms can better control their travel spending by ensuring greater compliance with travel policies and striking better deals with travel vendors.

Source: A. Tausz, "Easing Expenses," *CMA Management*, November 2001, pp. 48–49. Reprinted with permission from CMA Canada.

The Problem of Employee Morale

Employee resistance is a recurrent problem in process re-engineering. The cause of much of this resistance is the fear that employees may lose their jobs. Employees reason that if process re-engineering succeeds in eliminating non-value-added activities, there will be less work to do and management may be tempted to reduce the payroll. Process re-engineering, if carried out insensitively and without regard to such fears, can undermine morale and will ultimately fail to improve the bottom line (i.e., profits). As with other improvement projects, employees must be convinced that the result of the improvement will be more secure, rather than less secure, jobs. Real improvement can have this effect if management uses the improvement to generate more business, rather than to cut the workforce. If by improving processes the company is able to produce a better product at a lower cost, the company will have the competitive strength to prosper. And a prosperous company is a much more secure employer than a company that is in trouble.

The Theory of Constraints (TOC)

A **constraint** is a hurdle (or obstacle) that prevents people from getting more of what they want. For example, each day has only 24 hours, which appears to be a constraint for all of us (students, parents, working adults). We have to juggle our activities such that we are able to complete them (or not complete all of them) within the available time. Every individual and every organization faces at least one constraint. For example, Petro Canada has a limited number of pumps at each of its gas stations, which means customers have to wait for their turn or else go to a competitor.

The **theory of constraints (TOC)** framework focuses on effectively managing constraints as the key to success. For example, Petro Canada could consider one of several options: (1) install additional pumps (but this may be prohibitively expensive), (2) increase pumping speed, or (3) introduce fast checkout. All of these can help in reducing customer waiting time and potentially increase revenues.

An Example of TOC

ProSport Equipment, Inc. manufactures aluminum tennis racquets using the production process illustrated in Exhibit 1–4. The capacity of each workstation is stated in terms of the maximum number of racquets that can be processed in a week. For example, the aluminum extruding workstation can extrude enough aluminum each week to build as many as 2,500 tennis racquets. Referring to Exhibit 1–4, what is the maximum rate of output of tennis racquets that can be sustained in a week? The rate of output of the entire system is limited by the rate of output of the slowest workstation, which is frame assembly with a rate of output of only 1,800 racquets per week. Even though the other workstations can process more than 1,800 racquets per week, the entire production line can process only 1,800 racquets per week. The frame assembly workstation is the *bottleneck*. In addition, if demand exceeds 1,800 racquets per week, the frame assembly workstation is the constraint. How can management increase the output of the production process?

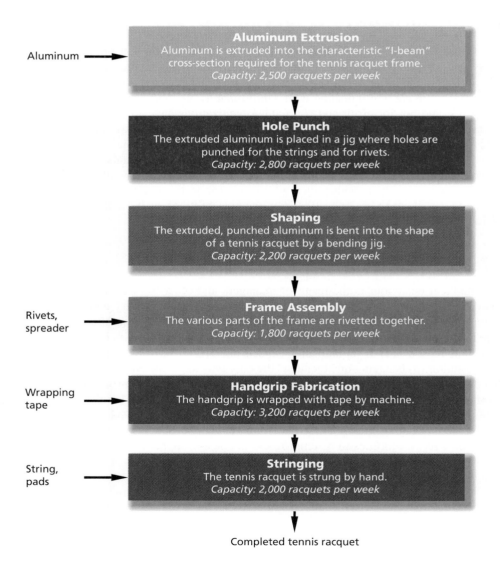

Exhibit 1–4
A Flowchart of an Aluminum
Tennis Racquet Production Line

TOC and Continuous Improvement

In TOC, an analogy is often drawn between a business process—such as the tennis racquet production line—and a chain. What is the most effective way to increase the strength of a chain? Should you concentrate your efforts on strengthening the strongest link, the largest link, all the links, or the weakest link? Clearly, focusing effort on the weakest link will bring the biggest benefit.

Continuing with this analogy, the procedure to follow in strengthening the chain is straightforward. First, identify the weakest link, which is the constraint. Second, do not place a greater strain on the system than the weakest link can handle. Third, concentrate the improvement efforts on strengthening the weakest link. Fourth, if the improvement efforts are successful, eventually the weakest link will improve to the point where it is no longer the weakest link. At this point, the new weakest link (i.e., the new constraint) must be identified, and the improvement efforts must be shifted over to that link. This simple sequential process provides a powerful strategy for continuous improvement. The TOC approach is a perfect complement to TQM and process re-engineering—it focuses improvement efforts where they are likely to be most effective.

Ethical Responsibility and Corporate Governance

 KNOW

CC5: Explain the importance of ethical responsibility, corporate governance, and codes of conduct.

As mentioned in the opening paragraph of this chapter, the conduct of organizations is an extremely important issue all over the world. As businesses interact more and more with organizations in different parts of the world, they must be cautious that the companies they deal with are worth dealing with. Unfortunately, we find that many businesses, governments, and not-for-profit and charitable organizations have engaged in questionable practices, which have affected their own reputations as well as those of other stakeholders (such as employees and investors). When government departments engage in such practices, it affects the taxpayer. Although these allegations and scandals have received considerable attention, it is important to remember that there are many other businesses and other organizations that conduct their affairs in a responsible manner. Nonetheless, no organization can claim to be 100% free from the possibility of such events taking place in the future.

Professional Ethics

Often, unethical behaviour is the result of managers and other top executives focusing exclusively on achieving short-term profits *at any cost*. This can be very dangerous as it can drive employees to act unethically in order to meet the expectations of their superiors. "Those who engage in unethical behavior often justify their actions with one or more of the following reasons: (1) the organization expects unethical behavior, (2) everyone else is unethical, and/or (3) behaving unethically is the only way to get ahead."[5]

To counter the first justification for unethical behaviour, many organizations have implemented formal ethical codes of conduct. For example, Manitoba Hydro's purchasing department expects all of its buyers to abide by the Purchasing Management Association of Canada's Code of Ethics. These codes are generally broad-based statements of an organization's responsibilities to its employees, customers, suppliers, and the communities in which it operates. Codes rarely spell out specific do's and don'ts or suggest proper behaviour in specific situations. Instead, they provide broad guidelines.

---

[5]Michael K. McCuddy, Karl E. Reichardt, and David Schroder, "Ethical Pressures: Fact or Fiction?" *Management Accounting*, April 1993, pp. 57–61.

Whistle-Blowing Policies

Recent media attention to scandals in businesses and other organizations has increased the importance of ethical policies and procedures, and codes of conduct. But employees in many organizations know when they are not followed. Should they "blow the whistle?" According to a 2003 survey conducted in the United States, 65% of the respondents reported that they will likely report misconduct (this number is up from 48% in 1994). Many large corporations, such as the Royal Bank of Canada and Shell Canada, have implemented whistle-blowing policies to protect individuals who speak up. Other organizations, such as Ottawa-based Democracy Watch, continue to press for whistle-blowing provisions in both government and business.

Source: Matthew McLearn, "A Snitch in Time," *Canadian Business*, Dec.–Jan. 2004, pp. 61–70. Reprinted with permission from Canadian Business.

Accountants are generally considered the *guardians* of an organization's money. But, what if accountants themselves behave in an irresponsible manner? To counter such behaviour, professional accounting bodies in most parts of the world have developed codes of conduct to guide appropriate behaviour of accounting professions. For example, each of the provincial offices of CMA Canada (one of the three professional accounting bodies in Canada) has developed ethical guidelines for practising **CMAs (certified management accountants)**.[6] Essentially, the Code of Ethics focuses on several key factors pertaining to an accountant's role. These include competence, responsibility, independence of thought and action, integrity, fairness, loyalty, confidentiality, and trust. Similarly, the *Code of Ethics for Professional Accountants*, issued in June 2005 by the International Federation of Accountants (IFAC), governs the activities of *all* professional accountants throughout the world, regardless of whether they are in public practice or employed in government service or private industry.

In addition to outlining ethical requirements in matters dealing with competence, objectivity, independence, and confidentiality, the IFAC's code also outlines the accountant's responsibilities in matters relating to taxes, fees and commissions, advertising and solicitation, the handling of monies, and cross-border activities. Where cross-border activities are involved, the IFAC ethical requirements must be followed if these requirements are stricter than the ethical requirements of the country in which the work is being performed. Canadian companies dealing with foreign governments are bound by the *Corruption of Foreign Public Officials Act*, which prohibits company executives from offering gifts, payments, or other benefits to foreign government officials in order to receive favourable business treatment.

The ethical standards provide sound, practical advice for management accountants and managers. Most of the rules in the ethical standards are motivated by a very practical consideration—if these rules were not generally followed in business, then the economy would come to a screeching halt.

---

[6]For the code of ethics developed by the Certified Management Accountants of Ontario, see Appendix 1A.

Who Is to Blame?

Don Keough, a retired Coca-Cola executive, recalls that, "In my time, CFOs [chief financial officers] were basically tough, smart, and mean. Bringing good news wasn't their function. They were the truth-tellers." But that had changed by the late 1990s in some companies. Instead of being truth-tellers, CFOs became corporate spokespeople, guiding stock analysts in their quarterly earnings estimates—and then making sure those earnings estimates were beaten using whatever means necessary, including accounting tricks and in some cases outright fraud. But does the buck stop there?

A survey of 179 CFOs published in May 2004 showed that only 38% of those surveyed believed that pressure to use aggressive accounting techniques to improve results had lessened relative to three years earlier. And 20% of those surveyed said the pressure had increased over the past three years. Where did the respondents say the pressure was coming from? Personal greed, weak boards of directors, and overbearing chief executive officers (CEOs) topped the list. Who is to blame? Perhaps that question is less important than focusing on what is needed—greater personal integrity and less emphasis on meeting quarterly earnings estimates.

Sources: Jeremy Kahn, "The Chief Freaked Out Officer," *Fortune*, December 9, 2002, pp. 197–202, and Don Durfee, "After the Scandals: It's Better (and Worse) Than You Think," *CFO*, May 2004, p. 29.

Corporate Governance

Corporate governance is the system by which an organization is directed and controlled. If properly implemented, it should provide incentives for the board of directors and top management to pursue objectives that are in the interests of the company's owners and it should provide for effective monitoring of performance.[7] Effective corporate governance enhances stakeholders' confidence that an organization is being managed in their best interests rather than solely in the interests of top management and certain key individuals.

Unfortunately, history has repeatedly shown that unscrupulous top managers, if unchecked, can exploit their power to defraud stakeholders. This unpleasant reality became all too clear in 2001 when the fall of Enron kicked off an unprecedented wave of corporate scandals. These scandals were characterized by financial reporting fraud and misuse of corporate funds at the very highest levels—including CEOs and CFOs. While this was disturbing in itself, it also indicated that the institutions intended to prevent such abuses weren't working, thus raising fundamental questions about the adequacy of the existing corporate governance system. In an attempt to respond to these concerns, the U.S. Congress passed the most important reform of corporate governance in many decades—the **Sarbanes-Oxley Act** of 2002, which is intended to protect the interests of those who invest in publicly traded companies by improving the reliability and accuracy of corporate financial reports and disclosures.

Sarbanes-Oxley: An Expensive Piece of Legislation

You wouldn't think 169 words could be so expensive! But that is the case with what is known as Section 404 of the Sarbanes-Oxley Act of 2002, which requires that a publicly

---

[7]This definition of corporate governance was adapted from the 2004 report titled *OECD Principles of Corporate Governance* published by the Organization for Economic Co-Operation and Development.

traded company's annual report contains an internal control report certified by its auditors. Although this may sound simple enough, estimates indicate that Sarbanes-Oxley compliance will cost the Fortune 1000 companies alone about $6 billion annually—much of which will go to public accounting firms in fees. With the increased demand for audit services, public accounting firms such as KPMG, PricewaterhouseCoopers, Ernst & Young, and Deloitte are returning to campuses to hire new auditors in large numbers and students are flocking to accounting classes.

Source: Holman W. Jenkins Jr., "Thinking Outside the Sarbox," *The Wall Street Journal*, November 24, 2004, p. A13.

Implications of the New Business Environment on Managerial Accounting

What are the implications of changes in the business environment previously described? Organizations cannot use systems designed in the early 1900s to implement their strategies and achieve their objectives. To compete in a global world, organizations must have well-designed management accounting systems to guide managers. Organizations must question the usefulness of their existing managerial accounting tool kit and replace obsolete tools/techniques with more relevant ones. For example, Chapter 6 explains a cost management method known as *activity-based costing/management* (*ABC/ABM*). In a nutshell, managers must employ methods that take into consideration the factors that drive costs, revenues, and profits. An excellent management accounting system will not by itself guarantee success, but a poorly designed system will certainly lead to failure.

Organization of the Text

This text is designed to give you a basic idea of the types of management (*or internal*) accounting information useful to managers in their role to ensure that the main purpose of their organization is achieved. In doing so, the text begins by introducing cost terminology that will be used throughout the text. It then proceeds to describe different systems that are used to determine the cost per unit of providing a service or manufacturing a product. The text then focuses on the information required for planning, decision making, and control. In explaining each topic (conceptually and procedurally), the text briefly examines the impact of the lean business model. Although each chapter may focus on one or more specific topics, you are encouraged to integrate topics in an attempt to understand the interrelationships among them.

Glossary

At the end of each chapter, a list of key terms for review is given, along with the definition of each term. (These terms are printed in boldface where they are defined in the chapter.) Carefully study each term to be sure you understand its meaning as the terms are used repeatedly in the chapters that follow. Here is the list for Chapter 1.

Benchmarking A study of organizations that are among the best in the world at performing a particular task. (p. 13)

Budget A detailed plan for the future, usually expressed in formal quantitative terms. (p. 6)

Business process A series of steps that are followed in order to carry out a task in a business. (p. 15)

CMA Certified management accountant. (p. 19)

Constraint A hurdle (or obstacle) that prevents people from getting more of what they want. (p. 16)

Control The process of instituting procedures and then obtaining feedback to ensure that all parts of the organization are functioning effectively and moving toward overall company goals. (p. 6)

Controlling Ensuring that the plan is actually carried out. (p. 5)

Corporate governance The system by which an organization is directed and controlled. (p. 20)

Directing and motivating Mobilizing people to carry out plans and run routine operations. (p. 5)

Feedback Accounting and other reports that help managers monitor performance and focus on problems and/or opportunities that might otherwise go unnoticed. (p. 6)

Financial accounting The discipline of accounting concerned with providing information to shareholders, creditors, and others outside the organization. (p. 4)

Generally accepted accounting principles (GAAP) Rules that indicate acceptable accounting practice. (p. 9)

Just-in-time (JIT) approach A production and inventory control system in which materials are purchased and units are produced only as needed to meet actual customer demand. (p. 12)

Lean business model A business model that focuses on continuous improvement by eliminating waste in an organization. (p. 10)

Managerial accounting The discipline of accounting concerned with providing information to managers for use in planning, directing and motivating, and controlling within the organization. (p. 4)

Non-value-added activity An activity that consumes resources or takes time, but does not add value for which customers are willing to pay. (p. 15)

Performance report A detailed report comparing budgeted results with actual results. (p. 6)

Plan-do-check-act (PDCA) cycle or **Deming Wheel** A systematic approach to continuous improvement that applies the scientific method to problem solving. (p. 13)

Planning Selecting a course of action and specifying how the action will be implemented. (p. 5)

Planning and control cycle The flow of management activities through planning, directing and motivating, and controlling, and then back again to planning. (p. 6)

Process re-engineering An approach to improvement that involves completely redesigning business processes in order to eliminate unnecessary steps, reduce errors, and reduce costs. (p. 15)

Sarbanes-Oxley Act U.S. legislation of 2002 that was intended to protect the interests of those who invest in publicly traded companies by improving reliability and accuracy of corporate financial reports and disclosures. (p. 20)

Segment Any part of an organization that can be evaluated independently of other parts and about which the manager seeks financial data. Examples include a product line, a sales territory, a division, or a department. (p. 8)

Strategy The general direction in which an organization plans to move to achieve its goals and objectives. (p. 4)

Theory of constraints (TOC) A management approach that emphasizes the importance of managing constraints. (p. 16)

Total quality management (TQM) An approach to continuous improvement that focuses on customers and using teams of front-line workers to systematically identify and solve problems. (p. 13)

Zero defects Having zero or as few as possible defects. (p. 13)

Questions

1–1   What is the basic difference in orientation between financial and managerial accounting?

1–2   What are the three major activities of a manager?

1–3   Describe the steps in the planning and control cycle.

1–4   What are the major differences between financial and managerial accounting?

1–5   Describe the lean business model and its corresponding management practices.

1–6   What are the pros and cons of a JIT system?

1–7   It is vital that management accountants abide by a code of ethics. Agree or disagree? Explain.

1–8   As a management accountant, you adhere to the code of ethics set forth by IFAC. Keeping in mind the IFAC Code, determine if are there any clear ethical considerations in the following scenarios:

a. Cleo Patra is the management accountant for a multinational company. An industry stock analyst has invited her to spend two weeks in Aruba at no cost to her. In return for this favour, Cleo would send him any financial press releases before it hits the public.

b. Your company is a large multinational with high investor opinion. The share price is overpriced in your opinion. As the management accountant, you know that the company's earnings cannot sustain investor expectations and within the next year you believe that the share price will fall dramatically. Your parents are thinking of investing a large part of their retirement income in the company. Do you tell them not to based on what you know?

Appendix 1A: Code of Ethics—Certified Management Accountants of Ontario

As professionals and pre-eminent specialists in the field of management accounting, CMAs are bound by the Society's Code of Professional Ethics. This code stipulates and binds them to the highest level of care, duty, and responsibility to their clients, the public, and their fellow professionals.

A synopsis of the Code of Professional Ethics is presented in the following table.

A CMA is required to adhere to, and exhibit the following:

Professionalism

1. Show responsibility for and fidelity to public needs.
2. Maintain fairness and loyalty to associates, clients, and employers.
3. Exhibit competence (high levels of personal honour and professional integrity).

Independence and Objectivity

4. Maintain independence of thought and action.
5. Communicate information in an objective and unbiased manner.
6. Provide full disclosure of all facts to avoid misleading reports.

Confidentiality/Disclosure

7. Refrain from disclosing or using confidential information in the course of performing one's duties.
8. Inform employer or client of any pertinent business or other connections.
9. Not receive any additional remuneration or benefit without the employer's or client's consent in the course of exercising duties on the employer's or client's behalf.
10. Establish a clear understanding of the scope and objectives of any work before it commences and furnish the client with an estimate of the cost before the work commences or soon thereafter.

Integrity

11. Conduct oneself with courtesy and good faith.
12. Not behave in a manner discreditable to the profession.
13. Not engage in any activity considered as incompatible with the professional ethics of a management accountant.
14. Not accept or pay a commission in securing work.
15. Uphold the principle of adequate compensation for work.
16. Not act maliciously or in a manner that may adversely reflect on the public or professional reputation or business of another member.

Competence

17. Maintain standards of competence expressed by the Board from time to time.
18. Disseminate knowledge and promote the advancement of the profession.
19. Undertake only work commensurate with one's level of competence.

Responsibility

20. Expose any incompetent, unethical, illegal, or unfair conduct by a member before the appropriate tribunals of the Society.
21. Endeavour to ensure that a professional partnership or company, of which the member is associated as a partner, director, or officer, abides by the Society's Code of Professional Ethics and Rules of Professional Conduct.

Source: http://ww3.cma-ontario.org/content.asp?id=800. Reprinted by permission of CMA.

CHAPTER TWO

Cost Concepts

CHAPTER COMPETENCIES

After studying Chapter 2, you should be able to demonstrate the following competencies:

Competency	Know	Apply
Understand cost classification by behaviour.		
CC1 Define variable and fixed costs.	○	
CC2 Give examples of variable and fixed costs.		○
Understand cost classification by traceability.		
CC3 Define direct and indirect costs.	○	
CC4 Give examples of direct and indirect costs.		○
Understand cost classification by relevance.		
CC5 Define differential costs, opportunity costs, and sunk costs.	○	
CC6 Give examples of differential costs, opportunity costs, and sunk costs.		○
Understand cost classification by function.		
CC7 Distinguish between manufacturing and nonmanufacturing costs.	○	
CC8 Identify and give examples of direct materials, direct labour, and manufacturing overhead costs.	○	○
CC9 Identify and give examples of marketing or selling and administrative costs.	○	○
CC10 Distinguish between product and period costs.	○	
CC11 Give examples of product and period costs.		○
CC12 Explain how costs are classified in financial statements of merchandising and manufacturing companies.	○	
Prepare financial reports.		
CC13 Prepare an income statement.		○
CC14 Prepare a schedule of cost of goods sold.		○
Understand and prepare manufacturing reports.		
CC15 Explain the basic inventory flow equation.	○	
CC16 Prepare a schedule of cost of goods manufactured, including the computation of the cost of direct materials used.		○

TELUS

the future is friendly®

DECISION FEATURE
Understanding Costs Important to TELUS

TELUS Corporation, headquartered in Vancouver, is the largest telecommunications company in Western Canada and the second largest in the country, offering a wide range of communication services. In 2006, TELUS's total revenue exceeded $8 billion and total assets exceeded $16 billion. Needless to say, the company's costs also run into the billions with operating expenses exceeding $5 billion. With increasing competitive challenges and slowing revenue growth, especially in its wireline operations, ongoing cost control is important to ensure continued financial success.

In recognition of the importance of cost control, TELUS embarked upon a major operational and capital efficiency program in 2002, which included some elements of the lean business model described in Chapter 1. Although TELUS incurred one-time costs of more than $500 million, management expected that these costs would be more than offset by the recurring annual expected savings in operating expenses of about $550 million, as well as a reduction in capital expenditures. As at the end of the first quarter of 2003, the program generated savings of $245 and $1,100 million, respectively, in operating expenses and capital expenditures.

Large telecommunication companies, such as TELUS, usually have a high proportion of fixed costs due to the infrastructure required to provide services to customers. Automating processes performed by humans usually means a reduction in recurring salary expenses but a corresponding increase in amortization expenses and maintenance costs. Understanding the nature of costs and the implications of alternative cost reduction programs is very important in order to decide which program to implement.

Sources: http://about.telus.com/investors/annualreport2002/english/downloads/annualreport2002.pdf, http://about.telus.com/investors/operation_efficiency.html, and http://about.telus.com/investors/annual report2005/downloads/telus_2005_financial_review.pdf.

A Look Back

In Chapter 1, we introduced the three main activities of a manager and the need for managerial accounting information. We then compared financial and managerial accounting information. We also addressed some of the challenges faced by management and described the lean business model.

A Look at This Chapter

We define many of the terms that managers use to classify costs. Because these terms are used throughout the text, be sure you are familiar with them.

A Look Ahead

Chapter 3 builds on the introduction to cost behaviour in the previous chapter. We further describe fixed and variable costs, and introduce the concepts of step-variable and mixed costs. Next, we discuss the analysis of mixed costs and cost estimation. We conclude the chapter by introducing the concept of contribution margin.

Costs are incurred by all kinds of organizations: governments (e.g., City of Victoria); hospitals (e.g., Ontario General Hospital); educational institutions (e.g., Brandon University); and merchandising, service, and manufacturing companies (e.g., Canadian Tire, Myers Norris Penny, and Toyota Canada). The costs incurred may be one-time or recurring, and may differ depending on the need. Managers find it useful to classify costs in different ways in order to facilitate their analysis. In general, costs can be classified using four broad categories: behaviour, traceability, relevance, and function. In this chapter, we will discuss each of the cost classification categories.

Cost Classification by Behaviour

 KNOW

CC1: Define variable and fixed costs.

Managers often need to understand how costs will behave in response to certain activities; such an understanding is useful for cost estimation, planning, and cost/profitability analysis. For instance, a manager at Air Canada may want to estimate the impact of a 10% increase in passengers on its catering costs. It seems reasonable to assume that an increase in the number of passengers will result in a proportionate increase in catering costs. The airline will have to acquire 10% more food and drinks. Therefore, we will say that catering costs *vary* with respect to the number of passengers. On the other hand, a 10% increase in the number of passengers will not require additional fuel or even additional flight attendants; this means that fuel and flight attendant costs do not vary, or are *fixed*, with respect to the number of passengers.

Cost behaviour is the way a cost will respond to changes in the level of an organization's business activity (such as the number of passengers flying Air Canada). As the level of activity rises or falls, a particular cost may rise or fall, respectively, or may remain constant. For planning purposes, a manager must be able to estimate how different costs will behave with respect to changes in business activity. Classifying costs as variable or fixed helps a manager make such predictions.

Variable Cost

 APPLY

CC2: Give examples of variable and fixed costs.

A **variable cost** is one that varies in direct proportion to changes in the level of activity. The activity can be expressed in many ways, such as output (units produced, units sold), miles driven, beds occupied, lines of print, hours worked, and so forth. As an example, consider the KIA car. Each auto requires one battery. As the output of autos increases and decreases, the number of batteries used will increase and decrease proportionately. If auto production goes up 10%, then the number of batteries used will also go up 10%. This means the total cost of batteries will also go up by 10%.

It is important to note that when we speak of a cost as being variable, we mean the *total* cost rises and falls as the activity level rises and falls. This idea is presented below, assuming that a KIA's battery costs $24:

Number of Autos Produced		Cost per Battery	Total Variable Cost— Batteries
1	. . . .	$24	$ 24
500	. . . .	24	12,000
1,000	. . . .	24	24,000

One interesting aspect of variable cost behaviour is that a variable cost is constant if expressed on a *per-unit* basis. Observe from the tabulation above that the per-unit cost of

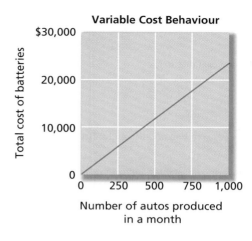

Variable Cost Behaviour

Total cost of batteries

$30,000

20,000

10,000

0

0   250   500   750   1,000

Number of autos produced
in a month

Fixed Cost Behaviour

Total cost of rent

$24,000

16,000

8,000

0

0   500   1,000 1,500 2,000

Number of lab tests performed
in a month

Exhibit 2–1
Variable and Fixed Cost
Behaviour

batteries remains constant at $24, even though the total amount of cost involved increases and decreases with activity. The concept of a variable cost is shown in graphical form in Exhibit 2–1.

There are many examples of costs that are variable with respect to the products and services provided by a company. In a merchandising company, variable costs include such items as cost of goods sold, commissions to salespersons, and billing costs. In a hospital, the variable costs of providing health care services to patients would include the costs of the supplies, drugs, meals, and perhaps nursing services. In a manufacturing company, variable costs include such items as materials used in the product, wages of operators, lubricants, supplies, shipping costs, and sales commissions.

The activity causing changes in a variable cost need not be how much output is produced or sold. For example, the wages paid to employees at a Blockbuster Video outlet will depend on the number of hours the store is open and not strictly on the number of videos rented. In this case, we would say that wage costs are variable with respect to the hours of operation. Nevertheless, when we say that a cost is variable, we ordinarily mean it is variable with respect to the volume of revenue-generating output—in other words, how many videos are rented, how many patients are treated, and so on.

Food Costs at a Luxury Hotel

IN BUSINESS TODAY

The Sporthotel Theresa (http://www.theresa.at/), owned and operated by the Egger family, is a four-star hotel located in Zell im Zillertal, Austria. The hotel features access to hiking, skiing, biking, and other activities in the Ziller Alps, as well as its own fitness facility and spa.

Three full meals a day are included in the hotel room charge. Breakfast and lunch are served buffet-style, while dinner is a more formal affair with as many as six courses. A sample dinner menu appears below:

Tyrolean cottage cheese with homemade bread

***

Salad bar

***

Broccoli-terrine with saddle of venison and smoked goose-breast

Or

Chicken liver pâté with gorgonzola cheese ravioli and port wine sauce

***

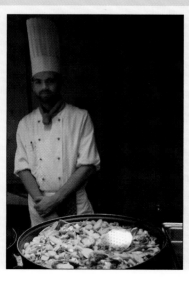

Clear vegetable soup with fine vegetable strips

Or

Whey-yoghurt juice

***

Roulade of pork with zucchini, ham, and cheese on pesto ribbon noodles and saffron sauce

Or

Roasted fillet of Irish salmon and prawns with spring vegetables and sesame mash

Or

Fresh white asparagus with scrambled egg, fresh herbs, and parmesan

Or

Steak of Tyrolean organic beef

***

Strawberry terrine with homemade chocolate ice cream

Or

Iced Viennese coffee

The chef, Stefan Egger, believes that food costs are roughly proportional to the number of guests staying at the hotel; that is, they are a variable cost. He must order food two or three days in advance from suppliers, but he adjusts his purchases to the number of guests who are currently staying at the hotel and their consumption patterns. In addition, guests make their selections from the dinner menu early in the day, which helps Stefan plan which foodstuffs will be required for dinner. Consequently, he is able to prepare just enough food so that all guests are satisfied and yet waste is held to a minimum.

Source: Conversation with Stefan Egger, chef at the Sporthotel Theresa.

Fixed Cost

A **fixed cost** is one that remains constant, regardless of changes in the level of activity. Unlike variable costs, fixed costs are not affected by changes in activity. Consequently, as the activity level rises and falls, the fixed costs remain constant in total amount unless influenced by some outside force, such as a price change or a substantial increase in demand leading to an increase in the resource requirement.

Rent is a good example of a fixed cost. Suppose the Hospital for Sick Children in Toronto rents for $8,000 per month a machine that tests blood samples for the presence of leukemia cells. The $8,000 monthly rental cost will be incurred regardless of the number of tests that may be performed during the month. The concept of a fixed cost is shown in graphical form in Exhibit 2–1.

Very few costs are completely fixed. Most will change if there is a large enough change in activity. For example, suppose that the capacity of the leukemia diagnostic machine at the hospital is 2,000 tests per month. If the hospital wishes to perform more than 2,000 tests in a month, it would be necessary to rent an additional machine, which would cause a jump in the fixed costs. When we say a cost is *fixed*, we mean it is fixed within some *relevant range*. The **relevant range** is the range of activity within which the assumptions about variable and fixed costs are valid. For example, the assumption that the rent for diagnostic machines is $8,000 per month is valid within the relevant range of 0 to 2,000 tests per month.

Fixed costs can create confusion if they are expressed on a per-unit basis. This is because the average fixed cost per unit increases and decreases *inversely* with changes in activity.

In the Hospital for Sick Children example, the average cost per test will fall as the number of tests performed increases because the $8,000 rental cost will be spread over more tests. Conversely, as the number of tests performed in the hospital declines, the average cost per test will rise, as the $8,000 rental cost is spread over fewer tests. This concept is illustrated in the table below:

Monthly Rental Cost	Number of Tests Performed	Average Cost per Test
$8,000	10	$800
8,000	500	16
8,000	2,000	4

Note that if the hospital performs only 10 tests each month, the rental cost of the equipment will average $800 per test. But if 2,000 tests are performed each month, the average cost will drop to only $4 per test. More will be said later about the problems created for both the accountant and the manager by this variation in unit costs.

Examples of fixed costs include straight-line amortization, insurance, property taxes, rent, supervisory salaries, administrative salaries, and advertising.[1]

A summary of both variable and fixed cost behaviour is presented in Exhibit 2–2.

	Behaviour of the Cost (within the relevant range)	
Cost	In Total	Per Unit
Variable cost	Total variable cost increases and decreases in proportion to changes in the activity level.	Variable cost remains constant per unit.
Fixed cost	Total fixed cost is not affected by changes in the activity level within the relevant range.	Fixed cost per unit decreases as the activity level rises and increases as the activity level falls.

Exhibit 2–2
Summary of Variable and Fixed Cost Behaviour

The Cost of a Call

IN BUSINESS TODAY

On average, the variable cost of physically transporting a telephone call is about 7% of the price a customer pays for the call. It now costs more to bill for the call than to provide it. Then why aren't telephone companies fabulously profitable? In short, they have extremely high fixed costs for equipment, buildings, and personnel. The prices the telephone companies charge to consumers must cover these fixed costs, as well as the relatively small variable costs of completing a particular call for a customer.

Source: Scott Woolley, "Meltdown," *Forbes*, July 3, 2000, pp. 70–71.

[1] *The Canadian Institute of Chartered Accountants (CICA) Handbook* uses the term "amortization"; however, Section 3061.29 states that the term "depreciation" can also be used.

DECISION MAKER

Financial Analyst

You are a financial analyst for several clients who are interested in making investments in stable companies. You become aware of a privately owned airline that has been in business for 20 years and needs to raise $75 million in new capital. When you call one of your clients, she replies that she avoids investing in airlines because of the high proportion of fixed costs in this industry. How would you respond to this statement?

Cost Classification by Traceability

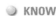 **KNOW**

CC3: Define direct and indirect costs.

In addition to understanding costs by behaviour, managers also need to know whether costs can be traced to specific cost objects; this helps managers in accurately assigning costs. A **cost object** is anything for which cost data are desired—department, division, product, product line, customer, geographical territory. Costs can be classified as either *direct* or *indirect* based on traceability.

Direct Cost

A **direct cost** is one that pertains to a certain cost object and can be easily and economically traced to that cost object. As an example, the salary of the secretary of the University of Saskatchewan's Accounting department is directly traceable to the department (the desired cost object).

APPLY

CC4: Give examples of direct and indirect costs.

Indirect Cost

An **indirect cost** is one that cannot be easily and conveniently traced to a particular cost object under consideration. For example, Air Canada flies to many different locations. Some costs such as the salaries of the pilots and flight attendants, and fuel costs, can be traced to individual flights and are therefore considered direct costs. However, other costs such as the salaries of the baggage handling staff, ticketing staff, and other office staff, or the expenses incurred in running the airline's marketing and accounting departments cannot be traced to specific flights and therefore are classified as indirect costs. This is because these costs are not driven by any one specific flight; they are incurred as a result of running the airline. *To be traced to a cost object, such as a specific flight, the cost must be caused by the cost object.* The airline's baggage handling, ticketing, and marketing costs are common to multiple flights. A **common cost** is one that is incurred to support a number of cost objects (e.g., different flights), but cannot be traced to individual cost objects.

A particular cost may be classified as direct or indirect depending upon the cost object. For example, although salaries of the baggage handling staff are indirect to individual flights offered by Air Canada, they are direct to the baggage handling department. In the second case, the cost object is the baggage handling department.

Cost Classification by Relevance

 KNOW

CC5: Define differential costs, opportunity costs, and sunk costs.

Given the importance of cost information for decision making, managers must be able to identify costs that are relevant for individual decisions. Cost classification by relevance helps in decision making. Only costs that are relevant to individual decisions must be used in the analysis preceding decision making. In general, *differential* and *opportunity* costs are relevant for most decisions, whereas *sunk* costs are irrelevant for any decision.

Differential Cost and Revenue

Decisions involve choosing between alternatives. In business decisions, each alternative will have certain costs and benefits that must be compared with the costs and benefits of the other available alternatives. A difference in costs between any two alternatives is known as a **differential cost.** A difference in revenues between any two alternatives is known as **differential revenue.**

A differential cost is also known as an **incremental cost,** although technically an incremental cost should refer only to an increase in cost from one alternative to another; decreases in cost should be referred to as **decremental costs.** Differential cost is a broader term, encompassing both cost increases (incremental costs) and cost decreases (decremental costs) between alternatives.

The accountant's differential cost concept can be compared to the economist's marginal cost concept. When speaking of changes in cost and revenue, the economist employs the terms *marginal cost* and *marginal revenue.* The revenue that can be obtained from selling one more unit of product is called marginal revenue, and the cost involved in producing one more unit of product is called marginal cost. The economist's marginal concept is basically the same as the accountant's differential concept applied to a single unit of output.

Differential costs can be either fixed or variable. To illustrate, assume that Nature Way Cosmetics, Inc. is considering changing its marketing method from distribution through retailers to distribution by door-to-door direct sale. Present costs and revenues are compared with projected costs and revenues in the following table:

● APPLY

CC6: Give examples of differential costs, opportunity costs, and sunk costs.

	Retailer Distribution (current)	Direct Sale Distribution (proposed)	Differential Costs and Revenues
Revenues (V)...............	$700,000	$800,000	$100,000
Cost of goods sold (V)	350,000	400,000	50,000
Advertising (F)	80,000	45,000	(35,000)
Commissions (V)	–0–	40,000	40,000
Warehouse amortization (F)	50,000	80,000	30,000
Other expenses (F)	60,000	60,000	–0–
Total	540,000	625,000	85,000
Net income	$160,000	$175,000	$ 15,000

V = Variable; F = Fixed.

According to the preceding analysis, the differential revenue is $100,000, and the differential costs total $85,000, leaving a positive differential net income of $15,000 under the proposed marketing plan. The financial analysis suggests that Nature Way Cosmetics should implement the proposed plan. However, before making any changes, management must also consider nonfinancial factors, such as the effect of the new distribution policy on brand image.

In general, only the differences between alternatives are relevant in decisions. Those items that are the same under all alternatives are not affected by the decision and can be ignored. For example, in the Nature Way Cosmetics example, the "Other expenses" category, which is $60,000 under both alternatives, can be ignored because it is not affected by the decision. If it were removed from the calculations, the door-to-door direct selling method would still be preferred by $15,000. This is an extremely important principle in management accounting that we will return to in later chapters.

The Cost of a Healthier Alternative

In recent years, McDonald's has received growing pressure from critics to address the health implications of its menu. In response, McDonald's announced plans to switch from the partially hydrogenated vegetable oil that it had been using to fry foods to a new soybean oil that would cut trans-fat levels by 48%. After making the announcement, McDonald's came to the realization that the unhealthy oil is much cheaper than the soybean oil and it lasts twice as long. What were the cost implications of this change? A typical McDonald's restaurant uses 500 pounds of the relatively unhealthy oil per week at a cost of about $186. In contrast, the same restaurant would need to use 1,000 pounds of the new soybean oil per week at a cost of about $571. This is a differential cost of $385 per restaurant per week. This may seem like a small amount of money until the calculation is expanded to include 13,000 McDonald's restaurants operating 52 weeks a year. Now, the total tab rises to about $260 million per year.

Source: Matthew Boyle, "Can You Really Make Fast Food Healthy?" *Fortune*, August 9, 2004, pp. 134–139.

Opportunity Cost

Opportunity cost is the potential benefit that is given up when one alternative is selected over another. To illustrate this important concept, consider the following examples:

EXAMPLE 1
Vicki has a part-time job that pays her $200 per week while attending college. She would like to spend a week at the beach during spring break, and her employer has agreed to give her the time off, but without pay. The $200 in lost wages would be an opportunity cost of taking the week off to be at the beach.

EXAMPLE 2
Suppose that Wal-Mart Canada is considering investing a large sum of money in land that may be a site for a future store. Rather than invest the funds in land, the company could invest the funds in high-grade securities. If the land is acquired, the opportunity cost will be the investment income that could have been realized if the securities had been purchased instead.

EXAMPLE 3
Steve is employed with a company that pays him a salary of $30,000 per year. He is thinking about leaving the company and returning to school. Since returning to school would require that he give up his $30,000 salary, the forgone salary would be an opportunity cost of seeking further education.

Opportunity cost is not usually recorded in the accounts of an organization, but it is a cost that must be explicitly considered in every decision a manager makes. Virtually every alternative has some opportunity cost attached to it. In Example 3, for instance, if Steve decides to stay at his job, there still is an opportunity cost involved: it is the greater income that could be realized in future years as a result of returning to school.

Your Decision to Attend Class

When you make the decision to attend class, what are the opportunity costs that are inherent in that decision?

Sunk Cost

A **sunk cost** is one that has already been incurred and that cannot be changed by any decision made now or in the future. Since sunk costs cannot be changed by any decision, they are not differential costs. Therefore, they can and should be ignored when making a decision; in other words, sunk costs are irrelevant.

To illustrate a sunk cost, assume that a company paid $50,000 several years ago for a special-purpose machine. The machine was used to make a product that is now obsolete and is no longer being sold. Even though in hindsight the purchase of the machine may have been unwise, no amount of regret can undo that decision. And, it would be foolish to continue making the obsolete product in a misguided attempt to "recover" the original cost of the machine. In short, the $50,000 originally paid for the machine has already been incurred and cannot be a differential cost in any future decision. For this reason, such costs are said to be sunk and should be ignored in decisions.

Cost Classification by Function

Another cost classification is based on function. Before discussing this further, it might be useful to understand that every organization carries out a sequence of activities to fulfill its mission.[2] Such a sequence of activities is known as the **value chain** of that organization.

Acadian Seaplants, located in Dartmouth, Nova Scotia, is a diversified, technology-based manufacturer of natural, specialty fertilizers, crop biostimulants, feed, food, food ingredients, and brewery supplies derived from select species of marine plants. Acadian is a fully integrated company involved in activities ranging from marine plant cultivation and the hand harvesting of pure seaweeds to product and application development, manufacturing, and technical customer support. Acadian's value chain is considerably broad (see Exhibit 2–3). In contrast, some competitors of Acadian may be less integrated—involved only in product and application development or in manufacturing. Such competitors must depend on other organizations for the cultivation and harvesting of seaweeds (front end of the value chain) and customer support (back end of the value chain); their value chains would be narrow.

Cost classification by function consists of associating costs with the type of activity for which that cost is incurred (e.g., manufacturing, marketing, or administration). For a retailer, such as Zellers, costs pertaining to the procurement and stacking of the goods to be sold would be classified as merchandising costs, whereas advertising costs and the costs of the accountants and legal personnel may be classified under selling and administrative costs. Such a distinction is more pronounced for manufacturing companies; we can distinguish between manufacturing and nonmanufacturing costs.

Exhibit 2–3
Acadian Seaplants' Value Chain

---

[2] The term "activity" was introduced in the section on cost behaviour and was used to denote a cost driver (i.e., something that causes costs to go up or down). However, activity in this section pertains to a series of tasks or steps that are carried out by an organization to fulfil its mission.

💿 **KNOW**

CC7: Distinguish between manufacturing and nonmanufacturing costs.

Manufacturing Costs

Similar to merchandising companies that must procure the goods they sell, manufacturing companies must produce the goods they sell; we use the term **manufacturing costs** to identify the costs associated with production activity. Typically, there are three types of manufacturing costs; we discuss each of these below as they might pertain to AmbuTech, a division of Winnipeg-based Melet Plastics, Inc., which produces a variety of canes for visually impaired and physically challenged customers.

DIRECT MATERIALS The materials that go into the final product are called **raw materials.** At the least, the raw materials required for one line of AmbuTech's canes would include aluminum for the body of the cane and plastic or wood for the handle.

The term "raw materials" is somewhat misleading because it seems to imply unprocessed natural resources. Actually, raw materials refer to any materials that are used in the final (finished) product of a company. Note, however, that the finished product of one company can be the raw material for another company. For example, AmbuTech might be purchasing "ready to assemble" plastic cane handles from a supplier, rather than producing them in-house. Whether to make the cane handles or buy them from outside can be

---

IN BUSINESS TODAY   **Benetton and the Value Chain**

United Colors of Benetton, an Italian apparel company headquartered in Ponzano, is unusual in that it is involved in all activities in the value chain from clothing design through manufacturing, distribution, and ultimate sale to customers in Benetton retail outlets. Most companies are involved in only one or two of these activities. Looking at this company allows us to see how costs are distributed across the entire value chain. A recent income statement from the company contained the following data:

	Millions of Euros	Percentage of Net Sales
Net sales	1,461	100.0%
Cost of sales	814	55.7%
Selling and general and administrative expenses:		
Payroll and related cost.	107	7.3
Distribution and transport.	23	1.6
Sales commissions	69	4.7
Advertising and promotion	82	5.6
Depreciation and amortization	74	5.1
Other expenses	109	7.5
Total selling and general and administrative expenses	464	31.8%

Even though this company spends large sums on advertising and runs its own shops, the cost of sales is still quite high in relation to the net sales—56% of net sales. And despite the company's lavish advertising campaigns, advertising and promotion costs amounted to only a little over 5% of net sales. (Note: One Euro was worth about Canadian $1.545 at the time of this financial report.)

an important decision which would influence AmbuTech's costs; we will examine such decisions in Chapter 12.

The aluminum sheets and plastic cane handles can also be called **direct materials,** since they become an integral part of the cane. As you can see, the quantity of direct materials required varies proportionately with the number of units produced. Therefore, direct materials is a variable cost with respect to production activity.

In addition to the direct materials, AmbuTech would also be using other **indirect materials** in the manufacturing process (e.g., screws, glue, solder, and other supplies) that are not integral parts of the cane. Indirect materials are relatively insignificant in value, and their costs are either not traceable to, or not worth tracing directly to, the finished product. The cost of indirect materials is included as part of manufacturing overhead, which is discussed later in this section.

● **APPLY**

CC8: Give examples of direct materials, direct labour, and manufacturing overhead costs.

DIRECT LABOUR   The term **direct labour** is reserved for those labour costs that can be easily (i.e., physically and conveniently) traced to individual units of product. Direct labour is sometimes called *touch labour*, since direct labour workers typically touch the product while it is being made. In the case of AmbuTech, this would include the wages and benefits of the individuals directly involved in rolling the aluminum sheets to form the body of the canes and those involved in assembling the canes. As you can see, direct labour costs are variable in nature, although this trend is changing.

Labour costs that cannot be physically traced to the creation of products, or that can be traced only at great cost and inconvenience, are termed **indirect labour** and treated as part of manufacturing overhead, along with indirect materials. Indirect labour includes the labour costs of janitors, supervisors, materials handlers, and night security guards. Although the efforts of these workers are essential to production, it would be either impractical or impossible to accurately trace their costs to specific units of product.

In some industries, major shifts are taking place in the structure of labour costs. Sophisticated automated equipment, run and maintained by skilled indirect workers, is increasingly replacing direct labour. In a few companies, direct labour has become such a minor element of cost that it has disappeared altogether as a separate cost category. More is said in later chapters about this trend and about the impact it is having on cost systems. However, the vast majority of manufacturing and service companies throughout the world continue to recognize direct labour as a separate cost category. In service companies, labour can often be a significant portion of the total cost of providing a service.

MANUFACTURING OVERHEAD   In addition to direct materials and direct labour, AmbuTech would also be incurring other costs related to manufacturing. These might include indirect materials and indirect labour (discussed previously), factory maintenance, utilities, property taxes, and amortization on equipment and factory buildings. Such costs are included in a separate category called **manufacturing overhead.** It is important to remember that AmbuTech will incur utility, maintenance, and amortization expenses associated with its selling and administrative functions; however, these costs are *not* recorded as part of manufacturing overhead. Only costs that are associated with the manufacturing function (i.e., operating the factory) are included in the manufacturing overhead category.

Various names are used for manufacturing overhead, such as *indirect manufacturing cost*, *factory overhead*, and *factory burden*. All of these terms are synonymous with *manufacturing overhead*.

Manufacturing overhead combined with direct labour is called **conversion cost.** This term stems from the fact that direct labour costs and overhead costs are incurred to convert raw materials into finished products. Direct labour combined with direct materials is called **prime cost.**

Nonmanufacturing Costs

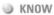 **APPLY**

CC9: Identify and give examples of marketing or selling and administrative costs.

Generally, nonmanufacturing costs are subclassified into two categories:

- marketing or selling costs
- administrative costs

Marketing or **selling costs** include all costs necessary to secure customer orders and get the finished product or service into the hands of the customer. These costs are often called *order-getting* and *order-filling costs.* Examples of marketing costs include advertising, shipping, sales travel, sales commissions, sales salaries, and costs of finished goods warehouses.

Administrative costs include all executive, organizational, and clerical costs associated with the general management of an organization, rather than with manufacturing, marketing, or selling. Examples of administrative costs include executive compensation, general accounting, secretarial, public relations, and similar costs involved in the overall, general administration of the organization *as a whole.*

Product Costs Versus Period Costs

Another classification by function that is often used synonymously with manufacturing versus nonmanufacturing costs is that of *product* versus *period* costs. To understand the distinction between the two, we must first refresh our understanding of the matching principle from financial accounting.

 KNOW

CC10: Distinguish between product and period costs.

The *matching principle* is based on the accrual concept and states that *costs incurred to generate a particular revenue should be recognized as expenses in the same period that the revenue is recognized.* This means that if a cost is incurred to acquire or make something that will eventually be sold, then the cost should be recognized as an expense only when the sale takes place—that is, when the benefit occurs. Such costs are called *product costs.*

Product Costs

For financial accounting purposes, **product costs** include all of the costs that are involved in acquiring or making a product. In the case of a merchandising firm, such as Hudson's Bay Company (HBC), product costs would include the costs associated with procuring (or acquiring) the merchandise HBC sells, whereas for a manufacturing company, product costs include direct materials and labour and manufacturing overhead. Product costs are *attached* to goods when they are acquired or produced, and are carried forward to an inventory account which appears on the balance sheet. Consequently, product costs are also known as **inventoriable costs.** HBC's 2006 annual report showed a merchandise inventory balance of about $1.47 billion (21% of revenue).

As and when the goods are sold, the amounts attached to the quantities sold are *expensed* (i.e., matched against sales revenue) and carried forward to the cost of goods sold account, which appears on the income statement. It is important to note that product costs may not be expensed in the period in which they are incurred; instead, the period when the goods are sold is critical for determining when to expense the product costs.

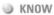 **APPLY**

CC11: Give examples of product and period costs.

Period Costs

Period costs are all the costs that are not included in product costs. These costs are expensed on the income statement in the period in which they are incurred, using the usual rules of accrual accounting you have already learned in financial accounting.

Period costs are not included as part of the cost of either purchased or manufactured goods. Sales commissions and office rent are good examples of the kind of costs we are talking about. Neither commission nor office rent is included as part of the cost of purchased or manufactured goods. Rather, both items are treated as expenses on the income statement in the period in which they are incurred. Thus, they are said to be period costs.

As suggested previously, *all selling and administrative expenses are considered to be period costs.* Therefore, advertising, executive salaries, sales commissions, public relations, and other nonmanufacturing costs discussed previously would all be period costs. They will appear on the income statement as expenses in the period in which they are incurred.

Exhibit 2–4 contains a summary of cost classifications by function.

Exhibit 2–4
Summary of Cost
Classifications by Function

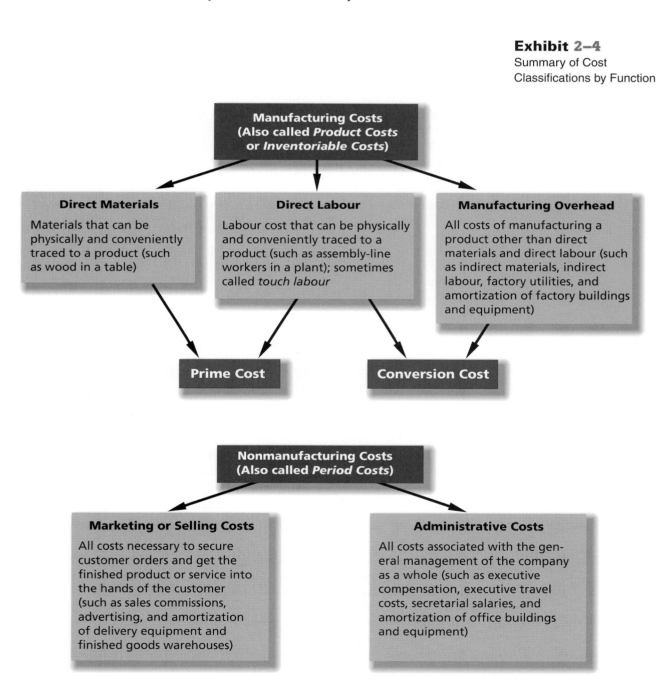

Manufacturing Costs
(Also called *Product Costs* **or *Inventoriable Costs*)**

Direct Materials

Materials that can be physically and conveniently traced to a product (such as wood in a table)

Direct Labour

Labour cost that can be physically and conveniently traced to a product (such as assembly-line workers in a plant); sometimes called *touch labour*

Manufacturing Overhead

All costs of manufacturing a product other than direct materials and direct labour (such as indirect materials, indirect labour, factory utilities, and amortization of factory buildings and equipment)

Prime Cost

Conversion Cost

Nonmanufacturing Costs
(Also called *Period Costs*)

Marketing or Selling Costs

All costs necessary to secure customer orders and get the finished product or service into the hands of the customer (such as sales commissions, advertising, and amortization of delivery equipment and finished goods warehouses)

Administrative Costs

All costs associated with the general management of the company as a whole (such as executive compensation, executive travel costs, secretarial salaries, and amortization of office buildings and equipment)

Cost Classifications on Financial Statements

In your prior accounting training, you learned that firms prepare periodic financial reports for creditors, shareholders, and others to show the financial condition of the firm and the firm's earnings performance over some specified interval.

The financial statements prepared by a *manufacturing* company are more complex than the statements prepared by, say, a *merchandising* company. Manufacturing companies are more complex organizations than merchandising companies because the manufacturing company must produce its goods as well as market them. The production process gives rise to many costs that do not exist in a merchandising company, and somehow these costs must be accounted for on the manufacturing company's financial statements. In this section, we focus our attention on how this accounting is carried out on the balance sheet and in the income statement.

The Balance Sheet

The balance sheet of a manufacturing company is similar to that of a merchandising company. However, the inventory accounts differ between the two types of companies. A merchandising company has only one class of inventory—goods purchased from suppliers that are awaiting resale to customers. In contrast, manufacturing companies have three classes of inventories—*raw materials*, *work in process*, and *finished goods*. Raw materials, as we have noted, are the materials that are used to make a product. **Work in process** consists of units of product that are only partially complete and will require further work before they are ready for sale to a customer. **Finished goods** consist of units of product that have been completed, but have not yet been sold to customers. The overall inventory figure is usually broken down into these three classes of inventories in a footnote to the financial statements.

We will use two companies—Halifax Manufacturing Corporation and Brandon Bookstore—to illustrate the concepts discussed in this section. Halifax Manufacturing Corporation makes precision brass fittings for yachts, and Brandon Bookstore specializes in books about Canadian history.

The footnotes to Halifax Manufacturing Corporation's annual report reveal the following information concerning its inventories:

HALIFAX MANUFACTURING CORPORATION
Inventory Accounts

	Beginning Balance	Ending Balance
Raw materials	$ 60,000	$ 50,000
Work in process	90,000	60,000
Finished goods	125,000	175,000
Total inventory accounts	$275,000	$285,000

Halifax Manufacturing Corporation's raw materials inventory would consist largely of brass rods and brass blocks. The work-in-process inventory would consist of partially completed brass fittings, and the finished goods inventory would consist of brass fittings that are ready to be sold to customers.

In contrast, the inventory account at Brandon Bookstore would consist entirely of the costs of books the company has purchased from publishers for resale to the public. In merchandising companies like Brandon, these inventories may be called *merchandise inventory*.

The beginning and ending balances in this account appear as follows:

BRANDON BOOKSTORE Inventory Accounts		
	Beginning Balance	**Ending Balance**
Merchandise inventory..........	$100,000	$150,000

The Income Statement

Exhibit 2–5 compares the income statements of Brandon Bookstore and Halifax Manufacturing Corporation. For purposes of illustration, these statements contain more detail about cost of goods sold than you will generally find in published financial statements.

Exhibit 2–5

Comparative Income Statements: Merchandising and Manufacturing Companies

		MERCHANDISING COMPANY **Brandon Bookstore**		
	Sales			$1,000,000
The cost of merchandise inventory purchased from outside suppliers during the period.	Cost of goods sold:			
	Beginning merchandise inventory		$100,000	
	Add: Purchases...........................		650,000	
	Goods available for sale		750,000	
	Deduct: Ending merchandise inventory		150,000	600,000
	Gross margin			400,000
	Less: Operating expenses:			
	Selling expense..........................		100,000	
	Administrative expense....................		200,000	300,000
	Net income			$ 100,000

		MANUFACTURING COMPANY **Halifax Manufacturing Corporation**		
	Sales			$1,500,000
The manufacturing costs associated with the goods that were finished during the period. (See Exhibit 2–7 for details.)	Cost of goods sold:			
	Beginning finished goods inventory...........		$125,000	
	Add: Cost of goods manufactured		850,000	
	Goods available for sale		975,000	
	Deduct: Ending finished goods inventory		175,000	800,00
	Gross margin			700,000
	Less: Operating expenses:			
	Selling expense..........................		250,000	
	Administrative expense....................		300,000	550,000
	Net income			$ 150,000

At first glance, the income statements of merchandising and manufacturing firms like Brandon Bookstore and Halifax Manufacturing Corporation are very similar. The only apparent difference is in the labels of some of the entries in the computation of the cost of goods sold. In Exhibit 2–5, the computation of cost of goods sold relies on the following basic equation for inventory accounts:

KNOW

CC15: Explain the basic inventory flow equation.

BASIC EQUATION FOR INVENTORY ACCOUNTS

$$\begin{array}{c} \text{Beginning} \\ \text{balance} \end{array} + \begin{array}{c} \text{Additions} \\ \text{to inventory} \end{array} = \begin{array}{c} \text{Withdrawals} \\ \text{from inventory} \end{array} + \begin{array}{c} \text{Ending} \\ \text{balance} \end{array}$$

The preceding equation provides the mathematics for calculating the cost of goods sold in both merchandising and manufacturing organizations. The logic underlying this equation, which applies to any inventory account, is illustrated in Exhibit 2–6A. During a period, additions to the inventory account come through purchases or other means. The sum of the additions to the account and the beginning balance represent the total amount of inventory that is available for use during the period. At the end of the period, some or all of the inventory may have been withdrawn from the inventory account.

To determine the cost of goods sold in a merchandising company like Brandon Bookstore, we only need to know the beginning and ending balances in the merchandise inventory account, and the purchases (see Exhibit 2–6B). Total purchases can be easily determined in a merchandising company by simply adding all purchases from suppliers.

To determine the cost of goods sold in a manufacturing company like Halifax Manufacturing Corporation, we need to know the cost of goods manufactured and the beginning and ending balances in the finished goods inventory account (see Exhibit 2–6B). The **cost of goods manufactured** consists of the manufacturing costs associated with goods that were *finished* during the period. The cost of goods manufactured figure for Halifax Manufacturing Corporation is computed in Exhibit 2–7, which contains a *schedule of cost of goods manufactured.*

Schedule of Cost of Goods Manufactured

APPLY

CC16: Prepare a schedule of cost of goods manufactured, including the computation of the cost of direct materials used.

At first glance, the **schedule of cost of goods manufactured** in Exhibit 2–7 appears complex and perhaps even intimidating. However, it is all quite logical. Notice that the schedule of cost of goods manufactured contains the three elements of product costs that we discussed earlier—direct materials, direct labour, and manufacturing overhead.

The cost of direct materials used is computed by taking into consideration the cost of direct materials in inventory at the start and the end of a period, and the cost of purchases during the period (see the schedule of direct materials used in Exhibit 2–6B). Once the cost of direct materials used is computed, direct labour and manufacturing overhead costs are added, which results in the total manufacturing costs incurred during the period ($820,000 in Exhibit 2–7). This amount, however, is *not* the cost of goods manufactured for the period.

Exhibit 2–6A
Inventory Flows

Exhibit 2–6B

Inventory Flows and Cost of Goods Sold

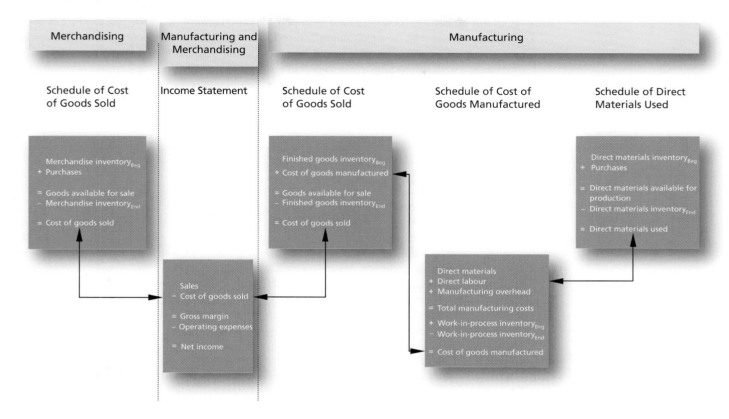

Exhibit 2–7

Schedule of Cost of Goods Manufactured

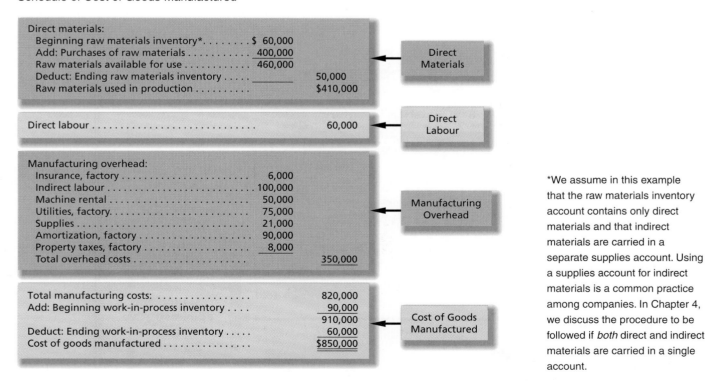

Direct materials:
Beginning raw materials inventory*........	$ 60,000	
Add: Purchases of raw materials	400,000	
Raw materials available for use	460,000	
Deduct: Ending raw materials inventory		50,000
Raw materials used in production		$410,000

Direct labour		60,000

Manufacturing overhead:
Insurance, factory	6,000	
Indirect labour	100,000	
Machine rental	50,000	
Utilities, factory.........................	75,000	
Supplies	21,000	
Amortization, factory	90,000	
Property taxes, factory	8,000	
Total overhead costs		350,000

Total manufacturing costs:	820,000
Add: Beginning work-in-process inventory	90,000
	910,000
Deduct: Ending work-in-process inventory	60,000
Cost of goods manufactured	$850,000

Direct
Materials

Direct
Labour

Manufacturing
Overhead

Cost of Goods
Manufactured

*We assume in this example that the raw materials inventory account contains only direct materials and that indirect materials are carried in a separate supplies account. Using a supplies account for indirect materials is a common practice among companies. In Chapter 4, we discuss the procedure to be followed if *both* direct and indirect materials are carried in a single account.

The total units manufactured in any period often include partially completed units carried forward from the previous period (called *beginning work-in-process inventory*); similarly, manufacturing activity in the current period often includes partially completed units that will be carried forward to the next period (called *ending work-in-process inventory*). To compute the cost of goods manufactured, prior period costs associated with the beginning work-in-process inventory must be added to the manufacturing costs, whereas costs associated with the ending work-in-process inventory must be deducted from the manufacturing costs (see the schedule of cost of goods manufactured in Exhibit 2–6B). This adjustment of the costs associated with the beginning and ending work-in-process inventories is also shown at the bottom of Exhibit 2–7, and results in the cost of goods manufactured for the current period amounting to $850,000.

Product Costs—A Closer Look

Previously in the chapter, we defined product costs as those costs that are involved in either the purchase or manufacture of goods. For manufactured goods, we stated that these costs consist of direct materials, direct labour, and manufacturing overhead. To understand product costs more fully, it will be helpful at this point to look briefly at the flow of costs in a manufacturing company. By doing so, we will be able to see how product costs move through the various accounts and affect the balance sheet and the income statement in the course of producing and selling products.

Exhibit 2–8 illustrates the flow of costs in a manufacturing company. Raw materials purchases are recorded in the raw materials inventory account. When raw materials are used in production, their costs are transferred to the work-in-process inventory account as direct materials. Notice that direct labour cost and manufacturing overhead cost are added directly to work in process. Work in process can be viewed most simply as an assembly line where workers are stationed and where products slowly take shape as they move from one end of the assembly line to the other. The direct materials, direct labour, and manufacturing overhead costs added to work in process in Exhibit 2–8 are the costs needed to complete these products as they move along this assembly line.

Exhibit 2–8
Cost Flows and Classifications in a Manufacturing Company

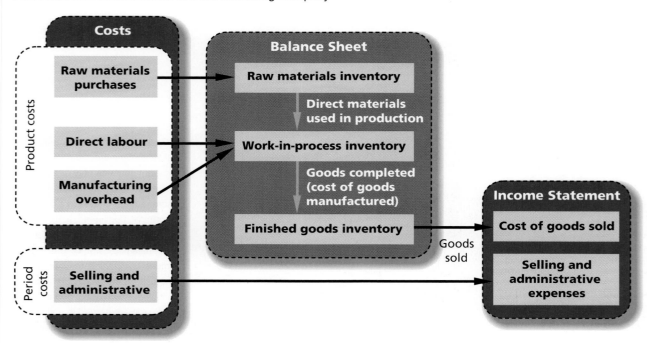

Notice from the exhibit that as goods are completed, their cost is transferred from work in process to finished goods. Here the goods await sale to a customer. As goods are sold, their cost is then transferred from finished goods to cost of goods sold. At this point, the various material, labour, and overhead costs that are required to make the product are finally treated as expenses.

As stated previously, product costs are often called *inventoriable costs* because these costs go directly into inventory accounts as they are incurred (first into work in process and then into finished goods), rather than going into expense accounts. *This is a key concept, since such costs can end up on the balance sheet as assets if goods are only partially completed or are unsold at the end of a period.*

Selling and administrative expenses are not involved in the manufacture of a product. For this reason, they are not treated as product costs but, rather, as period costs that go directly into expense accounts as they are incurred as shown in Exhibit 2–8.

Cost Manager   DECISION MAKER

Your company has recently implemented a just-in-time inventory program, and the company's operations manager questions your method of recording all purchases and production to the inventory account. According to her, the company's goal is zero inventories; therefore, the inventory account should be eliminated from the books. How would you respond?

An Example of Cost Flows

To provide a numerical example of cost flows in a manufacturing company, assume that a company's annual insurance cost is $2,000. Three-fourths of this amount ($1,500) applies to factory operations, and one-fourth ($500) applies to selling and administrative activities. Therefore, $1,500 of the $2,000 insurance cost would be a product (inventoriable) cost and would be added to the cost of the goods produced during the year. This portion of the year's insurance cost will not become an expense until the goods that are produced during the year are sold—which may not happen until the following year or even later. Until the goods are sold, the $1,500 will remain as part of inventory (either as part of work in process or as part of finished goods), along with the other costs of producing the goods.

By contrast, the $500 of insurance cost that applies to the company's selling and administrative activities will go into an expense account immediately as a charge against the period's revenue.

Product or Period Cost?—Not Just an Academic   IN BUSINESS TODAY
Distinction

Whether a cost is considered a product or period cost can have an important impact on a company's financial statements and can create conflicts inside an organization. Consider the following excerpts from a conversation recorded on the Institute of Management Accountants' Ethics Hot Line:

Caller: My problem basically is that my boss, the division general manager, wants me to put costs into inventory that I know should be expensed.

Counsellor: Have you expressed your doubts to your boss?

Caller: Yes, but he is basically a salesman and claims he knows nothing about GAAP. He just wants the "numbers" to back up the good news he keeps telling corporate [headquarters], which is what corporate demands. Also, he asks if I am ready to make the entries that I think are improper. It seems he wants to make it look like my idea all along. Our company had legal problems a few years ago with some government contracts, and it was the lower level people who were "hung out to dry" rather than the higher-ups who were really at fault.

Counsellor: What does he say when you tell him these matters need resolution?

Caller: He just says we need a meeting, but the meetings never solve anything.

Counsellor: Does your company have an ethics hot line?

Caller: Yes, but my boss would view use of the hot line as snitching or even whistle-blowing.

Counsellor: If you might face reprisals for using the hot line, perhaps you should evaluate whether or not you really want to work for a company whose ethical climate is one you are uncomfortable in.

Caller: I have already asked … for a transfer back to the corporate office.

Source: Curtis C. Verschoor, "Using a Hot Line Isn't Whistle-Blowing," *Strategic Finance*, April 1999, pp. 27–28. Used with permission from *Strategic Finance* and the Institute of Management Accountants.

Cost Classification Summary

As explained previously in the chapter, costs can be classified in various ways to meet the information needs of managers; Exhibit 2–9 provides a summary of these different classifications. Indeed, the same cost item may be classified in more than one way. For example, the salary of Holiday Inn's catering department manager is a fixed cost with respect to the number of guests staying the hotel. It is directly traceable to the catering department, but not to the sales department. It is a period cost because the individual's services cannot be *banked*. Finally, it is a relevant cost when deciding whether to eliminate the department and outsource catering. When to use which classification depends on the purpose of the classification. The purposes and corresponding cost classifications are summarized in Exhibit 2–10. You will find it useful to understand the notion of "different costs for different purposes" as you progress through the text.

Exhibit 2–9

Cost Classification Summary

Exhibit 2–10
Cost Classifications for Different Purposes

Purpose of Cost Classification	Cost Classifications

Preparing external financial statements	• Product costs (inventoriable)
	  • Direct materials
	  • Direct labour
	  • Manufacturing overhead
	• Period costs (expensed)
	  • Nonmanufacturing costs
	    • Marketing or selling costs
	    • Administrative costs

Predicting cost behaviour in response to changes in activity	• Variable cost (proportional to activity) • Fixed cost (constant in total)
Assigning costs to cost objects, such as departments or products	• Direct cost (can be easily traced) • Indirect cost (cannot be easily traced; must be allocated)
Making decisions	• Differential cost (differs between alternatives) • Sunk cost (past cost not affecting a decision) • Opportunity cost (forgone benefit)

Application Competency Summary

Application Competency	Deliverable	Source Documents and Key Information	Steps	Knowledge Competency
Compute net income for the period. ○ CC13	**Key Information** Gross margin and net income **Report/Document** Income statement	**Sales ledger** Actual sales revenue **Schedule of cost of goods sold** Actual cost of goods sold (COGS) **Selling, general, and administrative expenses ledgers** Actual selling, general, and administrative expenses	1. Obtain the sales revenues from the sales ledger. 2. Obtain the COGS from the schedule of cost of goods sold. 3. Obtain the selling, general, and administrative expenses from the ledgers. 4. Compute net income as sales revenue *minus* COGS minus selling, general, and administrative expenses.	Manufacturing versus nonmanufacturing costs ○ CC7 Product versus period costs ○ CC10
Compute the COGS for the period. ○ CC14	**Key Information** Cost of goods available for sale and COGS **Report/Document** Schedule of COGS	**Schedule of cost of goods manufactured** Cost of goods manufactured (COGM) **Finished goods inventory ledger** Cost of beginning and ending finished goods inventory	1. Obtain the beginning and ending finished goods inventory amounts from the finished goods inventory ledger. 2. Obtain the COGM from the schedule of the cost of goods manufactured. 3. Compute the COGS as beginning finished goods inventory *plus* COGM *Less* ending finished goods inventory.	Manufacturing versus nonmanufacturing costs ○ CC7 Product versus period costs ○ CC10 Inventory flow equation ○ CC15

continued

Application Competency	Deliverable	Source Documents and Key Information	Steps	Knowledge Competency
Compute the COGM for the period. ⊙ CC16	*Key Information* Manufacturing costs and the COGM *Report/Document* Schedule of COGM	*Schedule of cost of materials used* Cost of materials used *Direct labour ledger* Cost of direct labour *Various manufacturing overhead ledgers* Cost of manufacturing overhead *Work-in-process inventory ledger* Cost of beginning and ending work-in-process inventory	1. Obtain the cost of direct materials used from the schedule of cost of materials used. 2. Obtain the cost of direct labour from the labour cost ledger. 3. Obtain the cost of manufacturing overhead from the overhead cost ledger. 4. Obtain the beginning and ending work-in-process inventory amounts from the work-in-process inventory ledger. 5. Compute COGM as costs of direct materials used *plus* direct labour *plus* manufacturing overhead *plus* beginning work-in-process inventory *less* ending work-in-process inventory	Direct versus indirect costs ⊙ CC3 Materials, labour, and overhead costs ⊙ CC7, 8 Inventory flow equation ⊙ CC15
Compute the cost of direct materials used during the period. ⊙ CC16	*Key Information* Cost of direct materials used *Report/Document* Schedule of cost of materials used	*Raw materials inventory ledger* Cost of beginning and ending materials inventory *Materials purchases ledgers* Cost of materials purchased	1. Obtain the beginning and ending materials inventory amounts from the materials inventory ledger. 2. Obtain the cost of materials purchased from the cost of materials purchases ledger. 3. Compute the cost of direct materials used as the cost of beginning materials inventory *plus* the cost of purchases *less* the cost of ending materials inventory.	

Guidance Answers to Decision Maker and You Decide

FINANCIAL ANALYST (p. 30)

Fixed and *variable* are terms used to describe cost behaviour or how a given cost will react or respond to changes in the level of business activity. A fixed cost is a cost that remains constant, in total, regardless of changes in the level of activity. However, on a per-unit basis, a fixed cost varies inversely with changes in activity. The cost structures of a number of industries lean toward fixed costs because of the nature of their operations. Obviously, the cost of airplanes would be fixed, and within some relevant range, such costs would not change if the number of passengers flown changed. This would also be true in other industries, such as trucking and rail transportation. You might suggest that it would be worthwhile to research the prospects for growth in this industry and for this company. If a downturn in business is not anticipated, a cost structure weighted toward fixed costs should not be used as the primary reason for turning down the investment opportunity. On the other hand, if a period of decline is anticipated, your client's initial impression might be on target.

YOUR DECISION TO ATTEND CLASS (p. 32)
Every alternative has some opportunity cost attached to it. If you brainstormed a bit, you probably came up with a few opportunity costs that accompany your choice to attend class. If you had trouble answering the question, think about what you could be doing instead of attending class.

- You could have been working at a part-time job; you could quantify that cost by multiplying your pay rate by the time you spend in class.
- You could have spent the time studying for another class; the opportunity cost could be measured by the improvement in the grade that would result from spending more time on that class.
- You could have slept in or taken a nap; depending on your level of sleep deprivation, this opportunity cost might be priceless.

COST MANAGER (p. 43)
At a conceptual level, the physical flow of goods remains the same, regardless of the inventory levels maintained by a company (see Exhibit 2–6A). Until such time that the company continues to carry some inventory, it becomes necessary to maintain an inventory account. In a company with "near zero" inventory levels, additions to the inventory account are equal to the withdrawals from the account during a given period. In reality, although the goal of a just-in-time program is zero inventories, companies take a long time before that goal is achieved. Once the company can sustain a "near zero" inventory level, the company may consider eliminating the inventory account. In such a situation, all costs will be treated like period costs and expensed during the period in which they are incurred.

Review Problem 1: Cost Terms

You have been introduced to many new cost terms in this chapter. It will take you some time to learn what each term means and how to properly classify costs in an organization. Consider the following example: Porter Company manufactures furniture, including tables. Selected costs are given below:
1. The tables are made of wood that costs $100 per table.
2. The tables are assembled by workers, at a wage cost of $40 per table.
3. Workers assembling the tables are supervised by a factory supervisor who is paid $25,000 per year.
4. Electrical costs are $2 per machine-hour. Four machine-hours are required to produce a table.
5. The straight-line amortization cost of the machines used to make the tables totals $10,000 per year.
6. The salary of the president of Porter Company is $100,000 per year.
7. Porter Company spends $250,000 per year to advertise its products.
8. Salespersons are paid a commission of $30 for each table sold.
9. Instead of producing the tables, Porter Company could rent its factory space out at a rental income of $50,000 per year.

Required:
Classify these costs according to various cost terms used in the chapter. *Carefully study the classification of each cost.* If you do not understand why a particular cost is classified the way it is, reread the section of the chapter discussing the particular cost term. The terms *variable cost* and *fixed cost* refer to how costs behave with respect to the number of tables produced in a year.

SOLUTION TO REVIEW PROBLEM 1

| | To Units of Product Sold | | Period (selling and adminis- trative) Cost | Product Cost | | | To Units of Product Sold | | Sunk Cost | Oppor- tunity Cost |
	Variable Cost	Fixed Cost		Direct Materials	Direct Labour	Manufacturing Overhead	Direct	Indirect		
1. Wood used in a table ($100 per table)	X			X			X			
2. Labour cost to assemble a table ($40 per table) . . .	X				X		X			
3. Salary of the factory supervisor ($25,000 per year)		X				X		X		
4. Cost of electricity to produce tables ($2 per machine- hour)	X					X		X		
5. Amortization of machines used to produce tables ($10,000 per year)		X				X		X	X*	
6. Salary of the company president ($100,000 per year)		X	X					X		
7. Advertising expense ($250,000 per year)		X	X					X		
8. Commissions paid to sales persons ($30 per table sold)	X		X				X			
9. Rental income forgone on factory space ($50,000 per year)										X†

*This is a sunk cost, since the equipment has already been purchased.

†This is an opportunity cost, since it represents the potential benefit that is lost or sacrificed as a result of using the factory space to produce tables. Opportunity cost is a special category of cost that is not ordinarily recorded in an organization's accounting books. To avoid possible confusion with other costs, we will not attempt to classify this cost in any other way except as an opportunity cost.

Review Problem 2: Schedule of Cost of Goods Manufactured and Income Statement

The following information has been taken from the accounting records of Klear-Seal Company for last year:

Selling expenses	$ 165,000
Raw materials inventory, January 1	120,000
Raw materials inventory, December 31	82,000
Utilities, factory	38,500
Direct labour cost	157,300

Amortization, factory	155,000
Purchases of raw materials	723,000
Sales	2,500,000
Insurance, factory	42,000
Supplies, factory	14,000
Administrative expenses	283,000
Indirect labour	306,000
Maintenance, factory	89,000
Work-in-process inventory, January 1	180,000
Work-in-process inventory, December 31	100,000
Finished goods inventory, January 1	260,000
Finished goods inventory, December 31	210,000

Management wants these data organized in a better format so that financial statements can be prepared for the year.

Required:
1. Prepare a schedule of cost of goods manufactured, similar to Exhibit 2–7.
2. Compute the cost of goods sold.
3. Using data as needed from parts(1) and (2), prepare an income statement.

SOLUTION TO REVIEW PROBLEM 2

1.

KLEAR-SEAL COMPANY
Schedule of Cost of Goods Manufactured
For the Year Ended December 31

Direct materials:		
Raw materials inventory, January 1	$120,000	
Add: Purchases of raw materials	723,000	
Raw materials available for use	843,000	
Deduct: Raw materials inventory, December 31	82,000	
Raw materials used in production		$ 761,000
Direct labour		157,300
Manufacturing overhead:		
Utilities, factory	38,500	
Amortization, factory	155,000	
Insurance, factory	42,000	
Supplies, factory	14,000	
Indirect labour	306,000	
Maintenance, factory	89,000	
Total overhead costs		644,500
Total manufacturing costs		1,562,800
Add: Work-in-process inventory, January 1		180,000
		1,742,800
Deduct: Work-in-process inventory, December 31		100,000
Cost of goods manufactured		$1,642,800

2.

The cost of goods sold would be computed as follows:	
Finished goods inventory, January 1	$ 260,000
Add: Cost of goods manufactured	1,642,800
Goods available for sale	1,902,800
Deduct: Finished goods inventory, December 31	210,000
Cost of goods sold	$1,692,800

3.

KLEAR-SEAL COMPANY Income Statement For the Year Ended December 31		
Sales		$2,500,000
Less: Cost of goods sold (see above)		1,692,000
Gross margin.......................................		807,200
Less: Selling and administrative expenses:		
Selling expenses	$165,000	
Administrative expenses	283,000	
Total expenses.....................................		448,000
Net income		$ 359,200

Glossary

Administrative costs All executive, organizational, and clerical costs associated with the general management of an organization, rather than with manufacturing, marketing, or selling. (p. 36)

Common cost A cost that is incurred to support a number of cost objects, but cannot be traced to them individually. For example, the salary and benefit package of the receptionist in a bank is common to all the different services provided by that bank. (p. 30)

Conversion cost Direct labour cost plus manufacturing overhead cost. (p. 35)

Cost behaviour The way in which a cost reacts or responds to changes in the level of business activity. (p. 26)

Cost object Anything for which cost data are desired. Examples of possible cost objects are services, product lines, customers, jobs, and organizational subunits, such as departments or divisions of a company. (p. 30)

Cost of goods manufactured The manufacturing costs associated with the goods that were finished during the period. (p. 40)

Decremental cost A decrease in cost between two alternatives. (p. 31)

Differential cost A difference in cost between any two alternatives. Also see *decremental cost* and *incremental cost*. (p. 31)

Differential revenue The difference in revenue between any two alternatives. (p. 31)

Direct cost A cost that can be easily and conveniently traced to a particular cost object. (p. 30)

Direct labour Those factory labour costs that can be easily traced to individual units of product. Also called *touch labour*. (p. 35)

Direct materials Those materials that become an integral part of a finished product and can be conveniently traced to it. (p. 35)

Finished goods Units of product that have been completed, but have not yet been sold to customers. (p. 38)

Fixed cost A cost that remains constant, in total, regardless of changes in the level of activity within a relevant range. If a fixed cost is expressed on a per-unit basis, it varies inversely with the level of activity. (p. 28)

Incremental cost An increase in cost between two alternatives. Also see *decremental cost* and *differential cost*. (p. 31)

Indirect cost A cost that cannot be easily and conveniently traced to a particular cost object. (p. 30)

Indirect labour The labour costs of janitors, supervisors, materials handlers, and other factory workers that cannot be traced directly to particular products. (p. 35)

Indirect materials Small items of material, such as glue and nails. These items may become an integral part of a finished product but are traceable to the product only at great cost or inconvenience. (p. 35)

Inventoriable cost Cost that can be carried forward to inventory. Synonym for *product costs*. (p. 36)

Manufacturing cost Cost incurred in production during a certain period. Includes *direct materials*, *direct labour*, and *manufacturing overhead*. (p. 34)

Manufacturing overhead All costs associated with manufacturing, except direct materials and direct labour. Synonyms include *indirect manufacturing cost*, *factory overhead*, and *factory burden*. (p. 35)

Marketing or **selling costs** All costs necessary to secure customer orders and get the finished product or service into the hands of the customer. Also called *order-getting* and *order-filling costs*. (p. 36)

Opportunity cost The potential benefit that is given up when one alternative is selected over another. (p. 32)

Period costs All costs not included in product costs, e.g., all selling and administrative expenses. (p. 36)

Prime cost Direct materials cost plus direct labour cost. (p. 35)

Product costs All costs that are involved in acquiring or making a product. In the case of manufactured goods, these costs consist of direct materials, direct labour, and manufacturing overhead. Also see *inventoriable costs*. (p. 36)

Raw materials Materials that are used to make a product. (p. 34)

Relevant range The range of activity within which assumptions about variable and fixed cost behaviour are valid. (p. 28)

Schedule of cost of goods manufactured A schedule showing the direct materials, direct labour, and manufacturing overhead costs incurred for a period and assigned to work in process and finished goods. (p. 40)

Sunk cost Any cost that has already been incurred and that cannot be changed by any decision made now or in the future. (p. 33)

Value chain A sequence of major activities undertaken by an organization to fulfil its mission. (p. 33)

Variable cost A cost that varies, in total, in direct proportion to changes in the level of activity. (p. 26)

Work in process Units of product that are only partially complete and will require further work before they are ready for sale to a customer. (p. 38)

Questions

2–1 What is meant by the term *cost behaviour*?

2–2 "A variable cost is a cost that varies per unit of activity, whereas a fixed cost is constant per unit of activity." Do you agree? Explain.

2–3 How do fixed costs create difficulties in costing units of product?

2–4 Give two examples each of variable and fixed costs.

2–5 Fixed costs are inversely proportional to volume. As volume decreases fixed costs increase and as volume increases fixed costs decrease. Do you agree? Explain.

2–6 Why is manufacturing overhead considered an indirect cost of a unit of product?

2–7 Define the following terms: differential cost, opportunity cost, and sunk cost.

2–8 Only variable costs can be differential costs. Do you agree? Explain.

2–9 What are the three major elements of product costs in a manufacturing company?

2–10 Distinguish among the following: (a) direct materials, (b) indirect materials, (c) direct labour, (d) indirect labour, and (e) manufacturing overhead.

2–11 Given:
- Prime costs   = PC
- Conversion costs   = CC
- Direct materials costs   = DM
- Direct labour costs   = DL
- Manufacturing overhead costs   = MOH

Develop an equation that connects PC and CC.

2–12 Explain the difference between a product cost and a period cost.

2–13 Describe how the income statement of a manufacturing company differs from the income statement of a merchandising company.

2–14 Of what value is the schedule of cost of goods manufactured? How does it tie into the income statement?

2–15 Describe how the inventory accounts of a manufacturing company differ from the inventory account of a merchandising company.

2–16 Why are product costs sometimes called inventoriable costs? Describe the flow of such costs in a manufacturing company from the point of incurrence until they finally become expenses on the income statement.

2–17 Is it possible for such costs as salaries or amortization to end up as assets on the balance sheet? Explain.

Brief Exercises

BRIEF EXERCISE 2–1   Identifying Variable and Fixed Costs (CC1, 2)

Following are a number of costs that are incurred in a variety of organizations.

Required:

Classify each cost as variable or fixed with respect to the number of units of product sold or services provided by the organization by placing an *X* in the appropriate column.

	Cost Behaviour	
Cost Item	**Variable**	**Fixed**
1. X-ray film used in the radiology lab at your local hospital		
2. The costs of advertising a Madonna rock concert in Toronto		
3. Amortization on the Planet Hollywood restaurant building in Hong Kong		
4. The electrical costs of running a roller coaster at West Edmonton Mall		
5. Property taxes on your local cinema		
6. Commissions paid to salespersons at Wavelength Electronics		
7. Property insurance on a Coca-Cola bottling plant		
8. The costs of synthetic materials used to make Nike running shoes		
9. The costs of shipping Panasonic televisions to retail stores		
10. The cost of leasing an ultra-scan diagnostic machine at the American Hospital in Paris		

BRIEF EXERCISE 2–2   Identifying Direct and Indirect Costs (CC3, 4)

University Hospital is a full-service hospital that provides everything from major surgery and emergency room care to outpatient clinics.

Required:

For each cost incurred at University Hospital, indicate whether it would most likely be a direct cost or an indirect cost of the specified cost object by placing an *X* in the appropriate column.

Cost	Cost object	Direct Cost	Indirect Cost
Ex. Catered food served to patients	A particular patient	X	
1. The wages of pediatric nurses	The Pediatrics Department		
2. Prescription drugs	A particular patient		
3. Heating the hospital	The Pediatrics Department		
4. The salary of the head of Pediatrics	The Pediatrics Department		
5. The salary of the head of Pediatrics	A particular pediatric patient		
6. Hospital chaplain's salary	A particular patient		
7. Lab tests by outside contractor	A particular patient		
8. Lab tests by outside contractor	A particular department		

BRIEF EXERCISE 2–3   Differential, Opportunity, and Sunk Costs (CC5, 6)

University Hospital's Radiology Department is considering replacing an old inefficient X-ray machine with a state-of-the-art digital X-ray machine. The new machine would provide higher quality X-rays in less time and at a lower cost per X-ray. The new machine would require less power consumption and would use a colour laser printer to produce easily readable X-ray images. Instead of investing the funds in the new X-ray machine, the Laboratory Department is lobbying the hospital's management to buy a new DNA analyzer.

Required:

For each of the following items, indicate by placing an X in the appropriate column whether it should be considered a differential cost, an opportunity cost, or a sunk cost in the decision to replace the old X-ray machine with a new machine. If none of the categories applies for a particular item, leave all columns blank.

Item	Differential Cost	Opportunity Cost	Sunk Cost
Ex. Cost of X-ray film used in the old machine	X		
1. Cost of the old X-ray machine			
2. The salary of the head of the Radiology Department			
3. The salary of the head of the Pediatrics Department			
4. Cost of the new colour laser printer			
5. Rent on the space occupied by the Radiology Department			
6. The cost of maintaining the old machine			
7. Benefits from a new DNA analyzer			
8. Cost of electricity to run the X-ray machines			

BRIEF EXERCISE 2–4   Classifying Manufacturing Costs (CC7, 8, 9)

Your Computer, Inc. assembles custom computers from components supplied by various manufacturers. The company is very small and its assembly shop and retail sales store are housed in a single facility in North Vancouver. Following are some of the costs that are incurred at the company.

Required:

For each cost, indicate whether it would most likely be classified as direct labour, direct materials, manufacturing overhead, marketing and selling, or an administrative cost.
1. The cost of a hard drive installed in a computer
2. The cost of advertising in the *Puget Sound Computer User* newspaper
3. The wages of employees who assemble computers from components
4. Sales commissions paid to the company's salespeople
5. The wages of the assembly shop's supervisor
6. The wages of the company's accountant
7. Amortization on equipment used to test assembled computers before release to customers
8. Rent on the facility

BRIEF EXERCISE 2–5   Identifying Product and Period Costs (CC10, 11)

A product cost is also known as an *inventoriable cost*. Classify the following costs as either product (inventoriable) costs or period (noninventoriable) costs in a manufacturing company:
1. Amortization on salespersons' cars
2. Rent on equipment used in the factory
3. Lubricants used for maintenance of machines
4. Salaries of finished goods warehouse personnel
5. Soap and paper towels used by factory workers at the end of a shift
6. Factory supervisors' salaries
7. Heat, water, and power consumed in the factory
8. Materials used in boxing units of finished product for shipment overseas (Units are not normally boxed.)
9. Advertising outlays
10. Workers' compensation insurance on factory employees
11. Amortization on chairs and tables in the factory lunchroom
12. The salary of the switchboard operator for the company
13. Amortization on a Lear Jet used by the company's executives
14. Rent on rooms at a Florida resort for the annual sales conference
15. Attractively designed box for packaging breakfast cereal

BRIEF EXERCISE 2–6   Constructing an Income Statement (CC13, 14, 15)

Last month CyberGames, a computer game retailer, had total sales of $1,500,000, selling expenses of $215,000, and administrative expenses of $185,000. The company had beginning merchandise inventory of $300,000, purchased additional merchandise inventory for $800,000, and ending merchandise inventory of $200,000.

Required:

Prepare an income statement for the company for the month in good form.

BRIEF EXERCISE 2–7   Prepare a Schedule of Cost of Goods Manufactured (CC15, 16)
Lompac Products manufactures a variety of products in its factory. Data for the most recent month's operations follow:

Beginning raw materials inventory	$ 70,000
Purchases of raw materials	720,000
Ending raw materials inventory	50,000
Direct labour	145,000
Manufacturing overhead	380,000
Beginning work-in-process inventory	110,000
Ending work-in-process inventory	140,000

Required:
Prepare in good form a schedule of cost of goods manufactured for the company for the month.

Exercises

EXERCISE 2–1   Cost Identification (CC1, 2, 5, 6, 7, 8, 9, 10, 11)
Wollogong Group Ltd. of New South Wales, Australia, acquired its factory building about 10 years ago. For several years the company has rented out a small annex attached to the rear of the building. The company has received a rental income of $30,000 per year on this space. The renter's lease will expire soon, and rather than renew the lease, the company has decided to use the space itself to manufacture a new product.

Direct materials cost for the new product will total $80 per unit. To have a place to store finished units of product, the company will rent a small warehouse nearby. The rental cost will be $500 per month. In addition, the company must rent equipment for use in producing the new product; the rental cost will be $4,000 per month. Workers will be hired to manufacture the new product, with direct labour cost amounting to $60 per unit. The space in the annex will continue to be amortized on a straight-line basis, as in prior years. This amortization is $8,000 per year.

Advertising costs for the new product will total $50,000 per year. A supervisor will be hired to oversee production; her salary will be $1,500 per month. Electricity for operating machines will be $1.20 per unit. Costs of shipping the new product to customers will be $9 per unit.

To provide funds to purchase materials, meet payrolls, and so forth, the company will have to liquidate some temporary investments. These investments are presently yielding a return of about $3,000 per year.

Required:
Prepare an answer sheet with the following column headings:

Name of the Cost	Variable Cost	Fixed Cost	Product Cost			Period (selling and administrative) Cost	Opportunity Cost	Sunk Cost
			Direct Materials	Direct Labour	Manufacturing Overhead			

List the different costs associated with the new product decision down the extreme left column (under Name of the Cost). Then place an X under each heading that helps describe the type of cost involved. There may be Xs under several column headings for a single cost. (For example, a cost may be a fixed cost, a period cost, and a sunk cost; you would place an X under each of these column headings opposite the cost.)

EXERCISE 2–2   Definitions of Cost Terms (CC1, 2, 5, 6, 10, 11)
Following are a number of cost terms introduced in the chapter:

Variable cost	Product cost
Fixed cost	Sunk cost
Prime cost	Conversion cost
Opportunity cost	Period cost

Choose the term or terms that most appropriately describe the cost identified in each of the following situations. A cost term can be used more than once.

1. Lake Company produces a tote bag that is very popular with college students. The cloth going into the manufacture of the tote bag would be called direct materials and classified as a _____ cost. In terms of cost behaviour, the cloth could also be described as a _____ cost.

2. The direct labour cost required to produce the tote bags, combined with the manufacturing overhead cost involved, would be known as _____ cost.

3. The company could have taken the funds that it has invested in production equipment and invested them in interest-bearing securities instead. The interest forgone on the securities would be called _____ cost.

4. Taken together, the direct materials cost and the direct labour cost required to produce tote bags would be called _____ cost.

5. The company used to produce a smaller tote bag that was not very popular. Some three hundred of these smaller bags are stored in one of the company's warehouses. The amount invested in these bags would be called a _____ cost.

6. The tote bags are sold through agents who are paid a commission on each bag sold. These commissions would be classified by Lake Company as a _____ cost. In terms of cost behaviour, commissions would be classified as a _____ cost.

7. Amortization on the equipment used to produce tote bags would be classified by Lake Company as a _____ cost. However, amortization on any equipment used by the company in selling and administrative activities would be classified as a _____ cost. In terms of cost behaviour, amortization would probably be classified as a _____ cost.

8. A _____ cost is also known as an inventoriable cost, since such costs go into the work-in-process inventory account and then into the finished goods inventory account before appearing on the income statement as part of cost of goods sold.

9. The salary of Lake Company's president would be classified as a _____ cost, since the salary will appear on the income statement as an expense in the time period in which it is incurred.

10. Costs can often be classified in several ways. For example, Lake Company pays $5,000 rent each month on its factory building. The rent would be part of manufacturing overhead. In terms of cost behaviour, it would be classified as a _____ cost. The rent can also be classified as a _____ cost and as part of _____ cost.

EXERCISE 2–3   Classification of Variable, Fixed, Direct, and Indirect Costs (CC1, 2, 3, 4)
Various costs are associated with running a communications company dealing with the production of video commercials, as given below:
1. Account manager's salary
2. Rent on building
3. Videos used in the production of commercials
4. Marketing manager's salary
5. Wages of operators involved in editing
6. Amortization of equipment used in editing
7. Amortization on television sets used for viewing videos
8. Insurance on building

Required:
Classify each cost as being either variable or fixed with respect to the number of commercials produced. Also indicate whether each cost would typically be treated as a direct cost or an indirect cost with respect to the number of commercials produced. Prepare your answer sheet as shown below:

	Cost Behaviour		To Number of Commercials Produced	
Cost Item	Variable	Fixed	Direct	Indirect

EXERCISE 2–4   Classification of Variable, Fixed, Period, and Product Costs (CC1, 2, 10, 11)
Following are listed various costs that are found in organizations.
1. Hamburger buns in a McDonald's outlet
2. Advertising by a dental office
3. Apples processed and canned by Del Monte Corporation
4. Shipping canned apples from a Del Monte plant to customers
5. Insurance on a Bausch & Lomb factory producing contact lenses

6. Insurance on IBM's corporate headquarters
7. Salary of a supervisor overseeing production of circuit boards at Hewlett-Packard
8. Commissions paid to Encyclopedia Britannica salespersons
9. Amortization of factory lunchroom facilities at a General Electric plant
10. Steering wheels installed in BMWs

Required:

Classify each cost as being either variable or fixed with respect to the number of units sold. Also classify each cost as either a selling and administrative cost or a product cost. Prepare your answer sheet as shown below.

Cost Item	Cost Behaviour		Selling and Administrative Cost	Product Cost
	Variable	Fixed		

Place an *X* in the appropriate columns to show the proper classification of each cost.

EXERCISE 2–5 Determining Cost of Goods Sold (CC14, 15, 16)

The following cost and inventory data are taken from the accounting records of Mason Company for the year just completed:

Costs incurred:	
Direct labour cost	$ 70,000
Purchases of raw materials	120,000
Indirect labour	30,000
Maintenance, factory equipment	6,000
Advertising expense	90,000
Insurance, factory equipment	900
Sales salaries	50,000
Rent, factory facilities	24,000
Supplies	4,600
Amortization, office equipment	3,500
Amortization, factory equipment	21,000

	Beginning of the Year	End of the Year
Inventories:		
Raw materials	$ 8,000	$16,500
Work in process	10,300	5,150
Finished goods	23,250	38,100

Required:

1. Prepare a schedule of cost of goods manufactured in good form.
2. Prepare the cost of goods sold section of Mason Company's income statement for the year.

EXERCISE 2–6 Cost Flows (CC12)

The Devon Motor Company produces automobiles. During April, the company purchased 8,000 batteries at a cost of $10 per battery. Devon withdrew 7,600 batteries from the storeroom during the month. Of these, 100 were used to replace batteries in autos being used by the company's travelling sales staff. The remaining 7,500 batteries withdrawn from the storeroom were placed in autos being produced by the company. Of the autos in production during April, 90% were completed and transferred from work in process to finished goods. Of the cars completed during the month, 30% were unsold at April 30.

There were no inventories of any type on April 1.

Required:

1. Determine the cost of batteries that would appear in each of the following accounts at April 30:
   a. Raw materials
   b. Work in process
   c. Finished goods.
   d. Cost of goods sold
   e. Selling expense
2. Specify whether each of the previous accounts would appear on the balance sheet or on the income statement at April 30.

EXERCISE 2–7   Cost of Goods Manufactured (CC16)

The following cost information is presented for Phoenix Ltd. for the most recent period:

Cost of direct material used in manufacturing	$92,000
Direct labour costs	25,000
Manufacturing overhead	6,500
Sales commissions @ 8% of sales	32,000
Opening finished goods inventory	9,000
Opening work-in-process inventory	6,000
Ending finished goods inventory	22,000
Ending work-in-process inventory	17,000

What was the cost of goods manufactured for Phoenix?

EXERCISE 2–8   Cost of Goods Manufactured (CC14, 15, 16)

Sage Ltd. had the following results for the month of March:

Sales	$1,700,000
Opening finished goods inventory	30,000
Gross margin	800,000
Ending finished goods inventory	185,000

What was the cost of goods manufactured in March?

Problems

PROBLEM 2–1   Cost Identification (CC1, 2, 7, 8, 10, 11)

CHECK FIGURE
Clay and glaze: variable, direct materials

Staci Valek began dabbling in pottery several years ago as a hobby. Her work is quite creative, and it has been so popular with friends and others that she has decided to quit her job with an aerospace firm and manufacture pottery full time. The salary from Staci's aerospace job is $2,500 per month.

Staci will rent a small building near her home to use as a place for manufacturing the pottery. The rent will be $500 per month. She estimates that the cost of clay and glaze will be $2 for each finished piece of pottery. She will hire workers to produce the pottery at a labour rate of $8 per pot. To sell her pots, Staci feels that she must advertise heavily in the local area. An advertising agency states that it will handle all advertising for a fee of $600 per month. Staci's brother will sell the pots; he will be paid a commission of $4 for each pot sold. Equipment needed to manufacture the pots will be rented at a cost of $300 per month.

Staci has already paid the legal and filing fees associated with incorporating her business in the state. These fees amounted to $500. A small room has been located in a tourist area that Staci will use as a sales office. The rent will be $250 per month. A phone installed in the room for taking orders will cost $40 per month. In addition, a recording device will be attached to the phone for taking after-hours messages.

Staci has some money in savings that is earning interest of $1,200 per year. These savings will be withdrawn and used to get the business going. For the time being, Staci does not intend to draw any salary from the new company.

Required:

1. Prepare an answer sheet with the following column headings:

Name of the Cost	Variable Cost	Fixed Cost	Product Cost			Period (selling and administrative) Cost	Opportunity Cost	Sunk Cost
			Direct Materials	Direct Labour	Manufacturing Overhead			

List the different costs associated with the new company down the extreme left column (under Name of the Cost). Then place an X under each heading that helps describe the type of cost involved. There may be Xs under several column headings for a single cost. (That is, a cost may be a fixed cost, a period cost, and a sunk cost; you would place an X under each of these column headings opposite the cost.)

Under the Variable Cost column, list only those costs that would be variable with respect to the number of units of pottery that are produced and sold.

2. All of the costs you have listed above, except one, would be differential costs between the alternatives of Staci producing pottery or staying with the aerospace firm. Which cost is *not* differential? Explain.

CHECK FIGURE
Boxes for packaging: variable, direct

PROBLEM 2–2   Cost Classification (CC1, 2, 3, 4, 7, 9)

Following are a number of costs typically found in organizations:

1. Property taxes, factory
2. Boxes used for packaging detergent
3. Salespersons' commissions
4. Supervisor's salary, factory
5. Amortization, executive automobiles
6. Wages of workers assembling computers
7. Packing supplies for out-of-state shipments
8. Insurance, finished goods warehouses
9. Lubricants for machines
10. Advertising costs
11. "Chips" used in producing calculators
12. Shipping costs on merchandise sold
13. Magazine subscriptions, factory lunchroom
14. Thread in a garment factory
15. Billing costs
16. Executive life insurance
17. Ink used in textbook production
18. Fringe benefits, assembly-line workers
19. Yarn used in sweater production
20. Wages of receptionist, executive offices

Required:

Prepare an answer sheet with column headings as shown following. For each cost item, indicate whether it would be variable or fixed with respect to the number of units produced and sold; and then whether it would be a selling cost, an administrative cost, or a manufacturing cost. If it is a manufacturing cost, indicate whether it would typically be treated as a direct cost or an indirect cost with respect to units of product. Three sample answers are provided for illustration.

Cost Item	Variable or Fixed	Selling Cost	Administrative Cost	Manufacturing (Product) Cost	
				Direct	Indirect
Direct labour	V			X	
Executive salaries	F		X		
Factory rent	F				X

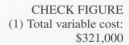

CHECK FIGURE
(1) Total variable cost:
$321,000

PROBLEM 2–3   Cost Identification and Cost Concepts (CC1, 2, 3, 4, 7, 9)
The Dorilane Company specializes in producing a set of wooden patio furniture consisting of a table and four chairs. The set enjoys great popularity, and the company has ample orders to keep production going at its full capacity of 2,000 sets per year. Annual cost data at full capacity follow:

Factory labour, direct............................	$118,000
Advertising	50,000
Factory supervision	40,000
Property taxes, factory building...................	3,500
Sales commissions................................	80,000
Insurance, factory	2,500
Amortization, office equipment....................	4,000
Lease cost, factory equipment....................	12,000
Indirect materials, factory	6,000
Amortization, factory building	10,000
General office supplies (billing)	3,000
General office salaries	60,000
Direct materials used (wood, bolts, etc.)............	94,000
Utilities, factory.................................	20,000

Required:
1. Prepare an answer sheet with the column headings shown following. Enter each cost item on your answer sheet, placing the dollar amount under the appropriate headings. As examples, this has been done already for the first two items in the preceding list. Note that each cost item is classified in two ways: first, as variable or fixed, with respect to the number of units produced and sold; and second, as a selling and administrative cost or a product cost. (If the item is a product cost, it should also be classified as being either direct or indirect as shown.)

	Cost Behaviour		Selling and Administrative Cost	Product Cost	
Cost Item	**Variable**	**Fixed**		**Direct**	**Indirect***
Factory labour, direct............	$118,000			$118,000	
Advertising		$50,000	$50,000		

*To units of product.

2. Total the dollar amounts in each of the columns in part (1). Compute the average product cost per patio set.
3. Assume that production drops to only 1,000 sets annually. Would you expect the average product cost per patio set to increase, decrease, or remain unchanged? Explain. No computations are necessary.
4. Refer to the original data. The president's brother-in-law has considered making himself a patio set and has priced the necessary materials at a building supply store. The brother-in-law has asked the president if he could purchase a patio set from the Dorilane Company "at cost," and the president agreed to let him do so.
   a. Would you expect any disagreement between the two men over the price the brother-in-law should pay? Explain. What price does the president probably have in mind? The brother-in-law?
   b. Since the company is operating at full capacity, what cost term used in the chapter might be justification for the president to charge the full, regular price to the brother-in-law and still be selling "at cost"?

PROBLEM 2–4   Classification of Salary Cost (CC10, 11)
You have just been hired by Ogden Company to fill a new position that was created in response to rapid growth in sales. It is your responsibility to coordinate shipments of finished goods from the factory to distribution warehouses located in various parts of Canada so that goods will be available as orders are received from customers.

The company is unsure how to classify your annual salary in its cost records. The company's cost analyst says that your salary should be classified as a manufacturing (product) cost; the controller says that it should be classified as a selling expense; and the president says that it does not matter which way your salary cost is classified.

Required:
1. Which viewpoint is correct? Why?
2. From the point of view of the reported net income for the year, is the president correct in his statement that it does not matter which way your salary cost is classified? Explain.

CHECK FIGURE
Case 1: Goods available
for sale = $19,000

PROBLEM 2–5   Supplying Missing Data (CC14, 15, 16))
Supply the missing data in the following cases. Each case is independent of the others.

	Case			
	1	**2**	**3**	**4**
Direct materials..................	$ 4,500	$ 6,000	$ 5,000	$ 3,000
Direct labour.....................	?	3,000	7,000	4,000
Manufacturing overhead...........	5,000	4,000	?	9,000
Total manufacturing costs..........	18,500	?	20,000	?
Beginning work-in-process inventory....................	2,500	?	3,000	?
Ending work-in-process inventory ...	?	1,000	4,000	3,000
Cost of goods manufactured........	18,000	14,000	?	?
Sales	30,000	21,000	36,000	40,000
Beginning finished goods inventory....................	1,000	2,500	?	2,000
Cost of goods manufactured........	?	?	?	17,500
Goods available for sale	?	?	?	?
Ending finished goods inventory	?	1,500	4,000	3,500
Cost of goods sold................	17,000	?	18,500	?
Gross margin....................	13,000	?	17,500	?
Operating expenses...............	?	3,500	?	?
Net income	$ 4,000	?	$ 5,000	$ 9,000

CHECK FIGURE
(1) COGM: $310,000

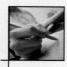

PROBLEM 2–6   Preparing Financial Statements for a Manufacturer (CC13, 14, 15, 16)
Swift Company was organized on March 1 of the current year. After five months of startup losses, management had expected to earn a profit during August, the most recent month. Management was disappointed, however, when the income statement for August also showed a loss. August's income statement follows:

SWIFT COMPANY **Income Statement** **For the Month Ended August 31**	
Sales	$450,000
Less: Operating expenses:	
Indirect labour cost	$ 12,000
Utilities	15,000
Direct labour cost	70,000
Amortization, factory equipment	21,000
Raw materials purchased	165,000
Amortization, sales equipment	18,000

continued

Insurance.....................................	4,000	
Rent on facilities............................	50,000	
Selling and administrative salaries..............	32,000	
Advertising	75,000	462,000
Net loss		$(12,000)

After seeing the $12,000 loss for August, Swift's president stated, "I was sure we'd be profitable within six months, but our six months are up and this loss for August is even worse than July's. I think it's time to start looking for someone to buy out the company's assets—if we don't, within a few months there won't be any assets to sell. By the way, I don't see any reason to look for a new controller. We'll just limp along with Sam for the time being."

The company's controller resigned a month ago. Sam, a new assistant in the controller's office, prepared the income statement above. Sam has had little experience in manufacturing operations. Additional information about the company follows:

a. Some 60% of the utilities cost and 75% of the insurance apply to factory operations. The remaining amounts apply to selling and administrative activities.

b. Inventory balances at the beginning and end of August were:

	August 1	August 31
Raw materials............	$ 8,000	$13,000
Work in process	16,000	21,000
Finished goods	40,000	60,000

c. Only 80% of the rent on facilities applies to factory operations; the remainder applies to selling and administrative activities.

The president has asked you to check over the income statement and make a recommendation as to whether the company should look for a buyer for its assets.

Required:

1. As one step in gathering data for a recommendation to the president, prepare a schedule of cost of goods manufactured in good form for August.
2. As a second step, prepare a new income statement for August.
3. On the basis of your statements prepared in parts (1) and (2), would you recommend that the company look for a buyer?

PROBLEM 2–7   Financial Statements; Cost Behaviour (CC1, 2, 13, 14, 15, 16)
Various cost and sales data for Meriwell Company for the just completed year follow:

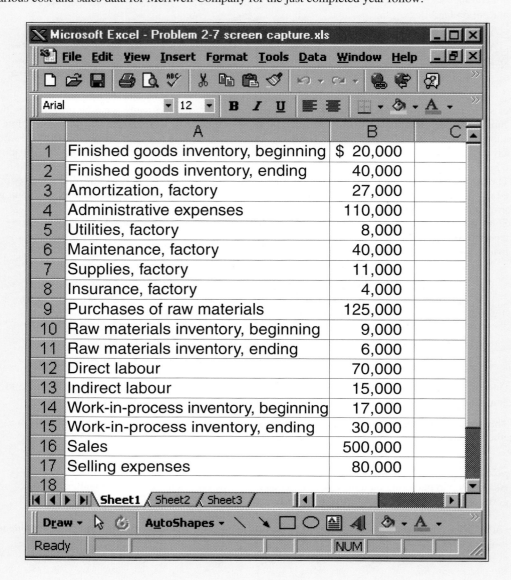

	A	B	C
1	Finished goods inventory, beginning	$ 20,000	
2	Finished goods inventory, ending	40,000	
3	Amortization, factory	27,000	
4	Administrative expenses	110,000	
5	Utilities, factory	8,000	
6	Maintenance, factory	40,000	
7	Supplies, factory	11,000	
8	Insurance, factory	4,000	
9	Purchases of raw materials	125,000	
10	Raw materials inventory, beginning	9,000	
11	Raw materials inventory, ending	6,000	
12	Direct labour	70,000	
13	Indirect labour	15,000	
14	Work-in-process inventory, beginning	17,000	
15	Work-in-process inventory, ending	30,000	
16	Sales	500,000	
17	Selling expenses	80,000	
18			

Required:
1. Prepare a schedule of cost of goods manufactured.
2. Prepare an income statement.
3. Assume that the company produced the equivalent of 10,000 units of product during the year just completed. What was the average cost per unit for direct materials? What was the average cost per unit for factory amortization?
4. Assume that the company expects to produce 15,000 units of product during the coming year. What average cost per unit and what total cost would you expect the company to incur for direct materials at this level of activity? For factory amortization? (In preparing your answer, assume that direct materials is a variable cost and that amortization is a fixed cost; also assume that amortization is computed on a straight-line basis.)
5. As the manager responsible for production costs, explain to the president any difference in the average cost per unit between parts (3) and (4).

PROBLEM 2–8   Financial Statements; Cost Behaviour (CC1, 2, 13, 14, 15, 16)
Selected account balances for the year ended December 31 are provided following for Superior Company:

CHECK FIGURE
(1) COGM: $690,000

Selling and administrative salaries	$110,000
Insurance, factory	8,000
Utilities, factory	45,000
Purchases of raw materials	290,000
Indirect labour	60,000
Direct labour	?
Advertising expense	80,000
Cleaning supplies, factory	7,000
Sales commissions	50,000
Rent, factory building	120,000
Maintenance, factory	30,000

Inventory balances at the beginning and end of the year were as follows:

	Beginning of the Year	End of the Year
Raw materials	$40,000	$10,000
Work in process	?	35,000
Finished goods	50,000	?

The total manufacturing costs for the year were $683,000; the goods available for sale totalled $740,000; and the cost of goods sold totalled $660,000.

Required:
1. Prepare a schedule of cost of goods manufactured in good form and the cost of goods sold section of the company's income statement for the year.
2. Assume that the dollar amounts given above are for the equivalent of 40,000 units produced during the year. Compute the average cost per unit for direct materials used and the average cost per unit for rent on the factory building.
3. Assume that in the following year the company expects to produce 50,000 units. What average cost per unit and total cost would you expect to be incurred for direct materials? For rent on the factory building? (In preparing your answer, you may assume that direct materials is a variable cost and that rent is a fixed cost.)
4. As the manager in charge of production costs, explain to the president the reason for any difference in average cost per unit between parts (2) and (3).

PROBLEM 2–9   Cost of Goods Manufactured, Sold (CC14, 15, 16)
You have the following information about the activities of Xavier Inc., for 2007:

CHECK FIGURE
(4) $44,600

Sales	$500,000
Factory maintenance	24,000
Indirect labour	19,000
Direct material purchases	98,000

continued

Factory utilities	17,000
Direct materials used in production	95,000
General and administrative expenses	71,200
Beginning work-in-process inventory	26,000
Beginning finished goods inventory	63,000
Ending work-in-process inventory	34,000
Beginning direct materials inventory	13,000
Selling expenses	67,600
Direct labour	83,000
Factory insurance	9,000
Indirect materials	7,600
Amortization — factory	30,000
Cost of goods sold	295,000

Required:
1. What was amount of the ending direct materials inventory?
2. What was the amount of the total manufacturing costs?
3. What was the cost of goods manufactured in 2007?
4. What was the amount of the ending finished goods inventory?

(Adapted © CGA-Canada)

CHECK FIGURE
(2) $60,500

PROBLEM 2–10   Computation of Manufacturing Costs (CC10, 11, 14)
Magnito Ltd. incurred the following costs last year:

Direct materials	$90,000
Direct labour	25,000
Indirect labour	3,000
Indirect materials	4,000

Other operating expenses pertaining to factory operations were as follows:

Utilities	$ 3,500
Maintenance	5,000
Supplies	2,000
Amortization	15,000
Property taxes	3,000

The only inventory was $7,000 of finished goods at year end.

Required:
1. What was the prime cost?
2. What was the conversion cost incurred?
3. What was the cost of goods sold?

(Adapted © CGA-Canada)

CHECK FIGURE
(1) $230,000

PROBLEM 2–11   Manufacturing Costs; Inventory Calculation (CC13, 14, 15, 16)
The following partial income statement information is available for Frodo Products for June 2008:

Sales	$600,000
Beginning finished goods inventory	300,000

continued

Cost of goods manufactured	270,000
Net income	60,000
Nonmanufacturing costs	200,000

Required:
1. What was the value of the ending inventory of finished goods?
2. If the beginning work-in-process inventory was $120,000 and there was no ending work-in-process inventory, what was the total manufacturing cost in June 2008?

(Adapted © CGA-Canada)

Building Your Skills

ANALYTICAL THINKING (CC13, 14, 15, 16)
Visic Company, a manufacturing firm, produces a single product. The following information has been taken from the company's production, sales, and cost records for the just completed year.

CHECK FIGURE
(1) COGM: $870,000

Production in units	29,000
Sales in units.....................................	?
Ending finished goods inventory in units	?
Sales in dollars	$1,300,000
Costs:	
Advertising	105,000
Entertainment and travel..........................	40,000
Direct labour.....................................	90,000
Indirect labour...................................	85,000
Raw materials purchased	480,000
Building rent (production uses 80% of the space; administrative and sales offices use the rest)	40,000
Utilities, factory	108,000
Royalty paid for use of production patent, $1.50 per unit produced	?
Maintenance, factory	9,000
Rent for special production equipment, $7,000 per year plus $0.30 per unit produced	?
Selling and administrative salaries.................	210,000
Other factory overhead costs	6,800
Other selling and administrative expenses	17,000

	Beginning of the Year	End of the Year
Inventories:		
Raw materials	$20,000	$30,000
Work in process.................	50,000	40,000
Finished goods	–0–	?

The finished goods inventory is being carried at the average unit production cost for the year. The selling price of the product is $50 per unit.

Required:
1. Prepare a schedule of goods manufactured for the year.
2. Compute the following:
   a. The number of units in the finished goods inventory at the end of the year
   b. The cost of the units in the finished goods inventory at the end of the year
3. Prepare an income statement for the year.

CHECK FIGURE
(2) COGM: $780,000

COMMUNICATING IN PRACTICE   (CC10, 11, 12, 13, 14, 15, 16)

"I was sure that when our battery hit the market it would be an instant success," said Roger Strong, founder and president of Solar Technology, Inc. "But just look at the gusher of red ink for the first quarter. It's obvious that we're better scientists than we are businesspeople." The data to which Roger was referring follow:

SOLAR TECHNOLOGY, INC. Income Statement For the Quarter Ended March 31		
Sales (32,000 batteries).............................		$960,000
Less: Operating expenses:		
Selling and administrative salaries	$110,000	
Advertising	90,000	
Maintenance, production	43,000	
Indirect labour cost	120,000	
Cleaning supplies, production..................	7,000	
Purchases of raw materials	360,000	
Rental cost, facilities........................	75,000	
Insurance, production	8,000	
Amortization, office equipment	27,000	
Utilities	80,000	
Amortization, production equipment	100,000	
Direct labour cost	70,000	
Travel, salespersons	40,000	
Total operating expenses........................		1,130,000
Net loss		$(170,000)

"At this rate we'll be out of business within a year," said Cindy Zhang, the company's accountant. "But I've double-checked these figures, so I know they're right."

Solar Technology was organized at the beginning of the current year to produce and market a revolutionary new solar battery. The company's accounting system was set up by Margie Wallace, an experienced accountant who recently left the company to do independent consulting work. The statement above was prepared by Zhang, her assistant.

"We may not last a year if the insurance company doesn't pay the $226,000 it owes us for the 8,000 batteries lost in the warehouse fire last week," said Roger. "The insurance adjuster says our claim is inflated, but he's just trying to pressure us into a lower figure. We have the data to back up our claim, and it will stand up in any court."

On April 3, just after the end of the first quarter, the company's finished goods storage area was swept by fire and all 8,000 unsold batteries were destroyed. (These batteries were part of the 40,000 units completed during the first quarter.) The company's insurance policy states that the company will be reimbursed for the "cost" of any finished batteries destroyed or stolen. Zhang has determined this cost as follows:

$$\frac{\text{Total costs for the quarter, } \$1,130,000}{\text{Batteries produced during the quarter, } 40,000} = \$28.25 \text{ per battery}$$

$$8,000 \text{ batteries} \times \$28.25 \text{ per battery} = \$226,000$$

The following additional information is available on the company's activities during the quarter ended March 31:

a. Inventories at the beginning and end of the quarter were as follows:

	Beginning of the Quarter	End of the Quarter
Raw materials	–0–	$10,000
Work in process	–0–	50,000
Finished goods	–0–	?

b. 80% of the rental cost for facilities and 90% of the utilities cost relate to manufacturing operations. The remaining amounts relate to selling and administrative activities.

Required:

1. Write a brief memorandum to the president identifying what conceptual errors, if any, were made in preparing the income statement above.
2. Prepare a schedule of cost of goods manufactured for the first quarter.
3. Prepare a corrected income statement for the first quarter. Your statement should show in detail how the cost of goods sold is computed.
4. Do you agree that the insurance company owes Solar Technology, Inc. $226,000? Explain your answer in another brief memorandum to the president.

ETHICS CHALLENGE   (CC10, 11)

M. K. Gallant is president of Kranbrack Corporation, a company whose shares are traded on a national exchange. In a meeting with investment analysts at the beginning of the year, Gallant had predicted that the company's earnings would grow by 20% this year. Unfortunately, sales have been less than expected for the year, and Gallant concluded within two weeks of the end of the fiscal year that it would be impossible to ultimately report an increase in earnings as large as predicted unless some drastic action was taken. Accordingly, Gallant has ordered that wherever possible, expenditures should be postponed to the new year—including cancelling or postponing orders with suppliers, delaying planned maintenance and training, and cutting back on end-of-year advertising and travel. Additionally, Gallant ordered the company's controller to carefully scrutinize all costs that are currently classified as period costs and reclassify as many as possible as product costs. The company is expected to have substantial inventories of work in process and finished goods at the end of the year.

Required:

1. Why would reclassifying period costs as product costs increase this period's reported earnings?
2. Do you believe Gallant's actions are ethical? Why or why not?

TEAMWORK IN ACTION   (CC1, 2)

Steel production involves a large amount of fixed costs. Since competition is defined primarily in terms of price, steel manufacturers (and many of their manufacturing and service industry counterparts) try to gain a competitive advantage by using economies of scale and investment in technology to increase productivity and drive unit costs lower. Their substantial fixed costs are the result of their size.

Required:

1. The team should discuss and then write descriptions of the definitions of fixed costs and variable costs.
2. Each member of the team should select one of the following types of businesses and perform the following: (a) give examples of fixed costs and variable costs that would be incurred by that type of business, (b) choose a relevant measure of production or service activity for that type of business, and (c) explain the relationship between the production (or service) output and each of the following: total fixed costs, fixed cost per unit, total variable costs, and variable cost per unit.
   a. Steel company
   b. Hospital
   c. University
   d. Auto manufacturer

Each team member should present his or her notes to the other teammates, who should confirm or correct the presentation. Then, work together as a team to complete steps 3 through 6 following.

3. Using the examples of fixed and variable costs for steel companies from (a) above, explain the relationship between production output at a steel company and each of the following: total fixed costs, fixed cost per unit, total variable costs, variable cost per unit, total costs, and average unit cost.

4. With an *X*-axis (horizontal axis) of tonnes produced and a *Y*-axis (vertical axis) of total costs, graph total fixed costs, total variable costs, and total costs against tonnes produced.

5. With an *X*-axis of tonnes produced and a *Y*-axis of unit costs, graph fixed cost per unit, variable cost per unit, and total (or average) cost per unit against tonnes produced.

6. Explain how costs (total and per unit) behave with changes in demand once capacity has been set.

Don't forget to visit the Online Learning Centre for self-study quizzes, practice exams, and more! Visit www.mcgrawhill.ca/olc/brewer.

CHAPTER *Three*

Cost Behaviour: Analysis and Use

CHAPTER COMPETENCIES

After studying Chapter 3, you should be able to demonstrate the following competencies:

Competency	Know	Apply
Understand cost behaviour.		
CC1 Describe the behaviour of variable costs.	●	
CC2 Describe the behaviour of step-variable costs.	●	
CC3 Describe the behaviour of fixed costs.	●	
CC4 Explain committed and discretionary fixed costs.	●	
CC5 Explain the importance of relevant range in understanding fixed costs.	●	
CC6 Describe the behaviour of mixed costs.	●	
Analyze and estimate costs.		
CC7 Construct a basic linear cost equation.		●
CC8 Explain the individual elements of the cost equation.	●	
CC9 Explain the importance of separating mixed costs into fixed and variable portions.	●	
CC10 Describe the high-low method of analyzing mixed costs.	●	
CC11 Set up a cost equation using the high-low method.		●
CC12 Explain the scattergraph method of analyzing mixed costs.	●	
CC13 Set up a cost equation using the scattergraph method.		●
CC14 Explain the least-squares regression method of analyzing mixed costs.	●	
CC15 Set up a cost equation using the least-squares regression method.		●
Compute contribution margin and income.		
CC16 Explain the concept of contribution margin and prepare a contribution margin income statement.	●	●

DECISION FEATURE
Back on Track

Imagine a company operating in the railroad industry derailing. After suffering a loss in 2001, management at Calgary-based Global Railway Industries Limited knew it was time to get back on track.

Global Railway is a fast-growing company that has pursued an aggressive "growth by acquisition" strategy; it offers its products and services to rail and transit carriers through its five operating subsidiaries: three Canadian and two American. This acquisition strategy allowed Global to expand its offerings and its customer base. Needless to say, this strategy has delivered the results. Sales increased from $7.1 million in 2001 to $29.9 million in 2005.

Just increasing sales was not enough to remain on track, and Mike Kohut, President and CEO, recognized this fact. With a view to increasing the gross margin, he encouraged his company to convert to a largely variable cost structure. This could translate into higher efficiencies because the company did not have a large amount of fixed resources, and what it had was not being fully utilized. A thorough understanding of costs with a focus on cost behaviour can position the company to better understand the implications of fixed versus variable cost structures on profitability. Kohut was bang on target; gross margin has remained steady at about 37% of sales over the last three years.

Sources: L. Yturralde, "Bay Street's Boarding Global Railway," www.investorfile.com, Special Report, November 7, 2003; Financial Reports of Global Railway available at www.globalrailway.com.

A Look Back

We introduced managerial accounting in Chapter 1, followed by various cost concepts in Chapter 2.

A Look at This Chapter

After reviewing the behaviour of variable and fixed costs in Chapter 2, in Chapter 3 we will discuss mixed costs, a third type of behavioural pattern, and provide an overview of the methods that can be used to break a mixed cost into its variable and fixed components. We also introduce the contribution format income statement, which is used for internal decision making.

A Look Ahead

Chapters 4, 5, and 6 describe costing systems that are used to compute product/service costs. Specifically, Chapters 4 and 5 describe two contrasting costing systems: job-order costing and process costing, whereas Chapter 6 describes activity-based costing, an approach to cost allocation and cost management.

█n our discussion of cost terms and concepts in Chapter 2, we stated that one way in which costs can be classified is by behaviour. We defined cost behaviour as the way a cost reacts or changes as changes take place in the level of business activity. An understanding of cost behaviour is the key to many decisions in an organization. Managers who understand how costs behave are better able to predict costs under various operating circumstances. Attempts at planning and decision making without a thorough understanding of the costs involved—and how these costs may change with the activity level—can lead to disaster. For example, a decision to cut back a particular product line might result in far less cost savings than managers had assumed if they confuse variable and fixed costs—leading to a decline in profits. To avoid such problems, a manager must be able to accurately predict what costs will be at various activity levels. In this chapter, we shall find that the key to effective cost prediction lies in understanding variable and fixed costs. (Planning and decision-making topics are covered in the later chapters of this text.)

We briefly review in this chapter the definitions of variable costs and fixed costs, and then discuss the behaviour of these costs in greater depth than we were able to do in Chapter 2. After this review and discussion, we turn our attention to the analysis of mixed costs. We conclude the chapter by introducing a new income statement format—called the *contribution format*—in which costs are organized by behaviour rather than by the traditional functions of production, sales, and administration.

Types of Cost Behaviour Patterns

In Chapter 2, we mentioned only variable and fixed costs. In this chapter, we will discuss a third behaviour pattern, generally known as a *mixed* cost. All three cost behaviour patterns—variable, fixed, and mixed—are found in most organizations. The relative proportion of each type of cost present in a firm is known as the firm's **cost structure.** For example, a firm might have many fixed costs, but few variable or mixed costs. Alternatively, it might have many variable costs, but few fixed or mixed costs. A firm's cost structure can have a significant impact on decisions. In this chapter, we will concentrate on getting a better understanding of the behaviour of each type of cost.

IN BUSINESS TODAY   **What Are the Costs?**

The fall of Nortel Networks Corporation left many shareholders and employees with a bad taste in their mouths. The telecommunications behemoth kept expanding as much as it could until the broadband capacity was no longer sustainable. The rates for long distance calls, wireless services, and data transmission were heading toward zero. Pricing was something the company should have taken into account, since it was obvious that there was too much capacity and too much competition in the marketplace. However, the market continued to expand rapidly.

Nortel's fatal mistake was not anticipating the huge collapse of the market. Specifically, it should have eliminated all its fixed costs and transformed the company into a variable costing operation in order for operating profits to not be hurt so badly. In other words, costs and revenues would drop little by little to mitigate the effects of the loss.

Source: Fred Lazar, "What's Next for Nortel?" *Financial Post (National Post)*, August 15, 2001, p. C15. Reprinted with permission from Fred Lazar.

Variable Costs

We explained in Chapter 2 that a variable cost is a cost whose total dollar amount varies in direct proportion to changes in the activity level. If the activity level doubles, the total dollar amount of the variable cost also doubles. If the activity level increases by only 10%, then the total dollar amount of the variable cost increases by 10% as well.

We also found in Chapter 2 that a variable cost remains constant when expressed on a *per-unit* basis. To provide an example, consider 50 Plus Expeditions, a Toronto-based company that organizes adventure travel for people over 50. Among other things, the company provides all of the necessary equipment and experienced guides, and serves meals to its guests. Assume that the meals cost $30 per person for a daylong excursion. If we look at the cost of the meals on a *per-person* basis, the cost remains constant at $30. This unit cost of $30 per person will not change, regardless of how many people participate in a daylong excursion. The behaviour of this variable cost, on both per-unit and total bases, is tabulated below:

● **KNOW**

CC1: Describe the behaviour of variable costs.

Number of Guests	Cost of Meals per Guest	Total Cost of Meals
250	$30	$ 7,500
500	30	15,000
750	30	22,500
1,000	30	30,000

The idea that a variable cost is constant per unit, but varies in total with the activity level, is crucial to an understanding of cost behaviour patterns. We shall rely on this concept again and again in this chapter and in the chapters ahead.

Exhibit 3–1 provides a graphical illustration of variable cost behaviour. Notice that the graph of the total cost of the meals slants upward to the right because the total cost of the meals is directly proportional to the number of guests. In contrast, the graph of the per-unit cost of meals is flat because the cost of the meals per guest is constant at $30 per guest.

Exhibit 3–1

Variable Cost Behaviour

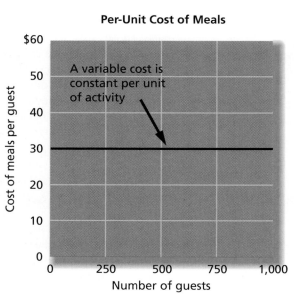

Westjet's Low Cost Strategy

From four destinations in Western Canada to 24 across Canada, and from 220 employees to about 6,000, WestJet Airlines Ltd. has come a long way in its twelve years of existence as a friendly, efficient, and low-fare airline. One of WestJet's highlights is that between 1997 and 2006 it made money ever year except just one! This can be considered exceptional given the increased challenges facing the airline industry, such as fuel, taxes, and safety.

The airline industry is one in which fixed costs are very high compared to the variable costs. What, then, is WestJet's secret? According to the company, its secret is that it has successfully implemented a low-cost strategy, meaning it has effectively managed its costs while still providing customers with a unique flying experience. Three key components underlie this strategy:

- Simplicity—using a single type of aircraft, maintaining a lean organizational structure, and employing a simplified route structure and operations
- Technology—using technology to lower costs
- Utilization—maximizing aircraft utilization (this is absolutely critical in generating revenues to offset the high fixed costs)

Source: www.westjet.com

THE ACTIVITY BASE   For a cost to be variable, it must be variable *with respect to something*. That "something" is its *activity base*. An **activity base** is a measure of whatever causes the incurrence of variable cost. An activity base is also sometimes referred to as a *cost driver*. Some of the most common activity bases are direct labour-hours, machine-hours, units produced, volume of goods sold or services provided, and number of customers served. Other activity bases (cost drivers) might include the number of miles driven by salespersons, the number of kilograms of laundry cleaned by a hotel, the number of letters typed by a secretary, and the number of beds occupied in a hospital.

To plan and control variable costs, a manager must be well acquainted with the various activity bases within the firm. People sometimes have the notion that if a cost does not vary with production or with sales, then it is not really a variable cost. This is not correct. As suggested by the range of bases listed above, costs are caused by many different activities within an organization. Whether a cost is considered to be variable depends on whether it is caused by the activity under consideration. For example, if a manager is analyzing the cost of service calls, the relevant activity measure will be the number of service calls made. Those costs that vary in total with the number of service calls made are the variable costs of making service calls.

Nevertheless, unless stated otherwise, you can assume that the activity base under consideration is the total volume of goods and services provided by the organization. So, for example, if we ask whether direct materials at Ford is a variable cost, the answer is yes, since the cost of direct materials is variable with respect to Ford's total volume of output. We will specify the activity base only when it is something other than total output.

Budget Analyst

You are the budget analyst for a firm that provides janitorial services to other companies. You have been asked to estimate the costs that will be incurred on the janitorial jobs that will be performed next year. What types of costs would you expect? How would you characterize these costs in terms of behaviour? What activity would you need to measure in order to estimate the costs?

EXTENT OF VARIABLE COSTS   The number and type of variable costs present in an organization will depend in large part on the organization's structure and purpose. A public utility, such as BC Hydro with large investments in equipment, will tend to have few variable costs. Most of the costs are associated with its plant, and these costs tend to be insensitive to changes in levels of service provided. A manufacturing company, such as Black & Decker, in contrast, will often have many variable costs; these costs will be associated with both the manufacture and distribution of its products to customers.

A merchandising company, such as Wal-Mart or Safeway will usually have a high proportion of variable costs in its cost structure. In most merchandising companies, the cost of merchandise purchased for resale, a variable cost, constitutes a large component of total cost. Service companies, by contrast, have diverse cost structures. On the one hand, some service companies, such as the Boston Pizza restaurant chain, have fairly large variable costs because of the costs of their raw materials. On the other hand, service companies involved in consulting, auditing, engineering, dental, medical, and architectural activities have very large fixed costs in the form of expensive facilities and highly trained salaried employees.

Some of the more frequently encountered variable costs are listed in Exhibit 3–2. This exhibit is not a complete listing of all costs that can be considered variable. Moreover, some of the costs listed in the exhibit may behave more like fixed than variable costs in some firms. We will see some examples of this later in the chapter. Nevertheless, Exhibit 3–2 provides a useful listing of many of the costs that normally would be considered variable with respect to the volume of output.

Exhibit 3–2
Examples of Variable Costs

Type of Organization	Costs that Are Normally Variable with Respect to Volume of Output
Merchandising company	Cost of goods (merchandise) sold

Manufacturing company	Manufacturing costs:
	    Direct materials
	    Direct labour*
	Variable portion of manufacturing overhead:
	    Indirect materials
	    Lubricants
	    Supplies

Both merchandising and manufacturing companies	Selling, general, and administrative costs:
	    Commissions
	    Clerical costs, such as invoicing
	    Shipping costs

Service organizations	Supplies, travel, clerical

*Direct labour may or may not be variable in practice. See the discussion later in this chapter.

True Variable Versus Step-Variable Costs

Not all variable costs have exactly the same behaviour pattern. Some variable costs behave in a *true variable* or *proportionately variable* pattern. Other variable costs behave in a *step-variable* pattern. Let us examine these costs using Boston Pizza as an example.

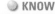
KNOW

CC2: Describe the behaviour of step-variable costs.

TRUE VARIABLE COSTS   **True variable costs** are those that vary in direct proportion to changes in the level of activity. Direct materials is a true or proportionately variable cost because the amount used during a period will vary in direct proportion to the number of customers served or pizzas served. Moreover, any amounts purchased but not used can be stored and carried forward to the next period as inventory (remember that JIT purchasing is extremely important in the restaurant business because direct materials are perishable items).

STEP-VARIABLE COSTS   A cost that is obtainable only in large chunks and increases or decreases only in response to fairly wide changes in the activity level is known as a **step-variable cost.** The behaviour of a step-variable cost, contrasted with the behaviour of a true variable cost, is illustrated in Exhibit 3–3.

For example, the need for waiters changes only with fairly wide changes in the number of customers, and when additional waiter time is obtained, it comes in large, indivisible chunks. The strategy of management in dealing with step-variable costs must be to obtain the fullest use of services possible for each step. Great care must be taken in working with these kinds of costs to prevent "fat" (or excess) from building up in an organization. There may be a tendency to employ additional help more quickly than needed, and there is a natural reluctance to lay people off when volume declines.

Exhibit 3–3
True Variable versus Step-Variable Costs

Direct Materials (true variable)

Cost

Volume

Waiters (step variable)

Cost

Volume

Coping with the Fallout from September 11

Costs can change for reasons having nothing to do with changes in volume. Filterfresh Coffee Service Inc. services office coffee machines, providing milk, sugar, cups, and coffee. The company's operations were profoundly affected by the security measures many companies initiated after the terrorist attacks on the World Trade Center and the Pentagon on September 11, 2001. Heightened security at customer locations means that Filterfresh's 250 deliverymen can no longer casually walk through a customer's lobby with a load of supplies. Now a guard typically checks the deliveryman's identification and paperwork at the loading dock and may search the van before permitting the deliveryman access to the customer's building. These delays have added an average of about an hour per day to each route, which means that Filterfresh needs 24 more delivery people to do the same work it did prior to September 11. That's a 10% increase in cost without any increase in the amount of coffee sold.

Source: Anna Bernasek, "The Friction Economy," *Fortune*, February 18, 2002, pp. 104–112.

The Linearity Assumption and the Relevant Range

In dealing with variable costs, we have assumed a strictly linear relationship between cost and volume, except in the case of step-variable costs. Economists correctly point out that many costs classified as variable by the accountant actually behave in a *curvilinear* fashion. The behaviour of a **curvilinear cost** is shown in Exhibit 3–4.

Although many costs are not strictly linear when plotted as a function of volume, a curvilinear cost can be satisfactorily approximated with a straight line within a narrow band of activity known as the *relevant range*. The **relevant range** is the range of activity within which the assumptions made about cost behaviour by the manager are valid. For example, notice that the dashed line in Exhibit 3–4 can be used as an approximation to the curvilinear cost with little loss of accuracy within the shaded relevant range. However, outside of the relevant range, this particular straight line is a poor approximation to the curvilinear cost relationship. Managers should always keep in mind that a particular assumption made about cost behaviour may be inappropriate if activity falls outside of the relevant range.

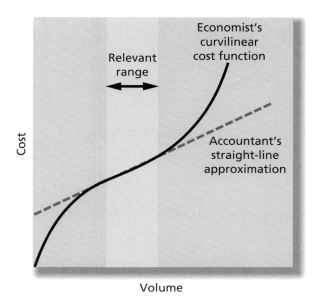

Exhibit 3–4
Curvilinear Costs and the Relevant Range

Fixed Costs

In our discussion of cost behaviour patterns in Chapter 2, we stated that fixed costs remain constant in total dollar amount within the relevant range of activity. To continue the 50 Plus Expeditions example, assume the company decides to rent a building for $500 per month to store its equipment. The *total* amount of rent paid is the same, regardless of the number of guests the company takes on its expeditions during any given month. This cost behaviour pattern is shown graphically in Exhibit 3–5.

Since fixed costs remain constant in total, the amount of fixed costs computed on a *per-unit* basis becomes progressively smaller as the level of activity increases. If 50 Plus Expeditions has only 250 guests in a month, the $500 fixed rental cost would amount to $2 per guest. If there are 1,000 guests, the fixed rental cost would amount to only 50 cents per guest. This aspect of the behaviour of fixed costs is also displayed in Exhibit 3–5. Observe that as the number of guests increases, the average unit cost drops, but it drops at a decreasing rate. The first guests have the biggest impact on unit costs.

As we noted in Chapter 2, this aspect of fixed costs can be confusing, although it is necessary in some contexts to express fixed costs on an average per-unit basis. Fixed costs are sometimes expressed on a per-unit basis (i.e., unitized). In such situations, users of the information must be cautioned that fixed costs have been unitized and should not be mistaken for variable costs. For example, if Boston Pizza allocates building rent at $0.25 per pizza, this does not mean that rent cost will increase by $0.25 each time a pizza is served. The amount of $0.25 per pizza is simply an average cost based on a certain volume of pizzas served and really has no meaning for decision-making purposes. This amount is allocated so that managers understand that the total cost of a pizza is *more than* the sum of all the variable costs. From a decision-making angle, this information can be useful for

KNOW

CC3: Describe the behaviour of fixed costs.

Exhibit 3–5
Fixed Cost Behaviour

pricing purposes; and from an analysis perspective, total cost information is useful to understand profitability.

Types of Fixed Costs

Fixed costs are sometimes referred to as *capacity costs*, since they result from outlays made for buildings, equipment, skilled professional employees, and other items needed to provide the basic capacity for sustained operations. For planning purposes, fixed costs can be viewed as being either *committed* or *discretionary*.

COMMITTED FIXED COSTS   **Committed fixed costs** relate to the investment in facilities, equipment, and the basic organizational structure of a firm. Examples of such costs include amortization of buildings and equipment, taxes on real estate, insurance, and salaries of top management and operating personnel.

Committed fixed costs are long term in nature and cannot be reduced to zero even for short periods without seriously impairing the profitability or long-term goals of the organization. Even if operations are interrupted or cut back, the committed fixed costs will still continue largely unchanged. During a recession, for example, a firm will not usually discharge key executives or sell off key facilities. The basic organizational structure and facilities ordinarily are kept intact. The costs of restoring them later are likely to be far greater than any short-term savings that might be realized.

Since it is difficult to change a committed fixed cost once the commitment has been made, management should approach these decisions with particular care. Decisions to acquire major equipment or to take on other committed fixed costs involve a long planning horizon. Management should make such commitments only after careful analysis of the available alternatives. Once a decision is made to build a certain size facility, a firm becomes locked into that decision for many years to come. Decisions relating to committed fixed costs will be examined in Chapter 12.

DISCRETIONARY FIXED COSTS   **Discretionary fixed costs** (often referred to as *managed fixed costs*) usually arise from *annual* decisions by management to spend in certain fixed cost areas. Examples of discretionary fixed costs include advertising, research, public relations, management development programs, and internships for students.

Basically, two key differences exist between discretionary fixed costs and committed fixed costs. First, the planning horizon for a discretionary fixed cost is fairly short term—usually a single year. By contrast, as previously indicated, committed fixed costs have a planning horizon that encompasses many years. Second, discretionary fixed costs can be cut for short periods with minimal damage to the long-term goals of the organization. For example, spending on management development programs can be cut back because of poor economic conditions. Although some unfavourable consequences may result from the cutback, it is doubtful that these consequences would be as great as those that would result if the company decided to economize during the year by laying off key personnel.

Whether a particular cost is regarded as committed or discretionary may depend on management's strategy. For example, during recessions when the level of home building is down, many construction companies lay off most of their workers and virtually disband operations. Other construction companies retain large numbers of employees on the payroll, even though the workers have little or no work to do. While these latter companies may be faced with short-term cash flow problems, it will be easier for them to respond quickly when economic conditions improve. And, the improved morale and loyalty of their employees may give these companies a significant competitive advantage.

The most important characteristic of discretionary fixed costs is that management is not locked into a decision regarding such costs. They can be adjusted from year to year, or even perhaps during the course of a year, if circumstances demand such a modification.

THE TREND TOWARD FIXED COSTS   The trend in many industries is toward greater fixed costs relative to variable costs. Chores that used to be performed by hand have been taken over by machines. For example, an H&R Block employee used to fill out tax returns for customers by hand and the advice given to a customer largely depended on the knowledge of that particular employee. Now, sophisticated computer software is used to complete tax returns, and the software provides the customer with tax planning and other advice tailored to the customer's needs on the basis of the accumulated knowledge of many experts. The move towards online banking and shopping has also necessitated these organizations to invest more in technology and support structure.

As machines take over more and more of the tasks that were performed by humans, the overall demand for human workers has not diminished. The demand for *knowledge workers*—those who work primarily with their minds, rather than their muscles—has grown tremendously. Knowledge workers tend to be salaried, highly trained, and difficult to replace. As a consequence, the costs of compensating knowledge workers are often relatively fixed and are committed, rather than discretionary, costs.

IS LABOUR A VARIABLE OR A FIXED COST?   As the preceding discussion suggests, wages and salaries may be fixed or variable. The behaviour of wage and salary costs will differ from one country to another, depending on labour regulations, labour contracts, and custom. In some countries, such as France, Germany, China, and Japan, management has little flexibility in adjusting the labour force to changes in business activity. In such countries as Canada, management typically has much greater latitude. However, even in less restrictive environments, managers may choose to treat employee compensation as a fixed cost for several reasons.

First, many organizations have become much more reluctant to adjust the workforce in response to short-term fluctuations in sales. Most organizations realize that their employees are an extremely valuable asset. More and more, highly skilled and trained employees are required to run a successful business, and these workers are not easy to replace. Trained workers who are laid off may never return, and layoffs undermine the morale of those workers who remain.

In addition, managers do not want to be caught with a bloated payroll in an economic downturn. Therefore, there is an increased reluctance to add workers when sales activity picks up. Many organizations are turning to temporary and part-time workers to pick up the slack when their permanent, full-time employees are unable to handle all of the demand for the company's products and services. In such companies, labour costs are a mixture of fixed and variable costs.

Many major organizations have undergone waves of downsizing in recent years in which large numbers of employees—particularly middle managers—have lost their jobs. It may seem that this downsizing proves that even management salaries should be regarded as variable costs, but this would not be a valid conclusion. Downsizing has been the result of attempts to re-engineer business processes and cut costs, rather than a response to a decline in sales activity. This underscores an important, but subtle, point. Fixed costs can change—they just do not change in response to small changes in activity.

In summary, we cannot provide a clear-cut answer to the question "Is labour a variable or fixed cost?" It depends on how much flexibility management has and management's strategy. *Nevertheless, we will assume in this text that, unless otherwise stated, direct labour is a variable cost*. This assumption is less likely to be valid for organizations in countries where employment laws permit much less flexibility.

IN BUSINESS TODAY   ## Labour at Southwest Airlines

Starting with a $10,000 investment in 1966, Herb Kelleher built Southwest Airlines Co. into the most profitable airline in the United States. Prior to stepping down as president and CEO of the airline in 2001, Kelleher wrote: "The thing that would disturb me most to see after I'm no longer CEO is layoffs at Southwest. Nothing kills your company's culture like layoffs. Nobody has ever been furloughed here, and that is unprecedented in the airline industry. It's been a huge strength of ours . . . We could have furloughed at various times and been more profitable, but I always thought that was shortsighted. You want to show your people that you value them and you're not going to hurt them just to get a little money in the short run."

Because of this commitment by management to the company's employees, all wages and salaries are basically committed fixed costs at Southwest Airlines.

Source: Herb Kelleher, "The Chairman of the Board Looks Back," *Fortune*, May 28, 2001, pp. 63–76.

Fixed Costs and the Relevant Range

⬤ KNOW

CC5: Explain the importance of relevant range in understanding fixed costs.

The concept of the relevant range, which was introduced in the discussion of variable costs, is also important in understanding fixed costs—particularly discretionary fixed costs. The levels of discretionary fixed costs are typically decided at the beginning of the year and depend on the support needs of planned programs, such as advertising and training. The scope of these programs will depend, in turn, on the overall anticipated level of activity for the year. At very high levels of activity, programs are usually broadened or expanded. For example, if a law firm hopes to increase revenues by 25%, it would probably plan for much larger advertising costs than if no increase were planned. So, the *planned* level of activity might affect total discretionary fixed costs. However, once the total discretionary fixed costs have been budgeted, they are unaffected by the *actual* level of activity. For example, once the advertising budget has been decided and has been spent, it will not be affected by the actual increase in revenues. Therefore, the cost is fixed with respect to the *actual* revenues.

Discretionary fixed costs are easier to adjust than committed fixed costs. They also tend to be less *lumpy*. Committed fixed costs consist of costs such as buildings, equipment, and the salaries of key personnel. It is difficult to buy half a piece of equipment or to hire a quarter of a sales manager; thus, the step pattern depicted in Exhibit 3–6 is typical for such costs. The relevant range of activity for a fixed cost is the range of activity over which the graph of the cost is flat as in Exhibit 3–6. As a company expands its level of activity, it may outgrow its present facilities, or the key management team may need to be expanded. The result, of course, will be increased committed fixed costs as larger facilities are built and as new management positions are created.

One reaction to the step pattern depicted in Exhibit 3–6 is to say that discretionary and committed fixed costs are really just step-variable costs. To some extent, this is true, since almost *all* costs can be adjusted in the long run. There are two major differences, however, between the step-variable costs depicted in Exhibit 3–3 and the fixed costs depicted in Exhibit 3–6.

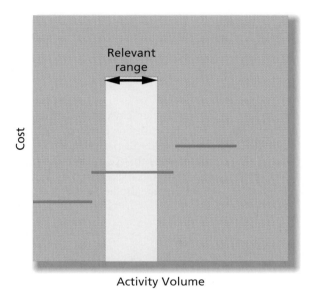

Exhibit 3–6
Fixed Costs and the Relevant Range

The first difference is that the step-variable costs can often be adjusted quickly as conditions change, whereas once fixed costs have been set, they often cannot be changed easily. A step-variable cost, such as waiters, can be adjusted upward or downward by hiring and laying off waiters. By contrast, once an organization has signed a lease for a building, it is locked into that level of lease cost for the life of the contract.

The second difference is that the *width of the steps* depicted for step-variable costs is much narrower than the width of the steps depicted for the fixed costs in Exhibit 3–6. The width of the steps relates to volume or level of activity. For step-variable costs, the width of a step might be 40 hours of activity or less if one is dealing, for example, with clerical labour cost. For fixed costs, however, the width of a step might be *thousands* or even *tens of thousands* of hours of activity. In essence, the width of the steps for step-variable costs is generally so narrow that these costs can be treated essentially as variable costs for most purposes. The width of the steps for fixed costs, in contrast, is so wide that these costs must generally be treated as entirely fixed within the relevant range.

Managing Sales and Marketing

Core Emballage Limited, based in western India, is a manufacturer and exporter of packaging materials—corrugated boxes, trays, and sheets—catering to varying packaging needs of customers. As with every organization, Core has also been finding ways to reduce costs across various functions. A thorough cost analysis suggested that there was some scope for reducing sales and marketing costs by at least 25%. After some analysis,

Core decided to close its sales offices in some locations and employ sales agents on a commission basis. As a result, the company eliminated the large fixed costs of maintaining sales offices. It now incurs only variable costs by way of commissions paid to the sales agents on the basis of sales revenues. Core saved about rupees (Rs.) 23,000 per month on sales of Rs. 200,000 (One dollar = approx. Rs. 34 at the time of writing this text), which translated into a reduction of about 31%. Core has not stopped its cost reduction efforts with these savings; instead, it continues to find other areas where costs can be saved.

Source: Personal correspondence with the Managing Director of Core Emballage Limited.

Mixed Costs

⬤ **KNOW**

CC6: Describe the behaviour of mixed costs.

A **mixed cost** is one that contains both variable and fixed cost elements. Mixed costs are also known as *semivariable costs*. To continue the 50 Plus Expeditions example, assume that the company must pay a licence fee of $25,000 per year plus $3 per rafting party to provincial authorities. If the company runs 1,000 rafting parties this year, then the total fees paid to the province would be $28,000, made up of $25,000 in fixed cost plus $3,000 in variable cost. The behaviour of this mixed cost is shown graphically in Exhibit 3–7.

Exhibit 3–7

Mixed Cost Behaviour

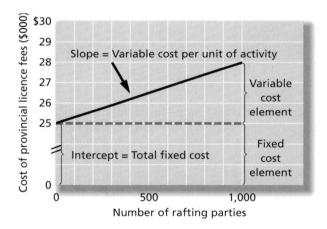

Even if 50 Plus fails to attract any customers, the company will still have to pay the licence fee of $25,000. This is why the cost line in Exhibit 3–7 intersects the vertical cost axis at the $25,000 point. For each rafting party the company organizes, the total cost of the provincial fees will increase by $3. Therefore, the total cost line slopes upward as the variable cost element is added to the fixed cost element.

⬤ **APPLY**

CC7: Construct a basic linear cost equation.

Since the mixed cost in Exhibit 3–7 is represented by a straight line, the following equation for a straight line can be used to express the relationship between mixed cost and the level of activity:

$$Y = a + bX$$

In this equation,

⬤ **KNOW**

CC8: Explain the individual elements of the cost equation.

Y = Total mixed cost
a = Total fixed cost (the vertical intercept of the line)
b = Variable cost per unit of activity (the slope of the line)
X = Level of activity

In the case of the provincial fees paid by 50 Plus Expeditions, the equation is written as follows:

$$Y = \$25,000 + \$3.00X$$

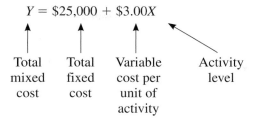

| Total mixed cost | Total fixed cost | Variable cost per unit of activity | Activity level |

This equation makes it easy to calculate the total mixed cost for any level of activity within the relevant range. For example, suppose that the company expects to organize 800 rafting parties in the next year. The total fees would be $27,400 calculated as follows:

$$Y = \$25,000 + (\$3.00 \text{ per rafting party} \times 800 \text{ rafting parties})$$

$$= \$27,400$$

Note that we have presented a rather simplistic linear cost equation. In Chapter 6, we will introduce additional X-variables (i.e., factors affecting costs). The cost equation will simply extend to include the additional variables (e.g., $Y = a + b_1X_1 + b_2X_2$ and so on). Moreover, as previously discussed, costs can behave in nonlinear patterns (e.g., curvilinear costs) that can be expressed in different forms (e.g., $Y = a + bX^2$ or $Y = a + bX_1{}^*X_2$).

The Analysis of Mixed Costs

In practice, mixed costs are quite common. For example, the cost of providing X-ray services to patients at the Toronto General Hospital is a mixed cost. There are substantial fixed costs for equipment amortization and for salaries of radiologists and technicians, but there are also variable costs for X-ray film, power, and supplies. At WestJet Airlines, maintenance costs are mixed costs. The company must incur fixed costs for renting maintenance facilities and for keeping skilled mechanics on the payroll, but the costs of replacement parts, lubricating oils, tires, and so on, are variable with respect to how often and how far the company's aircraft are flown.

The fixed portion of a mixed cost represents the basic, minimum cost of just having a service *ready and available* for use. The variable portion represents the cost incurred for *actual consumption* of the service. The variable element varies in proportion to the amount of service that is consumed.

Why should management be interested in separating the fixed and variable portions of a mixed cost? The simple answer is that a mixed cost is a combination of two cost types with exactly opposite behaviours. While one cost type varies in proportion to changes in activity volume, the other type does not. Therefore, when activity levels change within the organization, only the variable portion of the mixed cost will be affected (in terms of total cost going up or down). Approximating a mixed cost to one or the other will distort planning and decision making. For example, budgeting is an important activity in most organizations and requires a good understanding of cost behaviour. Managers who are unable to separate variable costs from fixed costs will not be able to make accurate predictions of future costs—this is not a desirable situation.

Now we know why separating the fixed and variable portions is important, but how does management go about estimating the fixed and variable elements? That really depends on the availability of historical data to guide the process. *Account analysis* and *engineering approach* are commonly used when there is little or no historical data available for analysis. However, when a considerable amount of historical data are available, managers can choose from the following three methods: *high-low*, *scattergraph*, and *regression analysis*.

KNOW

CC9: Explain the importance of separating mixed costs into fixed and variable portions.

Non-Quantitative Approaches to Cost Analysis

In **account analysis,** each account under consideration is classified as either variable or fixed on the basis of the analyst's knowledge of how the cost in the account behaves. For example, direct materials would be classified as variable, and a building lease cost would be classified as fixed because of the nature of those costs. The total fixed cost of an organization is the sum of the costs for the accounts that have been classified as fixed. The variable cost per unit is estimated by dividing the sum of the costs for the accounts that have been classified as variable by the total activity.

Account analysis works best when analyzing costs at a fairly aggregated level, such as the cost of serving patients in the emergency room (ER) of your local hospital. The costs of drugs, supplies, forms, wages, equipment, and so on, can be roughly classified as variable or fixed, and a mixed cost formula for the overall cost of the ER can be estimated fairly quickly.

The **engineering approach** to cost analysis involves a detailed analysis of what the cost behaviour should be, based on an industrial engineer's evaluation of the production methods to be used, the materials specifications, labour requirements, equipment usage, efficiency of production, power consumption, and so on. For example, Pizza Hut might use the engineering approach to estimate the cost of serving a particular take-out pizza. The cost of the pizza would be estimated by carefully costing the specific ingredients used to make the pizza, the power consumed to cook the pizza, and the cost of the container the pizza is delivered in. The engineering approach must be used in those situations where no past experience is available concerning activity and costs. In addition, it is sometimes combined with other methods to improve the accuracy of cost analysis.

Quantitative Approaches to Cost Analysis

This section will focus on how to estimate fixed and variable costs using quantitative methods. We do this using an example.

MANAGERIAL ACCOUNTING IN ACTION

The Issue

MID-TOWN MEDICAL CENTRE

Dr. Derek Chalmers, the chief executive officer of Mid-Town Medical Centre (MMC), motioned Kinh Nguyen, the chief financial officer of the hospital, into his office.

Derek: Kinh, come on in.
Kinh: What can I do for you?
Derek: Actually, I wanted to talk to you about our maintenance expenses. I don't usually pay attention to such things, but these expenses seem to be bouncing around a lot. Over the last half year or so, they have been as low as $7,400 and as high as $9,800 per month.
Kinh: Actually, that's a pretty normal variation in those expenses.
Derek: Well, we budgeted a constant $8,400 a month. Can't we do a better job of predicting what these costs are going to be? And how do we know when we've spent too much in a month? Shouldn't there be some explanation for these variations?
Kinh: Now that you mention it, we are in the process right now of tightening up our budgeting process. Our first step is to break all of our costs down into fixed and variable components.
Derek: How will that help?
Kinh: Well, that will permit us to predict what the level of costs will be. Some costs are fixed and shouldn't change much. Other costs go up and down as our activity level goes up and down. The trick is to figure out what is driving the variable component of the costs.
Derek: What about the maintenance costs?

Kinh: My guess is that the variations in maintenance costs are being driven by our overall level of activity. When we treat more patients, our equipment is used more intensively, which leads to more maintenance expense.

Derek: How would you measure the level of overall activity? Would you use patient-days?

Kinh: I think so. Each day a patient is in the hospital counts as one patient-day. The greater the number of patient-days in a month, the busier we are. Besides, our budgeting is all based on projected patient-days.

Derek: Okay, so suppose you are able to break the maintenance costs down into fixed and variable components. What will that do for us?

Kinh: Basically, I will be able to predict what maintenance costs should be as a function of the number of patient-days.

Derek: I can see where that would be useful. We could use it to predict costs for budgeting purposes.

Kinh: We could also use it as a benchmark. On the basis of the actual number of patient-days for a period, I can predict what the maintenance costs should have been. We can compare this with the actual spending on maintenance.

Derek: Sounds good to me. Let me know when you get the results.

We will examine three methods that Kinh Nguyen might use to break down mixed costs into their fixed and variable elements—the *high-low method*, the *scattergraph method*, and the *least-squares regression method*. All three methods are based on analyzing cost and activity records from a number of prior periods. In the case of MMC, we will use the following records of maintenance costs and patient-days for the previous year to estimate the fixed and variable elements of maintenance costs:

Month	Activity Level: Patient-Days	Maintenance Cost Incurred
January	5,600	$7,900
February	7,100	8,500
March	5,000	7,450
April	6,500	8,200
May...........	7,300	9,070
June...........	8,000	9,800
July	6,200	7,800
August.........	7,200	8,600
September......	6,100	8,000
October........	5,900	7,950
November......	6,200	8,120
December	5,800	7,970

The High-Low Method

To analyze mixed costs with the **high-low method,** you begin by identifying the period with the lowest level of activity and the period with the highest level of activity. The difference in cost corresponding to the two extreme activity levels is divided by the difference between the high and low activity levels to estimate the variable cost per unit of activity.

 KNOW

CC10: Describe the high-low method of analyzing mixed costs.

Since total maintenance cost at MMC appears to generally increase as the activity level increases, it is likely that some variable cost element is present. Using the high-low method, we first identify the periods with the highest and lowest *activity*—in this case, June and March. We then use the activity and cost data from these two periods to estimate the variable cost component as follows:

	Patient-Days	Maintenance Cost Incurred
High activity level (June)	8,000	$9,800
Low activity level (March)	5,000	7,450
Change	3,000	$2,350

APPLY

CC11: Set up a cost equation using the high-low method.

$$\text{Variable cost} = \frac{\text{Change in cost}}{\text{Change in activity}} = \frac{\$2,350}{3,000 \text{ patient-days}} = \$0.783 \text{ per patient-day}$$

Having determined that the variable rate for maintenance cost is 78.3 cents per patient-day, we can now determine the amount of fixed cost. This is done by taking total cost at *either* the high or the low activity level and deducting the variable cost element. In the computation following, total cost at the high activity level is used in computing the fixed cost element:

$$\text{Fixed cost element} = \text{Total cost} - \text{Variable cost element}$$
$$= \$9,800 - (\$0.783 \text{ per patient-day} \times 8,000 \text{ patient-days})$$
$$= \$3,536$$

Both the variable and fixed cost elements have now been isolated. The cost of maintenance can be expressed as $3,536 per month plus 78.3 cents per patient-day.

The cost of maintenance can also be expressed in terms of the equation for a straight line as follows:

$$Y = \$3,536 + \$0.783X$$

Total
maintenance
cost

Total
patient-days

The data used in this illustration are shown graphically in Exhibit 3–8. Three things should be noted in relation to this exhibit:

1. The total maintenance cost, *Y*, is plotted on the vertical axis. Cost is known as the **dependent variable,** since the amount of cost incurred during a period depends on the level of activity for the period. (That is, as the level of activity increases, total cost will also increase.)
2. The activity, *X* (patient-days in this case), is plotted on the horizontal axis. Activity is known as the **independent variable,** since it causes variations in the cost.
3. A straight line has been drawn through the points corresponding to the low and high levels of activity. In essence, that is what the high-low method does—it draws a straight line through those two points.[1]

---

[1]The formula for the variable cost, $\dfrac{\text{Change in cost (i.e., change in } Y)}{\text{Change in activity (i.e., change in } X)}$, is basically the same as the

formula for the slope of the line, $\dfrac{\text{Rise (i.e., change in } Y)}{\text{Run (i.e., change in } X)}$, that you are familiar with from high school

algebra. This is because the slope of the line is the variable cost per unit. The higher the variable cost per unit, the steeper the line.

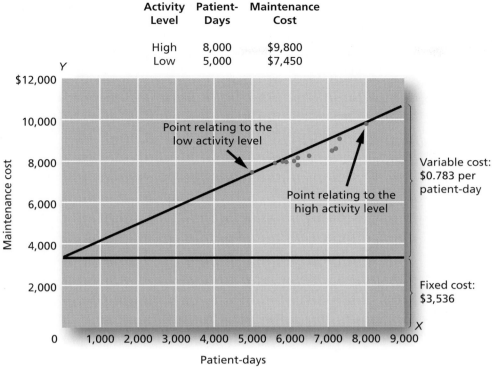

Activity Level	Patient-Days	Maintenance Cost
High	8,000	$9,800
Low	5,000	$7,450

Exhibit 3–8
High-Low Method of Cost Analysis

Sometimes, the high and low levels of activity do not coincide with the high and low amounts of cost. For example, the period that has the highest level of activity may not have the highest amount of cost. Nevertheless, the highest and lowest levels of *activity* and the corresponding costs are used to analyze a mixed cost under the high-low method. The reason is that the activity presumably causes costs, and so the analyst would like to use data that reflect the greatest possible variation in activity.

The high-low method is simple to apply, but it suffers from a major (and sometimes critical) defect—it utilizes only two data points. Generally, two points are not enough to produce accurate results in cost analysis work. Additionally, periods in which the activity level is unusually low or unusually high will tend to produce inaccurate results. A cost formula that is estimated solely using data from these unusual periods may seriously misrepresent the true cost relationship that holds during normal periods. Such a distortion is evident in Exhibit 3–8. The straight line should probably be shifted down somewhat so that it is closer to more of the data points. For these reasons, other methods of cost analysis that utilize a greater number of points will generally be more accurate than the high-low method. If a manager chooses to use the high-low method, he or she should do so with a full awareness of the method's limitations.

The Scattergraph Method

A more accurate way of analyzing mixed costs is to use the **scattergraph method,** which takes into account all of the cost data. A graph like the one that we used in Exhibit 3–8 is constructed, in which cost is shown on the vertical axis and the level of activity is shown on the horizontal axis. Costs observed at various levels of activity are then plotted on the graph, and a line is fitted to the plotted points. However, rather than just fitting the line to the high and low points, all points are considered when the line is drawn. This is done through simple visual inspection of the data, with the analyst taking care that the placement of the line is representative of all points, not just the high and low ones. Typically, the line is placed so that approximately equal numbers of points fall above and below it.

 KNOW

CC12: Explain the scattergraph method of analyzing mixed costs.

APPLY

CC13: Set up a cost equation using the scattergraph method.

A graph of this type is known as a *scattergraph*, and the line *fitted* to the plotted points is known as a **regression line.**

The scattergraph approach using the MMC maintenance data is illustrated in Exhibit 3–9. Notice that the regression line has been placed in such a way that approximately equal numbers of points fall above and below it. Also, notice that the line has been drawn so that it goes through one of the points. This is not absolutely necessary, but it makes subsequent calculations a little easier.

Since the regression line strikes the vertical cost axis at $3,750, this amount represents the fixed cost element. The variable cost element can be computed by subtracting the fixed cost of $3,750 from the total cost for any point lying on the regression line. Since the point representing 5,900 patient-days lies on the regression line, we can use it. The variable cost (to the nearest tenth of a cent) would be 71.2 cents per patient-day, computed as follows:

Total cost for 5,900 patient-days (a point falling on the regression line).......	$7,950
Less: Fixed cost element	3,750
Variable cost element......................	$4,200

$4,200 ÷ 5,900 patient-days = $0.712 per patient-day

Thus, the cost formula using the regression line in Exhibit 3–9 would be $3,750 per month plus 71.2 cents per patient-day. In terms of the linear equation $Y = a + bX$, the cost formula can be written as follows:

$$Y = \$3,750 + \$0.712X$$

where activity (X) is expressed in patient-days.

In this example, there is not a great deal of difference between the cost formula derived using the high-low method and the cost formula derived using the scattergraph method. However, sometimes, there *will* be a big difference. In such situations, more reliance should ordinarily be placed on the results of the scattergraph approach.

Also, observe that all of the points in Exhibit 3–9 lie reasonably close to the straight line. In other words, the estimates of the fixed and variable costs are reasonably accurate

Exhibit 3–9

Scattergraph Method of Cost Analysis

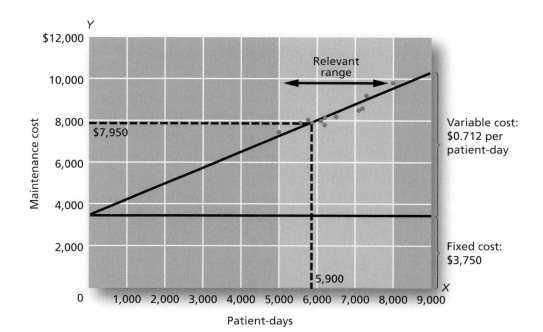

within this range of activity, and so the relevant range extends at least from 5,000 to 8,000 patient-days. It may also be accurate below 5,000 patient-days and above 8,000 patient-days—we cannot tell for sure without looking at more data.

A scattergraph can be an extremely useful tool in the hands of an experienced analyst. Quirks in cost behaviour due to strikes, bad weather, breakdowns, and so on, become immediately apparent to the trained observer, who can make appropriate adjustments to the data when fitting the regression line. Some cost analysts would argue that a scattergraph should be the starting point in all cost analyses, due to the benefits to be gained from having the data visually available in graph form.

However, the scattergraph method has two major drawbacks. First, it is subjective. No two analysts who look at the same scattergraph are likely to draw exactly the same regression line. Second, the estimates are not as precise as they are with other methods. Some managers are uncomfortable with these elements of subjectivity and imprecision, desiring a method that will yield a precise answer that will be the same no matter who does the analysis. Fortunately, modern computer software makes it easy to use sophisticated statistical methods, such as *least-squares regression*, that are capable of providing much more information than just the estimates of variable and fixed costs. The details of these statistical methods are beyond the scope of this text, but the basic approach is discussed following. Nevertheless, even if the least-squares regression approach is used, it is always a good idea to plot the data in a scattergraph. By simply looking at the scattergraph, you can quickly verify whether it makes sense to fit a straight line to the data using least-squares regression or some other method.

The Least-Squares Regression Method

The **least-squares regression method** is a more objective and precise approach to estimating the regression line than the scattergraph method. Rather than fitting a regression line through the scattergraph data by visual inspection, the least-squares regression method uses mathematical formulas to fit the regression line. Also, unlike the high-low method, the least-squares regression method takes all of the data into account when estimating the cost formula.

The basic idea underlying the least-squares regression method is illustrated in Exhibit 3–10 using hypothetical data points. Notice that the deviations from the plotted points to the regression line are measured vertically on the graph. These vertical deviations are called the *regression errors* and are the key to understanding least-squares regression. There is nothing mysterious about the least-squares regression method. It simply computes the regression line that minimizes the sum of these squared errors. The formulas that accomplish this are fairly complex and involve numerous calculations, but the principle is simple.

Fortunately, computers are adept at carrying out the computations required by the least-squares regression formulas. The data—the observed values of X and Y—are entered into the computer, and software does the rest. In the case of MMC's maintenance cost data, we used a statistical software package. Most spreadsheet package can also be used to carry out regression analysis on a personal computer. The following table presents selected results using the Regression tool in Microsoft Excel:

Regression Statistics	
Multiple R.	0.94
R Square	0.88
Adjusted R Square	0.87
Standard Error	229.38
Observations.	12

◔ KNOW

CC14: Explain the least-squares regression method of analyzing mixed costs.

◔ APPLY

CC15: Set up a cost equation using the least-squares method.

	Coefficients	t Stat	P-value
Intercept	3752	7.11	0.000
X Variable 1	0.707	8.65	0.000

Therefore, using the least-squares regression method, the fixed element of the maintenance cost is $3,752 per month and the variable portion is 70.7 cents per patient-day.

In terms of the linear equation $Y = a + bX$, the cost formula can be written as

$$Y = \$3,752 + \$0.707X$$

where activity (X) is expressed in patient-days.

One very important statistic generated as part of the regression analysis is R^2. The R^2 in this example is 0.88 or 88%. This simply means that 88% of the variation in maintenance cost is accounted for (or explained) by the variation in patient-days. In other words, only 12% of the variation in maintenance cost is not explained by the variation in patient-days. Knowing this is important for the managers to decide whether the basis upon which the cost estimates are developed (e.g., patient-days) is reliable. In other words, if the R^2 is low, the manager must look for some other base to estimate costs.

Exhibit 3–10

The Concept of Least-Squares Regression

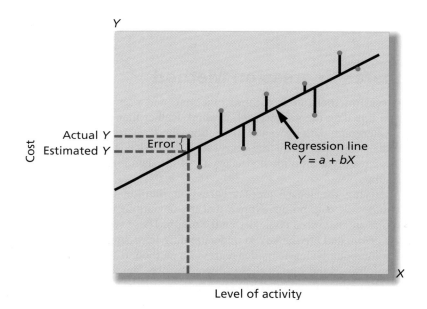

Therefore, using the least-squares regression method, the fixed element of the maintenance cost is $3,752 per month and the variable portion is 70.7 cents per patient-day.

MANAGERIAL ACCOUNTING
IN ACTION

The Wrap-Up

After completing the analysis of maintenance costs, Kinh Nguyen met with Dr. Derek Chalmers to discuss the results.

Kinh: We used least-squares regression analysis to estimate the fixed and variable components of maintenance costs. According to the results, the fixed cost per month is $3,752 and the variable cost per patient-day is 70.7 cents.

Derek: Okay, so if we plan for 7,800 patient-days next month, what is your estimate of the maintenance costs?

Kinh: That will take just a few seconds to figure out. [Kinh wrote the following calculations on a pad of paper.]

Fixed costs	$3,752
Variable costs:	
7,800 patient-days × $0.707 per patient-day	5,515
Total expected maintenance costs.	$9,267

Derek: Nine thousand two hundred and sixty-seven dollars; isn't that a bit *too* precise?
Kinh: Sure. I don't really believe the maintenance costs will be exactly this figure.
However, based on the information we have, this is the best estimate we can come
up with.
Derek: Don't let me give you a hard time. Even though it is an estimate, it will be a
lot better than just guessing like we have done in the past. It will surely help us in our
budgeting efforts. Thanks. I hope to see more of this kind of analysis.

Entrepreneur

YOU DECIDE

You are the owner of a small manufacturing firm. You are thinking about expanding your
production capacity and are wondering about the implications of this on your costs. You
therefore need a better understanding of your costs. How do you proceed?

Contribution Margin

What do you do after separating costs on the basis of behaviour? We have already partially answered this question by saying that this separation can be used to estimate costs.
Another important use of the separation of costs into fixed and variable is that managers can use the information to compute the contribution margin and prepare an income
statement using a different format than the one presented in the previous chapter (the
traditional income statement).

The **contribution margin** is the difference between sales revenues and all variable costs
based on the number of units sold; it is the amount remaining once all the variable costs
have been deducted from sales revenues. Consider a pizza place whose average monthly
sales amount to $200,000 (10,000 pizzas served at $20 per pizza). The variable costs of
making a pizza (i.e., materials and labour) amount to $6, sales commissions amount to
$0.80 per pizza sold, and other variable costs total $1.20 per pizza. Monthly fixed expenses
amount to $65,000. Total variable costs for the month will amount to $80,000 (10,000 pizzas at $8 per pizza), resulting in a contribution margin of $120,000 ($200,000 − $80,000)
or $12 per pizza. Income for the month will amount to $55,000 ($200,000 − $80,000
− $65,000). We can use a different format, known as the *contribution margin income state-
ment*, to report income (see following).

● KNOW ● APPLY

CC16: Explain the concept of
contribution margin and prepare
a contribution margin income
statement.

	Total	Per unit	Percentage
Sales Revenues:			
(10,000 pizzas @ $20)	$200,000	$20.00	100
Less: Variable Costs:			
Materials and labour (10,000 @ $6)	60,000	6.00	30
Sales commissions (10,000 @ $0.80) . . .	8,000	0.80	4
Other costs (10,000 @ $1.20)	12,000	1.20	6
Total variable costs	$ 80,000	$ 8.00	40

continued

	Total	Per unit	Percentage
Contribution margin	$120,000	$12.00	60
Less: Fixed expenses.	65,000		
Net income	$ 55,000		

The concepts of contribution margin and the contribution margin income statement are useful for the purposes of planning and decision making, but our intent was simply to introduce these concepts. We will revisit them again in Chapters 11 and 12.

Application Competency Summary

Application Competency	Deliverable	Source Documents and Key Information	Steps	Knowledge Competency
Construct a basic linear cost equation. ◗ CC7	**Key Information** Cost equation **Report/Document** No specific report Can be used in preparing other reports for planning and decision making (e.g., flexible budget performance report)	**Cost records** Fixed portion of the total cost (constant term) Variable portion of the total cost (slope of the equation) Activity causing costs (independent variable)	1. Identify the fixed and variable portions of the cost, and express the cost equation in the form $Y = a + bX$	Mixed costs ◗ CC6
Set up a cost equation using the high-low method. ◗ CC11	**Key Information** Cost equation **Report/Document** No specific report Can be used in preparing other reports for planning and decision making (e.g., standard cost card)	**Historical cost records** Actual historical data of the volume of the independent variable (X-values) and the corresponding cost (Y-values) over a period (e.g., daily, weekly, monthly)	1. Identify the high and low observations of the independent variable and the corresponding costs associated with each observation. 2. Compute the slope (b) as follows: divide the difference in the two cost numbers by the difference between the quantity of the high and low observations of the independent variable. 3. Compute the intercept (a) as follows: multiply the slope by the high (or low) observation of the independent variable and deduct this amount from the total cost corresponding to the independent variable. 4. Using the slope and the intercept, construct a cost equation to estimate future costs.	Mixed costs ◗ CC6 Elements of the cost equation ◗ CC8 High-low method ◗ CC10

continued

Application Competency	Deliverable	Source Documents and Key Information	Steps	Knowledge Competency
Set up a cost equation using the scattergraph method. ⦿ CC13	*Key Information* Cost equation *Report/Document* No specific report Can be used in preparing other reports for planning and decision-making situations (e.g., profitability report)	*Historical cost records* Actual historical data of the volume of the independent variable (X-values) and the corresponding cost (Y-values) over a period (e.g., daily, weekly, monthly)	1. Plot the data with the x-axis representing the independent variable and the y-axis the cost. 2. Visually, draw a straight line through the points on the plot that best fits the data and extend it to intersect the y-axis. The above intersection point on the y-axis represents the intercept (fixed portion) of the cost equation. 3. Draw vertical lines from any two points on the x-axis such that they intersect the y-axis. Draw lines from the intersecting points on the line to the y-axis. Compute the slope as follows: divide the difference between the two points on the y-axis by the difference between the two points on the x-axis. 4. Using the slope and the intercept, construct a cost equation to estimate future costs.	Mixed costs ⦿ CC6 Elements of the cost equation ⦿ CC8 Scattergraph method ⦿ CC12
Set up a cost equation using the least-squares regression method. ⦿ CC15	*Key Information* Cost equation *Report/Document* No specific report Can be used in preparing other reports for planning and decision-making situations (e.g., budget)	*Historical cost records* Actual historical data of the volume of the independent variable (X-values) and the corresponding cost (Y-values) over a period (e.g., daily, weekly, monthly)	1. Enter the data using statistics software or a spreadsheet, then run the least-squares regression method. 2. Identify the value of the slope and intercept from the output generated by the software. 3. Using the slope and the intercept, construct a cost equation to estimate future costs.	Mixed costs ⦿ CC6 Elements of the cost equation ⦿ CC8 Least-squares regression technique ⦿ CC12
Prepare a contribution margin income statement. ⦿ CC16	*Key Information* Contribution margin and net income *Report/Document* Contribution margin income statement	*Sales ledger* Actual sales revenue *Various cost ledgers* Actual costs of variable and fixed costs	1. Obtain the sales revenue from the sales ledger, and the variable and fixed costs from various cost ledgers. 2. Deduct all variable costs from sales revenues to compute the contribution margin, and deduct fixed costs to compute net income.	Variable and fixed costs ⦿ CC1, 3

Guidance Answers to Decision Maker and You Decide

BUDGET ANALYST (p. 74)
A janitorial service company is likely to incur most of the following types of costs:

Cost	Type	Activity Base (if variable)
Cleaning supplies	Variable	Square footage of client's spaces
Amortization (vacuum cleaners, etc.)......	Fixed	Not applicable
Reimbursement of employee mileage......	Variable	Distance (kilometres) to client
Salary of supervisor(s)	Fixed	Not applicable
Wages of janitorial employees	Variable	Square footage of client's spaces

ENTREPRENEUR (p. 91)
One good way to begin to understand your costs is by understanding the behaviour of the individual costs. A variety of approaches can be used to understand cost behaviour, including account analysis, engineering approach, high-low method, scattergraph method, and least-squares regression method.

Review Problem 1: Cost Behaviour

Neptune Rentals offers a boat rental service. Consider the following costs of the company over the relevant range of 5,000 to 8,000 hours of operating time for its boats:

	Hours of Operating Time			
	5,000	6,000	7,000	8,000
Total costs:				
Variable costs	$ 20,000	$?	$?	$?
Fixed costs	168,000	?	?	?
Total costs	$188,000	$?	$?	$?
Cost per hour:				
Variable cost	$?	$?	$?	$?
Fixed cost	?	?	?	?
Total cost per hour.........	$?	$?	$?	$?

Required:
Compute the missing amounts, assuming that cost behaviour patterns remain unchanged within the relevant range of 5,000 to 8,000 hours.

SOLUTION TO REVIEW PROBLEM 1
The variable cost per hour can be computed as follows:

$$\$20,000 \div 5,000 \text{ hours} = \$4 \text{ per hour}$$

Therefore, in accordance with the behaviour of variable and fixed costs, the missing amounts are as follows:

	Hours of Operating Time			
	5,000	6,000	7,000	8,000
Total costs:				
Variable costs	$ 20,000	$ 24,000	$ 28,000	$ 32,000
Fixed costs	168,000	168,000	168,000	168,000
Total costs	$188,000	$192,000	$196,000	$200,000

continued

Cost per hour:				
Variable cost	$ 4.00	$ 4.00	$ 4.00	$ 4.00
Fixed cost	33.60	28.00	24.00	21.00
Total cost per hour. . . .	$37.60	$32.00	$28.00	$25.00

Observe that the total variable costs increase in proportion to the number of hours of operating time, but that these costs remain constant at $4 if expressed on a per-hour basis.

In contrast, the total fixed costs do not change with changes in the level of activity. They remain constant at $168,000 within the relevant range. With increases in activity, however, the fixed costs decrease on a per-hour basis, dropping from $33.60 per hour when the boats are operated 5,000 hours a period to only $21 per hour when the boats are operated 8,000 hours a period. *Because of this troublesome aspect of fixed costs, they are most easily (and most safely) dealt with on a total basis, rather than on a unit basis, in cost analysis work.*

Review Problem 2: High-Low Method

The manager of Golf Warehouse would like a cost formula linking the costs involved in processing orders to the number of orders received during a month. The order entry department's costs and the number of orders received during the immediately preceding eight months are given in the following table:

Month	Number of Orders Received	Order Entry Department Costs
May.	1,000	$11,980
June.	1,700	16,000
July	1,400	14,200
August.	1,650	15,500
September.	900	11,520
October	1,150	12,500
November	1,200	13,000
December	1,320	13,800

Required:
1. Use the high-low method to establish the fixed and variable components of order processing costs.
2. Express the fixed and variable components of order processing costs as a cost formula in the linear equation form $Y = a + bX$.

SOLUTION TO REVIEW PROBLEM 2
1. The first step in the high-low method is to identify the periods of the highest and lowest activity. Those periods are June (1,700 orders received) and September (900 orders received).
   The second step is to compute the variable cost per unit using those two points:

Month	Number of Orders Received	Order Entry Department Costs
High activity level (June).	1,700	$16,000
Low activity level (September)	900	11,520
Change.	800	$ 4,480

$$\text{Variable cost} = \frac{\text{Change in cost}}{\text{Change in activity}} = \frac{\$4,480}{800 \text{ orders received}} = \$5.60 \text{ per order received}$$

The third step is to compute the fixed cost element by deducting the variable cost element from the total cost at either the high or low activity. In the computation below, the high point of activity is used:

Fixed cost element = Total cost − Variable cost element
= $16,000 − ($5.60 per patient admitted × 1,700 orders received)
= $6,480

2. The cost formula expressed in the linear equation form is $Y = \$6,480 + \$5.60X$.

Glossary

Account analysis A method for analyzing cost behaviour in which each account is classified as either variable or fixed on the basis of the analyst's knowledge of how the cost in the account behaves. (p. 84)
Activity base A measure of whatever causes the incurrence of a variable cost. (For example, the total cost of X-ray film in a hospital will increase as the number of X-rays taken increases. Therefore, the number of X-rays is an activity base for explaining the total cost of X-ray film.) (p. 74)
Committed fixed cost A fixed cost that is difficult to adjust and relates to the investment in facilities, equipment, and the basic organizational structure of a firm. (p. 78)
Contribution margin The amount remaining from sales revenues after all variable expenses have been deducted. (p. 91)
Cost structure The relative proportion of fixed, variable, and mixed costs found within an organization. (p. 72)
Curvilinear costs A relationship between cost and activity that is a curve, rather than a straight line. (p. 76)
Dependent variable A variable that reacts or responds to some causal factor; total cost is the dependent variable, as represented by the letter Y, in the equation $Y = a + bX$. (p. 86)
Discretionary fixed cost A fixed cost that arises from annual decisions by management to spend in certain fixed cost areas, such as advertising and research. (p. 78)
Engineering approach A detailed analysis of cost behaviour based on an industrial engineer's evaluation of the inputs that are required to carry out a particular activity and of the prices of those inputs. (p. 84)
High-low method A method of separating a mixed cost into its fixed and variable elements by analyzing the change in cost between the high and low levels of activity. (p. 85)
Independent variable A variable that acts as a causal factor; activity is the independent variable, as represented by the letter X, in the equation $Y = a + bX$. (p. 86)
Least-squares regression method A method of separating a mixed cost into its fixed and variable elements by fitting a regression line that minimizes the sum of the squared errors. (p. 89)
Mixed cost A cost that contains both variable and fixed cost elements. (p. 82)
Regression line A line fitted to an array of plotted points. The slope of the line, denoted by the letter b in the linear equation $Y = a + bX$, represents the variable cost per unit of activity. The point where the line intersects the cost axis, denoted by the letter a in the above equation, represents the total fixed cost. (p. 88)
Relevant range The range of activity within which assumptions about variable and fixed cost behaviour are valid. (p. 77)
Scattergraph method A method of separating a mixed cost into its fixed and variable elements. Under this method, a regression line is fitted to an array of plotted points by drawing a line with a straight-edge. (p. 87)
Step-variable cost A cost (such as the cost of a maintenance worker) that is obtainable only in large chunks and that increases and decreases only in response to fairly wide changes in activity. (p. 76)
True variable cost A cost that varies in direct proportion to changes in the level of activity. (p. 75)

Questions

3–1 Distinguish among (a) a variable cost, (b) a fixed cost, and (c) a mixed cost.
3–2 What effect does an increase in volume have on:
   a. Unit fixed costs?
   b. Unit variable costs?
   c. Total fixed costs?
   d. Total variable costs?
3–3 Define the following terms: (a) cost behaviour and (b) relevant range.
3–4 What is meant by an *activity base* when dealing with variable costs? Give several examples of activity bases.

3–5 Distinguish among (a) a variable cost, (b) a mixed cost, and (c) a step-variable cost. Chart the three costs on a graph, with activity plotted horizontally and cost plotted vertically.

3–6 Managers often assume a strictly linear relationship between cost and volume. How can this practice be defended in light of the fact that many costs are curvilinear?

3–7 Distinguish between discretionary fixed costs and committed fixed costs.

3–8 Classify the following fixed costs as normally being either committed or discretionary:
   a. Amortization on buildings
   b. Advertising
   c. Research
   d. Long-term equipment leases
   e. Pension payments to the firm's retirees
   f. Management development and training

3–9 Does the concept of the relevant range apply to fixed costs? Explain.

3–10 What is the major disadvantage of the high-low method?

3–11 What methods are available for separating a mixed cost into its fixed and variable elements using past records of cost and activity data? Which method is considered to be most accurate? Why?

3–12 What is meant by a regression line? Give the general formula for a regression line. Which term represents the variable cost? The fixed cost?

3–13 Once a regression line has been drawn, how do you determine the fixed cost element? The variable cost element?

3–14 What is meant by least-squares regression?

3–15 Why is the least-squares regression method preferred to the high-low method when analyzing mixed costs?

3–16 What is the difference between the scattergraph method and the least-squares regression method?

3–17 The higher the R^2 of a regression equation, the better the likelihood that X is an appropriate cost driver for Y. True or false? Explain.

3–18 What is the contribution margin?

3–19 What is the difference between the contribution margin approach to the income statement and the traditional approach to the income statement?

Brief Exercises

BRIEF EXERCISE 3–1   Fixed and Variable Cost Behaviour (CC1, 3)
Espresso Express operates a number of espresso coffee stands in busy suburban malls. The fixed weekly expense of a coffee stand is $1,200 and the variable cost per cup of coffee served is $0.22.

Required:
1. Fill in the following table with your estimates of total costs and cost per cup of coffee at the indicated levels of activity for a coffee stand. Round off the cost of a cup of coffee to the nearest tenth of a cent.

	Cups of Coffee Served in a Week		
	2,000	**2,100**	**2,200**
Fixed cost	?	?	?
Variable cost	?	?	?
Total cost.	?	?	?
Cost per cup of coffee served	?	?	?

2. Does the cost per cup of coffee served increase, decrease, or remain the same as the number of cups of coffee served in a week increases? Explain.

BRIEF EXERCISE 3–2   High-Low Method (CC10, 11)
The Royal Canadian Lodge in Banff, Alberta, has accumulated records of the total electrical costs of the hotel and the number of occupancy-days over the last year. An occupancy-day represents a room rented out for one day. The hotel's business is highly seasonal, with peaks occurring during the ski season and in the summer.

Month	Occupancy-Days	Electrical Costs
January	1,736	$4,127
February	1,904	4,207
March	2,356	5,083
April	960	2,857
May.	360	1,871
June.	744	2,696
July	2,108	4,670
August.	2,406	5,148
September.	840	2,691
October.	124	1,588
November	720	2,454
December	1,364	3,529

Required:

1. Using the high-low method, estimate the fixed cost of electricity per month and the variable cost of electricity per occupancy-day. Round off the fixed cost to the nearest whole dollar and the variable cost to the nearest whole cent.
2. What factors other than occupancy-days are likely to affect the monthly variation in electrical costs?

BRIEF EXERCISE 3–3   Scattergraph Method (CC12, 13)

Oki Products, Ltd. has observed the following processing costs at various levels of activity over the last 15 months:

Month	Units Produced	Processing Cost
1	4,500	$38,000
2	11,000	52,000
3	12,000	56,000
4	5,500	40,000
5	9,000	47,000
6	10,500	52,000
7	7,500	44,000
8	5,000	41,000
9	11,500	52,000
10	6,000	43,000
11	8,500	48,000
12	10,000	50,000
13	6,500	44,000
14	9,500	48,000
15	8,000	46,000

Required:

1. Prepare a scattergraph by plotting these data on a graph. Plot cost on the vertical axis and activity on the horizontal axis. Fit a line to your plotted points by visual inspection.
2. What is the approximate monthly fixed cost? The approximate variable cost per unit processed? Show your computations.

BRIEF EXERCISE 3–4   Least-Squares Regression Method (CC14, 15)

Using the data in the previous exercise, repeat #2 using least-squares regression (using any spreadsheet software). Is Units Produced a reliable basis for estimating processing costs?

BRIEF EXERCISE 3–5   Cost Behaviour: Fixed Costs (CC1, 3)

Cyclop Inc. manufactures top quality laser printers. The selling price per printer is $445 and the variable cost per printer is $145. The sales volume of $431,650 is necessary to produce a net income of $195,500 before taxes. What are Cyclop's total fixed costs?

(Adapted © CGA-Canada)

BRIEF EXERCISE 3–6   Cost Behaviour: Mixed Costs (CC6, 7, 8)

Which of the following are linear cost functions? Which are mixed cost functions? Given Y=total costs, X_1 = production volume and X_2 = number of batches produced.

1. $Y=\$4{,}000+3X_1 + 45X_2$
2. $Y=\$1{,}500+6X_1 * 4X_2$
3. $Y=\$16{,}780$
4. $Y=\$4.5X_2$
5. $Y=\$12{,}450 + 3.20\ X_1X_2$

BRIEF EXERCISE 3–7   High-Low Method (CC10, 11)

Wolfsbane Serum produced 50,000 pounds in January at a cost of $1,000,000. In March 40,000 pounds were produced at a cost of $850,000. Using these two data points, compute the cost function for Wolfsbane Serum.

BRIEF EXERCISE 3–8   Contribution Margin Income Statement (CC16)

The Alpine House, Inc. is a large retailer of winter sports equipment. An income statement for the company's Ski Department for a recent quarter is presented following:

THE ALPINE HOUSE, INC.		
Income Statement—Ski Department		
For the Quarter Ended March 31		
Sales.		$150,000
Less: Cost of goods sold		90,000
Gross margin		60,000
Less: Operating expenses:		
Selling expenses.	$30,000	
Administrative expenses	10,000	40,000
Net income.		$ 20,000

On average, skis sell for $750 per pair. Variable selling expenses are $50 per pair of skis sold. The remaining selling expenses are fixed. The administrative expenses are 20% variable and 80% fixed. The company does not manufacture its own skis; it purchases them from a supplier for $450 per pair.

Required:

1. Prepare a contribution margin income statement for the quarter.
2. For every pair of skis sold during the quarter, what was the contribution toward covering fixed expenses and toward earning profits?

Exercises

EXERCISE 3–1   High-Low Method; Predicting Cost (CC10, 11)

The Lakeshore Hotel's guest-days of occupancy and custodial supplies expense over the last seven months were as follows:

Month	Guest-Days of Occupancy	Custodial Supplies Expense
March.	4,000	$ 7,500
April.	6,500	8,250
May	8,000	10,500
June	10,500	12,000
July.	12,000	13,500
August	9,000	10,750
September	7,500	9,750

Guest-days is a measure of the overall activity at the hotel. For example, a guest who stays at the hotel for three days is counted as three guest-days.

Required:
1. Using the high-low method, estimate a cost formula for custodial supplies expense.
2. Using the cost formula you derived above, what amount of custodial supplies expense would you expect to be incurred at an occupancy level of 11,000 guest-days?

EXERCISE 3–2   Least-Squares Regression Method (CC14, 15)
Repeat parts (1) and (2) of Exercise 3–1 using least-squares regression (you may use a spreadsheet to compute the fixed and variable costs). Comment on the reliability of using guest-days as an allocation base.

EXERCISE 3–3   High-Low and Scattergraph Methods (CC8, 10, 11, 12, 13)
Refer to the data in Exercise 3–1.

Required:
1. Prepare a scattergraph using the data from Exercise 3–1. Plot cost on the vertical axis and activity on the horizontal axis. Fit a regression line to your plotted points by visual inspection.
2. What is the approximate monthly fixed cost? The approximate variable cost per guest-day?
3. Scrutinize the points on your graph, and explain why the high-low method would or would not yield an accurate cost formula in this situation.

EXERCISE 3–4   High-Low and Scattergraph Methods (CC10, 11, 12, 13)
The following data relating to units shipped and total shipping expense have been assembled by Archer Company, a manufacturer of large, custom-built air-conditioning units for commercial buildings:

Month	Units Shipped	Total Shipping Expense
January............	3	$1,800
February...........	6	2,300
March.............	4	1,700
April.............	5	2,000
May	7	2,300
June	8	2,700
July	2	1,200

Required:
1. Using the high-low method, estimate a cost formula for shipping expense.
2. For the scattergraph method, do the following:
   a. Prepare a scattergraph, using the data given above. Plot cost on the vertical axis and activity on the horizontal axis. Fit a regression line to your plotted points by visual inspection.
   b. Using your scattergraph, estimate the approximate variable cost per unit shipped and the approximate fixed cost per month.
3. What factors, other than the number of units shipped, are likely to affect the company's total shipping expense? Explain.

EXERCISE 3–5   High-Low Method; Predicting Cost (CC7, 10, 11)
Hoi Chong Transport, Ltd. operates a fleet of delivery trucks in Singapore. The company has determined that if a truck is driven 105,000 kilometres during a year, the average operating cost is 11.4 cents per kilometre. If a truck is driven only 70,000 kilometres during a year, the average operating cost increases to 13.4 cents per kilometre. (The Singapore dollar is the currency used in Singapore.)

Required:
1. Using the high-low method, estimate the variable and fixed cost elements of the annual cost of truck operation.
2. Express the variable and fixed costs in the form $Y = a + bX$.
3. If a truck were driven 80,000 kilometres during a year, what total cost would you expect to be incurred?

EXERCISE 3–6   Cost Behaviour and Contribution Margin Income Statement (CC1, 3, 16)
Harris Company manufactures and sells a single product. A partially completed schedule of the company's total and per-unit costs over the relevant range of 30,000 to 50,000 units produced and sold annually is given below:

	Units Produced and Sold		
	30,000	40,000	50,000
Total costs:			
Variable costs	$180,000	?	?
Fixed costs	300,000	?	?
Total costs..............	$480,000	?	?
Cost per unit:			
Variable cost	?	?	?
Fixed cost	?	?	?
Total cost per unit	?	?	?

Required:
1. Complete the schedule of the company's total and unit costs.
2. Assume that the company produces and sells 45,000 units during a year at a selling price of $16 per unit. Prepare a contribution margin income statement for the year.

Problems

PROBLEM 3–1   High-Low Method; Predicting Cost (CC10, 11)
St. Mark's Hospital contains 450 beds. The average occupancy rate is 80% per month. In other words, on average, 80% of the hospital's beds are occupied by patients. At this level of occupancy, the hospital's operating costs are $32 per occupied bed per day, assuming a 30-day month. This $32 figure contains both variable and fixed cost elements.
    During June, the hospital's occupancy rate was only 60%. A total of $326,700 in operating costs were incurred during the month.

Required:
1. Using the high-low method, estimate:
    a. The variable cost per occupied bed on a daily basis
    b. The total fixed operating costs per month
2. Assume an occupancy rate of 70% per month. What amount of total operating cost would you expect the hospital to incur?

CHECK FIGURE
(1) $270,000 per month
plus $7 per bed-day

PROBLEM 3–2   Scattergraph Method (CC12, 13)
Molina Company is a value-added computer resaler that specializes in providing services to small companies. The company owns and maintains several autos for use by its sales staff. All expenses of operating these autos have been entered into an Automobile Expense account on the company's books. Along with this record of expenses, the company has also kept a careful record of the number of kilometres the autos have been driven each month.
    The company's records of miles driven and total auto expenses over the past 10 months are given below:

Month	Total Mileage (000)	Total Cost
January.................	4	$3,000
February................	8	3,700
March..................	7	3,300
April...................	12	4,000

continued

May	6	3,300
June	11	3,900
July.	14	4,200
August	10	3,600
September	13	4,100
October	15	4,400

Molina Company's president wants to know the cost of operating the fleet of cars in terms of the fixed monthly cost and the variable cost per mile driven.

Required:
1. Prepare a scattergraph using the data provided. Place cost on the vertical axis and activity (kilometres driven) on the horizontal axis. Fit a regression line to the plotted points by simple visual inspection.
2. By analyzing your scattergraph, estimate fixed cost per month and the variable cost per kilometre driven.

CHECK FIGURE
(1) $1,000 per month plus
$20 per scan

PROBLEM 3–3   High-Low, Scattergraph, and Least-Squares Regression Methods (CC8, 10, 11, 12, 13)

Pleasant View Hospital of British Columbia has just hired a new chief administrator who is anxious to employ sound management and planning techniques in the business affairs of the hospital. Accordingly, she has directed her assistant to summarize the cost structure existing in the various departments to secure data for planning purposes.

The assistant is unsure how to classify the utilities costs in the Radiology Department, since these costs do not exhibit either strictly variable or fixed cost behaviour. Utilities costs are very high in the department due to a CAT scanner that draws a large amount of power and is kept running at all times. The scanner cannot be turned off due to the long warm-up period required for its use. When the scanner is used to scan a patient, it consumes an additional burst of power. The assistant has accumulated the following data on utilities costs and use of the scanner since the first of the year.

Month	Number of Scans	Utilities Cost
January.	60	$2,200
February.	70	2,600
March.	90	2,900
April.	120	3,300
May	100	3,000
June	130	3,600
July.	150	4,000
August	140	3,600
September	110	3,100
October	80	2,500

The chief administrator has informed her assistant that the utilities cost is probably a mixed cost that will have to be broken down into its variable and fixed cost elements by use of a scattergraph. The assistant feels, however, that if an analysis of this type is necessary, then the high-low method should be used because it is easier and quicker to use than other methods. The controller has suggested that there may be a better approach.

Required:
1. Using the high-low method, estimate a cost formula for utilities. Express the formula in the form $Y = a + bX$. (The variable rate should be stated in terms of cost per scan.)
2. Prepare a scattergraph by plotting the above data on a graph. (The number of scans should be placed on the horizontal axis, and utilities cost should be placed on the vertical axis.) Fit a regression line to the plotted points by visual inspection and estimate a cost formula for utilities.
3. Estimate a cost formula using least-squares regression (use a spreadsheet).
4. Comment on the differences between the three cost formulas estimated above. Which one would you use?

PROBLEM 3–4   Cost Behaviour; High-Low Analysis; Contribution Margin Income Statement
(CC1, 3, 6, 10, 11)
Morrisey & Brown, Ltd., of Sydney, is a merchandising firm that is the sole distributor of a product that is increasing in popularity among Australian consumers. The company's income statements for the three most recent months follow:

MORRISEY & BROWN, LTD.
Income Statements
For the Three Months Ending September 30

	July	August	September
Sales in units....................	4,000	4,500	5,000
Sales revenue....................	A$400,000	A$450,000	A$500,000
Less: Cost of goods sold...........	240,000	270,000	300,000
Gross margin....................	160,000	180,000	200,000
Less: Operating expenses:			
Advertising expense	21,000	21,000	21,000
Shipping expense	34,000	36,000	38,000
Salaries and commissions........	78,000	84,000	90,000
Insurance expense..............	6,000	6,000	6,000
Amortization expense	15,000	15,000	15,000
Total operating expenses...........	154,000	162,000	170,000
Net income	A$ 6,000	A$ 18,000	A$ 30,000

(Note: Morrisey & Brown, Ltd.'s Australian-formatted income statement has been recast in the format common in Canada. The Australian dollar is denoted by A$.)

Required:
1. Identify each of the company's expenses (including cost of goods sold) as being variable, fixed, or mixed.
2. Using the high-low method, separate each mixed expense into variable and fixed elements. State the cost formula for each mixed expense.
3. Redo the company's income statement at the 5,000-unit level of activity using the contribution format.

PROBLEM 3–5   Identifying Cost Behaviour Patterns (CC1, 2, 3, 6)
A number of graphs displaying cost behaviour patterns that might be found in a company's cost structure are shown following. The vertical axis on each graph represents total cost and the horizontal axis represents the level of activity (volume).

Required:
1. For each of the following situations, identify the graph below that illustrates the cost pattern involved. Any graph may be used more than once.
   a. Cost of raw materials used.
   b. Electricity bill—a flat fixed charge, plus a variable cost after a certain number of kilowatt-hours are used.
   c. City water bill, which is computed as follows:

First 1,000,000 litres or less..........	$1,000 flat fee
Next 10,000 litres...................	0.003 per litre used
Next 10,000 litres...................	0.006 per litre used
Next 10,000 litres...................	0.009 per litre used
Etc...............................	Etc.

   d. Amortization of equipment, where the amount is computed by the straight-line method. When the amortization rate was established, it was anticipated that the obsolescence factor would be greater than the wear-and-tear factor.

e. Rent on a factory building donated by the city, where the agreement calls for a fixed fee payment unless 200,000 labour-hours or more are worked, in which case no rent need be paid.

f. Salaries of maintenance workers, where one maintenance worker is needed for every 1,000 hours of machine-hours or less (that is, 0 to 1,000 hours requires one maintenance worker, 1,001 to 2,000 hours requires two maintenance workers, etc.)

g. Cost of raw materials, where the cost starts at $7.50 per unit and then decreases by 5 cents per unit for each of the first 100 units purchased, after which it remains constant at $2.50 per unit.

h. Rent on a factory building donated by the county, where the agreement calls for rent of $100,000 less $1 for each direct labour-hour worked in excess of 200,000 hours, but a minimum rental payment of $20,000 must be paid.

i. Use of a machine under a lease, where a minimum charge of $1,000 is paid for up to 400 hours of machine time. After 400 hours of machine time, an additional charge of $2 per hour is paid up to a maximum charge of $2,000 per period.

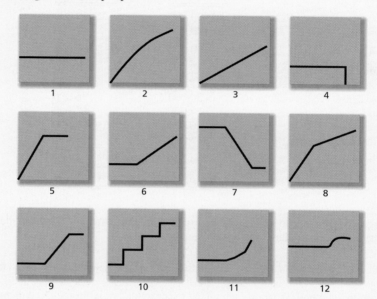

2. How would knowing cost behaviour patterns, such as those above, be of help to a manager in analyzing the cost structure of his or her firm?

(CPA adapted)

CHECK FIGURE
(2) ¥1,500,000 per year
plus ¥35 per DLH

PROBLEM 3–6   High-Low Method and Cost Behaviour (CC10, 11)

Sawaya Co., Ltd., of Japan, is a manufacturing company whose total factory overhead costs fluctuate considerably from year to year according to increases and decreases in the number of direct labour-hours worked in the factory. Total factory overhead costs (in Japanese yen, denoted ¥) at high and low levels of activity for recent years are provided following:

	Level of Activity	
	Low	High
Direct labour-hours	50,000	75,000
Total factory overhead costs	¥14,250,000	¥17,625,000

The factory overhead costs above consist of indirect materials, rent, and maintenance. The company has analyzed these costs at the 50,000-hour level of activity as follows:

Indirect materials (V)	¥ 5,000,000
Rent (F)	6,000,000
Maintenance (M)	3,250,000
Total factory overhead costs	¥14,250,000

V = variable; F = fixed; M = mixed.

To have data available for planning, the company wants to break down the maintenance cost into its variable and fixed cost elements.

Required:
1. Estimate how much of the ¥17,625,000 factory overhead cost at the high level of activity consists of maintenance cost. (Hint: To do this, it may be helpful to first determine how much of the ¥17,625,000 consists of indirect materials and rent. Think about the behaviour of variable and fixed costs!)
2. By means of the high-low method of cost analysis, estimate a cost formula for maintenance.
3. What total factory overhead costs would you expect the company to incur at an operating level of 70,000 direct labour-hours?

PROBLEM 3–7   High-Low Method and Predicting Cost (CC10, 11)

Nova Company's total overhead costs at various levels of activity follow:

CHECK FIGURE
(2) $9,000 per month plus $1.60 per machine-hour

Month	Machine-Hours	Total Overhead Costs
April	70,000	$198,000
May.	60,000	174,000
June.	80,000	222,000
July	90,000	246,000

Assume that the total overhead costs consist of utilities, supervisory salaries, and maintenance. The breakdown of these costs at the 60,000 machine-hour level of activity is:

Utilities (V).	$ 48,000
Supervisory salaries (F)	21,000
Maintenance (M)	105,000
Total overhead costs	$174,000

V = variable; F = fixed; M = mixed.

Nova Company's management wants to break down the maintenance cost into its basic variable and fixed cost elements.

Required:
1. As shown, overhead costs in July amounted to $246,000. Determine how much of this consisted of maintenance cost. (Hint: To do this, it may be helpful to first determine how much of the $246,000 consisted of utilities and supervisory salaries. Think about the behaviour of variable and fixed costs!)
2. By means of the high-low method, estimate a cost formula for maintenance.
3. Express the company's *total* overhead costs in the linear equation form $Y = a + bX$.
4. What *total* overhead costs would you expect to be incurred at an operating activity level of 75,000 machine-hours?

PROBLEM 3–8   High-Low Method; Cost of Goods Manufactured (CC10, 11)

Amfac Company manufactures a single product. The company keeps careful records of manufacturing activities from which the following information has been extracted:

CHECK FIGURE
(2) $30,000 per month plus $8 per unit

	Level of Activity	
	March-Low	June-High
Number of units produced	6,000	9,000
Cost of goods manufactured	$168,000	$257,000
Work-in-process inventory, beginning.	9,000	32,000
Work-in-process inventory, ending	15,000	21,000
Direct materials cost per unit.	6	6
Direct labour cost per unit	10	10
Manufacturing overhead cost, total	?	?

The company's manufacturing overhead cost consists of both variable and fixed cost elements. To have data available for planning, management wants to determine how much of the overhead cost is variable with units produced and how much of it is fixed per month.

Required:
1. For both March and June, determine the amount of manufacturing overhead cost added to production. (Hint: A useful way to proceed might be to construct a schedule of cost of goods manufactured.)
2. By means of the high-low method of cost analysis, estimate a cost formula for manufacturing overhead. Express the variable portion of the formula in terms of a variable rate per unit of product.
3. If 7,000 units are produced during a month, what would be the cost of goods manufactured? (Assume that work-in-process inventories do not change for the month.)

CHECK FIGURE
(1) 1,034,100

PROBLEM 3–9   Mixed Cost Analysis (CC10, 11, 12, 13, 14)

Cypher Company is a manufacturer of board games. The management accountant at Cypher has been having some difficulty estimating overhead costs. He wishes to determine a systematic method for associating overhead costs with production levels. To facilitate this association, he has assembled data on the monthly overhead costs and monthly production levels for 2007.

Month	Production (Units)	Overhead Cost
1.............	75,000	$ 925,800
2.............	90,000	876,000
3.............	65,000	910,000
4.............	80,000	946,000
5.............	55,000	879,000
6.............	50,000	825,000
7.............	85,000	960,000
8.............	105,000	1,055,000
9.............	102,000	1,020,000
10	68,000	905,000
11	75,000	938,000
12	95,000	995,000

Required
1. Using the high-low method, calculate next month's overhead costs, assuming the company is planning to produce 100,000 units.
2. Sketch a scattergraph showing the overhead costs plotted against the production in units.
3. Briefly describe the relationship you observe in the scattergraph between overhead costs and units produced in terms of R^2.

(Adapted © CGA-Canada)

CHECK FIGURE
(1) Monthly cost equation:
   $881 + $5.43 per
   machine-hour

PROBLEM 3–10   High-Low Method, Least-Squares Regression (CC5, 10, 11, 14, 15)

The following cost and activity data are available for KeeKaaKoo Enterprises for 2007.

Month	Machine-hours	Electricity costs
January	2,500	$ 18,400
February	2,900	21,000
March	1,900	11,200
April	3,100	20,100
May..............	3,800	29,250
June..............	3,300	24,000
July	4,100	24,750
August............	3,500	22,750
September.........	2,000	19,700
October...........	3,700	26,000
November.........	4,700	26,400
December	4,200	27,750

Required

1. Using the high-low method, develop a cost equation for the electricity costs per month. What will the cost equation be for the *annual* electricity costs?
2. Estimate the electricity costs for months in which 4,000 and 7,000 machine-hours are consumed.
3. Using a regression analysis, KeeKaaKoo developed the following cost equation for its monthly electricity costs: Y = $6,513.10 + $4.86 per machine hour. The R^2 came out to be under 74%. Compute the electricity costs for a month in which 4,000 machine-hours are consumed.
4. KeeKaaKoo produces five different products (A to E), which consume the same number of machine-hours per unit. However, each product requires a different set of machines (set A for product A, set B for product B and so on). Machine sets A and D are highly energy efficient (they consume little power per machine-hour), set E is moderately energy efficient, and sets B and C are not energy efficient. Do you believe machine-hours is a good basis on which to develop the cost equation for electricity hours? Why or why not?

Building Your Skills

ANALYTICAL THINKING   (CC5, 10, 11, 12, 13)

The Ramon Company manufactures a wide range of products at several plant locations. The Franklin plant, which manufactures electrical components, has been experiencing difficulties with fluctuating monthly overhead costs. The fluctuations have made it difficult to estimate the level of overhead that will be incurred for any one month.

Management wants to be able to estimate overhead costs accurately in order to better plan its operational and financial needs. A trade association publication to which Ramon Company subscribes indicates that for companies manufacturing electrical components, overhead tends to vary with direct labour-hours.

One member of the accounting staff has proposed the cost behaviour pattern of the overhead costs be determined. Then overhead costs could be predicted from the budgeted direct labour-hours.

Another member of the accounting staff has suggested that a good starting place for determining the cost behaviour pattern of overhead costs would be an analysis of historical data. The historical cost behaviour pattern would provide a basis for estimating future overhead costs. Ramon Company has decided to employ the high-low method and the scattergraph method. Data on direct labour-hours and the respective overhead costs incurred have been collected for the past two years. The raw data are as follows:

CHECK FIGURE
(1) Cost formula,
Y = $41,500 + $2.30X

| Month | Prior Year | | Current Year | |
	Direct Labour-Hours	Overhead Costs	Direct Labour-Hours	Overhead Costs
January	20,000	$84,000	21,000	$86,000
February	25,000	99,000	24,000	93,000
March	22,000	89,500	23,000	93,000
April	23,000	90,000	22,000	87,000
May............	20,000	81,500	20,000	80,000
June............	19,000	75,500	18,000	76,500
July	14,000	70,500	12,000	67,500
August..........	10,000	64,500	13,000	71,000
September	12,000	69,000	15,000	73,500
October	17,000	75,000	17,000	72,500
November	16,000	71,500	15,000	71,000
December	19,000	78,000	18,000	75,000

All equipment in the Franklin plant is leased under an arrangement calling for a flat fee up to 19,500 direct labour-hours of activity in the plant, after which lease charges are assessed on an hourly basis. Lease expense is a major item of overhead cost.

Required:

1. Using the high-low method, estimate the cost formula for overhead in the Franklin plant.
2. Prepare a scattergraph, including on it all data for the two-year period. Fit a regression line or lines to the plotted points by visual inspection. In this part, it is not necessary to compute the fixed and variable cost elements.

3. Assume that the Franklin plant works 22,500 direct labour-hours during a month. Compute the expected overhead cost for the month using the cost formulas developed above with:
   a. The high-low method
   b. The scattergraph method [read the expected costs directly off the graph prepared in part (2)]
4. Of the two proposed methods, which one should the Ramon Company use to estimate monthly overhead costs in the Franklin plant? Explain fully, indicating the reasons why the other method is less desirable.
5. Would a relevant range concept probably be more or less important in the Franklin plant than in most companies?

(CMA adapted)

COMMUNICATING IN PRACTICE   (CC1, 2, 3, 5, 6)

Maria Chavez owns a catering company that serves food and beverages at parties and business functions. Chavez's business is seasonal, with a heavy schedule during the summer months and holidays and a lighter schedule at other times.

One of the major events requested by Chavez's customers is a cocktail party. She offers a standard cocktail party and has estimated the total cost per guest as follows:

Food and beverages	$15.00
Labour (0.5 hours @ $10.00 per hour).	5.00
Overhead (0.5 hours @ $13.98 per hour).	6.99
Total cost per guest.	$26.99

The standard cocktail party lasts three hours, and she hires one worker for every six guests, which works out to one-half hour of direct labour per guest. The servers work only as needed and are paid only for the hours they actually work.

When bidding on cocktail parties, Chavez adds a 15% markup to yield a price of $31 per guest. Chavez is confident about her estimates of the costs of food and beverages and labour, but is not as comfortable with the estimate of overhead cost. The overhead cost per guest was determined by dividing total overhead expenses for the last 12 months by total labour-hours for the same period. Her overhead includes such costs as annual rent for office space, administrative costs (including those relating to hiring and paying workers), and so on.

Chavez has received a request to bid on a large fundraising cocktail party to be given next month by an important local charity. (The party would last three hours.) She would really like to win this contract—the guest list for this charity event includes many prominent individuals she would like to land as future clients. Other caterers have also been invited to bid on the event, and she believes that one, if not more, of those companies will bid less than $31 per guest. She is not willing to lose money on the event and needs your input before making any decisions.

Required:

Write a memorandum to Ms. Chavez that addresses the validity of her concern about her estimate of overhead costs and whether she should base her bid on the estimated cost of $26.99 per guest. (Hint: Start by discussing the need to consider cost behaviour when estimating costs. You can safely assume that she will not incur any additional fixed costs if she wins the bid on this cocktail party.)

TEAMWORK IN ACTION   (CC1, 3, 5)

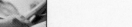

Assume that your team is going to form a company that will manufacture chocolate chip cookies. The team is responsible for preparing a list of all product components and costs necessary to manufacture this product.

Required:

1. The team should discuss and then write a brief description of the definitions of variable, fixed, and mixed costs. All team members should agree with and understand the definitions.
2. After preparing a list of all product components and costs necessary to manufacture your cookies, identify each of the product costs as direct materials, direct labour, or factory overhead. Then, identify each of those costs as variable, fixed, or mixed.
3. Prepare to report this information in class. (Each teammate can assume responsibility for a different part of the presentation.)

Don't forget to visit the Online Learning Centre for self-study quizzes, practice exams, and more! Visit www.mcgrawhill.ca/olc/brewer.

CHAPTER *Four*

Systems Design: Job-Order Costing

CHAPTER COMPETENCIES

After studying Chapter 4, you should be able to demonstrate the following competencies:

Competency		Know	Apply
Understand the context for costing systems.			
CC1	Distinguish between process costing and job-order costing by identifying companies that would use each costing method.	●	
CC2	Describe the key decisions management must make when applying a system to determine costs.	●	
CC3	Distinguish between absorption and variable costing, and between normal and actual costing.	●	
Compute the costs of a specific job.			
CC4	Determine the cost of a specific job in a job-order costing system.		●
CC5	Identify the source documents used in a job-order costing system.	●	
Understand the importance of the concept of overhead cost and its computation.			
CC6	Compute predetermined overhead rates.		●
CC7	Determine the amount of overhead to be applied to a job using a predetermined rate.		●
CC8	Explain why estimated overhead costs, not actual overhead costs, are preferred to be used in the costing process.	●	
CC9	Explain the importance of an overhead allocation base when allocating overhead costs to products and services.	●	
Determine costs incurred in a job-order production system over a specified period and describe the flow of costs through the cost accounting system.			
CC10	Explain why the unit cost of a product is an average cost, not the cost of making another unit of the product.	●	
CC11	Describe the relationship between the flow of documents in a job-order costing system.	●	
CC12	Provide an accounting of the costs incurred over a specific period of operations by preparing journal entries to record costs in a job-order costing system.		●
CC13	Differentiate between the process for determining the cost of a specific product and the accounting for the costs incurred in a job-order costing system during a specific period of operations.	●	
Understand the incurrence and application of overhead costs.			
CC14	Describe how incurred overhead costs are recorded in the accounting system.	●	
CC15	Apply overhead costs to work in process using a predetermined overhead rate.		●
CC16	Explain the concept of a clearing account.	●	
Prepare accounting schedules documenting the costs incurred.			
CC17	Prepare T-accounts to show the flow of costs in a job-order costing system.		●
CC18	Prepare schedules of COGM and COGS.		●
Reconcile the difference between actual and applied overhead cost.			
CC19	Compute under- or over-applied overhead cost, and prepare the journal entry to close the balance in manufacturing overhead to the appropriate accounts.		●
CC20	Describe the causes of under- and over-applied overhead.	●	
CC21	Explain why the under- or over-applied overhead balance must be disposed of at period end.	●	
CC22	Distinguish between a plantwide overhead rate and a multiple overhead rate.	●	
Prepare profitability reports for management using information from the cost accounting system.			
CC23	Determine the profitability of operations over a specific period by preparing an income statement from the information accumulated in a job-order costing system.		●

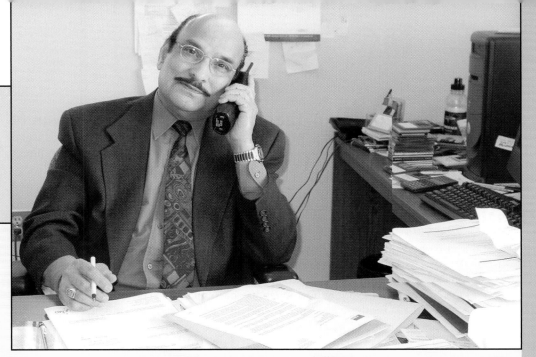

DECISION FEATURE
Leveraging Brain Power: System Ecotechnologies

System Ecotechnologies Inc., a Canadian success story, is located in Saskatoon, Saskatchewan. The company founder and owner, Dr. G. Lakshman designs ingenious customized engineering solutions for such clients as the governments of Egypt and El Salvador; public and private for-profit companies, such as Seagram's and EnviroSeed Technologies Inc.; not-for-profit organizations, such as Cities of Estevan, Whitehorse, and Prince George; and SaskPower and Saskatchewan Water Corporation.

Consider these two examples. He devised a way for Seagram's to convert "mash"— a by-product of the process of turning grain into 100% ethanol, which has high concentrations of "heavy metals"—into environmentally friendly waste water. In El Salvador, Dr. Lakshman showed how the "pulp" by-product of coffee production could be treated to extract caffeine and release harmless waste water.

System Ecotechnologies Inc.'s revenues are driven by the stream of contracts and projects— *jobs*—that Dr. Lakshman is able to attract *and* deliver on. He runs a lean operation from a small lab and office in a research park on the grounds of the University of Saskatchewan. Upon obtaining a project, Dr. Lakshman devotes the bulk of his time to designing the engineering and chemical solution and protocol to the client's problem. He outsources all of the complex chemical and lab work, and bills the client. His approach typically is to model a solution on a scale that can be analyzed and studied in the lab. Following this, a full-scale implementation is designed and applied.

Dr. Lakshman's reputation would not be what it is if his own operations and the engineered solutions were not also *cost efficient*. His management system enables him to ride the ups and downs of an uncertain revenue stream. Cost management is a key component in being "lean." His business has many of the classic characteristics of a "job-shop"—a type of production system, which is the subject of this chapter. In such systems, the business depends on "artisanship." The skills offered and leveraged relate to thinking creatively and *crafting* a solution. Quality and timely delivery are key success factors. Each project or job is unique and the price charged comes down specifically to the work done to develop the solution. And, as just mentioned, *cost management* is absolutely critical.

Source: Site visit and personal interviews conducted by the authors, and promotional materials furnished by Dr. Lakshman.

A Look Back
Chapter 1 described the three major activities of managers, comparing and contrasting financial and managerial accounting. In Chapter 2, we defined many of the terms that are used to classify costs in business. We used many of these terms in Chapter 3. Now would be a good time to check your understanding of these terms by referring to the glossary at the end of Chapters 2 and 3.

A Look at This Chapter
Chapter 4 distinguishes between two costing systems, job-order and process costing, and then provides an in-depth look at a job-order costing system. We describe how direct material and direct labour costs are accumulated on jobs. Then, we address manufacturing overhead, an indirect cost that must be allocated (or applied) to jobs. Finally, we take a more detailed look at the flow of costs through a company's accounting system using journal entries.

A Look Ahead
Chapter 5 continues the discussion of cost determination in the process costing system. We show that many of the issues relating to cost accumulation in a job-order costing system also carry over to the process costing system. Nonetheless, there are important differences that are highlighted in that chapter.

Product costing is the process of assigning costs to

a company's products and services. An understanding of this process is vital to managers because the cost data provided by the costing systems will help them plan, control, direct, and make decisions.

The Purpose of Costing Systems

The purpose of costing systems is to accumulate and record the incurrence of costs and to assign the costs to the cost objects—products and activities that lead to their incurrence. Every costing system must accomplish two things: (1) it should tell you which costs are *traceable* to the cost object, including how much has been incurred. These are the cost object's *direct costs*. And, (2) for those costs that cannot be traced directly to a product or activity—such as the costs of using physical facilities, utility and power costs, shop supplies, and so on—the costing system or approach must tell you how to *allocate* those costs to the product or activity whose cost you are trying to compute. These are the *indirect costs*.

Types of Costing Systems

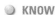 **KNOW**

CC1: Distinguish between process costing and job-order costing by identifying companies that would use each costing method.

Costs are typically incurred when the company makes goods for or provides services to customers. Therefore, the nature of the costing system is intimately tied to the type of production system used by a company. Two types of production systems are common: job shops and flow shops. The two types of costing systems that correspond to the job shop and the flow shop are respectively the **job-order costing system** and **process costing system**.

Job Shops and Job-Order Costing

Job shops typically make a large variety of products in small quantities called *batches*. Each order or batch is also referred to as a *job*. *Flow shops* produce a much smaller variety of products in large volumes, using a standardized and fixed sequence of operations. Job shops usually *produce to order*. These production facilities are capable of making special one-of-a-kind custom orders. Small metal fabrication companies, for example, can make custom components for use in machinery. Golf equipment maker MacGregor Golf, for example, can custom forge its irons by grinding the top-line and the sole of the club in addition to setting the lie angle according to the specification of the customer. Examples of companies that use this type of production system include Bombardier, De Havilland, Hallmark (the greeting card maker), and LSG Sky Chefs (who prepare airline meals).

Flow Shops and Process Costing

Flow shops typically *produce to stock*, and the products that are made by these systems are sold from inventory. Examples include J. G. Schneider Foods in Kitchener, Ontario, which makes processed meats; any soft-drink bottler; the Potash Corporation of Saskatchewan; and Reynolds Aluminium. Television and appliance makers also fall into this category as do flour mills, cement manufacturers, and oil refiners. The difference between an appliance maker and an oil refiner is that oil refining is a *continuous* process, meaning the output is one continuous stream. You cannot distinguish between the first litre and the last litre of oil. Appliance production, however, is a *discrete* process, which means that it is possible to identify the first unit from the last unit.

Because production occurs continuously in large volumes in a flow shop, the concept of a batch is not meaningful over a period of time. Therefore, in process costing, costs of production over a period are accumulated first within a process and then divided by the volume of production to compute unit costs. This costing technique results in a broad average unit cost figure that applies to homogeneous units flowing in a continuous stream out of the production process. Process costing will be considered in the next chapter.

Approaches to Costing—Key Management Decisions

Absorption Versus Variable Costing Approaches

Before a costing system is used to determine product costs, management must make certain important decisions. A firm will incur both fixed and variable costs when engaged in providing goods and services. One important decision for managers to make is whether product costs should include *both* fixed and variable costs. If a firm decides the cost of each unit of product will include a portion of the fixed as well as variable costs, the unit of product is said to *fully absorb* manufacturing costs. This approach to product costing is called **absorption** (or **full**) **costing**: all manufacturing costs are completely assigned to products. In certain circumstances, when management determines that fixed costs are *not relevant* to the purpose for which product cost information is desired, a different approach called **variable costing** is used. In the variable costing approach, only variable costs of the product are considered in the analysis of the product's contribution to the firm's profits.

The absorption costing approach is common to many businesses since (1) external financial reporting and tax reporting requirements dictate the use of this approach and (2) many companies have found this approach useful for management accounting purposes. For this reason, in this chapter and in the two that follow, we will use the absorption costing approach to determine product costs. Variable costing will be considered in later chapters.

● **KNOW**

CC2: Describe the key decisions management must make when applying a system to determine costs.

● **KNOW**

CC3: Distinguish between absorption and variable costing, and between normal and actual costing.

Normal Versus Actual Costing Approaches

Consider that the actual cost of a product is not known until the product is made. However, managers often require cost information to make important decisions before a product is made (e.g., in a situation where the company might be bidding for a contract). Managers might be able to estimate and predict the incurrence of direct costs before these costs are incurred. But what about the incurrence of indirect costs—overhead costs? Should managers wait until after the overhead costs have been incurred and then allocate these *actual* overhead costs to the product? Or should managers first *budget* the manufacturing overhead costs, then *apply* these *budgeted* manufacturing overhead costs to the products? If managers allocate *actual* manufacturing overhead costs to products, they are said to be using the **actual costing system**. If managers use the *budgeted* manufacturing overhead costs and apply them to the product, they are said to be using a **normal costing system.**

Managers must decide whether to use a normal costing system or the actual costing system. For our purposes, we will follow a normal costing approach in this chapter and the next two. In a normal costing system, actual overhead costs are never assigned to products and these costs do not flow through the inventory accounts. Instead of actual costs, budgeted overhead costs are applied to products and it is these budgeted overhead costs that flow through to the inventory accounts.

Certainly, managers are aware that the amount of the actual manufacturing costs can vary (more or less) from the amount budgeted. Such differences will have to be reconciled at period end to bring normal costs in line with actual costs, especially when preparing and reporting financial results. The choice of a method of reconciliation is another decision for managers to make, and there are several approaches that can be used for adjusting normal costs. Regardless of the method of adjustment chosen, product costs are never adjusted in a normal costing system in the reconciliation process. In this text we will adjust the cost of goods sold at the end of the operating cycle for the difference between actual and applied manufacturing overhead costs.

Manufacturing Overhead Cost Allocation Approaches

One of the main challenges for management accountants is the problem of overhead allocation. Indirect costs—budgeted or actual—by their very nature are not traceable to the product and therefore have to be allocated to products using an allocation method. The choice of the allocation method is another important decision for managers because different methods can lead to different allocations of manufacturing overhead. This topic will be considered later in this chapter and in other chapters in this text. For now, you should note that the debate about the choice of the allocation method is distinct from the debate regarding the merits of normal versus actual costing systems.

We are now ready to proceed to a detailed look at the job-order costing system. Our illustration of the job-order costing system will deal with a manufacturing firm, but the same concepts and procedures may be used by many service organizations like hospitals, movie studios, and professional service firms like law offices and accounting firms. We will assume that management has decided to follow the absorption costing approach and the normal costing system.

Job-Flow Systems in Canada

How many Canadian manufacturing companies are designed as job-flow systems? According to a survey of manufacturing companies, over 26% were organized as job-flow systems, whereas over 8% were organized as process-flow systems. What about the remaining 66% (two-thirds)? It is important to remember that job-flow and process-flow systems are two pure systems—two ends of a continuum—whereas in practice many companies may adopt some combination of the two. Another interesting point is that over 55% of the companies indicated that they were using a just-in-time (JIT) production system, one component of the lean business model.

Source: Murray Lindsay and Suresh Kalagnanam, *The Adoption of Just-in-Time Production Systems in Canada and Their Association with Management Control Practices*. Society of Management Accountants of Canada, 1993. Reprinted with permission from CMA Canada.

An Overview of Job-Order Costing—Determine the Cost of a Specific Job

APPLY

CC4: Determine the cost of a specific job in a job-order costing system.

To introduce job-order costing, we will follow a specific job as it progresses through the manufacturing process. Yost Precision Manufacturing has agreed to manufacture two experimental couplings for Loops Unlimited, a manufacturer of roller coasters. A coupling connects the cars on the roller coaster and is a critical component in the performance and safety of the ride. Loops Unlimited wants to test a new design and requires only two units. Yost Precision considers the job as an investment; it wants to show Loops that it can make the couplings according to the required specifications and quality. If the tests are successful, Yost will be in a commanding position to win the order to supply couplings for the whole ride.

To secure Loops' business, Yost has agreed to supply the experimental couplings at its cost of goods sold. This means that Yost must carefully document its costs during the manufacturing process. This is the responsibility of Yost's job-order costing system. The cost of manufacturing the couplings will be determined by recording and accumulating the costs of direct materials, direct labour, and manufacturing overhead incurred to complete the job.

Measuring Direct Materials Cost

The costing system kicks into gear when a production order is issued authorizing production. The production department then prepares a *materials requisition form* for the job. The **materials requisition form** is a detailed source document that (1) specifies the type and quantity of materials to be drawn from the storeroom, and (2) identifies the job to which the costs of materials are to be charged. The form is used to control the flow of materials into production and also for making entries in the accounting records. The information on the materials requisition form about the quantity and type of materials required is typically taken from the product's *bill of materials*. The **bill of materials** is a document that lists the type of and quantity of each item of materials required to complete one unit of product. The bill of materials itself is determined initially from blueprints and engineering specifications and will undergo many revisions as the product goes through its development cycle.

Each coupling will require one M46 housing and two G7 connectors. This means that the order will require four G7 connectors and two M46 housings in total to make two couplings. This information is shown in the materials requisition form in Exhibit 4–1 prepared by the company's milling department. This completed form is presented to the storeroom clerk, who then issues the necessary raw materials. The storeroom clerk is not allowed to release materials without such a form bearing an authorized signature.

● KNOW

CC5: Identify the source documents used in a job-order costing system.

Materials Requisition
Number _____ 14873 _____   Date ___ March 2 ___
Job Number to Be Charged ___ 2847 ___
Department _Milling_____

Description	Quantity	Unit Cost	Total Cost
M46 Housing	2	$124	$248
G7 Connector	4	103	412
			$660
			To Job Cost Sheet (Job #2847)

Authorized
Signature _____ Bill White _____

Exhibit 4–1
Materials Requisition Form

Job Cost Sheet

After being notified that the production order has been issued, the accounting department prepares a *job cost sheet* similar to the one presented in Exhibit 4–2. A **job cost sheet** is a form prepared for each separate job that records the materials, labour, and overhead costs charged to the job.

In addition to serving as a means for charging costs to jobs, the job cost sheet also serves as a key part of a firm's accounting records. The job cost sheets form a subsidiary ledger to the work-in-process account. They are detailed records for the jobs in process that add up to the balance in work in process.

Measuring Direct Labour Cost

Direct labour cost is handled in much the same way as direct materials cost. Direct labour consists of labour charges that are easily traced to a particular job. Labour charges that

Exhibit 4–2
Job Cost Sheet

JOB COST SHEET

Job Number ___2847___   Date Initiated ___March 2___

Date Completed _____

Department ___Milling___   Units Completed _____

Item ___Special order coupling___

For Stock _____

Direct Materials		Direct Labour			Manufacturing Overhead		
Req. No.	Amount	Ticket	Hours	Amount	Hours	Rate	Amount
From Materials Requisition Forms	From Materials Requisition Forms	From Time Tickets	From Time Tickets	From Time Tickets			

Cost Summary		Units Shipped		
Direct Materials	$	Date	Number	Balance
Direct Labour	$			
Manufacturing Overhead	$			
Total Cost	$			
Unit Cost	$			

cannot be easily traced directly to any job are treated as part of manufacturing overhead. As discussed in the previous chapter, this latter category of labour costs is called *indirect labour* and includes such tasks as maintenance, supervision, and clean-up.

Workers use *time tickets* to record the time they spend on each job and task. A completed **time ticket** is an hour-by-hour summary of the employee's activities throughout the day. An example of an employee time ticket is shown in Exhibit 4–3. When working on a specific job, the employee enters the job number on the time ticket and notes the amount of time spent on that job. When not assigned to a particular job, the employee records the nature of the indirect labour task (such as clean-up and maintenance) and the amount of time spent on the task.

Exhibit 4–3
Employee Time Ticket

Time Ticket No. ___843___   Date ___March 3___

Employee ___Mary Holden___   Station ___4___

Started	Ended	Time Completed	Rate	Amount	Job Number
7:00	12:00	5.0	$9	$45 (To various job cost sheets)	2847
12:30	2:30	2.0	9	18	2B50
2:30	3:30	1.0	9	9	Maintenance
Totals		8.0		$72	

Supervisor ___R.W. Pace___

Is Sending Jobs Overseas Always a Good Idea?   IN BUSINESS TODAY

In recent years, many companies have sent jobs from high labor cost countries such as the United States to lower labor cost countries such as India and China. But is chasing labor cost savings always the right thing to do? In manufacturing, the answer is no. Typically, total direct labor costs are around 7% to 15% of cost of goods sold. Since direct labor is such a small part of overall costs, the labor savings realized by "offshoring" jobs can easily be overshadowed by a decline in supply chain efficiency that occurs simply because production facilities are located farther from the ultimate customers. The increase in inventory carrying costs and obsolescence costs coupled with slower response to customer orders, not to mention foreign currency exchange risks, can more than offset the benefits of employing geographically dispersed low-cost labor.

One manufacturer of casual wear in Los Angeles, California, understands the value of keeping jobs close to home in order to maintain a tightly knit supply chain. The company can fill orders for as many as 160,000 units in 24 hours. In fact, the company carries less than 30 days' inventory and is considering fabricating clothing only after orders are received from customers rather than attempting to forecast what items will sell and making them in advance. How would they do this? The company's entire supply chain—including weaving, dyeing, and sewing—is located in downtown Los Angeles, eliminating shipping delays.

Source: Robert Sternfels and Ronald Ritter, "When Offshoring Doesn't Make Sense," *The Wall Street Journal*, October 19, 2004, p. B8.

At the end of the day, the time tickets are gathered and the accounting department enters the direct labour-hours and costs on individual job cost sheets. (See Exhibit 4–2 for an example of how direct labour costs are entered on the job cost sheet.) The daily time tickets are source documents that are used as the basis for labour cost entries into the accounting records.

The system we have just described is a manual method. Many companies now rely on computerized systems. Computers, coupled with such technology as bar codes, can eliminate much of the drudgery involved in routine bookkeeping activities while increasing timeliness and accuracy.

The Potential for Inaccurate Product Costs   IN BUSINESS TODAY

Labour costs were a large portion of total manufacturing costs as recently as 20 years ago. However, increasing price competition and a strong focus on quality and reliability have forced many manufacturers to automate many of their processes. A 2002–2003 Management Issues survey conducted by Canadian Manufacturers & Exporters suggests that Canadian manufacturers are rapidly adopting computer technology in such areas as design and engineering, fabrication and assembly, materials handling, and control and communication. A direct result of automation is that direct labour is becoming less important and also represents a smaller portion of total manufacturing costs. This raises two issues: (1) whether companies should maintain elaborate systems to track direct labour-hours and costs, and (2) whether direct labour is still an appropriate base to allocate manufacturing overhead costs.

Source: Canadian Manufacturers & Exporters, Dr. Jason Myers, PhD, Chief Economist, http://www.cme-mec.ca/national/documents/management_issues_survey_oct_07_2002.pdf

Application of Manufacturing Overhead

Manufacturing overhead must be included with direct materials and direct labour on the job cost sheet since manufacturing overhead is also a product cost. However, assigning manufacturing overhead to units of product can be a difficult task. There are three reasons for this.

- Manufacturing overhead is an *indirect cost*. This means that it is either impossible or difficult to trace these costs to a particular product or job.
- Manufacturing overhead consists of many different items ranging from the grease used in machines to the annual salary of the production manager.
- Even though output may fluctuate due to seasonal or other factors, manufacturing overhead costs tend to remain relatively constant due to the presence of fixed costs.

Given these problems, about the only way to assign overhead costs to products is to use an allocation process. This allocation of overhead costs is accomplished by selecting an **allocation base** that is common to all of the company's products and services. Examples include direct labour-hours and machine-hours.

The allocation base is used to compute the **predetermined overhead rate** in the following formula:

$$\text{Predetermined overhead rate} = \frac{\text{Estimated total manufacturing overhead cost}}{\text{Estimated total units in the allocation base}}$$

Notice that the predetermined overhead rate is based on *estimates*, rather than actual results. This is because the *predetermined* overhead rate is computed *before* the period begins and is used to *apply* overhead cost to jobs throughout the period. The process of assigning overhead cost to jobs is called **overhead application.** The formula for determining the amount of overhead cost to apply to a particular job is as follows:

$$\begin{array}{c}\text{Overhead applied to}\\\text{a particular job}\end{array} = \begin{array}{c}\text{Predetermined}\\\text{overhead rate}\\\text{per unit of allocation base}\end{array} \times \begin{array}{c}\text{Amount of the allocation}\\\text{base incurred by the job}\end{array}$$

When the allocation base is direct labour-hours (i.e., DLH), the formula becomes:

$$\begin{array}{c}\text{Overhead applied to}\\\text{a particular job}\end{array} = \begin{array}{c}\text{Predetermined}\\\text{overhead rate per DLH}\end{array} \times \begin{array}{c}\text{Actual DLHs}\\\text{charged to the job}\end{array}$$

For example, if the predetermined overhead rate is $8 per direct labour-hour, then $8 of overhead cost is *applied* to a job for each direct labour-hour incurred by the job.

USING THE PREDETERMINED OVERHEAD RATE   To illustrate the steps involved in computing and using a predetermined overhead rate, let us return to Yost Precision Machining. The company has estimated its total manufacturing overhead costs to be $320,000 for the year and its total direct labour-hours to be 40,000. Its predetermined overhead rate for the year would be $8 per direct labour-hour, as shown below:

$$\text{Predetermined overhead rate} = \frac{\text{Estimated total manufacturing overhead cost}}{\text{Estimated total units in the allocation base}}$$

$$\frac{\$320,000}{40,000 \text{ DLHs}} = \$8 \text{ per DLH}$$

The job cost sheet in Exhibit 4–4 indicates that 27 direct labour-hours were charged to job 2847. Therefore, a total of $216 of overhead cost would be applied to the job:

$$\begin{array}{c}\text{Overhead applied to}\\\text{job 2847}\end{array} = \begin{array}{c}\text{Predetermined}\\\text{overhead rate}\end{array} \times \begin{array}{c}\text{Actual DLHs}\\\text{charged to job 2847}\end{array}$$

$$\$8 \text{ per DLH} \times 27 \text{ DLHs} = \$216 \text{ of overhead applied to job 2847}$$

Exhibit 4–4
A Completed Job Cost Sheet

JOB COST SHEET

Job Number __2847__   Date Initiated __March 2__
                                        Date Completed __March 8__

Department __Milling__
Item __Special order coupling__   Units Completed __2__
For Stock _____

Direct Materials		Direct Labour			Manufacturing Overhead		
Req. No.	Amount	Ticket	Hours	Amount	Hours	Rate	Amount
14873	$ 660	843	5	$ 45	27	$8/DLH	$216
14875	506	846	8	60			
14912	238	850	4	21			
	$1,404	851	10	54			
			27	$180			

Cost Summary		Units Shipped		
Direct Materials	$1,404	Date	Number	Balance
Direct Labour	$ 180	March 8	—	2
Manufacturing Overhead	$ 216			
Total Cost	$1,800			
Unit Cost	$ 900*			

*$1,800 ÷ 2 units = $900 per unit.

This amount of overhead has been entered on the job cost sheet in Exhibit 4–4. Note that this is *not* the actual amount of overhead caused by the job. There is no attempt to trace actual overhead costs to jobs—if that could be done, the costs would be direct costs, not overhead. The overhead assigned to the job is simply a share of the total overhead that was estimated at the beginning of the year. When a company applies overhead cost to jobs as we have done—that is, by multiplying actual activity by the predetermined overhead rate—it is called a *normal costing system.*

The overhead may be applied when direct labour-hours are charged to jobs, or all of the overhead can be applied at once when the job is completed. The choice is up to the company. If a job is not completed at year-end, however, overhead should be applied to value the work in process inventory.

THE NEED FOR A PREDETERMINED RATE   Instead of using a predetermined rate, a company could wait until the end of the accounting period to compute an actual overhead rate based on the *actual* total manufacturing costs and the *actual* total units in the allocation base for the period. However, managers cite several reasons for using predetermined overhead rates instead of actual overhead rates:

- Managers would like to know the accounting system's valuation of completed jobs *before* the end of the accounting period. Suppose, for example, that Yost Precision Machining waits until the end of the year to compute its overhead rate. Then there would be no way for managers to know the cost of goods sold for job 2847 until the close of the year, even though the job was completed and shipped to the customer in March. The seriousness of this problem can be reduced to some extent by computing the actual overhead more frequently, but that immediately leads to another problem you shall see following.

 KNOW

CC8: Explain why estimated overhead costs, not actual overhead costs, are preferred to be used in the costing process.

- If actual overhead rates are computed frequently, seasonal factors in overhead costs or in the allocation base can produce fluctuations in the overhead rates. Managers generally feel that such fluctuations in overhead rates serve no useful purpose and are misleading.
- The use of a predetermined overhead rate simplifies recordkeeping. To determine the overhead cost to apply to a job, the accounting staff at Yost Precision Machining simply multiplies the direct labour-hours recorded for the job by the predetermined overhead rate of $8 per direct labour-hour.

For these reasons, most companies use predetermined overhead rates, rather than actual overhead rates, in their cost accounting systems.

Choice of an Allocation Base for Overhead Cost

Ideally, the allocation base should be a *cost driver* of the overhead cost. A **cost driver** is a factor, such as machine-hours, beds occupied, computer time, or flight-hours, that causes overhead costs. If a base is used to compute overhead rates that does not "drive" overhead costs, then the result will be inaccurate overhead rates and distorted product costs. For example, if direct labour and overhead costs have been moving in opposite directions in a company because of a shift toward automation and the increased use of highly skilled indirect labour, such as engineers, direct labour should not be used as the allocation base. If direct labour is used in this situation, then products with high direct labour-hour requirements will be over-costed and products with low direct labour-hours requirement will be under-costed. The debate about which allocation base is appropriate has spurred the redesign of costing systems according to the principles of *activity-based costing* (ABC). ABC is a costing technique that is designed to more accurately reflect the demands that products, customers, and other cost objects make on overhead resources. The ABC approach is the topic of Chapter 6.

IN BUSINESS TODAY **Waist Management**

New research from the University of Michigan suggests that an important cost driver for a company's health care costs is the weight of its employees. In fact, the research indicates that workers who have added a few too many pounds can cost companies as much as $1,500 more annually to insure. So what is a company to do? Park Place Entertainment, a casino operator with more than 7,000 employees, decided to attack the problem by holding a weight-loss contest. Over two years, the company's workforce dropped 20 tons of weight. After the contest, 12 diabetics were able to stop using medications that cost $13,300 per year per employee. Additionally, the company believes that its contest has caused a decline in absenteeism and an increase in productivity.

Source: Jill Hecht Maxwell, "Worker Waist Management," *Inc.*, August 2004, p. 32; Jessi Hempel, "Dieting for Dollars," *BusinessWeek*, November 3, 2003, p. 10.

IN BUSINESS TODAY **Understanding Cost Drivers Can Be Tricky Business**

In recent years, hospitals have developed a keen interest in controlling their costs. Conventional wisdom in the health care industry was that costs could be reduced by reducing a patient's length of stay in a hospital. It seemed logical that reducing the number of days that a patient spends in the hospital should reduce the cost of treating that patient. However, researchers John Evans, Yuhchang Hwang, and Nandu Nagarajan provide evidence within one hospital that when doctors were motivated to reduce length of stay, it did not reduce costs. The researchers found that doctors compensated for a reduction in length of stay by increasing the number of procedures performed per patient per day. Thus, any potential savings from reducing one cost driver—length of stay—were offset by cost increases caused by increasing another cost driver—number of procedures performed per patient per day.

Source: John H. Evans, Yuhchang Hwang, and Nandu J. Nagarajan, "Management Control and Hospital Cost Reduction: Additional Evidence," *Journal of Accounting and Public Policy*, Spring 2001, pp. 73–88.

Computation of Unit Costs

With the application of Yost Precision Machining's $216 manufacturing overhead to the job cost sheet in Exhibit 4–4, the job cost sheet is almost complete. There are two final steps. First, the totals for direct materials, direct labour, and manufacturing overhead are transferred to the Cost Summary section of the job cost sheet and added together to obtain the total cost for the job. Then the total cost ($1,800) is divided by the number of units (2) to obtain the unit cost ($900). As indicated previously, *this unit cost is an average cost and should not be interpreted as the cost that would actually be incurred if another unit were produced.* Much of the actual overhead would not change at all if another unit were produced, and so the incremental cost of an additional unit is something less than the average unit cost of $900.

The completed job cost sheet is now ready to be transferred to the finished goods inventory account, where it will serve as the basis for valuing unsold units in ending inventory and determining cost of goods sold.

The sequence of events discussed previously is summarized in Exhibit 4–5. A careful study of the flow of documents in this exhibit will provide a good overview of the overall operation of a job-order costing system.

> 🌑 **KNOW**
>
> CC10: Explain why the unit cost of a product is an average cost, not the cost of making another unit of the product.

> 🌑 **KNOW**
>
> CC11: Describe the relationship between the flow of documents in a job-order costing system.

Treasurer of the Class Reunion Committee   DECISION MAKER

It is hard to believe that 10 years have passed so quickly since your graduation from high school. Take a minute to reflect on what has happened in that time frame. After high school, you attended the local community college, transferred to a university, and graduated on time. You are juggling a successful career, classes in an evening MBA program, and a new family. And now, after reminiscing with one of your high school classmates, you have somehow agreed to handle the financial arrangements for your 10-year reunion. What were you thinking? Well, at least you can fall back on those accounting skills.

You call the restaurant where the reunion will be held and jot down the most important information. The meal cost (including beverages) will be $30 per person plus a 15% gratuity. An additional $200 will be charged for a banquet room with a dance floor. (You do not remember dancing in high school.) A band has been hired for $500. One of the members of the reunion committee informs you that there is just enough money left in the class bank account to cover the printing and mailing costs. He mentions that at least one-half of the class of 400 will attend the reunion and wonders if he should add the 15% gratuity to the $30 per person meal cost when he drafts the invitation, which will indicate that a cheque must be returned with the reply card.

DECISION MAKER   **continued**

How should you respond? How much will you need to charge to cover the various costs? After making your decision, label your answer with the managerial accounting terms covered in this chapter. Finally, identify any issues that should be investigated further.

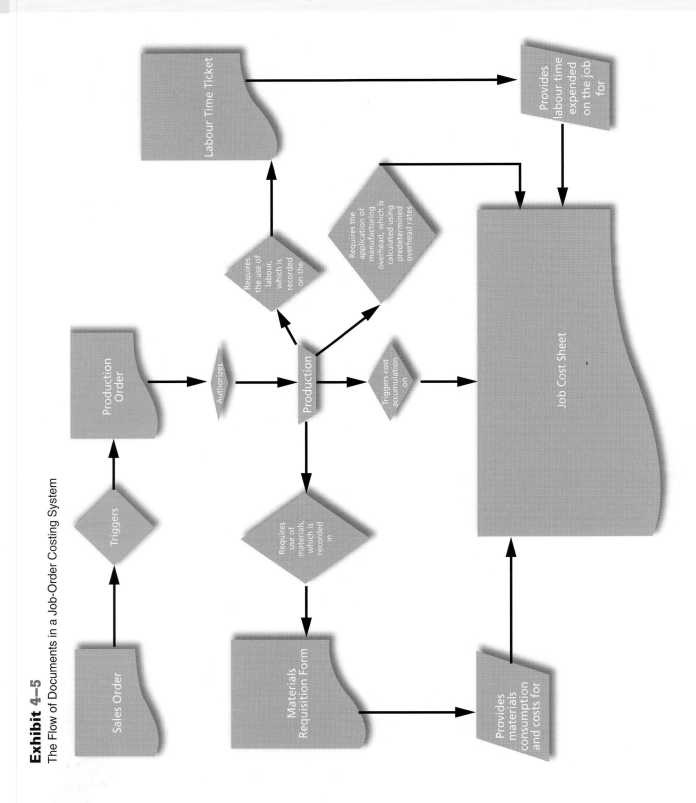

Exhibit 4–5
The Flow of Documents in a Job-Order Costing System

Cost Accounting in a Job-Order System

We are now ready to look at the *flow of costs* through the company's formal accounting system. To illustrate, we shall consider a single month's activity for Rand Company, a producer of gold and silver commemorative medallions. Rand Company has two jobs in process during April, the first month of its fiscal year. Job A, a special minting of 1,000 gold medallions commemorating the invention of motion pictures, was started during March. By the end of March, $30,000 in manufacturing costs had been recorded for the job. Job B, an order for 10,000 silver medallions commemorating the fall of the Berlin Wall, was started in April.

● **APPLY**

CC12: Provide an accounting of the costs incurred over a specific period of operations by preparing journal entries to record costs in a job-order costing system.

The Purchase and Issue of Materials

On April 1, Rand Company had $7,000 in raw materials on hand. During the month, the company purchased an additional $60,000 in raw materials. The purchase is recorded in journal entry (1) below:

● **KNOW**

CC13: Differentiate between the process for determining the cost of a specific product and the accounting for the costs incurred in a job-order costing system during a specific period of operations.

(1)

| Raw Materials . . . . | 60,000 | |
| Accounts Payable. . . . . | | 60,000 |

As explained in the previous chapter, raw materials is an asset account. Thus, when raw materials are purchased, they are initially recorded as an asset—not as an expense.

ISSUE OF DIRECT AND INDIRECT MATERIALS During April, $52,000 in raw materials were requisitioned from the storeroom for use in production. Entry (2) records the issue of the materials to the production departments.

(2)

Work in Process.	50,000	
Manufacturing Overhead.	2,000	
Raw Materials.		52,000

The materials charged to work in process represent direct materials for specific jobs. As these materials are entered into the work-in-process account, they are also recorded on the appropriate job cost sheets. This point is illustrated in Exhibit 4–6, where $28,000 of the $50,000 in direct materials is charged to job A's cost sheet and the remaining $22,000 is charged to job B's cost sheet. (In this example, all data are presented in summary form, and the job cost sheet is abbreviated.)

The $2,000 charged to manufacturing overhead in entry (2) represents indirect materials used in production during April. Observe that the manufacturing overhead account is separate from the work-in-process account. The purpose of the manufacturing overhead account is to accumulate all manufacturing overhead costs as they are incurred during a period.

Before leaving Exhibit 4–6, we need to point out one additional thing. Notice that the job cost sheet for job A contains a beginning balance of $30,000. We stated previously that this balance represents the cost of work done during March that has been carried forward to April. Also notice that the work-in-process account contains the same $30,000 balance. *The reason the $30,000 appears in both places is that the work-in-process account is a control account and the job cost sheets form a subsidiary ledger. Thus, the work-in-process account contains a summarized total of all costs appearing on the individual job cost sheets for all jobs in process at any given point in time.* Since Rand Company had only job A in process at the beginning of April, job A's $30,000 balance on that date is equal to the balance in the work-in-process account.

Exhibit 4–6
Raw Materials Cost Flows

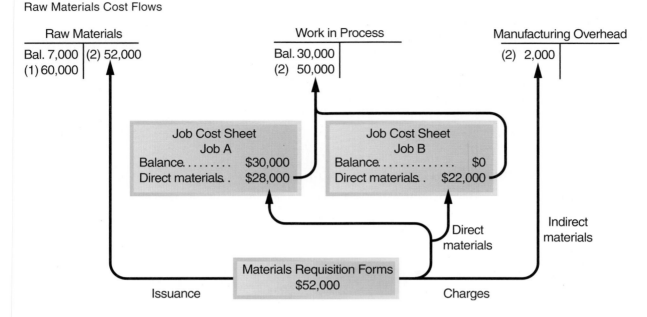

ISSUE OF DIRECT MATERIALS ONLY Sometimes, the materials drawn from the raw materials inventory account are all direct materials. In this case, the entry to record the issue of the materials into production would be as follows:

Work in Process...............................	XXX	
Raw Materials		XXX

Labour Cost

As work is performed each day in various departments of Rand Company, employee time tickets are filled out by workers, collected, and forwarded to the accounting department. In the accounting department, the tickets are costed according to the various employee wage rates, and the resulting costs are classified as either direct or indirect labour. This costing and classification for April resulted in the following summary entry:

(3)

Work in Process............................	60,000	
Manufacturing Overhead.....................	15,000	
Salaries and Wages Payable		75,000

Only direct labour is added to the work-in-process account. For Rand Company, this amounted to $60,000 for April.

At the same time that direct labour costs are added to work in process, they are also added to the individual job cost sheets, as shown in Exhibit 4–7. During April, $40,000 of direct labour cost was charged to job A and the remaining $20,000 was charged to job B.

The labour costs charged to manufacturing overhead represent the indirect labour costs of the period, such as supervision, janitorial work, and maintenance.

Manufacturing Overhead Costs

Recall that all costs of operating the factory other than direct materials and direct labour are classified as manufacturing overhead costs. We will follow a simplified approach to

Exhibit 4-7
Labour Cost Flows

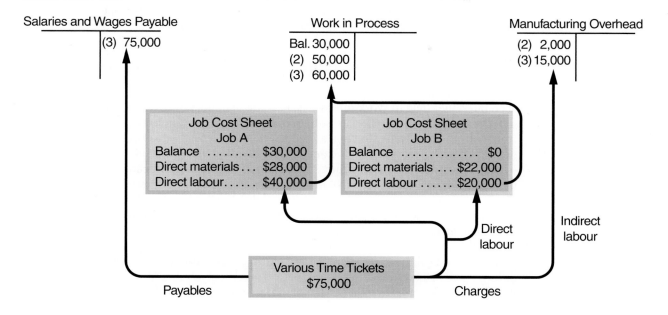

recording the incurrence of these costs by entering them directly into the manufacturing overhead account as they are incurred. To illustrate, assume that Rand Company *incurred* the following general factory costs during April:

Utilities (heat, water, and power)	$21,000
Rent on factory equipment	16,000
Miscellaneous factory costs	3,000
Total	$40,000

● KNOW

CC14: Describe how incurred overhead costs are recorded in the accounting system.

The following entry records the incurrence of these costs:

(4)

Manufacturing Overhead	40,000	
Accounts Payable.		40,000

In addition, let us assume that during April, Rand Company recognized $13,000 in accrued property taxes and that $7,000 in prepaid insurance expired on factory buildings and equipment. The following entry records these items:

(5)

Manufacturing Overhead	20,000	
Property Taxes Payable		13,000
Prepaid Insurance.		7,000

Finally, let us assume that the company recognized $18,000 in amortization on factory equipment during April. The following entry records the accrual of this amortization:

(6)

Manufacturing Overhead	18,000	
Accumulated Amortization		18,000

In short, *all* manufacturing overhead costs are recorded directly into the manufacturing overhead account as they are incurred day by day throughout a period. It is important to understand that in actuality, manufacturing overhead is a control account for many—perhaps thousands—of subsidiary accounts, such as indirect materials, indirect labour, factory utilities, and so on. In the preceding example and also in the end-of-chapter material for this chapter, we omit the entries to the subsidiary accounts for the sake of brevity.

The Application of Manufacturing Overhead

Since actual manufacturing costs are charged to the Manufacturing Overhead control account, rather than to Work in Process, how are manufacturing overhead costs assigned to Work in Process? The answer is, by means of the predetermined overhead rate. Recall from our previous discussion that a predetermined overhead rate is established at the beginning of each year. The rate is calculated by dividing the estimated total manufacturing overhead cost for the year by the estimated total units in the allocation base (measured in machine-hours, direct labour-hours, or some other base). The predetermined overhead rate is then used to apply overhead costs to jobs. For example, if direct labour-hours is the allocation base, overhead cost is applied to each job by multiplying the number of direct labour-hours charged to the job by the predetermined overhead rate.

To illustrate, assume that Rand Company has used machine-hours to compute its predetermined overhead rate and that this rate is $6 per machine-hour. Also, assume that during April, 10,000 machine-hours were worked on job A and 5,000 machine-hours were worked on job B (a total of 15,000 machine-hours). Thus, $90,000 in overhead cost (15,000 machine-hours × $6 per machine-hour = $90,000) would be applied to work in process. The following entry records the application of manufacturing overhead to work in process:

(7)

Work in Process............................	90,000	
Manufacturing Overhead		90,000

The flow of costs through the manufacturing overhead account is shown in Exhibit 4–8.

The "actual overhead costs" in the manufacturing overhead account in Exhibit 4–8 are the costs that were added to the account in entries (2)–(6). Observe that the incurrence of these actual overhead costs [entries (2)–(6)] and the application of overhead to work in process [entry (7)] represent two separate and entirely distinct processes.

THE CONCEPT OF A CLEARING ACCOUNT The manufacturing overhead account operates as a clearing account. As we have noted, actual factory overhead costs are debited to the accounts as they are incurred day by day throughout the year. At certain intervals during the year, usually when a job is completed, overhead cost is applied to the work-in-process account by means of the predetermined overhead rate. This sequence of events is illustrated as follows:

Manufacturing Overhead
(a clearing account)

Actual overhead costs are charged to the account as these costs are incurred day by day throughout the period.	Overhead is applied to work in process using the predetermined overhead rate.

As we emphasized previously, the predetermined overhead rate is based entirely on estimates of what overhead costs are *expected* to be, and it is established before the year begins. As a result, the overhead cost applied during a year will almost certainly turn out to be different from the overhead cost that is actually incurred. For example, note from Exhibit 4–8 that Rand Company's actual overhead costs for the period are $5,000 greater

Exhibit 4–8
The Flow of Costs in Overhead Application

than the overhead cost that has been applied to work in process. The resulting $5,000 debit balance in the manufacturing overhead account is called *under-applied overhead* because the applied cost ($90,000) is less than the actual cost ($95,000). We will reserve discussion of what to do with this $5,000 balance until the next section, *Problems of Overhead Application.*

For the moment, we can conclude from Exhibit 4–8 that the cost of a completed job consists of the actual materials cost of the job, the actual labour cost of the job, and the overhead cost *applied* to the job. Pay particular attention to the following subtle but important point: *Actual overhead costs are not charged to jobs; actual overhead costs do not appear on the job cost sheet, nor do they appear in the work-in-process account. Only the applied overhead cost, based on the predetermined overhead rate, appears on the job cost sheet and in the work-in-process account.*

Cost of Goods Manufactured

When a job has been completed, the finished output is transferred from the production departments to the finished goods warehouse. By this time, the accounting department will have charged the job with direct materials and direct labour cost, and manufacturing overhead will have been applied using the predetermined rate. A transfer of these costs must be made within the costing system that *parallels* the physical transfer of the goods to the finished goods warehouse. The costs of the completed job are transferred out of the work-in-process account and into the finished goods account. The sum of all amounts transferred between these two accounts represents the cost of goods manufactured (COGM) for the period. (This point was illustrated earlier in Exhibit 2–7 in Chapter 2.)

In the case of Rand Company, let us assume that job A was completed during April. The following entry transfers the cost of job A from work in process to finished goods:

(8)

Finished Goods	158,000	
Work in Process.........................		158,000

The $158,000 represents the completed cost of job A, as shown on the job cost sheet in Exhibit 4–8. Since job A was the only job completed during April, the $158,000 also represents the cost of goods manufactured for the month.

Job B was not completed by month-end, and so its cost will remain in the work-in-process account, carrying over to the next month. If a balance sheet is prepared at the end of April, the cost accumulated thus far on job B will appear as *work-in-process inventory* in the assets section.

Cost of Goods Sold

As units in finished goods are shipped to fill customers' orders, the unit cost appearing on the job cost sheets is used as a basis for transferring the cost of the items sold from the finished goods account into the cost of goods sold account. If a complete job is shipped, as in the case where a job has been done to a customer's specifications, then it is a simple matter to transfer the entire cost appearing on the job cost sheet into the cost of goods sold account. In most cases, however, only a portion of the units involved in a particular job will be immediately sold. In these situations, the unit cost must be used to determine how much product cost should be removed from finished goods and charged to cost of goods sold.

For Rand Company, we will assume 750 of the 1,000 gold medallions in job A were shipped to customers by the end of the month for total sales revenue of $225,000. Since 1,000 units were produced and the total cost of the job from the job cost sheet was $158,000, the unit product cost was $158. The following journal entries would record the sale (all sales are on account):

(9)

Accounts Receivable.....................	225,000	
Sales		225,000

(10)

Cost of Goods Sold.......................	118,500	
Finished Goods		118,500
($158 per unit × 750 units = $118,500)		

With entry (10), the flow of costs through our job-order costing system is completed.

Summary of Manufacturing Cost Flows

To pull the entire example together, journal entries (1) through (10) are summarized in Exhibit 4–9. The flow of costs through the accounts is presented in T-account form in Exhibit 4–10. The corresponding model summarizing the cost flows in a job-order system appears in Exhibit 4–11. Study Exhibits 4–10 and 4–11 together.[1] A good grasp of

APPLY

CC17: Prepare T-accounts to show the flow of costs in a job-order costing system.

APPLY

CC18: Prepare schedules of COGM and COGS.

---

[1]Note that in Exhibit 4–10, we have shown for completeness some of the entries to the accounts that will have been made prior to start of the manufacturing process. The end-of-chapter material will not require that such entries be presented and explained.

Exhibit 4–9
Summary of Rand Company
Journal Entries

(1)

| Raw Materials...................................... | 60,000 | |
| Accounts Payable............................. | | 60,000 |

(2)

Work in Process	50,000	
Manufacturing Overhead	2,000	
Raw Materials		52,000

(3)

Work in Process	60,000	
Manufacturing Overhead	15,000	
Salaries and Wages Payable....................		75,000

(4)

| Manufacturing Overhead .... | 40,000 | |
| Accounts Payable............................. | | 40,000 |

(5)

Manufacturing Overhead	20,000	
Property Taxes Payable		13,000
Prepaid Insurance............................		7,000

(6)

| Manufacturing Overhead .... | 18,000 | |
| Accumulated Amortization .... | | 18,000 |

(7)

| Work in Process .... | 90,000 | |
| Manufacturing Overhead..................... | | 90,000 |

(8)

| Finished Goods................................ | 158,000 | |
| Work in Process............................. | | 158,000 |

(9)

| Accounts Receivable........................... | 225,000 | |
| Sales..................................... | | 225,000 |

(10)

| Cost of Goods Sold............................ | 118,500 | |
| Finished Goods .... | | 118,500 |

the logic of the cost flows will be very helpful in understanding how an income statement for a manufacturing concern is constructed. We have illustrated this process in Exhibit 4–12. This exhibit presents the supporting cost schedules as a series of "waterfalls" which cascade down into the income statement. It is easy to see how the various schedules articulate with each other and where the data in the schedules come from. To illustrate, compare the T-accounts in Exhibit 4–10 to the schedules in Exhibit 4–12. Note that the direct materials used is calculated from the raw materials T-account. Direct materials used then flows into the work-in-process account. The entries in the work-in-process account provide the basis for determining cost of goods manufactured. Then the cost of goods manufactured flows into the finished goods account. The inventory balances in finished goods along with cost of goods manufactured determines cost of goods sold, which finally flows into the income statement.

Exhibit 4–10

Flow of Costs through T-Accounts: Rand Company

(continued)

(continued)

Work in Process		Finished Goods			Cost of Goods Sold

Work in Process

Opening Bal.: 30,000
(2)   50,000   158,000   (8) → CoGM

(3)   60,000

(7)   90,000

Ending Bal.: 72,000

Finished Goods

Opening Bal.: 10,000   118,500   (10) → (10)   CoGS
(8)   158,000
Ending Bal.:   49,500

Cost of Goods Sold

(10)   118,500

Sales

225,00   (9) → (9)

Accounts Receivable

XX
225,000

Explanation of Symbols.

* Debit entry occurs when payment is made. Credit entry is to cash.

** Debit entry is made at start of period when payment was made. Cash is credited.

*** Debit entry is on disposal of asset.

XX Normal balance in account.

Exhibit 4–11
A General Model of Cost Flows

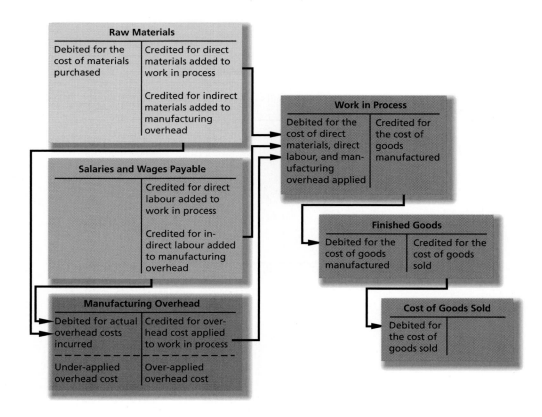

Problems of Overhead Application

You will note from Exhibit 4–10 that the manufacturing overhead account shows a debit balance of $5,000. The cost of goods sold amount of $118,500 does not reflect this $5,000, since it only contains the *applied* manufacturing overhead. Since the *actual* manufacturing overhead costs incurred amount to $95,000 and only $90,000 has been *applied*, the debit balance of $5,000 in manufacturing overhead account represents **under-applied overhead.** The opposite result can also occur in some circumstances. This is where there will be a credit balance in the manufacturing overhead account indicating that *applied* overhead costs are greater than the *actual* manufacturing overhead costs incurred. In this case the credit balance in the manufacturing overhead account is called **over-applied overhead.**

Since the predetermined overhead rate is established before a period begins and is based entirely on estimated data, there generally will be either under-applied or over-applied overhead at the end of the period. To illustrate how this can happen, consider another example. Suppose that two companies—Turbo Crafters and Black and Howell—have prepared the following estimated data for the coming year:

	Company	
	Turbo Crafters	**Black and Howell**
Predetermined overhead rate based on	Machine-hours	Direct materials cost
Estimated manufacturing overhead	$300,000 (a)	$120,000 (a)
Estimated machine-hours	75,000 (b)	—
Estimated direct materials costs	—	$80,000 (b)
Predetermined overhead rate, (a) ÷ (b)	$4 per machine-hour	150% of direct materials cost

Exhibit 4–12

Flow of Supporting Cost Schedules to the Income Statement

Direct Materials

Opening balance:	$7,000
Plus: Purchases	$60,000
RM available for use	$67,000
Less: Ending balance:	$15,000
RM used	$52,000
Less: Indirect RM	$2,000
DM used	$50,000 >>>>>>

COGM

DM	$50,000
DL	$60,000
Applied MOH	$90,000
Total Mfg. Costs	$200,000
Plus: Beginning WIP	$30,000
Mfg. cost to account	$230,000
Less: Ending WIP	$72,000
COGM	$158,000 >>>>>>

COGS

Opening bal. FG	$10,000
COGM	$158,000
Goods avail. for sale	$168,000
Less: End. Bal. FG	$49,500
COGS	$118,500 >>>>>>

Income Statement

Sales	$225,000
COGS	$118,500
GM	$106,500
Less: Non-mfg costs	
Net Income	

Note: The schedules shown in this exhibit are *not* in good form. They are presented in the format shown only to illustrate how the various schedules relate to each other. RM = raw materials; DM = direct materials; DL = direct labour; MOH = manufacturing overhead; WIP = work in process; FG = finished goods; COGM = cost of goods manufactured; COGS = (unadjusted) cost of goods sold; GM = gross margin.

Now, assume that *actual* overhead cost and *actual* activity recorded during the year in each company are as follows:

	Company	
	Turbo Crafters	**Black and Howell**
Actual manufacturing overhead costs	$290,000	$130,000
Actual machine-hours	68,000	—
Actual direct materials costs	—	$90,000

For each company, the actual data for both cost and activity differ from the estimates used in computing the predetermined overhead rate. This leads to under-applied and over-applied overhead as follows:

	Company	
	Turbo Crafters	**Black and Howell**
Actual manufacturing overhead costs	$290,000	$130,000
Manufacturing overhead costs applied to work in process: 68,000 *actual* machine-hours × $4 per machine-hour	$272,000	—
$90,000 *actual* direct materials cost × 150%		$135,000
Under-applied (over-applied) overhead	$18,000	$(5,000)

For Turbo Crafters, the overhead that was applied to work in process ($272,000) is less than the actual overhead cost for the year ($290,000). Therefore, overhead is under-applied. The opposite is true for Black and Howell. The applied overhead to work in process ($135,000) is greater than the actual overhead cost for the year ($130,000). So, the overhead is over-applied.

In summary, note that the impact of the original estimate of the overhead cost is felt only through the predetermined overhead rate that is used. The original estimate is not directly involved in the computation of the under-applied or over-applied overhead.

Causes of Under- and Over-applied Overheads

 KNOW

CC20: Describe the causes of under- and over-applied overhead.

What causes under-applied or over-applied overhead? From the example of Turbo Crafters and Black and Howell, it would seem that under-applied overhead or over-applied overhead will exist because the estimates of the manufacturing overhead cost for the year and the quantity of the allocation base made at the beginning of the period will differ from the actual amounts at the end of the year. This can happen if there are unexpected changes in overhead spending and in demand for the companies' products. This way of understanding the cause for under-applied or over-applied overhead suggests that the only problem is with the inputs used, not with the method itself.

The *method* of applying overhead to jobs using a predetermined rate assumes that actual overhead costs will be *proportional in the amount of the predetermined rate* to the actual amount of the allocation base incurred during the period. At Turbo Crafters, for example, this means that the managers of the company believe (1) that changes in manufacturing overhead are proportional to the change in machine-hours, and (2) that the rate of increase in manufacturing overhead is $4 per machine-hour. Let us consider this carefully. Look at Exhibit 4–13, which summarizes the process of determining the predetermined overhead rate, the allocation of overhead to work in process and the

At the beginning of the period:

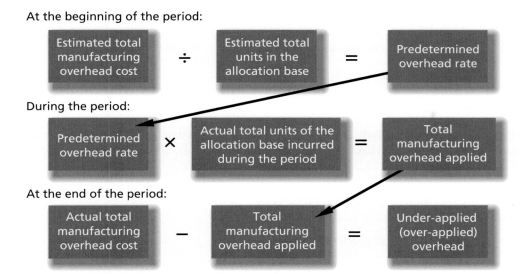

Exhibit 4–13
Summary of Overhead Concepts

computation of the under-applied and over-applied overhead. It can be seen that if the actual total overhead cost is not the same as the amount that was estimated at the start of the period, a discrepancy will result between actual overhead and applied overhead, even if there was no error in estimating the quantity of the allocation base. Manufacturing overhead costs can contain a significant amount of nondiscretionary or unavoidable costs. If this is so, these costs will not be proportional to changes in the allocation base. Therefore, when management estimates the total overhead costs at the start of the period assuming that overhead costs are, in fact, related to the quantity of the allocation base, it is making a mistake in using the predetermined rate method when applying overhead. It will discover, at the end of the period, that there is either under- or over-applied overhead.

Even if management is correct in its belief that actual manufacturing overhead cost is proportional to the actual number of units of the allocation base used during the period, there can be errors in estimating the quantities of the allocation base and total amount of manufacturing cost at the beginning of the period. This was previously mentioned. The company can end up actually spending either more or less than what was planned or expected due to circumstances beyond its control (sudden increase in energy costs) or because of poor management (wasteful work practices). Similarly, the company can end up actually using either more or less units of the allocation base than what was planned. Examples of why this is true include unexpected increases in demand, loss of experienced employees, poor maintenance, and so on.

Since a company is certain to have under- or over-applied overhead at the end of the period, how can management tell if it is because overhead cost is not proportional to the units of the allocation base or if it is because of errors in estimating the data inputs for calculating the predetermined rate? A complete answer is beyond the scope of this text, but we will return to consider this question further in a later chapter.

Disposition of Under- or Over-applied Overhead Balances

Our previous discussion included why over- or under-applied overhead balances exist. We have yet to consider what to do with these balances: What disposition of any under- or over-applied balance remaining in the manufacturing overhead account should managers make at the end of the period? The simplest method is to close out the balance to cost of

 KNOW

CC21: Explain why the under- or over-applied overhead balance must be disposed of at period end.

goods sold. Other complicated methods exist, but these are beyond the scope of this text. To illustrate the simplest method, recall that Rand Company had under-applied overhead of $5,000. The entry to close this under-applied overhead to cost of goods sold would be:

(11)

Cost of Goods Sold	5,000	
Manufacturing Overhead..................		5,000

Observe that since the manufacturing overhead account has a debit balance, manufacturing overhead must be credited to close out the account. This has the effect of increasing cost of goods sold for April to $123,500:

Unadjusted cost of goods sold [from entry (10)]..........	$118,500
Add under-applied overhead [entry (11) above]	5,000
Adjusted cost of goods sold........................	$123,500

After this adjustment has been made, Rand Company's Schedule of Cost of Goods Manufactured and Cost of Goods Sold for April will appear as shown in Exhibit 4–14.

Exhibit 4–14

Schedules of Cost of Goods Manufactured and Cost of Goods Sold

Cost of Goods Manufactured

Direct materials:		
Raw materials inventory, beginning	$ 7,000	
Add: Purchases of raw materials................	60,00	
Total raw materials available	67,000	
Less: Raw materials inventory, ending	15,000	
Raw materials used in production...............	52,000	
Less: Indirect materials included in manufacturing		
overhead	2,000	$ 50,000
Direct labour		60,000
Manufacturing overhead applied to work in process...		90,000
Total manufacturing costs		200,000
Add: Beginning work-in-process inventory..........		30,000
		230,000
Less: Ending work-in-process inventory		72,000
Cost of goods manufactured		$158,000

Cost of Goods Sold

Finished goods inventory, beginning	$ 10,000
Add: Cost of goods manufactured	158,000
Goods available for sale.........................	168,000
Less: Finished goods inventory, ending.............	49,500
Unadjusted cost of goods sold	118,500
Add: Under-applied overhead	5,000
Adjusted cost of goods sold......................	$123,500

*Note that the under-applied overhead is added to cost of goods sold. If overhead were over-applied, it would be deducted from cost of goods sold.

Remaining Balance in the Overhead Account   YOU DECIDE

The simplest method for disposing of any balance remaining in the overhead account is to close it out to cost of goods sold. If there is a debit balance (that is, overhead has been under-applied), the entry to dispose of the balance would include a debit to cost of goods sold. This debit would increase the balance in the cost of goods sold account. On the other hand, if there is a credit balance, the entry to dispose of the balance would include a credit to cost of goods sold. That credit would decrease the balance in the cost of goods sold account. If you were the company's controller, would you want a debit balance, a credit balance, or no balance in the overhead account at the end of the period?

Multiple Predetermined Overhead Rates

Our discussion in this chapter has assumed that there is a single predetermined overhead rate for an entire factory called a **plantwide overhead rate.** This is, in fact, a common practice—particularly in smaller companies. But in larger companies, *multiple predetermined overhead rates* are often used. In a **multiple predetermined overhead rate** system, each production department will usually have a different overhead rate. Such a system, while more complex, is considered to be more accurate, since it can reflect differences in how overhead costs are incurred across departments. For example, overhead might be allocated on the basis of direct labour-hours in departments that are relatively labour intensive and machine-hours in departments that are relatively machine intensive. When multiple predetermined overhead rates are used, overhead is applied in each department according to its own overhead rate as a job proceeds through the department.

> ◗ KNOW
>
> CC22: Distinguish between a plantwide overhead rate and a multiple overhead rate.

Nonmanufacturing Costs

In addition to manufacturing costs, companies also incur marketing and selling costs. As explained in the previous chapter, these costs should be treated as period expenses and charged directly to the income statement. *Nonmanufacturing costs should not go into the manufacturing overhead account.* To illustrate the correct treatment of nonmanufacturing costs, assume that Rand Company incurred the following selling and administrative costs during April:

Top-management salaries	$21,000
Other office salaries	9,000
Total salaries	$30,000

The following entry records these salaries:

(12)

Salaries Expense	30,000	
Salaries and Wages Payable		30,000

Assume that amortization on office equipment during April was $7,000. The entry would be:

(13)

Amortization Expense	7,000	
Accumulated Amortization		7,000

Pay particular attention to the difference between this entry and entry (6) where we recorded amortization on factory equipment. In journal entry (6), amortization on factory equipment was debited to manufacturing overhead and is therefore a product cost. In journal entry (9), amortization on office equipment was debited to amortization expense. Amortization on office equipment is considered to be a period expense, rather than a product cost.

Finally, assume that advertising was $42,000 and that other selling and administrative expenses in April totalled $8,000. The following entry records these items:

(14)

Advertising Expense.	42,000	
Other Selling and Administrative Expense.	8,000	
Accounts Payable.		50,000

● **APPLY**

CC23: Determine the profitability of operations over a specific period by preparing an income statement from the information accumulated in a job-order costing system.

Since the amounts in entries (12) through (14) all go directly into expense accounts, they will have no effect on the costing of Rand Company's production for April. The same will be true of any other selling and administrative expenses incurred during April, including sales commissions, amortization on sales equipment, rent on office facilities, insurance on office facilities, and related costs. The income statement showing these costs appears in Exhibit 4–15.

Exhibit 4–15
Income Statement Including Nonmanufacturing Costs

RAND COMPANY		
Income Statement		
For the Month Ending April 30		
Sales		$225,000
Less: Cost of goods sold ($118,50 + $5,000)		123,500
Gross margin.		101,500
Less: Selling and administrative expenses:		
Salaries expense	$30,000	
Amortization expense	7,000	
Advertising expense.	42,000	
Other expense.	8,0000	87,000
Net Income		$14,500

Job-Order Costing in Service Companies

Job-order costing is also used in service organizations such as law firms, movie studios, hospitals, and repair shops, as well as in manufacturing companies. In a law firm, for example, each client is considered to be a *job*, and the costs of that job are accumulated day by day on a job cost sheet as the client's case is handled by the firm. Legal forms and similar inputs represent the direct materials for the job; the time expended by attorneys represents the direct labor; and the costs of secretaries, clerks, rent, amortization, and so forth, represent the overhead.

In a movie studio such as Columbia Pictures, each film produced by the studio is a job, and costs for direct materials (costumes, props, film, etc.) and direct labor (actors, directors, and extras) are charged to each film's job cost sheet. A share of the studio's overhead costs, such as utilities, amortization of equipment, wages of maintenance workers, and so forth, is also charged to each film. However, there is considerable controversy about the methods used by some studios to distribute overhead costs among movies, and these controversies sometimes result in lawsuits.

In summary, job-order costing is a versatile and widely used costing method that may be encountered in virtually any organization that provides diverse products or services.

A Fair Share of Profits

"Net profit participation" contracts in which writers, actors, and directors share in the net profits of movies are common in Hollywood. For example, Winston Groom, the author of the novel *Forrest Gump*, has a contract with Paramount Pictures Corp. that calls for him to receive 3% of the net profits on the movie. However, Paramount claims that *Forrest Gump* has yet to show any profits, even though it has the third-highest gross receipts of any film in history. How can this be?

Movie studios assess a variety of overhead charges including a charge of about 15% on production costs for production overhead, a charge of about 30% of gross rentals for distribution overhead, and a charge for marketing overhead that amounts to about 10% of advertising costs. After all of these overhead charges and other hotly contested accounting practices, it is a rare film that shows a profit. Fewer than 5% of released films show a profit for net profit participation purposes. Examples of "money-losing" films include *Rain Man*, *Batman*, and *Who Framed Roger Rabbit?*, as well as *Forrest Gump*. Disgruntled writers and actors are increasingly suing studios, claiming unreasonable accounting practices that are designed to cheat them of their share of profits.

Source: Ross Engel and Bruce Ikawa, "Where's the Profit?" Reprinted with permission from *Management Accounting*, January 1997, pp. 40–47.

Application Competency Summary

Application Competency	Deliverable	Source Documents and Key Information	Steps	Knowledge Competency
Determine the cost of a job (including computing and applying a predetermined overhead allocation rate). ○ CC4 ○ CC6 ○ CC7	*Key Information* Cost of the job and the cost of each unit produced in the job *Report/Document* Job cost sheet	*Materials Requisition Forms* Direct materials costs incurred by individual jobs *Labour Time Tickets* Direct labour hours supplied by each employee to individual jobs Employee wage rate *Annual Budget Documents* Budgeted amount of annual manufacturing overhead Budgeted quantity of overhead allocation base	1. Record the costs of direct materials from the various materials requisition forms on job cost sheet and calculate total material cost. 2. Record the wage costs of each employee from his/her employee ticket on the job cost sheet and calculate total direct labour cost. 3. Calculate predetermined overhead allocation rate per unit of allocation base (by dividing the budgeted overhead amount by the budgeted quantity of the overhead allocation base).	Actual costing and normal costing ○ CC3

continued

Application Competency	Deliverable	Source Documents and Key Information	Steps	Knowledge Competency
		Inventory and Production Records Number of units produced of each job, and number of units in WIP inventory Actual consumption of machine hours and other resources that are used as bases to allocated overhead	4. Apply the predetermined rate to the quantity of the overhead allocation base consumed by the job (multiply the actual quantity of the allocation base consumed by the predetermined overhead allocation rate). 5. Add the costs of actual direct materials and labour and the applied overhead to compute the total costs of a job.	
Account for the cost of jobs worked on and completed during an operating cycle (e.g., a year). ⚫ CC12 ⚫ CC15 ⚫ CC17	*Key Information* Description of manufacturing cost flows occurring during the period and the calculation of the COGM *Report/Document* T-account analysis of cost flows Schedule of COGM	*Materials Requisition Forms* Direct materials (DM) requisitioned and used during the period for the jobs Indirect materials used during the period *Labour Time Tickets* Cost of direct labour consumed during the period Indirect labour cost incurred during the period *Various Accounts in the General Ledger* Other manufacturing overhead (MOH) costs incurred during the period *Individual Job Cost Sheets* Quantity of overhead allocation base consumed in the period	1. Post transactions to T-accounts: • use of DM in jobs • use of indirect materials • use of direct labour • use of indirect labour • incurrence of actual overhead costs • application of MOH to WIP • cost of jobs completed and transferred from WIP to finished goods inventory	Costing of a specific job versus accounting for the all the manufacturing cost flows occurring during a selected operating period ⚫ CC13, 14
Determine the over-applied or under-applied overhead for the period. ⚫ CC19	*Key Information* Amount of over- or under-applied overhead *Report/Document* None	*Manufacturing Overhead Account in the General Ledger* Actual MOH costs incurred—sum of all debit entries *Individual Job Cost Sheets* Total of MOH applied to various jobs—sum of all the credit entries in the MOH account. Applied MOH is the predetermined MOH rate times the quantity of overhead allocation base consumed by jobs in the period.	1. Calculate the balance in the MOH account at the end of the period: a debit balance is the amount of under-applied MOH and a credit balance is the amount of over-applied MOH.	Actual and normal costing ⚫ CC3 Predetermined overhead rate ⚫ CC6 Disposition of balance in MOH account ⚫ CC16, 19, 21
Prepare schedules of COGM and COGS. ⚫ CC18	*Key Information* The cost of jobs sold *Report/Document* Schedule of COGS	*Individual Job Cost Sheets* Cost of each unit (or job, if entire job is sold) sold	1. Total the cost of all the jobs sold and the cost of the units sold from jobs (normal costs).	Actual and normal costing ⚫ CC3 Application of overhead ⚫ CC7

continued

Application Competency	Deliverable	Source Documents and Key Information	Steps	Knowledge Competency
Determine the profitability of operations for the period given the nonmanufacturing costs

⚫ CC23 | *Key Information* Net income for the period

Report/Document Income Statement | *Sales/Revenue Account in the General Ledger* Revenue from sales in the period

Schedule of COGS COGS before disposition of over- or under- applied overhead

MOH Account in the General Ledger Actual and applied overhead amounts, and the amount of over- or under-applied manufacturing overhead for the period

Nonmanufacturing Accounts in the General Ledger All nonmanufacturing costs incurred in the period | 1. Dispose of the over- or under-applied MOH by closing it out to COGS.

2. Make appropriate entry (debit or credit) to MOH to reduce MOH balance to zero.

3. Make the opposite entry to COGS and determine revised balance in the COGS account.

4. Enter this amount for COGS on the income statement.

5. Complete the income statement. | Actual and normal costing

⚫ CC3

Disposition of under- or over-applied overhead

⚫ CC16, 19, 21 |

Guidance Answers to Decision Maker and You Decide

TREASURER OF THE CLASS REUNION COMMITTEE (p. 121)
You should charge $38 per person to cover the costs calculated as follows:

Meal cost	$30.00	Direct cost
Gratuity ($30 × 0.15)	4.50	Direct cost
Room charge ($200 ÷ 200 expected attendees)	1.00	Overhead cost
Band cost ($500 ÷ 200 expected attendees)	2.50	Overhead cost
Total cost	$38.00	

The number of expected attendees (or estimated units in the allocation base) was used to allocate the band cost. Attendees who plan to leave immediately after dinner might object to this allocation. However, this personal choice probably should not override the decision to base the allocation on this very simple base.

If exactly 200 classmates attend the reunion, the $7,600 of receipts (200 @ $38) will cover the expenditures of $7,600 [meal cost of $6,000 (or 200 @ $30) plus gratuity cost of $900 (or $6,000 × 0.15) plus the $200 room charge plus the $500 band cost]. Unfortunately, if less than 200 attend, the Reunion Committee will come up short in an amount equal to the difference between the 200 estimated attendees and the actual number of attendees multiplied by $3.50 (the overhead charge per person). As such, you should talk to the members of the Reunion Committee to ensure that (1) the estimate is as reasonable as possible, and (2) there is a plan to deal with the shortage. However, if more than 200 attend, the Reunion Committee will collect more money than it needs to disburse. The amount would be equal to the difference between the actual number of attendees and the 200 estimated attendees multiplied by $3.50. Again, a plan should be in place to deal with this situation. (Perhaps the funds could be used to cover the mailing costs for the next reunion.)

REMAINING BALANCE IN THE OVERHEAD ACCOUNT (p. 137)
A quick response on your part might have been that you would prefer a credit balance in the Overhead account. The entry to dispose of the balance would decrease the balance in the cost of goods sold

account, causing the company's gross margin and net income to be higher than might have otherwise been expected. However, the impact on decision making during the period should be carefully considered.

Ideally, a controller would want the balance in the overhead account to be zero. If there is no remaining balance in the overhead account at the end of the period, that means that the actual overhead costs for the period (which are debited to the overhead account) exactly equalled the overhead costs that were applied (or allocated to the products made by being added to the work-in-process account) during the period. As a result, the products made during the period would have had the *correct* amount of overhead assigned as they moved from the factory floor to the finished goods area to the customer. This would not usually be the case because the predetermined overhead rate (used to apply or allocate overhead to the products made) is developed using two estimates (the total amount of overhead expected and the total units in the allocation base expected during the period). It would be difficult, if not impossible, to accurately predict one or both estimates.

If there is a remaining balance in the overhead account, then the products manufactured during the period either received too little overhead (if there is a debit or under-applied balance) or too much overhead (if there is a credit or over-applied balance). As such, units carried along with them inaccurate product costs as the costs flowed through system. Decisions that relied on those inaccurate product costs may have been faulty.

Review Problem: Job-Order Costing

Hogle Company is a manufacturing firm that uses job-order costing. On January 1, the beginning of its fiscal year, the company's inventory balances were as follows:

Raw materials	$20,000
Work in process	15,000
Finished goods	30,000

The company applies overhead cost to jobs on the basis of machine-hours worked. For the current year, the company estimated that it would work 75,000 machine-hours and incur $450,000 in manufacturing overhead cost. The following transactions were recorded for the year:

a. Raw materials were purchased on account, $410,000.

b. Raw materials were requisitioned for use in production, $380,000 ($360,000 direct materials and $20,000 indirect materials).

c. The following costs were incurred for employee services: direct labour, $75,000; indirect labour, $110,000; sales commissions, $90,000; and administrative salaries, $200,000.

d. Sales travel costs were incurred, $17,000.

e. Utility costs were incurred in the factory, $43,000.

f. Advertising costs were incurred, $180,000.

g. Amortization was recorded for the year, $350,000 (80% relates to factory operations, and 20% relates to selling and administrative activities).

h. Insurance expired during the year, $10,000 (70% relates to factory operations, and the remaining 30% relates to selling and administrative activities).

i. Manufacturing overhead was applied to production. Due to greater than expected demand for its products, the company worked 80,000 machine-hours during the year.

j. Goods costing $900,000 to manufacture according to their job cost sheets were completed during the year.

k. Goods were sold on account to customers during the year at a total selling price of $1,500,000. The goods cost $870,000 to manufacture according to their job cost sheets.

Required:

1. Prepare journal entries to record the preceding transactions.

2. Post the entries in part (1) to T-accounts (do not forget to enter the opening balances in the inventory accounts).
3. Is manufacturing overhead under-applied or over-applied for the year? Prepare a journal entry to close any balance in the manufacturing overhead account to cost of goods sold.
4. Prepare an income statement for the year.

SOLUTION TO REVIEW PROBLEM

1. *a.* Raw Materials 410,000
       Accounts Payable.   410,000

   b. Work in Process. 360,000
       Manufacturing Overhead.   20,000
       Raw Materials   380,000

   c. Work in Process. 75,000
       Manufacturing Overhead. 110,000
       Sales Commissions Expense 90,000
       Administrative Salaries Expense 200,000
       Salaries and Wages Payable.   475,000

   d. Sales Travel Expense. 17,000
       Accounts Payable.   17,000

   e. Manufacturing Overhead. 43,000
       Accounts Payable.   43,000

   f. Advertising Expense 180,000
       Accounts Payable.   180,000

   g. Manufacturing Overhead. 280,000
       Amortization Expense 70,000
       Accumulated Amortization   350,000

   h. Manufacturing Overhead. 7,000
       Insurance Expense 3,000
       Prepaid Insurance.   10,000

   i. The predetermined overhead rate for the year would be computed as follows:

$$\frac{\text{Estimated manufacturing overhead, \$450,000}}{\text{Estimated machine-hours, 75,000}} = \$6 \text{ per machine-hour}$$

   Based on the 80,000 machine-hours actually worked during the year, the company would have applied $480,000 in overhead cost to production: 80,000 machine-hours × $6 per machine-hour = $480,000. The following entry records this application of overhead cost:

   Work in Process. 480,000
       Manufacturing Overhead.   480,000

   j. Finished Goods 900,000
       Work in Process   900,000

   k. Accounts Receivable 1,500,000
       Sales.   1,500,000

   Cost of Goods Sold 870,000
       Finished Goods   870,000

2.

Accounts Receivable		
(k) 1,500,000		

Prepaid Insurance		
	(h)	10,000

Raw Materials		
Bal. 20,000	(b)	380,000
(a) 410,000		
Bal. 50,000		

Work in Process		
Bal. 15,000	(j)	900,000
(b) 360000		
(c) 75,000		
(i) 480,000		
Bal. 30,000		

Finished Goods		
Bal. 30,000	(k)	870,000
(j) 900,000		
Bal. 60,000		

Manufacturing Overhead		
(b) 20,000	(i)	480,000
(c) 110,000		
(e) 43,000		
(g) 280,000		
(h 7,000		
460,000		480,000
	Bal.	20,000

Accumulated Amortization		
	(g)	350,000

Accounts Payable		
	(a)	410,000
	(d)	17,000
	(e)	43,000
	(f)	180,000

Salaries and Wages Payable		
	(c)	475,000

Sales		
	(k)	1,500,000

Cost of Goods Sold		
(k) 870,000		

Commissions Expense		
(c) 90,000		

Administrative Salary Expense		
(c) 200,000		

Sales Travel Expense		
(d) 17,000		

Advertising Expense		
(f) 180,000		

Amortization Expense		
(g) 70,000		

Insurance Expense		
(h) 3,000		

3. Manufacturing overhead is over-applied for the year. The entry to close it out to cost of goods sold is as follows:

Manufacturing Overhead	20,000	
Cost of Goods Sold............................		20,000

4.

HOGLE COMPANY
Income Statement
For the Year Ended December 31

Sales		$1,500,000
Less: Cost of goods sold ($870,000 − $20,000)		850,000
Gross margin		650,000
Less: Selling and administrative expenses:		
Commissions expense........................	$ 90,000	
Administrative salaries expense	200,000	
Sales travel expense	17,000	
Advertising expense	180,000	
Amortization expense.......................	70,000	
Insurance expense..........................	3,000	560,000
Net income		$ 90,000

Absorption (or **full**) **costing** A costing method that includes all manufacturing costs—direct materials, direct labour, and both variable and fixed overhead—as part of the cost of a finished unit of product. This term is synonymous with *full costing*. (p. 113)

Actual costing system A costing system in which actual overhead costs are applied to jobs by multiplying the actual overhead rate by the actual amount of the allocation base incurred by the job. (p. 113)

Allocation base A measure of activity, such as direct labour-hours or machine-hours, that is used to assign costs to cost objects. (p. 118)

Bill of materials A document that shows the type and quantity of each major item of materials required to make a product. (p. 115)

Cost driver A factor, such as machine-hours, beds occupied, computer time, or flight-hours, that causes overhead costs. (p. 120)

Full costing See *absorption costing*. (p. 113)

Job cost sheet A form prepared for each job that records the materials, labour, and overhead costs charged to the job. (p. 115)

Job-order costing system A costing system used in situations where many different products, jobs, or services are produced each period. (p. 112)

Materials requisition form A detailed source document that specifies the type and quantity of materials that are to be drawn from the storeroom and identifies the job to which the costs of materials are to be charged. (p. 115)

Multiple predetermined overhead rates A costing system in which there are multiple overhead cost pools with different predetermined rates for each cost pool, rather than a single predetermined overhead rate for the entire company. Frequently, each production department is treated as a separate overhead cost pool. (p. 137)

Normal costing system A costing system in which overhead costs are applied to jobs by multiplying a predetermined overhead rate by the actual amount of the allocation base incurred by the job. (p. 113)

Over-applied overhead A credit balance in the manufacturing overhead account that arises when the amount of overhead cost applied to work in process is greater than the amount of overhead cost actually incurred during a period. (p. 132)

Overhead application The process of charging manufacturing overhead cost to job cost sheets and to the work-in-process account. (p. 118)

Plantwide overhead rate A single predetermined overhead rate that is used throughout a plant. (p. 137)

Predetermined overhead rate A rate used to charge overhead cost to jobs in production; the rate is established in advance for each period by use of estimates of total manufacturing overhead cost and of the total allocation base for the period. (p. 118)

Process costing system A costing system used in those manufacturing situations where a single, homogeneous product (such as cement or flour) is produced for long periods. (p. 112)

Time ticket A detailed source document used to record an employee's hour-by-hour activities during a day. (p. 116)

Under-applied overhead A debit balance in the manufacturing overhead account that arises when the amount of overhead cost actually incurred is greater than the amount of overhead cost applied to work in process during a period. (p. 132)

Variable costing A costing method that includes only variable manufacturing costs—direct materials, direct labour, and variable overhead—as part of the finished unit of product. (p. 113)

Questions

4–1   Why are actual overhead costs not traced to jobs just as direct materials and direct labour costs are traced to jobs?

4–2   When would job-order costing be used in preference to process costing?

4–3   What is the purpose of the job cost sheet in a job-order costing system?

4–4   What is a predetermined overhead rate, and how is it computed?

4–5   Explain how a sales order, a production order, a materials requisition form, and a labour time ticket are involved in producing and costing products.

4–6   Explain why some production costs must be assigned to products through an allocation process. Name several such costs. Would such costs be classified as *direct* or as *indirect* costs?

4–7   Why do firms use predetermined overhead rates, rather than actual manufacturing overhead costs, in applying overhead to jobs?

4–8 What factors should be considered in selecting a base to be used in computing the predetermined overhead rate?

4–9 If a company fully allocates all of its overhead costs to jobs, does this guarantee that a profit will be earned for the period?

4–10 What account is credited when overhead cost is applied to work in process? Would you expect the amount applied for a period to equal the actual overhead costs of the period? Why, or why not?

4–11 What is under-applied overhead? Over-applied overhead? What disposition is made of these amounts at the end of the period?

4–12 Give two reasons why overhead might be under-applied in a given year.

4–13 What adjustment is made for under-applied overhead on the schedule of cost of goods sold? What adjustment is made for over-applied overhead?

4–14 Sigma Company applies overhead cost to jobs on the basis of direct labour cost. Job A, which was started and completed during the current period, shows charges of $5,000 for direct materials, $8,000 for direct labour, and $6,000 for overhead on its job cost sheet. Job B, which is still in process at year-end, shows charges of $2,500 for direct materials and $4,000 for direct labour. Should any overhead cost be added to job B at year-end? Explain.

4–15 A company assigns overhead cost to completed jobs on the basis of 125% of direct labour cost. The job cost sheet for job 313 shows that $10,000 in direct materials has been used on the job and that $12,000 in direct labour cost has been incurred. If 1,000 units were produced in job 313, what is the cost per unit?

4–16 What is a plantwide overhead rate? Why are multiple overhead rates, rather than a plantwide rate, used in some companies?

4–17 What happens to overhead rates based on direct labour when automated equipment replaces direct labour?

Brief Exercises

BRIEF EXERCISE 4–1   Process Versus Job-Order Costing (CC1)

Which method of determining product costs, job-order costing or process costing, would be more appropriate in each of the following situations?

a. An Elmer's glue factory
b. A textbook publisher, such as McGraw-Hill
c. A Husky oil refinery
d. A facility that makes Minute Maid frozen orange juice
e. A Scott paper mill
f. A custom home builder
g. A shop that customizes vans
h. A manufacturer of specialty chemicals
i. An auto repair shop
j. A Firestone tire manufacturing plant
k. An advertising agency
l. A law office

BRIEF EXERCISE 4–2   Job-Order Costing Documents (CC5)

Cycle Gear Corporation has incurred the following costs on job number W456, an order for 20 special sprockets to be delivered at the end of next month.

Direct materials:

> On April 10, requisition number 15673 was issued for 20 titanium blanks to be used in the special order. The blanks cost $15 each.

> On April 11, requisition number 15678 was issued for 480 hardened nibs also to be used in the special order. The nibs cost $1.25 each.

Direct labour:

> On April 12, Jamie Unser worked from 11:00 AM until 2:45 PM on Job W456. He is paid $9.60 per hour.

> On April 18, Melissa Chan worked from 8:15 AM until 11:30 AM on Job W456. She is paid $12.20 per hour.

Required:

1. On what documents would these costs be recorded?
2. How much cost should have been recorded on each of the documents for job W456?

BRIEF EXERCISE 4–3   Compute the Predetermined Overhead Rate (CC6)

Harris Fabrics computes its predetermined overhead rate annually on the basis of direct labour hours. At the beginning of the year, it estimated that its total manufacturing overhead would be $134,000 and the total direct labour would be 20,000 hours. Its actual total manufacturing overhead for the year was $123,900, and its actual total direct labour was 21,000 hours.

Required:

Compute the company's predetermined overhead rate for the year.

BRIEF EXERCISE 4–4   Prepare Journal Entries (CC12)

Larned Corporation recorded the following transactions for the past month.

a. $80,000 in raw materials were purchased on account.

b. $71,000 in raw materials were requisitioned for use in production. Of this amount, $62,000 was for direct materials and the remainder was for indirect materials.

c. Total labour wages of $112,000 were incurred. Of this amount, $101,000 was for direct labour and the remainder was for indirect labour.

d. Additional manufacturing overhead costs of $175,000 were incurred.

Required:

Record the preceding transactions in journal entries.

BRIEF EXERCISE 4–5   Apply Overhead (CC15)

Luthan Company uses a predetermined overhead rate of $23.40 per direct labour-hour. This predetermined rate was based on 11,000 estimated direct labour-hours and $257,400 of estimated total manufacturing overhead.

The company incurred actual total manufacturing overhead costs of $249,000 and 10,800 total direct labour-hours during the period.

Required:

Determine the amount of manufacturing overhead that would have been applied to units of product during the period.

BRIEF EXERCISE 4–6   Prepare T-Accounts (CC17, 19)

Jurvin Enterprises recorded the following transactions for the past month. The company had no beginning inventories.

a. $94,000 in raw materials were purchased for cash.

b. $89,000 in raw materials were requisitioned for use in production. Of this amount, $78,000 was for direct materials and the remainder was for indirect materials.

c. Total labour wages of $132,000 were incurred and paid. Of this amount, $112,000 was for direct labour and the remainder was for indirect labour.

d. Additional manufacturing overhead costs of $143,000 were incurred and paid.

e. Manufacturing overhead costs of $152,000 were applied to jobs using the company's predetermined overhead rate.

f. All of the jobs in progress at the end of the month were completed and shipped to customers.

g. The under-applied or over-applied overhead for the period was closed out to Cost of Goods Sold.

Required:

1. Post the preceding transactions to T-accounts.

2. Determine the cost of goods sold for the period.

BRIEF EXERCISE 4–7   Under- and Over-applied Overhead (CC19)

Osborn Manufacturing uses a predetermined overhead rate of $18.20 per direct labour-hour. This predetermined rate was based on 12,000 estimated direct labour-hours and $218,400 of estimated total manufacturing overhead.

The company incurred actual total manufacturing overhead costs of $215,000 and 11,500 total direct labour-hours during the period.

Required:

1. Determine the amount of under-applied or over-applied manufacturing overhead for the period.

2. Assuming that the entire amount of the under-applied or over-applied overhead is closed out to cost of goods sold, what would be the effect of the under-applied or over-applied overhead on the company's gross margin for the period?

Exercises

EXERCISE 4–1 Applying Overhead in a Service Firm (CC5, 6, 7)

Leeds Architectural Consultants began operations on January 2. The following activity was recorded in the company's work-in-process account for the first month of operations:

Work in Process

Costs of subcontracted work	250,000	To completed projects	445,000
Direct staff costs	100,000		
Studio overhead	135,000		

Leeds Architectural Consultants is a service firm; thus, the names of its accounts differ from those used in manufacturing firms. Costs of subcontracted work is basically the same thing as direct materials; direct staff costs is the same as direct labour; studio overhead is the same as manufacturing overhead; and completed projects is the same as finished goods. Apart from the difference in terms, the accounting methods used by the company are identical to the methods used by manufacturing companies.

Leeds Architectural Consultants uses a job-order costing system, applying studio overhead to work in process on the basis of direct staff costs. At the end of January, only one job was still in process. This job (Lexington Gardens Project) had been charged with $7,000 in direct staff costs.

Required:
1. Compute the predetermined overhead rate that was in use during January.
2. Complete the following job cost sheet for the partially completed Lexington Gardens Project.

Job Cost Sheet—Lexington Gardens Project
As of January 31

Costs of subcontracted work	$?
Direct staff costs	?
Studio overhead	?
Total cost to January 31	$?

EXERCISE 4–2 Varying Predetermined Overhead Rates (CC6, 7)

Kingsport Containers, Ltd. of the Bahamas experiences wide variation in demand for the 200-litre steel drums it fabricates. The leakproof, rustproof steel drums have a variety of uses from storing liquids and bulk materials to serving as makeshift musical instruments. The drums are made to order and are painted according to the customer's specifications—often in bright patterns and designs. The company is well known for the artwork that appears on its drums. Unit costs are computed on a quarterly basis by dividing each quarter's manufacturing costs (materials, labour, and overhead) by the quarter's production in units. The company's estimated costs, by quarter, for the coming year follow:

	Quarter			
	First	Second	Third	Fourth
Direct materials.	$240,000	$120,000	$ 60,000	$180,000
Direct labour	128,000	64,000	32,000	96,000
Manufacturing overhead	300,000	220,000	180,000	260,000
Total manufacturing costs	$668,000	$404,000	$272,000	$536,000
Number of units to be produced	80,000	40,000	20,000	60,000
Estimated cost per unit	$8.35	$10.10	$13.60	$8.93

Management finds the variation in unit costs to be confusing and difficult to work with. It has been suggested that the problem lies with manufacturing overhead, since it is the largest element of cost. Accordingly, you have been asked to find a more appropriate way of assigning manufacturing overhead cost to units of product. After some analysis, you have determined that the company's overhead costs are mostly fixed and therefore show little sensitivity to changes in the level of production.

Required:
1. The company uses a job-order costing system. How would you recommend that manufacturing overhead cost be assigned to production? Be specific, and show computations.
2. Recompute the company's unit costs in accordance with your recommendations in part (1).

EXERCISE 4–3   Journal Entries and T-Accounts (CC7, 12, 15, 17)

The Polaris Company uses a job-order costing system. The following data relate to October, the first month of the company's fiscal year:

a. Raw materials purchased on account, $210,000.
b. Raw materials issued to production, $190,000 ($178,000 direct materials and $12,000 indirect materials).
c. Direct labour cost incurred, $90,000; indirect labour cost incurred, $110,000.
d. Amortization recorded on factory equipment, $40,000.
e. Other manufacturing overhead costs incurred during October, $70,000 (credit accounts payable).
f. The company applies manufacturing overhead cost to production on the basis of $8 per machine-hour. There were 30,000 machine-hours recorded for October.
g. Production orders costing $520,000 according to their job cost sheets were completed during October and transferred to finished goods.
h. Production orders that had cost $480,000 to complete according to their job cost sheets were shipped to customers during the month. These goods were sold at 25% above cost. The goods were sold on account.

Required:
1. Prepare journal entries to record the preceding information.
2. Prepare T-accounts for manufacturing overhead and work in process. Post the relevant information above to each account. Compute the ending balance in each account, assuming that work in process has a beginning balance of $42,000.

EXERCISE 4–4   Applying Overhead; Cost of Goods Manufactured (CC18, 19)

The following cost data relate to the manufacturing activities of Chang Company during the past year:

Manufacturing overhead costs incurred:	
Indirect materials.............................	$ 17,000
Indirect labour................................	130,000
Property taxes, factory........................	9,500
Utilities, factory..............................	72,000
Amortization, factory..........................	240,000
Insurance, factory	11,000
Total actual costs incurred	$479,500
Other costs incurred:	
Purchases of raw materials (both direct and indirect) ..	$400,000
Direct labour cost.............................	65,000
Inventories:	
Raw materials, beginning	30,000
Raw materials, ending	40,000
Work in process, beginning	50,000
Work in process, ending........................	80,000

The company uses a predetermined overhead rate to apply overhead cost to production. The rate for the year was $23 per machine-hour. A total of 20,000 machine-hours was recorded for the year.

Required:
1. Compute the amount of under- or over-applied overhead cost for the year.
2. Prepare a schedule of cost of goods manufactured for the year.

EXERCISE 4–5   Applying Overhead with Differing Bases (CC6, 7, 19)
Estimated cost and operating data for three companies for the upcoming year follow:

	Company		
	X	Y	Z
Direct labour-hours............	80,000	45,000	60,000
Machine-hours	30,000	70,000	21,000
Direct materials cost..........	$400,000	$290,000	$300,000
Manufacturing overhead cost ...	536,000	315,000	480,000

Predetermined overhead rates are computed using the following bases in the three companies:

Company	Overhead Rate Based on—
X	Direct labour-hours
Y	Machine-hours
Z	Direct materials cost

Required:
1. Compute the predetermined overhead rate to be used in each company during the upcoming year.
2. Assume that Company X works on three jobs during the upcoming year. Direct labour-hours recorded by job are: job 418, 12,000 hours; job 419, 36,000 hours; job 420, 30,000 hours. How much overhead cost will the company apply to work in process for the year? If actual overhead costs total $530,000 for the year, will overhead be under- or over-applied? By how much?

EXERCISE 4–6   Journal Entries; Applying Overhead (CC12, 19)
The following information is taken from the accounts of Latta Company. The entries in the T-accounts are summaries of the transactions that affected those accounts during the year.

Manfacturing Overhead		
(a)	460,000	(b)	390,000
Bal.	70,000	

Work in Process		
Bal.	5,000	(c)	710,000
	270,000	
	85,000	
(b)	390,000	
Bal.	40,000	

Finished Goods		
Bal.	50,000	(d)	640,000
(c)	710,000	
Bal.	120,000	

Cost of Goods Sold		
(d)	640,000	

The overhead that was applied to work in process during the year is distributed among the ending balances in the accounts as follows:

Work in Process, ending	$ 19,500
Finished Goods, ending..........................	58,500
Cost of Goods Sold	312,000
Overhead applied..............................	$390,000

For example, of the $40,000 ending balance in work in process, $19,500 was overhead that had been applied during the year.

Required:
1. Identify reasons for entries (a) through (d).
2. Assume that the company closes any balance in the manufacturing overhead account directly to cost of goods sold. Prepare the necessary journal entry.

EXERCISE 4–7   Applying Overhead; Journal Entries; T-Accounts (CC4, 6, 7, 12, 17)

Dillon Products manufactures various machined parts to customer specifications. The company uses a job-order costing system and applies overhead cost to jobs on the basis of machine-hours. At the beginning of the year, it was estimated that the company would work 240,000 machine-hours and incur $4,800,000 in manufacturing overhead costs.

The company spent the entire month of January working on a large order for 16,000 custom-made machined parts. The company had no work in process at the beginning of January. Cost data relating to January follow:

a. Raw materials purchased on account, $325,000.
b. Raw materials requisitioned for production, $290,000 (80% direct materials and 20% indirect materials).
c. Labour cost incurred in the factory, $180,000 (one-third direct labour and two-thirds indirect labour).
d. Amortization recorded on factory equipment, $75,000.
e. Other manufacturing overhead costs incurred, $62,000 (credit accounts payable).
f. Manufacturing overhead cost was applied to production on the basis of 15,000 machine-hours actually worked during the month.
g. The completed job was moved into the finished goods warehouse on January 31 to await delivery to the customer. (In computing the dollar amount for this entry, remember that the cost of a completed job consists of direct materials, direct labour, and *applied* overhead.)

Required:
1. Prepare journal entries to record items (a) through (f) above [ignore item (g) for the moment].
2. Prepare T-accounts for manufacturing overhead and work in process. Post the relevant items from your journal entries to these T-accounts.
3. Prepare a journal entry for item (g).
4. Compute the unit cost that will appear on the job cost sheet.

EXERCISE 4–8   Pre-determined Overhead Rate, Overhead Application, Job Cost, Over- or Under-applied Overhead, Journal Entries (CC4, 6, 7, 19)

Answer each question independently of the other.

Required:
1. Mirage Mirror's predetermined overhead rate for manufacturing overhead is $18 per direct labour-hour. The direct labour rate is $24 per hour. If the budgeted direct labour cost was $300,000, what was the budgeted manufacturing overhead?
2. Zion wants to compute the total cost for preparing a corporate tax return for his client. His labour is the only direct cost at $65 per hour. He estimates monthly overhead costs at $7,500 for 150 direct labour-hours. If the tax return requires 13 hours to prepare, what would be the total direct cost, indirect cost, and job cost, respectively?
3. Kyle Corporation had the following account balances at the end of 2007:

Direct materials inventory............	$1,000
Work in progress..................	680
Finished goods	450
Manufacturing overhead control.......	122 credit
Cost of goods sold	800

Assuming that over- or under-applied overhead is written off to cost of goods sold, prepare the appropriate journal entry and compute the adjusted balance in the cost of goods sold account.

EXERCISE 4–9   Job Costs and Price (CC4)

Magma Inc. uses a job-order costing system and applies manufacturing overhead using multiple overhead rates. Selling price is calculated on the basis of cost plus a 55% markup on cost. Cost information on the product is as follows:

Direct materials cost per kilogram	$45.00
Direct labour per hour..............	25.00

Overhead estimates at the beginning of the year:

Overhead Cost Pool	Budgeted Level	Budgeted Overhead Cost
Machine setups	1,000 setups	$400,000
Quality inspections	13,500 inspections	259,200

One job order consists of 271 units and uses the following:

> 600 kilograms of direct materials
> 150 direct labour-hours
> 5 machine setups
> 25 quality inspections

What is the selling price of one unit of product?

(Adapted © CGA-Canada)

Problems

PROBLEM 4–1   Departmental Overhead Rates (CC6, 7, 9, 22)

White Company has two departments, Cutting and Finishing. The company uses a job-order cost system and computes a predetermined overhead rate in each department. The Cutting Department bases its rate on machine-hours, and the Finishing Department bases its rate on direct labour cost. At the beginning of the year, the company made the following estimates:

	Department	
	Cutting	Finishing
Direct labour-hours	5,000	33,000
Machine-hours.	45,000	3,000
Manufacturing overhead cost.	$382,500	$499,500
Direct labour cost.	50,000	270,000

Required:

1. Compute the predetermined overhead rate to be used in each department.
2. Assume that the overhead rates that you computed in part (1) are in effect. The job cost sheet for job 203, which was started and completed during the year, showed the following:

	Department	
	Cutting	Finishing
Direct labour-hours	6	20
Machine-hours.	80	4
Materials requisitioned	$500	$310
Direct labour cost.	70	150

Compute the total overhead cost applied to job 203.

3. Would you expect substantially different amounts of overhead cost to be assigned to some jobs if the company used a plantwide overhead rate based on direct labour cost, rather than using departmental rates? Explain. No computations are necessary.

PROBLEM 4–2   Applying Overhead; T-Accounts; Journal Entries (CC6, 7, 12, 15, 17, 19, 20)

Harwood Company is a manufacturing firm that operates a job-order costing system. Overhead costs are applied to jobs on the basis of machine-hours. At the beginning of the year, management estimated that the company would incur $192,000 in manufacturing overhead costs and work 80,000 machine-hours.

Required:

1. Compute the company's predetermined overhead rate.

2. Assume that during the year the company works only 75,000 machine-hours and incurs the following costs in the manufacturing overhead and work in process accounts:

Manufacturing Overhead		
(Maintenance)	21,000	?
(Indirect materials)	8,000	
(Indirect labour)	60,000	
(Utilities)	32,000	
(Insurance)	7,000	
(Amortization)	56,000	

Work in Process		
(Direct materials)	710,000	
(Direct labour)	90,000	
(Overhead)	?	

Copy the data in the previous T-accounts onto your answer sheet. Compute the amount of overhead cost that would be applied to work in process for the year and make the entry in your T-accounts.

3. Compute the amount of under- or over-applied overhead for the year and show the balance in your manufacturing overhead T-account. Prepare a general journal entry to close out the balance in this account to cost of goods sold.

4. Explain why the manufacturing overhead was under- or over-applied for the year.

PROBLEM 4–3   Applying Overhead in a Service Firm; Journal Entries (CC7, 12, 15, 19)

CHECK FIGURE
(3) Balance in WIP: $18,000

Vista Landscaping uses a job-order costing system to track the costs of its landscaping projects. The company provides garden design services, as well as actually carrying out the landscaping for the client. The table below provides data concerning the three landscaping projects that were in progress during April. There was no work in process at the beginning of April.

	Project		
	Harris	**Chan**	**James**
Designer-hours	150	120	100
Direct materials cost	$4,800	$4,000	$1,800
Direct labour cost	9,600	8,000	7,200

Actual overhead costs were $35,000 for April. Overhead costs are applied to projects on the basis of designer-hours since most of the overhead is related to the costs of the garden design studio. The predetermined overhead rate is $90 per designer-hour. The Harris and Chan projects were completed in April; the James project was not completed by the end of the month.

Required:

1. Compute the amount of overhead cost that would have been charged to each project during April.
2. Prepare a journal entry showing the completion of the Harris and Chan projects and the transfer of costs to the completed projects (i.e., finished goods) account.
3. What is the balance in the work-in-process account at the end of the month?
4. What is the balance in the overhead account at the end of the month? What is this balance called?

PROBLEM 4–4   Comprehensive Problem (CC12, 17, 19, 23)

CHECK FIGURE
(3) Over-applied by
Rmb7,000
(4) NI: Rmb247,000

Gold Nest Company of Guandong, China, is a family-owned enterprise that makes birdcages for the South China market. A popular pastime among older Chinese men is to take their pet birds on daily excursions to teahouses and public parks where they meet with other bird owners to talk and play mahjong. A great deal of attention is lavished on these birds, and the birdcages are often elabourately constructed from exotic woods and contain porcelain feeding bowls and silver roosts. Gold Nest Company makes a broad range of birdcages that it sells through an extensive network of street vendors who receive commissions on their sales. The Chinese currency is the renminbi, which is denoted by RMB. All of the company's transactions with customers, employees, and suppliers are conducted in cash; there is no credit.

The company uses a job-order costing system in which overhead is applied to jobs on the basis of direct labour cost. At the beginning of the year, it was estimated that the total direct labour cost for the year would be RMB200,000 and the total manufacturing overhead cost would be RMB330,000. At the beginning of the year, the inventory balances were as follows:

Raw materials	RMB25,000
Work in process	10,000
Finished goods................................	40,000

During the year, the following transactions were completed:

a. Raw materials purchased for cash, RMB275,000.
b. Raw materials requisitioned for use in production, RMB280,000 (materials costing RMB220,000 were charged directly to jobs; the remaining materials were indirect).
c. Costs for employee services were incurred as follows:

Direct labour	RMB180,000
Indirect labour	72,000
Sales commissions............................	63,000
Administrative salaries	90,000

d. Rent for the year was RMB18,000 (RMB13,000 of this amount related to factory operations, and the remainder related to selling and administrative activities).
e. Utility costs incurred in the factory, RMB57,000.
f. Advertising costs incurred, RMB140,000.
g. Amortization recorded on equipment, RMB100,000. (RMB88,000 of this amount was on equipment used in factory operations; the remaining RMB12,000 was on equipment used in selling and administrative activities.)
h. Manufacturing overhead cost was applied to jobs, RMB ___?___.
i. Goods that cost RMB675,000 to manufacture according to their job cost sheets were completed during the year.
j. Sales for the year totalled RMB1,250,000. The total cost to manufacture these goods according to their job cost sheets was RMB700,000.

Required:

1. Prepare journal entries to record the transactions for the year.
2. Prepare T-accounts for inventories, manufacturing overhead, and cost of goods sold. Post relevant data from your journal entries to these T-accounts (do not forget to enter the beginning balances in your inventory accounts). Compute an ending balance in each account.
3. Is manufacturing overhead under-applied or over-applied for the year? Prepare a journal entry to close any balance in the manufacturing overhead account to cost of goods sold.
4. Prepare an income statement for the year. (Do not prepare a schedule of cost of goods manufactured; all of the information needed for the income statement is available in the journal entries and T-accounts you have prepared.)

CHECK FIGURE
(3) Indirect labour: $30,000
(7) Over-applied: $10,000

PROBLEM 4–5   T-Account Analysis of Cost Flows (CC17, 19)

Selected ledger accounts of Moore Company are given below for the past year:

Raw Materials

Bal. 1/1	15,000	Credits	?
Debits	120,000		
Bal. 12/31	25,000		

Manufacturing Overhead

Debits	230,000	Credits	?

Work in Process

Bal. 1/1	20,000	Credits	470,000
Direct materials	90,000		
Direct labour	150,000		
Overhead	240,000		
Bal. 12/31	?		

Factory Wages Payable

Debts	185,000	Bal. 1/1	9,000
		Credits	180,000
		Bal. 12/31	4,000

Finished Goods				Cost of Goods Sold		
Bal. 1/1	40,000	Credits	?	Debits	?	
Debits	?					
Bal. 12/31	60,000					

Required:
1. What was the cost of raw materials put into production during the year?
2. How much of the materials in part (1) consisted of indirect materials?
3. How much of the factory labour cost for the year consisted of indirect labour?
4. What was the cost of goods manufactured for the year?
5. What was the cost of goods sold for the year (before considering under- or over-applied overhead)?
6. If overhead is applied to production on the basis of direct labour cost, what rate was in effect during the year?
7. Was manufacturing overhead under- or over-applied? By how much?
8. Compute the ending balance in the work-in-process inventory account. Assume that this balance consists entirely of goods started during the year. If $8,000 of this balance is direct labour cost, how much of it is direct materials cost? Manufacturing overhead cost?

PROBLEM 4–6   Overhead Analysis; Schedule of Cost of Goods Manufactured (CC6, 7, 18, 19)
Gitano Products operates a job-order cost system and applies overhead cost to jobs on the basis of direct materials *used in production* (*not* on the basis of raw materials purchased). In computing a predetermined overhead rate at the beginning of the year, the company's estimates were as follows: manufacturing overhead cost, $800,000; and direct materials to be used in production, $500,000. The company's inventory accounts at the beginning and end of the year were as follows:

CHECK FIGURE
(2) COGM: $1,340,000

	A	B	C	D	E
1		Beginning	Ending		
2	Raw Materials	$ 20,000	$ 80,000		
3	Work in Process	150,000	70,000		
4	Finished Goods	260,000	400,000		
5					
6	The following actual costs were incurred during the year:				
7	Purchase of raw materials (all direct)		$510,000		
8	Direct labour cost		90,000		
9	Manufacturing overhead costs:				
10	Indirect labour		170,000		
11	Property taxes		48,000		
12	Amortization of equipment		260,000		
13	Maintenance		95,000		
14	Insurance		7,000		
15	Rent, building		180,000		
16					

Required:
1. a. Compute the predetermined overhead rate for the year.
   b. Compute the amount of under- or over-applied overhead for the year.
2. Prepare a schedule of cost of goods manufactured for the year.
3. Compute the cost of goods sold for the year. (Do not include any under- or over-applied overhead in your cost of goods sold figure.)
4. Job 215 was started and completed during the year. What price would have been charged to the customer if the job required $8,500 in direct materials and $2,700 in direct labour cost and the company priced its jobs at 25% above cost to manufacture?

5. Direct materials made up $24,000 of the $70,000 ending work-in-process inventory balance. Supply the information missing below:

Direct materials	$24,000
Direct labour	?
Manufacturing overhead	?
Work-in-process inventory.	$70,000

CHECK FIGURE
(3) $78.16 per unit

PROBLEM 4–7   Multiple Departments; Applying Overhead (CC4, 6, 7, 19)

High Desert Potteryworks makes a variety of pottery products that it sells to retailers, such as Home Depot. The company uses a job-order costing system in which predetermined overhead rates are used to apply manufacturing overhead cost to jobs. The predetermined overhead rate in the Moulding Department is based on machine-hours, and the rate in the Painting Department is based on direct labour cost. At the beginning of the year, the company's management made the following estimates:

	Department	
	Moulding	**Painting**
Direct labour-hours	12,000	60,000
Machine-hours	70,000	8,000
Direct materials cost	$510,000	$650,000
Direct labour cost.	130,000	420,000
Manufacturing overhead cost.	602,000	735,000

Job 205 was started on August 1 and completed on August 10. The company's cost records show the following information concerning the job:

	Department	
	Moulding	**Painting**
Direct labour-hours	30	85
Machine-hours	110	20
Materials placed into production	$470	$332
Direct labour cost.	290	680

Required:

1. Compute the predetermined overhead rate used during the year in the Moulding Department. Compute the rate used in the Painting Department.
2. Compute the total overhead cost applied to job 205.
3. What would be the total cost recorded for job 205? If the job contained 50 units, what would be the cost per unit?
4. At the end of the year, the records of High Desert Potteryworks revealed the following actual cost and operating data for all jobs worked on during the year:

	Department	
	Moulding	**Painting**
Direct labour-hours	10,000	62,000
Machine-hours	65,000	9,000
Direct materials cost	$430,000	$680,000
Direct labour cost.	108,000	436,000
Manufacturing overhead cost.	570,000	750,000

What was the amount of under- or over-applied overhead in each department at the end of the year?

PROBLEM 4–8   T-Accounts; Applying Overhead (CC17, 19, 23)

Hudson Company's trial balance as of January 1, the beginning of the fiscal year, follows:

CHECK FIGURE
(2) WIP balance: $17,300
(4) NI: $18,700

Cash	$ 7,000	
Accounts Receivable	18,000	
Raw Materials	9,000	
Work in Process	20,000	
Finished Goods	32,000	
Prepaid Insurance	4,000	
Plant and Equipment	210,000	
Accumulated Amortization		$ 53,000
Accounts Payable		38,000
Capital Shares		160,000
Retained Earnings		49,000
Total	$300,000	$300,000

Hudson Company is a manufacturing firm and employs a job-order costing system. During the year, the following transactions took place:
a. Raw materials purchased on account, $40,000.
b. Raw materials were requisitioned for use in production, $38,000 (85% direct and 15% indirect).
c. Factory utility costs incurred, $19,100.
d. Amortization was recorded on plant and equipment, $36,000. Three-fourths of the amortization related to factory equipment, and the remainder related to selling and administrative equipment.
e. Advertising expense incurred, $48,000.
f. Costs for salaries and wages were incurred as follows:

Direct labour	$45,000
Indirect labour	10,000
Administrative salaries	30,000

g. Prepaid insurance expired during the year, $3,000 (80% related to factory operations, and 20% related to selling and administrative activities).
h. Miscellaneous selling and administrative expenses incurred, $9,500.
i. Manufacturing overhead was applied to production. The company applies overhead on the basis of $8 per machine-hour; 7,500 machine-hours were recorded for the year.
j. Goods that cost $140,000 to manufacture according to their job cost sheets were transferred to the finished goods warehouse.
k. Sales for the year totalled $250,000 and were all on account. The total cost to manufacture these goods according to their job cost sheets was $130,000.
l. Collections from customers during the year totalled $245,000.
m. Payments to suppliers on account during the year, $150,000; payments to employees for salaries and wages, $84,000.

Required:
1. Prepare a T-account for each account in the company's trial balance, and enter the opening balances shown above.
2. Record the preceding transactions directly into the T-accounts. Prepare new T-accounts as needed. Key your entries to the letters (a) through (m). Find the ending balance in each account.
3. Is manufacturing overhead under-applied or over-applied for the year? Make an entry in the T-accounts to close any balance in the manufacturing overhead account to cost of goods sold.
4. Prepare an income statement for the year. (Do not prepare a schedule of cost of goods manufactured; all of the information needed for the income statement is available in the T-accounts.)

PROBLEM 4–9   Journal Entries; T-Accounts; Cost Flows (CC12, 17, 19, 23)

Almeda Products, Inc. uses a job-order cost system. The company's inventory balances on April 1, the start of its fiscal year, were as follows:

CHECK FIGURE
(3) Under-applied by $4,000
(4) NI: $57,000

Raw materials	$32,000
Work in process	20,000
Finished goods	48,000

During the year, the following transactions were completed:
a. Raw materials were purchased on account, $170,000.
b. Raw materials were issued from the storeroom for use in production, $180,000 (80% direct and 20% indirect).
c. Employee salaries and wages were accrued as follows: direct labour, $200,000; indirect labour, $82,000; and selling and administrative salaries, $90,000.
d. Utility costs were incurred in the factory, $65,000.
e. Advertising costs were incurred, $100,000.
f. Prepaid insurance expired during the year, $20,000 (90% related to factory operations, and 10% related to selling and administrative activities).
g. Amortization was recorded, $180,000 (85% related to factory assets, and 15% related to selling and administrative assets).
h. Manufacturing overhead was applied to jobs at the rate of 175% of direct labour cost.
i. Goods that cost $700,000 to manufacture according to their job cost sheets were transferred to the finished goods warehouse.
j. Sales for the year totalled $1,000,000 and were all on account. The total cost to manufacture these goods according to their job cost sheets was $720,000.

Required:
1. Prepare journal entries to record the transactions for the year.
2. Prepare T-accounts for raw materials, work in process, finished goods, manufacturing overhead, and cost of goods sold. Post the appropriate parts of your journal entries to these T-accounts. Compute the ending balance in each account. (Do not forget to enter the beginning balances in the inventory accounts.)
3. Is manufacturing overhead under-applied or over-applied for the year? Prepare a journal entry to close this balance to cost of goods sold.
4. Prepare an income statement for the year. (Do not prepare a schedule of cost of goods manufactured; all of the information needed for the income statement is available in the journal entries and T-accounts you have prepared.)

CHECK FIGURE
(3) Over-applied by $9,400
(4) NI: $78,400

PROBLEM 4–10   Cost Flows; T-Accounts; Income Statement (CC6, 7, 15, 17, 19, 23)
Supreme Videos, Inc. produces short musical videos for sale to retail outlets. The company's balance sheet accounts as of January 1, the beginning of the fiscal year, follow:

SUPREME VIDEOS, INC. Balance Sheet January 1		
Assets		
Current assets:		
Cash		$ 63,000
Accounts receivable		102,000
Inventories:		
Raw materials (film, costumes)	$ 30,000	
Videos in process	45,000	
Finished videos awaiting sale	81,000	156,000
Prepaid insurance		9,000
Total current assets		330,000
Studio and equipment	730,000	
Less: Accumulated amortization	210,000	520,000
Total assets		$850,000
Liabilities and Shareholders' Equity		
Accounts payable		$160,000
Capital shares	$420,000	
Retained earnings	270,000	690,000
Total liabilities and shareholders' equity		$850,000

Since the videos differ in length and complexity of production, the company uses a job-order costing system to determine the cost of each video produced. Studio (manufacturing) overhead is charged to videos on the basis of camera-hours of activity. At the beginning of the year, the company estimated that it would work 7,000 camera-hours and incur $280,000 in studio overhead cost. The following transactions were recorded for the year:

a. Film, costumes, and similar raw materials purchased on account, $185,000.
b. Film, costumes, and other raw materials issued to production, $200,000 (85% of this material was considered direct to the videos in production, and the other 15% was considered indirect).
c. Utility costs incurred in the production studio, $72,000.
d. Amortization recorded on the studio, cameras, and other equipment, $84,000. Three-fourths of this amortization related to actual production of the videos, and the remainder related to equipment used in marketing and administration.
e. Advertising expense incurred, $130,000.
f. Costs for salaries and wages were incurred as follows:

Direct labour (actors and directors)............	$ 82,000
Indirect labour (carpenters to build sets, costume designers, and so forth)............	110,000
Administrative salaries	95,000

g. Prepaid insurance expired during the year, $7,000 (80% related to production of videos, and 20% related to marketing and administrative activities).
h. Miscellaneous marketing and administrative expenses incurred, $8,600.
i. Studio (manufacturing) overhead was applied to videos in production. The company recorded 7,250 camera-hours of activity during the year.
j. Videos that cost $550,000 to produce according to their job cost sheets were transferred to the finished videos warehouse to await sale and shipment.
k. Sales for the year totalled $925,000 and were all on account. The total cost to produce these videos according to their job cost sheets was $600,000.
l. Collections from customers during the year totalled $850,000.
m. Payments to suppliers on account during the year, $500,000; payments to employees for salaries and wages, $285,000.

Required:

1. Prepare a T-account for each account on the company's balance sheet, and enter the opening balances.
2. Record the transactions directly into the T-accounts. Prepare new T-accounts as needed. Key your entries to the letters (a) through (m). Find the ending balance in each account.
3. Is the studio (manufacturing) overhead account under-applied or over-applied for the year? Make an entry in the T-accounts to close any balance in the studio overhead account to cost of goods sold.
4. Prepare an income statement for the year. (Do not prepare a schedule of cost of goods manufactured; all of the information needed for the income statement is available in the T-accounts.)

PROBLEM 4–11   Cost Flows, T-Accounts (CC17)
Information for Polaris Manufacturing Ltd. at September 1, 2008 is as follows:

CHECK FIGURE
Work in process,
September 30, $8,680

Inventories:
Raw materials (all direct)	$2,700
Work in process	1,240
Finished goods	2,090

Transactions in September 2008:

1. Purchased $24,400 of direct materials on account.
2. Transferred $22,800 of direct materials into production.
3. Production wages totalled $7,500, of which direct labour accounted for $6,000.
4. Salary in September for the production supervisor was $4,000.
5. Total utility cost was $640, of which $400 was variable and $240 was fixed.
6. Transferred $1,200 of indirect material from factory supplies into production.
7. Amortization on factory assets for September was $23,500.
8. Amortization of prepaid insurance on factory assets was $1,800.

continued

Other information:

9. The company transfers actual overhead costs during each month to the work-in-process inventory account. It uses separate accounts to record the incurrence of fixed and variable overhead.
10. During September, goods with a value of $54,000 were completed and transferred to finished goods.
11. During September, finished goods with a value of $51,315 were sold on account for $74,670.

Required:
Using T-accounts, show the flow of costs into and out of the factory overhead, inventory, and cost of goods sold accounts for the month of September. Also, compute the value of each of the raw materials, work in process, and finished goods inventories at the end of September 2008. Be sure to use separate accounts as necessary.

(Adapted © CGA-Canada)

CHECK FIGURE
Finished goods inventory,
April 30, $47,040

PROBLEM 4–12   Job Costs, T-Accounts (CC 4, 17)
Juggernaut Ltd. is in the business of manufacturing cabinets, computer stands, and countertops. Most of its jobs are contracts for new-home builders. The following information is available for the month of April:

	Costs Incurred to April 1		Added in April		
Job Number	Direct Materials	Direct Labour	Direct Materials	Direct Labour	Status at April 30
02-101	$18000	$4,000	$ —	$2,000	Completed but not sold
02-103	5,000	3,000	?	?	Not completed
02-111	1200	200	1000	6,000	Completed but not sold
02-115	—	—	1600	400	Not completed

Activity in accounts:

Account	Opening Balance April 1	Purchased in April	Issued/Used in April	Ending Balance April 30
Direct materials	$6,000	$12,000	$9,800	$?
Direct labour			16,000	

On April 1, finished goods inventory consisted of one job, 02-105, with a total cost of $36,000. This job was sold during April. Note: Manufacturing overhead is applied at 120% of the direct labour cost.

Required:
Calculate the costs of completed jobs 02-101 and 02-111, and also the inventories account balances in direct materials, work in process, and finished goods, as of April 30. Show T-Accounts.

(Adapted © CGA-Canada)

Building Your Skills

ANALYTICAL THINKING   (CC4, 6, 7, 8, 9, 23)
Kelvin Aerospace, Inc. manufactures parts, such as rudder hinges, for the aerospace industry. The company uses a job-order costing system with a plantwide predetermined overhead rate based on direct labour-hours. On December 16, 2007, the company's controller made a preliminary estimate of the predetermined overhead rate for the year 2008. The new rate was based on the estimated total manufacturing overhead cost of $3,402,000 and the estimated 63,000 total direct labour-hours for 2008:

$$\text{Predetermined overhead rate} = \frac{\$3,402,000}{63,000 \text{ direct labour-hours}}$$
$$= \$54 \text{ per direct labour-hours}$$

This new predetermined overhead rate was communicated to top managers in a meeting on December 19. The rate did not cause any comment because it was within a few pennies of the overhead rate that had been used during 2007. One of the subjects discussed at the meeting was a proposal by the production manager to purchase an automated milling machine built by Sunghi Industries. The president of Kelvin Aerospace, Harry Arcany, agreed to meet with the sales representative from Sunghi Industries to discuss the proposal.

On the day following the meeting, Harry Arcany met with Jasmine Chang, Sunghi Industries' sales representative. The following discussion took place:

Arcany: Wally, our production manager, asked me to meet with you, since he is interested in installing an automated milling machine. Frankly, I'm sceptical. You're going to have to show me this isn't just another expensive toy for Wally's people to play with.

Chang: This is a great machine with direct bottom-line benefits. The automated milling machine has three major advantages. First, it is much faster than the manual methods you are using. It can process about twice as many parts per hour as your present milling machines. Second, it is much more flexible. There are some upfront programming costs, but once those have been incurred, almost no setup is required to run a standard operation. You just punch in the code for the standard operation, load the machine's hopper with raw material, and the machine does the rest.

Arcany: What about cost? Having twice the capacity in the milling machine area won't do us much good. That centre is idle much of the time anyway.

Chang: I was getting there. The third advantage of the automated milling machine is lower cost. Wally and I looked over your present operations, and we estimated that the automated equipment would eliminate the need for about 6,000 direct labour-hours a year. What is your direct labour cost per hour?

Arcany: The wage rate in the milling area averages about $32 per hour. Fringe benefits raise that figure to about $41 per hour.

Chang: Don't forget your overhead.

Arcany: Next year, the overhead rate will be $54 per hour.

Chang: So, including fringe benefits and overhead, the cost per direct labour-hour is about $95.

Arcany: That's right.

Chang: Since you can save 6,000 direct labour-hours per year, the cost savings would amount to about $570,000 a year. And our 60-month lease plan would require payments of only $348,000 per year.

Arcany: That sounds like a no-brainer. When could you install the equipment?

Shortly after this meeting, Harry Arcany informed the company's controller of the decision to lease the new equipment, which would be installed over the Christmas vacation period. The controller realized that this decision would require a recomputation of the predetermined overhead rate for the year 2008, since the decision would affect both the manufacturing overhead and the direct labour-hours for the year. After talking with both the production manager and the sales representative from Sunghi Industries, the controller discovered that in addition to the annual lease cost of $348,000, the new machine would also require a skilled technician/programmer who would have to be hired at a cost of $50,000 per year to maintain and program the equipment. Both of these costs would be included in factory overhead. There would be no other changes in total manufacturing overhead cost, which is almost entirely fixed. The controller assumed that the new machine would result in a reduction of 6,000 direct labour-hours for the year from the levels that had initially been planned.

When the revised predetermined overhead rate for the year 2008 was circulated among the company's top managers, there was considerable dismay.

Required:

1. Recompute the predetermined rate assuming that the new machine will be installed. Explain why the new predetermined overhead rate is higher (or lower) than the rate that was originally estimated for the year 2008.
2. What effect (if any) would this new rate have on the cost of jobs that do not use the new automated milling machine?
3. Why would managers be concerned about the new overhead rate?
4. After seeing the new predetermined overhead rate, the production manager admitted that he probably would not be able to eliminate all of the 6,000 direct labour-hours. He had been hoping to accomplish the reduction by not replacing workers who retire or quit, but that had not been possible. As a result, the real labour savings would be only about 2,000 hours—one worker. In the light of this additional

information, evaluate the original decision to acquire the automated milling machine from Sunghi Industries.

COMMUNICATING IN PRACTICE   (CC1, 6, 7, 9, 22)

Look in the Yellow Pages or contact your local chamber of commerce or local chapter of CMA-Canada to find the names of manufacturing companies in your area. Call or make an appointment to meet with the controller or chief financial officer of one of these companies.

Required:

Ask the following questions and write a brief memorandum to your instructor that addresses what you found out.

1. What are the company's main products?
2. Does the company use job-order costing, process costing, or some other method of determining product costs?
3. How is overhead assigned to products? What is the overhead rate? What is the basis of allocation? Is more than one overhead rate used?
4. Has the company recently changed its cost system, or is it considering changing its cost system? If so, why? What changes were made, or what changes are being considered?

ETHICS CHALLENGE   (CC6, 7, 9, 23)

Terri Ronsin had recently been transferred to the Home Security Systems Division of National Home Products. Shortly after taking over her new position as divisional controller, she was asked to develop the division's predetermined overhead rate for the upcoming year. The accuracy of the rate is of some importance, since it is used throughout the year and any over-applied or under-applied overhead is closed out to cost of goods sold only at the end of the year. National Home Products uses direct labour-hours in all of its divisions as the allocation base for manufacturing overhead.

To compute the predetermined overhead rate, Terri divided her estimate of the total manufacturing overhead for the coming year by the production manager's estimate of the total direct labour-hours for the coming year. She took her computations to the division's general manager for approval, but was quite surprised when he suggested a modification in the base. Her conversation with the general manager of the Home Security Systems Division, Harry Irving, went like this:

Ronsin: Here are my calculations for next year's predetermined overhead rate. If you approve, we can enter the rate into the computer on January 1 and be up and running in the job-order costing system right away this year.

Irving: Thanks for coming up with the calculations so quickly, and they look just fine. There is, however, one slight modification I would like to see. Your estimate of the total direct labour-hours for the year is 440,000 hours. How about cutting that to about 420,000 hours?

Ronsin: I don't know if I can do that. The production manager says she will need about 440,000 direct labour-hours to meet the sales projections for the year. Besides, there are going to be over 430,000 direct labour-hours during the current year, and sales are projected to be higher next year.

Irving: Teri, I know all of that. I would still like to reduce the direct labour-hours in the base to something like 420,000 hours. You probably don't know that I had an agreement with your predecessor as divisional controller to shave 5% or so off the estimated direct labour-hours every year. That way, we kept a reserve that usually resulted in a big boost to net income at the end of the fiscal year in December. We called it our Christmas bonus. Corporate headquarters always seemed as pleased as punch that we could pull off such a miracle at the end of the year. This system has worked well for many years, and I don't want to change it now.

Required:

1. Explain how shaving 5% off the estimated direct labour-hours in the base for the predetermined overhead rate usually results in a big boost in net income at the end of the fiscal year.
2. Should Terri Ronsin go along with the general manager's request to reduce the direct labour-hours in the predetermined overhead rate computation to 420,000 direct labour-hours?

TEAMWORK IN ACTION   (CC6, 7, 12, 15, 17, 19)

CHECK FIGURE
(3) WIP inventory: $14,300

In an attempt to conceal a theft of funds, Snake N. Grass, controller of Bucolic Products, Inc., placed a bomb in the company's record vault. The ensuing explosion left only fragments of the company's factory ledger, as shown below:

Raw Materials

Bal. 6/1	8,000		

Manufacturing Overhead

Actual costs for June	79,000		
		Over-applied overhead	6,100

Work in Process

Bal. 6/1	7,200		

Accounts Payable

		Bal. 6/30	16,000

Finished Goods

Bal. 6/30	21,000		

Cost of Goods Sold

To bring Mr. Grass to justice, the company must reconstruct its activities for June. Your team has been assigned to perform the task of reconstruction. After interviewing selected employees and sifting through charred fragments, you have determined the following additional information:

a. According to the company's treasurer, the accounts payable are for purchases of raw materials only. The company's balance sheet, dated May 31, shows that accounts payable had a $20,000 balance at the beginning of June. The company's bank has provided photocopies of all cheques that cleared the bank during June. These photocopies show that payments to suppliers during June totalled $119,000. (All materials used during the month were direct materials.)

b. The production superintendent states that manufacturing overhead cost is applied to jobs on the basis of direct labour-hours. However, he does not remember the rate currently being used by the company.

c. Cost sheets kept in the production superintendent's office show that only one job was in process on June 30, at the time of the explosion. The job had been charged with $6,600 in materials, and 500 direct labour-hours at $8 per hour had been worked on the job.

d. A log is kept in the finished goods warehouse showing all goods transferred in from the factory. This log shows that the cost of goods transferred into the finished goods warehouse from the factory during June totalled $280,000.

e. The company's May 31 balance sheet indicates that the finished goods inventory totalled $36,000 at the beginning of June.

f. A charred piece of the payroll ledger, found after sifting through piles of smoking debris, indicates that 11,500 direct labour-hours were recorded for June. The company's Human Resources Department has verified that, as a result of a union contract, all factory employees earn the same $8 per hour rate.

g. The production superintendent states that there was no under- or over-applied overhead in the manufacturing overhead account at May 31.

Required:

1. Each member of the team should determine what types of transactions would be posted to one of the following sets of accounts:
   a. Raw materials and accounts payable
   b. Work in process and manufacturing overhead
   c. Finished goods and cost of goods sold

   Each team member should present a summary of the types of transactions that would be posted to the accounts to the other team members, who should confirm or correct the summary. Then, the team should work together to complete steps 2 through 8.

2. Determine the transaction that should be reflected in the manufacturing overhead account, and then determine the company's predetermined overhead rate.
3. Determine the June 30 balance in the company's work-in-process account.
4. Determine the transactions that should be reflected in the work-in-process account.
5. Determine the transactions that should be reflected in the finished goods account.
6. Determine the transactions that should be reflected in the cost of goods sold account.
7. Determine the transactions that should be reflected in the accounts payable account.
8. Determine the transactions that should be reflected in the raw materials account.
   (Hint: A good method for determining the transactions that were recorded in a given account is to update the related fragmented T-account by posting whatever entries can be developed from the information provided above.)

Don't forget to visit the Online Learning Centre for self-study quizzes, practice exams, and more! Visit www.mcgrawhill.ca/olc/brewer.

CHAPTER *Five*

Process Costing

CHAPTER COMPETENCIES

After studying Chapter 5, you should be able to demonstrate the following competencies:

Competency	Know	Apply
Understand the distinction between job-order and process costing systems.		
CC1 Compare and contrast job-order and process costing systems.	○	
CC2 Explain a production report.	○	
CC3 Describe a processing department.	○	
CC4 Describe the flow of costs through a process costing system.	○	
Describe the cost concepts relevant to process costing and the flow of costs through the costing system.		
CC5 Define transferred-in costs.	○	
CC6 Describe the cost categories commonly used in process costing.	○	
CC7 Explain the use of the conversion cost category in process costing.	○	
CC8 Prepare journal entries to record the incurrence and flow of costs through a process costing system.		○
Understand the concept of equivalent units of production and its computation.		
CC9 Explain the concepts of degree of completion and equivalent units of production.	○	
CC10 Explain the concept of equivalent units of production and the role of WIP inventories in the weighted average method.	○	
CC11 Compute the equivalent units of production for each cost category using the weighted average method.		○
CC12 Explain the concept of equivalent units of production including the roles of the number of units started and completed in a given period and WIP inventories in the FIFO method.	○	
CC13 Compute the equivalent units of production for each cost category using the FIFO method.		○
Prepare a production cost report using the weighted average method to account for the flow of production and the production cost.		
CC14 Account for the flow of production by preparing a quantity schedule using the weighted average method.		○
CC15 Compute the cost per equivalent unit of production using the weighted average method.		○
CC16 Account for the costs of production in a given period by preparing a cost reconciliation using the weighted average method.		○
Prepare a production cost report using the FIFO method to account for the flow of production and the production cost		
CC17 Account for the flow of production by preparing a quantity schedule using the FIFO method.		○
CC18 Compute the cost per equivalent unit of production using the FIFO method.		○
CC19 Account for the costs of production in a given period by preparing a cost reconciliation using the FIFO method.		○
CC20 Distinguish between the FIFO and weighted average methods to costing.	○	

DECISION FEATURE
Quality and Costs Are Important in Beer Making, Too!

Whether you are drinking Grasshopper Wheat Ale, Traditional Ale, or Black Amber Ale, you care about deriving value for the money you spend. For Big Rock Brewery of Calgary, value means offering distinctive premium quality beers at competitive prices.

So, is there a difference in the way the different beers are made? The process they follow is essentially the same. The raw ingredients are first crushed or milled and then mashed. The wort, resulting from the mashing process is the liquid that will eventually become the beer. This liquid is then boiled to be sterilized. The next step in the process is fermentation, but this requires that the sterilized liquid be cooled before it is sent for fermentation. The fermentation process is important in terms of maintaining the desired consistency and quality of the beer. After the fermentation process, the beer is aged, filtered, packaged (bottled and labelled), and then sent off to distributors.

Like many other industries, the beer industry is also fiercely competitive. However, such companies as Big Rock Brewery have thrived in the marketplace by developing specialty beers, which offer superior quality and taste and by controlling costs. And management's efforts have certainly paid off! In the last five years, sales grew by over 83%, and the net income as a percentage of sales increased from −3.3% in 1999 to over 7.5% in 2003.

Big Rock, however, understands that it cannot afford to be complacent. In an effort to further control costs, the company has invested in a computer system that allows managers to implement more effective cost controls in many areas. The system generates detailed cost information on weekly and monthly bases. This is important, given the number of different processes that add to the costs of brewing a good beer. Knowing the cost added at each stage of the entire process is essential to identify potential avenues for cost management. Managers at Big Rock may also decide to adopt the lean business model to improve quality and efficiency (cost), two important factors in enhancing the value that the company's beers offer its drinkers.

Source: 2003 Annual Report, obtained at http://www.bigrockbeer.com/investors.htm. Big Rock Brewery © 2007.

A Look Back

We described a basic job-order costing system in Chapter 4. We used a single plantwide overhead rate to apply overhead costs to jobs. This is a normal costing approach: only *applied* (as opposed to *actual*) overhead costs flow through work in process to finished goods and then to cost of goods sold.

A Look at this Chapter

In Chapter 5, we continue the discussion of the accumulation of product cost by describing a basic process costing system. This is applicable to production environments in which essentially homogeneous units of product are produced in large volumes. We stick to the normal costing approach to the allocation of manufacturing overhead costs.

A Look Ahead

In Chapter 6, we will look at activity-based costing, a more sophisticated technique that uses a variety of allocation bases to assign overhead costs to products.

As explained in Chapter 4, two basic costing systems are in use: job-order costing and process costing. A job-order costing system is used in situations where many different jobs or products are worked on in each period. Examples of industries that would typically use job-order costing include furniture manufacturers, special-order printing, shipbuilding, and many types of service organizations.

A **process costing** system is used in industries that produce essentially homogeneous (i.e., uniform) products on a continuous basis, such as bricks, corn flakes, or paper. Process costing is used in such companies as Reynolds Aluminum (aluminum ingots), Scott Paper (toilet paper), General Mills (flour), Petro Canada (gasoline and lubricating oils), Coppertone (sunscreens), and Kellogg (breakfast cereals). In addition, process costing is often used in companies with assembly operations, such as Panasonic (video monitors), Compaq (personal computers), General Electric (refrigerators), Toyota (automobiles), Amana (washing machines), and Sony (CD players). As suggested by the length of this list, process costing is in wide use.

In this chapter we will explain how product costing occurs in a process costing system.

Comparison of Job-Order and Process Costing

Similarities between Job-Order and Process Costing

 KNOW

CC1: Compare and contrast job-order and process costing systems.

The similarities between job-order and process costing can be summarized as follows:

- Both systems share a common purpose, which is to assign material, labour, and overhead cost to products and to provide a mechanism for computing unit costs.
- Both systems maintain and use the same basic accounts, including manufacturing overhead, raw materials, work in process, and finished goods, and the flow of costs through the accounts is basically the same in both systems.

As can be seen from this comparison, much of the knowledge that we have already acquired about job-order costing is applicable to process costing. Our task now is simply to refine and extend this knowledge to process costing.

Differences between Job-Order and Process Costing

The differences between job-order and process costing are caused by two factors: (1) the flow of units in a process costing system is more or less continuous, and (2) these units are indistinguishable from one another. Under process costing, it makes no sense to try to identify materials, labour, and overhead costs with a particular order from a customer (as we did with job-order costing), since each order is just one of many that are filled from a continuous flow of virtually identical units from the production line. Therefore, under process costing, we accumulate costs *by department*, or process, rather than by order, and assign these costs uniformly to all units that pass through the department during a period.

The job cost sheet is not used in process costing because the focal point of this method is on departments. Instead of using job cost sheets, a **production report** is prepared for each department in which work is done on products. The production report serves several functions. It provides a summary of the number of units moving through a department during a period, and also provides a computation of unit costs. In addition, it shows the costs that were charged to the department and the disposition made of these costs. The department production report is the key document in a process costing system.

KNOW

CC2: Explain a production report.

The major differences between job-order and process costing are summarized in Exhibit 5–1.

Job-Order Costing	Process Costing
1. Many different jobs are worked on during each period, with each job having different production requirements.	1. A single product is produced either on a continuous basis or for long periods. All units of product are identical.
2. Costs are accumulated by individual job.	2. Costs are accumulated by department or process.
3. The *job cost sheet* is the key document controlling the accumulation of costs by a job.	3. The *department production report* is the key document showing the accumulation and disposition of costs by department.
4. Unit costs are computed *by job* on the job cost sheet.	4. Unit costs are computed *by department* on the department production report.

Exhibit 5–1
Differences between Job-Order and Process Costing

A Perspective of Process Cost Flows

Before presenting a detailed example of process costing, we will show how manufacturing costs flow through a process costing system.

Processing Departments

A **processing department** is any location in an organization where work is performed on a product and where materials, labour, or overhead costs are added to the product. For example, a potato chip factory might have three processing departments—one for preparing potatoes, one for cooking, and one for inspecting and packaging. A company can have as many or as few processing departments as are needed to complete a product or service. Some products and services may go through several processing departments, while others may go through only one or two. Regardless of the number of departments involved, all processing departments have three essential features. First, the activity performed in the processing department must be performed uniformly on all of the units passing through it. This means that each unit must be treated in an identical fashion. Second, the output of the processing department must be homogeneous. This means that each unit must be indistinguishable from the other units. Third, the processing departments involved would probably be organized in a *sequential* pattern. By *sequential processing*, we mean that units flow in sequence from one department to another as shown in Exhibit 5–2.

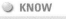

KNOW

CC3: Describe a processing department.

Exhibit 5–2
Sequential Processing Departments

Costing the "Quicker-Picker-Upper"

If you have ever spilled milk, there is a good chance that you used Bounty paper towels to clean up the mess. Procter & Gamble (P&G) manufactures Bounty in two main processing departments—Paper Making and Paper Converting. In the Paper Making Department, wood pulp is converted into paper and then spooled into 2,000-pound rolls that are inventoried and retrieved as needed to supply the paper converting process. In the Paper Converting Department, two 2,000-pound rolls of paper are simultaneously unwound into a machine that creates a two-ply paper towel that is decorated, perforated, and embossed to create texture. The large sheets of paper towels that emerge from this process are wrapped around a cylinder-shaped cardboard core measuring eight feet in length. Once enough sheets wrap around the core, the eight-foot roll is cut into individual rolls of Bounty that are sent down a conveyor to be wrapped, packed, and shipped.

In this type of manufacturing environment, costs cannot be readily traced to individual rolls of Bounty; however, given the homogeneous nature of the product, the total costs incurred in the Paper Making Department can be spread uniformly across its output of 2,000-pound rolls of paper. Similarly, the total costs incurred to produce a particular style of Bounty in the Paper Converting Department (including the cost of the 2,000-pound rolls that are transferred in from the Paper Making Department) can be spread uniformly across the number of cases produced of that style.

P&G uses a similar costing approach for many of its products such as Tide, Crest toothpaste, and Pringles.

Source: Conversation with Brad Bays, retired financial executive from Procter & Gamble.

The Flow of Materials, Labour, and Overhead Costs

Cost accumulation is simpler in a process costing system than in a job-order costing system. In a process costing system, instead of having to trace costs to hundreds of different jobs, costs are traced to only a few processing departments.

A T-account model of materials, labour, and overhead cost flows in a process costing system is given in Exhibit 5–3. Several key points should be noted from this exhibit. First, note that a separate work-in-process account is maintained for *each processing department*. In contrast, in a job-order costing system, there may be only a single work-in-process account for the entire company. Second, notice that the costs of completed production of the first processing department (Department A in the exhibit) is transferred into the work-in-process account of the second processing department (Department B). In Department B, completed production received from Department A undergoes additional work, leading to costs being incurred in Department B. After this additional work, the completed units are then transferred into finished goods. (In Exhibit 5–3, we show only two processing departments, but there can be many such departments in a company.)

Third, note that materials, labour, and overhead costs can be added in *any* processing department—not just the first. Costs in Department B's work-in-process account would consist of the materials, labour, and overhead costs incurred in Department B plus the costs attached to partially completed units transferred in from Department A (called **transferred-in costs**).

Finally, note that the flow of costs through the processing departments parallels the physical flow of production through these departments as shown in Exhibits 5–2 and 5–3.

Exhibit 5–3
T-Account Model of Process Costing Flows

Efficiency Boosts Production Levels   IN BUSINESS TODAY

Leamington, Ontario, the "Tomato Capital of Canada," is where H.J. Heinz Company of Canada Ltd. has established its operations for ketchup manufacturing. Since its establishment at Leamington, the company has processed close to 300,000 tons of ketchup per year at its 20-acre site that employs 1,000 people. Due to the vast size of the plant, it is important for the company to find ways for maximum efficiency. Line 59 within the facility moves at least 100 containers per minute, thanks to the capital investment of $3.5 million to better fill and package the containers. As well, the Leamington plant's changeover times are faster than in the production facilities in the United States, even though Heinz Canada can take up to five hours, depending on the complexity of the changeover. The company also claims its superiority over the competition in cleaning and sterilizing its machines by utilizing circulating air filters to keep the product edible. In terms of environmental responsibility, the plant produces its own energy from a co-generating system using natural gas. The spare heat goes back into a boiler package to produce free steam used during manufacturing, which increases production levels.

Source: "No Other Kinds," *Canadian Packaging*, December 2001, Volume 54 (12), p. 19. Reprinted by permission of Rogers Publishing Ltd.

Product Cost Categories in a Process Costing System

The example described in the *In Business Today* feature illustrates that production environments that use a process costing system for determining product costs are typically highly capital intensive. Labour will usually comprise a small proportion of total manufacturing cost. In such environments, it may not be economical to track three separate product cost categories. Labour costs and manufacturing overhead are commonly combined into a single cost category called **conversion cost.** It is important to realize that this is usually relevant for cost reporting on a production report, and illustrates the management accounting philosophy of "different costs for different purposes." The company's cost accounts will record labour and manufacturing overhead cost incurrence separately, and managers will be able to obtain this information, if needed. The manufacturing overhead cost component of conversion cost will still come from assigning it using an overhead allocation rate.

IN BUSINESS TODAY **Cutting Conversion Costs**

CEMEX S.A., the world's third largest cement maker, owns 54 plants that each consumes 800 tons of fuel a day heating kilns to 2,700 degrees Fahrenheit. Not surprisingly, energy costs account for 40% of the company's overall conversion costs. Historically, Cemex relied exclusively on coal to heat its kilns; however, faced with soaring coal prices and shrinking profits, the company desperately needed a lower cost heat source. Cemex turned its attention to an oil industry waste product called petroleum coke that burns hotter than coal and costs half as much. The company spent about $150 million to convert its manufacturing processes to accommodate petroleum coke and set up an office in Houston, Texas, to negotiate bulk petroleum coke purchases from locally headquartered oil companies. Overall, Cemex has cut its energy bills by 17%, thus helping it earn higher profit margins than its biggest rivals.

Source: John Lyons, "Expensive Energy? Burn Other Stuff, One Firm Decides," *The Wall Street Journal*, September 1, 2004, pp. A1 and A8.

Materials, Labour, and Overhead Cost Entries

To complete our discussion of cost flows in a process costing system, in the following paragraphs we show journal entries relating to materials, labour, and overhead costs.

MATERIALS COSTS As in job-order costing, materials are drawn from the storeroom using a materials requisition form. As stated previously, materials can be added in any processing department, although it is not unusual for materials to be added only in the first processing department, with subsequent departments adding only labour and overhead costs as the partially completed units move along toward completion.

Assuming that the first processing department in a company is Department A, the journal entry for placing materials into production is as follows:

Work in Process—Department A	XXX	
Raw Materials		XXX

If other materials are subsequently added in Department B, the entry is the following:

Work in Process—Department B	XXX	
Raw Materials		XXX

LABOUR COSTS In process costing, it is necessary to keep track of only the amount of labour cost incurred in each department because labour costs do not have to be traced to specific jobs. The following journal entry will record the labour costs for a period in Department A:

> Work in Process—Department A   XXX
>   Salaries and Wages Payable   XXX

OVERHEAD COSTS In process costing, predetermined overhead rates are usually used to apply overhead costs to departments (or processes); each department receives a portion of the total overhead based on this rate. Overhead cost is then charged to units of product as the units move through the department using a journal entry, such as the following for Department A:

> Work in Process—Department A   XXX
>   Manufacturing Overhead Applied   XXX

COMPLETING THE COST FLOWS Once processing has been completed in a department, the units are transferred to the next department for further processing, as illustrated previously in the T-accounts in Exhibit 5–3. The following journal entry is used to transfer the costs of partially completed units from Department A to Department B:

> Work in Process—Department B   XXX
>   Work in Process—Department A   XXX

After processing has been completed in Department B, the costs of the completed units are then transferred to the finished goods inventory account:

> Finished Goods   XXX
>   Work in Process—Department B   XXX

Finally, when a customer's order is filled and units are sold, the cost of the units is transferred to cost of goods sold:

> Cost of Goods Sold   XXX
>   Finished Goods   XXX

To summarize, cost flows between accounts are basically the same in a process costing system as they are in a job-order costing system. The only noticeable difference at this point is that in a process costing system there is a separate work-in-process account for each department.

Samantha Trivers, president of Double Diamond Skis, was worried about the future of her company. After a rocky start, the company had come out with a completely redesigned ski called The Ultimate, made of exotic materials and featuring flashy graphics. Exhibit 5–4 illustrates how this ski is manufactured. The ski was a runaway bestseller—particularly among younger skiers—and had provided the company with much-needed cash for two years. However, last year, a dismal snowfall in the Canadian Rockies had depressed sales, and Double Diamond was once again short of cash. Samantha was worried that another bad ski season would force Double Diamond into bankruptcy.

Just before starting production of next year's model of The Ultimate, Samantha called Jerry Madison, the company controller, into her office to discuss the reports she would need in the coming year.

MANAGERIAL ACCOUNTING IN ACTION

The Issue

Exhibit 5–4
The Production Process at
Double Diamond Skis*

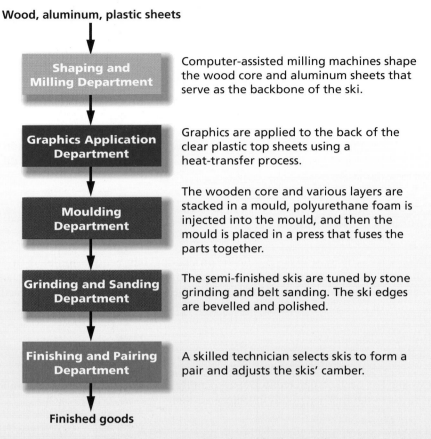

Wood, aluminum, plastic sheets

Shaping and Milling Department
Computer-assisted milling machines shape the wood core and aluminum sheets that serve as the backbone of the ski.

Graphics Application Department
Graphics are applied to the back of the clear plastic top sheets using a heat-transfer process.

Moulding Department
The wooden core and various layers are stacked in a mould, polyurethane foam is injected into the mould, and then the mould is placed in a press that fuses the parts together.

Grinding and Sanding Department
The semi-finished skis are tuned by stone grinding and belt sanding. The ski edges are bevelled and polished.

Finishing and Pairing Department
A skilled technician selects skis to form a pair and adjusts the skis' camber.

Finished goods

Source: *Adapted from Bill Gout, Jesse James Doquilo, and Studio M D, "Capped Crusaders," *Skiing*, October 1993, pp. 138–144.

Samantha: Jerry, I am going to need more frequent cost information this year. I really have to stay on top of things.

Jerry: What do you have in mind?

Samantha: I'd like reports at least once a month that detail our production costs for each department and for each pair of skis.

Jerry: That shouldn't be much of a problem. We already compile almost all of the necessary data for the annual report. The only complication is our work-in-process inventories. They haven't been a problem in our annual reports, since our fiscal year ends at a time when we have finished producing skis for the last model year and haven't yet started producing for the new model year. Consequently, there aren't any work-in-process inventories to value for the annual report. But that won't be true for monthly reports.

Samantha: I'm not sure why that is a problem, Jerry. But I'm confident you can figure out how to solve it.

Jerry: You can count on me.

The Costing Challenge in a Process Costing Environment

Jerry Diamond, the controller of Double Diamond, has the fundamental problem faced by all management accountants in a process costing environment. How can a department's output be determined? Until Samantha asked for more frequent cost reports, Jerry had no difficulty preparing reports annually. During this period, all production initiated in the company was *fully completed*. There never was unfinished, that is, work-in-process, inventory at the end of the period. This makes it easy to determine the output of a processing department and the cost per unit of that output.

Consider the data shown in Exhibit 5–5 for a fictitious processing department. Situation 1 in this exhibit illustrates a scenario similar to what Jerry Diamond had faced until now. During a given period, direct material costs of $100 and conversion costs of $80 are incurred to initiate and fully complete 20 units. There are no units in process at the beginning and end of the period. This means that all of the work performed and all of the costs incurred must have been to start and complete 20 full units—the output of the department for the period. The material cost per unit will be $5 ($100 ÷ 20), and the conversion cost per unit will be $4 ($80 ÷ 20). The total cost per unit is $9.

But now Samantha has asked for cost reports to be prepared more frequently. This means that at the end of a subperiod (and therefore also at the beginning of the following subperiod) when a cost report is prepared, it is likely that there will be partially completed units in inventory at Double Diamond. This makes the costing problem challenging. How? Consider the data shown in situation 2 in Exhibit 5–5. There are 10 units in ending work-in-process inventory. These are units yet to be fully completed. Only 10 of the 20 units started have been fully completed. What costs will you assign to the 20 physical units on which work has been performed—and costs incurred—by this department?

If you decide to treat partially completed units and fully completed units as though they were identical, you would assign, like in situation 1, $5 per unit of direct materials cost and $4 per unit of conversion costs. Or, you can completely ignore the partially completed units and assign all of the incurred costs only to the 10 units fully finished. This would lead to direct materials cost per unit of $10 and conversion cost of $8 per unit. *Both* these approaches are unreasonable and violate a host of fundamental accounting principles. In the first case, the fully finished units are getting an unfair advantage; these units have been assigned less than their fair share of the incurred costs because you are treating the partially completed units as if they were fully finished. In the second case, the partially finished units are getting an unfair advantage because none of the costs incurred during the period has been assigned to them even though some of the costs incurred were due to the fact that work was performed on them.

Situation 3 illustrates what is often found in a processing department when a cost report is required. There will be both beginning and ending work-in-process inventories.

Exhibit 5–5
Units of Production and Work-in-Process Inventories

Business Situations Regarding Work-in-Process Inventories

	(1) No WIP		(2) Zero Beginning WIP and Nonzero Ending WIP		(3) Nonzero Beginning and Ending WIP	
	DM	Conversion	DM	Conversion	DM	Conversion
Costs incurred this period	$100	$80	$100	$80	$100	$80
Units in beginning WIP.	0	0	0	0	5	5
Units started this period	20	20	20	20	20	20
Units completed this period	20	20	10	10	10	10
Units in ending WIP	0	0	10	10	15	15
Cost per unit	$5 ($100 ÷ 20)	$4 ($80 ÷ 20)	?	?	?	?

When there are no WIP inventories at both the beginning and end of a period, determining the cost per unit is easy (situation 1). But if there are WIP inventories, then determining the cost per unit of product becomes challenging (situations 2 and 3). This is indicated by a "?" in the table.

The added complication now is that the units in beginning work-in-process inventory will bring the prior period costs assigned to them into the current period. These costs must be somehow folded into the current period costs incurred to finish these units.

The precise procedure for handling the complications just described, which would exist in cases similar to situations 2 and 3, is the subject of the remainder of this chapter. We will first learn how to resolve the problem that the partially completed units are not the same as fully completed units. We will then examine the physical flow of units in a processing department to learn about the approaches available to incorporate prior period costs contained in units in beginning work-in-process inventory, and finally, we will tie it all together by showing you how to prepare a production cost report.

Degree of Completion and Equivalent Units of Production

From the previous discussion, you know that it is wrong to treat each partially completed unit as if it were one fully completed unit. However, each partially completed unit can be thought of as being equivalent to a percentage of a fully completed unit. Using this idea, we can express the units of partially completed product in terms of the number of **equivalent units** fully completed. This is done using the following formula:

$$\text{Equivalent units} = \text{Number of partially completed units} \times \text{Percentage complete}$$

● KNOW

CC9: Explain the concepts of degree of completion and equivalent units of production.

The **percentage completion** of a partially completed unit describes how much work has been done on the product. The figure of 100% describes a fully completed unit, whereas 0% says that no work has been done. There will be percentage completion data *for each cost category*. Before we explain why this must be so, let us show you how to apply the formula. Suppose you know that units in ending work in process are just 60% complete with respect to conversion costs in the sense that only 60% of the work related to conversion has been performed on them. Then, *with respect to conversion costs*, each unit in ending work in process is equivalent to 60% of a fully completed unit. In situation 2 of Exhibit 5–5, there are 10 units in ending work in process. These 10 partially completed units are equivalent to $10 \times 0.6 = 6$ *fully completed units*. There are already 10 units fully completed. So, adding the 6 equivalent units in ending work in process to the 10 fully finished units gives a total of 16 *equivalent units of production*. Now it is easy to determine *the conversion cost per unit*. Given that $80 of conversion costs were incurred during the period, the conversion cost *per equivalent unit of production* is $80 \div 16 = \$5$.

The previous illustration of the concept of equivalent units and its use in calculating cost per unit was in the context of conversion costs. The same process must be applied to the other cost category to calculate the direct materials cost per equivalent unit of production. Consider situation 2 in Exhibit 5–5 once more. Now suppose that the 10 units in ending work in process are 25% complete with respect to the direct materials. This leads us to determine that there are $0.25 \times 10 = 2.5$ equivalent units in ending work in process with respect to direct materials. Adding the 10 fully completed units to 2.5 equivalent units gives a total of 12.5 equivalent units of production. Given that $100 of direct materials costs were incurred during the period, the direct material cost per equivalent unit of production is $100 \div 12.5 = \$8$. With these calculations in hand, you can say that the total cost per equivalent unit of production is $5 + \$8 = \$13$.

The concept of equivalent units of production is the solution to resolving the problem of partially completed units and fully completed units. Equivalent units of production are the sum of the number of fully completed units and the number of equivalent units in work-in-process inventories.

Before proceeding further, note that we *first* calculated the cost per unit *separately for each cost category* and *then* assembled the total unit cost by summing the unit costs from each cost category. Why? The *degree of completion* with respect to direct materials can be different from that for conversion costs. For example, when baking bread, normally all of the ingredients are assembled before mixing and baking. In this case, you can see that all the required direct materials are added right at the beginning of the bread making process. Thus, the degree of completion of partially made bread with respect to the direct materials can be said to be 100%, whereas the degree of completion with respect to conversion costs will not be 100%. Instead, it will be some percentage less than 100%. Do not be misled into thinking that direct materials will always be added at the beginning of a production process. The application of materials and conversion to units of product will obviously be determined by the requirements of the production process. Here is an example where the degree of completion for direct materials is less than 100%—a cake making process. When preparing a cake, even though most of the ingredients are introduced at the beginning, the icing is not put on until after the cake has been baked. Some direct materials are added only toward the end, and therefore, in the case of a partially completed cake, the degree of completion with respect to direct materials (as well conversion costs) will not be 100%. In conclusion, each cost category must be considered separately when calculating its equivalent units of production.

The Flow of Physical Units

Consider situation 3 in Exhibit 5–5. There are 5 units in beginning work-in-process inventory; 20 units were started from scratch during the period; 10 units were fully completed, and there are 15 units in ending work-in-process inventory. Note that these data obey the inventory balance relationship for physical units:

$$\begin{array}{ccccccc} \text{Number} & & & & & & \text{Number} \\ \text{of units in} & & \text{Number} & & \text{Number} & & \text{of units in} \\ \text{beginning work} & + & \text{of units} & = & \text{of units} & + & \text{ending work} \\ \text{in process} & & \text{started} & & \text{finished} & & \text{in process} \\ \\ 5 & + & 20 & = & 10 & + & 15 \end{array}$$

On the left-hand side, there are 25 units to be accounted for. These are the units on which work *is being* performed. The right-hand side shows what happened to the 25 units on the left-hand side: work was fully completed on 10 of these units, leaving 15 units yet to be fully completed. Therefore, the right-hand side is an accounting of all of the units in the department during the period.

We want to understand how to calculate the equivalent units of production in this situation. The introduction of beginning work-in-process inventory is an important complication. To illustrate the issues involved, suppose that the units in work-in-process inventories are partially finished, as follows:

		Percentage Complete	
Situation 3	Units	Materials	Conversion
WIP, Beginning....................	5	80%	40%
Units started	20	n.a.*	n.a.*
Units finished	10	100%	100%
WIP, Ending	15	60%	40%
*Not applicable.			

There are two alternative approaches for calculating equivalent units of production for each cost category: (1) the **weighted average method,** and (2) the **first-in-first-out (FIFO) method.** Each method must tell us how to calculate the equivalent units of production corresponding to the total 25 *physical* units that exist.

WEIGHTED AVERAGE METHOD   This method considers only the right-hand side of the balance relationship. There are 10 units fully completed. You can see that these must be 100% complete, and thus, there are 10 equivalent units of production here, regardless of the cost category. There are 15 units in ending work in process. Using the data on degree of completion, the total **equivalent units of production** for each cost category is calculated as before, using the following formula:

Weighted Average Method Formula
(A separate calculation is made for each cost category in each processing department):

Equivalent units of production	=	Number of units fully completed (i.e., transferred to the next department or to finished goods)
		+ Number of equivalent units in ending work in process

The formula is illustrated in Exhibit 5–6. The circle on the left represents the units completed in the current period (10 units). These units are complete and therefore, they represent full units. The only partial units in the department are those in ending work in process. These units are shown in the shaded portion of the circle on the right. There are 15 units in this area. These partial units must be expressed in terms of equivalent units of production for each cost category. The computations are shown in Exhibit 5–7 following. There are 19 equivalent units of production with respect to direct materials and 16 equivalent units of production with respect to conversion costs. Note that the work that

Exhibit 5–6
Flow of Physical Units: The Weighted Average Method View

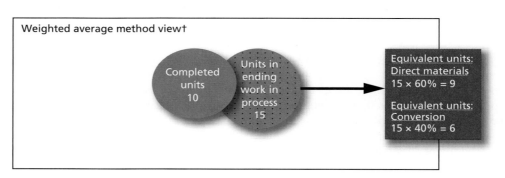

† Units in beginning work-in-process inventory are ignored in this method and thus not shown
Equivalent units of production: Direct materials 10 + 9 = 19
Equivalent units of production: Conversion 10 + 6 = 16

Exhibit 5–7
Calculation of Equivalent Units of Production: Weighted Average Method

Cost Category	(1) Physical Units Processed this Period	(2) Units in Ending WIP Inventory	(3) Degree of Completion	(4) Equivalent Units (2) × (3)	(5) Units Completed this Period	(6) Equivalent Units of Production (4) + (5)
Direct materials	25	15	60%	9	10	19
Conversion	25	15	40%	6	10	16

was done in the previous period on the units in beginning work in process, and hence, the work that was done in the current period to bring these units to completion is not explicitly accounted for. The weighted average method blends the work done (and the costs incurred) from the previous period with the work done and the costs incurred in the current period.

FIFO METHOD   The FIFO method recognizes that current period's production activity involves three types of work: (1) work to finish off the partially completed units from the previous period, (2) work done on units that were started from scratch and fully completed, and (3) work done on units that were started but were not completed. Costs during the period must have been incurred because these three distinct types of work were performed in the period, and therefore, the FIFO method provides the procedure by which the incurred costs can be allocated among the three types of work. This type of detailed accounting of the costs can be valuable to managers.

The procedure to calculate equivalent units of production consists of three steps. The physical units in beginning work in process are converted to equivalent units using the degree of completion information from the previous period. For example, the data on degree of completion with respect to direct materials tell you that the 5 units in beginning work in process are 80% complete. This is at the start of the period, and thus, these data actually represent work done previously. If 80% of work has already been done, then there must be 20% (100% − 80%) remaining to be done in the current period. Therefore, we can say that the work required and the costs incurred to bring 5 physical units in beginning work in process to completion, with respect to direct materials, is equivalent to work required and costs incurred to make 20% × 5 = 1 fully completed unit. For the case of conversion costs, the number of equivalent units will be (100%−40%) × 5 = 3.

The second step involves finding out how many units were started from scratch and fully completed. This involves answering either of the following questions: (1) How many of the 20 units started this period were fully completed? Answer: 20 units were started, there are 15 physical units in ending work in process, and therefore, 20 − 15 = 5 units were started and fully completed in this period. (2) How many of the 10 units that are fully complete and ready to transfer out were started this period (and, therefore, started and finished this period)? Answer: There were 5 units in beginning work in process, and according to the FIFO concept, these 5 physical units must have been completed *first*. Therefore, out of the 10 units that are fully completed, if 5 are the units from beginning work in process, then the remaining 10 − 5 = 5 units must be units that were started and finished during this period.

Note the application of the FIFO principle in answering the questions. With the first question, the principle allows us to infer that the department will not begin to work on new units until the units in beginning work in process have been completed. Therefore, any units in ending work in process cannot be units from beginning work in process still waiting to be completed and consequently must be units that were started during this period. With the second question, looking at the fully finished units, the principle allows us to infer that these must contain the units that were in beginning work in process because these would have been the units completed first. Thus, the balance, as was stated before, must represent the units that were started in the current period. We have now developed the following formula to calculate the number of units that are started from scratch and fully completed in a given period:

Number of units started and finished = Number of units started this period
                                                        − Number of units in ending work-in-process inventory

or,

Number of units started and finished = Number of units completed this period
                                                        − Number of units in beginning work-in-process inventory

⊘ KNOW

CC12: Explain the concept of equivalent units of production including the roles of the number of units started and completed in a given period and WIP inventories in the FIFO method.

◔ KNOW

CC13: Compute the equivalent
units of production for each cost
category using the FIFO method.

Exhibit 5–8 illustrates this formula. The circle on the left represents the units completed this period (10 units). This circle has two pieces: a piece with horizontal stripes representing the units in beginning work in process (5 units), and a darkly shaded portion shaped like a lens representing the units that were started and fully completed (5 units). The circle on the right represents the units that were started during this period (20 units). This circle has two pieces. A piece with vertical stripes representing ending work in process (15 units) and the lens-shaped area representing the units were started and fully finished in the period (5 units). The purpose of the formula is to help you calculate the units in the lens area. This can be found either by taking the units in the left circle and subtracting the units in the area with the horizontal stripes or by taking the units in the right circle and subtracting the units in the area with vertical stripes.

The final step involves calculating the equivalent units in ending work in process. There are 15 units here. These are 60% complete with respect to direct material. Thus, the number of equivalent units in ending work in process is 9 (60% × 15) with respect to direct materials. The 15 units in ending work-in-process inventory are 40% complete with respect to conversion costs. Therefore, there are 6 (40% × 15) equivalent units in ending work-in-process inventory with respect to conversion costs. Combining the results of the three steps, the total equivalent units of production is $1 + 5 + 9 = 15$ for direct materials and $3 + 5 + 6 = 14$. This computation of equivalent units of production under the FIFO method is shown in Exhibit 5–9.

Exhibit 5–8
Flow of Physical Units: FIFO View

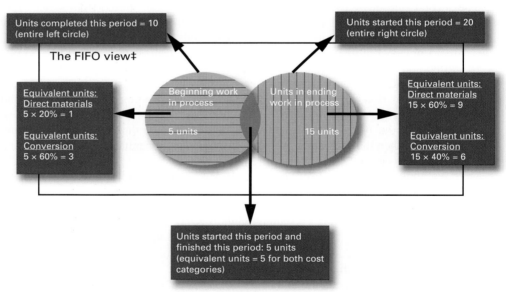

‡ Units in beginning work-in-process inventory are analyzed for the work done in the current period to complete them, also the costs incurred to complete these units are considered separately from costs incurred in prior periods.

Equivalent units of production: Direct materials 1 + 5 + 9 = 15

Equivalent units of production: Conversion 3 + 5 + 6 = 14

Exhibit 5–9
Calculation of Equivalent Units of Production: FIFO Method

Cost Category	(1) Physical Units Processed this Period	(2) Units in Beginning WIP Inventory	(3) Degree of Completion this Period*	(4) Equivalent Units in Beginning WIP Inventory (2) × (3)	(5) Units in Ending WIP Inventory	(6) Degree of Completion this Period	(7) Equivalent Units in Ending WIP Inventory (5) × (6)	(8) Units Started this Period and Finished this Period†	(9) Equivalent Units of Production (4)+(7)+(8)
Direct materials	25	5	20%	1	15	60%	9	5	15
Conversion	25	5	60%	3	15	40%	6	5	14

*Units in work-in-process inventory at the start of period are already 80% complete with respect to direct materials and 40% complete with respect to conversion cost. This implies the degree of completion for this period will be 20% with respect to direct materials and 60% with respect to conversion.
†Units started this period and finished this period = Units brought into production − Units in ending work in process = 20 − 15 = 5 (Or equivalently: Units finished and transferred out − Units in beginning work in process = 10 − 5 = 5).

Writer of Term Papers

YOU DECIDE

Assume that all of your professors have assigned short papers this term. In fact, you have to turn in four separate five-page papers early next month. During the month, you purchased all of the paper that you will need, began and finished two papers, and wrote the first two and one-half pages of the other two papers. You turned in the papers that you had finished to your instructors on the last day of the month.

If instead you had focused all your efforts into starting *and* completing papers this month, how many papers would you have written this month? After answering that question, reconfigure your answer as a computation of equivalent units of production by (1) preparing a quantity schedule, and (2) computing the number of equivalent units for labour.

Production Report—Weighted Average Method

The production report developed in this section contains the information requested by the president of Double Diamond Skis. The purpose of the production report is to summarize for management all of the activity that takes place in a department's work-in-process account for a period. This activity includes the units and costs that flow through the work-in-process account. A separate production report is prepared for each department.

Previously, when we outlined the differences between job-order costing and process costing, we stated that the production report takes the place of a job cost sheet in a process costing system. The production report is a key management document. The production report has three separate (though highly interrelated) parts:

- a quantity schedule, which shows the flow of units through the department and a computation of equivalent units
- a computation of costs per equivalent unit
- a reconciliation of all cost flows into and out of the department during the period

Home Runs Galore

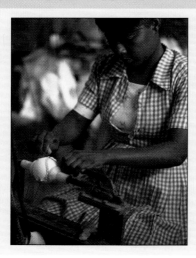

Remember the summer of 1999? Rawlings, the ball manufacturer, was forced to open its Turrialba facility in Costa Rica to a delegation from Major League Baseball to dispel rumors that Rawlings balls were behind the record numbers of home runs.

The delegation found that the production process is unchanged from earlier years. The red pills (rubber-coated corks purchased from a company in Mississippi) are wound three times with wool yarn and then once with cotton string. The balls are weighed, measured, and inspected after each wind. The covers, cut from sheets of rawhide, are hand-stitched and then machine-rolled. After a trip through a drying room to remove the moisture that kept the leather soft during the sewing process, the balls are stamped with logos. After they are weighed, measured, and inspected once again, the balls are wrapped in tissue and packed in boxes. Balls that don't meet Major League specifications (5–5⁄ ounces and 9–9⁄ inches in circumference) are sold commercially.

A trip to Mississippi is next on the agenda.

Source: "Behind-the-Seams Look Rawlings Throws Open Baseball Plant Door," *USA Today*, May 24, 2000, pp. 1C–2C. Copyright 2000, *USA TODAY*. Reprinted with permission.

Cost Analyst

Assume that you are a cost analyst in the Rawlings plant in Costa Rica that supplies baseballs to Major League Baseball. Your assignment is to identify the production departments in that facility. How many production reports will be needed to summarize the activity in each department?

We will use the data that follow for the May operations of the Shaping and Milling Department of Double Diamond Skis to illustrate the production report. Keep in mind that this report is only one of the five reports that would be prepared for the company, since the company has five processing departments.

Shaping and Milling Department		
Work in process, beginning:		
Units in process		200
Stage of completion with respect to materials		50%
Stage of completion with respect to conversion		30%
Costs in the beginning inventory:		
Materials cost	$	3,000
Conversion cost		1,000
Total cost in process	$	4,000
Units started into production during May		5,000
Units completed and transferred out		4,800
Costs added to production during May:		
Materials cost	$	74,000
Conversion cost		70,000
Total cost added in the department	$	144,000
Work in process, ending:		
Units in process		400
Stage of completion with respect to materials		40%
Stage of completion with respect to conversion		25%

In this section, we show how a production report is prepared when the weighted average method is used to compute equivalent units and unit costs.

Step 1: Prepare a Quantity Schedule and Compute the Equivalent Units

The first part of a production report consists of a **quantity schedule,** which shows the flow of units through the department and a computation of equivalent units.

Shaping and Milling Department
Quantity Schedule and
Computation of Equivalent Units

	Quantity Schedule
Units to be accounted for:	
Work in process, May 1 (50% materials;	
30% conversion added last month)	200
Started into production	5,000
Total units	5,200

		Equivalent Units	
		Materials	Conversion
Units accounted for as follows:			
Transferred to the next department . . .	4,800	4,800	4,800
Work in process, May 31 (40% materials;			
25% conversion added this month)	400	160*	100†
Total units and equivalent units			
of production.	5,200	4,960	4,900

*40% × 400 units = 160 equivalent units.
†25% × 400 units = 100 equivalent units.

The quantity schedule shows how many units moved through the department during the period, as well as the stage of completion of any in-process units. In addition to providing this information, the quantity schedule serves as an essential guide in preparing and tying together the remaining parts of a production report.

Step 2: Compute Costs per Equivalent Unit

As stated previously, the weighted average method blends together the work that was accomplished in the prior period with the work that was accomplished in the current period. That is why it is called the *weighted average method*; it averages together units and costs from both the prior and current periods by adding the cost in the beginning work-in-process inventory to the current period costs. These computations are shown following for the Shaping and Milling Department for May:

Shaping and Milling Department

	Total Cost	Materials	Conversion	Whole Unit
Cost to be accounted for:				
Work in process, May 1	$ 4,000	$ 3,000	$ 1,000	
Cost added in the Shaping				
and Milling Department ...	144,000	74,000	70,000	
Total cost (a)	$148,000	$77,000	$71,000	
Equivalent units of production				
(Step 1 above) (b)		4,960	4,900	
Cost per EU, (a) ÷ (b)		$15.524 +	$14.490 =	$30.014

The cost per equivalent unit (EU) that we have computed for the Shaping and Milling Department will be used to apply cost to units that are transferred to the next department, graphics application, and will also be used to compute the cost in the ending work-in-process inventory. For example, each unit transferred out of the Shaping and Milling Department to the Graphics Application Department will carry with it a cost of $30.014. Since the costs are passed on from department to department, the unit cost of the last department, Finishing and Pairing, will represent the final unit cost of a completed unit of product.

Step 3: Prepare a Cost Reconciliation

The purpose of a **cost reconciliation** is to show how the costs that have been charged to a department during a period are accounted for. Generally, the costs charged to a department will consist of the following:

- Cost in the beginning work-in-process inventory
- Materials, labour, and overhead costs added during the period
- Cost (if any) transferred in from the preceding department

In a production report, these costs are generally titled "Cost to be accounted for." They are accounted for in a production report by computing the following amounts:

- Cost transferred out to the next department (or to finished goods)
- Cost remaining in the ending work-in-process inventory

In short, when a cost reconciliation is prepared, the "Cost to be accounted for" from step 2 is reconciled with the sum of the cost transferred out during the period plus the cost in the ending work-in-process inventory. This concept is shown graphically in Exhibit 5–10. Study this exhibit carefully before going on to the cost reconciliation for the Shaping and Milling Department.

Exhibit 5–10

Graphical Illustration of the Cost Reconciliation Part of a Production Report

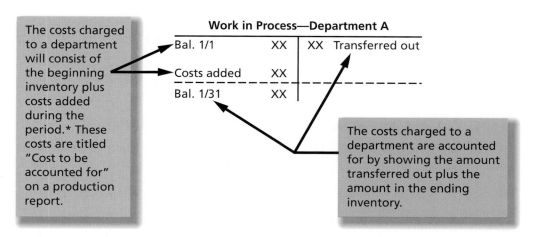

* Departments that follow Department A (Department B and so on) will need to show the amount of cost transferred in from the preceding department.

EXAMPLE OF A COST RECONCILIATION   To prepare a cost reconciliation, follow the quantity schedule line for line and show the cost associated with each group of units. This is done in Exhibit 5–11 following, where we present a completed production report for the Shaping and Milling Department.

The quantity schedule in the exhibit shows that 200 units were in process on May 1 and that an additional 5,000 units were started into production during the month. Looking at the "Cost to be accounted for" in the middle part of the exhibit, notice that the units in process on May 1 had $4,000 in cost attached to them and that the Shaping and Milling Department added another $144,000 in cost to production during the month. Thus, the department has $148,000 ($4,000 + $144,000) in cost to be accounted for.

This cost is accounted for in two ways. As shown on the quantity schedule, 4,800 units were transferred to the Graphics Application Department, the next department in the production process. Another 400 units were still in process in the Shaping and Milling Department at the end of the month. Thus, part of the $148,000 "Cost to be accounted for" goes with the 4,800 units to the Graphics Application Department, and part of it remains with the 400 units in the ending work-in-process inventory in the Shaping and Milling Department.

Each of the 4,800 units transferred to the Graphics Application Department is assigned $30.014 in cost, for a total $144,067. The 400 units still in process at the end of the month are assigned costs according to their stage of completion. To determine the stage of completion, we refer to the equivalent units computation and bring the equivalent unit figures down to the cost reconciliation part of the report. We then assign costs to these units, using the cost per equivalent unit figures already computed.

After cost has been assigned to the ending work-in-process inventory, the total cost that we have accounted for ($148,000) agrees with the amount that we had to account for ($148,000). Thus, the cost reconciliation is complete.

Production Report—FIFO Method

In this section, we will develop the production cost report for the Shaping and Milling Department at Double Diamond Skis using the FIFO method. The steps we will follow are identical to those shown previously for the weighted cost approach; only the details of the calculation of the equivalent units of production and the preparation of the cost reconciliation will be slightly different.

Step 1: Prepare a Quantity Schedule and Compute the Equivalent Units

Refer to Exhibit 5–12. The first part of the production report consists of the quantity schedule, which shows the flow of units through the department, and a computation of equivalent units. According to the schedule, 200 units were in process on May 1, and 5,000 units were started into production during the month. Thus, a total of 5,200 units must be accounted for. This is accomplished as follows. In terms of the physical units, applying the FIFO principle, we recognize that the 200 units from work in process on May 1, were fully completed. Since we also know that a total of 4,800 units were fully completed during May, we recognize that 4,600 units were started and fully completed during May. On May 31, there are 400 units in ending work-in-process inventory. Thus, we have 200 + 4,600 + 400 = 5,200 units all accounted for.

The quantity schedule also shows the computation of the equivalent units of production with respect to each of the two cost categories. In the FIFO method, we must calculate equivalent units in beginning work-in-process inventory, in addition to the equivalent units in ending work-in-process inventory. This recognizes that effort and costs are incurred to bring the units in process at the beginning to completion. Remember that when applying the degree of completion percentage to units in beginning work-in-process inventory, it has to be

APPLY

CC17: Account for the flow of production by preparing a quantity schedule using the FIFO method.

Exhibit 5–11
Production Report—Weighted Average Method

DOUBLE DIAMOND SKIS
Shaping and Milling Department Production Report
(weighted average method)

Quantity Schedule and Equivalent Units

	Quantity Schedule
Units to be accounted for:	
Work in process, May 1 (50% materials; 30% conversion added last month)............	200
Started into production........................	5,000
Total units...................................	5,200

	Quantity Schedule	Equivalent Units (EU) Materials	Equivalent Units (EU) Conversion
Units accounted for as follows:			
Transferred to the next department..............	4,800	4,800	4,800
Work in process, May 31 (40% materials; 25% conversion added this month)............	400	160*	100†
Total units and equivalent units of production.............................	5,200	4,960	4,900

*40% × 400 units = 160 equivalent units.
†25% × 400 units = 100 equivalent units.

Costs per Equivalent Unit

	Total Cost	Materials	Conversion	Whole Unit
Cost to be accounted for:				
Work in process, May 1.........................	$ 4,000	$ 3,000	$ 1,000	
Cost added in the Shaping and Milling Department..............................	144,000	74,00	70,000	
Total cost (a)...............................	$148,000	$77,000	$71,000	
Equivalent units of production (above) (b)..........		4,960	4,900	
Cost per EU, (a) ÷ (b)........................		$15.524 +	$14.490 =	$30.014

EU = Equivalent unit.

Cost Reconciliation

	Total Cost	Equivalent Units (above) Materials	Equivalent Units (above) Conversion
Cost accounted for as follows:			
Transferred to next department:			
4,800 units × $30.014 per unit..............	$144,067	4,800	4,800
Work in process, May 31:			
Materials, at $15.524 per EU..................	2,484	160	
Conversion, at $14.490 per EU................	1,449		100
Total work in process, May 3.................	3,933		
Total cost..................................	$148,000		

Exhibit 5–12
Production Report—FIFO Method

DOUBLE DIAMOND SKIS
Shaping and Milling Department—Production Report
(FIFO Method)

Quantity Schedule and Equivalent Units

Quantity Schedule

Units to be accounted for:

Work in process, May 1 (50% materials, 30% conversion added last month)	200
Started into production	5,000
Total Units	5,200

Equivalent Units (EU)

	Physical Units	Eqivalent Units Materials	Eqivalent Units Conversion
Units accounted for:			
Work in process, May 1 (50% materials, 70% conversion added this month)*	200	100†	140‡
Units brought into production and fully completed during May	4,600§	4,600	4,600
Work in process, May 31 (40% materials, 25% conversion added this month)	400	160ǁ	100#
Total units and equivalent units of production	5,200	4,860	4,840

*From the quantity schedule, work in process, May 1 was 50% complete with respect to materials, therefore during May, 100 − 50 = 50% materials was added. Similarly 100 − 30 = 70% of conversion was added during May.
†50% × 200 units = 100 equivalent units.
‡70% × 200 units = 140 equivalent units.
§Units started minus units in work in process May 31 = 5,000 − 400 = 4,600 units or alternatively
 Units completed in May minus units in work in process May 1 = 4,800 − 200 = 4,600 units.
ǁ40% × 400 units = 160 equivalent units.
#25% × 400 units = 100 equivalent units.

Cost per Equivalent Unit

	Total costs	Materials	Conversion	Whole Unit
Costs to be accounted for:				
Prior period cost in work in process, May 1	$4,000	$3,000	$1,000	
Costs incurred during May (a)	144,000	74,000	70,000	
Total cost.	$148,000	$77,000	$71,000	
Equivalent units of production (b)		4,860 units	4,840 units	
Cost per EU (a) ÷ (b)		$15.226	$14.463	$29.689
EU = Equivalent unit				

continued

Exhibit 5–12 (continued)

Cost Reconciliation

	Total Costs	Equivalent Units	
		Materials	Conversion
Cost accounted for:			
Prior period cost in work in process, May 1 (1)	$4,000		
Cost incurred during May:			
To complete units in work in process, May 1			
Direct material at $15.226 per EU	1,522.60	100	
Conversion at $14.463 per EU	2,024.82		140
Total (2).	$3,547.42		
To bring into production and fully complete 4,600			
units during May at $29.689 per unit (3)	$136,569.40		
To partially complete units in work in process, May 31			
Direct material at $15.226 per EU	2,436.16	160	
Conversion at $14.463 per EU	1,446.30		100
Total (4)	$3,882.46		
Total cost	$147,999.28*		
Cost transferred out to Graphics Application			
Department, May 31 (1) + (2) + (3)	$144,116.82		

*Total does not add up to $148,000 due to rounding.

ensured that it represents the work *to be done* in the current period (May) and not the work that was *already done* in the previous period (April).

The calculation proceeds as follows. First, we take the 200 units in beginning work in process and express these as equivalent units of production for each cost category. The percentage completion for the current period is obtained as 100% less the percentage completed in the previous period. For materials, the percentage completion for the current period is 100% − 50% = 50%; and for conversion, it is 100% − 30% = 70%. The equivalent units in beginning work in process for direct materials is 200 units × 50% = 100. The equivalent units in beginning work in process for conversion is 200 units × 70% = 140.

Second, we calculate the units that were started and fully completed in the current period. This is 4,600 units (5,000 units started − 400 units in ending work in process or 4,800 units completed and transferred out − 200 units in beginning work in process). These represent equivalent units for both cost categories.

Third, we calculate the equivalent units corresponding to the 400 physical units in ending work in process for each cost category. For direct materials, the number of equivalent units in ending work in process is 400 units × 40% = 160. For conversion, the number of equivalent units in ending work in process is 400 units × 25% = 100.

Combining the three calculations, the total equivalent units of production for direct materials and conversion are 4,860 (100 + 4,600 + 160) and 4,840 (140 + 4,600 + 100), respectively.

Step 2: Compute Costs per Equivalent Unit

APPLY

CC18: Compute the cost per equivalent unit using the FIFO method.

The second part of the production report shows the calculation of cost per equivalent unit. Only the current period costs enter into this calculation. We ignore the $4,000 ($3,000 direct materials cost plus $1,000 conversion cost) incurred in the previous period. Double Diamond incurred direct materials cost of $74,000 during May. Given the 4,860 equivalent units of production for direct materials, the direct material cost per equivalent unit is $74,000 ÷ 4,860 = $15.226. For conversion cost the cost per equivalent unit is $70,000 ÷ 4,840 = $14.463. The total cost per unit of product is $15.226 + $14.463 = $29.689.

Step 3: Prepare a Cost Reconciliation

The purpose of a cost reconciliation is to show how the costs that have been charged to the department are accounted for. The costs charged to a department will consist of the following:

- Cost in the beginning work-in-process inventory
- Materials and conversion costs added during the period
- Cost (if any) transferred in from the preceding department

In the FIFO method, we account for the above costs as follows:

1. Costs in the beginning work in process inventory.
2. Materials and conversion costs added to complete the units in beginning work-in-process inventory.
3. Materials and conversion costs incurred to start and fully complete units in the current period.
4. Materials and conversion costs added to partially complete the units in ending work-in-process inventory.

The costs transferred out to the next department (or to finished goods) will be the sum of the costs (1) + (2) + (3). The cost in (4) will remain with the units in ending work-in-process inventory and will flow into the following period as the cost of the beginning work-in-process inventory.

The cost reconciliation is the bottom portion of the production report in Exhibit 5–12. This portion provides an accounting of the total incurred cost itemized in the quantity schedule. Remember, the costs to account for are an itemization by cost category and by period. The costs are accounted for by itemizing by category and by the type of the work done to incur the cost.

We begin by recording the prior period cost (1). Next, we determine the material costs and conversion costs incurred to complete the units in process at the start of May by valuing the equivalent units in beginning work-in-process inventory using the rate per equivalent unit, with respect to each category. This gives us the cost in (2). Next, the cost of completing 4,600 units from scratch is calculated by multiplying 4,600 by the total cost per equivalent unit, $29.689—this gives us the cost in (3) in the above list. Finally, the equivalent units in ending work in process are valued with respect to each cost category using the cost per equivalent unit. This is the cost in (4). The total of the costs in (1) through (4) agrees with the amount that we had to account for. Thus, the cost reconciliation is complete. The last line shows that the costs that are transferred out to the Graphics Application Department, which is the next department in the production process. This cost is in the amount of $144,116.82.

APPLY

CC19: Account for the costs of production in a given period by preparing a cost reconciliation using the FIFO method.

Jerry: Here are two examples of the kind of report I can put together for you each month. These particular reports are for the Shaping and Milling Department. Each report follows a fairly standard format for industries like ours and is called a *production report*. I hope that the information they provide is what you had in mind.

Samantha: The quantity schedule makes sense to me. I can see we had a total of 5,200 units to account for in the department for May. We completed 4,800 units and had 400 units remaining to be finished in April. I can also see from the FIFO-based report that we completed the 200 units that were in process at the beginning of May and then began processing 5,000 units from scratch in May. So, we must have started and completed 4,600 units during May. What are these "equivalent units?"

Jerry: That is the problem I mentioned earlier. The 400 units still in process at the end of May, for example, are far from complete. When we compute unit costs, it wouldn't make sense to count each of these as a whole unit.

MANAGERIAL ACCOUNTING IN ACTION

Samantha: I suppose not. Since the 400 units in process at May end are only 25% complete with respect to our conversion costs, we should count these as 100 units when we compute the conversion cost per unit.

Jerry: That's right. I hope the rest of each of the reports is clear.

Samantha: Yes, they seem pretty clear, although I need to study each of them to decide which method I prefer. It appears that the weighted average method calculates the costs per unit by including the prior period costs with the current period costs, whereas the FIFO method only considers the current period costs when determining the cost per unit.

Jerry: You are right again! The FIFO method gives you a better idea of how the work done and the costs incurred as a result, in a period, are allocated between units in process at the beginning, units brought into production and completed, and units in process at the end of the period. But the weighted average method is less complicated and depending on your specific needs it may be sufficient. The less inventory we have in our system at the end of each month, the less it will matter as to which method we use.

Samantha: In any event, I think I have enough information to help me understand our cost side better. I can focus my efforts on cost control knowing more about how our costs are determined. This information will also help me for planning purposes. Thanks, Jerry.

A Comparison of Costing Methods

⚪ **KNOW**

CC20: Distinguish between the FIFO and weighted average methods to costing.

This chapter has presented two methods of determining the cost of output in a processing department: the weighted average method and the FIFO method. Which method is better? The answer, not surprisingly, is "it depends." The weighted average method is slightly less complicated, but it combines the cost incurred in the prior period that is attached to the units in beginning work-in-process inventory with those incurred in the present period and the entire total is assigned to the units processed by the department. This lack of detail might be undesirable for some managers. The FIFO method keeps prior period costs in the beginning work-in-process inventory separate from the costs incurred in the current period. Only current period costs are assigned to the units that were processed during the period. The FIFO method is also more intuitive in that the physical flow of units is easier to follow. The idea that work done by a department in a period, logically, has to be for completing units from beginning work in process, for starting and finishing units, and for starting some units is very appealing. This more detailed accounting of the costs is attractive, but the method is more involved. Ultimately, it all comes down to how much inventory remains in the department at the end of each period. If these inventories are insignificant, it will not matter which method is chosen. But if work-in-process inventories are substantial, the FIFO method, despite its greater complexity, might well be preferred for its more detailed accounting of the costs.

A Comment about Rounding Errors

If you use a calculator or computer spreadsheet and do not round off the costs per equivalent unit, there should not be any discrepancy between the "Cost to be accounted for" and the "Cost accounted for" in the cost reconciliation. However, if you round off the costs per equivalent unit, the two figures will not always exactly agree. In all of the end-of-chapter material and other materials, we follow two rules: (1) all the costs per equivalent unit are rounded off to three decimal places, and (2) any adjustment needed to reconcile the "Cost accounted for" with the "Cost to be accounted for" is made to the cost "transferred" amount, rather than to the ending inventory (weighted average method), or to the cost of "bringing into production and fully complete" amount (FIFO).

Application Competency Summary

Application Competency	Deliverable	Source Documents and Key Information	Steps	Knowledge Competency
Prepare journal entries to record the incurrence and flow of costs through a process costing system. ◉ CC8	*Key Information* Transactional information describing the incurrence of costs in a processing department *Report/Document* T-accounts analysis with appropriately journalized entries	*Materials Requisition Forms* Direct material (DM) costs for individual departments *Labour Time Tickets* Labour hours and wage rates for individual departments *Annual Budget Documents* Quantity of OH driver consumed and the OH allocation rate	1. Record the issuance of DM (dr. WIP and cr. DM), the application of labour to production (dr. WIP and cr. wages payable), and the application of MOH to production (dr. WIP and cr. MOH control).	Actual and normal costing ◉ CC3 (Ch. 4) Overhead cost driver and allocation base; overhead application rate ◉ CC6 (Ch. 4) Applied versus actual overhead ◉ CC9 (Ch. 4)
Compute the equivalent units (EU) of production for each cost category using the weighted average method. ◉ CC11	*Key Information* EU for each cost category as per the weighted average method *Report/Document* No specific document	*Inventory and Production Records* Percentage of completion information with respect to each cost category of the units in ending WIP inventory Quantity completed and transferred out of the department; Number of units in ending WIP	1. EU for a cost category is the sum of the percentage completion for the cost category for the units in ending WIP multiplied by the number of units in ending WIP plus the number of units completed and transferred out from the department.	Cost categories ◉ CC6 Degree of completion ◉ CC9 EUs of production and the role of WIP inventories in the weighted average method ◉ CC10
Compute the EUs of production for each cost category using the FIFO method. ◉ CC13	*Key Information* EU for each cost category as per the FIFO method *Report/Document* No specific document	*Inventory and Production Records* Percentage of completion information with respect to each cost category of: (1) the units in beginning WIP inventory, and (2) the units in ending WIP inventory Quantity completed and transferred out of the department; Number of units in beginning WIP and the number in ending WIP	1. Compute the units that were started and finished during the period. 2. Compute the percentage remaining to be completed of the units in beginning in WIP for each cost category. 3. EU for a cost category is the sum of the percentage remaining multiplied by units in beginning WIP, the percentage completion for the cost category of the units in ending WIP multiplied by the number of units in ending WIP, and the number of units begun and finished during the period.	Cost categories ◉ CC6 Degree of completion ◉ CC9 EUs of production and the role of WIP inventories in the FIFO method ◉ CC12

continued

Application Competency	Deliverable	Source Documents and Key Information	Steps	Knowledge Competency
Account for the flow of production by preparing a quantity schedule using the weighted average method. ◕ CC14	*Key Information* The number of units in beginning WIP and the number of units brought into production during the period The number of units completed and transferred out during the period and the number of units in ending WIP The number of EUs for each cost category *Report/Document* Quantity Schedule	*Inventory Records and Production Records* Number of units in beginning WIP Number of units brought into production Number of units completed and transferred out Number of units in ending WIP Percentage completion of production for each cost category	1. Determine the number of physical units to account for; this will be units in beginning WIP and the units brought into production. 2. Account for the above total of physical units by determining that it equals the number of physical units completed and transferred out plus the number of physical units in ending WIP. 3. Compute the number of EUs for each category (multiply the physical units by the corresponding degree of completion for each cost category).	Cost categories ◕ CC6 Degree of completion ◕ CC9 EUs ◕ CC10, 11
Compute the cost per EU of production using the weighted average method. ◕ CC15	*Key Information* Per EU cost for each type of cost *Report/Document* Schedule of the cost per EU	*Quantity Schedule* Flow of production during the period *Cost Records* Cost of DM, labour, and MOH accumulated to perform the period's production activity Cost of DM, labour, and MOH accumulated in the previous period and assigned to units in beginning WIP	1. Compute the total DM cost (sum of DM cost in beginning WIP and DM cost added in the department during the period). 2. Combine direct labour and MOH costs to obtain the conversion cost. 3. Compute the total conversion cost. (Use the approach used for DM.) 4. Compute the cost per EU for DM and for conversion by dividing the total cost in each category by the corresponding EUs. 5. Add the cost per EU for each cost category to compute the total cost per EU.	Cost categories ◕ CC6 Conversion costs ◕ CC7 EUs of production ◕ CC10, 11

continued

Application Competency	Deliverable	Source Documents and Key Information	Steps	Knowledge Competency
Account for the costs of production in a given period by preparing a cost reconciliation using the weighted average method. ● CC16	*Key Information* The costs charged to the department and an accounting of these costs broken down into the portion transferred out and the portion remaining in ending WIP and carried forward to the next period *Report/Document* Cost Reconciliation Schedule (part of a production report)	*Quantity Schedule* Flow of production during the period Number of units completed and transferred out during the period and the number of units in ending WIP Number of EUs for each cost category *Schedule of the Cost per EU* Cost per EU for each cost category	1. Determine the costs to account for. These are (a) costs in beginning WIP and (b) costs added in the department during the period. 2. Determine the cost of the units completed and transferred out (total cost per EU multiplied by the number of units completed and transferred out). 3. Determine cost of DM in ending WIP (DM cost per EU multiplied by the number of EUs for DM in ending WIP). 4. Determine conversion costs in ending WIP (conversion cost per EU multiplied by the number of EUs for DM in ending WIP). 5. Reconcile the costs to account for with the sum of the costs assigned to the units transferred out and the EUs in ending WIP.	Cost categories ● CC6 EUs of production ● CC10, 11 Flow of production ● CC14 Cost per EU ● CC15
Account for the flow of production by preparing a quantity schedule using the FIFO method. ● CC17	*Key Information* The number of units in beginning WIP and the number of units brought into production during the period The number of units completed and transferred out during the period and the number of units in ending WIP The number of EUs for each cost category *Report/Document* Quantity Schedule	*Inventory Records and Production Records* Number of units in beginning WIP Number of units brought into production Number of units completed and transferred out Number of units in ending WIP Percentage completion of production for each cost category	1. Determine the number of physical units to account for. This will be the physical units in beginning WIP and the physical units brought into production. 2. Account for the above total by determining that it equals (a) the number of physical units in beginning WIP, (b) the number of units started and completed during the period, and (c) the number of units in ending WIP. 3. Compute the number of EUs for each cost category (for beginning WIP, multiply the physical units by the portion remaining to be completed; for units started and completed and the ending WIP, multiply the physical units by the percentage of completion).	Cost categories ● CC6 Degree of completion ● CC9 EUs ● CC12, 13

continued

Application Competency	Deliverable	Source Documents and Key Information	Steps	Knowledge Competency
Compute the cost per EU of production using the FIFO method. ⚪ CC18	**Key Information** Per EU cost for each type of cost **Report/Document** Schedule showing the calculation of cost per EU	**Quantity Schedule** Flow of production during the period **Cost Records** Cost of DM, labour and MOH accumulated to perform the period's production activity Cost of DM, labour, and MOH accumulated in the previous period and assigned to units in beginning WIP	1. Compute the total DM cost (sum of DM cost in beginning WIP and DM cost added in the department during the period), 2. Combine direct labour and MOH costs to obtain the conversion cost, 3. Compute the total conversion cost. (Use the approach used for DM.) 4. Compute the cost per EU for DM and for conversion by dividing the total cost in each category by the corresponding EUs. 5. Add the cost per EU for each cost category to compute the total cost per EU.	Cost categories ⚪ CC6 Conversion costs ⚪ CC7 EUs of production ⚪ CC12, 13
Account for the costs of production in a given period by preparing a cost reconciliation using the FIFO method. ⚪ CC19	**Key Information** The costs charged to the department and an accounting of these costs broken down into the portion transferred out and the portion remaining in ending WIP and carried forward to the next period. **Report/Document** Cost Reconciliation Schedule	**Quantity Schedule** Flow of production during the period Number of units completed and transferred out during the period and the number of units in ending WIP Number of EUs for each cost category **Schedule of the Cost per EU** Cost per EU for each cost category	1. Determine the costs to account for. These are (a) costs in beginning WIP and (b) costs added in the department during the period. 2. Determine the cost of the units completed and transferred out (total cost per EU multiplied by the number of units completed and transferred out). 3. Determine the cost of DM in ending WIP (DM cost per EU multiplied by the number of EUs for DM in ending WIP). 4. Determine conversion costs in ending WIP (conversion cost per EU multiplied by the number of EUs for DM in ending WIP). 5. Reconcile the costs to account for with the sum of the costs assigned to the units transferred out and the EUs in ending WIP.	Cost categories ⚪ CC6 EUs of production ⚪ CC12, 13 Flow of production ⚪ CC17 Cost per EU ⚪ CC18

Guidance Answers to You Decide and Decision Maker

WRITER OF TERM PAPERS (p. 181)
You wrote a total of 15 pages (5 + 5 + 2.5 + 2.5) this month. If you had placed all of your efforts into starting *and* completing papers, you could have written three complete five-page papers.

	Quantity Schedule
Units (papers) to be accounted for:	
Work in process, beginning of month	
Started into production	4
Total units	4

		Equivalent Units
		Labour
Units accounted for as follows:		
Transferred (handed in) to instructors	2	2
Work in process, end of month (all materials and 50% of labour and overhead added this month)	2	1*
Total units and equivalent units of production	4	3

*2 units (papers) × 50% (or 2.5 pages out of 5) = 1

COST ANALYST (p. 182)
The Rawlings baseball production facility in Costa Rica might include the following production departments: winding, cutting, stitching, rolling, drying, stamping, inspecting, and packaging. Each department would have its own production report.

Review Problem: Process Cost Flows and Reports

Luxguard Home Paint Company produces exterior latex paint, which it sells in four-litre containers. The company has two processing departments—Base Fab and Finishing. White paint, which is used as a base for all the company's paints, is mixed from raw ingredients in the Base Fab Department. Pigments are added to the basic white paint, the pigmented paint is squirted under pressure into four-litre containers, and the containers are labelled and packed for shipping in the Finishing Department. Information relating to the company's operations for April follows:

a. Raw materials were issued for use in production: Base Fab Department, $851,000; and Finishing Department, $629,000.
b. Direct labour costs were incurred: Base Fab Department, $330,000; and Finishing Department, $270,000.
c. Manufacturing overhead cost was applied: Base Fab Department, $665,000; and Finishing Department, $405,000.
d. The cost of basic white paint transferred from the Base Fab Department to the Finishing Department was $1,850,000.
e. Paint that had been prepared for shipping was transferred from the Finishing Department to finished goods. Its cost according to the company's cost system was $3,200,000.

Required:

1. Prepare journal entries to record items (a) through (e).
2. Post the journal entries from part (1) to T-accounts. The balance in the Base Fab Department's work-in-process account on April 1 was $150,000; the balance in the Finishing Department's work-in-process account was $70,000. After posting entries to the T-accounts, find the ending balance in each department's work-in-process account.
3. Prepare a production report (weighted average method) for the Base Fab Department for April using the additional information given below:

Production data:

Units* in process, April 1: 100% complete as to materials, 60% complete as to labour and overhead	30,000
Units started into production during April	420,000
Units completed and transferred to the Finishing Department	370,000
Units in process, April 30: 50% complete as to materials, 25% complete as to labour and overhead	80,000

Cost data:

Work-in-process inventory, April 1:

Materials	$	92,000
Labour		21,000
Overhead		37,000
Total cost	$	150,000

Cost added during April:

Materials	$	851,000
Labour		330,000
Overhead		665,000
Total cost		$1,846,000

*One unit represents four litres.

4. Prepare a FIFO-based production report after combining labour and manufacturing overhead into conversion costs.

SOLUTION TO REVIEW PROBLEM

1. a.	Work in Process—Base Fab Department	851,000	
	Work in Process—Finishing Department	629,000	
	Raw Materials		1,480,000
b.	Work in Process—Base Fab Department	330,000	
	Work in Process—Finishing Department	270,000	
	Salaries and Wages Payable		600,000
c.	Work in Process—Base Fab Department	665,000	
	Work in Process—Finishing Department	405,000	
	Manufacturing Overhead		1,070,000
d.	Work in Process—Finishing Department	1,850,000	
	Work in Process—Base Fab Department		1,850,000
e.	Finished Goods	3,200,000	
	Work in Process—Finishing Department		3,200,000

2.

Raw Materials			
Bal.	XXX	(a)	1,480,000

Salaries and Wages Payable		
	(b)	600,000

Work in Process—Base Fab Department			
Bal.	150,000	(d)	1,850,000
(a)	851,000		
(b)	330,000		
(c)	665,000		
Bal.	146,000		

Manufacturing Overhead			
(Various actual costs)		(c)	1,070,000

Work in Process—Finishing Department			
Bal.	70,000	(e)	3,200,000
(a)	629,000		
(b)	270,000		
(c)	405,000		
(d)	1,850,000		
Bal	24,000		

Finished Goods		
Bal.	XXX	
(e)	3,200,000	

3.

LUXGUARD HOME PAINT COMPANY
Production Report—Base Fab Department
For the Month Ended April 30
(Weighted Average Method)

Quantity Schedule and Equivalent Units

	Quantity Schedule
Units to be accounted for:	
Work in process, April 1 (all materials, 60% labour and overhead added last month)	30,000
Started into production	420,000
Total units	450,000

	Quantity Schedule	Equivalent Units (EU)		
		Materials	Labour	Overhead
Units accounted for as follows:				
Transferred to Finishing Department	370,000	370,000	370,000	370,000
Work in process, April 30 (50% materials, 25% labour and overhead added this month)	80,000	40,000*	20,000*	20,000*
Total units and EUs of production..................	450,000	410,000	390,000	390,000

Costs per EU

	Total Cost	Materials	Labour	Overhead	Whole Unit
Cost to be accounted for:					
Work in process, April 1	$ 150,000	$ 92,000	$ 21,000	$ 37,000	
Cost added by the Base Fab Department	1,846,000	851,000	330,000	665,000	
Total cost (a)	$1,996,000	$943,000	$351,000	$702,000	
EUs of production (b)		410,000	390,000	390,000	
Cost per EU, (a) ÷ (b)		$2.30 +	$0.90 +	$1.80 =	$5.00

Cost Reconciliation

	Total Cost	Equivalent Units (above)		
		Materials	Labour	Overhead
Cost accounted for as follows:				
Transferred to Finishing Department:				
370,000 units × $5.00 each	$1,850,000	370,000	370,000	370,000
Work in process, April 30:				
Materials, at $2.30 per EU	92,000	40,000		
Labour, at $0.90 per EU	18,000		20,000	
Overhead, at $1.80 per EU	36,000			20,000
Total work in process	146,000			
Total cost	$1,996,000			

*Materials: 80,000 units × 50% =40,000 EUs; labour and overhead: 80,000 units × 25% =20,000 EUs.

4.

LUXGUARD HOME PAINT COMPANY
Base Fab Department Production Report
(FIFO Method)

Quantity Schedule and Equivalent Units

	Quantity Schedule
Units to be accounted for:	
Work in process, April 1 (all materials, 60% conversion added last month)	30,000
Started into production	420,000
Total Units (litres)	450,000

Equivalent Units (EU)

	Physical Units	EUs Materials	EUs Conversion
Units accounted for:			
Work in process, April 1 (0% materials, 40% conversion added this month)	30,000	0*	12,000†
Units brought into production and fully complete during April.	340,000‡	340,000	340,000
Work in process, April 30 (50% materials, 25% conversion added this month)	80,000	40,000§	20,000‖
Total units and EUs of production	450,000	380,000	372,000

*Work in process on April 1 was fully complete with respect to materials and 60% complete with respect to conversion. Therefore, no work related to materials was performed (100 − 100 = 0%) and 100 − 60 = 40% conversion was added.
†40% × 30,000 units = 12,000 equivalent units.
‡Units started minus units in work in process April 30 = 420,000 − 80,000 = 340,000 units, or Units completed in April minus units in work in process April 1 = 370,000 − 30,000 = 340,000 units
§50% × 80,000 units = 40,000 equivalent units.
‖25% × 80,000 units = 20,000 equivalent units.

Cost per EU

	Total Cost	Materials	Conversion	Whole Unit
Cost to be accounted for:				
Prior period cost in work in process, April 1	$ 150,000	$ 92,000	$ 58,000	
Costs incurred during April (a)	1,846,000	851,000	995,000	
Total cost.	$1,996,000	$943,000	$1,053,000	
EUs of production (b)		380,000 units	372,000 units	
Cost per EU (a) ÷ (b)		$2.24	$2.675	$4.915

Cost Reconciliation

	Total Costs	Equivalent Units	
		Materials	Conversion
Cost accounted for:			
Prior period cost in work in process, April 1 (1)	$150,000		
Cost incurred during April:..............			
To complete units in work in process, April 1			
Direct material at $2.24 per EU	0	0	
Conversion at $2.675 per EU	32,100		12,000
Total (2)........................	$32,100		
To bring into production and fully complete 340,000 units during April at $4.915 per unit (3)	$1,671,100		
To partially complete units in work in process, April 30			
Direct material at $2.24 per EU	89,600	40,000	
Conversion at $2.675 per EU	53,500		20,000
Total (4)	$143,100		
Total cost	$1,996,300*		
Cost transferred out to Graphics Application Department, April 30 (1) + (2) + (3)	$1,853,200		

*Total exceeds $1,996,000 due to rounding errors.

Glossary

Conversion cost Direct labour cost plus manufacturing overhead cost. (p. 172)

Cost reconciliation The part of a department's production report that shows the cost to be accounted for during a period and how those costs are accounted for. (p. 184)

Equivalent units (EUs) The product of the number of partially completed units and their percentage of completion with respect to a particular cost. EUs are the number of complete whole units you can obtain from the materials and effort contained in partially completed units. (p. 176)

Equivalent units of production The units transferred to the next department (or to finished goods) during the period plus the equivalent units in the department's ending work-in-process inventory. (p. 178)

FIFO method A method of accounting for cost flows in a process costing system in which equivalent units and unit costs relate only to work done during the current period. (p. 177)

Percentage completion The extent to which a physical unit is complete for each cost category. (p. 176)

Process costing A costing method used in situations where essentially homogeneous products are produced on a continuous basis. (p. 168)

Processing department Any location in an organization where work is performed on a product and where materials, labour, or overhead costs are added to the product. (p. 169)

Production report A report that summarizes all activity in a department's work-in-process account during a period and that contains three parts: a quantity schedule and a computation of equivalent units, a computation of total and unit costs, and a cost reconciliation. (p. 168)

Quantity schedule The part of a production report that shows the flow of units through a department during a period and a computation of equivalent units. (p. 183)

Transferred-in cost The cost attached to products that have been received from a prior processing department. (p. 170)

Weighted average method A method of process costing that blends together units and costs from both the current and prior periods. (p. 177)

Questions

5–1 Under what conditions would it be appropriate to use a process costing system?

5–2 In what ways are job-order and process costing similar?

5–3 Costs are accumulated by job in a job-order costing system; how are costs accumulated in a process costing system?

5–4 Why is cost accumulation easier under a process costing system than it is under a job-order costing system?

5–5 How many work-in-process accounts are maintained in a company using process costing?

5–6 Assume that a company has two processing departments, Mixing and Firing. Prepare a journal entry to show a transfer of partially completed units from the Mixing Department to the Firing Department.

5–7 Assume again that a company has two processing departments, Mixing and Firing. Explain what costs might be added to the Firing Department's work-in-process account during a period.

5–8 What is meant by the term *equivalent units of production* when the weighted average method is used?

5–9 What is a quantity schedule, and what purpose does it serve?

5–10 Under process costing, it is often suggested that a product is like a rolling snowball as it moves from department to department. Why is this an apt comparison?

5–11 Watkins Trophies, Inc. produces thousands of medallions made of bronze, silver, and gold. The medallions are identical except for the materials used in their manufacture. What costing system would you advise the company to use?

Brief Exercises

BRIEF EXERCISE 5–1 Process Costing Journal Entries (CC8)

Quality Brick Company produces bricks in two processing departments—moulding and firing. Information relating to the company's operations in March follows:

a. Raw materials were issued for use in production: Moulding Department, $25,000; and Firing Department, $10,000.

b. Direct labour costs were incurred: Moulding Department, $15,000; and Firing Department, $10,000.

c. Manufacturing overhead was applied: Moulding Department, $29,000; and Firing Department, $40,000.

d. Unfired, moulded bricks were transferred from the Moulding Department to the Firing Department. According to the company's process costing system, the cost of the unfired, moulded bricks was $61,000.

e. Finished bricks were transferred from the Firing Department to the finished goods warehouse. According to the company's process costing system, the cost of the finished bricks was $110,000.

f. Finished bricks were sold to customers. According to the company's process costing system, the cost of the finished bricks sold was $107,000.

Required:
Prepare journal entries to record items (a) through (f).

BRIEF EXERCISE 5–2 Computation of Equivalent Units—Weighted Average Method (CC11)

Clonex Labs, Inc. uses a process costing system. The following data are available for one department for October:

	Units	Percentage Completed	
		Materials	Conversion
Work in process, October 1..........	45,000	65%	30%
Work in process, October 31.........	20,000	80%	50%

The department started 185,000 units into production during the month and transferred 200,000 completed units to the next department.

Required:
Compute the equivalent units of production for October assuming that the company uses the weighted average method of accounting for units and costs.

BRIEF EXERCISE 5–3   Preparation of Quantity Schedule—Weighted Average Method (CC14)

Hielta Oy, a Finnish company, processes wood pulp for various manufacturers of paper products. Data relating to tonnes of pulp processed during June are provided below:

	Tonnes of Pulp	Percent Completed	
		Materials	Labour and Overhead
Work in process, June 1	20,000	90%	80%
Work in process, June 30	30,000	60%	40%
Started into processing during June	190,000	—	—

Required:
1. Compute the number of tonnes of pulp completed and transferred out during June.
2. Prepare a quantity schedule for June assuming that the company uses the weighted average method.

BRIEF EXERCISE 5–4   Preparation of Quantity Schedule—FIFO Method (CC17)

Refer to the data in Brief Exercise 5–3. Prepare a quantity schedule for June assuming that Hielta Oy uses the FIFO method.

BRIEF EXERCISE 5–5   Cost per Equivalent Unit—Weighted Average Method (CC15)

Superior Micro Products uses the weighted average method in its process costing system. Data for the Assembly Department for May appear following:

	Materials	Labour	Overhead
Work in process, May 1	$36,000	$11,000	$55,000
Cost added during May..............	$238,900	$80,300	$485,000
Equivalent units of production	38,000	36,000	36,000

Required:
1. Compute the cost per equivalent unit for materials, labour, and overhead.
2. Compute the total cost per equivalent whole unit.

BRIEF EXERCISE 5–6   Cost Reconciliation—Weighted Average Method (CC15)

Superior Micro Products uses the weighted average method in its process costing system. During January, the Delta Assembly Department completed its processing of 25,000 units and transferred them to the next department. The cost of beginning inventory and the costs added during January amounted to $599,780 in total. The ending inventory in January consisted of 3,000 units, which were 80% complete with respect to materials and 60% complete with respect to labour and overhead. The costs per equivalent unit for the month were as follows:

	Materials	Labour	Overhead
Cost per equivalent unit	$12.50	$3.20	$6.40

Required:
1. Compute the total cost per equivalent unit for the month.
2. Compute the equivalent units of material, labour, and overhead in the ending inventory for the month.
3. Prepare the cost reconciliation portion of the department's production report for January.

BRIEF EXERCISE 5–7   Cost of Units: Weighted Average Method (CC16)

In June, 4,600 units were completed and transferred out of the mixing process at Avalanche Industries Ltd. The ending work-in-process inventory was 400 units, 30% complete as to conversion costs and 100% complete as to materials costs. The month's charges were $18,880 for conversion costs and $12,500 for materials costs. There was no beginning inventory in June.

Required:
What is the cost of the units completed and transferred out during June?

(Adapted © CGA-Canada)

BRIEF EXERCISE 5–8 Inventory Valuation: FIFO Method (CC10, 13, 18)

Bedlam Company made an error in computing the percentage of completion of the current year's beginning work-in-process inventory. The error resulted in the assignment of a lower percentage of completion to each unit of the inventory than actually was the case. There was no ending work-in-process inventory this year end. The company uses the FIFO cost flow method.

Required:

What is the effect in the current year of the error on the computation of equivalent units produced and the computation of costs per equivalent unit?

	EUs Produced	Cost per EU
1)	Understated	Understated
2)	Understated	Overstated
3)	Overstated	Understated
4)	Overstated	Overstated

(Adapted © CGA-Canada)

BRIEF EXERCISE 5–9 Cost of Units: Weighted Average Method (CC15)

Sauron Company incurred $140,000 in direct materials costs during May. Additionally, the 12,000 units in the work-in-process inventory on May 1 had a direct materials balance of $40,000, but were only 5% complete as to direct materials. No additional units were transferred into work-in-process inventory during May, and there was no work-in-process inventory at the end of May.

Required:

What is the cost per equivalent unit for materials for May, assuming Sauron uses the weighted average method of costing?

Exercises

EXERCISE 5–1 Process Costing Journal Entries (CC8)

Chocolaterie de Geneve, SA, is located in a French-speaking canton in Switzerland. The company makes chocolate truffles that are sold in popular embossed tins. The company has two processing departments—Cooking and Moulding. In the Cooking Department, the raw ingredients for the truffles are mixed and then cooked in special candy-making vats. In the Moulding Department, the melted chocolate and other ingredients from the Cooking Department are carefully poured into moulds and decorative flourishes are applied by hand. After cooling, the truffles are packed for sale. The company uses a process costing system. The following T- accounts show the flow of costs through the two departments in April (all amounts are in Swiss francs):

Work in Process—Cooking

Bal. 4/1	8,000	Transferred out	160,000
Direct materials	42,000		
Direct labour	50,000		
Overhead	75,000		

Work in Process—Moulding

Bal. 4/1	4,000	Transferred out	240,000
Transferred in	160,000		
Direct labour	36,000		
Overhead	45,000		

Required:

Prepare journal entries showing the flow of costs through the two processing departments during April.

EXERCISE 5–2　Quantity Schedule and Equivalent Units—Weighted Average Method (CC11, 14)

The Alaskan Fisheries, Inc. processes salmon for various distributors. Two departments are involved—Department 1 and Department 2. Data relating to pounds of salmon processed in Department 1 during July are presented below:

	Pounds of Salmon	Percentage Completed*
Work in process, July 1	20,000	30%
Started into processing during July	380,000	—
Work in process, July 31	25,000	60%

*Labour and overhead only.

All materials are added at the beginning of processing in Department 1. Labour and overhead (conversion) costs are incurred uniformly throughout processing.

Required:

Prepare quantity schedules and a computation of equivalent units for July for Department 1 according to the weighted average method of accounting for units.

EXERCISE 5–3　Quantity Schedule and Equivalent Units—FIFO Method (CC13, 17)

Refer to the data in Exercise 5–2. Prepare a quantity schedule and a computation of equivalent units for July for Department 1 assuming that the company uses the FIFO method of accounting for units.

EXERCISE 5–4　Equivalent Units and Cost per Equivalent Unit—Weighted Average Method (CC11, 15)

Helox, Inc. manufactures a product that passes through two production processes. A quantity schedule for a recent month for the first process follows:

	Quantity Schedule
Units to be accounted for:	
Work in process, May 1 (all materials, 40% conversion cost added last month) ...	10,000
Started into production	190,000
Total units	200,000

	Quantity Schedule	EUs Materials	EUs Conversion
Units accounted for as follows:			
Transferred to the next process	185,000	?	?
Work in process, May 31 (all materials, 30% conversion cost added this month) ...	15,000	?	?
Total units	200,000	?	?

Costs in the beginning work-in-process inventory of the first processing department were materials, $2,000; and conversion cost, $4,200. Costs added during the month were materials, $56,000; and conversion cost, $360,000.

Required:

1. Assume that the company uses the weighted average method of accounting for units and costs. Determine the equivalent units for the month for the first process.
2. Compute the costs per equivalent unit for the month for the first process.

EXERCISE 5–5　Cost Reconciliation—Weighted Average Method (CC16)

(*This exercise should be assigned only if Exercise 5–4 is also assigned.*) Refer to the data for Helox, Inc. in Exercise 5–4 and to the equivalent units and costs per equivalent unit you have computed there.

Required:

Complete the following cost reconciliation for the first process:

Cost Reconciliation

	Total Cost	EUs Materials	Conversion
Cost accounted for as follows:			
Transferred to the next process: (? units × $?).....	$?		
Work in process, May 31:			
Materials, at _____ per EU.................	?	?	
Conversion, at _____ per EU	?		?
Total work in process	?		
Total cost.....................	$?		

EXERCISE 5–6   Quantity Schedule, Equivalent Units, and Cost per Equivalent Unit—Weighted Average Method and FIFO Method (CC11, 13, 14, 15, 17, 18)

Pureform, Inc. manufactures a product that passes through two departments. Data for a recent month for the first department follow:

	Units	Materials	Labour	Overhead
Work in process, beginning......	5,000	$ 4,500	$ 1,250	$ 1,875
Units started in process.........	45,000			
Units transferred out	42,000			
Work in process, ending	8,000			
Cost added during the month	—	52,800	21,500	32,250

The beginning work-in-process inventory was 80% complete as to materials and 60% complete as to processing. The ending work-in-process inventory was 75% complete as to materials and 50% complete as to processing.

Required:

1. Assume that the company uses the weighted average method of accounting for units and costs. Prepare a quantity schedule and a computation of equivalent units for the month.
2. Determine the costs per equivalent unit for the month.
3. Repeat the requirements of parts (1) and (2) assuming the FIFO method of accounting is used.

EXERCISE 5–7   Equivalent Units: Weighted Average Method (CC11, 15)

Forge Inc. manufactures paint in a highly automated process. Its costing system uses two cost categories: direct materials and conversion costs. Each batch of product must pass through the Mixing Department and the Testing Department. Direct materials are all added at the beginning of the production process and conversion costs are incurred evenly throughout production. Forge uses the weighted average method for costing.

Data for the Mixing Department for September:
Work in process, beginning inventory:
  500 units
Conversion costs: 50% complete
Units started during September: 1,600 units
Work in process, ending inventory: 300 units
Conversion costs: 75% complete

Costs for September
Cost of work in process, beginning:
  Direct materials: $360,000
  Conversion costs: $540,000

Costs added in September:
Direct materials: $2,000,000
Conversion costs: $2,000,000

Required:
1. What are the equivalent units for direct materials for September?
2. What is the conversion cost per equivalent unit during September?

(Adapted © CGA-Canada)

EXERCISE 5–8   Equivalent Units: FIFO Method (CC12, 18)
Rictor Company had 30,000 units in process on December 31, 2007, 80% complete as to materials and 40% complete as to conversion costs. The company's records show that 60,000 units were transferred to the finished goods inventory during 2008. Furthermore, 22,500 units were on hand at the end of 2008, 60% complete as to materials and 30% complete as to conversion costs.

Required:
What is the equivalent work done in 2008 for the conversion costs using the FIFO method?

(Adapted © CGA-Canada)

EXERCISE 5–9   Equivalent Units and Cost per Equivalent Unit (CC11, 13, 15, 18)
The Mixing Department of Cerise Ltd., a producer of fabric for Broadway shows, has the following information regarding costs and output for March 2008:

Units:
Opening work-in-process inventory: 0 units
Started and completed: 140,000 units
Started and still in process at March 31:
   50,000 units
Direct materials: 100% complete
Conversion costs: 30% complete

Costs:
Direct materials: $836,000
Direct labour: $86,800
Factory overhead: $347,200

The company uses the FIFO method of process costing.

Required:
1. What was the conversion cost per equivalent unit of production in March 2008?
2. What was the cost of direct materials in the ending work-in-process inventory?

(Adapted © CGA-Canada)

EXERCISE 5–10   Cost Flows: Weighted Average Method (CC16)
Omerta Inc. uses the weighted average method in its process costing system. Information for Department A for July is as follows:

	Materials	Conversion
Work in process, beginning	$8,000	$6,000
Current costs added	$40,000	$32,000
Equivalent units	100,000 units	95,000 units
Costs per equivalent unit	$0.48	$0.40

Goods completed: 90,000 units
Work in process, ending: 10,000 units

Materials are all added at the beginning of the process. The ending work-in-process inventory is 50% complete with respect to conversion costs.

Required:
How would the "total costs accounted for" be distributed between units completed and transferred out, and units in ending work-in-process inventory?

	Costs Completed and Transferred out	Ending Work in Process
1)	$ 79,200	$ 6,800
2)	79,200	8,800
3)	86,000	0
4)	88,000	6,800

(Adapted © CGA-Canada)

EXERCISE 5–11   Equivalent Units: Weighted Average Method (CC11, 14, 15)

Micromax Co. uses a weighted average process costing system. The following data are for the Production Department for December.

	Materials		Conversion
	Units	Percentage complete	Percentage complete
Work in process, beginning.	4,000	$ 9,000 (60%)	$ 9,600 (60%)
Units started into production.	68,000		
Costs added in December		$140,000	$140,000

The December ending work-in-process inventory was 75% complete with respect to both materials and conversion costs.

Required:

1. What is the number of units in the December ending work-in-process inventory, assuming that 60,000 units were transferred out?
2. Assume that 60,000 units were transferred out and the number of units in the December ending work-in-process inventory was 16,000. What is the equivalent number of units produced for materials for December?
3. Assume that the equivalent number of units produced for materials for December was 71,100. What is the unit cost of production for December (rounded to the nearest cent)?

(Adapted © CGA-Canada)

EXERCISE 5–12   Equivalent Units: Weighted Average and FIFO Methods (CC11, 13)

Last month, the Finishing Department of Theoden Inc. started 12,000 units into production. The department had 3,600 units in process at the beginning of the month and these units were 50% complete with respect to conversion costs. There were 4,800 units in process at the end of the month and these units were 40% complete with respect to conversion costs. A total of 10,800 units were completed and transferred to the next department during the month.

Required:

1. For the last month, compute the equivalent units for conversion using the weighted average method.
2. For the last month, compute the equivalent units for conversion using the FIFO method.

(Adapted © CGA-Canada)

Problems

PROBLEM 5–1   Equivalent Units; Cost Reconciliation—Weighted Average Method and FIFO Method (CC 11, 16, 13, 19)

CHECK FIGURE
(2) 6/30 WIP: $9,020

Martin Company manufactures a single product. The company uses the weighted average method in its process costing system. Activity for June has just been completed. An incomplete production report for the first processing department follows:

Quantity Schedule and Equivalent Units

	Quantity Schedule
Units to be accounted for:	
Work in process, June 1 (all materials, 75% labour and overhead added last month)	16,000
Started into production	90,000
Total units	106,000

	EUs		
	Materials	**Labour**	**Overhead**
Units accounted for as follows:			
Transferred to the next department 96,000	?	?	?
Work in process, June 30 (all materials, 40% labour and overhead added this month)....... 10,000	?	?	?
Total units....................... 106,000	?	?	?

Costs per EU

	Total Cost	Materials	Labour	Overhead	Whole Unit
Cost to be accounted for:					
Work in process, June 1	$ 14,260	$ 10,300	$ 1,320	$ 2,640	
Cost added by the department........	117,640	58,600	19,680	39,360	
Total cost (a)	$131,900	$68,900	$21,000	$42,000	
Equivalent units (b).................		106,000	100,000	100,000	
Cost per EU, (a) ÷ (b)		$0.65 +	$0.21 +	$0.42 =	$1.28

Cost Reconciliation

	Total Cost	
Cost accounted for as follows:		
?	?	

Required:

1. Prepare a schedule showing how the equivalent units were computed for the first processing department.
2. Complete the Cost Reconciliation part of the production report for the first processing department.
3. Repeat parts (1) and (2) assuming that the company uses the FIFO method.

CHECK FIGURE
(1) Materials: 220,000 equivalent units
(2) Conversion: $1.30 per unit
(3) 160,000 units

PROBLEM 5–2   Interpreting a Production Report—Weighted Average Method (CC11, 14, 15, 16)
Cooperative San José of southern Sonora state in Mexico makes a unique syrup using cane sugar and local herbs. The syrup is sold in small bottles and is prized as a flavouring for drinks and desserts. The bottles are sold for $12 each. (The Mexican currency is the peso and is denoted by $.) The first stage in the production process is carried out in the Mixing Department, which removes foreign matter from the raw materials and mixes them in the proper proportions in large vats. The company uses the weighted average method in its process costing system.

A hastily prepared report for the Mixing Department for April follows:

Quantity Schedule	
Units to be accounted for:	
Work in process, April 1 (90% materials, 80% conversion cost added last month)	30,000
Started into production	200,000
Total units	230,000
Units accounted for as follows:	
Transferred to the next department	190,000
Work in process, April 30 (75% materials, 60% conversion cost added this month)	40,000
Total units	230,000

Total Cost

Cost to be accounted for:

Work in process, April 1	$ 98,000
Cost added during the month.	827,000
Total cost	$925,000

Cost Reconciliation

Cost accounted for as follows:

Transferred to the next department	$805,600
Work in process, April 30	119,400
Total cost	$925,000

Cooperative San José has just been acquired by another company, and the management of the acquiring company wants some additional information about Cooperative San José's operations.

Required:
1. What were the equivalent units for the month?
2. What were the costs per equivalent unit for the month? The beginning inventory consisted of the following costs: materials, $67,800; and conversion cost, $30,200. The costs added during the month consisted of: materials, $579,000; and conversion cost, $248,000.
3. How many of the units transferred to the next department were started and completed during the month?
4. The manager of the Mixing Department, anxious to make a good impression on the new owners, stated, "Materials prices jumped from about $2.50 per unit in March to $3 per unit in April, but due to good cost control, I was able to hold our materials cost to less than $3 per unit for the month." Should this manager be rewarded for good cost control? Explain.

PROBLEM 5–3   Production Report—Weighted Average Method (CC11, 14, 15, 16)

Sunspot Beverages, Ltd. of Fiji makes blended tropical fruit drinks in two stages. Fruit juices are extracted from fresh fruits and then blended in the Blending Department. The blended juices are then bottled and packed for shipping in the Bottling Department. The following information pertains to the operations of the Blending Department for June. (The currency in Fiji is the Fijian dollar (FJ$).)

CHECK FIGURE
6/30 WIP: $87,500

	A	B	C	D
1			*Percent Completed*	
2		*Units*	*Materials*	*Conversion*
3	Work in process, beginning	20,000	100%	75%
4	Started into production	180,000		
5	Completed and transferred out	160,000		
6	Work in process, ending	40,000	100%	25%
7				
8			*Materials*	*Conversion*
9	Work in process, beginning		FJ$ 25,200	FJ$ 24,800
10	Cost added during June		334,800	238,700
11				

Required:
Prepare a production report for the Blending Department for June assuming that the company uses the weighted average method.

PROBLEM 5–4   Step-by-Step Production Report—Weighted Average Method and FIFO Method
(CC11, 13, 14, 15, 16, 17, 18, 19)
Builder Products, Inc. manufactures a caulking compound that goes through three processing stages prior to completion. Information on work in the first department, Cooking, is given below for May:

Production data:
Units in process, May 1: 100% complete
as to materials and 80% complete
as to labour and overhead 15,000
Units started into production during May 110,000
Units completed and transferred out 100,000
Units in process, May 31: 60% complete
as to materials and 20% complete
as to labour and overhead .... ?
Cost data:
Work in process inventory, May 1:
Materials cost............................. $ 2,000
Labour cost 2,400
Overhead cost 6,000
Cost added during May:
Materials cost............................. 160,000
Labour cost 24,000
Overhead cost 70,000

Materials are added at several stages during the cooking process, whereas labour and overhead costs are incurred uniformly. The company uses the weighted average method.

Required:
Prepare a production report for the Cooking Department for May. Use the following three steps in preparing your report:
1. Prepare a quantity schedule and a computation of equivalent units.
2. Compute the costs per equivalent unit for the month.
3. Using the data from parts (1) and (2), prepare a cost reconciliation.
4. Prepare a production report for the Cooking Department for May assuming the company uses the FIFO method. Follow parts (1) to (3).

PROBLEM 5–5   Preparation of Production Report from Analysis of Work in Process—Weighted Average Method (CC11, 14, 15, 16)
Weston Products manufactures an industrial cleaning compound that goes through three processing departments—Grinding, Mixing, and Cooking. All raw materials are introduced at the start of work in the Grinding Department, with conversion costs being incurred evenly throughout the grinding process. The work-in-process T-account for the Grinding Department for a recent month follows:

Work in Process—Grinding Department

Inventory, May 1 (18,000 kgs, 1/3 processed)	$21,800	Completed and transferred to mixing (? kgs)	$?
May costs added:			
Raw materials (167,000 kgs)	133,400		
Labour and overhead	226,800		
Inventory, May 31 (15,000 kgs, 2/3 processed)	$?		

The May 1 work-in-process inventory consists of $14,600 in materials cost and $7,200 in labour and overhead cost. The company uses the weighted average method to account for units and costs.

Required:
1. Prepare a production report for the Grinding Department for the month.
2. What criticism can be made of the unit costs that you have computed on your production report?

CHECK FIGURE
(1) Labour: $2.64 per unit
(2) 12/31 WIP: $903,000
(4) COGS: $3,434,400

PROBLEM 5–6   Costing Inventories; Journal Entries; Cost of Goods Sold—Weighted Average Method (CC8, 11, 14, 15, 16)

You are employed by Spirit Company, a manufacturer of digital watches. The company's chief financial officer is trying to verify the accuracy of the ending work in process and finished goods inventories prior to closing the books for the year. You have been asked to assist in this verification. The year-end balances shown on Spirit Company's books are as follows:

	Units	Costs
Work in process, December 31 (50% complete as to labour and overhead)	250,000	$ 660,960
Finished goods, December 31.	150,000	1,009,800

Materials are added to production at the beginning of the manufacturing process, and overhead is applied to each product at the rate of 60% of direct labour cost. There was no finished goods inventory at the beginning of the year. A review of Spirit Company's inventory and cost records has disclosed the following data, all of which are accurate:

		Costs	
	Units	Materials	Labour
Work in process, January 1 (80% complete as to labour and overhead).	100,000	$ 200,000	$ 315,000
Units started into production.	900,000		
Cost added during the year:			
Materials cost		1,300,000	
Labour cost			1,995,000
Units completed during the year.	750,000		

The company uses the weighted average cost method.

Required:
1. Determine the equivalent units and costs per equivalent unit for materials, labour, and overhead for the year.
2. Determine the amount of cost that should be assigned to the ending work-in-process and finished goods inventories.
3. Prepare the necessary correcting journal entry to adjust the work-in-process and finished goods inventories to the correct balances as of December 31.
4. Determine the cost of goods sold for the year assuming there is no under- or over-applied overhead.

(CPA adapted)

PROBLEM 5–7   Comprehensive Process Costing Problem—Weighted Average Method and FIFO Method (CC8, 11, 13, 14, 15, 16, 17, 18, 19)

Lubricants, Inc. produces a special kind of grease that is widely used by race car drivers. The grease is produced in two processes: refining and blending.

Raw oil products are introduced at various points in the Refining Department; labour and overhead costs are incurred evenly throughout the refining operation. The refined output is then transferred to the Blending Department.

CHECK FIGURE
(2) 3/31 Refining Dept.
WIP: $46,000

The following incomplete work-in-process account is available for the Refining Department for March:

Work in Process—Refining Department

March 1 inventory (20,000 litres; 100% complete as to materials; 90% complete as to labour and overhead)	38,000	Completed and transferred to blending (? litres)	?
March costs added:			
Raw oil materials (390,000 litres)	495,000		
Direct labour	72,000		
Overhead	181,000		
March 31 inventory (40,000 litres; 75% complete as to materials; 25% complete as to labour and overhead)	?		

The March 1 work-in-process inventory in the Refining Department consists of the following cost elements: raw materials, $25,000; direct labour, $4,000; and overhead, $9,000.

Costs incurred during March in the Blending Department were as follows: materials used, $115,000; direct labour, $18,000; and overhead cost applied to production, $42,000. The company accounts for units and costs by the weighted average method.

Required:
1. Prepare journal entries to record the costs incurred in both the Refining Department and Blending Department during March. Key your entries to the items (a) through (g) following:
   a. Raw materials were issued for use in production.
   b. Direct labour costs were incurred.
   c. Manufacturing overhead costs for the entire factory were incurred, $225,000. (Credit accounts payable.)
   d. Manufacturing overhead cost was applied to production using a predetermined overhead rate.
   e. Units that were complete as to processing in the Refining Department were transferred to the Blending Department, $740,000.
   f. Units that were complete as to processing in the Blending Department were transferred to finished goods, $950,000.
   g. Completed units were sold on account, $1,500,000. The cost of goods sold was $900,000.
2. Post the journal entries from part (1) to T-accounts. The following account balances existed at the beginning of March. (The beginning balance in the Refining Department's work-in-process account is given above.)

Raw Materials	$618,000
Work in Process—Blending Department.	65,000
Finished Goods	20,000

After posting the entries to the T-accounts, find the ending balance in the inventory accounts and the manufacturing overhead account.
3. Prepare a production report for the Refining Department for March, using the weighted average method.
4. Prepare a production report for the Refining Department for March assuming that the company uses the FIFO method.

CHECK FIGURE
(2) 5/31 Cooking
Dept. WIP:
$66,000

PROBLEM 5–8   Comprehensive Process Costing Problem—Weighted Average Method and FIFO Method (CC8, 11, 13, 14, 15, 16, 17, 18, 19)
Hilox, Inc. produces an antacid product that goes through two departments—Cooking and Bottling. The company has recently hired a new assistant accountant, who has prepared the following summary of production and costs for the Cooking Department for May using the weighted average method.

Cooking Department costs:

Work-in-process inventory, May 1: 70,000 litres, 60% complete as to materials and 30% complete as to labour and overhead........	$ 61,000*
Materials added during May......................	570,000
Labour added during May	100,000
Overhead applied during May	235,000
Total departmental costs........................	$966,000

Cooking Department costs assigned to:

Litres completed and transferred to the Bottling Department: 400,000 litres at ? per litre.........	$?
Work-in-process inventory, May 31: 50,000 litres, 70% complete as to materials and 40% complete as to labour and overhead...........	?
Total departmental costs assigned..................	$?

*Consists of materials, $39,000; labour, $5,000; and overhead, $17,000.

The new assistant accountant has determined the cost per litre transferred to be $2.415, as follows:

$$\frac{\text{Total departmental costs, } \$966{,}000}{\text{Litres completed and transferred, } 400{,}000} = \$2.415 \text{ per litre}$$

However, the assistant accountant is unsure how to use this unit cost figure in assigning cost to the ending work in process inventory. In addition, the company's general ledger shows only $900,000 in cost transferred from the Cooking Department to the Bottling Department, which does not agree with the $966,000 figure above.

The general ledger also shows the following costs incurred in the Bottling Department during May: materials used, $130,000; direct labour cost incurred, $80,000; and overhead cost applied to products, $158,000.

Required:

1. Prepare journal entries as follows to record activity in the company during May. Key your entries to the letters (a) through (g) following.
   a. Raw materials were issued to the two departments for use in production.
   b. Direct labour costs were incurred in the two departments.
   c. Manufacturing overhead costs were incurred, $400,000. (Credit accounts payable.) The company maintains a single manufacturing overhead account for the entire plant.
   d. Manufacturing overhead cost was applied to production in each department using predetermined overhead rates.
   e. Units completed as to processing in the Cooking Department were transferred to the Bottling Department, $900,000.
   f. Units completed as to processing in the Bottling Department were transferred to finished goods, $1,300,000.
   g. Units were sold on account, $2,000,000. The cost of goods sold was $1,250,000.
2. Post the journal entries from part (1) to T-accounts. Balances in selected accounts on May 1 follow:

Raw Materials	$710,000
Work in Process—Bottling Department	85,000
Finished Goods	45,000

After posting the entries to the T-accounts, find the ending balance in the inventory accounts and the manufacturing overhead account.
3. Prepare a production report for the Cooking Department for May using the weighted average method.
4. Prepare a production report for the Cooking Department for May assuming that the company uses the FIFO method.

PROBLEM 5–9   Cost per Equivalent Unit: FIFO Method (CC18, 19)

The following information pertains to production activities in the refining department of
Storm Corporation. All units in work in process were costed using the FIFO cost flow assumption.

Refining Department	Units	Percentage of Conversion Completion	Costs
WIP, November 1	18,750	80%	$ 16,500
Units started and cost incurred during November	101,250		$ 107,250
Units completed and transferred to the mixing department	75,000		
WIP, November 28	?	50%	$??

Required:
1. What were the conversion costs per equivalent unit of production last period and this period, respectively?
2. What was the conversion cost in the work in process inventory account at November 28?
3. What was the per-unit conversion cost of the units started last period and completed this period?

PROBLEM 5–10   Production Report: FIFO Method (CC13, 17, 18, 19)

Callisto Company manufactures chemical additives for industrial applications. As the new cost accountant
for Callisto, you have been assigned the task of completing the production cost report for the most recent
period. Callisto uses the FIFO method of process costing. The following information pertains to the most
recent period:

Beginning WIP inventory:	16,000 units (75% complete as to materials; 70% complete as to conversion costs)
Units started into production this period:	27,000 units
Units completed and transferred out:	33,000 units
Ending WIP inventory:	10,000 units (60% complete as to materials; 50% complete as to conversion costs)
Costs in beginning inventory:	$132,000 materials; $164,000 conversion costs
Current period costs:	$252,000 materials; $440,000 conversion costs

Required:
Prepare a complete production report for the period using the FIFO method. (Round the cost per equivalent
unit to three decimal places; round the costs in the cost report to the nearest dollar.)

PROBLEM 5–11   Equivalent Units and Costs: FIFO Method (CC13, 17)

Below is information about Gandelf, a chemical producer, for October:

Work in process, beginning inventory	50,000 units
Transferred-in	100% complete
Direct materials	0% complete
Conversion costs	80% complete
Transferred in during October	200,000 units
Completed and transferred out during October	210,000 units
Work in process, ending inventory	? units
Transferred-in	100% complete
Direct materials	0% complete
Conversion costs	40% complete

Required:
1. Compute the number of units in work-in-process inventory at the end of the month.

2. Using the FIFO method, compute the equivalent units of production for the month with respect to materials.
3. Using the FIFO method, compute the equivalent units of production for the month with respect to conversion costs.

PROBLEM 5–12   Cost Reconciliation: FIFO Cost Method (CC19)

CHECK FIGURE: Cost per EU, Direct labour; $0.05

The BerryPhoenix BrickWorks, in Saskatoon, Saskatchewan, manufactures high-quality bricks used in residential and commercial construction. The firm is small but highly automated and typically produces about 300,000 bricks per month. A brick is created in a continuous production operation. In the initial step, the raw material, a mixture of soils and water, is forced into a brick mould moving along a conveyer belt. No other materials are actually required in the manufacture of a brick. Each brick takes about three days to complete. Approximately the last 36 hours on the conveyer belt are spent in an oven that removes moisture from the product. The conveyer belt speed is monitored and controlled by computer. The firm uses a process costing system based on actual costs in three cost pools—direct materials, direct labour, and factory overhead—to assign production costs to output. Following are cost and production data for May 2008:

Beginning work-in-process inventory   25,000 bricks
100% complete as to direct materials
60% complete as to direct labour
36% complete as to factory overhead

Started this period   305,000 bricks

Ending work-in-process inventory   30,000 bricks
100% complete as to direct materials
50% complete as to direct labour
40% complete as to factory overhead

| | Costs | | |
	Materials	Direct Labour	Overhead
Beginning inventory , , , , , ,	$ 1,330	$ 835	$ 552
Costs added in May , , , , , ,	16,200	15,000	18,180

Required:
Determine the cost of bricks transferred to finished goods inventory and the cost of bricks in ending work-in-process inventory for May 2008. Assume the company uses the FIFO method of process costing.

Building Your Skills

ANALYTICAL THINKING   (CC11, 14, 15, 16)
"I think we goofed when we hired that new assistant controller," said Ruth Scarpino, president of Provost Industries. "Just look at this production report that he prepared for last month for the Finishing Department. I can't make heads or tails out of it."

Finishing Department costs:
Work-in-process inventory, April 1, 450 units; 100% complete as to materials; 60% complete as to conversion costs . . . . $ 8,208*
Costs transferred in during the month from the preceding department, 1,950 units 17,940
Materials cost added during the month (materials are added when processing is 50% complete in the Finishing Department) 6,210
Conversion costs incurred during the month 13,920
Total departmental costs $46,278

Finishing Department costs assigned to:	
Units completed and transferred to finished	
goods, 1,800 units at $25.71 per unit	$46,278
Work-in-process inventory, April 30, 600	
units; 0% complete as to materials;	
35% complete as to processing.	–0–
Total departmental costs assigned.	$46,278

*Consists of: cost transferred in, $4,068; materials cost, $1,980; and conversion cost, $2,160.

"He's struggling to learn our system," replied Frank Harrop, the operations manager. "The problem is that he's been away from process costing for a long time, and it's coming back slowly."

"It's not just the format of his report that I'm concerned about. Look at that $25.71 unit cost that he's come up with for April. Doesn't that seem high to you?" said Ms. Scarpino.

"Yes, it does seem high; but on the other hand, I know we had an increase in materials prices during April, and that may be the explanation," replied Mr. Harrop. "I'll get someone else to redo this report and then we may be able to see what's going on."

Provost Industries manufactures a ceramic product that goes through two processing departments—Moulding and Finishing. The company uses the weighted average method to account for units and costs. *Hint: Include transferred-in costs as a separate cost category and let the percentage of completion for this category be 100% [Why?].*

Required:
1. Prepare a revised production report for the Finishing Department.
2. Explain to the president why the unit cost on the new assistant controller's report is so high.

COMMUNICATING IN PRACTICE   (CC8, 16)
Assume that you are the cost analyst who prepared the production report that appears in Exhibit 5–11. You receive a call from Minesh Patel, a new hire in the company's accounting staff, who is not sure what needs to be done with the cost reconciliation portion of the report. He wants to know what journal entries should be prepared and what balances need to be checked in the company's accounts.

Required:
Write a memorandum to Mr. Patel that explains the steps that should be taken. Refer to specific amounts on the Cost Reconciliation portion of the production report to ensure that he properly completes the steps.

ETHICS CHALLENGE   (CC9, 16)
Gary Stevens and Mary James are production managers in the Consumer Electronics Division of General Electronics Company, which has several dozen plants scattered in locations throughout the world. Mary manages the plant located in Hamilton, Ontario, while Gary manages the plant in El Segundo, California. Production managers are paid a salary and get an additional bonus equal to 5% of their base salary if the entire division meets or exceeds its target profits for the year. The bonus is determined in March after the company's annual report has been prepared and issued to shareholders.

Shortly after the beginning of the new year, Mary received a phone call from Gary that went like this:

Gary: How's it going, Mary?
Mary: Fine, Gary. How's it going with you?
Gary: Great! I just got the preliminary profit figures for the division for last year and we are within $200,000 of making the year's target profits. All we have to do is to pull a few strings, and we'll be over the top!
Mary: What do you mean?
Gary: Well, one thing that would be easy to change is your estimate of the percentage completion of your ending work-in-process inventories.
Mary: I don't know if I can do that, Gary. Those percentage completion figures are supplied by Tom Winthrop, my lead supervisor, who I have always trusted to provide us with good estimates. Besides, I have already sent the percentage completion figures to the corporate headquarters.

Gary: You can always tell them there was a mistake. Think about it, Mary. All of us managers are doing as much as we can to pull this bonus out of the hat. You may not want the bonus cheque, but the rest of us sure could use it.

The final Processing Department in Mary's production facility began the year with no work-in-process inventories. During the year, 210,000 units were transferred in from the prior Processing Department and 200,000 units were completed and sold. Costs transferred in from the prior department totalled $39,375,000. No materials are added in the final processing department. A total of $20,807,500 of conversion cost was incurred in the final processing department during the year.

Required:
1. Tom Winthrop estimated that the units in ending inventory in the final processing department were 30% complete with respect to the conversion costs of the final processing department. If this estimate of the percentage completion is used, what would be the cost of goods sold for the year?
2. Does Gary Stevens want the estimated percentage completion to be increased or decreased? Explain why.
3. What percentage completion would result in increasing reported net income by $200,000 over the net income that would be reported if the 30% figure were used?
4. Do you think Mary James should go along with the request to alter estimates of the percentage completion?

TEAMWORK IN ACTION   (CC11, 14, 15, 16)
The production report includes a quantity schedule, the computation of equivalent costs and costs per equivalent units, and a cost reconciliation.

Required:
1. *Learning teams* of three (or more) members should be formed. Each team member must select one of the following sections of the production report (as illustrated in Exhibit 5–9) as an area of expertise (each team must have at least one expert in each section).
   a. Quantity schedule and equivalent units
   b. Costs per equivalent unit
   c. Cost reconciliation
2. *Expert teams* should be formed from the individuals who have selected the same area of expertise. Expert teams should discuss and write a brief summary that each expert will present to his/her learning team that addresses the following:
   a. The purpose of the section of the production report
   b. The manner in which the amounts appearing in this section of the report are determined
3. Each expert should return to his/her learning team. In rotation, each member should present his/her expert team's report to the learning team.

Don't forget to visit the Online Learning Centre for self-study quizzes, practice exams, and more! Visit www.mcgrawhill.ca/olc/brewer.

CHAPTER *Six*

Activity-Based Costing

CHAPTER COMPETENCIES

After studying Chapter 6, you should be able to demonstrate the following competencies:

Competency	Know	Apply
Explain the basics of activity-based costing (ABC).		
CC1 Outline the limitations of plantwide and departmental overhead allocation.	●	
CC2 Describe the basic approach underlying ABC.	●	
CC3 Describe the hierarchical classification of activities.	●	
CC4 Distinguish between unit-, batch-, product-, and facility-level activities.	●	
Apply ABC.		
CC5 Design an ABC system.		●
CC6 Compute activity rates used to allocate costs to cost objects.		●
CC7 Assign activity costs to cost objects, and compute unit costs.		●
CC8 Describe the use of ABC in nonmanufacturing organizations.	●	
Understand the benefits and limitations of ABC.		
CC9 Explain the benefits and limitations of ABC.	●	
Explain cost flows in an ABC system.		
CC10^A Describe the flow of costs in an ABC system.	●	
CC11^A Record the flow of costs in an ABC system.		●
Understand quality costs.		
CC12^B Identify the four types of quality costs.	●	
CC13^B Explain how the different quality costs interact.	●	
CC14^B Prepare a cost of quality report.		●

Note: A and B refer to Appendix 6A and Appendix 6B respectively; both appendices are available online at www.mcgrawhill.ca/olc/brewer.

DECISION FEATURE
Understanding Costs with Cutting-Edge Tools

Understanding costs is fundamental to better planning and decision making, as realized by Quebec- based RONA Inc. Founded in 1939, RONA is the largest Canadian distributor and retailer of hardware, home renovation, and gardening products. In 2005, it operated a network of just under 600 stores, and generated over $4 billion in sales and over $175 million in net earnings.

A secret of RONA's success is its efficient and effective handling of supply chain management—distribution and purchasing activities. However, to operate efficiently, managers needed a better understanding of costs. Using an average costing system to allocate costs and determine the cost per supplier provided little information. Managers knew that something was wrong; costs could not be uniform across products and suppliers. Therefore, in 2003, the company turned to activity-based management (ABM) for help. Activity-based costing (ABC), which is the topic of this chapter and a critical component of ABM, helps organizations better manage activities. Implementing the ABM system allowed managers to obtain details on the costs that were previously not available.

What is the value of such an investment? It has a direct impact on decision making: managers, armed with more accurate cost information, are in a better position to negotiate with suppliers. Understanding the value chain allows managers to contemplate changes in distribution channels. According to Martin Beauregard, the then-chief financial analyst, "You can make better distribution decisions by knowing their financial impact; [moreover it helps] bring cost transparency to [RONA's] supply chain."

Source: R. Colman and J. Demers, "Route-to-Market Knowledge Builders," *CMA Management*, February 2004, pp. 14–15; 2003 and 2005 annual reports of RONA, Inc. available online (see http://www.rona.ca).

A Look Back

The previous two chapters introduced two contrasting systems: job-order and process costing. The approach in both the systems to overhead allocation was the use of a single plantwide overhead rate.

A Look at This Chapter

Chapter 6 continues the discussion of overhead cost allocation; it introduces the concept of activity-based costing, a technique that uses a number of allocation bases to assign overhead costs to cost objects.

A Look Ahead

The next four chapters deal with the concepts of planning and control. Chapter 7 describes budgeting, a key element of the planning process.

As previously discussed, direct materials and direct

labour costs can be easily traced to the desired cost object (e.g., product, job, or process). Overhead costs, in contrast, cannot be traced to cost objects and must be allocated. Chapter 4 introduced the concept of overhead allocation using direct labour as an allocation base. This chapter further elaborates on the concept and process of cost allocation. In doing so, it questions the practice described in Chapter 4 (that is, allocation using a plant-wide overhead rate) and introduces activity-based costing.

Assigning Overhead Costs to Cost Objects

Organizations must find an appropriate method to assign overhead costs to cost objects. The most common cost object to which costs are assigned is product (or service). Other cost objects may include process, customer, distribution channel, and product line. Regardless of the cost object, overhead costs cannot be directly traced to them and must therefore be allocated (or assigned) to the cost object. This section describes three different methods of overhead cost allocation (the focus of this chapter is on the third method). The discussion of overhead allocation is largely couched within a manufacturing context, although the principles can easily be applied to nonmanufacturing settings too, as we will see later in this chapter.

Plantwide Overhead Rate

⊙ **KNOW**

CC1: Outline the limitations of plantwide and departmental overhead allocation.

The simplest method of assigning overhead, introduced in Chapter 4, involves using a single allocation base and rate, known as a *plantwide overhead rate*. This method is based on the convenience it offers in that the cost accounting system must capture only two pieces of information: total overhead costs and the volume of the allocation base (such as total direct labour-hours). As suggested in Chapter 4, direct labour-hours were widely used largely because direct labour was a significant component of the total conversion costs (i.e., labour and overhead) and the designers of cost accounting systems believed that direct labour influenced overhead costs. Moreover, direct labour-hours were always meticulously recorded, which means that the information was readily available.

Conceptually, the use of a plantwide rate assumes the following: (1) all overhead costs in the organization are *driven* (or caused) by the single allocation base that is used, and (2) cost objects (e.g., products) consume overhead resources in the same proportion in which they consume the allocation base. Both assumptions are weak; therefore, using a single plantwide overhead rate has serious limitations, which can lead to cost distortions. A manager using distorted cost information can make flawed decisions that may have serious implications for the future of the organization.

Departmental Overhead Rate

As a first step to improving the allocation method, many companies use multiple overhead rates along departmental lines. As an example, consider a manufacturing company with three departments: materials, machining, and assembly. Overhead costs *within* each department are accumulated in a single *overhead cost pool*; thus, there will be three overhead cost pools in our example. An appropriate allocation base for each pool must then be identified and a predetermined overhead rate computed for each of the three pools. The allocation bases typically depend upon the nature of the work performed in each department. For example, direct material costs may be used to assign overhead incurred by the materials department, whereas direct labour may be used to allocate the assembly department's overhead costs.

Unfortunately, even departmental overhead allocation makes the same assumptions made in the case of plantwide overhead allocation (but at a departmental, rather than a plantwide, level). These assumptions may not hold true in situations where a company offers a diverse product range and has a complex set of overhead costs. As a result, this method of overhead allocation can also lead to product cost distortions.

Activity-Based Costing

A serious limitation in the case of both plantwide and departmental overhead allocation is the failure by both methods to recognize two facts: (1) the total overhead cost pool in an organization is an accumulation of the costs of numerous resources that are consumed by the organization to serve its customers, and (2) the individual overhead costs are driven by different factors. While some overhead costs may be caused by the level of production or service volume, others may be caused by the number of transactions processed, and still others may be caused by other drivers. Second, the two previous methods also fail to recognize that different cost objects (i.e., products, services, and customers) may consume resources in different proportions.

For example, consider two customers of a large organization—both customers may consume the same amount of resources with respect to order processing, but there may be significant differences between the two customers in terms of the consumption of resources relating to after-sales service. A (traditional) cost allocation system using a single allocation base (and rate) will not be able to capture these differences in the resource consumption patterns of the two customers. A good cost allocation system must recognize these differences and must consider them when assigning costs.

Also, as explained in Chapter 1, the business environment has changed considerably over the last 25 years. In adopting the lean business model, many organizations have automated their operations to a significant extent. This has resulted in a shift in the cost structure within organizations—the proportion of overhead costs has increased at the expense of direct labour costs. Therefore, it is essential that managers reconsider using traditional cost accounting systems that allocate overhead costs using a plantwide rate or even departmental rates. Moreover, increased competition has resulted in organizations offering a diverse range of products and services to their customers. Often, these diverse products/services consume overhead resources in different proportions; this diversity cannot be captured by traditional costing systems.

Activity-based costing (ABC) is a method of cost allocation that attempts to assign overhead costs to cost objects more accurately than the methods discussed so far. The basic idea underlying ABC is illustrated in Exhibit 6–1. A customer order for a product or a service triggers a number of activities. For example, if Hudson's Bay Company (HBC) orders a line of women's skirts from Calvin Klein, a production order is generated, materials are ordered, patterns are created, textiles are cut to pattern and then sewn, and the finished products are packed for shipping. These activities consume resources. For example, ordering the appropriate materials consumes clerical time—a resource the company must pay for. In activity-based costing, an attempt is made to trace these costs directly to the activities that cause them.

Rather than a single allocation base, such as direct labour-hours or machine-hours, in ABC, a company uses a number of allocation bases for assigning costs to products. Each allocation base in an ABC system represents a major *activity* that causes overhead costs. An **activity** in activity-based costing is an event that causes the consumption of resources. Examples of activities in various organizations include the following:

KNOW

CC2: Describe the basic approach underlying ABC.

- Setting up machines
- Admitting patients to a hospital
- Scheduling production
- Performing blood tests at a clinic
- Billing customers
- Maintaining equipment

- Ordering materials or supplies
- Stocking shelves at a store
- Meeting with clients at a law firm
- Preparing shipments
- Inspecting materials for defects
- Opening an account at a bank

Exhibit 6–1
The ABC Model

Activity-based costing centres on these activities. Each major activity has its own overhead cost pool (also known as an *activity cost pool*), its own *activity measure*, and its own predetermined overhead rate (also known as an *activity rate*). An **activity cost pool** is a *cost bucket* in which costs related to a particular activity are accumulated. The **activity measure** expresses how much of the activity is carried out, and is used as the allocation base for applying overhead costs to products and services. For example, *the number of patients admitted* is a natural choice of an activity measure for the activity *admitting patients to the hospital*. An **activity rate** is a predetermined overhead rate in an ABC system. Each activity has its own activity rate that is used to apply overhead costs.

For example, the activity *setting up machines* to process a batch of 100 units of a product would have its own activity cost pool. If the total cost in this activity cost pool is $150,000 and the total expected activity is 1,000 machine setups, the predetermined overhead rate (i.e., activity rate) for this activity would be $150 per machine setup ($150,000 ÷ 1,000 machine setups = $150 per machine setup). Note that this amount does not depend on how many units are produced after the machine is set up. A small job requiring a machine setup would be charged $150—just the same as a large job.

Taking each activity in isolation, this system works exactly like the job-order costing system described in Chapter 4. A predetermined overhead rate is computed for each activity and then applied to cost objects based on the amount of activity required by that cost object. The ABC system can be used by organizations with a job-order costing system or a process costing system. In job-order costing, the desired cost object is a specific job, whereas in a process-costing system, it is a process (or a department).

Designing an Activity-Based Costing System

In most companies, hundreds or even thousands of different activities cause overhead costs. These activities range from taking a telephone order to training new employees. Setting up and maintaining a complex costing system that includes all of these activities would be prohibitively expensive.

The challenge in designing an activity-based costing system is to identify a reasonably small number of activities that explain the bulk of the variation in overhead costs. This is usually done by interviewing a broad range of managers in the organization to find out what activities they think are important and that consume most of the resources they manage. This often results in a long list of potential activities that could be included in the ABC system. This list is refined and pruned in consultation with top managers. Related activities are frequently combined to reduce the amount of detail and record-keeping cost.

For example, several actions may be involved in handling and moving raw materials, but these may be combined into a single activity called *materials handling*. The end result of this stage of the design process is an *activity dictionary* that defines each of the activities that will be included in the ABC system and how the activities will be measured.

Hierarchy of Activities

Once an activity dictionary is created, the next challenge is to determine what causes these activities. In a manufacturing firm, should we expect all activities to be directly related to production volume? In other words, must the organization perform every activity listed in the activity dictionary each time an additional unit of a product is manufactured? The answer is no. While some activities will be performed each time an additional unit of product is manufactured, others will not be.

Generally speaking, a manufacturing organization can classify its activities into four types: (1) unit-level, (2) batch-level, (3) product-level, and (4) facility-level. Exhibit 6-2 lists commonly found activities in a manufacturing company using this four-level hierarchical classification scheme. Using such a classification scheme allows designers of an ABC system to examine whether activities can be meaningfully combined to simplify the system, as well as to identify appropriate activity measures that can be used to allocate activity costs to cost objects.

KNOW
CC3: Describe the hierarchical classification of activities.

Level	Activities	Activity Measures
Unit-level	Processing units on machines	Machine-hours
	Processing units by hand	Direct labour-hours
	Consuming factory supplies	Units produced
Batch-level	Processing purchase orders	Purchase orders processed
	Processing production orders	Production orders processed
	Setting up equipment	Number of setups; setup hours
	Handling material	Kilograms of material handled; number of times material moved
Product-level	Testing new products	Hours of testing time
	Administering parts inventories	Number of part types
	Designing products	Hours of design time
Facility-level	General factory administration	Direct labour-hours*
	Plant building and grounds	Direct labour-hours*

*Facility-level costs cannot be traced on a cause-and-effect basis to individual products. Nevertheless, these costs are usually allocated to products using some arbitrary basis, such as direct labour-hours. Note, however, that these costs will represent a small portion of the total overhead costs. Therefore, the distortion, which might result from the use of an arbitrary basis for allocating these costs, will not be significant.

Exhibit 6–2
Examples of Activities and Activity Measures in Manufacturing Companies

Unit-level activities are performed each time a unit is produced. The costs of unit-level activities should be proportional to the number of units produced. For example, providing power to run processing equipment would be a unit-level activity, since power tends to be consumed in proportion to the number of units produced.

Batch-level activities consist of tasks that are performed each time a batch (or lot) is processed, such as processing purchase orders, setting up equipment, packing shipments to customers, and handling material. Costs at the batch level depend on *the number of batches processed*, rather than on the number of units produced. For example, the cost of processing a purchase order is the same, regardless of whether one unit or 5,000 units of an item are ordered. Thus, the total cost of a batch-level activity, such as purchasing, is a function of the *number* of orders placed.

Product-level activities (sometimes called *product-sustaining activities*) relate to specific products and typically must be carried out regardless of how many batches or units of the product are manufactured. Product-level activities include maintaining inventories of parts for a product (also known as *parts administration*), issuing engineering change notices to modify a product to meet a customer's specifications, and developing special test routines when a product is first placed into production. These activities generally depend on the number of different products that a company produces.

Facility-level activities (also called *organization-sustaining activities*) are activities that are carried out regardless of which products are produced, how many batches are run, or how many units are made. Facility-level costs include such items as factory management salaries, insurance, property taxes, and building amortization. The costs of facility-level activities are often combined into a single cost pool and allocated to products using an arbitrary base such as direct labour-hours. As we will see later in the book, allocating such costs to products will result in misleading data that can lead to bad decisions. However, facility-level costs must be allocated to meet external reporting requirements.

IN BUSINESS TODAY   Dining in the Canyon

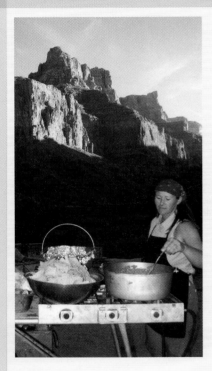

Western River Expeditions (www.westernriver.com) runs river rafting trips on the Colorado, Green, and Salmon Rivers. One of its most popular trips is a six-day trip down the Grand Canyon, which features famous rapids such as Crystal and Lava Falls, as well as the awesome scenery accessible only from the bottom of the Grand Canyon. The company runs trips of one or two rafts, each of which carries two guides and up to 18 guests. The company provides all meals on the trip, which are prepared by the guides.

In terms of the hierarchy of activities, a guest can be considered as a unit and a raft as a batch. In that context, the wages paid to the guides are a batch-level cost, since each raft requires two guides regardless of the number of guests in the raft. Each guest is given a mug to use during the trip and to take home at the end of the trip as a souvenir. The cost of the mug is a unit-level cost since the number of mugs given away is strictly proportional to the number of guests on a trip.

What about the costs of food served to guests and guides—is this a unit-level cost, a batch-level cost, a product-level cost, or an organization-sustaining cost? At first glance, it might be thought that food costs are a unit-level cost—the greater the number of guests, the higher the food costs. However, that is not quite correct. Standard menus have been created for each day of the trip. For example, the first night's menu might specify shrimp cocktail, steak, cornbread, salad, and cheesecake. The day before a trip begins, all of the food needed for the trip is taken from the central warehouse and packed in modular containers. It isn't practical to finely adjust the amount of food for the actual number of guests planned to be on a trip—most of the food comes prepackaged in large lots. For example, the shrimp cocktail menu may call for two large bags of frozen shrimp per raft and that many bags will be packed regardless of how many guests are expected on the raft. Consequently, the costs of food are not a unit-level cost that varies with the number of guests actually on a trip. Instead, the costs of food are a batch-level cost.

Source: Conversations with Western River Expeditions personnel.

⬤ **APPLY**

CC5: Design an ABC system.

An Example of an ABC System Design

Exhibit 6–3 illustrates an ABC system flow chart, which consists of a two-stage allocation procedure. The first stage includes the following steps:

1. Estimated costs of the various overhead resources are assigned (or allocated) to each of the eight activity cost pools.
2. Activity measure for each pool is identified.

Exhibit 6–3

Example of an ABC System Flow Chart

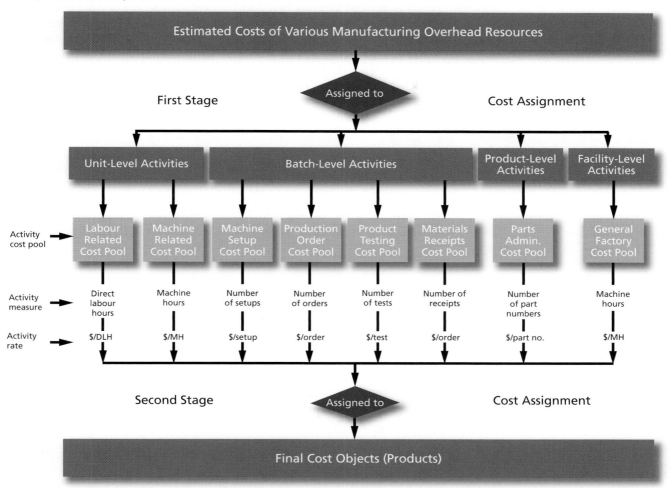

3. Total activity volume for each activity measure is estimated.
4. Predetermined overhead allocation rate (i.e., activity rate) for each pool is computed.

In the second stage, costs from the different pools are allocated to the desired cost objects using the activity rate and the volume of activity measure consumed by that cost object.

As an example, consider the Materials Receipts cost pool. The resources consumed by the activities included in this pool would be labour (receiving clerks), supplies (shipping documents), and equipment (computers and other material tracking devices). There may be other "common" resources that are consumed by multiple activities, such as the building, central information system, and so on. *In this text, we will not go into the details of how these resource costs are assigned to activity cost pools. Notice that in all the examples and assignments, these cost assignments have already been made.*

Once the amount of cost assigned to the Materials Receipts cost pool is known, we must identify an activity measure; in Exhibit 6–3, the activity measure chosen is Number of Receipts. Next, we estimate the total volume for this measure for a given period, and then compute a predetermined activity rate as explained on page 118. The procedure for computing a predetermined activity rate is the same as that explained in Chapter 4. Assume that an amount of $50,000 was allocated to the Materials Receipts cost pool at the beginning of the period and that the total activity volume was estimated at 2,500 receipts. The predetermined activity rate is then computed as $20 per receipt ($50,000 ÷ 2,500).

In the second stage, the $20 rate is used to assign costs to the desired cost objects (say, products). If Product A required three shipments of incoming raw materials (i.e., three material receipts), $60 will be assigned to this product ($20 × 3). Note that this procedure is similar to what was explained in Chapter 4; the only difference is that the ABC system has multiple overhead cost pools that are based on activities. This means that activity consumption information must be collected for individual cost objects.

Using Activity-Based Costing

Different products place different demands on overhead resources. This difference in demand on resources is not recognized by traditional costing systems, which assume that overhead resources are consumed in direct proportion to a single allocation base, such as direct labour-hours. The following example illustrates the distortions in product costs that can result from using a traditional costing system and the improvements made possible by ABC.

**MANAGERIAL
ACCOUNTING
IN ACTION**

The Issue

Comtek Sound, Inc. makes two products, a built-in DVD player (called a *DVD unit*) and a radio with a built-in compact disc player (called a *CD unit*). Both these products are sold to automobile manufacturers for installation in new vehicles. The president of the company, Sarah Kastler, recently returned from a management conference at which activity-based costing was discussed. Following the conference, she called a meeting of the top managers in the company to discuss what she had learned. Attending the meeting were the production manager, Frank Hines; the marketing manager, Nicole Sermone; and the accounting manager, Tom Frazier.

Sarah: I learned some things at the conference I just attended that may help resolve some long-standing puzzles here at Comtek Sound.
Nicole: Did they tell you why we've been losing all those bids lately on our bread-and-butter CD units and winning every bid on our specialty DVD units?
Sarah: Nicole, you probably weren't expecting this answer, but yes, there may be a simple explanation. We may have been shooting ourselves in the foot.
Nicole: How so? I don't know about anyone else, but we have been hustling like crazy to get more business for the company.
Sarah: Nicole, when you talk with our customers, what reasons do they give for taking their CD unit business to our competitors? Is it a problem with quality or on-time delivery?
Nicole: No, our customers readily admit that we're among the best in the business.
Sarah: Then what's the problem?
Nicole: Price. The competition is undercutting our price on the CD units and then bidding high on the DVD units. As a result, they're stealing our high-volume CD business and leaving us with just the low-volume DVD business.
Sarah: Why is our price so high for the tape units that the competition is able to undercut us?
Nicole: Our price isn't too high. Theirs is too low. Our competitors must be pricing below their costs on the CD units.
Sarah: Why do you think that?
Nicole: Well, if we charged the prices for our CD units that our competitors are quoting, we'd be pricing below *our* cost, and I know we're just as efficient as any competitor.
Frank: Nicole, why would our competitors price below their cost?
Nicole: They're out to grab market share.

Frank: Does that make any sense? What good does more market share do them if they're pricing below their cost?

Sarah: I think Frank has a point. Tom, you're the expert with the numbers. Can you suggest another explanation?

Tom: I was hoping you'd ask that. Those product cost figures my department reports to you are primarily intended to be used to value inventories and determine cost of goods sold for our external financial statements. I am awfully uncomfortable about using them for bidding. In fact, I have mentioned this several times, but no one was interested.

Sarah: Now I'm interested. Tom, are you telling us that the product cost figures we have been using for bidding may be wrong? Are you suggesting that we really don't know what the manufacturing cost is for either the CD units or the DVD units?

Tom: Yes, that could be the problem. Our cost system isn't designed to recognize that our two products place different demands on our resources, especially overhead. The CD units are simple to manufacture, and the DVD units are more complex. We need a cost system that recognizes this difference in demand on resources.

Sarah: That's exactly the point made at the conference. The conference speakers suggested we recost our products using something called activity-based costing. Tom, can we do this?

Tom: You bet! But we need to do it as a team. Can each person in the room appoint one of their top people to work with me?

Sarah: Let's do it! I'd like the special ABC team to report back to this group as soon as possible. If there's a problem with our costs, we need to know it before the competition plows us under.

Comtek Sound Inc.'s Basic Data

Tom Frazier and the ABC team immediately began gathering basic information relating to the company's two products. As a basis for its study, the team decided to use the cost and other data planned for the current year. A summary of some of this information follows. For the current year, the company's budget provides for selling 50,000 DVD units and 200,000 CD units. Both products require two direct labour-hours to complete. Therefore, the company plans to work 500,000 direct labour-hours (DLHs) during the current year, computed as follows:

	Hours
DVD units: 50,000 units × 2 DLHs per unit	100,000
CD units: 200,000 units × 2 DLHs per unit.	400,000
Total direct labour-hours.	500,000

Costs for materials and labour for one unit of each product are given below:

	DVD Units	CD Units
Direct materials.	$90	$50
Direct labour (at $10 per DLH)	20	20

The company's estimated manufacturing overhead costs for the current year total $10,000,000. The ABC team discovered that both products use the same amount of DLHs per unit, but the DVDs use more machine-hours per unit and require greater testing. Moreover, the DVDs are produced in much smaller lot (batch) sizes than the CDs. As a result, machines are required to be set up more frequently thereby requiring more setups.

The company has always used DLHs as the base for assigning overhead costs to its products.

With these data in hand, the ABC team was prepared to begin the design of the new activity-based costing system. But first, they wanted to compute the cost of each product using the company's existing cost system.

Direct Labour-Hours as a Base

Under the company's existing costing system, the company's predetermined overhead rate would be $20 per direct labour-hour. The rate is computed as follows:

$$\text{Predetermined overhead rate} = \frac{\text{Estimated total manufacturing overhead}}{\text{Estimated total direct labour-hours (DLHs)}}$$

$$= \frac{\$10,000,000}{500,000 \text{ DLHs}} = \$20 \text{ per DLH}$$

Using this rate, the ABC team then computed the unit product costs as given below:

	DVD Units	CD Units
Direct materials (above)	$90	$50
Direct labour (above)	20	20
Manufacturing overhead (2 DLHs × $20 per DLH)	40	40
Unit product cost.	$150	$110

Tom Frazier explained to the ABC team that the problem with this costing approach is that it relies entirely on labour time in assigning overhead cost to products and does not consider the impact of other factors—such as setups and testing—on the overhead costs of the company. Since these other factors are being ignored and the two products require equal amounts of labour time, they are assigned equal amounts of overhead cost.

Tom explained that while this method of computing costs is fast and simple, it is accurate only in those situations where other factors affecting overhead costs are not significant. Tom stated that he believed these other factors are significant in the case of Comtek Sound, Inc., and he was anxious for the team to analyze the various activities of the company to see their impact on costs.

Computing Activity Rates

APPLY

CC6: Compute activity rates used to allocate costs to cost objects.

The ABC team then analyzed Comtek Sound, Inc.'s operations and identified eight major activities to be included in the new activity-based costing system. (These eight activities are identical to those illustrated previously in Exhibit 6–3.) Cost and other data relating to the activities are presented in Exhibit 6–4.

As shown in the Basic Data panel at the top of Exhibit 6–4, the ABC team estimated the amount of overhead cost for each activity cost pool, along with the expected activity volume for the current year. The machine setups activity cost pool, for example, has been assigned $1,600,000 in overhead cost. The company expects to complete 4,000 setups during the year, of which 3,000 will be for DVD units and 1,000 will be for CD units. Data for other activities are also shown in the exhibit.

The ABC team then computed an activity rate for each activity. (See the middle panel in Exhibit 6–4.) The rate for machine setups, for example, was computed by dividing the total estimated overhead cost in the activity cost pool, $1,600,000, by the expected amount of activity, 4,000 setups. The result was the activity rate of $400 per setup. This process was repeated for each of the other activities in the ABC system.

Exhibit 6–4
Comtek Sound's Activity-Based Costing System

Basic Data

Activities and Activity Measures	Estimated Overhead Cost	Expected Activity Volume		
		CD Units	DVD Units	Total
Labour related (direct labour-hours).......	$ 800,000	400,000	100,000	500,000
Machine related (machine-hours).........	2,100,000	700,000	300,000	1,000,000
Machine setups (setups)	1,600,000	1,000	3,000	4,000
Production orders (orders)	450,000	800	400	1,200
Product testing (tests)	1,700,000	4,000	16,000	20,000
Material receipts (receipts).............	1,000,000	3,200	1,800	5,000
Parts administration (part types).........	350,000	300	400	700
General factory (machine-hours)	2,000,000	700,000	300,000	1,000,000
	$10,000,000			

Computation of Activity Rates

Activities	(a) Estimated Overhead Cost	(b) Total Expected Activity Volume	(a) ÷ (b) Activity Rate
Labour related...................	$ 800,000	500,000 DLHs	$ 1.60 per DLH
Machine related..................	2,100,000	1,000,000 MHs	2.10 per MH
Machine setups	1,600,000	4,000 setups	400.00 per setup
Production orders	450,000	1,200 orders	375.00 per order
Product testing	1,700,000	20,000 tests	85.00 per test
Material receipts	1,000,000	5,000 receipts	200.00 per receipt
Parts administration	350,000	700 part numbers	500.00 per part no.
General factory	2,000,000	1,000,000 MHs	2.00 per MH

Computation of the Overhead Cost per Unit of Product

Activities and Activity Rates	DVD Units		CD Units	
	Expected Activity Volume	Amount	Expected Activity Volume	Amount
Labour related, at $1.60 per DLH...........	100,000 DLH	$ 160,000	400,000 DLH	$ 640,000
Machine related, at $2.10 per MH	300,000 MH	630,000	700,000 MH	1,470,000
Machine setups, at $400 per setup	3,000 setups	1,200,000	1,000 setups	400,000
Production orders, at $375 per order........	400 orders	150,000	800 orders	300,000
Product testing, at $85 per test	16,000 tests	1,360,000	4,000 tests	340,000
Materials receipts, at $200 per receipt	1,800 receipts	360,000	3,200 receipts	640,000
Parts administration, at $500 per part no.	400 part nos.	200,000	300 part nos.	150,000
General factory, at $2.00 per MH	300,000 MH	600,000	700,000 MH	1,400,000
Total overhead costs assigned (a)		$4,660,000		$5,340,000
Number of units produced (b).............		50,000		200,000
Overhead cost per unit (a) ÷ (b)...........		$93.20		$26.70

Computing Product Costs

Once the activity rates were determined, it was then an easy matter to compute the overhead cost that would be allocated to each product. (See the bottom panel of Exhibit 6–4.) For example, the amount of machine setup cost allocated to DVD units was determined by multiplying the activity rate of $400 per setup by the 3,000 expected setups for DVD units during the year. This yielded a total of $1,200,000 in machine setup costs to be assigned to the DVD units.

Observe from the exhibit that the use of an activity approach has resulted in $93.20 in overhead cost being assigned to each DVD unit and $26.70 to each CD unit. The ABC team then used these amounts to determine unit product costs under activity-based costing, as presented in the table below. For comparison, the table also shows the unit costs derived earlier when direct labour was used as the base for assigning overhead costs to the products.

	Activity-Based Costing		Direct Labour-Based Costing	
	DVD Units	**CD Units**	**DVD Units**	**CD Units**
Direct materials..........	$ 90.00	$50.00	$ 90.00	$ 50.00
Direct labour.............	20.00	20.00	20.00	20.00
Manufacturing overhead...	93.20	26.70	40.00	40.00
Unit product cost.........	$203.20	$96.70	$150.00	$110.00

The ABC team members were shocked by their findings, which Tom Frazier summarized as follows in the team's report:

> In the past, the company has been charging $40 in overhead cost per DVD and CD product, whereas it should have been charging $93.20 in overhead cost to each DVD unit and only $26.70 to each CD unit. Thus, as a result of using direct labour as the base for overhead costing, unit product costs had been badly distorted. The company may even have been suffering a loss on the DVD units without knowing it because the cost of these units has been so vastly understated. Through activity-based costing, we have been able to better identify the overhead costs of each product and thus derive more accurate cost data.

The pattern of cost distortion shown by the ABC team's findings is quite common. Such distortion can happen in any company that relies on a single allocation base in assigning overhead cost to products, ignoring other significant factors affecting overhead cost incurrence. When a company implements activity-based costing, overhead cost often shifts from high-volume products to low-volume products, with a higher unit product cost resulting for the low-volume products. This results from the existence of batch-level and product-level costs, which do not vary with the number of units produced.

The ABC team presented the results of its work in a meeting attended by all of the top managers of Comtek Sound including the president, Sarah Kastler; the production manager, Frank Hines; the marketing manager, Nicole Sermone; and the accounting manager, Tom Frazier. After the formal presentation by the ABC team, the following discussion took place:

Sarah: I would like to personally thank the ABC team for all the work they have done. I am now beginning to wonder about some of the decisions we have made in the past using our old cost accounting system.

Nicole: It's obvious from this ABC information that we had everything backwards. We thought the competition was pricing below cost on the CD units, but in fact, *we* were overcharging for these units because our costs were overstated. And, we thought the competition was overpricing DVD units, but in fact, *our* prices were way too low because our costs for these units were understated. I'll bet the competition has really been laughing behind our backs!

Sarah: You can bet they won't be laughing when they see our next bids.

Activity-Based Costing in Nonmanufacturing Organizations

Although initially developed as a tool for computing product costs in manufacturing companies, activity-based costing is now also being used to assign their marketing and administrative costs to desired cost objects. For example, many companies assign marketing costs to different customer groups to analyze customer profitability. Activity-based costing has also been implemented by various service organizations, such as banks, hospitals, cities, and data service companies. Successful implementation of an activity-based costing system depends on identifying the key activities that generate costs and tracking how many of those activities are performed for each service the organization provides.

> **KNOW**
>
> CC8: Describe the use of ABC in nonmanufacturing organizations.

An Example of Using Activity-Based Costing in a Bank[1]

RBC Royal Bank, the largest bank in Canada, uses activity-based costing to assign its costs to various cost objects such as products, customers, distribution channels, and regions. An example of a product is a mortgage. RBC Royal Bank offers mortgage financing to clients through a variety of channels, including its bank branches. Exhibit 6-5 maps the branch activities involved in approving a mortgage for a client. The mortgage approval process consists mainly of three activities:

- Delivering financial advice to the client—Branch staff discuss mortgage options with clients, such as interest rates, amortization, payment frequency, insurance, etc.
- Application process—Mortgage applications are prepared and analyzed by branch staff. If the application scores within their authorities, they can approve or decline at that point. If it is beyond their authority, then the application would be sent to a centralized credit adjudication group to determine the creditworthiness of the client, deciding whether the mortgage should be approved or declined. Branch staff performs verification and due diligence.
- Fulfilment—Applications are forwarded to a processing centre for processing and funding.

An additional task found in the Application process activity—contacting the client—may be involved in the process if errors or omissions are detected during the mortgage processing activity (this is essentially a quality problem and necessitates rework, which consists of obtaining the required information from the client).

Exhibit 6-6 lists the activities using the hierarchy of activities described previously, the resource requirements for each activity, the allocation basis, and the amount allocated to the service provided (i.e., mortgage). Notice that all three activities listed in Exhibit 6-6 are unit-level activities; mortgages cannot be processed in batches. Regardless of the fact that all the activities are unit-based, costs are assigned using three different allocation bases (and not one like in a traditional costing system). Doing so enhances the accuracy of cost allocation. All activity cost pools consist of salaries, premises, computer equipment, and other costs for branch staff.

In addition to the amounts shown in Exhibit 6-6, the following costs are also directly assigned to the product (mostly product-specific costs):

- Business development costs—Marketing and advertising costs:
  - Costs of specific mortgage-related advertisements are directly traced to the product.

---

[1]The authors would like to thank RBC Financial Group for its assistance in providing this example. All the numbers presented in the example are fictitious.

Exhibit 6–5
Activities Involved in Mortgage Approval Process

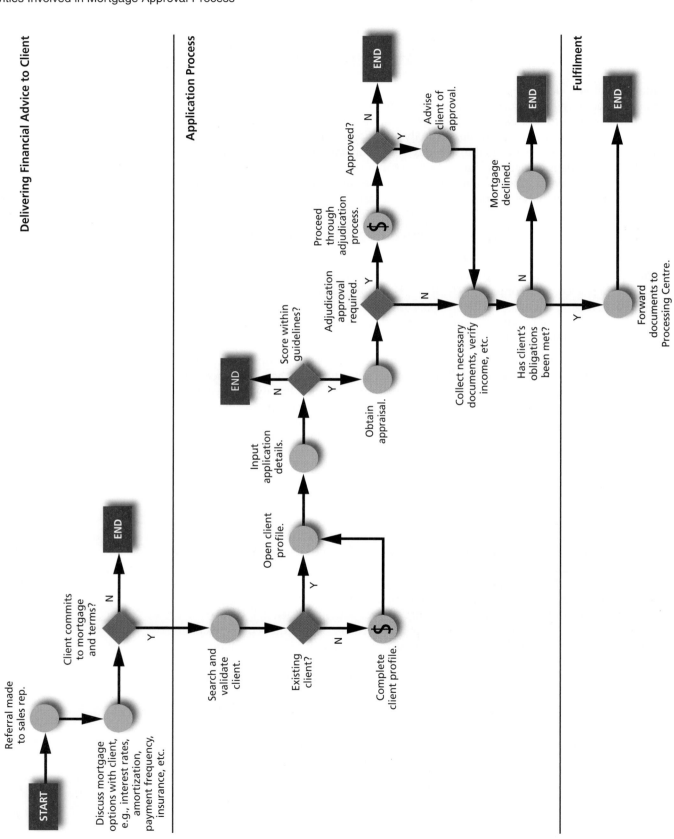

Activity hierarchy	Activity	Resource(s) required	Allocation basis	Amount allocated
Unit-level	Delivering financial advice to client	Branch labour (personal banker)	Time	$50,000
Unit-level	Application Process	Branch labour (personal banker)	Time	31,500
Unit-level	Fulfilment	Branch labour (personal banker)	Time	10,000
				$91,500

Exhibit 6–6
Activities and Costs for Mortgages Processed in a Quarter

- Costs of general advertisements are allocated on the basis of product mix (percentage of product mix represented by each product).
- Corporate overhead costs – allocated on the basis of the operating expenses assigned to the product.

Suppose the product-specific level costs assigned to mortgages during the quarter amount to $51,500, and that 250 mortgages were processed. The total (full) costs of $143,000 ($91,500 + $51,500) are then divided by the number of mortgages processed to compute the average unit cost per mortgage; in this case, it amounts to $572 per mortgage.

Unlike in manufacturing where it is easy to measure activity volume (e.g., machine-hours, number of setups), it may not be easy to accurately record the time that branch employees spend in carrying out each activity (such as client interviews). In such situations, employees are surveyed to determine the portion of the time that they spend on different activities (e.g., 15% on client interviews) during a representative 37.5-hour week. This information is then used to assign employee costs to activities.

RBC devotes considerable resources to accurately collecting activity cost information, which management uses to assign costs to different cost objects, conduct profitability analyses, and make decisions to increase efficiencies and reduce costs. For example, managers can compare the unit cost of $572 to industry data to know how they rank compared to competing financial institutions. Once they know, they can initiate improvement processes, such as total quality management or process re-engineering, to increase efficiencies and decrease errors, thereby reducing costs.

Evaluating Activity-Based Costing

Although the prior discussion of activity-based costing appears to suggest that it might be a useful tool for managers, it is important to examine ABC in greater detail, along with its potential limitations.

◔ **KNOW**

CC9: Explain the benefits and limitations of ABC.

Benefits of Activity-Based Costing

There are at least three different benefits of implementing an activity-based costing system, as shown following.

ACCURATE COSTING   The initial purpose of implementing an activity-based costing system was to improve the accuracy of costs assigned to cost objects (say, product costs). ABC improves the accuracy of product costs in three ways. First, it usually accumulates overhead costs in multiple activity cost pools, which represent the major activities instead of just one or two pools. As a result, the allocation is based on a better matching of the consumption of resources by cost objects.

Second, the activity cost pools are more homogeneous than departmental cost pools. In principle, all of the costs in a single activity cost pool pertain to a single activity. In the event that multiple activities are grouped in a single cost pool, these activities are usually related and, therefore, homogeneous. In contrast, departmental cost pools contain costs of many different activities carried out in a department.

Third, ABC does not rely just on *volume-based* allocation bases (such as direct labour-hours or machine-hours) to assign overhead. Instead, managers use a combination of *volume-based* and *non–volume-based* activity measures to assign overhead costs to cost objects. The non–volume-based activity measures include the batch-level and product-level activity measures illustrated previously in the chapter. The focus of ABC is to identify the activities or factors that cause or drive costs and use them as allocation bases. In doing so, the system attempts to establish a *cause-effect* relationship between the overhead costs and the allocation bases.

COST ESTIMATION   Increased accuracy in overhead allocation means that companies can do a better job of estimating costs. In today's competitive world, many companies are finding that they have less flexibility in setting their prices; they are largely market driven. Consequently, managers in these companies must identify a target cost, which they can work toward to generate a desired profit margin. Activity-based costing can be a valuable tool in providing relevant cost information to managers in identifying the target costs and also in monitoring a company's progress toward achieving the target costs. It can also help in estimating costs related to quality. See Appendix 6A on the Online Learning Centre at www.mcgrawhill.ca/olc/brewer.

ACTIVITY-BASED MANAGEMENT   An important benefit from using ABC is that it allows managers to identify activities that would benefit from improvement, thereby resulting in greater efficiency and lower costs. Indeed, this is the most widely cited benefit of activity-based costing by managers.[2] When used in this manner, it is often called *activity-based management*. Essentially, **activity-based management (ABM)** involves focusing on activities to eliminate waste. In other words, ABM is a tool that can supplement management practices, such as total quality management and process re-engineering described in Chapter 1.

The first step in any improvement program is to decide what to improve. The theory of constraints (TOC) approach discussed in Chapter 1 is a powerful tool for targeting the area

---

IN BUSINESS TODAY   **ABM in the Service Industry**

Reducing the costs to serve clients is a prime objective when using ABM. Mutual Life of Canada decided to use ABM to improve its understanding of the costs of its shared services which provide valuable service to internal customers (departments), such as finance, corporate affairs, strategic development, and human resources. Prior to the implementation, the shared services function for the retail insurance company accounted for one-third of total non–sales-related costs. In addition, many of the internal customers questioned the cost-benefit of the shared services. Mutual Life went through an activity identification process and then mapped those activities to products provided: for example, mapping payroll activity to the payroll product. But more detail was required. ABM revealed where activities could be combined, eliminated, or outsourced. As a result of the ABM effort, service-level agreements were set up with internal customers, along with monthly invoices to bill back to business units for services provided.

Source: Content adapted from: Tad Leahy, "Beyond Traditional Product Costing," *Business Finance Magazine*, 2003.

---

[2] D. Swenson, "The Benefits of Activity-Based Cost Management to the Manufacturing Industry," *Journal of Management Accounting Research* 7, Fall 1995, pp. 167–80.

in an organization whose improvement will yield the greatest benefit. An ABC system can provide valuable information. For example, Comtek's managers may wonder why it costs $375, on average, to process a purchase order (see Exhibit 6–4). Such a question arises when organizations decide on **benchmarking** their costs against the costs of similar organizations known for their outstanding performance. Once the activity is targeted for improvement, managers can use the ABM approach to study the activity in greater detail and identifying ways to eliminate the wasteful consumption of resources. Some activities that are deemed to not add any value are targeted for elimination. However, managers must be careful to ensure that eliminating a certain activity does not negatively impact other activities.

Benchmarking Beyond Borders   IN BUSINESS TODAY

Molson Inc. completed an intensive five-month global benchmarking study in December 2001 to measure its corporate performance globally against other brewers. Areas that were measured included packaging line productivity, maintenance costs, utilities consumption, and product shrinkage. The company's representatives examined over 20 manufacturing facilities and compared its performance with that of eight global brewers. In order to be "the best in its class around the world," Molson had to significantly reduce costs and identified that it could potentially save $50 million, as follows:

- $18 million by reducing maintenance costs,
- $14 million by improving bottling line productivity, and
- $9 million each by lowering utilities consumption and reducing shrinkage.

Source: 2002 Annual Report, available at http://www.sedar.com.

Limitations of Activity-Based Costing

Any discussion of activity-based costing is incomplete without some cautionary warnings. First, the cost of implementing and maintaining an ABC system may outweigh the benefits. Second, it would be naïve to assume that product costs provided even by an activity-based costing are always relevant when making decisions. These limitations are discussed following.

THE COST OF IMPLEMENTING ACTIVITY-BASED COSTING   Implementing ABC is a major project that involves a great deal of effort. First, the cost system must be designed—preferably—by a cross-functional team. This requires taking valued employees away from other tasks for a major project. In addition, the data used in the ABC system must be collected and verified. In some cases, this requires collecting data that have never been collected before. In short, implementing and maintaining an ABC system can present a formidable challenge, and management may decide that the costs are too great to justify the expected benefits. Nevertheless, keep in mind that the costs of collecting and processing data have dropped dramatically over the last several decades due to bar coding and other technologies, and these costs can be expected to continue to fall.

When are the benefits of activity-based costing most likely to be worth the cost? Companies that have some of the following characteristics are most likely to benefit from ABC:

1. Products differ substantially in volume, lot size, and in the activities they require.
2. Conditions have changed substantially since the existing cost system was established.
3. Overhead costs are high and increasing, and no one seems to understand why.
4. Management does not trust the existing cost system and ignores cost data from the system when making decisions.

LIMITATIONS OF THE ABC MODEL   The ABC model relies on a number of critical assumptions. Perhaps the most important of these assumptions is that the cost in each activity cost pool is strictly proportional to its activity measure. The issue of whether overhead costs are proportional to the driver is of universal concern. What little evidence we have on this issue suggests that overhead costs are less than proportional to activity.[3] As a practical matter, this means that product costs will be overstated for the purposes of making decisions. The product costs generated by activity-based costing are almost certainly more accurate than those generated by a conventional costing system, but the product costs should nevertheless be viewed with caution. Managers should be particularly alert to product costs that contain allocations of facility-level costs. As we shall see later in the text, such product costs can easily lead managers astray in decisions.

MODIFYING THE ABC MODEL   The discussion in this chapter has assumed that the primary purpose of the ABC system is to provide more accurate product costs for inventory valuation in external reports. If the product costs are to be used by managers for internal decisions, some modifications should be made. For example, for decision-making purposes, the distinction between manufacturing costs on the one hand and selling and general administrative expenses on the other hand is unimportant. Managers need to know what costs a product causes, and it does not matter whether the costs are manufacturing costs or selling and general administrative expenses. Consequently, for decision-making purposes, some selling and general administrative expenses should be assigned to products. Moreover, as mentioned previously, facility-level costs should be removed from product costs when making decisions. Nevertheless, the techniques covered in this chapter provide a good basis for understanding the mechanics of activity-based costing. For a more complete coverage of the use of ABC in decisions, see more advanced texts.

IN BUSINESS TODAY   ## And the Surveys Say ...

What methods do companies use to compute product costs? To allocate overhead? Surveys reveal mixed results. A survey of about 2,000 U.S. organizations conducted jointly by Ernst & Young and the Institute of Management Accounts revealed that 76% of the responding organizations use full absorption costing and that 70% use direct labour as the base to allocate overhead, thereby, revealing the potentially limited use of activity-based costing (ABC). However, other surveys provide slightly different results. In their survey of 85 Fortune 500 corporations in the U.S., researchers Kiani and Sangeladji found that over 51% of the respondents used ABC, although less than 10% had used it for over five years. Similarly, another survey of organizations in India revealed that 48% of the manufacturing and 79% of the nonmanufacturing firms used activity-based costing.

Sources: The State of Management Accounting: The Ernst & Young and IMA Survey (2003); R. Kiani and M. Sangeladji (2003), "An Empirical Study About the Use of the ABC/ABM Models by Some of the Fortune 500 Largest Industrial Corporations in the USA," *Journal of American Academy of Business*, Vol. 3, ½, pp. 174–82; R. Cable, C. Li and P. Healy (2006), "An Investigation into the Management Accounting Tools in India," in A. Neely, M. Kennerley and A. Walters (eds.), *Performance Measurement and Management 2006: Public and Private*, Conference Proceedings, pp. 139–46.

YOU DECIDE   ## Entrepreneur

You are the owner of a small manufacturing firm. You are implementing a cost accounting system and wondering whether you should use direct labour as the base for assigning overhead or implement activity-based costing. How would you go about making this decision?

---

[3]Eric Noreen and Naomi Soderstrom, "The Accuracy of Proportional Cost Models: Evidence from Hospital Service Departments," *Review of Accounting Studies* 2, 1997; and Eric Noreen and Naomi Soderstrom, "Are Overhead Costs Proportional to Activity? Evidence from Hospital Service Departments," *Journal of Accounting and Economics*, January 1994, pp. 253–278.

City Controller

You are the controller of your city office. The managers responsible for utilities and property taxes have complained to you regarding the charges from support services departments, such as information systems and maintenance. The city recently decided to "charge" the internal users of support services an "appropriate" amount to reflect the cost of these services. After meeting with the cost analyst for the city, you discover that the city uses a single "citywide" rate to allocate overhead costs. You are puzzled because you know that the support services departments are quite different from one another and that it does not make sense to combine the overhead costs into one single pool. How do you proceed to resolve the issue?

Application Competency Summary

Application Competency	Deliverable	Source Documents and Key Information	Steps	Knowledge Competency
Design an ABC system. CC5	*Key Information* Activities Costs assigned to individual activities Activity cost rates *Report/Document* No specific document	*Work Flow Chart* Work flow *Interview Transcripts* Notes from interviews regarding work done and activities	1. Identify activities and prepare an activity dictionary. 2. Identify activities as unit, batch, product, and facility-level activities. 3. Identify the appropriate activity measure (allocation base) for each activity.	
Compute activity rates used to allocate costs to cost objects. CC6	*Key Information* Activity cost rates *Report/Document* No specific document	*Annual Budget Documents* Budgeted activity costs Budgeted activity volume for each activity measure	1. Assign costs to individual activities. 2. Estimate the activity volume for the corresponding activity measure. 3. Divide activity costs by the activity volume to determine the activity cost rate.	Basic approach underlying ABC CC2 Unit, batch, product, facility-level classification of activities CC3, 4
Assign activity costs to cost objects, and compute unit costs. CC7	*Key Information* Total activity costs assigned to individual cost objects Cost per unit of individual cost objects *Report/Document* Product cost report	*Activity Consumption Report* Activity rates Activity volume consumed by individual cost objects Volume of the cost object (e.g., production volume)	1. Identify the activity volume consumed by individual cost objects (e.g., individual products). 2. Multiply the activity volume for each cost object by the corresponding activity cost rate to determine the total activity costs assigned to each cost object. 3. Divide total activity costs by the volume of the cost object (e.g., production volume) to determine the cost per unit of the cost object.	

Guidance Answers to You Decide and Decision Maker

ENTREPRENEUR (p. 236)

You are a small firm, which likely means that your overhead costs are less complex than those of a large firm. However, your firm's overhead may still account for a significant portion of your total costs. This, in itself, may require you to think twice about using a plantwide overhead rate. You must also consider the diversity of your product line and whether individual products consume overhead resources differently. If your products are diverse, using a plantwide overhead rate can lead to product cost distortions. Moreover, regularly adding new products will increase your overhead costs. It is perhaps best for you to implement an ABC system that allows the flexibility of adding new overhead cost items and activity measures, as needed. Of course, implementing such a system will be initially expensive because you may not fully use the system. Therefore, you must carefully weigh all the factors before implementing a system (once implemented, it may take extra effort to change).

CITY CONTROLLER (p. 237)

You already took the first step by talking to the cost analyst. Your next step is to put together a small four- to six-person team consisting of individuals from support services, user departments, and the cost accounting department. You should instruct the team to do a special overhead cost accounting project consisting of at least three major steps: (1) compiling a list of overhead cost items and the factors that cause them, (2) analyzing the data to identify appropriate allocation bases, and (3) testing the system by applying it to one user department. Whether you implement ABC citywide will depend on such issues as cost-benefit and behavioural consequences of the new system.

Review Problem: Activity-Based Costing

Fine Deck, Inc. manufactures and sells two types of wooden deck chairs: Deluxe and Tourist. Annual sales in units, direct labour-hours (DLHs) per unit, and total direct labour-hours per year are provided below:

	Total Hours
Deluxe deck chair: 2,000 units × 5 DLHs per unit..............	10,000
Tourist deck chair: 10,000 units × 4 DLHs per unit.............	40,000
Total DLHs	50,000

Costs for materials and labour for one unit of each product are given below:

	Deluxe	Tourist
Direct materials	$25	$17
Direct labour (at $12 per DLH)...........	60	48

Manufacturing overhead costs total $800,000 each year. The breakdown of these costs among the company's six activity cost pools is given below. The activity measures are shown in parentheses.

Activities and Activity Measures	Estimated Overhead Cost	Expected Activity		
		Deluxe	Tourist	Total
Labour related (DLHs)	$ 80,000	10,000	40,000	50,000
Machine setups (number of setups)	150,000	3,000	2,000	5,000
Parts administration (number of parts)..........	160,000	50	30	80
Production orders (number of orders)...........	70,000	100	300	400
Material receipts (number of receipts)	90,000	50	600	750
Generalfactory (machine-hours)...............	250,000	12,000	28,000	40,000
	$800,000			

Required:
1. Classify each of Fine Deck's activities as either unit-level, batch-level, product-level, or facility-level.
2. Assume that the company applies overhead cost to products on the basis of direct labour-hours.
   a. Compute the predetermined overhead rate that would be used.
   b. Determine the unit product cost of each product, using the predetermined overhead rate computed in (2)(a).
3. Assume that the company uses ABC to compute overhead rates.
   a. Compute the activity rate (i.e., predetermined overhead rate) for each of the six activity centres listed above.
   b. Using the rates developed in (3)(a), determine the amount of overhead cost that would be assigned to a unit of each product.
   c. Determine the unit product cost of each product and compare this cost with the cost computed in (2)(b).

SOLUTION TO REVIEW PROBLEM

1.

Activity Cost Pool	Type of Activity
Labour related..............................	Unit level
Machine setups.............................	Batch level
Parts administration	Product level
Production orders	Batch level
Material receipts..........................	Batch level
General factory...........................	Facility level

2. a.

$$\text{Predetermined overhead rate} = \frac{\text{Estimated total manufacturing overhead}}{\text{Estimated total direct labour-hours (DLHs)}} = \frac{\$800,000}{50,000 \text{ DLHs}} = \$16 \text{ per DLH}$$

b.

	Deluxe	Tourist
Direct materials......................	$ 25	$ 17
Direct labour........................	60	48
Manufacturing overhead applied:		
Deluxe: 5 DLHs × $16 per DLH......	80	
Tourist: 4 DLHs × $16 per DLH		64
Unit product cost....................	$165	$129

3. a.

Activities	(a) Estimated Overhead Cost	(b) Total Expected Activity	(a) ÷ (b) Activity Rate
Labour related..................	$ 80,000	50,000 DLHs	$1.60 per DLH
Machine setups	150,000	5,000 setups	$30.00 per setup
Parts administration	160,000	80 parts	$2,000.00 per part
Production orders	70,000	400 orders	$175.00 per order
Material receipts	90,000	750 receipts	$120.00 per receipt
General factory	250,000	40,000 MHs	$6.25 per MH

b.

Activities and Activity Rates	Deluxe Expected Activity	Deluxe Amount	Tourist Expected Activity	Tourist Amount
Labour related, at $1.60 per DLH............	10,000	$ 16,000	40,000	$ 64,000
Machine setups, at $30 per setup	3,000	90,000	2,000	60,000
Parts administration, at $2,000 per part	50	100,000	30	60,000
Production orders, at $175 per order.........	100	17,500	300	52,500
Material receipts, at $120 per receipt	150	18,000	600	72,000
General factory, at $6.25 per MH............	12,000	75,000	28,000	175,000
Total overhead cost assigned (a)............		$316,500		$483,500
Number of units produced (b)..............		2,000		10,000
Overhead cost per unit, (a) ÷ (b)		$158.25		$48.35

c.

	Deluxe	Tourist
Direct materials.....................	$ 25.00	$ 17.00
Direct labour......................	60.00	48.00
Manufacturing overhead (see above)	158.25	48.35
Unit product cost...................	$243.25	$113.35

Under ABC, the unit product cost of the Deluxe deck chair is much greater than the cost computed in (2)(b), and the unit product cost of the Tourist deck chair is much less. Using volume (direct labour-hours) in (2)(b) as a basis for applying overhead cost to products has resulted in too little overhead cost being applied to the Deluxe deck chair (the low-volume product) and too much overhead cost being applied to the Tourist deck chair (the high-volume product).

Glossary

Activity An event that causes the consumption of overhead resources in an organization. (p. 221)
Activity-based costing (ABC) A two-stage costing method in which overhead costs are assigned to products on the basis of the activities they require. (p. 221)
Activity-based management (ABM) A management approach that focuses on managing activities as a way of eliminating waste and reducing delays and defects. (p. 234)
Activity cost pool A "bucket" in which costs are accumulated that relate to a single activity in the activity-based costing system. (p. 222)
Activity measure An allocation base in an activity-based costing system; ideally, a measure of whatever causes the costs in an activity cost pool. (p. 222)
Activity rate A predetermined overhead rate in activity-based costing. Each activity cost pool has its own activity rate which is used to apply overhead to products and services. (p. 222)
Batch-level activities Activities that are performed each time a batch of goods is handled or processed, regardless of how many units are in a batch. The amount of resources consumed depends on the number of batches run, rather than on the number of units in the batch. (p. 223)
Benchmarking A systematic approach to identifying the activities with the greatest room for improvement. It is based on comparing the performance in an organization with the performance of other, similar organizations known for their outstanding performance. (p. 235)
Facility-level activities Activities that relate to overall production and therefore cannot be traced to specific products. Costs associated with these activities pertain to a plant's general manufacturing process. (p. 224)
Product-level activities Activities that relate to specific products that must be carried out regardless of how many units are produced and sold or batches run. (p. 223)
Unit-level activities Activities that arise as a result of the total volume of goods and services that are produced and that are performed each time a unit is produced. (p. 223)

Questions

6–1 What are the three common approaches for assigning overhead costs to products?
6–2 Why is ABC growing in popularity?
6–3 Why do departmental overhead rates sometimes result in inaccurate product costs?
6–4 What are the four hierarchical levels of activity discussed in the chapter?
6–5 Why is ABC described as a "two-stage" costing method?
6–6 Why do overhead costs often shift from high-volume products to low-volume products when a company switches from a traditional costing method to ABC?
6–7 What are the three major ways in which ABC improves the accuracy of product costs?
6–8 What are the major limitations of ABC?

Brief Exercises

BRIEF EXERCISE 6–1   ABC Cost Hierarchy (CC3, 4)
The following activities occur at Greenwich Corporation, a company that manufactures a variety of products.
a. Receive raw materials from suppliers.
b. Manage parts inventories.
c. Do rough milling work on products.
d. Interview and process new employees in the human resources department.
e. Design new products.
f. Perform periodic preventative maintenance on general-use equipment.
g. Use the general factory building.
h. Issue purchase orders for a job.

Required:
Classify each of the activities as a unit-level, batch-level, product-level, or facility-level cost activity.

BRIEF EXERCISE 6–2   Compute Activity Rates (CC1, 6)
Kramer Corporation is a diversified manufacturer of consumer goods. The company's activity-based costing system has the following seven activity cost pools:

Activity Cost Pool	Estimated Overhead Cost	Expected Activity
Labour related.............	$ 48,000	20,000 direct labour-hours
Machine related............	67,500	45,000 machine-hours
Machine setups	84,000	600 setups
Production orders	112,000	400 orders
Product testing	58,500	900 tests
Packaging	90,000	6,000 packages
General factory	672,000	20,000 direct labour-hours

Required:
1. Compute the activity rate for each activity cost pool.
2. Compute the company's predetermined overhead rate, assuming that the company uses a single plantwide predetermined overhead rate based on direct labour-hours.

BRIEF EXERCISE 6–3   Compute ABC Product Costs (CC2, 5, 6, 7)
Klumper Corporation is a diversified manufacturer of industrial goods. The company's ABC system has the following six activity cost pools and activity rates:

Activity Cost Pool	Activity Rates
Labour related.....................	$ 12.00 per direct labour-hour
Machine related	8.00 per machine-hour

continued

Machine setups	100.00 per setup
Production orders	180.00 per order
Shipments	28.00 per shipment
General factory	18.00 per direct labour-hour

Cost and activity data have been supplied for the following products:

	K425	M67
Direct materials cost per unit	$26.00	$112.00
Direct labour cost per unit	$11.20	$7.00
Number of units produced per year	400	4,000

	Total Expected Activity	
	K425	M67
Direct labour-hours	160	1,000
Machine-hours	200	3,000
Machine setups	2	8
Production orders	2	8
Shipments	2	20

Required:
Compute the unit product cost of each of the products listed above.

BRIEF EXERCISE 6–4   Contrast ABC and Traditional Product Costs (CC2, 5, 6, 7)
Midwest Industrial Products Corporation makes two products, Product H and Product L. Product H is expected to sell 50,000 units next year and Product L is expected to sell 10,000 units. A unit of either product requires 0.2 direct labour-hours.
    The company's total manufacturing overhead for the year is expected to be $1,920,000.

Required:
1. The company currently applies manufacturing overhead to products using direct labour-hours as the allocation base. If this method is followed, how much overhead cost would be applied to each product? Compute both the overhead cost per unit and the total amount of overhead cost that would be applied to each product. (In other words, how much overhead cost is applied to a unit of Product H? Product L? How much overhead cost is applied in total to all the units of Product H? Product L?)
2. Management is considering an activity-based costing system and would like to know what impact this change might have on product costs. For purposes of discussion, it has been suggested that all of the manufacturing overhead be treated as a product-level cost. The total manufacturing overhead would be divided in half between the two products, with $960,000 assigned to Product H and $960,000 assigned to Product L.
       If this suggestion is followed, how much overhead cost per unit would be applied to each product?
3. Explain the impact on unit product costs of the switch in costing systems.

Exercises

EXERCISE 6–1   ABC Cost Hierarchy (CC2, 3, 4, 5)
The following activities are carried out in Greenberry Company, a manufacturer of consumer goods.
a. Direct labour workers assemble a product.
b. Engineers design a new product.
c. A machine is set up to process a batch.
d. Numerically controlled machines cut and shape materials.
e. The HR department trains new employees concerning company policies.
f. Raw materials are moved from the receiving dock to the production line.
g. A random sample of 10 units is inspected for defects in each batch.

Required:
1. Classify each activity as a unit-level, batch-level, product-level, or facility-level cost.
2. Provide at least one example of an allocation base (i.e., activity measure) that could be used to allocate the cost of each activity listed above.

EXERCISE 6–2   Contrast ABC and Traditional Product Costs (CC1, 2, 6, 7)

Harrison Company makes two products and uses a conventional costing system in which a single plant-wide predetermined overhead rate is computed based on direct labour-hours. Data for the two products for the upcoming year follow:

	Rascon	Parcel
Direct materials cost per unit	$19.50	$33.00
Direct labour cost per unit	$9.00	$4.50
Direct labour-hours per unit	0.60	0.30
Number of units produced	30,000	120,000

These products are customized to some degree for specific customers.

Required:
1. The company's manufacturing overhead costs for the year are expected to be $864,000. Using the company's traditional costing system, compute the unit product costs for the two products.
2. Management is considering an ABC system in which half of the overhead would continue to be allocated on the basis of direct labour-hours and half would be allocated on the basis of engineering design time. This time is expected to be distributed as follows during the upcoming year:

	Rascon	Parcel	Total
Engineering design time (in hours).	4,500	4,500	9,000

Compute the unit product costs for the two products using the proposed ABC system.

3. Explain why the product costs differ between the two systems.

EXERCISE 6–3   Computing Activity Rates and Assigning Activity Costs (CC6, 7, 10, 11)

Sylvan Company uses activity-based costing to determine product costs for external financial reports. Some of the entries have been completed to the Manufacturing Overhead account for the current year, as shown by entry (a) below:

Manufacturing Overhead

(a) 1,302,000	

Required:
1. What does entry (a) represent?
2. At the beginning of the year, the company made the following estimates of cost and activity for its five activity cost pools:

Activity Cost Pool	Activity Measure	Estimated Overhead Cost	Expected Activity
Labour related.	Direct labour-hours	$280,000	40,000 DLHs
Purchase orders.	Number of orders	90,000	1,500 orders
Parts management. . . .	Number of part types	120,000	400 part types
Board etching	Number of boards	360,000	2,000 boards
General factory	Machine-hours	400,000	80,000 MHss

Compute the activity rate (i.e., predetermined overhead rate) for each of the activity cost pools.

3. During the year, actual activity was recorded as follows:

Activity Cost Pool	Actual Activity
Labour related...........	41,000 DLHs
Purchase orders..........	1,300 orders
Parts management........	420 part types
Board etching...........	2,150 boards
General factory..........	82,000 MHs

Determine the amount of manufacturing overhead cost applied to production for the year.
4. Determine the amount of under-applied or over-applied overhead cost for the year.

EXERCISE 6–4   Assigning Overhead to Products in ABC (CC7)

Refer to the data in Exercise 6–3 for Sylvan Company. The activities during the year were distributed across the company's four products as follows:

Activity Cost Pool	Actual Activity	Product A	Product B	Product C	Product D
Labour related....	41,000 DLHs	9,000	11,000	12,500	8,500
Purchase orders...	1,300 orders	100	300	400	500
Parts management	420 part types	30	85	190	115
Board etching	2,150 boards	300	1,200	650	–0–
General factory ...	82,000 MHs	16,000	24,000	30,000	12,000

Required:
Compute the amount of overhead cost applied to each product during the year.

EXERCISE 6–5   Activity-based Costing in Marketing and Sales (CC1, 2, 6, 7, 8)

Kramer Corporation is an office supplier dealing in a number of different products. It currently allocates its ordering and delivery costs to its residential and business customer groups on the basis of order value. However, the company has recently decided to implement activity-based costing starting in 2009 to assign these costs to customers. Key data for 2008 are as follows:

Activity	Activity Cost	Activity Base	Activity Volume Residential	Activity Volume Business	Total Activity Volume
Sales (order value)			$2,600,000	$2,000,000	$4,600,000
Order processing	$ 480,000	# of orders	8,000	2,000	10,000
Getting sales	1,000,000	# of sales calls	1,000	4,000	5,000
Sales follow-up	540,000	# of follow-ups	100	500	600
Processing change orders	120,000	# of change orders	200	100	300
Delivery	850,000	# of deliveries	8,000	2,000	10,000

Kramer has 2,000 residential customers and 500 business customers.

Required:
1. Compute the cost per customer for residential and business customers for 2008, using the current system of cost allocation.
2. Assume that the 2008 data will hold for 2009. Compute the cost per customer for residential and business customers for 2009, using the proposed system of cost allocation. In doing so, compute the overhead allocation rate for each activity, and use these rates to assign costs to the two customer groups.
3. Explain the difference between the two cost allocation systems.

EXERCISE 6–6   Assigning Overhead Cost to Products in ABC (CC5, 6, 7)

PoseiDon Inc. (PDI) recently started operations to obtain a share of the growing golfing market. PDI manufactures two models of specialty drivers: the Thunderbolt model and the Earthquake model. The company was formed as a partnership by two professional engineers and a professional golfer, none of whom had any accounting experience. The business has been very successful, and to cope with the increased level of activity, the partners have hired a professional accountant as their controller. One of the first improvements that the controller wants to make is to update the costing system by changing from a single overhead application rate using direct labour-hours to activity-based costing. The controller has identified the following three activities as cost drivers, along with the related cost pools:

Model	Number of Materials Requisitions	Number of Product Inspections	Number of Orders Shipped
Thunderbolt	46	23	167
Earthquake	62	31	129
Total costs in the cost pool	$54,000	$8,200	$103,000

Required:
Using ABC, prepare a schedule that shows the allocation of the costs of each cost pool for each model. Show your calculations.

EXERCISE 6–7   ABC Overview (CC1, 2, 5, 6, 7, 9)
The following question is related to an ABC system.

Required:
1. Identify the four steps involved in an ABC system.
2. Identify *one* benefit of ABC compared with a traditional costing system.
3. Identify *one* limitation of ABC.

Problems

PROBLEM 6–1   ABC Cost Hierarchy (CC3, 4, 5)
Juneau Company manufactures a variety of products in a single facility. Consultants hired by the company to do an ABC analysis have identified the following activities carried out in the company on a routine basis:
a. Machines are set up between batches of different products.
b. The company's grounds crew maintains planted areas surrounding the factory.
c. A percentage of all completed goods are inspected on a random basis.
d. Milling machines are used to make components for products.
e. Employees are trained in general procedures.
f. Purchase orders are issued for materials required in production.
g. The maintenance crew does routine periodic maintenance on general-purpose equipment.
h. The plant controller prepares periodic accounting reports.
i. Material is received on the receiving dock and moved to the production area.
j. The engineering department makes modifications in the designs of products.
k. The human resources department screens and hires new employees.
l. Production orders are issued for jobs.

Required:
1. Classify each of the previous activities as a unit-level, batch-level, product-level, or facility-level activity.
2. For each of the above activities, suggest an activity measure that could be used to allocate its costs to products.

PROBLEM 6–2   Contrasting ABC and Traditional Product Costs (CC1, 5, 6, 7)
Siegel Corporation manufactures a product that is available in both a deluxe and a regular model. The company has made the regular model for years; the deluxe model was introduced several years ago to tap a new segment of the market. Since the introduction of the deluxe model, the company's profits have steadily declined, and management has become concerned about the accuracy of its costing system. Sales of the deluxe model have been increasing rapidly.

Overhead is applied to products on the basis of direct labour-hours. At the beginning of the current year, management estimated that $2,000,000 in overhead costs would be incurred and the company would produce and sell 5,000 units of the deluxe model, and 40,000 units of the regular model. The deluxe model

CHECK FIGURE
(3b) Regular: $152 per unit

requires 1.6 hours of direct labour time per unit, and the regular model requires 0.8 hours. Materials and labour costs per unit follow:

	Deluxe	Regular
Direct materials cost per unit	$150	$112
Direct labour cost per unit	16	8

Required:
1. Compute the predetermined overhead rate using direct labour-hours as the basis for allocating overhead costs to products. Compute the unit product cost for one unit of each model.
2. An intern suggested that the company use activity-based costing to cost its products. A team was formed to investigate this idea, and it came back with the recommendation that four activity cost pools be used. These cost pools and their associated activities follow:

Activity Cost Pool and Activity Measure	Estimated Overhead Cost	Activity		
		Deluxe	Regular	Total
Purchase orders (number of orders)	$ 84,000	400	800	1,200
Rework requests (number of requests) ...	216,000	300	600	900
Product testing (number of tests)	450,000	4,000	11,000	15,000
Machine-related (machine-hours).......	1,250,000	20,000	30,000	50,000
	$2,000,000			

Compute the activity rate (i.e., predetermined overhead rate) for each of the activity cost pools.
3. Assume that actual activity is as expected for the year. Using activity-based costing, do the following:
   a. Determine the total amount of overhead that would be applied to each model for the year.
   b. Compute the unit product cost for one unit of each model.
4. Can you identify a possible explanation for the company's declining profits? If so, what is it?

CHECK FIGURE
(2d) Total overhead over-applied: $22,500

PROBLEM 6–3   Unit Product Costs in ABC and Cost Flows (CC6, 7, 10[A], 11[A])
Hunter Corporation uses ABC to determine product costs for external financial reports. At the beginning of the year, management made the following cost and activity estimates in the company's five activity cost pools:

Activity Cost Pool	Activity Measure	Estimated Overhead Cost	Expected Activity
Labour related........	Direct labour-hours	$405,000	45,000 DLHs
Production orders	Number of orders	90,000	1,125 orders
Material receipts	Number of receipts	270,000	1,800 receipts
Relay assembly.......	Number of relays	480,000	12,000 relays
General factory	Machine-hours	1,260,000	90,000 MHs

Required:
1. Compute the activity rate (i.e., predetermined overhead rate) for each of the activity cost pools.
2. During the year, actual overhead cost and activity were recorded as follows:

Activity Cost Pool	Actual Overhead Cost	Actual Activity
Labour related	$ 418,500	48,000 DLHs
Production orders............	87,000	1,050 orders
Material receipts	285,000	1,950 receipts
Relay assembly	480,000	11,850 relays
General factory	1,270,500	91,500 MHs
Total overhead cost	$2,541,000	

a. Prepare a journal entry to record the incurrence of actual manufacturing overhead cost for the year (credit Accounts Payable). Post the entry to the company's manufacturing overhead T-account.
b. Determine the amount of overhead cost applied to production during the year.
c. Prepare a journal entry to record the application of manufacturing overhead cost to work in process for the year. Post the entry to the company's manufacturing overhead T-account.
d. Determine the amount of under-applied or over-applied manufacturing overhead for the year.

3. The actual activity for the year was distributed among the company's four products as follows:

Activity Cost Pool	Actual Activity	Product A	Product B	Product C	Product D
Labour related.........	48,000 DLHs	12,000	16,500	6,000	13,500
Production orders	1,050 orders	240	300	195	315
Materials receipts	1,950 receipts	150	690	360	750
Relay assembly........	11,850 relays	4,050	–0–	7,800	–0–
General factory........	91,500 MHs	19,500	27,000	21,000	24,000

a. Determine the total amount of overhead cost applied to each product.
b. Does the total amount of overhead cost applied to the products above tie in to the T-accounts in any way? Explain.

PROBLEM 6–4   Contrast Activity-Based Costing and Traditional Product Costs (CC1, 5, 6, 7)
Ellix Company manufactures two models of ultra-high-fidelity speakers, the X200 model and the X99 model. Data regarding the two products follow:

CHECK FIGURE
(2b) X200 unit product
cost: $213

	Direct Labour-Hours per Unit	Annual Production	Total Direct Labour-Hours
Model X200.........	1.8	5,000 units	9,000
Model X99..........	0.9	30,000 units	27,000
			36,000

Additional information about the company follows:
a. Model X200 requires $72 in direct materials per unit, and model X99 requires $50.
b. The direct labour wage rate is $10 per hour.
c. The company has always used direct labour-hours as the base for applying manufacturing overhead cost to products.
d. Model X200 is more complex to manufacture than model X99 and requires the use of special equipment. Consequently, the company is considering the use of activity-based costing to apply manufacturing overhead cost to products for external financial reports. Three activity cost pools have been identified as follows:

Activity Cost Pool	Activity Measure	Estimated Overhead Cost
Machine setups	Number of setups	$ 360,000
Special processing........	Machine-hours	180,000
General factory	Direct labour-hours	1,260,000
		$1,800,000

Activity Measure	Expected Activity		
	Model X200	Model X99	Total
Number of setups........	50	100	150
Machine-hours..........	12,000	–0–	12,000
Direct labour-hours	9,000	27,000	36,000

Required:

1. Assume that the company continues to use direct labour-hours as the base for applying overhead cost to products.
   a. Compute the predetermined overhead rate.
   b. Compute the unit product cost of each model.
2. Assume that the company decides to use activity-based costing to apply manufacturing overhead cost to products.
   a. Compute the predetermined overhead rate for each activity cost pool and determine the amount of overhead cost that would be applied to each model using the activity-based costing system.
   b. Compute the unit product cost of each model.
3. Explain why the manufacturing overhead cost shifts from Model X99 to Model X200 under activity-based costing.

CHECK FIGURE
(2d) Total overhead
under-applied:
$14,410

PROBLEM 6–5 Activity-Based Costing Cost Flows (CC6, 7, 10ᴬ, 11ᴬ)

Munoz Corporation uses ABC to determine product costs for external financial reports. At the beginning of the year, management made the following cost and activity estimates in the company's five activity cost pools:

Activity Cost Pool	Activity Measure	Estimated Overhead Cost	Expected Activity
Labour related......	Direct labour-hours	$178,500	29,750 DLHs
Purchase orders.....	Number of orders	61,200	765 orders
Product testing	Number of tests	142,800	1,190 tests
Template etching....	Number of templates	267,750	8,925 templates
General factory	Machine-hours	714,000	59,500 MHs

Required:

1. Compute the activity rate (i.e., predetermined overhead rate) for each of the activity cost pools.
2. During the year, actual overhead cost and activity were recorded as follows:

Activity Cost Pool	Actual Overhead Cost	Actual Activity
Labour related.....................	$ 174,250	27,200 DLHs
Purchase orders....................	62,900	808 orders
Product testing	136,000	1,105 tests
Template etching..................	287,300	9,775 templates
General factory	701,250	57,800 MHs
Total overhead cost................	$1,361,700	

   a. Prepare a journal entry to record the incurrence of actual manufacturing overhead cost for the year (credit Accounts Payable). Post the entry to the company's Manufacturing Overhead T-account.
   b. Determine the amount of overhead cost applied to production during the year.
   c. Prepare a journal entry to record the application of manufacturing overhead cost to work in process for the year. Post the entry to the company's Manufacturing Overhead T-account.
   d. Determine the amount of under-applied or over-applied manufacturing overhead for the year.
3. The actual activity for the year was distributed among the company's four products as follows:

Activity Cost Pool	Actual Activity	Product A	Product B	Product C	Product D
Labour related.......	27,200 DLHs	2,500	7,500	9,700	7,500
Purchase orders......	808 orders	150	200	148	310
Product testing	1,105 tests	315	125	165	500
Template etching.....	9,775 templates	–0–	4,500	–0–	5,275
General factory	57,800 MHs	7,800	18,000	17,000	15,000

   a. Determine the total amount of overhead cost applied to each product.
   b. Does the total amount of overhead cost applied to the products above relate to the T-accounts in any way? Explain.

CHECK FIGURE
(3a) Mono-relay overhead
cost: $10.80

PROBLEM 6–6   Contrasting ABC and Traditional Product Costs (CC5, 6, 7)

For many years, Zapro Company manufactured a single product called a mono-relay. Then, three years ago, the company automated a portion of its plant and at the same time introduced a second product called a bi-relay that has become increasingly popular. The bi-relay is a more complex product, requiring one hour of direct labour time per unit to manufacture and extensive machining in the automated portion of the plant. The mono-relay requires only 0.75 hour of direct labour time per unit and only a small amount of machining. Manufacturing overhead costs are currently assigned to products on the basis of direct labour-hours.

Despite the growing popularity of the company's new bi-relay, profits have been declining steadily. Management is beginning to believe that there may be a problem with the company's costing system. Material and labour costs per unit are as follows:

	Mono-Relay	Bi-Relay
Direct materials.	$35	$48
Direct labour (0.75 hour and 1.0 hour @ $12 per hour).	9	12

Management estimates that the company will incur $1,000,000 in manufacturing overhead costs during the current year and 40,000 units of the mono-relay and 10,000 units of the bi-relay will be produced and sold.

Required:

1. Compute the predetermined manufacturing overhead rate assuming that the company continues to apply manufacturing overhead cost on the basis of direct labour-hours. Using this rate and other data from the problem, determine the unit product cost of each product.
2. Management is considering using ABC to apply manufacturing overhead cost to products for external financial reports. The ABC system would have the following four activity cost pools:

Activity Cost Pool	Activity Measure	Estimated Overhead Cost
Maintaining parts inventory	Number of part types	$ 180,000
Processing purchase orders.	Number of purchase orders	90,000
Quality control	Number of tests run	230,000
Machine related.	Machine-hours	500,000
		$1,000,000

	Expected Activity		
Activity Measure	Mono-Relay	Bi-Relay	Total
Number of part types	75	150	225
Number of purchase orders.	800	200	1,000
Number of tests run.	2,500	3,250	5,750
Machine-hours	4,000	6,000	10,000

Determine the activity rate (i.e., predetermined overhead rate) for each of the four activity cost pools.
3. Using the activity rates you computed in (2) above, do the following:
   a. Compute the total amount of manufacturing overhead cost that would be applied to each product using the activity-based costing system. After these totals have been computed, determine the amount of manufacturing overhead cost per unit of each product.
   b. Compute the unit product cost of each product.
4. From the data you have developed in (1) through (3) above, identify factors that may account for the company's declining profits.

PROBLEM 6–7   Compute and Use Activity Rates to Determine the Costs of Serving Customers (CC1, 5, 6, 7, 8)

Jordan's Lakeside is a popular restaurant located on Lake Muskoka in Ontario. The owner of the restaurant has been trying to better understand costs at the restaurant and has hired a student intern to conduct an ABC study. The intern, in consultation with the owner, identified the following major activities:

CHECK FIGURE
(3b) $11.95 per diner

Activity Cost Pool	Activity Measure
Serving a party of diners	Number of parties served
Serving a diner.	Number of diners served
Serving drinks	Number of drinks ordered

A group of diners who ask to sit at the same table are counted as a party. Some costs, such as the costs of cleaning linen, are the same whether one person is at a table or the table is full. Other costs, such as washing dishes, depend on the number of diners served.

Data concerning these activities are displayed below.

Prior to the ABC study, the owner knew very little about the costs of the restaurant. She knew that the total cost for the month was $195,000 and that 15,000 diners had been served. Therefore, the average cost per diner was $13 ($195,000 ÷ 15,000 diners = $13 per diner).

Required:

1. Compute the activity rates for each of the three activities.
2. According to the ABC system, what is the total cost of serving each of the following parties of diners?
   a. A party of four diners who order three drinks in total.
   b. A party of two diners who do not order any drinks.
   c. A lone diner who orders two drinks.
3. Convert the total costs you computed in part (1) to costs per diner. In other words, what is the average cost per diner for serving each of the following parties of diners?
   a. A party of four diners who order three drinks in total.
   b. A party of two diners who do not order any drinks.
   c. A lone diner who orders two drinks.
4. Why do the costs per diner for the three different parties differ from each other and from the overall average cost of $13 per diner?

CHECK FIGURE
(1) Total overhead costs allocated to Scrubbies, $6,875

PROBLEM 6–8   Assigning Costs to Product Lines (CC7)

Grey Inc. manufactures and distributes two types of household items. The items, Scrubbies and Squeegies, are manufactured on a common assembly line by the same direct labourers. Different direct materials are used in each type and the machinery is retooled for each product. Until now, manufacturing overhead costs have been allocated on the basis of direct labour-hours using a plantwide rate. However, the production manager has been reading about ABC and wishes to institute it for Grey's production operations. To that end, she has assembled the following information regarding production activities and manufacturing overhead costs for the month of September:

Activity Cost Pool	Cost Driver (Activity Base)	Allocation Rate	Activity Usage Scrubbies	Activity Usage Squeegies
Materials handling	Number of parts	$1.00 per part	2,000 parts	1,300 parts
Machining	Machine hours	$15.00 per machine-hour	205 machine-hours	300 machine-hours
Assembly	Units started	$1.60 per unit	1,000 units	1,300 units
Inspection	Units tested	$2.00 per unit	100 units	1,200 units

continued

Direct materials	$ 5,200	$ 2,600
Direct labour	$12,000	$12,000

Each product consumed 600 direct labour-hours.

Required:
1. Using ABC, determine the total manufacturing cost and cost per unit for each of the two product lines for September, assuming that all units were started and completed in September.
2. One of the benefits of ABC often cited is the elimination of any cross-subsidization. With reference to the results of the analysis in part (1), which of the two products is (i) under-costed, and (ii) over-costed? Briefly explain your reasoning.

(Adapted © CGA-Canada)

PROBLEM 6–9   Contrasting ABC and Traditional Product Costs (CC1, 5, 6, 7)

CHECK FIGURE
(1) Overhead allocated to Intermediate, $35,120

Water Ride Inc. manufactures and distributes three types of water skis: beginner, intermediate, and advanced. Production is highly automated for the beginner model, whereas the intermediate and advanced models require increasing degrees of labour, depending on the shaping and finishing processes. Water Ride applies all indirect costs to production using a single predetermined overhead (OH) rate based on direct labour-hours. A consultant recently suggested that Water Ride switch to an ABC system, and assembled the following information:

Activity	Recommended Activity Measure	Estimated Overhead Cost	Volume of Activity Measure
Order processing	Number of orders	$ 52,500	100 orders
Materials handling	Materials used (kilos)	585,000	122,385 kilos
Machine amortization and maintenance	Machine hours	322,000	16,000 hours
Quality control	Number of inspections	94,000	40 inspections
		$1,053,500	

In addition, management estimates that 30,000 DLHs will be used in the upcoming year, at a rate of $14 per hour. Assume that the following activity took place in the first month of the upcoming year:

	Beginner	Intermediate	Advanced
Number of units produced ...	20,000	8,000	3,000
Direct material costs........	$20,800	$13,000	$8,000
Direct labour-hours.........	500	1,000	2,000
Number of orders	6	4	3
Number of production runs...	2	2	3
Kilograms of material used...	8,000	3,200	1,500
Machine-hours	1,200	300	200
Number of inspections	3	3	3
Number of units shipped.....	18,000	7,500	2,500

Required:
1. Compute the production costs for each product in the first month of the upcoming year, using DLHs as the allocation base. (Round calculations to the nearest cent.)
2. Compute the production costs for each product in the first month of the upcoming year, using ABC. (Round calculations to the nearest cent.)
3. Compare your answers in parts (1) and (2). Is the overhead charged to each product the same under the two methods? Explain.

(Adapted © CGA-Canada)

PROBLEM 6–10   Contrasting ABC and Traditional Product Costs (CC1, 5, 6, 7)

CHECK FIGURE
(1) $200,000 to Model A

Mayers Temp Inc. (MTI) uses a traditional approach to overhead allocation. The company produces two different models of thermometers for use in homes, Model A (an analogue temperature scale) and model D (a digital temperature readout). Prices for the two products are based on full costs of production. In 2007, MTI incurred $300,000 of factory overhead and produced 40,000 units of model A and 20,000 units of model D. Overhead was applied based on a predetermined overhead rate of $10 per direct labour-hour. Based on this rate, the cost per unit of each product in 2007 was as follows:

	Model A	Model D
Direct materials..........	$ 6	$ 10
Direct labour............	5	5
Factory overhead.........	5	5
Total	$ 16	$ 20

The market is becoming more competitive and MTI is looking into refining its costing system by introducing ABC next year. Analysis of the 2007 data showed that the $300,000 of overhead costs could be assigned to three activities as follows:

Overhead costs assigned in 2007	
Setups	$ 20,000
Material handling	60,000
Equipment operations	220,000
	$300,000

Management determined that the following activity drivers were appropriate for each overhead category:

Activity	Driver	2007 Activity Level
Setups	Number of setups	160 setups
Materials handling	Quantity of material (kg)	120,000 kg
Equipment operations	Machine-hours (MHs)	40,000 MHs

Activity drivers and units produced in 2007 for each model are:

	Model A	Model D
Number of units	40,000	20,000
Number of setups	100	60
Quantity of material handled (in kg).....	60,000	60,000
Machine-hours	14,000	26,000

Required:
1. In 2007, MTI used a single predetermined overhead rate based on DLHs to allocate overhead. How much factory overhead was allocated to the Model A product line and to the Model D product line?
2. In 2007, if ABC had been used, how much factory overhead would have been allocated to the Model A product line and to the Model D product line? Calculate the total unit cost for Model A and Model D under ABC.

(Adapted © CGA-Canada)

CHECK FIGURE
Overhead allocation rate
for Inspection, $100 per
hour

PROBLEM 6–11   Assigning Overhead Cost to Products in ABC (CC5, 6, 7)
Mahal Co. produces two products—standard and deluxe—and allocates its fixed manufacturing costs using a predetermined overhead rate based on estimated total overhead for the year and estimated machine-hours for the year. The estimates are as follows:

Estimated total overhead for the year..................	$2,000,000
Estimated total machine-hours to be worked in the year ...	20,000

The controller is not sure that the estimated costs of the two products reflect the actual costs for which each product is responsible. She is thinking about switching to ABC. An analysis performed by the accounting department came up with the following information about activities and associated cost drivers for the two products:

Activity	Activity Measure	Estimated Activity Cost	Estimated Volume of Activity Measure
Materials purchasing	Quantity of materials (kg)	$200,000	100,000 kg
Machine setups	Number of machine setups	800,000	400 setups
Inspection	Inspection hours	400,000	4,000 hours
Machine operations	Machine-hours	600,000	20,000 MHs

The following data pertain to Mahal for October, the most recent month:

	Standard Product	Deluxe Product
Purchasing materials	6,000 kg	4,000 kg
Machine setups	10	30
Inspection	200 hours	200 hours
Machine operations	1,500 hours	500 hours

Required:

Prepare an analysis of the overhead costs allocated to the standard and deluxe products for October, using the ABC method.

(Adapted © CGA-Canada)

Building Your Skills

ANALYTICAL THINKING* (CC1, 2, 5, 6, 7)

"A dollar of gross margin per briefcase? That's ridiculous!" roared Art Dejans, president of CarryAll, Inc. "Why do we go on producing those standard briefcases when we're able to make over $15 per unit on our specialty items? Maybe it's time to get out of the standard line and focus the whole plant on specialty work."

Mr. Dejans is referring to a summary of unit costs and revenues that he had just received from the company's Accounting Department:

CHECK FIGURE
(2) Standard model unit product cost: $29.98 per unit

	Standard Briefcases	Specialty Briefcases
Selling price per unit.	$36	$40
Unit product cost.	35	25
Gross margin per unit	$ 1	$15

CarryAll produces briefcases from leather, fabric, and synthetic materials in a single plant. The basic product is a standard briefcase that is made from leather lined with fabric. The standard briefcase is a high-quality item and has sold well for many years.

Last year, the company decided to expand its product line and produce specialty briefcases for special orders. These briefcases differ from the standard in that they vary in size, they contain the finest synthetic materials, and they are imprinted with the buyer's name. To reduce labour costs on the specialty briefcases, most of the cutting and stitching is done by automated machines. These machines are used to a much lesser degree in the production of standard briefcases.

"I agree that the specialty business is looking better and better," replied Sally Henrie, the company's marketing manager. "And there seems to be plenty of specialty work out there, particularly since the competition hasn't been able to touch our price. Did you know that Armor Company, our biggest competitor, charges over $50 a unit for its specialty items? Now that's what I call gouging the customer!"

---

*Adapted from a case written by Harold P. Roth and Imogene Posey, "Management Accounting Case Study: CarryAll Company," *Management Accounting Campus Report*, Institute of Management Accountants (Fall 1991), p. 9. Used by permission.

A breakdown of the manufacturing cost for each of CarryAll's product lines follows:

	Standard Briefcases		Specialty Briefcases
Units produced each month ..		10,000		2,500
Direct materials:				
Leather	1.0 sq. m	$15.00	0.5 sq. m	$ 7.50
Fabric	1.0 sq. m	5.00	1.0 sq. m	5.00
Synthetic.		—		5.00
Total materials		20.00		17.50
Direct labour.	0.5 hr. @ $12	6.00	0.25 hr. @ $12	3.00
Manufacturing overhead.	0.5 hr. @ $18	9.00	0.25 hr. @ $18	4.50
Unit product cost		$35.00		$25.00

Manufacturing overhead is applied to products on the basis of direct labour-hours. The rate of $18 per direct labour-hour is determined by dividing the total manufacturing overhead cost for a month by the direct labour-hours:

$$\frac{\text{Manufacturing overhead cost, } \$101,250}{\text{Direct labour-hours, } 5,625} = \$18 \text{ per DLH}$$

The following additional information is available about the company and its products:
a. Standard briefcases are produced in batches of 200 units, and specialty briefcases are produced in batches of 25 units. Thus, the company does 50 setups for the standard items each month and 100 setups for the specialty items. A setup for the standard items requires one hour of time, whereas a setup for the specialty items requires two hours of time.
b. All briefcases are inspected to ensure that quality standards are met. A total of 300 hours of inspection time is spent on the standard briefcases and 500 hours of inspection time is spent on the specialty briefcases each month.
c. A standard briefcase requires 0.5 hour of machine time, and a specialty briefcase requires two hours of machine time.
d. The company is considering using ABC as an alternative to its traditional costing system for computing unit product costs. Since these unit product costs will be used for external financial reporting, all manufacturing overhead costs are to be allocated to products and nonmanufacturing costs are to be excluded from product costs. The ABC system has already been designed and costs allocated to the activity cost pools. The activity cost pools and activity measures follow:

Activity Cost Pool	Activity Measure	Estimated Overhead Cost
Purchasing.	Number of orders	$ 12,000
Material handling	Number of receipts	15,000
Production orders and setup	Setup hours	20,250
Inspection	Inspection-hours	16,000
Frame assembly	Assembly-hours	8,000
Machine related.	Machine-hours	30,000
		$101,250

	Expected Activity		
Activity Measure	Standard Briefcase	Specialty Briefcase	Total
Number of orders:			
Leather	34	6	40
Fabric	48	12	60
Synthetic material.	—	100	100

continued

Number of receipts:			
Leather	52	8	60
Fabric	64	16	80
Synthetic material	—	160	160
Setup hours	?	?	?
Inspection-hours	?	?	?
Assembly-hours	800	800	1,600
Machine-hours	?	?	?

Required:

1. Using ABC, determine the amount of manufacturing overhead cost that would be applied to each standard briefcase and each specialty briefcase.
2. Using the data computed in part (1) and other data from the case as needed, determine the unit product cost of each product line from the perspective of the ABC system.
3. Within the limitations of the data that have been provided, evaluate the president's concern about the profitability of the two product lines. Would you recommend that the company shift its resources entirely to production of specialty briefcases? Explain.
4. Sally Henrie stated that "the competition hasn't been able to touch our price" on specialty business. Why do you suppose that is?

COMMUNICATING IN PRACTICE   (CC1, 2)

You often provide advice to Maria Graham, a client who is interested in diversifying her company. Maria is considering the purchase of a small manufacturing concern that assembles and packages its many products by hand. She plans to automate the factory and her projections indicate that the company will once again be profitable within two to three years. During her review of the company's records, she discovered that the company currently uses direct labour-hours to allocate overhead to its products. Because of its simplicity, Maria hopes that this approach can continue to be used.

Required:

Write a memorandum to Maria that addresses whether DLHs should continue to be used as an allocation base for overhead.

ETHICS CHALLENGE   (CC1, 2, 8)

You and your friends go to a restaurant as a group. At the end of the meal, the issue arises of how the bill for the group should be shared. One alternative is to figure out the cost of what each individual consumed and divide up the bill accordingly. Another alternative is to split the bill equally among the individuals.

Required:

Which system for dividing the bill is more equitable? Which system is easier to use? How does this issue relate to the material covered in this chapter?

TEAMWORK IN ACTION   (CC2)

This activity requires teamwork to reinforce the understanding of the hierarchy of activities commonly found in ABC systems in manufacturing companies.

Required:

1. The team should discuss and then draft a brief description of how the ABC system allocates overhead to products. All team members should agree with and understand the description.
2. Without referring to the related section in the text, each member of the team should choose one of the following levels of activities, define the level of activity chosen, and provide one or more examples of the tasks that are performed at that level of activity in a manufacturing firm:
   a. Unit-level activities
   b. Batch-level activities
   c. Product-level activities
   d. Facility-level activities
3. Each team member should present his or her answers from part (2) to the other teammates who should confirm or correct those answers.

Don't forget to visit the Online Learning Centre for self-study quizzes, practice exams, and more! Visit www.mcgrawhill.ca/olc/brewer.

CHAPTER *Seven*

Budgeting

CHAPTER COMPETENCIES

After studying Chapter 7, you should be able to demonstrate the following competencies:

Competency	Know	Apply
Understand the concept of budgets and budgeting.		
CC1 Explain the role of budgeting.	●	
CC2 Explain why organizations budget.	●	
CC3 Describe a master budget and the relationships among its components.	●	
CC4 Explain zero-based budgeting.	●	
Understand the preparation of each component budget of the master budget.		
CC5 Prepare a sales budget including a schedule of cash collections.		●
CC6 Prepare a production budget.		●
CC7 Prepare a direct materials budget, including a schedule of cash disbursements for purchases of raw materials.		●
CC8 Prepare a direct labour budget.		●
CC9 Prepare a manufacturing overhead budget.		●
CC10 Prepare an ending finished goods inventory budget.		●
CC11 Prepare a selling and administrative expense budget.		●
CC12 Prepare a cash budget.		●
Develop budgeted financial statements using the information from the component budgets of the master budget.		
CC13 Prepare a budgeted income statement.		●
CC14 Prepare a budgeted balance sheet.		●
Understand the practical issues surrounding the budgeting process and the role of the beyond budgeting model in addressing such issues.		
CC15 Describe the practical issues that should be considered in the budgeting process including the concepts of participative budgeting and responsibility accounting.	●	
CC16 Explain the beyond budgeting model and its approach to budgeting.	●	

Note: Appendix 7A is available online (see www.mcgrawhill.ca/olc/brewer).

DECISION FEATURE
Lilo & Stitch on Budget

The full-length feature cartoon *Tarzan* grossed about $450 million worldwide for The Walt Disney Company. However, production costs got out of control. The company traditionally manages film production by focusing on meeting the planned release date—paying little attention to costs. In the case of *Tarzan*, production fell behind schedule due to the tendency of animation teams to add more eye-dazzling complexity to each production. At one point, it was estimated that 190,000 individual drawings would be needed to complete the film in contrast to the 130,000 drawings needed to complete *The Lion King*. To meet *Tarzan*'s release date, workers were pulled off other productions and were often paid at overtime rates. The size of the film crew eventually reached 573, which was nearly twice the size of the crew that had made *The Lion King*. With animators earning salaries in the hundreds of thousands of dollars, the cost implications were staggering.

Thomas S. Schumacher, Disney's feature-animation chief, was charged with dramatically reducing the cost of future films while making sure that the audience wouldn't notice any decline in quality. *Lilo & Stitch* was the first film to be produced with this goal in mind. The process began by prioritizing where the money was to be spent. The budget for music was kept generous; animation costs were cut by controlling the small details that add big costs with little effect on the quality of the film. For example, animators wanted to draw cute designs on the shirts worn by Nani, Lilo's big sister. However, adding this level of detail on every frame in which Nani appears in the film would have added about $250,000 in cost. By controlling such details, *Lilo & Stitch* was finished on time and at a cost of about $80 million. This contrasted with a cost of more than $150 million for *Tarzan*.

Source: Bruce Orwall, "Comics Stripped: At Disney, String of Weak Cartoons Leads to Cost Cuts," *The Wall Street Journal*, June 18, 2002, pp. A1 and A8.

A Look Back

In Chapter 6, we completed our discussion of costing systems by examining the concept of activity-based costing. We considered how the challenge of overhead allocation was addressed in ABC systems through the use of a number of allocation bases to assign overhead to cost objects.

A Look at This Chapter

After discussing why organizations prepare budgets, Chapter 7 provides an overview of each of the individual budgets that constitute a firm's master budget. We also address the preparation of the cash budget, the budgeted income statement, and the budgeted balance sheet. The chapter concludes with a discussion of the processes organizations use to create budgets and some of the issues that arise in practice.

A Look Ahead

In Chapter 8 we focus on management control and performance measures by considering the use of standard costs and variances.

In a **mission, vision, and values statement**, an organization captures the answers to such questions as: Where do we want to be five years from now? What should we be to our customers, our employees, and other stakeholders? Which markets do we want to dominate? The broad intent and aims stated in a mission statement are translated into specific goals and objectives to be achieved by the organization in the next few years by the process of strategic planning. **Strategic planning** involves making decisions about how the organization should position itself in the marketplace to compete successfully with its rivals for customers and resources. These decisions and their implications for resource acquisition and deployment are captured in the **strategic plan,** which is the principal output from the strategic planning process. The strategic plan is then used to develop the specific tactics that will be used to guide the short-term operations of the organization. This process of **operational planning** is where the process of *budgeting* enters the picture. **Budgeting** is the process used by businesses to describe, in financial terms, how they intend to achieve their desired financial and nonfinancial objectives.

In this chapter, we focus on budgeting. Budgeting is accomplished through the preparation of a number of budgets, which collectively form an integrated business plan known as the **master budget.** The budgeting process culminates with the preparation of a cash budget, detailing the planned cash receipts and disbursements, including short-term borrowing requirements, a budgeted income statement, and a budgeted balance sheet.

Budgets and Budgeting

�〕 **KNOW**

CC1: Explain the role of budgeting.

The key tool in the budgeting process is the **budget.** A budget is a quantitative plan for acquiring and using financial and other resources. It is a medium to communicate, quantitatively, management's objectives for sales, production, purchasing, distribution, and financing activities. It is also the instrument that guides and coordinates the firm's activities among all of these areas. Exhibit 7–1 provides a context to understand this role of budgeting. As you can see, the budget gives voice to what the organization intends to achieve financially during the upcoming operations period. And, in doing so, it becomes the basis for management's actions, as well as the reference point for performance measurement (what is measured) and performance evaluation (how the measures are used).

Budgets: Planning versus Control

Planning involves developing objectives and the various budgets to achieve these objectives. Budgeting serves to flesh out the conceptual plans and strategies by expressing the plans in financial terms. The use of budgets to guide and coordinate activities across the firm to ensure that objectives are attained is called *budgetary control.* The concept of **control** refers to the steps taken to increase the likelihood that the objectives and targets described in the budgets are attained and all parts of the organization function in a manner consistent with organizational policies.

Planning and control are distinct concepts, which are often thought to suggest the same thing. The confusion arises from the fact that budgets are common to both. To avoid this confusion, keep in mind that budgets are the *result* of planning and the *basis* for control. To be effective, a good budgeting system must provide for both planning and control. Good planning without effective control is time wasted.

Advantages of Budgeting

�〕 **KNOW**

CC2: Explain why organizations budget.

Why should we budget? The simplest answer is scarcity of resources. If resources were unlimited and free, we would be unconcerned about waste and there would be no need for planning and control. There would be no need for communication of plans throughout the

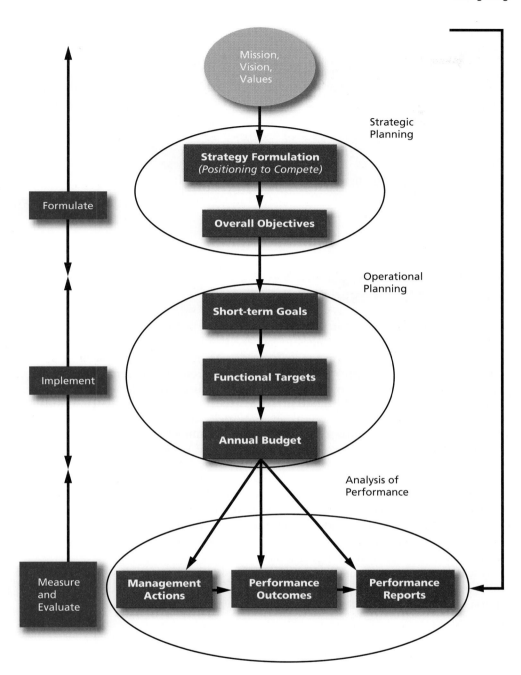

Exhibit 7–1
The Budget in the Context of Strategy and Planning

organization. Nothing would impede achieving our objectives. In short, there would be no need to think about how to achieve our objectives in a systematic, organized, and coordinated manner.

But, scarcity of resources is a fundamental reality confronting businesses and individuals. Therefore, organizations and individuals must:

- Think about and plan for the future systematically.
- Uncover potential impediments to achieving goals and objectives, such as resource constraints and bottlenecks.
- Communicate plans carefully and clearly.
- Coordinate the planned actions across the various parts of the organization.
- Ensure that scarce resources are employed to best benefit the organization.

- Define goals and objectives that can serve as benchmarks for subsequent performance.

Budgeting and budgets enable organizations to accomplish all of these items.

How can organizations ensure that the potential benefits from budgeting and preparing budgets are actually realized? This is an extremely important question, the answer to which requires us to consider the *individuals* involved in budgeting, the *steps* taken to accomplish the budgeting, and the manner in which the organization *intends to use* the budgets. We must also consider how the organization communicates those intentions and whether the budgets are, in fact, used as intended. To fully appreciate these important issues, you will find the following budgeting example to be helpful. Therefore, we will address these issues after we have illustrated the preparation of the master budget.

IN BUSINESS TODAY

Budgets Can Suggest What Must Be Controlled to Improve the Bottom Line

With the technology industry in decline, Nortel Networks Corporation (Nortel) realized that it needed to make some changes to halt the rapid slide toward extinction. Until it was toppled from its position as an industry leader, Nortel was a major player in the telecommunications industry, providing a wide range of products and services that support communication through networks. However, a major misreading of the future growth in demand for its products led Nortel to invest in excess network capacity. Unfortunately, the unanticipated economic downturn caused Nortel's customers to reduce their capital spending significantly. The result? Nortel's shares plummeted from a high of $124.50 to a mere 67¢. Nortel restructured drastically to reduce overhead and make operations more efficient.

Nortel was able to reduce its selling, general, and administrative expenses by $257 million, from $744 million to $487 million, from the first quarter of 2002 to the first quarter of 2003. In all segments of the business, Nortel reduced its workforce by more than 60%, from 96,000 to only 36,000. Nortel further streamlined operations by selling off certain optical components assets, and terminating and expiring certain credit facilities and amendments to its security agreements.

Research and development (R&D) was refocused toward investments that would allow Nortel to maintain its industry leader status. Nortel lowered its R&D expenditures by $106 million in one year to bring them in line with the overall cost structure of the company.

Sources: Nortel Networks Corporation. *2003 First Quarter Shareholders Report*, Brampton, ON. 2003; and Andrew Wahl, "Groovin' up quickly," *Canadian Business*, September 29–October 14, 2003, pp. 37–39. Reprinted with permission from *Canadian Business*.

An Overview of the Master Budget

KNOW

CC3: Describe a master budget and the relationships among its components.

The master budget is the principal output of the budgeting process. Exhibit 7–2 provides an overview of the various parts of the master budget and how they are related. The type of organization—is it a manufacturer or a merchandiser or a service provider?—will determine if some of the component budgets are necessary. A merchandiser will not require a *production budget*, for example. Instead, the merchandising company will prepare a *merchandise purchases budget*. A service provider will require neither a production budget nor a merchandise purchases budget. Service organizations, such as law offices or health services departments, will rely on the *operating expenses budget*.

Exhibit 7–2
The Master Budget Interrelationships

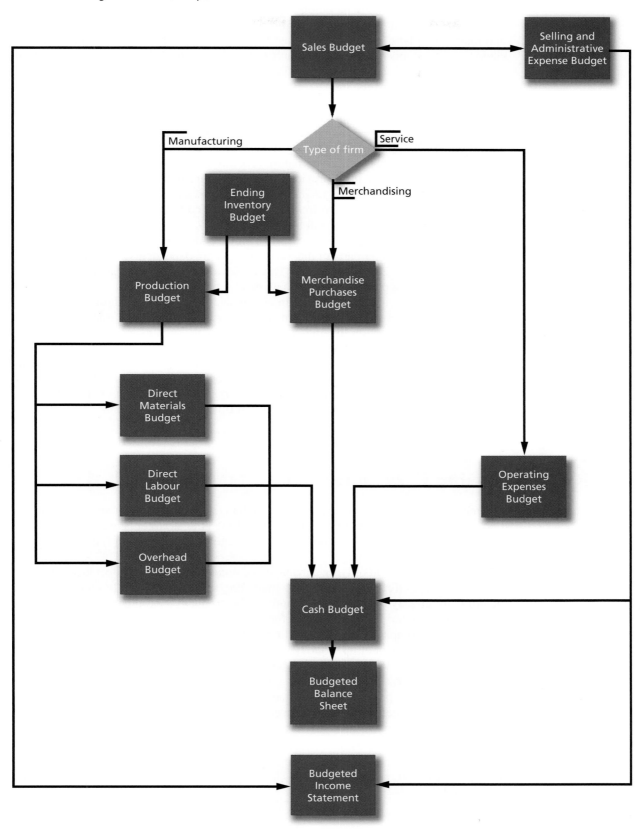

THE SALES BUDGET   A **sales budget** is a detailed schedule showing the expected sales—expressed both in dollars and units of product (or service)—for the budget period. The sales budget is usually based on the company's *sales forecast*. In addition, the manager may examine the company's unfulfilled back orders, the company's pricing policy and marketing plans, trends in the industry, and general economic conditions. Sophisticated statistical tools may be used to analyze the data and to build models that are helpful in predicting key factors influencing the company's sales. These tools and models are more appropriately covered in marketing courses, and so we will not go into the details of how sales forecasts are made.

Service organizations must estimate the demand for their services. Professional accountants, for example, have to estimate the revenues they expect to earn from their consulting practice. These estimates are typically derived from projections of the number of consulting engagements and the nature (tax advice, auditing engagements, business consulting) of the service to be provided. The projections will also depend on the rates to be charged. These rates, in turn, might be established on a cost-plus basis where the exact figure is set on the basis of the desired margin over the costs. In such cases, cost measurement, management, and control will be critical.

An accurate sales budget is the key to the entire budgeting process in for-profit organizations. All of the other parts of the master budget are dependent on the sales budget in some way, as illustrated in Exhibit 7–2. Thus, if the sales budget is sloppily done, then the rest of the budgeting process is largely a waste of time.

Not-for-profit organizations face different challenges. In many of these organizations, the concept of revenue generated from *selling* services will not be relevant. Many of these organizations rely on external sources of funding, such as a parent organization, individual and corporate donors, and/or local and higher levels of government. The programs and services these organizations offer consume financial resources. Budgeting for these organizations controls their operating expenses by controlling the variety and volume of services—the consumer of financial resources—offered so as to be in line with their financial endowments. See the following In Business Today feature.

IN BUSINESS TODAY   **Biasing Forecasts**

A manager's compensation is often tied to the budget. Typically, no bonus is paid unless a minimum performance hurdle such as 80% of the budget target is attained. Once that hurdle is passed, the manager's bonus increases until a cap is reached. That cap is often set at 120% of the budget target.

This common method of tying a manager's compensation to the budget has some serious negative side effects. For example, a marketing manager for a big beverage company intentionally grossly understated demand for the company's products for an upcoming major holiday so that the budget target for revenues would be low and easy to beat. Unfortunately, the company tied its production to this biased forecast and ran out of products to sell during the height of the holiday selling season.

As another example, near the end of the year another group of managers announced a price increase of 10% effective January 2 of the following year. Why would they do this? By announcing this price increase, managers hoped that customers would order before the end of the year, helping managers meet their sales targets for the current year. Sales in the following year would, of course, drop. What trick would managers pull to meet their sales targets next year in the face of this drop in demand?

Sources: Michael C. Jensen, "Corporate Budgeting Is Broken—Let's Fix It," *Harvard Business Review*, November, 2001; and Michael C. Jensen, "Why Pay People to Lie?" *The Wall Street Journal*, January 8, 2001, p. A32.

The remainder of the discussion will assume that we are concerned with a for-profit manufacturing organization.

THE INTERDEPENDENCY OF THE BUDGETS   The sales budget will help determine the number of units to be produced. Thus, the production budget is prepared after the sales budget. The production budget, in turn, is used to determine the budgets for the manufacturing costs, including the direct materials budget, the direct labour budget, and the manufacturing overhead budget. These budgets are then combined with the data from the sales budget and the selling and administrative expense budget to determine the cash budget.

THE CASH BUDGET   The term *operating budget* is used to refer to the budget that pertains to such activities as sales, production, purchasing, selling, and administration that the firm undertakes in the course of operating the business. A **cash budget** is a *financial* budget. It is a detailed plan showing how cash resources will be acquired and used over some specified period. Observe from Exhibit 7–2 that all of the operating budgets have an impact on the cash budget. Operations run, ultimately, on money! The sales budget provides the basis for the planned cash receipts from sales. In the case of the other budgets, the impact on the cash budget comes from the planned expenditures with the budgets themselves.

Choosing a Budget Period

Operating budgets, including the cash budget, ordinarily cover the company's fiscal year. Many companies divide their budget year into four quarters. The first quarter is then subdivided into months, and monthly budgets are developed. The last three quarters are carried in the budget at quarterly totals only. As the year progresses, the figures for the second quarter are broken down into monthly amounts, then the third-quarter figures are broken down, and so on. This approach has the advantage of requiring periodic review and reappraisal of budget data throughout the year.

In this chapter, we will focus on *one-year operating budgets*. However, using basically the same techniques, operating budgets can be prepared for periods that extend over many years. It may be difficult to accurately forecast sales and required data much beyond a year, but even rough estimates can be invaluable in uncovering potential problems and opportunities that would otherwise be overlooked.

Zero-Based Budgeting

In the traditional approach to budgeting, the manager starts with last year's budget and adds to it (or subtracts from it) according to anticipated needs. This is an incremental approach to budgeting, in which the previous year's budget is taken for granted as a baseline.

Zero-based budgeting is an alternative approach that is sometimes used—particularly in the governmental and not-for-profit sectors of the economy. Under a **zero-based budget,** managers are required to justify *all* budgeted expenditures, not just changes in the budget from the previous year. The baseline is zero, rather than last year's budget.

A zero-based budget requires considerable documentation. In addition to all of the schedules in the usual master budget, the manager must prepare a series of *decision packages* in which all of the activities of the department are ranked according to their relative importance and the cost of each activity is identified. Higher-level managers can then review the decision packages, cutting back in those areas that appear to be less critical or whose costs do not appear to be justified.

 KNOW

CC4: Explain zero-based budgeting.

Nearly everyone would agree that zero-based budgeting is a good idea. The only issue is the frequency with which a zero-based review is carried out. Under zero-based budgeting, the review is performed every year. Critics of zero-based budgeting charge that properly executed zero-based budgeting is too time consuming and too costly to justify on an annual basis. In addition, many argue that annual reviews soon become mechanical and that the whole purpose of zero-based budgeting is then lost.

Whether or not a company should use an annual review is a matter of judgment. In some situations, annual zero-based reviews may be justified; in other situations, they may not because of the time and cost involved. However, most managers would at least agree that on occasion zero-based reviews can be very helpful.

Better than Budgets?

Borealis is a company headquartered in Copenhagen, Denmark, that produces polymers for the plastics industry. Thomas Boesen, the company's financial controller, felt that the traditional budgeting process had outlived its usefulness—markets were changing so fast that the budget was out of date within weeks of its publication. Moreover, since budgets were used to control and evaluate the performance of managers, they were subject to considerable gaming behavior that reduced their accuracy and usefulness. So over a five-year period the company phased out its traditional budgets and replaced them with rolling forecasts and several other management tools. Instead of holding managers to a budget, targets based on competitors' performance were set for variable costs, fixed costs, and operating margins. Managers were given the freedom to spend money as needed to meet these competitive benchmarks. Since the rolling forecasts of financial results were not used to control spending or to evaluate managers' performance, managers had little incentive to "game the system," and hence the forecasts were more accurate than those obtained through the traditional budgeting process.

Source: Professor Bjorn Jorgensen, *Borealis*, Harvard Business School Case 9-102-048, Rev: May 9, 2002.

DECISION MAKER

Sales Manager

You were recently hired as the sales manager for a company that designs and manufactures hard-soled casual and dress shoes for sale to department stores. The vice-president of sales recently decided that the company will add athletic footwear to its catalogue, and asked you to prepare a sales budget for that product line for the coming year. How would you forecast sales for this product line?

Preparing the Master Budget

MANAGERIAL ACCOUNTING IN ACTION

The Issue

Tom Wills is the majority shareholder and chief executive officer of Hampton Freeze, Inc., a company he started in 2006. The company makes premium popsicles using only natural ingredients and featuring exotic flavours, such as tangy tangerine and minty mango. The company's business is highly seasonal, with most of the sales occurring in spring and summer.

In 2007, the company's second year of operations, a major cash crunch in the first and second quarters almost forced the company into bankruptcy. In spite of this cash crunch, 2007 turned out to be a very successful year in both overall cash flow and net income. Partly as a result of that harrowing experience, Tom decided to hire a professional financial manager toward the end of 2007. Tom interviewed several promising candidates for the job and settled on Larry Giano, who had considerable experience in the packaged foods industry. In the job interview, Tom questioned Larry about the steps he would take to prevent a recurrence of the 2007 cash crunch:

Tom: As I mentioned earlier, we are going to wind up 2007 with a very nice profit. What you may not know is that we had some very big financial problems this year.

Larry: Let me guess. You ran out of cash sometime in the first or second quarter.

Tom: How did you know?

Larry: Most of your sales are in the second and third quarters, right?

Tom: Sure, everyone wants to buy popsicles in the spring and summer, but nobody wants them when the weather turns cold.

Larry: So, you don't have many sales in the first quarter?

Tom: Right.

Larry: And in the second quarter, which is the spring, you are producing like crazy to fill orders?

Tom: Sure.

Larry: Do your customers, the grocery stores, pay you the day you make your deliveries?

Tom: Are you kidding? Of course not.

Larry: So, in the first quarter, you don't have many sales. In the second quarter, you are producing like crazy, which eats up cash, but you aren't paid by your customers until long after you have paid your employees and suppliers. No wonder you had a cash problem. I see this pattern all the time in food processing because of the seasonality of the business.

Tom: So, what can we do about it?

Larry: The first step is to predict the magnitude of the problem before it occurs. If we can predict early in the year what the cash shortfall is going to be, we can go to the bank and arrange for credit before we really need it. Bankers tend to be leery of panicky people who show up begging for emergency loans. They are much more likely to make the loan if you look like you know what you are doing, you have done your homework, and you are in control of the situation.

Tom: How can we predict the cash shortfall?

Larry: You can put together a cash budget. While you're at it, you might as well do a master budget. You'll find it is well worth the effort.

Tom: I don't like budgets. They are too confining. My wife budgets everything at home, and I can't spend what I want.

Larry: Can I ask a personal question?

Tom: What?

Larry: Where did you get the money to start this business?

Tom: Mainly from our family's savings. I get your point. We wouldn't have had the money to start the business if my wife hadn't been forcing us to save every month.

Larry: Exactly. I suggest you use the same discipline in your business. It is even more important here because you can't expect your employees to spend your money as carefully as you would.

Tom: I'm sold. Welcome aboard.

With the full backing of Tom Wills, Larry Giano set out to create a master budget for the company for the year 2008. In his planning for the budgeting process, Larry drew up the following list of documents that would be a part of the master budget:

1. A sales budget, including a schedule of expected cash collections.
2. A production budget (a merchandise purchases budget would be used in a merchandising company).
3. A direct materials budget, including a schedule of expected cash disbursements for raw materials (this would not be needed for a merchandising company).
4. A direct labour budget (this would not be needed for a merchandising company).
5. A manufacturing overhead budget.
6. An ending finished goods inventory budget.
7. A selling and administrative expense budget.
8. A cash budget.

   9. A budgeted income statement.

  10. A budgeted balance sheet.

Larry felt it was important to have everyone's cooperation in the budgeting process, and so he asked Tom to call a companywide meeting in which the budgeting process would be explained. At the meeting, there was initially some grumbling, but Tom was able to convince nearly everyone of the necessity for planning and getting better control over spending. It helped that the cash crisis earlier in the year was still fresh in everyone's minds.

In the months that followed, Larry worked closely with all of the managers involved in the master budget, gathering data from them and making sure that they understood and fully supported the parts of the master budget that would affect them. In subsequent years, Larry hoped to turn the whole budgeting process over to the managers and to take on a more advisory role.

The interdependent documents that Larry Giano prepared for Hampton Freeze are Schedules 1 through 10 of his company's master budget. In this section, we will study these schedules.

The Sales Budget

⬤ **APPLY**

CC5: Prepare a sales budget, including a schedule of cash collections.

The sales budget is the starting point in preparing the master budget. As shown previously in Exhibit 7–2, all other items in the master budget, including production, purchases, inventories, and expenses, depend on it in some way.

The sales budget is constructed by multiplying the budgeted sales in units by the selling price. Schedule 1 on the next page contains the sales budget for Hampton Freeze for the year 2008, by quarters. Notice from the schedule that the company plans to sell 100,000 cases of popsicles during the year, with sales peaking in the third quarter.

SCHEDULE OF EXPECTED CASH COLLECTIONS   A schedule of expected cash collections, such as the one that appears in Schedule 1 for Hampton Freeze, is prepared after the sales budget. This schedule will be needed later to prepare the cash budget. Cash collections consist of collections on sales made to customers in prior periods plus collections on sales made in the current budget period. At Hampton Freeze, experience has shown that 70% of sales are collected in the quarter in which the sale is made and the remaining 30% are collected in the following quarter. For example, 70% of the first quarter sales of $200,000 (or $140,000) are collected during the first quarter, and 30% (or $60,000) are collected during the second quarter.

The Production Budget

⬤ **APPLY**

CC6: Prepare a production budget.

The production budget is prepared after the sales budget. The **production budget** lists the number of units that must be produced during each budget period to meet sales needs and to provide for the desired ending inventory. Production needs can be determined as follows:

Budgeted sales in units	XXXX
Add: Desired ending inventory	XXXX
Total needs	XXXX
Less: Beginning inventory	XXXX
Required production	XXXX

Schedule 2 contains the production budget for Hampton Freeze.

Note that production requirements for a quarter are influenced by the desired level of the ending inventory. Inventories should be carefully planned. Excessive inventories tie up funds and create storage problems. Insufficient inventories can lead to lost sales or crash production efforts in the following period. At Hampton Freeze, management believes that an ending inventory equal to 20% of the next quarter's sales strikes the appropriate balance.

Schedule 1—Sales Budget and Schedule of Expected Cash Collections

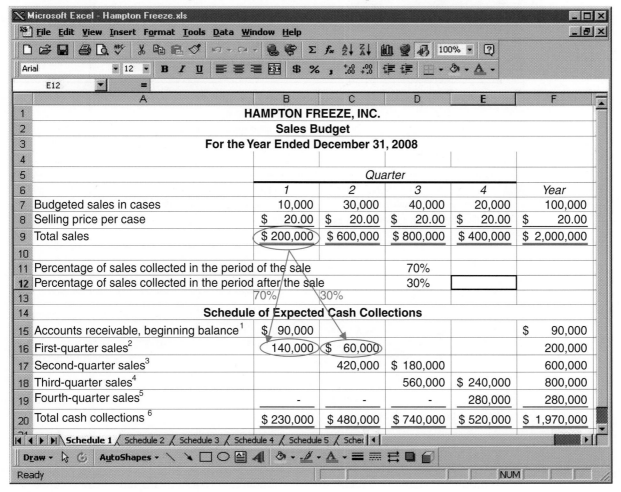

[1]Cash collections from last year's fourth-quarter sales. See the beginning-of-year balance sheet on page 278.

[2]$200,000 × 70%; $200,000 × 30%.

[3]$600,000 × 70%; $600,000 × 30%.

[4]$800,000 × 70%; $800,000 × 30%.

[5]$400,000 × 70%.

[6]Uncollected fourth-quarter sales appear as accounts receivable on the company's end-of-year balance sheet (see Schedule 10 on page 277).

Inventory Purchases—Merchandising Firm

Hampton Freeze prepares a production budget, since it is a *manufacturing* firm. If it were a *merchandising* firm, it would prepare a **merchandise purchases budget** showing the amount of goods to be purchased from its suppliers during the period. The merchandise purchases budget follows the same basic format as the production budget, as shown following:

Budgeted cost of goods sold (in units or in dollars)............	XXXXX
Add: Desired ending merchandise inventory	XXXXX
Total needs	XXXXX
Less: Beginning merchandise inventory....................	XXXXX
Required purchases (in units or in dollars).................	XXXXX

Schedule 2—Production Budget

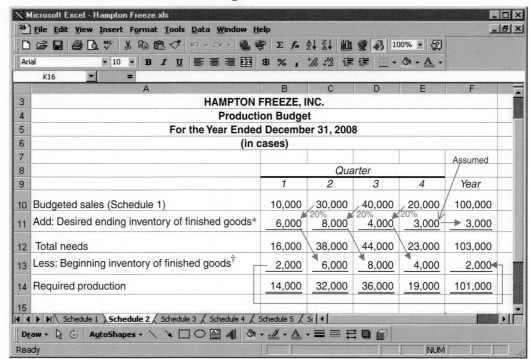

*20% of the next quarter's sales. The ending inventory of 3,000 cases is assumed.

†The beginning inventory in each quarter is the same as the prior quarter's ending inventory.

The spreadsheet shown:

HAMPTON FREEZE, INC.
Production Budget
For the Year Ended December 31, 2008
(in cases)

	1	2	3	4	Year (Assumed)
10 Budgeted sales (Schedule 1)	10,000	30,000	40,000	20,000	100,000
11 Add: Desired ending inventory of finished goods*	6,000	8,000	4,000	3,000	3,000
12 Total needs	16,000	38,000	44,000	23,000	103,000
13 Less: Beginning inventory of finished goods†	2,000	6,000	8,000	4,000	2,000
14 Required production	14,000	32,000	36,000	19,000	101,000

A merchandising firm would prepare an inventory purchases budget, such as the preceding one, for each item carried in stock.

The Direct Materials Budget

APPLY

CC7: Prepare a direct materials budget, including a schedule of cash disbursements for purchases of materials.

Returning to Hampton Freeze, after the production requirements have been computed, a direct materials budget can be prepared. The **direct materials budget** details the raw materials that must be purchased to fulfill the production budget and to provide for adequate inventories. The required purchases of raw materials are computed as follows:

Raw materials needed to meet the production schedule.........	XXXXX
Add: Desired ending inventory of raw materials	XXXXX
Total raw materials needs	XXXXX
Less: Beginning inventory of raw materials.................	XXXXX
Raw materials to be purchased	XXXXX

Schedule 3 contains the direct materials budget for Hampton Freeze. The only raw material included in that budget is high-fructose sugar, which is the major ingredient in popsicles other than water. The remaining raw materials are relatively insignificant and are included in variable manufacturing overhead. Note that materials requirements are first determined in units (kilograms, litres, and so on) and then translated into dollars by multiplying the appropriate unit cost. Also, notice that the management of Hampton Freeze desires to maintain ending inventories of sugar equal to 10% of the following quarter's production needs.

SCHEDULE OF EXPECTED CASH DISBURSEMENTS FOR RAW MATERIALS   The direct materials budget is usually accompanied by a schedule of expected cash disbursements for raw materials. This schedule is needed to prepare the overall cash

Schedule 3—Direct Materials Budget and Schedule of Expected Cash Disbursements for Materials

```
X Microsoft Excel - Hampton Freeze.xls                                    _ □ X
  File  Edit  View  Insert  Format  Tools  Data  Window  Help              _ 8 X
  [toolbar]   Σ fx ↓ ↓  92%  ▾
  Arial     ▾ 10 ▾  B I U  ≡ ≡ ≡  $ % , .0 .00  ▾ ▾ A ▾
  H30        =
```

	A	B	C	D	E	F	G
3		HAMPTON FREEZE, INC.					
4		Direct Materials Budget					
5		For the Year Ended December 31, 2008					
6						Assumed	
7			Quarter				
8		1	2	3	4	Year	
9	Required production in cases (Schedule 2)	14,000	32,000	36,000	19,000	101,000	
10	Raw materials needed per case (kilograms)	15	15	15	15	15	
11	Production needs (kilograms)	210,000	480,000	540,000	285,000	1,515,000	
12	Add: Desired ending inventory of raw materials¹	48,000	54,000	28,500	22,500	22,500	
13	Total needs	258,000	534,000	568,500	307,500	1,537,500	
14	Less: Beginning inventory of raw materials	21,000	48,000	54,000	28,500	21,000	
15	Raw materials to be purchased	237,000	486,000	514,500	279,000	1,516,500	
16	Cost of raw materials per kilogram	$ 0.20	$ 0.20	$ 0.20	$ 0.20	$ 0.20	
17	Cost of raw materials to be purchased	$ 47,400	$ 97,200	$ 102,900	$ 55,800	$ 303,300	
18							
19	Percentage of purchases paid for in the period of the purchase		50%				
20	Percentage of purchases paid for in the period after purchase		50%				
21		50%	50%				
22	Schedule of Expected Cash Disbursements for Materials						
23							
24	Accounts payable, beginning balance²	$ 25,800				$ 25,800	
25	First-quarter purchases³	23,700	$ 23,700			47,400	
26	Second-quarter purchases⁴		48,600	$ 48,600		97,200	
27	Third-quarter purchases⁵			51,450	$ 51,450	102,900	
28	Fourth-quarter purchases⁶	-	-	-	27,900	27,900	
29	Total cash disbursements	$ 49,500	$ 72,300	$ 100,050	$ 79,350	$ 301,200	

```
 ◄ ◄ ► ►  Schedule 1 / Schedule 2 \ Schedule 3 / Schedule 4 / Schedule 5 / Sche ◄
 Draw ▾  AutoShapes ▾ \ \ □ ○ ▨ ◢ ▾ ▾ A ▾ ≡ ≡ ≡ □ ▢
```

¹10% of the next quarter's production needs. For example, the second-quarter production needs are 480,000 kilograms. Therefore, the desired ending inventory for the first quarter would be 10% × 480,000 kilograms = 48,000 kilograms. The ending inventory of 22,500 kilograms for the quarter is assumed.

²Cash payments for last year's fourth-quarter material purchases. See the beginning-of-year balance sheet on page 278.
³$47,400 × 50%; $47,400 × 50%.
⁴$97,200 × 50%; $97,200 × 50%.
⁵$102,900 × 50%; $102,900 × 50%.
⁶$55,800 × 50%. Unpaid fourth-quarter purchases appear as accounts payable on the company's end-of-year balance sheet.

budget. Disbursements for raw materials consist of payments for purchases on account in prior periods plus any payments for purchases in the current budget period. Schedule 3 contains such a schedule of cash disbursements.

The Direct Labour Budget

The **direct labour budget** is also developed from the production budget. Direct labour requirements must be computed so that the company will know whether sufficient labour time is available to meet production needs. By knowing in advance just what will be needed in the way of labour time throughout the budget year, the company can develop plans to adjust the labour force as required. Firms that neglect to budget labour run the risk of facing labour shortages or having to hire and lay off at awkward times. Erratic labour policies lead to insecurity and inefficiency on the part of employees.

 APPLY

CC8: Prepare a direct labour budget.

Schedule 4—Direct Labour Budget

	A	B	C	D	E	F
		HAMPTON FREEZE, INC.				
1		HAMPTON FREEZE, INC.				
2		Direct Labour Budget				
3		For the Year Ended December 31, 2008				
4						
5				Quarter		
6		1	2	3	4	Year
7	Required production in cases (Schedule 2)	14,000	32,000	36,000	19,000	101,000
8	Direct labour-hours per case	0.80	0.80	0.80	0.80	0.80
9	Total direct labour-hours needed	11,200	25,600	28,800	15,200	80,800
10	Direct labour cost per hour	$ 7.50	$ 7.50	$ 7.50	$ 7.50	$ 7.50
11	Total direct labour cost*	$ 84,000	$ 192,000	$ 216,000	$ 114,000	$ 606,000

Schedule 1 / Schedule 2 / Schedule 3 \ **Schedule 4** / Schedule 5 / Schedul

*This schedule assumes that the direct labour workforce will be fully adjusted to the total direct labour-hours needed each quarter.

To compute direct labour requirements, the number of units of finished product to be produced each period (month, quarter, and so on) is multiplied by the number of direct labour-hours required to produce a single unit. The direct labour requirements can then be translated into expected direct labour costs. How this is done will depend on the labour policy of the firm. In Schedule 4, the management of Hampton Freeze has assumed that the direct labour force will be adjusted as the work requirements change from quarter to quarter. In that case, the total direct labour cost is computed by simply multiplying the direct labour-hour requirements by the direct labour rate per hour.

However, many companies have employment policies or contracts that prevent them from laying off and rehiring workers, as needed. Suppose, for example, that Hampton Freeze has 50 workers who are classified as direct labour and each of them is guaranteed at least 480 hours of pay each quarter at a rate of $7.50 per hour. In that case, the minimum direct labour cost for a quarter would be as follows:

50 workers × 480 hours per worker × $7.50 per hour = $180,000

Notice that in Schedule 4, the direct labour costs for the first and fourth quarters would have to be increased to the $180,000 level if Hampton Freeze's labour policy did not allow it to adjust the workforce.

The Manufacturing Overhead Budget

 APPLY

CC9: Prepare a manufacturing overhead budget.

The **manufacturing overhead budget** provides a schedule of all costs of production other than direct materials and direct labour. Schedule 5 shows the manufacturing overhead budget for Hampton Freeze. Note how the production costs are separated into variable and fixed components. The variable component is $2 per direct labour-hour. The fixed component is $60,600 per quarter.

Schedule 5 for Hampton Freeze shows its budgeted cash disbursements for manufacturing overhead. Since some of the overhead costs are not cash outflows, the total budgeted manufacturing overhead costs must be adjusted to determine the cash disbursements for manufacturing overhead. At Hampton Freeze, the only significant noncash manufacturing

Schedule 5—Manufacturing Overhead Budget

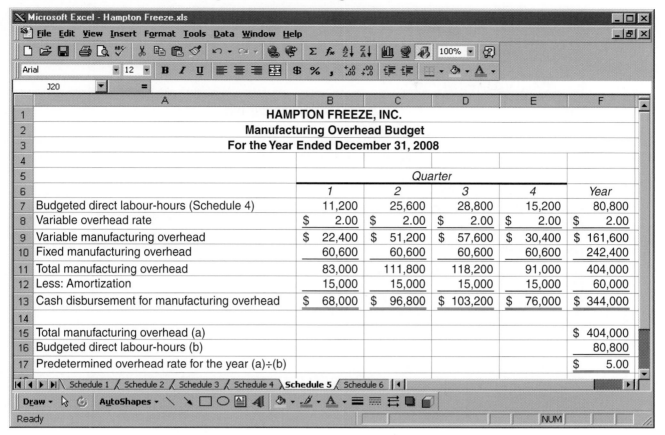

HAMPTON FREEZE, INC.
Manufacturing Overhead Budget
For the Year Ended December 31, 2008

	Quarter				
	1	2	3	4	Year
Budgeted direct labour-hours (Schedule 4)	11,200	25,600	28,800	15,200	80,800
Variable overhead rate	$ 2.00	$ 2.00	$ 2.00	$ 2.00	$ 2.00
Variable manufacturing overhead	$ 22,400	$ 51,200	$ 57,600	$ 30,400	$ 161,600
Fixed manufacturing overhead	60,600	60,600	60,600	60,600	242,400
Total manufacturing overhead	83,000	111,800	118,200	91,000	404,000
Less: Amortization	15,000	15,000	15,000	15,000	60,000
Cash disbursement for manufacturing overhead	$ 68,000	$ 96,800	$ 103,200	$ 76,000	$ 344,000
Total manufacturing overhead (a)					$ 404,000
Budgeted direct labour-hours (b)					80,800
Predetermined overhead rate for the year (a)÷(b)					$ 5.00

overhead cost is amortization, which is $15,000 per quarter. These noncash amortization charges are deducted from the total budgeted manufacturing overhead to determine the expected cash disbursements. Hampton Freeze pays all overhead costs involving cash disbursements in the quarter incurred. Notice that the company's predetermined overhead rate for the year will be $5 per direct labour-hour.

The Ending Finished Goods Inventory Budget

After completing Schedules 1–5, Larry Giano had all of the data he needed to compute unit product costs. This computation was needed for two reasons: first, to determine cost of goods sold on the budgeted income statement; and second, to know what amount to put on the balance sheet inventory account for unsold units. The carrying cost of the unsold units is computed on the **ending finished goods inventory budget.**

Larry Giano considered using variable costing in preparing Hampton Freeze's budget statements, but he decided to use absorption costing instead, since the bank would very likely require that absorption costing be used.[1] He also knew that it would be easy to convert the absorption costing financial statements to a variable costing basis later. At this point, the primary concern was to determine what financing, if any, would be required in the year 2008 and then to arrange for that financing from the bank.

The unit product cost computations are shown in Schedule 6. For Hampton Freeze, the absorption costing unit product cost is $13 per case of popsicles—consisting of $3 of direct materials, $6 of direct labour, and $4 of manufacturing overhead. Manufacturing

○ APPLY

CC10: Prepare an ending finished goods inventory budget.

---

[1]See Chapters 4 and 11.

Schedule 6—Ending Finished Goods Inventory Budget

HAMPTON FREEZE, INC.
Ending Finished Goods Inventory Budget
(absorption costing basis)
For the Year Ended December 31, 2008

Item	Quantity		Cost		Total
Production cost per case:					
Direct materials	15.00	kilograms	$ 0.20	per kilogram	$ 3.00
Direct labour	0.80	hours	7.50	per hour	6.00
Manufacturing overhead	0.80	hours	5.00	per hour	4.00
Unit product cost					$ 13.00
Budgeted finished goods inventory:					
Ending finished goods inventory in cases (Schedule 2)					3,000
Unit product cost (see above)					$ 13.00
Ending finished goods inventory in dollars					$ 39,000

overhead is applied to units of product on the basis of direct labour-hours. The budgeted carrying cost of the expected ending inventory is $39,000.

The Selling and Administrative Expense Budget

● APPLY

CC11: Prepare a selling and administrative expense budget.

The **selling and administrative expense budget** lists the budgeted expenses for areas other than manufacturing. In large organizations, this budget would be a compilation of many smaller, individual budgets submitted by department heads and other persons responsible for selling and administrative expenses. For example, the marketing manager in a large organization would submit a budget detailing the advertising expenses for each budget period.

Schedule 7 contains the selling and administrative expense budget for Hampton Freeze.

IN BUSINESS TODAY   Keeping Current

Jim Bell, Hunstman Corp.'s director of corporate finance, says that his company must frequently update its budgets and its forecasts to meet the demands of investors, creditors, and others. The company updates its annual budget each month, using the most recent data, to provide greater accuracy as the year unfolds. The budget is also used together with sophisticated modeling software to evaluate what effects decisions and various changes in input prices and other parameters might have on future results.

Source: Tim Reason, "Partial Clearing," *CFO*, December 2002, pp. 73–76.

Schedule 7—Selling and Administrative Expense Budget

		Quarter				
		1	2	3	4	Year

HAMPTON FREEZE, INC.
Selling and Administrative Expense Budget
For the Year Ended December 31, 2008

	1	2	3	4	Year
Budgeted sales in cases (Schedule 1)	10,000	30,000	40,000	20,000	100,000
Variable selling and administrative expense per case	$ 1.80	$ 1.80	$ 1.80	$ 1.80	$ 1.80
Total budgeted variable selling and administrative expense	$ 18,000	$ 54,000	$ 72,000	$ 36,000	$ 180,000
Budgeted fixed selling and administrative expenses:					
Advertising	20,000	20,000	20,000	20,000	80,000
Executive salaries	55,000	55,000	55,000	55,000	220,000
Insurance*		1,900	37,750		39,650
Property taxes*				18,150	18,150
Amortization	10,000	10,000	10,000	10,000	40,000
Total budgeted fixed selling and administrative expense	85,000	86,900	122,750	103,150	397,800
Total budgeted selling and administrative expenses	103,000	140,900	194,750	139,150	577,800
Less: Amortization	10,000	10,000	10,000	10,000	40,000
Cash disbursements for selling and administrative expenses	$ 93,000	$ 130,900	$ 184,750	$ 129,150	$ 537,800

*These amounts are shown on a cash basis. Ordinarily, the matching principle would require $39,650 and $18,150 be allocated equally to the four quarters, if quarterly financial statements were prepared.

The Cash Budget

As illustrated in Exhibit 7–2, the cash budget pulls together much of the data developed in the preceding schedules. It is a good idea to restudy Exhibit 7–2 to get the big picture firmly in mind before moving on.

 APPLY

CC12: Prepare a cash budget.

The cash budget is composed of four major sections:

- receipts
- disbursements
- cash excess or deficiency
- financing

The receipts section consists of a listing of all of the cash inflows, except for financing, expected during the budget period. Generally, the major source of receipts will be from sales.

The disbursements section consists of all cash payments that are planned for the budget period. These payments will include raw materials purchases, direct labour payments, manufacturing overhead costs, and so on, as contained in their respective budgets. In addition, other cash disbursements, such as equipment purchases, dividends, and other cash withdrawals by owners are listed. For instance, we see in Schedule 8 that management plans to spend $137,000 during the budget period on equipment purchases and $32,000 on dividends to the owners. This is additional information that does not appear on any of the previous schedules.

Schedule 8—Cash Budget

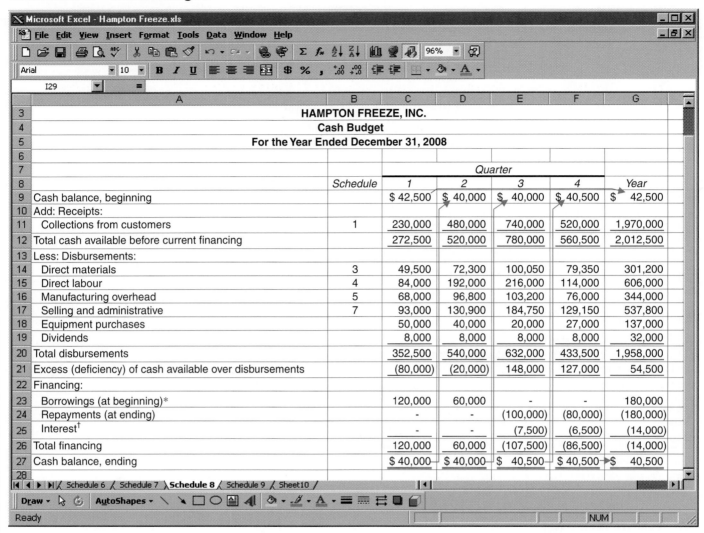

*The company requires a minimum cash balance of $40,000. Therefore, borrowing must be sufficient to cover the cash deficiency of $80,000 in quarter 1 and to provide for the minimum cash balance of $40,000. All borrowings and repayments of principal are in round $1,000 amounts.

†The interest payments relate only to the principal being repaid at the time it is repaid. For example, the interest in quarter 3 relates only to the interest due on the $100,000 principal being repaid from quarter 1 borrowing: $100,000 × 10% per year × 3/4 year = $7,500; the interest paid in quarter 4 is computed as follows:

$20,000 × 10% per year × 1 year.....	$2,000	(interest on amount repaid from quarter 1)
$60,000 × 10% per year × 3/4 year....	4,500	(interest on amount repaid from quarter 2)
Total interest paid..................	$6,500	

The cash excess or deficiency section is computed as follows:

Cash balance, beginning....................................	XXXX
Add: Receipts...	XXXX
Total cash available before financing	XXXX
Less: Disbursements......................................	XXXX
Excess (deficiency) of cash available over disbursements	XXXX

If there is a cash deficiency during any budget period, the company will need to borrow funds. If there is a cash excess during any budget period, funds borrowed in previous periods can be repaid or the excess funds can be invested.

The financing section provides a detailed account of the borrowings and repayments projected to take place during the budget period. It also includes a detail of interest payments that will be due on money borrowed.[2]

Generally speaking, the cash budget should be broken down into time periods that are as short as feasible. Considerable fluctuations in cash balances may be hidden by looking at a longer time period. While a monthly cash budget is most common, many firms budget cash on a weekly or even daily basis. Larry Giano has prepared a quarterly cash budget for Hampton Freeze that can be further refined, as necessary. This budget appears in Schedule 8. Larry has assumed in the budget that an open line of credit can be arranged with the bank that can be used, as needed, to bolster the company's cash position. He has also assumed that any loans taken out with this line of credit would carry an interest rate of 10% per year. Larry has assumed that all borrowings and repayments are in round $1,000 amounts and that all borrowing occurs at the beginning of a quarter and all repayments are made at the end of a quarter. The details on the interest calculation can be found at the Online Learning Centre at www.mcgrawhill.ca/olc/brewer.

In the case of Hampton Freeze, all loans have been repaid by year end. If all loans are not repaid and a budgeted income statement or balance sheet is being prepared, then interest must be accrued on the unpaid loans. This interest will *not* appear on the cash budget (since it has not yet been paid), but will appear as part of interest expense on the budgeted income statement and as a liability on the budgeted balance sheet.

The Budgeted Income Statement

A budgeted income statement can be prepared from the data developed in Schedules 1 to 8. *The budgeted income statement is one of the key schedules in the budget process.* It shows the company's planned profit for the upcoming budget period, and it serves as a benchmark against which subsequent company performance can be measured.

Schedule 9 contains the budgeted income statement for Hampton Freeze. The cost of goods sold is determined from schedules 1 and 6 as follows: Hampton Freeze has

 APPLY

CC13: Prepare a budgeted income statement.

Schedule 9—Budgeted Income Statement

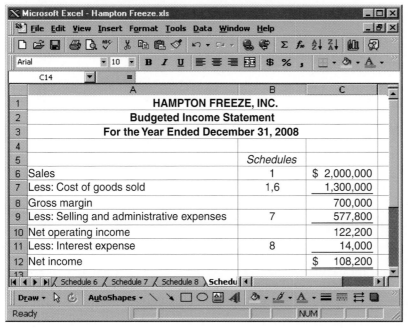

		Schedules	
1	HAMPTON FREEZE, INC.		
2	Budgeted Income Statement		
3	For the Year Ended December 31, 2008		
4			
5		*Schedules*	
6	Sales	1	$ 2,000,000
7	Less: Cost of goods sold	1,6	1,300,000
8	Gross margin		700,000
9	Less: Selling and administrative expenses	7	577,800
10	Net operating income		122,200
11	Less: Interest expense	8	14,000
12	Net income		$ 108,200

---

[2]The format for the cash flow statement, which is discussed in Chapter 15, may also be used for the cash budget.

planned to sell 100,000 cases during 2008. The cost of each case, from schedule 6 is $13. Therefore, the cost of goods sold is $1,300,000. Although this calculation is simple, it is important to realize it hides many details that may be of interest. For example, detail regarding manufacturing costs incurred and the cost of goods manufactured has been collapsed into the cost of goods sold. It is not difficult to extract this information from the schedules developed. An income statement showing this detail appears below.

HAMPTON FREEZE, INC.
Income Statement
For the year ended December 31, 2008

Sales (Schedule 1)...			$2,000,000
Cost of goods sold:			
Beginning finished goods inventory (2,000 cases, Schedule 2 × $13/case, Schedule 6).....			26,000
Add Cost of goods manufactured:			
Total manufacturing costs:			
Direct materials (Schedule 3):			
Beginning inventory of direct materials	$ 4,200		
Add: Purchases of direct materials	303,300		
Less: Ending inventory of direct materials	$4,500		
Direct materials used in production	303,000		
Direct labour (Schedule 4)	606,000		
Manufacturing overhead (Schedule 5)	404,000		
Manufacturing costs incurred	$1,313,000		
Cost of goods manufactured:		1,313,000	
Goods available for sale		1,339,000	
Less: Ending finished goods inventory (3,000 cases, Schedule 2 × $13/case, Schedule 6)		39,000	
Cost of goods sold..		1,300,000	
Gross margin...		700,000	
Selling and administrative expenses (Schedule 7)		577,800	
Net operating income		122,200	
Interest expense (Schedule 8)................................		14,000	
Net Income		$ 108,200	

Hampton Freeze does not have work-in-process inventory; therefore, the cost of goods manufactured and manufacturing costs incurred are equal. Study this income statement carefully and make sure you can see how the information from the various schedules has been used in its construction.

The Budgeted Balance Sheet

⚪ **APPLY**

CC14: Prepare a budgeted balance sheet.

The budgeted balance sheet is developed by beginning with the current balance sheet and adjusting it for the data contained in the other budgets. Hampton Freeze's budgeted balance sheet is presented in Schedule 10. Some of the data on the budgeted balance sheet have been taken from the company's end-of-year balance sheet for 2007, which appears on page 280.

Explanation of December 31, 2008, balance sheet figures:

a. The ending cash balance, as projected by the cash budget in Schedule 8.

b. 30% of fourth-quarter sales, from Schedule 1 ($400,000 × 30% = $120,000).

Schedule 10—Budgeted Balance Sheet

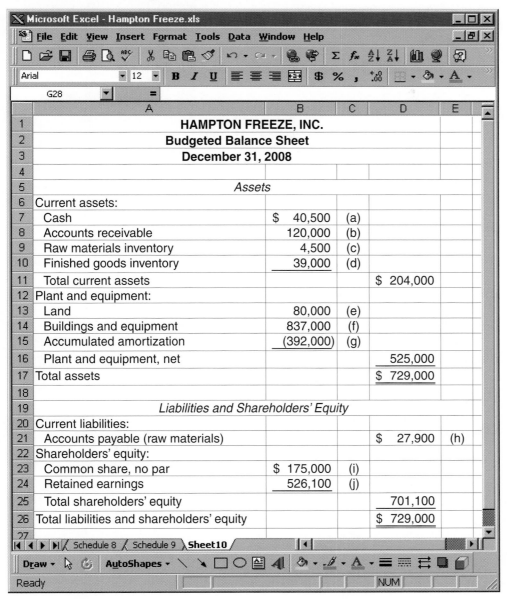

HAMPTON FREEZE, INC.
Budgeted Balance Sheet
December 31, 2008

Assets

Current assets:			
Cash	$ 40,500	(a)	
Accounts receivable	120,000	(b)	
Raw materials inventory	4,500	(c)	
Finished goods inventory	39,000	(d)	
Total current assets			$ 204,000
Plant and equipment:			
Land	80,000	(e)	
Buildings and equipment	837,000	(f)	
Accumulated amortization	(392,000)	(g)	
Plant and equipment, net			525,000
Total assets			$ 729,000

Liabilities and Shareholders' Equity

Current liabilities:			
Accounts payable (raw materials)			$ 27,900 (h)
Shareholders' equity:			
Common share, no par	$ 175,000	(i)	
Retained earnings	526,100	(j)	
Total shareholders' equity			701,100
Total liabilities and shareholders' equity			$ 729,000

c. From Schedule 3, the ending raw materials inventory will be 22,500 kilograms. This material costs $0.20 per kilogram. Therefore, the ending inventory in dollars will be 22,500 kilograms × $0.20 per kilogram = $4,500.

d. From Schedule 6.

e. From the December 31, 2007, balance sheet (no change).

f. The December 31, 2007, balance sheet indicated a balance of $700,000. During 2008, $137,000 additional equipment will be purchased (see Schedule 8), bringing the December 31, 2008, balance to $837,000.

g. The December 31, 2007, balance sheet indicated a balance of $292,000. During 2008, $100,000 of amortization will be taken ($60,000 on Schedule 5 and $40,000 on Schedule 7), bringing the December 31, 2008, balance to $392,000.

h. 50% of the fourth-quarter raw materials purchases, from Schedule 3.

i. From the December 31, 2007, balance sheet (no change).

j. December 31, 2007 balance $449,900
   Add net income, from Schedule 9   108,200
                                                          558,100
   Deduct dividends paid, from Schedule 8   32,000
   December 31, 2008, balance $526,100

HAMPTON FREEZE, INC.
Balance Sheet
December 31, 2007

Assets

Current assets:		
Cash	$42,500	
Accounts receivable	90,000	
Raw materials inventory (21,000 kilograms)	4,200	
Finished goods inventory (2,000 cses)	26,000	
Total current assets		$162,700
Plant and equipment:		
Land	80,000	
Buildings and equipment	700,000	
Accumulated amortization	(292,000)	
Plant and equipment, net		488,000
Total assets		$650,700

Liabilities and Shareholders' Equity

Current liabilities:		
Accounts payable (raw materials)		$25,800
Shareholders' equity:		
Common shares, no par	$175,000	
Retained earnings	449,900	
Total shareholders' equity		624,900
Total liabilities and shareholders' equity		$650,700

MANAGERIAL ACCOUNTING IN ACTION

The Wrap Up

Hampton Freeze, Inc.

After completing the master budget, Larry Giano took the documents to Tom Wills, chief executive officer of Hampton Freeze, for his review.

Larry: Here's the budget. Overall, the net income is excellent, and the net cash flow for the entire year is positive.

Tom: Yes, but I see on this cash budget that we have the same problem with negative cash flows in the first and second quarters that we had last year.

Larry: That's true. I don't see any way around that problem. However, there is no doubt in my mind that if you take this budget to the bank today, they'll approve an open line of credit that will allow you to borrow enough to make it through the first two quarters without any problem.

Tom: Are you sure? They didn't seem very happy to see me last year when I came in for an emergency loan.

Larry: Did you repay the loan on time?

Tom: Sure.

Larry: I don't see any problem. You won't be asking for an emergency loan this time. The bank will have plenty of warning. And, with this budget, you have a solid plan that shows when and how you are going to pay off the loan. Trust me, they'll go for it.

Tom: Fantastic! It would sure make life a lot easier this year.

A Fiscally Responsible Student

You are a new student who will be footing part of the bill for your education. You saved quite a bit of money but are sure that you will need to earn more to cover your expenses. Before you look for a part-time job, you need to decide how many hours per week you will work and what hourly wage you will need in order to pay your expenses. You decide to prepare a budget for your college education. How should you proceed?

Practical Issues in Budgeting: Use and Abuse

How can organizations ensure that the benefits of budgeting and budgets can be attained in practice? This important question suggests that it is possible for budgeting and budgets to have dysfunctional effects on an organization. In this part of the chapter, we will discuss the issues that organizations must consider in order to attain the advantages of budgeting and avoiding the dysfunctional effects.

> ⚪ **KNOW**
>
> CC15: Describe the practical issues that should be considered in the budgeting process including the concepts of participative budgeting and responsibility accounting.

The example of Larry Giano at Hampton Freeze provides an insightful starting point. Recall how Larry accomplished his mandate to introduce and develop a budgeting system.

1. Larry had the full backing of Tom Wills in developing the budgeting system at Hampton Freeze.
2. At the outset, Larry communicated the need for a budgeting system and obtained the cooperation of those whose involvement was essential to the development and *application* of the budgets.
3. Finally, Larry worked closely with all the managers involved and ensured that they understood and supported the parts of the budget that affected them, thus preparing them to take ownership of the budgeting system in the future.

Apparently, Larry knows a thing or two about managing. His experience illustrates the importance of top management support, communication, and cooperation for developing budgets that will be accepted by those who will have to follow them. We now examine these aspects further.

The Self-Imposed Budget

The success of a budget program will be determined, in large part, by the way in which the budget is developed. In the most successful budget programs, managers with cost control responsibilities actively participate in preparing their own budgets. This is in contrast to the approach in which budgets are imposed from above. The participative approach to preparing budgets is particularly important if the budget is to be used to control and evaluate a manager's performance. If a budget is imposed on a manager from above, it will probably generate resentment and ill-will, rather than cooperation and commitment.

This budgeting approach in which managers prepare their own budget estimates—called a *self-imposed budget*—is generally considered to be the most effective method of budget preparation. A **self-imposed budget** or **participative budget** is a budget that is prepared with the full cooperation and participation of managers at all levels. Exhibit 7–3 illustrates this approach to budget preparation.

A number of advantages are commonly cited for such self-imposed budgets:

- Individuals at all levels of the organization are recognized as members of the team whose views and judgments are valued by top management.
- Budget estimates prepared by front-line managers can be more accurate and reliable than estimates prepared by top managers who are more remote from day-to-day activities and who have less intimate knowledge of markets and operating conditions.

Exhibit 7–3
The Initial Flow of Budget Data
in a Self-Imposed (Participative)
Budgeting System

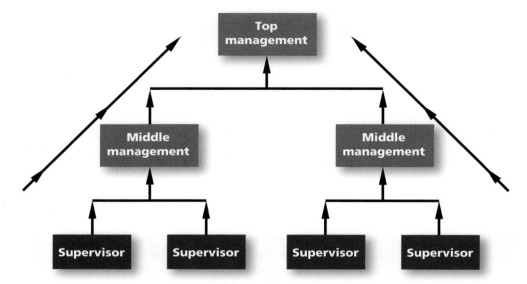

The initial flow of budget data in a participative system is from lower levels of responsibility to higher levels of responsibility. Each person with responsibility for cost control will prepare his or her own budget estimates and submit them to the next higher level of management. These estimates are reviewed and consolidated as they move upward in the organization.

- Motivation is generally higher when an individual participates in setting his or her own goals than when management imposes the goals. Self-imposed budgets create commitment.
- If a manager is unable to meet a budget that was imposed from above, the manager can always say that the budget was unreasonable or unrealistic to start with and therefore was impossible to meet. With a self-imposed budget, this excuse is not available.

Once self-imposed budgets are prepared, are they subject to any kind of review? The answer is yes. Budget estimates prepared by lower-level managers cannot necessarily be accepted without question by higher levels of management. If no system of checks and balances is present, self-imposed budgets may be too loose and allow too much *budgetary slack*. The result will be inefficiency and waste. Therefore, before budgets are accepted, they must be carefully reviewed by immediate superiors. If changes from the original budget seem desirable, the items in question are discussed and modified, as necessary.

In essence, all levels of an organization should work together to produce the budget. Since top management is generally unfamiliar with detailed, day-to-day operations, it should rely on subordinates to provide detailed budget data. However, top management has a perspective on the company as a whole that is also vital. Each level of responsibility in an organization should *cooperate* to develop an integrated budget.

We have described an ideal budgetary process that involves self-imposed budgets prepared by the managers who are directly responsible for revenues and costs. Most companies deviate from this ideal. Typically, top managers initiate the budget process by issuing broad guidelines in terms of overall target profits or sales. Lower-level managers are directed to prepare budgets that meet those targets. The difficulty is that the targets set by top managers may be unrealistically high or may allow too much slack. If the targets are too high and employees know they are unrealistic, motivation will suffer. If the targets allow too much slack, waste will occur. And, unfortunately, top managers are often not in a position to know whether the targets they have set are appropriate. Admittedly, however, a pure self-imposed budgeting system may lack sufficient strategic direction, and lower-level managers may be tempted to build a great deal of budgetary slack into their budgets. Nevertheless, because of the motivational advantages of self-imposed budgets, top managers should be cautious about setting inflexible targets.

The Matter of Human Relations

The success of a budget program also depends on the following: (1) the degree to which top management accepts the budget program as a vital part of the company's activities, and (2) the way in which top management uses budgeted data.

If a budget program is to be successful, it must have the complete acceptance and support of the persons who occupy key management positions. If lower or middle management personnel sense that top management is lukewarm about budgeting, or if they sense that top management simply tolerates budgeting as a necessary evil, then their own attitudes will reflect a similar lack of enthusiasm. Budgeting is hard work, and if top management is not enthusiastic about and committed to the budget program, then it is unlikely that anyone else in the organization will be either.

RESPONSIBILITY ACCOUNTING   The basic idea behind **responsibility accounting** is that a manager should be held responsible for those items—and *only* those items— that the manager can actually control to a significant extent. Each line item (i.e., revenue or cost) in the budget is made the responsibility of a manager, and that manager is held responsible for subsequent deviations between budgeted goals and actual results. In effect, responsibility accounting *personalizes* accounting information by looking at costs from a *personal control* standpoint. This concept is central to any effective profit planning and control system. Someone must be held responsible for each cost, or else no one will be responsible, and the cost will inevitably grow out of control.

Being held responsible for costs does not mean that the manager is penalized if the actual results do not measure up to the budgeted goals. However, the manager should take the initiative to correct any unfavourable discrepancies, should understand the source of significant favourable or unfavourable discrepancies, and should be prepared to explain the reasons for discrepancies to higher management. The point of an effective responsibility system is to make sure that nothing "falls through the cracks," that the organization reacts quickly and appropriately to deviations from its plans, and that the organization learns from the feedback it gets by comparing budgeted goals to actual results. The point is *not* to penalize individuals for missing targets. Top management must not use the budget as a punishment to pressure employees or as a way to find someone to blame if something goes wrong. Using budgets in such negative ways will simply breed hostility, tension, and mistrust, rather than greater cooperation and productivity. Unfortunately, research suggests that the budget is often used as a pressure device and that great emphasis is placed on "meeting the budget" under all circumstances.[3]

Rather than being used as a pressure device, the budget should be used as a positive instrument to assist in establishing goals, measuring operating results, and isolating areas that are in need of extra effort or attention. Any misgivings that employees have about a budget program can be overcome by meaningful involvement at all levels and by proper use of the program over time. Administration of a budget program requires a great deal of insight and sensitivity on the part of management. The budget program should be designed to be a positive aid in achieving both individual and company goals.

Management must keep clearly in mind that the human dimension in budgeting is of key importance. It is easy to become preoccupied with the technical aspects of the budget program to the exclusion of the human aspects. Indeed, the use of budget data in a rigid

---

[3]Paul J. Carruth, Thurrell O. McClendon, and Milton R. Ballard, "What Supervisors Don't Like about Budget Evaluations," *Management Accounting* 64, no. 8 (February 1983), p. 42.

and inflexible manner is the greatest single complaint of those whose performance is being evaluated using the budget process.[4] Management should remember that the purposes of the budget are to motivate employees and to coordinate efforts. Preoccupation with the dollars and cents in the budget, or being rigid and inflexible, can only lead to frustration of these purposes.

IN BUSINESS TODAY   **Using Budgets and Financials to Engage Employees**

According to Robert Meggy, CMA, FMCA, President and CEO of the Great Little Box Company (GLBC), "being named best place to work in B.C. is the highlight of my career." This recognition is just one of several accorded in recent years to GLBC which was named one of Canada's 50 best-managed companies for three years in a row. The company under the leadership of Mr. Meggy has made it a priority to connect with its employees by providing them with the information they need and empowering them to make decisions. The company's budget, financials, and financial statements comprise an important element of the information that is shared with employees. Every two years the employees are taught the basics of understanding financial statements using analogies drawn from personal finances. Personal vehicles, homes, mortgages are used to illustrate balance sheet concepts and costs and revenues are illustrated in terms of a simple business setting like a lemonade stand. According to Mr. Meggy "By doing this, I hope to create a sense of trust around our reporting." As this chapter has shown you, the budget is a repository of comprehensive information about the financial and operating plans of the company among other things. Sharing this information with employees can lead employees to increase their identification with their company and their commitment to work for its success. This is borne out by the experience of GLBC: "In our annual survey of employees, when we ask the question 'do you care about the future of the company,' it garners the highest positive response of any question."

Source: Robert Colman, "Packing the Perfect HR Punch," *CMA Management,* March 2007, pp. 40–43.

The Budget Committee

A standing **budget committee** will usually be responsible for overall policy matters relating to the budget program and for coordinating the preparation of the budget itself. This committee generally consists of the president; vice-presidents in charge of various functions, such as sales, production, and purchasing; and the controller. Difficulties and disputes between segments of the organization in matters relating to the budget are resolved by the budget committee. In addition, the budget committee approves the final budget and receives periodic reports on the progress of the company in attaining budgeted goals.

Disputes can (and do) erupt over budget matters. Because budgets allocate resources, the budgeting process to a large extent determines which departments get more resources and which get relatively less. Also, the budget sets the benchmarks by which managers and their departments will be at least partially evaluated. Therefore, it should not be surprising that managers take the budgeting process seriously, investing considerable energy and even emotion in ensuring that their interests and those of their departments are protected. Because of this, the budgeting process can easily degenerate into an interoffice brawl in which the ultimate goal of working together toward common goals is forgotten.

Running a successful budgeting program that avoids interoffice battles requires considerable interpersonal skills in addition to purely technical skills. But even the best

---

[4]Carruth et al., "What Supervisors Don't Like . . . ," p. 91.

interpersonal skills will fail if, as discussed previously, top management uses the budget process inappropriately as a club or as a way to find blame.

Budgets are Action Plans for Improving Financial Health

Grant MacEwan College in Edmonton, Alberta in 2003 was faced with higher operating costs than it could handle. Confronted with tight government financing, the college had to find ways to increase its revenues by June 2003 in order to avoid cost overruns, which outpaced the government grants received. For Grant MacEwan, the anticipated $2 million shortfall represents about 2% of the college's total annual budget of $115 million, that has to be recovered to avoid shrinking faculty and programs. Junior colleges like Grant MacEwan are strictly prohibited by law to run deficits unlike their university counterparts such as the University of Alberta and University of Calgary. In the case of Grant MacEwan, one step taken by the college was to increase 2004 tuition fees by 9.7%. The budget is typically the outlet for organizations like Grant MacEwan, especially public sector and not-for-profit organizations, to describe actions planned for improving the financial situation and an important planning tool to identify alternative financial health improving strategies. The exact courses of action and the financial consequences are often revealed to appropriate oversight departments and the public only when the budget is submitted.

Source: "Cash-strapped Edmonton College Must Come Up with Money or Make Cuts." *Canadian Press Newswire*. March 8, 2003.

Beyond Budgeting[5]

Is budgeting worth the trouble that organizations must endure to introduce and apply it successfully? This controversial question is at the heart of a new philosophy about budgeting being developed by the Beyond Budgeting Round Table (BBRT)—a program of a European think tank, the Consortium for Advanced Manufacturing-International (Europe). Traditional budgeting is viewed as a tool more appropriate in "command and control" organizations. Increased globalization, greater customer involvement, and intense competition have required that firms be more flexible and responsive. This, in turn, requires that firms move away from the "command and control" type structures to ones that disperse more authority to the front lines. Traditional budgeting is ill-suited to this type of organizations. It cannot be tweaked or modified. It has to go.

 KNOW

CC16: Explain the beyond budgeting model and its approach to budgeting.

WEAKNESSES OF TRADITIONAL BUDGETING   According to the BBRT, the traditional budgeting model has several weaknesses. Managers tend to view a budget as being "cast in stone." Therefore, performance evaluation using the budget as a benchmark is often feared and resented, since the actual performance invariably will differ from planned performance. This fear and resentment can often lead to *gaming*. Managers may *lowball* (understate) estimates or overstate the funding needs. Meeting the budget becomes an overarching objective even at the expense of long-term goals. Unnecessary spending can occur where managers end up spending surpluses to zero out the budget to avoid funding clawbacks for the next operating cycle. Finally, managers might understate

---

[5]This section is based on a two-part article "Budgeting—an Unnecessary Evil: How BBRT Envisions a World Without Traditional Budgeting," by Theresa Libby and R. Murray Lindsay, CMA *Management*, March, 2003 and April 2003, www.managementmag.com/index.cfm/ci_id/483/la_id/l.htm.

the actual performance and profits when they exceed targets to avoid the threat of upward ratcheting of performance targets.

Traditional budgets are considered to be financial representations of operational details of the firm's costs and revenues and, as such, are viewed as having little to do with implementing the firm's strategic objectives. It is argued that the traditional budgeting process disconnects the budget participants from the firm's long-term strategic imperatives. Resource allocation is viewed as a zero-sum game and managers become obsessed with ensuring that they get the funds they need. They end up drowning in the details of the budgeting process and the budgets and lose sight of the goals.

Think back to the master budget for Hampton Freeze. Recall that the various budgets comprising the master budget have a *functional* orientation: sales, production, selling and administration, purchasing, and so on. This orientation is considered to be out of step with recent developments in modern management, which emphasizes a *process* orientation. Management of processes is the cornerstone of value creation. Where will budgeting fit in this picture?

Finally, still staying with the Hampton Freeze example, note that Larry Giano could not have created the budget *overnight*. Budgets take time and effort to complete. While this is going on, what do you do if the data used as inputs change? Larry required the involvement and cooperation of many individuals throughout the company. This consumes time and attention. BBRT argues that up to 10 to 30% of a senior executives' time can be consumed by the budgeting process. Is this expenditure of resources worthwhile?

So, what is answer? According to the supporters of the Beyond Budgeting Model, the answer simply is, "Get rid of budgets." The argument is that budgets must play many roles: they have to capture plans and act as a coordinating mechanism for actions; they must provide benchmarks for performance evaluation; and they must motivate and guide management actions and behaviour. These are conflicting roles. No one knows how these conflicts can be resolved.

THE BEYOND BUDGETING MODEL   If traditional budgeting and budgets are to be done away, what should fill the gap? BBRT has proposed a model that eschews the fixed, performance-contract-based command-and-control framework of traditional budgeting. The BBRT model recommends the use of *relative* performance targets and emphasizes the principles of effective strategic management and empowering employees. The following are the key principles of this new model.

1. *Set challenging relative performance targets.* Benchmarks can be relative to industry, specific competitors, internal business units, and so on. The idea is that there is now a basis for evaluating performance. A manager would be hard pressed to explain away poor performance if targets were attained or exceeded by his or her counterparts in similar settings.
2. *Adopt continuous and inclusive planning.* The key here is the *inclusive* aspect. By devolving corporate objectives systematically down the various layers of the organization, a clear link is established between lower-level objectives and targets and the overall strategic imperatives. Now lower-level units of the organization can see and understand the connection between their actions and the attainment of corporate objectives. Front-line managers can make better informed decisions because they will be aware of the impact these decisions can have for the organization.
3. *Use rolling forecasts.* Forecasts are updated regularly and frequently. As the environment changes, forecasts are changed to respond to the changes. This allows managers to be aware of the current situation and manage accordingly. In this model, forecasts are separated from performance targets, measures, and rewards.
4. *Use market-like structures for coordination.* The free market structure is still the best coordinating mechanism. The discipline of the market in promoting efficiency and effectiveness is unequalled. The BBRT model proposes that the centralized coordination be replaced by a set of customer–supplier relationships. There is the external set

between the firm and its customers and suppliers. Within the firm, central services serve and support operating units through service agreements often based on market prices. Operating units and service units are subject to the discipline of the market.

5. *Decentralize resource management.* The BBRT model proposes that front-line units be allowed the freedom to manage their own resources and be held accountable for their actions. This eliminates many layers of bureaucracy, speeds up resource and funding approval requests, and enables managers to respond quickly to changing circumstances.

6. *Control through self-regulation and transparent information.* This principle advocates that managers be provided with strategic, competitive, and market-based information so that they can self-regulate. Information is the basis for making decisions and so should be available to everyone.

7. *Use low-powered incentives lined to group or organizational performance.* Rather than emphasizing individually tailored incentive and compensation schemes based on fixed targets negotiated in advance, this principle recommends the use of collective measures and the inclusion of everyone in the reward program. The idea is to promote a holistic view and teamwork, reducing peer pressure.

There is no doubt that the BBRT model will stimulate lively debate as proponents on both sides try to persuade you and others like you of the merits of their respective positions. Some organizations, such as Borealis, have adopted these principles and have claimed success. There is still a lot to discover and understand about how budgets are prepared and used. Are organizations and individuals prepared to take the leap without the safety parachute of budgets and embrace a management model that does not rely on traditional budgets? The authors of the article on which this discussion has been based have written a major research program to improve our understanding of these issues. We invite you to read their article available at the website referenced in the footnote at the beginning of this section.

Application Competency Summary

Application Competency	Deliverable	Source Documents and Key Information	Steps	Knowledge Competency
Prepare a sales budget including a schedule of cash receipts. ⊙ CC5	*Key Information* Projected quantity of and revenue from sales per period for the planning horizon and projected cash collections per period *Report/Document* Sales budget and schedule of cash receipts	*Sales Forecast Documents* • Projected sales quantities for each period *Pricing Documents* • Selling price of the product/service *Collection Policy Documents* • Expected collections pattern	1. Compute projected sales revenue as projected sales quantity multiplied by the unit selling price. 2. Compute cash receipts for the current period by multiplying the collection percentages for the sales made in prior periods (including the current period) by the respective period's sales and summing the results.	Cash collected in a period need not equal the sales revenue of the period due to timing differences between sales and collections. Accounts receivable represents uncollected sales revenue. Master budget relationships ⊙ CC3

continued

Application Competency	Deliverable	Source Documents and Key Information	Steps	Knowledge Competency
Prepare a production budget. ⊙ CC6	*Key Information* The number of units budgeted for production or purchase each period to satisfy sales, inventory, and other requirements *Report/Document* Production or purchases budget	*Sales Budget* • Projected sales *Inventory Policy Documents and Inventory Records* • Inventory requirements • Actual inventory balance at the beginning of budget planning period	1. Compute estimated production for each period as follows: • Budgeted sales in units plus desired ending inventory less beginning inventory.	Basic inventory flow equation ⊙ CC15 (Ch. 2)
Prepare a direct materials (DM) budget including a schedule of cash disbursements for purchases of raw materials. ⊙ CC7	*Key Information* Raw materials purchases required to support the budgeted production Projected cash disbursements for the purchase of direct materials *Report/Document* Direct materials budget and schedule of expected cash disbursements	*Production Budget* • Production quantity for each period *Materials Requirement and Cost Documents* • Direct materials required per unit of product • Cost per unit of direct materials *Materials Inventory Records* • Actual inventory balance at the beginning of budget planning period *Payables Policy Documents* • Expected payment patterns for materials purchases	1. Compute the quantity of DM required for production as follows: production quantity multiplied by the units of DM required per unit of production. 2. Add beginning DM inventories to obtain quantity of DM needs. 3. Subtract beginning DM inventory balance to obtain DM quantity to purchase. 4. Compute the cost of DM to be purchased as follows: quantity of DM purchase multiplied by the cost per unit of DM. 5. Compute cash payments for the current period by multiplying the payment percentages for the purchases made in prior periods (including the current period) by the respective period's purchases and summing the results.	Cash payments in a period need not equal the value of purchases made in the period due to timing difference between payments made on account and purchases Accounts payable represents purchases unpaid and remaining on account Basic inventory flow equation ⊙ CC15 (Ch. 2)
Prepare a direct labour (DL) budget. ⊙ CC8	*Key Information* DL hours required to support the planned production and the cost of the labour *Report/Document* Direct labour budget	*Production Budget* • Production quantity for each period *Labour Requirement Documents* • DL hours required for each unit *Wage Contract Documents* • DL cost per hour	1. Multiply the budgeted production quantity by the number of DLHs required per unit to compute the total estimated DLHs for the budget period. 2. Multiply the DLHs by the DL cost per hour to compute the total DL cost.	Budget depends on the assumption of period-by-period adjustment of the workforce to yield the required hours. If the firm maintains a constant workforce, this will change the budgeted cost: the cost will be the same for each period.

continued

Application Competency	Deliverable	Source Documents and Key Information	Steps	Knowledge Competency
Prepare a manufacturing overhead (MOH) budget. ⬤ CC9	**Key Information** Budgeted amount of MOH costs per period Cash disbursements for MOH MOH allocation rate per unit of the allocation base **Report/Document** Manufacturing overhead budget	**Activity/Resource Planning Documents** • Budgeted amounts of fixed and variable MOH • Budgeted amounts of overhead allocation base(s) – text example uses DLH as the base but other bases can be used. **Plant Property and Equipment Budget and the Existing Account in the General Ledger** • Current and estimated amortization amount	1. Calculate the budgeted variable MOH: quantity of allocation base multiplied by the variable MOH allocation rate. 2. Add the fixed MOH cost to obtain the total MOH cost. 3. Divide the total MOH by total quantity of the allocation base used over the budget period to get the MOH allocation rate per unit of allocation base. 4. Subtract amortization from total MOH to compute the cash disbursement for MOH.	MOH allocation base Variable MOH allocation rate Predetermined MOH rate ⬤ CC6, 7 (Ch. 4)
Prepare an ending finished goods inventory budget. ⬤ CC10	**Key Information** Budgeted value of ending finished goods inventory at year end (end of budget period) assuming absorption costing. **Report/Document** Ending finished goods inventory budget	**Production Budget** • Ending balance of finished goods inventory in units **Direct Materials Budget** • DM quantity need per unit of product • Cost of DM per unit of DM **Direct Labour Budget** • DL hours required per unit of product • Cost per DL hour **MOH Budget** • MOH allocation base required per unit of product • Predetermined rate per unit of allocation base	1. Calculate cost per unit of product by adding the DM cost, DL cost and MOH cost per unit of product 2. Calculate the value of ending finished goods inventory by multiplying the quantity of goods in ending inventory with the cost per unit calculated as shown in the previous step	Absorption costing ⬤ CC3 (Ch. 4)
Prepare a selling and administrative (S&A) expense budget. ⬤ CC11	**Key Information** Budgeted expenses for selling activities like advertising and for administration such as office salaries, insurance, and property taxes. Cash disbursements for S&A expenses **Report/Document** Selling and administrative expense budget	**Sales Budget** • Sales quantity and revenues **Documents Estimating the Fixed S&A Expenses** • Fixed expenses budgeted for various fixed S&A items including any amortization **Documents Describing Computation of the Variable S&A Expenses** • Variable S&A rate per unit of sales	1. Calculate the variable S&A expense per period: Sales quantity multiplied by the variable S&A expense rate. 2. Itemize the budgeted cost of the fixed components of S&A activities and determine the total fixed S&A expense per period. 3. Add the variable and fixed amounts to obtain total budgeted S&A expenses. 4. Subtract amortization from the total budgeted S&A expense to obtain cash disbursements for S&A expenses.	Variable versus fixed costs Amortization is a noncash expense. ⬤ CC1, 2 (Ch. 2)

continued

Application Competency	Deliverable	Source Documents and Key Information	Steps	Knowledge Competency
Prepare a cash budget. CC12	*Key Information* Expected cash receipts per period before financing; Expected cash disbursements per period before financing payments; Excess of cash or deficiency per period before financing; Financing inflows period and payments for financing charges; Cash balance at the end of each period projected after financing *Report/Document* Cash budget	*Prior Period Estimated Balance Sheet* • Estimated cash balance at the beginning of the budget period *Sales Budget and Schedule of Cash Receipts* • Cash receipts per period *DM Budget and Schedule of Disbursements for Materials Purchases* • Cash disbursements for DM purchases *DL, MOH, and S&A Budgets* • DL, MOH expense, and S&A expenses *Payment Policies Documents* • Disbursement policy for DL, MOH, and S&A related expenses *Capital Purchases Budget* • Amounts related to capital purchases *Documents Pertaining to Financing Available* • Interest rate on borrowing *Cash Policy Documents* • Minimum cash balance requirements *Dividend Policy Documents* • Expected dividend payments	1. Add cash receipts to the beginning cash balance to obtain the cash available before disbursements. 2. Itemize the disbursements and determine total disbursements for the period including expected payments of dividends and capital investment (equipment, etc.). 3. Calculate the difference between the total receipts and disbursements to determine the excess (or deficiency) of cash available over disbursements. 4. If there is a deficiency, calculate the amount of financing required by adding the desired ending cash balance to the amount of the shortfall. 5. If there is an excess of cash, determine the amount to repay on previous borrowings (if any) including interest charges.	Simple and compound interest
Prepare a budgeted income statement. CC13	*Key Information* Projected net income for the budget period *Report/Document* Income statement	*Sales Budget* • Sales revenue *DM, DL, MOH, and Ending Finished Goods Inventory Budgets* • COGS *S&A Expense Budget* • S&A expenses *Cash Budget* • Interest expense	1. Determine the annual sales revenue from the sales budget. 2. Determine the COGS: Multiply the total units sold by the cost per unit obtained from the finished goods ending inventory budget. 3. Calculate gross margin as sales less COGS. 4. Subtract the total S&A expense to obtain operating income. 5. Subtract annual interest expense to obtain net income. [Note: A detailed COGS including COGM schedule can also be prepared from this same information.]	COGS CC14 (Ch. 2) COGM CC16 (Ch. 2) Product and period costs CC10 (Ch. 2)

continued

Application Competency	Deliverable	Source Documents and Key Information	Steps	Knowledge Competency
Prepare a budgeted balance sheet. CC14	*Key Information* Budgeted balance sheet account information *Report/Document* Balance sheet	*Prior Period Balance Sheet* • Retained earnings for the prior period *Ending Finished Goods Inventory Budget* • Value of ending finished goods inventory *DM Budget and Schedule of Cash Disbursements for Purchases* • Value of ending balance in raw materials inventory • Unpaid purchases at the end of the budgeting period *Cash Budget* • Cash balance at the end of the budgeting period *Sales Budget and Schedule of Cash Receipts* • Uncollected sales revenue at the end of the budgeting period *Budgeted Income Statement* • Net income for the year • Total amortization for the budgeting period *Capital Purchases Budget* • Additions to plant and equipment in the current period *Dividend Policy Documents* • Estimated dividends to be declared during the budgeting period	1. From cash budget obtain the ending cash balance. 2. From the schedule of cash receipts, determine the uncollected sales revenue at year end—this is accounts receivable. 3. From the DM budget, determine the value of ending balance in raw materials inventory. 4. From the ending finished goods inventory budget, determine the value of ending balance in finished goods inventory. 5. Add the cash disbursements for equipment purchases from the cash budget to the prior period value of plant and equipment to obtain the year-end value of plant and equipment. 6. Add the total amortization from the MOH budget and the S&A budget to accumulated amortization from the prior period. 7. Subtract accumulated amortization from the value of plant and equipment to obtain plant and equipment net. 8. Determine total assets for the current year. 9. Obtain the amount on account for purchases of DM—this is accounts payable. 10. Add net income from income statement to the retained earnings balance from the prior period. 11. Subtract dividends paid from the total above to obtain year-end balance of retained earnings. 12. Determine total liabilities and equity for the current year. [Note: The preceding material is based on text example where all borrowings are paid by year end; therefore, there is no debt in this example. As well, there are no new share issues or redemptions.]	Master budget and its component budgets and the relationships between the budgets CC3 Understanding how the figures on the balance sheet are derived from the various budgets and schedules Uncollected sales revenue represents accounts receivable Unpaid purchases represents accounts payables Total amortization on the balance sheet includes amortization in MOH and in S&A expense budgets

Guidance Answers to Decision Maker and You Decide

SALES MANAGER (p. 264)

You probably cannot rely on the sales forecasts for casual and dress shoes to forecast the sales of athletic footwear. You should meet with the vice-president of sales to become knowledgeable about the factors that were considered when the decision was made to add this product line. It is hoped that the decision-making process included an extensive analysis of that market. If not, such market research will need to be undertaken at this time. In either case, you should review the results of that research to gain a better understanding of the market for athletic footwear. In addition, you should meet with the marketing department to become familiar with their plans for promoting the product and any goals that have been set in terms of unit sales or market share. Because this is a new product line, you should carefully state the assumptions used to forecast sales.

A FISCALLY RESPONSIBLE STUDENT (p. 279)

To prepare a personal budget, start by estimating your expenses. To ensure that you do not overlook any expenses, you can visit your college's financial aid office to request an estimate of student expenses for the coming school year. Your school might also offer a course designed to help students succeed in college. The textbooks for such courses often include strategies for managing money while in college and may include sample budgets. Consider sharing your list of expenses with someone knowledgeable (a faculty member, advisor, or adult relative) and asking for feedback. After you have estimated your expenses, you can determine the amount of income you will need in addition to the money you have saved. (Do not forget to set aside some of your savings for unforeseen emergencies.)

Many, if not most, college professors expect you to put in two to three hours outside of class per week for every hour that you are in class. If you find that the number of hours that you will need to work is excessive, you should consider restricting your spending in some areas. Keep in mind your long-term goal, which is to succeed in college!

Review Problem: Budget Schedules

Mylar Company manufactures and sells a product that has seasonal variations in demand, with peak sales coming in the third quarter. The following information concerns operations for Year 2—the coming year—and for the first two quarters of Year 3:

a. The company's single product sells for $8 per unit. Budgeted sales in units for the next six quarters are as follows:

	Year 2 Quarter				Year 3 Quarter	
	1	2	3	4	1	2
Budgeted sales in units . . .	40,000	60,000	100,000	50,000	70,000	80,000

b. Sales are collected in the following pattern: 75% in the quarter the sales are made and the remaining 25% in the following quarter. On January 1, Year 2, the company's balance sheet showed $65,000 in accounts receivable, all of which will be collected in the first quarter of the year. Bad debts are negligible and can be ignored.

c. The company desires an ending inventory of finished units on hand at the end of each quarter equal to 30% of the budgeted sales for the next quarter. This requirement was met on December 31, Year 1, in that the company had 12,000 units on hand to start the new year.

d. Five kilograms of raw materials are required to complete one unit of product. The company requires an ending inventory of raw materials on hand at the end of each quarter equal to 10% of the production needs of the following quarter. This requirement was met on December 31, Year 1, in that the company had 23,000 kilograms of raw materials on hand to start the new year.

e. The raw material costs $0.80 per kilogram. Purchases of raw material are paid for in the following pattern: 60% paid in the quarter the purchases are made, and the remaining 40% paid in the following quarter. On January 1, Year 2, the company's balance sheet showed $81,500 in accounts payable for raw material purchases, all of which will be paid for in the first quarter of the year.

Required:

Prepare the following budgets and schedules for the year, showing both quarterly and total figures:

1. A sales budget and a schedule of expected cash collections.
2. A production budget.
3. A direct materials purchases budget and a schedule of expected cash payments for material purchases.

SOLUTION TO REVIEW PROBLEM

1. The sales budget is prepared as follows:

	Year 2 Quarter				
	1	2	3	4	Year
Budgeted sales in units ..	40,000	60,000	100,000	50,000	250,000
Selling price per unit....	× $8	× $8	× $8	× $8	× $8
Total sales	$320,000	$480,000	$800,000	$400,000	$2,000,000

On the basis of the budgeted sales above, the schedule of expected cash collections is prepared as follows:

	Year 2 Quarter				
	1	2	3	4	Year
Accounts receivable, beginning balance........	$ 65,000				$ 65,000
First-quarter sales ($320,000 × 75%, 25%).....	240,000	$ 80,000			320,000
Second-quarter sales ($480,000 × 75%, 25%)...		360,000	$120,000		480,000
Third-quarter sales ($800,000 × 75%, 25%)....			600,000	$200,000	800,000
Fourth-quarter sales ($400,000 × 75%)........				$300,000	300,000
Total cash collections	$305,000	$440,000	$720,000	$500,000	$1,965,000

2. On the basis of the sales budget in units, the production budget is prepared as follows:

	Year 2 Quarter					Year 3 Quarter	
	1	2	3	4	Year	1	2
Budgeted sales (units)........................	40,000	60,000	100,000	50,000	250,000	70,000	80,000
Add: Desired ending inventory of finished goods* .	18,000	30,000	15,000	21,000†	21,000	24,000	
Total needs	58,000	90,000	115,000	71,000	271,000	94,000	
Less: Beginning inventory of finished goods	12,000	18,000	30,000	15,000	12,000	21,000	
Required production	46,000	72,000	85,000	56,000	259,000	73,000	

*30% of the following quarter's budgeted sales in units.
†30% of the budgeted Year 3 first-quarter sales.

3. On the basis of the production budget figures, raw materials will need to be purchased as follows during the year:

	Year 2 Quarter					Year 3 Quarter
	1	2	3	4	Year 2	1
Required production (units)	46,000	72,000	85,000	56,000	259,000	73,000
Raw materials needed per unit (kilograms)	× 5	× 5	× 5	× 5	× 5	× 5
Production needs (kilograms)........................	230,000	360,000	425,000	280,000	1,295,000	365,000
Add: Desired ending inventory of raw materials (kilograms)*.......................	36,000	42,500	28,000	36,500†	36,500	
Total needs (kilograms).	266,000	402,500	453,000	316,500	1,331,500	
Less: Beginning inventory of raw materials (kilograms)	23,000	36,000	42,500	28,000	23,000	
Raw materials to be purchased (kilograms)	243,000	366,500	410,500	288,500	1,308,500	

*10% of the following quarter's production needs in kilograms.
†10% of the Year 3 first-quarter production needs in kilograms.

On the basis of the raw material purchases above, expected cash payments are computed as follows:

| | Year 2 Quarter | | | | |
	1	2	3	4	Year 2
Cost of raw materials to be purchased at $0.80 per kilogram	$194,400	$293,200	$328,400	$230,800	$1,046,800
Accounts payable, beginning balance	$ 81,500				$ 81,500
First-quarter purchases ($194,400 × 60%, 40%)	116,640	$ 77,760			194,400
Second-quarter purchases ($293,200 × 60%, 40%)		175,920	$117,280		293,200
Third-quarter purchases ($328,400 × 60%, 40%)			197,040	$131,360	328,400
Fourth-quarter purchases ($230,800 × 60%)				138,480	138,480
Total cash disbursements	$198,140	$253,680	$314,320	$269,840	$1,035,980

Glossary

Budget A detailed plan for acquiring and using financial and other resources over a specified period. (p. 258)

Budget committee A group of key management persons who are responsible for overall policy matters relating to the budget program and for coordinating the preparation of the budget. (p. 282)

Budgeting The process used by businesses to describe, in financial terms, how they intend to achieve their desired financial and nonfinancial objectives. (p. 258)

Cash budget A detailed plan showing how cash resources will be acquired and used over some specific time period. (p. 263)

Control Those steps taken by management to increase the likelihood that the objectives and targets described in the budgeting stage are attained and to ensure that all parts of the organization function in a manner consistent with organizational policies. (p. 258)

Direct labour budget A detailed plan showing labour requirements over a specific period. (p. 269)

Direct materials budget A detailed plan showing the amount of raw materials that must be purchased during a period to meet both production and inventory needs. (p. 268)

Ending finished goods inventory budget A budget showing the dollar amount of cost expected to appear on the balance sheet for unsold units at the end of a period. (p. 271)

Manufacturing overhead budget A detailed plan showing the production costs, other than direct materials and direct labour, that will be incurred over a specified period. (p. 270)

Master budget A summary of a company's plans in which specific targets are set for sales, production, distribution, and financing activities and that generally culminates in a cash budget, budgeted income statement, and budgeted balance sheet. (p. 258)

Merchandise purchases budget A budget used by a merchandising company that shows the amount of goods that must be purchased from suppliers during the period. (p. 267)

Mission, vision, and values statement A statement that captures the answers to such question as: Where do we want to be five years from now? What should we be to our customers, our employees, and other stakeholders? Which markets do we want to dominate? (p. 258)

Operational planning The process in which the broad goals and objectives of the strategic plan are distilled into specific goals and targets to guide the operations of the organization in the short term (typically one year). (p. 258)

Participative budget See *self-imposed budget.* (p. 279)

Planning Developing objectives and preparing budgets to achieve these objectives. (p. 258)

Production budget A detailed plan showing the number of units that must be produced during a period in order to meet both sales and inventory needs. (p. 266)

Responsibility accounting A system of accountability in which managers are held responsible for those items of revenue and cost—and only those items—over which the manager can exert significant control. The managers are held responsible for differences between budgeted goals and actual results. (p. 281)

Sales budget A detailed schedule showing the expected sales for coming periods; these sales are typically expressed in both dollars and units. (p. 262)

Self-imposed budget A method of preparing budgets in which managers prepare their own budgets. These budgets are then reviewed by the manager's supervisor, and any issues are resolved by mutual agreement. (p. 279)

Selling and administrative expense budget A detailed schedule of planned expenses that will be incurred in areas other than manufacturing during a budget period. (p. 272)

Strategic plan A document that captures the decisions that the organization has made regarding its strategic position in the marketplace. It is the principal output of the strategic planning process. (p. 258)

Strategic planning The process of deciding how the organization should position itself in the marketplace to compete successfully with its rivals for customers and resources. (p. 258)

Zero-based budget A method of budgeting in which managers are required to justify all costs as if the programs involved were being proposed for the first time. (p. 263)

Questions

7–1 What is a budget? What is budgetary control?

7–2 What are some of the major benefits to be gained from budgeting?

7–3 What is meant by *responsibility accounting?*

7–4 What is a master budget? Briefly describe its contents.

7–5 Why is the sales forecast the starting point in budgeting?

7–6 "As a practical matter, planning and control mean exactly the same thing." Do you agree? Explain.

7–7 What is a self-imposed budget? What are the major advantages of self-imposed budgets? What caution must be exercised in their use?

7–8 How can budgeting assist a firm in its employment policies?

7–9 "The principal purpose of the cash budget is to see how much cash the company will have in the bank at the end of the year." Do you agree? Explain.

Brief Exercises

BRIEF EXERCISE 7–1   Budget Process (CC1, 2, 15)

The following terms pertain to the budgeting process:

Benchmarks	Bottlenecks
Budget	Budget committee
Control	Imposed from above
Motivation	Planning
Responsibility accounting	Self-imposed budget

Required:

Fill in the blanks with the most appropriate word or phrase from the above list.

1. _____ is generally higher when an individual participates in setting his or her own goals than when the goals are imposed from above.

2. If a manager is not able to meet the budget and it has been _____, the manager can always say that the budget was unreasonable or unrealistic to start with and therefore was impossible to meet.

3. A _____ is a detailed quantitative plan for acquiring and using financial and other resources over a specified period.

4. _____ involves developing objectives and preparing various budgets to achieve those objectives.

5. The budgeting process can uncover potential _____ before they occur.

6. _____ involves the steps taken by management to increase the likelihood that the goals and targets set down in the budgeting stage are attained.

7. Budgets define goals and objectives that can serve as _____ for evaluating subsequent performance.

8. In _____, a manager is held accountable for those items, and only those items, over which he or she has significant control.

9. A _____ is one that is prepared with the full cooperation and participation of managers at all levels of the organization.

10. A _____ is usually responsible for overall policy matters relating to the budget program and for coordinating the preparation of the budget itself.

BRIEF EXERCISE 7–2   Schedule of Expected Cash Collections (CC5)

Silver Company makes a product that is very popular as a Mother's Day gift. Thus, peak sales occur in May of each year. These peak sales are shown in the following sales budget for the second quarter:

	April	May	June	Total
Budgeted sales	$400,000	$600,000	$300,000	$1,100,000

From past experience, the company has learned that 25% of a month's sales are collected in the month of sale, that another 65% is collected in the month following sale, and that the remaining 10% is collected in the second month following sale. Bad debts are negligible and can be ignored. February sales totalled $380,000, and March sales totalled $360,000.

Required:

1. Prepare a schedule of expected cash collections from sales, by month and in total, for the second quarter.
2. Assume that the company will prepare a budgeted balance sheet as of June 30. Compute the accounts receivable as of that date.

BRIEF EXERCISE 7–3   Production Budget (CC6)

Down Under Products, Ltd., of Australia, has budgeted sales of its popular boomerang for the next four months as follows:

	Sales in Units
April.	50,000
May	75,000
June	90,000
July	80,000

The company is now in the process of preparing a production budget for the second quarter. Past experience has shown that end-of-month inventory levels must equal 10% of the following month's sales. The inventory at the end of March was 5,000 units. (Australia's currency is Australian dollars.)

Required:

Prepare a production budget for the second quarter; in your budget, show the number of units to be produced each month and for the quarter in total.

BRIEF EXERCISE 7–4   Materials Purchases Budget (CC7)

Three grams of musk oil are required for each bottle of Mink Caress, a popular perfume made by a small company in western Siberia. The cost of the musk oil is 150 roubles per gram. (Siberia is located in Russia, whose currency is the rouble.) Budgeted production figures of Mink Caress follow by quarters for Year 2 and for the first quarter of Year 3.

	Year 2 Quarter				Year 3 Quarter
	First	Second	Third	Fourth	First
Budgeted production, in bottles . . .	60,000	90,000	150,000	100,000	70,000

Musk oil has become so popular as a perfume base that it has become necessary to carry large inventories as a precaution against stockouts. For this reason, the inventory of musk oil at the end of a quarter must be equal to 20% of the following quarter's production needs. Some 36,000 grams of musk oil will be on hand to start the first quarter of Year 2.

Required:

Prepare a materials purchases budget for musk oil, by quarter and in total, for Year 2. At the bottom of your budget, show the amount of purchases in roubles for each quarter and for the year in total.

BRIEF EXERCISE 7–5   Direct Labour Budget (CC8)

The Production Department of Rordan Corporation has submitted the following forecast of units to be produced by quarter for the upcoming fiscal year.

	1st Quarter	2nd Quarter	3rd Quarter	4th Quarter
Units to be produced.....	9,000	7,500	8,000	8,500

Each unit requires 0.55 direct labour-hours, and direct labour-hour workers are paid $12.00 per hour.

Required:
1. Construct the company's direct labour budget for the upcoming fiscal year, assuming that the direct labour workforce is adjusted each quarter to match the number of hours required to produce the forecasted number of units produced.
2. Construct the company's direct labour budget for the upcoming fiscal year, assuming that the direct labour workforce is not adjusted each quarter. Instead, assume that the company's direct labour workforce consists of permanent employees who are guaranteed to be paid for at least 2,800 hours of work each quarter. If the number of required direct labour-hours is less than this number, the workers are paid for 2,800 hours anyway. Any hours worked in excess of 2,800 hours in a quarter are paid at the rate of 1.5 times the normal hourly rate for direct labour.

BRIEF EXERCISE 7–6   Manufacturing Overhead Budget (CC9)

The direct labour budget of Yuvwell Corporation for the upcoming fiscal year contains the following details concerning budgeted direct labour-hours.

	1st Quarter	2nd Quarter	3rd Quarter	4th Quarter
Budgeted direct labour-hours	8,000	8,200	8,500	7,800

The company's variable manufacturing overhead rate is $3.25 per direct labour-hour and the company's fixed manufacturing overhead is $48,000 per quarter. The only noncash item included in the fixed manufacturing overhead is amortization, which is $16,000 per quarter.

Required:
1. Construct the company's manufacturing overhead budget for the upcoming fiscal year.
2. Compute the company's manufacturing overhead rate (including both variable and fixed manufacturing overheads) for the upcoming fiscal year. Round off to the nearest whole cent.

BRIEF EXERCISE 7–7   Selling and Administrative Budget (CC11)

The budgeted unit sales of Weller Company for the upcoming fiscal year are as follows:

	1st Quarter	2nd Quarter	3rd Quarter	4th Quarter
Budgeted unit sales......	15,000	16,000	14,000	13,000

The company's variable selling and administrative expense per unit is $2.50. Fixed selling and administrative expenses include advertising expenses of $8,000 per quarter, executive salaries of $35,000 per quarter, and amortization of $20,000 per quarter. In addition, the company makes insurance payments of $5,000 in the first quarter and $5,000 in the third quarter. Finally, property taxes of $8,000 are paid in the second quarter.

Required:
Prepare the company's selling and administrative expense budget for the upcoming fiscal year.

BRIEF EXERCISE 7–8   Cash Budget (CC12)

Garden Depot is a retailer that is preparing its budget for the upcoming fiscal year. Management has prepared the following summary of its budgeted cash flows:

	1st Quarter	2nd Quarter	3rd Quarter	4th Quarter
Total cash receipts.......	$180,000	$330,000	$210,000	$230,000
Total cash disbursements	260,000	230,000	220,000	240,000

The company's beginning cash balance for the upcoming fiscal year will be $20,000. The company requires a minimum cash balance of $10,000 and may borrow any amount needed from a local bank at an annual interest rate of 12%. The company may borrow any amount at the beginning of any quarter and may repay its loans, or any part of its loans, at the end of any quarter. Interest payments are due on any principal at the time it is repaid.

Required:
Prepare the company's cash budget for the upcoming fiscal year.

BRIEF EXERCISE 7–9　Budgeted Income Statement (CC13)

Gig Harbour Boating is the wholesale distributor of small recreational catamaran sailboats. Management has prepared the following summary data to use in its annual budgeting process:

Budgeted sales (in units).............................	460
Selling price per unit.................................	$1,950
Cost per unit	$1,575
Variable selling and administrative expenses (per unit)	$75
Fixed selling and administrative expenses (per year).......	$105,000
Interest expense for the year.........................	$14,000

Required:
Prepare the company's budgeted income statement.

BRIEF EXERCISE 7–10　Budgeted Balance Sheet (CC14)

The management of Mecca Copy, a photocopying centre located on University Avenue, has compiled the following data to use in preparing its budgeted balance sheet for next year:

	Ending Balances
Cash	?
Accounts receivable	$ 8,100
Supplies inventory	3,200
Equipment.....................................	34,000
Accumulated amortization	16,000
Accounts payable	1,800
Common shares	5,000
Retained earnings	?

The beginning balance of retained earnings was $28,000, net income is budgeted to be $11,500, and dividends are budgeted to be $4,800.

Required:
Prepare the company's budgeted balance sheet.

BRIEF EXERCISE 7–11　Cash Collections and Disbursements (CC5, 7, 12)

The following information relates to Young Company for September 2008:

Opening cash balance.............	$ 16,000
Amortization expense.............	3,350
Dividends paid	5,750
Cash collections	35,500
Equipment purchased for cash	6,800
Cash operating expenses	14,900
Merchandise paid for	21,150

Required:
What is Young's cash balance on September 30, 2008?

(Adapted © CGA-Canada)

BRIEF EXERCISE 7–12   Production Budget (CC6)

A company has the following incomplete production budget data for the first quarter:

	January	February	March
Expected unit sales	2,000	6,000	8,000

In the previous December, ending inventory was 200 units, which was the minimum required, at 10% of projected sales units in the coming month.

Required:
What is the expected production in February?

(Adapted © CGA-Canada)

Exercises

EXERCISE 7–1   Schedules of Expected Cash Collections and Disbursements (CC5, 7, 12)

You have been asked to prepare a December cash budget for Ashton Company, a distributor of exercise equipment. The following information is available about the company's operations:
a. The cash balance on December 1 will be $40,000.
b. Actual sales for October and November and expected sales for December are as follows:

	October	November	December
Cash sales	$ 65,000	$ 70,000	$ 83,000
Sales on account	400,000	525,000	600,000

Sales on account are collected over a three-month period in the following ratio: 20% collected in the month of sale, 60% collected in the month following sale, and 18% collected in the second month following sale. The remaining 2% is uncollectible.
c. Purchases of inventory will total $280,000 for December. 30% of a month's inventory purchases are paid during the month of purchase. The accounts payable remaining from November's inventory purchases total $161,000, all of which will be paid in December.
d. Selling and administrative expenses are budgeted at $430,000 for December. Of this amount, $50,000 is for amortization.
e. A new Web server for the Marketing Department costing $76,000 will be purchased for cash during December, and dividends totalling $9,000 will be paid during the month.
f. The company must maintain a minimum cash balance of $20,000. An open line of credit is available from the company's bank to bolster the cash position, as needed.

Required:
1. Prepare a schedule of expected cash collections for December.
2. Prepare a schedule of expected cash disbursements for materials during December to suppliers for inventory purchases.
3. Prepare a cash budget for December. Indicate in the financing section any borrowing that will be needed during the month.

EXERCISE 7–2   Sales and Production Budgets (CC5, 6)

The Marketing Department of Jessi Corporation has submitted the following sales forecast for the upcoming fiscal year.

	1st Quarter	2nd Quarter	3rd Quarter	4th Quarter
Budgeted sales (units). . . .	8,000	10,000	12,000	11,000

The selling price of the company's product is $20.00 per unit. Management expects to collect 65% of sales in the quarter in which the sales are made, 30% in the following quarter, and 5% of sales are expected to be uncollectible. The beginning balance of accounts receivable, all of which is expected to be collected in the first quarter, is $80,500.

The company expects to start the first quarter with 2,000 units in finished goods inventory. Management desires an ending finished goods inventory in each quarter equal to 15% of the next quarter's budgeted sales. The desired ending finished goods inventory for the fourth quarter is 2,250 units.

Required:
1. Prepare the company's sales budget and schedule of expected cash collections.
2. Prepare the company's production budget for the upcoming fiscal year.

EXERCISE 7–3   Production and Direct Materials Budgets (CC6, 7)

The Marketing Department of Gaeber Industries has submitted the following sales forecast for the upcoming fiscal year.

	1st Quarter	2nd Quarter	3rd Quarter	4th Quarter
Budgeted sales (units). . . .	8,000	7,000	6,000	7,000

The company expects to start the first quarter with 1,600 units in finished goods inventory. Management desires an ending finished goods inventory in each quarter equal to 20% of the next quarter's budgeted sales. The desired ending finished goods inventory for the fourth quarter is 1,700 units.

   In addition, the beginning raw materials inventory for the first quarter is budgeted to be 3,120 kilograms and the beginning accounts payable for the first quarter is budgeted to be $14,820.

   Each unit requires two kilograms of raw material that costs $4 per kilogram. Management desires to end each quarter with an inventory of raw materials equal to 20% of the following quarter's production needs. The desired ending inventory for the fourth quarter is 3,140 kilograms. Management plans to pay for 75% of raw material purchases in the quarter acquired and 25% in the following quarter.

Required:
1. Prepare the company's production budget for the upcoming fiscal year.
2. Prepare the company's direct materials budget and schedule of expected cash disbursements for materials for the upcoming fiscal year.

EXERCISE 7–4   Direct Materials and Direct Labour Budgets (CC7, 8)

The Production Department of Hareston Company has submitted the following forecast of units to be produced by quarter for the upcoming fiscal year.

	1st Quarter	2nd Quarter	3rd Quarter	4th Quarter
Units to be produced.	7,000	8,000	6,000	5,000

In addition, the beginning raw materials inventory for the first quarter is budgeted to be 1,400 kilograms and the beginning accounts payable for the first quarter is budgeted to be $2,940.

   Each unit requires two kilograms of raw material that costs $1.40 per kilogram. Management desires to end each quarter with an inventory of raw materials equal to 10% of the following quarter's production needs. The desired ending inventory for the fourth quarter is 1,500 kilograms. Management plans to pay for 80% of raw material purchases in the quarter acquired and 20% in the following quarter. Each unit requires 0.60 direct labour-hours, and direct labour-hour workers are paid $14 per hour.

Required:
1. Prepare the company's direct materials budget and schedule of expected cash disbursements for materials for the upcoming fiscal year.
2. Prepare the company's direct labour budget for the upcoming fiscal year, assuming that the direct labour workforce is adjusted each quarter to match the number of hours required to produce the forecasted number of units produced.

EXERCISE 7–5   Direct Labour and Manufacturing Overhead Budgets (CC8, 9)

The production department of Raredon Corporation has submitted the following forecast of units to be produced by quarter for the upcoming fiscal year.

	1st Quarter	2nd Quarter	3rd Quarter	4th Quarter
Units to be produced.	24,000	28,000	26,000	22,000

Each unit requires 1.4 direct labour-hours, and direct labour-hour workers are paid $21.00 per hour.

   In addition, the variable manufacturing overhead rate is $1.30 per direct labour-hour. The fixed manufacturing overhead is $160,000 per quarter. The only noncash element of manufacturing overhead is amortization, which is $44,000 per quarter.

Required:
1. Prepare the company's direct labour budget for the upcoming fiscal year, assuming that the direct labour workforce is adjusted each quarter to match the number of hours required to produce the forecasted number of units produced.
2. Prepare the company's manufacturing overhead budget.

EXERCISE 7–6   Cash Budget Relations (CC12)
A cash budget, by quarters, follows for a retail company. Fill in the missing amounts (000 omitted). The company requires a minimum cash balance of at least $5,000 to start each quarter.

	1	2	3	4	Year
Cash balance, beginning	$ 6	$?	$?	$?	$?
Add: Collections from customers	?	?	96	?	323
Total cash available before current financing	71	?	?	?	?
Less: Disbursements:					
Purchase of inventory	35	45	?	35	?
Operating expenses	?	30	30	?	113
Equipment purchases	8	8	10	?	36
Dividends	2	2	2	2	?
Total disbursements.	?	85	?	?	?
Excess (deficiency) of cash available over disbursements	(2)	?	11	?	?
Financing:					
Borrowings	?	15	—	—	?
Repayments (including interest)*	—	—	(?)	(17)	(?)
Total financing	?	?	?	?	?
Cash balance, ending	$?	$?	$?	$?	$?

*Interest will total $1,000 for the year.

EXERCISE 7–7   Cash Budget (CC12)
The controller of Ultramint Company wishes to improve the company's control system by preparing a monthly cash budget. The following information relates to the month ending July 31, 2008.

June 30, 2008 cash balance	$ 90,000
Dividends to be declared on July 15*	24,000
Cash expenditures to be paid in July for operating expenses	73,600
Amortization expense	9,000
Cash collections to be received	178,000
Merchandise purchases to be paid in cash	112,400
Equipment to be purchased for cash	41,000
Ultramint Company wishes to maintain a minimum cash balance of	50,000

*Dividends are payable to shareholders of record on declaration date, 30 days after declaration.

Required:
1. Prepare a cash budget for the month ended July 31, 2008, indicating how much, if anything, Ultramint will need to borrow to meet its minimum cash requirement.
2. Explain how cash budgeting can reduce the cost of short-term borrowing.

(Adapted © CGA-Canada)

EXERCISE 7–8   Cash Budget and Materials Purchase Budget (CC5, 7, 12)
All sales of Gamma Electronics Supply are made on credit. Sales are billed twice monthly, on the 10th of the month for sales made in the last half of the prior month, and on the 20th of the month for sales made in

the first half of the current month. The terms of sales are 2/10, net 30. The expected collection experience of accounts receivable is as follows:

Within the discount period	80%
On the 30th day	18%
Uncollectible	2%

Sales for the month of May were $750,000. Forecast sales for the next four months are as follows:

June	$400,000
July	450,000
August	450,000
September	300,000

Gamma's average markup on its products is 20% of the sales price. Gamma purchases sufficient merchandise for resale to meet the current month's sales and to have an ending inventory of 25% of the next month's forecast sales. All purchases are on credit with terms of net 30. Gamma pays for one-half of a month's purchases in the month of purchase and the other half in the month following purchase. All purchases and sales occur evenly throughout the month.

Required:
1. How much will be collected in September from sales made in August?
2. What is the amount of expected collections during July?
3. How much merchandise should Gamma purchase in August?
4. State *two* benefits of cash budgeting.

(Adapted © CGA-Canada)

Problems

CHECK FIGURE
(1) July: $317,500
(2) July 31 cash balance:
    $28,000

PROBLEM 7–1   Schedule of Expected Cash Collections; Cash Budget (CC5, 7, 12)
Herbal Care Corp., a distributor of herb-based sunscreens, is ready to begin its third quarter, in which peak sales occur. The company has requested a $40,000, 90-day loan from its bank to help meet cash requirements during the quarter. Since Herbal Care has experienced difficulty in paying off its loans in the past, the loan officer at the bank has asked the company to prepare a cash budget for the quarter. In response to this request, the following data have been assembled:
a. On July 1, the beginning of the third quarter, the company will have a cash balance of $44,500.
b. Actual sales for the last two months and budgeted sales for the third quarter follow:

May (actual)	$250,000
June (actual)	300,000
July (budgeted)	400,000
August (budgeted).........	600,000
September (budgeted)	320,000

Past experience shows that 25% of a month's sales are collected in the month of sale, 70% in the month following sale, and 3% in the second month following sale. The remainder is uncollectible.
c. Budgeted merchandise purchases and budgeted expenses for the third quarter follow:

	July	August	September
Merchandise purchases..........	$240,000	$350,000	$175,000
Salaries and wages	45,000	50,000	40,000
Advertising	130,000	145,000	80,000
Rent payments................	9,000	9,000	9,000
Amortization.................	10,000	10,000	10,000

Merchandise purchases are paid in full during the month following purchase. Accounts payable for merchandise purchases on June 30, which will be paid during July, total $180,000.

d. Equipment costing $10,000 will be purchased for cash during July.

e. In preparing the cash budget, assume that the $40,000 loan will be made in July and repaid in September. Interest on the loan will total $1,200.

Required:

1. Prepare a schedule of expected cash collections for July, August, and September and for the quarter in total.

2. Prepare a cash budget, by month and in total, for the third quarter.

3. If the company needs a minimum cash balance of $20,000 to start each month, can the loan be repaid as planned? Explain.

PROBLEM 7–2 Production and Purchases Budgets (CC6, 7)

CHECK FIGURE
(1) July: 45,000 units

Daisy Products Limited of Shenzhen, China, manufactures and distributes toys throughout Southeast Asia. Three cubic centimetres (cc) of solvent Q80 are required to manufacture each unit of Fineclay, one of the company's products. The company is now planning raw materials needs for the third quarter, the quarter in which peak sales of Fineclay occur. To keep production and sales moving smoothly, the company has the following inventory requirements:

a. The finished goods inventory on hand at the end of each month must be equal to 3,750 units of Fineclay plus 20% of the next month's sales. The finished goods inventory on June 30 is budgeted to be 12,500 units.

b. The raw materials inventory on hand at the end of each month must be equal to one-half of the following month's production needs for raw materials. The raw materials inventory on June 30 is budgeted to be 67,500 cc of solvent Q80.

c. The company maintains no work-in-process inventories.

A sales budget for Fineclay for the last six months of the year follows:

	Budgeted Sales in Units
July	43,750
August	50,000
September	62,500
October	37,500
November	25,000
December	12,500

Required:

1. Prepare a production budget for Fineclay for the months July–October.

2. Examine the production budget that you prepared in part (1). Why will the company produce more units than it sells in July and August, and fewer units than it sells in September and October?

3. Prepare a budget showing the quantity of solvent Q80 to be purchased for July, August, and September, and for the quarter in total.

PROBLEM 7–3 Cash Budget; Income Statement; Balance Sheet (CC5, 7, 12, 13, 14)

CHECK FIGURE
(1) May 31 cash balance: $8,900
(2) NI: $15,900

Minden Company is a wholesale distributor of premium European chocolates. The company's balance sheet as of April 30 is as follows:

MINDEN COMPANY
Balance Sheet
April 30

Assets

Cash	$ 9,000
Accounts receivable, customers	54,000
Inventory	30,000
Buildings and equipment, net of amortization	207,000
Total assets	$300,000

continued

Liabilities and Shareholders' Equity

Accounts payable, suppliers..........................	$ 63,000
Note payable..	14,500
Capital shares, no par...............................	180,000
Retained earnings...................................	42,500
Total liabilities and shareholders' equity	$300,000

The company is in the process of preparing budget data for May. A number of budget items have already been prepared, as follows:

a. Sales are budgeted at $200,000 for May. Of these sales, $60,000 will be for cash; the remainder will be credit sales. One-half of a month's credit sales are collected in the month the sales are made, and the remainder is collected in the following month. All of the April 30 receivables will be collected in May.

b. Purchases of inventory are expected to total $120,000 during May. These purchases will all be on account. 40% of all purchases are paid for in the month of purchase; the remainder is paid in the following month. All of the April 30 accounts payable to suppliers will be paid during May.

c. The May 31 inventory balance is budgeted at $40,000.

d. Operating expenses for May are budgeted at $72,000, exclusive of amortization. These expenses will be paid in cash. Amortization is budgeted at $2,000 for the month.

e. The note payable on the April 30 balance sheet will be paid during May, with $100 in interest. (All of the interest relates to May.)

f. New refrigerating equipment costing $6,500 will be purchased for cash during May.

g. During May, the company will borrow $20,000 from its bank by giving a new note payable to the bank for that amount. The new note will be due in one year.

Required:

1. Prepare a cash budget for May. Support your budget with schedules showing budgeted cash receipts from sales and budgeted cash payments for inventory purchases.
2. Prepare a budgeted income statement for May. Use the traditional income statement format.
3. Prepare a budgeted balance sheet as of May 31.

CHECK FIGURE
(2) July: 36,000 units

PROBLEM 7–4   Integration of the Sales, Production, and Purchases Budgets (CC5, 6, 7)

Milo Company manufactures beach umbrellas. The company is now preparing detailed budgets for the third quarter and has assembled the following information to assist in the budget preparation:

a. The Marketing Department has estimated sales as follows for the remainder of the year (in units):

July.............	30,000	October..........	20,000
August..........	70,000	November........	10,000
September	50,000	December........	10,000

The selling price of the beach umbrellas is $12 per unit.

b. All sales are on account. On the basis of past experience, sales are collected in the following pattern:

30% in the month of sale
65% in the month following sale
5% uncollectible

Sales for June totalled $300,000.

c. The company maintains finished goods inventories equal to 15% of the following month's sales. This requirement will be met at the end of June.

d. Each beach umbrella requires four metres of Gilden, a material that is sometimes hard to get. Therefore, the company requires that the inventory of Gilden on hand at the end of each month be equal to 50% of the following month's production needs. The inventory of Gilden on hand at the beginning and end of the quarter will be:

June 30 .... 72,000 metres
September 30 ...... ? metres

e. Gilden costs $0.80 per metre. One-half of a month's purchases of Gilden is paid for in the month of purchase; the remainder is paid for in the following month. The accounts payable on July 1 for purchases of Gilden during June will be $76,000.

Required:

1. Prepare a sales budget, by month and in total, for the third quarter. (Show your budget in both units and dollars.) Also, prepare a schedule of expected cash collections, by month and in total, for the third quarter.
2. Prepare a production budget for each of the months July–October.
3. Prepare a materials purchases budget for Gilden, by month and in total, for the third quarter. Also prepare a schedule of expected cash payments for Gilden, by month and in total, for the third quarter.

PROBLEM 7–5   Cash Budget with Supporting Schedules (CC5, 7, 12)

Garden Sales, Inc. sells garden supplies. Management is planning its cash needs for the second quarter. The company usually has to borrow money during this quarter to support peak sales of lawn care equipment, which occur during May. The following information has been assembled to assist in preparing a cash budget for the quarter:

a. Budgeted monthly income statements for April–July are as follows:

	April	May	June	July
Sales	$480,000	$720,000	$400,000	$320,000
Cost of goods sold	336,000	504,000	280,000	224,000
Gross margin	144,000	216,000	120,000	96,000
Less: Operating expenses:				
Selling expense	63,200	96,000	49,600	40,800
Administrative expense*	36,000	41,600	32,800	30,400
Total operating expenses	99,200	137,600	82,400	71,200
Net income	$ 44,800	$ 78,400	$ 37,600	$ 24,800

*Includes $20,000 amortization each month.

b. Sales are 20% for cash and 80% on account.
c. Sales on account are collected over a three-month period in the following ratio: 10% collected in the month of sale; 70% collected in the first month following the month of sale; and the remaining 20% collected in the second month following the month of sale. February's sales totalled $160,000, and March's sales totalled $240,000.
d. Inventory purchases are paid for within 15 days. Therefore, 50% of a month's inventory purchases are paid for in the month of purchase. The remaining 50% is paid in the following month. Accounts payable at March 31 for inventory purchases during March total $100,800.
e. At the end of each month, inventory must be on hand equal to 20% of the cost of the merchandise to be sold in the following month. The merchandise inventory at March 31 is $67,200.
f. Dividends of $39,200 will be declared and paid in April.
g. Equipment costing $12,800 will be purchased for cash in May.
h. The cash balance at March 31 is $41,600; the company must maintain a cash balance of at least $32,000 at all times.
i. The company can borrow from its bank, as needed, to bolster the cash account. Borrowings and repayments must be in multiples of $800. All borrowings take place at the beginning of a month, and all repayments are made at the end of a month. The annual interest rate is 12%. Compute interest on whole months ($1/12$, $2/12$, and so forth).

Required:

1. Prepare a schedule of expected cash collections from sales for each of the months April, May, and June, and for the quarter in total.
2. Prepare the following for merchandise inventory:
    a. An inventory purchases budget for each of the months April, May, and June.
    b. A schedule of expected cash disbursements for inventory for each of the months April, May, and June, and for the quarter in total.

CHECK FIGURE
(2a) May purchases:
$459,200
(3) June 30 cash balance:
$57,880

3. Prepare a cash budget for the third quarter, by month as well as in total for the quarter. Show borrowings from the company's bank and repayments to the bank, as needed, to maintain the minimum cash balance.

PROBLEM 7–6   Cash Budget with Supporting Schedules (CC5, 7, 11, 12)

Westex Products is a wholesale distributor of industrial cleaning products. When the treasurer of Westex Products approached the company's bank in late 2007 seeking short-term financing, he was told that money was very tight and that any borrowing over the next year would have to be supported by a detailed statement of cash receipts and disbursements. The treasurer also was told that it would be very helpful to the bank if borrowers would indicate the quarters in which they would be needing funds, as well as the amounts that would be needed, and the quarters in which repayments could be made.

   Since the treasurer is unsure as to the particular quarters in which the bank financing will be needed, he has assembled the following information to assist in preparing a detailed cash budget:

a. Budgeted sales and merchandise purchases for the year 2008, as well as actual sales and purchases for the last quarter of 2007, are:

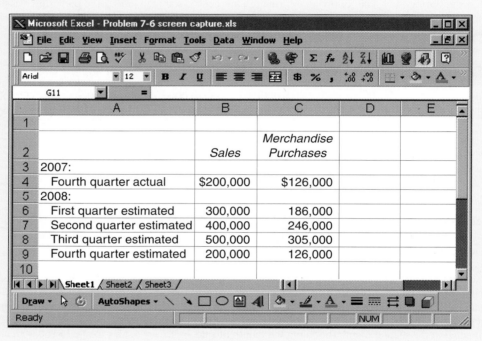

	Sales	Merchandise Purchases
2007:		
Fourth quarter actual	$200,000	$126,000
2008:		
First quarter estimated	300,000	186,000
Second quarter estimated	400,000	246,000
Third quarter estimated	500,000	305,000
Fourth quarter estimated	200,000	126,000

b. The company normally collects 65% of a quarter's sales before the quarter ends and another 33% in the following quarter. The remainder is uncollectible. This pattern of collections is now being experienced in the 2007 fourth-quarter actual data.

c. 80% of a quarter's merchandise purchases are paid for within the quarter. The remainder is paid in the following quarter.

d. Operating expenses for the year 2008 are budgeted quarterly at $50,000 plus 15% of sales. Of the fixed amount, $20,000 each quarter is depreciation.

e. The company will pay $10,000 in dividends each quarter.

f. Equipment purchases of $75,000 will be made in the second quarter, and purchases of $48,000 will be made in the third quarter. These purchases will be for cash.

g. The cash account contained $10,000 at the end of 2007. The treasurer feels that this represents a minimum balance that must be maintained.

h. Any borrowing will take place at the beginning of a quarter, and any repayments will be made at the end of a quarter at an annual interest rate of 10%. Interest is paid only when principal is repaid. All borrowings and all repayments of principal must be in round $1,000 amounts. Interest payments can be in any amount. (Compute interest on whole months, e.g., $1/12$, $2/12$.)

i. At present, the company has no loans outstanding.

Required:

1. Prepare the following by quarter and in total for the year 2008:
   a. A schedule of expected cash collections.
   b. A schedule of budgeted cash disbursements for merchandise purchases.

2. Compute the expected cash payments for operating expenses, by quarter and in total, for the year 2008.
3. Prepare a cash budget, by quarter and in total, for the year 2008. Show clearly in your budget the quarter(s) in which borrowing will be necessary and the quarter(s) in which repayments can be made, as requested by the company's bank.

PROBLEM 7–7   Comprehensive Master Budget (CC5, 7, 11, 12, 13, 14)
Hillyard Company, an office supplies specialty store, prepares its master budget on a quarterly basis. The following data have been assembled to assist in preparation of the master budget for the first quarter:
a. As of December 31 (the end of the prior quarter), the company's general ledger showed the following account balances:

CHECK FIGURE
(2a) February purchases: $315,000
(4) February ending cash balance: $30,800

	Debits	Credits
Cash	$ 48,000	
Accounts receivable	224,000	
Inventory	60,000	
Buildings and equipment (net)	370,000	
Accounts payable		$ 93,000
Capital shares		500,000
Retained earnings		109,000
	$702,000	$702,000

b. Actual sales for December and budgeted sales for the next four months are as follows:

December (actual)	$280,000
January	400,000
February	600,000
March	300,000
April	200,000

c. Sales are 20% for cash and 80% on credit. All payments on credit sales are collected in the month following sale. The accounts receivable at December 31 are a result of December credit sales.
d. The company's gross margin is 40% of sales.
e. Monthly expenses are budgeted as follows: salaries and wages, $27,000 per month: advertising, $70,000 per month; shipping, 5% of sales; amortization, $14,000 per month; other expenses, 3% of sales.
f. At the end of each month, inventory is to be on hand equal to 25% of the following month's sales needs, stated at cost.
g. One-half of a month's inventory purchases is paid for in the month of purchase; the other half is paid for in the following month.
h. During February, the company will purchase a new copy machine for $1,700 cash. During March, other equipment will be purchased for cash at a cost of $84,500.
i. During January, the company will declare and pay $45,000 in cash dividends.
j. The company must maintain a minimum cash balance of $30,000. An open line of credit is available at a local bank for any borrowing that may be needed during the quarter. All borrowing is done at the beginning of a month, and all repayments are made at the end of a month. Borrowings and repayments of principal must be in multiples of $1,000. Interest is paid only at the time of payment of principal. The annual interest rate is 12%. (Figure interest on whole months, e.g., $1/12, 2/12$.)

Required:
Using the preceding data, complete the following statements and schedules for the first quarter:
1. Schedule of expected cash collections:

	January	February	March	Quarter
Cash sales	$ 80,000			
Credit sales	224,000			
Total cash collections	$304,000			

2. a. Inventory purchases budget:

	January	February	March	Quarter
Budgeted cost of goods sold.....	$240,000*	$360,000		
Add: Desired ending inventory...	90,000†			
Total needs	330,000			
Less: Beginning inventory	60,000			
Required purchases...........	$270,000			

*For January sales: $400,000 sales × 60% cost ratio = $240,000.
†$360,000 × 25% = $90,000.

b. Schedule of cash disbursements for purchases:

	January	February	March	Quarter
December purchases...........	$ 93,000			$ 93,000
January purchases ($270,000)....	135,000	135,000		270,000
February purchases...........				
March purchases.............				
Total cash disbursements for purchases..............	$228,000			

3. Schedule of cash disbursements for expenses:

	January	February	March	Quarter
Salaries and wages	$ 27,000			
Advertising	70,000			
Shipping	20,000			
Other expenses	12,000			
Total cash disbursements for operating expenses	$129,000			

4. Cash budget:

	January	February	March	Quarter
Cash balance, beginning	$ 48,000			
Add: Cash collections	304,000			
Total cash available............	352,000			
Less: Disbursements:				
Purchases of inventory	228,000			
Operating expenses..........	129,000			
Purchases of equipment	—			
Cash dividends	45,000			
Total disbursements...........	402,000			
Excess (deficiency) of cash......	(50,000)			
Financing:				
Etc.				

5. Prepare an income statement for the quarter ending March 31 as shown in Schedule 9 in the chapter.
6. Prepare a balance sheet as of March 31.

PROBLEM 7–8   Comprehensive Master Budget (CC5, 7, 11, 12, 13, 14)

Following is selected information relating to the operations of Shilow Company, a wholesale distributor:

Current assets as of March 31:

Cash....................	$ 8,000
Accounts receivable........	20,000
Inventory	36,000
Plant and equipment, net....	120,000
Accounts payable	21,750
Capital shares	150,000
Retained earnings	12,250

a. Gross margin is 25% of sales.
b. Actual and budgeted sales data:

March (actual)............	$50,000
April.....................	60,000
May	72,000
June	90,000
July	48,000

c. Sales are 60% for cash and 40% on credit. Credit sales are collected in the month following sale. The accounts receivable at March 31 are a result of March credit sales.
d. At the end of each month, inventory is to be on hand equal to 80% of the following month's sales needs, stated at cost.
e. One-half of a month's inventory purchases is paid for in the month of purchase; the other half is paid for in the following month. The accounts payable at March 31 are a result of March purchases of inventory.
f. Monthly expenses are as follows: salaries and wages, 12% of sales; rent, $2,500 per month; other expenses (excluding amortization), 6% of sales. Assume that these expenses are paid monthly. Amortization is $900 per month (includes amortization on new assets).
g. Equipment costing $1,500 will be purchased for cash in April.
h. The company must maintain a minimum cash balance of $4,000. An open line of credit is available at a local bank. All borrowing is done at the beginning of a month, and all repayments are made at the end of a month; borrowing must be in multiples of $1,000. The annual interest rate is 12%. Interest is paid only at the time of repayment of principal; figure interest on whole months ($1/12$, $2/12$, and so forth).

Required:
Using the preceding data:
1. Complete the following schedule:

Schedule of Expected Cash Collections

	April	May	June	Quarter
Cash sales	$36,000			
Credit sales	20,000			
Total collections	$56,000			

2. Complete the following:

Inventory Purchases Budget

	April	May	June	Quarter
Budgeted cost of goods sold......	$45,000*	$54,000		
Add: Desired ending inventory....	43,200†			
Total needs	88,200			
Less: Beginning inventory	36,000			
Required purchases.............	$52,200			

*For April sales: $60,000 sales × 75% cost ratio = $45,000.
†$54,000 × 80% = $43,200.

Schedule of Expected Cash Disbursements—Purchases

	April	May	June	Quarter
March purchases	$21,750			$21,750
April purchases	26,100	$26,100		52,200
May purchases				
June purchases				
Total disbursements	$47,850			

3. Complete the following:

Schedule of Expected Cash Disbursements—Operating Expenses

	April	May	June	Quarter
Salaries and wages	$ 7,200			
Rent	2,500			
Other expenses	3,600			
Total disbursements	$13,300			

4. Complete the following cash budget:

Cash Budget

	April	May	June	Quarter
Cash balance, beginning	$ 8,000			
Add: Cash collections	56,000			
Total cash available	64,000			
Less: Cash disbursements:				
For inventory	47,850			
For expenses	13,300			
For equipment	1,500			
Total cash disbursements	62,650			
Excess (deficiency) of cash	1,350			
Financing:				
Etc.				

5. Prepare an income statement for the quarter ended June 30. (Use the functional format in preparing your income statement, as shown in Schedule 9 in the text.)
6. Prepare a balance sheet as of June 30.

CHECK FIGURE
(2) October 31 cash
balance: $42,550

PROBLEM 7–9   Purchases of Material and Cash Budget (CC7, 12)
GTC Ltd.'s September balance sheet contains the following information:

Cash	$ 37,500 (dr)
Accounts receivable	126,000 (dr)
Allowance for doubtful accounts	2,800 (cr)
Merchandise inventory	26,250 (dr)

Management has designated $37,500 as the firm's minimum monthly cash balance. Other information about the firm and its operations is as follows:
a. Sales revenues of $350,000, $420,000, and $312,500 are expected for October, November, and December, respectively. All goods are sold on account.
b. The collection pattern for accounts receivable is 55% in the month of sale, 44% in the month following the month of sale, and 1% uncollectible, which is set up as an allowance.
c. Cost of goods sold is 60% of sales revenues.

d. Management's target ending balance of merchandise inventory is 10% of the current month's sales.
e. All accounts payable for inventory are paid in the month of purchase.
f. Other monthly expenses are $47,250, which includes $3,500 of amortization but does not include bad debt expense.
g. In the event of a shortfall, the company borrows money. In contrast, in the event of excess cash the company invests in short-term investments. Borrowings and investments are assumed to be made at the end of a month in increments of $6,250.
h. Interest on borrowings is 10% per year, payable every quarter, on the accumulated amount of loan; similarly, interest earned on investments is 8% per year on the accumulated investments and is received every quarter. Investments can be matured and the principal amount redeemed in June or December of a year.

Required:
1. Prepare a merchandise purchases budget for October and November.
2. Prepare the cash budgets for October and November including the effects of financing (borrowing or investing). Interest is earned or paid quarterly.

(Adapted © CGA-Canada)

CHECK FIGURE
(1) November cash collections: $4,344,000

PROBLEM 7–10 Schedule of Cash Collections and Disbursements (CC5, 7, 12)
It is mid-September and a company has just approached its bank with a request for a $300,000 90-day loan, to meet its working capital requirements. Inventories peak in October in anticipation of holiday sales, and the treasurer believes the company can repay the loan in full by the end of the 90-day loan period. In support of the loan application, the bank has requested a three-month cash budget for October, November, and December. If the loan is granted, it will be made in October and repaid in December, and have an interest cost of $24,000 payable at the time of repayment. The following data are available to assist in the preparation of the cash budget:
a. The loan will be granted on October 1. The cash balance at the beginning of October is $520,000. Of the accounts receivable at September 30, the company expects to collect $2,820,000 in October and $144,000 in November. Some receivables will become uncollectible.
b. Past collection experience indicates that 20% of a month's sales will be collected in the month of the sales, 75% the next month, 4% the second month after the sale, and 1% will never be collected and represents bad debts.
c. Merchandise purchases are paid in full in the month after purchase. September purchases were $2,160,000.
d. The following are budgeted sales and expenses for the three-month loan period:

	October	November	December
Sales.	$ 4,000,000	$ 6,000,000	$ 5,000,000
Merchandise purchases	2,400,000	3,200,000	3,000,000
Wages paid.	180,000	180,000	160,000
Lease payments	1700,000	1900,000	1500,000
Equipment purchases.	160,000	—	—
Amortization	200,000	200,000	200,000

Required:
1. Prepare a schedule of expected cash collections for the months of October, November, and December, and for the three months in total.
2. Prepare a cash budget, by month and in total, for the three-month period.
3. Explain whether the loan can be repaid as planned if the company needs a minimum starting cash balance of $400,000 each month.

(Adapted © CGA-Canada)

Building Your Skills

ANALYTICAL THINKING   (CC5, 7, 12, 13, 14)

CHECK FIGURE
(1c) April purchases: 79,000 units
(2) June 30 cash balance: $94,700

You have just been hired as a new management trainee by Earrings Unlimited, a distributor of earrings to various retail outlets located in shopping malls across the country. In the past, the company has done very little in the way of budgeting and at certain times of the year has experienced a shortage of cash.

Since you are well trained in budgeting, you have decided to prepare comprehensive budgets for the upcoming second quarter in order to show management the benefits that can be gained from an integrated budgeting program. To this end, you have worked with accounting and other areas to gather the following information assembled.

The company sells many styles of earrings, but all are sold for the same price—$10 per pair. Actual sales of earrings for the last three months and budgeted sales for the next six months follow (in pairs of earrings):

January (actual).............	20,000	June (budget)	50,000
February (actual)...........	26,000	July (budget)..............	30,000
March (actual).............	40,000	August (budget)	28,000
April (budget)	65,000	September (budget).........	25,000
May (budget)..............	100,000		

The concentration of sales before and during May is due to Mother's Day. Sufficient inventory should be on hand at the end of each month to supply 40% of the earrings sold in the following month.

Suppliers are paid $4 for a pair of earrings. One-half of a month's purchases is paid for in the month of purchase; the other half is paid for in the following month. All sales are on credit, with no discount, and payable within 15 days. The company has found, however, that only 20% of a month's sales are collected in the month of sale. An additional 70% is collected in the following month, and the remaining 10% is collected in the second month following sale. Bad debts have been negligible.

Monthly operating expenses for the company follow:

Variable:	
Sales commissions........................	4% of sales
Fixed:	
Advertising..............................	$200,000
Rent	18,000
Salaries..................................	106,000
Utilities	7,000
Insurance expired.........................	3,000
Amortization	14,000

Insurance is paid on an annual basis, in November of each year.

The company plans to purchase $16,000 in new equipment during May and $40,000 in new equipment during June; both purchases will be for cash. The company declares dividends of $15,000 each quarter, payable in the first month of the following quarter.

A listing of the company's ledger accounts as of March 31 is given below:

Assets

Cash......................................	$ 74,000
Accounts receivable ($26,000 February sales;	
$320,000 March sales).....................	346,000
Inventory	104,000
Prepaid insurance.........................	21,000
Property and equipment (net)	950,000
Total assets...............................	$1,495,000

Liabilities and Shareholders' Equity

Accounts payable..........................	$ 100,000
Dividends payable	15,000
Capital shares.............................	800,000
Retained earnings	580,000
Total liabilities and shareholders' equity..........	$1,495,000

Part of the use of the budgeting program will be to establish an ongoing line of credit at a local bank. Therefore, determine the borrowing that will be needed to maintain a minimum cash balance of $50,000. All borrowing will be done at the beginning of a month; any repayments will be made at the end of a month.

The annual interest rate will be 12%. Interest will be computed and paid at the end of each quarter on all loans outstanding during the quarter. Compute interest on whole months ($^1/_{12}$, $^2/_{12}$, and so forth).

Required:

Prepare a master budget for the three-month period ending June 30. Include the following detailed budgets:

1. a. A sales budget, by month and in total.
    b. A schedule of expected cash collections from sales, by month and in total.
    c. A merchandise purchases budget in units and in dollars. Show the budget by month and in total.
    d. A schedule of expected cash disbursements for merchandise purchases, by month and in total.
2. A cash budget. Show the budget by month and in total.
3. A budgeted income statement for the three-month period ending June 30. Use the contribution approach.
4. A budgeted balance sheet as of June 30.

COMMUNICATING IN PRACTICE   (CC1, 2, 12)

Risky Rolling, Inc. is a rapidly expanding manufacturer of skateboards that have been modified for use on ski slopes during the off-season. This year's sales are considerably higher than last year's sales, and sales are expected to double next year. The unexpected growth in sales has presented numerous challenges to the company's management team, and the stress is really starting to show. Laura Dennan, the company's president, believes that the management time required to prepare a cash budget should be devoted to other, more pressing matters.

Required:

Write a memorandum to the president that states why cash budgeting is particularly important to a rapidly expanding company, such as Risky Rolling.

ETHICS CHALLENGE   (CC1, 2, 15)

Norton Company, a manufacturer of infant furniture and carriages, is in the initial stages of preparing the annual budget for next year. Scott Ford has recently joined Norton's accounting staff and is interested to learn as much as possible about the company's budgeting process. During a recent lunch with Marge Atkins, sales manager, and Pete Granger, production manager, Ford initiated the following conversation:

Ford: Since I'm new around here and am going to be involved with the preparation of the annual budget, I'd be interested to learn how the two of you estimate sales and production numbers.

Atkins: We start out very methodically by looking at recent history, discussing what we know about current accounts, potential customers, and the general state of consumer spending. Then, we add that usual dose of intuition to come up with the best forecast we can.

Granger: I usually take the sales projections as the basis for my projections. Of course, we have to make an estimate of what this year's ending inventories will be, which is sometimes difficult.

Ford: Why does that present a problem? There must have been an estimate of ending inventories in the budget for the current year.

Granger: Those numbers aren't always reliable, since Marge makes some adjustments to the sales number before passing them on to me.

Ford: What kind of adjustments?

Atkins: Well, we don't want to fall short of the sales projections, and so we generally give ourselves a little breathing room by lowering the initial sales projection anywhere from 5% to 10%.

Granger: So, you can see why this year's budget is not a very reliable starting point. We always have to adjust the projected production rates as the year progresses, and of course, this changes the ending inventory estimates. By the way, we make similar adjustments to expenses by adding at least 10% to the estimates; I think everyone around here does the same thing.

Required:

1. Marge Atkins and Pete Granger have described the use of what is sometimes called *budgetary slack*.
    a. Explain why Atkins and Granger behave in this manner and describe the benefits they expect to realize from the use of budgetary slack.
    b. Explain how the use of budgetary slack can adversely affect Atkins and Granger.

2. As a management accountant, Scott Ford believes that the behaviour described by Marge Atkins and Pete Granger may be unethical. Refer to the Standards of Ethical Conduct for Practitioners of Management Accounting and Financial Management in Chapter 1, and explain why the use of budgetary slack may be unethical.

(CMA adapted)

TEAMWORK IN ACTION   (CC1, 2, 15)

Tom Emory and Jim Morris strolled back to their plant from the administrative offices of Ferguson & Son Mfg. Company. Tom is manager of the machine shop in the company's factory; Jim is manager of the equipment maintenance department.

The men had just attended the monthly performance evaluation meeting for plant department heads. These meetings had been held on the third Tuesday of each month since Robert Ferguson, Jr., the president's son, had become plant manager a year earlier.

As they were walking, Tom Emory spoke: "Boy, I hate those meetings! I never know whether my department's accounting reports will show good or bad performance. I'm beginning to expect the worst. If the accountants say I saved the company a dollar, I'm called 'Sir,' but if I spend even a little too much— boy, do I get into trouble. I don't know if I can hold on until I retire."

Tom had just been given the worst evaluation he had ever received in his long career with Ferguson & Son. He was the most respected of the experienced machinists in the company. He had been with Ferguson & Son for many years and was promoted to supervisor of the machine shop when the company expanded and moved to its present location. The president (Robert Ferguson, Sr.) had often stated that the company's success was due to the high quality of the work of machinists like Tom. As supervisor, Tom stressed the importance of craftsmanship and told his workers that he wanted no sloppy work coming from his department.

When Robert Ferguson, Jr., became the plant manager, he directed that monthly performance comparisons be made between actual and budgeted costs for each department. The departmental budgets were intended to encourage the supervisors to reduce inefficiencies and to seek cost reduction opportunities. The company controller was instructed to have his staff tighten the budget slightly whenever a department attained its budget in a given month; this was done to reinforce the plant manager's desire to reduce costs. The young plant manager often stressed the importance of continued progress toward attaining the budget; he also made it known that he kept a file of these performance reports for future reference when he succeeded his father.

Tom Emory's conversation with Jim Morris continued as follows:

Emory: I really don't understand. We've worked so hard to meet the budget, and the minute we make it, they tighten the budget on us. We can't work any faster and still maintain quality. I think my men are ready to quit trying. Besides, those reports don't tell the whole story. We always seem to be interrupting the big jobs for all those small rush orders. All that setup and machine adjustment time is killing us. And quite frankly, Jim, you were no help. When our hydraulic press broke down last month, your people were nowhere to be found. We had to take it apart ourselves and got stuck with all that idle time.

Morris: I'm sorry about that, Tom, but you know my department has had trouble making budget, too.

We were running well behind at the time of that problem, and if we'd spent a day on that old machine, we would never have made it up. Instead, we made the scheduled inspections of the forklift trucks because we knew we could do those in less than the budgeted time.

Emory: Well, Jim, at least you have some options. I'm locked into what the scheduling department assigns to me, and you know they're being harassed by sales for those special orders. Incidentally, why didn't your report show all the supplies you guys wasted last month when you were working in Bill's department?

Morris: We're not out of the woods on that deal yet. We charged the maximum we could to other work and haven't even reported some of it yet.

Emory: Well, I'm glad you have a way of getting out of the pressure. The accountants seem to know everything that's happening in my department, sometimes even before I do. I thought all that budget and accounting stuff was supposed to help, but it just gets me into trouble. It's all a big pain. I'm trying to put out quality work; they're trying to save pennies.

Required:

The team should discuss and then respond to the following two questions. All team members should agree with and understand the answers and be prepared to explain the solutions in class. (Each teammate can assume responsibility for a different part of the presentation.)

1. Identify the problems that appear to exist in Ferguson & Son Mfg. Company's budgetary control system, and explain how the problems are likely to reduce the effectiveness of the system.

2. Explain how Ferguson & Son Mfg. Company's budgetary control system could be revised to improve its effectiveness.

(CMA adapted)

Don't forget to visit the Online Learning Centre for self-study quizzes, practice exams, and more! Visit www.mcgrawhill.ca/olc/brewer.

CHAPTER *Eight*

Standard Costs

CHAPTER COMPETENCIES

After studying Chapter 8, you should be able to demonstrate the following competencies:

Competency	Know	Apply
Understand standard costing and compute standard costs.		
CC1 Explain the concept of standards and standard costs.	●	
CC2 Distinguish between ideal and practical standards.	●	
CC3 Develop standard costs for direct materials.		●
CC4 Develop standard costs for direct labour.		●
CC5 Develop standard costs for variable overhead.		●
CC6 Prepare a standard cost card.		●
Understand variance analysis and compute variances.		
CC7 Explain the concept of variances.	●	
CC8 Distinguish between price and quantity variances.	●	
CC9 Explain and compute direct materials variances.	●	●
CC10 Explain and compute direct labour variances.	●	●
CC11 Explain and compute variable overhead variances.	●	●
Understand management control in a standard costing environment.		
CC12 Describe the principle of management by exception.	●	
CC13 Describe the benefits and limitations of using standard costing for the purposes of control.	●	
Understand cost flows in a standard costing environment.		
CC14[A] Explain the cost flows in a standard costing system.	●	
CC15[A] Prepare journal entries to record standard costs and variances.		●

Note: A refers to Appendix 8A available online (see www.mcgrawhill.ca/olc/brewer).

DECISION FEATURE
Auto Service Standards

Keith Atchinson and Herb Friesen, two co-workers in a Saskatoon-based auto service business, took over the business in 1961 and renamed it Keith & Herb Alignment and Brake, specializing in brakes, wheel alignments, and front-end repairs. After over 40 years, it is still very much in business and going strong. In 2000, Richard Semchyshen, a young mechanic with eight years of experience at Keith & Herb, bought out the business and is running it successfully with Heather, his business partner and wife.

Richard fully understands the value of the Keith & Herb's reputation and is working hard to maintain it by providing value to the customer—quality service at a reasonable price. At the same time, however, being profitable is also important to Richard, and this is where standards come into the picture. For most jobs (such as a wheel alignment for a four-wheel-drive jeep), his charges to customers are based on standard times that he has developed over the years; for others, he uses the standard times published in labour guides. Richard and his employees pay close attention to the standards—completing a job in less than the standard time means more money for the business.

Given the small size of his business, Richard does not need an elaborate standard costing system to monitor his performance. He has been doing this long enough and just knows when a job takes longer than it is supposed to! However, this does not mean that there are no avenues for improvement to close any gaps between standard and actual times for a job. Although the primary source of learning is "on-the-job" training and experience, that is, learning by doing more of the same, there are times when he attends training seminars organized by parts dealers and even contacts other mechanics when he needs a second opinion (especially on less frequent jobs). He is very careful about accepting jobs outside of his specialty areas, especially complicated ones, such as replacing a water pump on a Rolls Royce.

According to him, "there is never a dull moment in the shop," as he always has his hands full—literally speaking. Richard is as passionate about his work as he is about hockey, and, above all, his family!

8

A Look Back
We discussed the budgeting process in Chapter 7 and reviewed each of the budgets that constitute the master budget.

A Look at This Chapter
We begin a discussion of management control by focusing on standard costing systems in Chapter 8. Management by exception and variance analysis are described, as are the computations of material, labour, and overhead variances.

A Look Ahead
We compare and contrast the static budget approach and flexible budget approach in Chapter 9 and discuss the preparation of performance reports, using a flexible budget approach to analyze overhead variances.

I n this chapter, we will continue our focus on planning and extend it to control (the other side of the coin). We learned that budgeting can be a useful tool for planning purposes. However, in order to prepare budgets, managers must know the amount of resources (inputs) required to carry out different tasks or activities. For example, the manager of your local pizzeria knows that on average, it takes seven minutes to enter a customer's order on her computer system. She then uses this average time to compute the total time that should be budgeted for the order-taking activity during a certain period (week, month, quarter, or year). In other words, she strongly believes that seven minutes is an acceptable *standard* time for the order-taking activity.

We will now explain the concept of standard costs, illustrating how they are useful both in planning and control.

Standard Costs

⊙ KNOW

CC1: Explain the concept of standards and standard costs.

A *standard* is a benchmark or norm that is used as a basis for determining the quantity of resources required to carry out a certain activity (or set of activities). The same standard is also used as the base against which managers can compare actual performance at the end of the budgeting period. The use of standards is by no means restricted to businesses. Colleges and universities use admission standards to decide which students are eligible for admission into their programs. Your doctor evaluates your weight using standards that have been established for individuals of your age, height, and gender. Similarly, the food we eat in restaurants and the buildings we live in must also conform to certain standards. The absence of standards could result in adverse consequences.

IN BUSINESS TODAY   ## Standards in the Spanish Royal Tobacco Factory

Standards have been used for centuries. For example, the Spanish Royal Tobacco Factory in Seville used standards to control costs in the 1700s. The Royal Tobacco Factory had a monopoly over snuff and cigar production in Spain and was the largest industrial building in Europe. Employee theft of tobacco was a particular problem, due to its high value. Careful records were maintained for each worker of the amount of tobacco leaf issued to the worker, the number of cigars expected to be made based on standards, and the actual production. The worker was not paid if the actual production was less than expected. To minimize theft, tobacco was weighed after each production step to determine the amount of waste.

Source: Salvador Carmona, Mahmoud Ezzamel, and Fernando Gutiérrez, "Control and Cost Accounting Practices in the Spanish Royal Tobacco Factory," *Accounting Organizations and Society*, Vol. 22, pp. 411–446.

Managers and administrators of various organizations generally conform to some set of standards for carrying out their activities and defining their output specifications. For example, educational institutions set course completion standards, manufacturing companies set quality standards for their products, and hospital emergency units follow standard operating procedures. Similarly, these organizations develop standards for the inputs required to complete their tasks. For example, the auto service centre of Petro-Canada would set specific labour time standards for the completion of such tasks as replacing the timing belt, performing an oil change, and so on. Manufacturing companies use their product and process knowledge to determine standards for the inputs required to produce the output. These inputs typically consist of raw materials, labour, and manufacturing overhead. Such standards are known as *quantity standards*.

In addition, managers also like to compute the costs associated with the quantity standards; these are known as *cost (or price) standards*. A **standard cost** is computed as the standard quantity of input required to produce one unit of a product or provide one unit of service to a customer multiplied by the standard price of the input. For example, a tax consultant can compute the standard cost of preparing a normal tax return (i.e., one without too many complications).

Manufacturing companies often have highly developed standard costing systems in which standards relating to materials, labour, and overhead are developed in detail for each separate product. We now provide details of setting standards and the preparation of a standard cost card.

Setting Standard Costs

Setting price and quantity standards is more an art than a science. It requires the combined expertise of all persons who have responsibility over input prices and over the effective use of inputs. In a manufacturing setting, this might include accountants, purchasing managers, engineers, production supervisors, line managers, and production workers. Historical data, i.e., past records of purchase prices and input usage, can be helpful in setting standards. However, the standards should be designed to encourage efficient *future* operations, not a repetition of past inefficient operations.

Ideal Versus Practical Standards

Should standards be attainable all of the time, should they be attainable only part of the time, or should they be so tight that they become, in effect, "the impossible dream"? Opinions among managers vary, but standards tend to fall into one of two categories—either ideal or practical.

Ideal standards are those that can be attained only under the best circumstances. They allow for no machine breakdowns or other work interruptions, and they call for a level of effort that can be attained only by the most skilled and efficient employees working at peak effort 100% of the time. Some managers feel that such standards have a motivational value. These managers argue that even though employees know they will rarely meet the standard, it is a constant reminder of the need for ever-increasing efficiency and effort. For example, many "lean" organizations set "stretch targets" to encourage their employees to "take the extra step" toward achieving perfection. However, managers must make a conscious effort to ensure that employees are not discouraged by such standards/targets that might otherwise ruin morale within the organization. Deviations from ideal standards may be hard to interpret and must therefore be interpreted with caution.

Practical standards are defined as those that are "tight but attainable." They allow for normal machine downtime and employee rest periods, and they can be attained through reasonable, though highly efficient, efforts by the average worker. Variances from such a standard represent deviations that fall outside of normal operating conditions and signal a need for management attention. Furthermore, practical standards can serve multiple purposes. In addition to signalling abnormal conditions, they can also be used in forecasting cash flows and in planning inventory. By contrast, ideal standards cannot be used in forecasting and planning; they do not allow for normal inefficiencies, and therefore they result in unrealistic planning and forecasting figures.

KNOW

CC2: Distinguish between ideal and practical standards.

Hockey Coach

YOU DECIDE

During the winter, you coach a team of 8- to 10-year-olds, in your neighbourhood. One of the parents has approached you with a list of NHL records that he believes should be used as benchmarks or standards of performance for the kids. The parent suggests that players who meet the benchmarks be recognized and rewarded for their efforts. How do you respond?

Throughout the remainder of this chapter, we will assume the use of practical, rather than ideal, standards.

MANAGERIAL ACCOUNTING IN ACTION

The Issue

The Colonial Pewter Company was organized a year ago. The company's only product is a reproduction of an 18th century set of pewter bookends. The bookends are made largely by hand, using traditional metal-working tools. Consequently, the manufacturing process is labour intensive and requires a high level of skill.

Colonial Pewter has recently expanded its workforce to take advantage of unexpected demand for the bookends as gifts. The company started with a small cadre of experienced pewter workers, but has had to hire less experienced workers as a result of the expansion. The president of the company, J. D. Wriston, has called a meeting to discuss production problems. Attending the meeting are Tom Kuchel, the production manager; Janet Warner, the purchasing manager; and Terry Sherman, the corporate controller.

J. D.: I've got a feeling that we aren't getting the production we should out of our new people.

Tom: Give us a chance. Some of the new people have been on board for less than a month.

Janet: Let me add that production seems to be wasting an awful lot of material—particularly pewter. That stuff is very expensive.

Tom: What about the shipment of defective pewter you bought a couple of months ago—the one with the iron contamination? That caused us major problems.

Janet: That's ancient history. How was I to know it was off-grade? Besides, it was a great deal.

J. D.: Calm down everybody. Let's get the facts before we start sinking our fangs into each other.

Tom: I agree. The more facts, the better.

J. D.: Okay, Terry, it's your turn. Facts are the controller's department.

Terry: I'm afraid I can't provide the answers off the top of my head, but it won't take me too long to set up a system that can routinely answer questions relating to worker productivity, material waste, and input prices.

J. D.: How long is "not too long"?

Terry: I will need all of your cooperation, but how about a week from today?

J. D.: That's okay with me. What about everyone else?

Tom: Sure.

Janet: Fine with me.

J. D.: Let's mark it on our calendars.

Setting Direct Materials Standards

APPLY

CC3: Develop standard costs for direct materials.

Terry Sherman's first task was to prepare price and quantity standards for the company's only significant raw material, pewter ingots. The **standard price per unit** for direct materials should reflect the final, delivered cost of the materials, net of any discounts taken. After consulting with purchasing manager Janet Warner, Terry prepared the following documentation for the standard price of a kilogram of pewter in ingot form:

Purchase price, top-grade pewter ingots, in 18-kg ingots..........	$7.90
Freight, by truck, from the supplier's warehouse	1.00
Receiving and handling	0.10
Less: Purchase discount	(0.20)
Standard price per kilogram	$8.80

Notice that the standard price reflects a particular grade of material (top grade), purchased in particular lot sizes (18-kg ingots), and delivered by a particular type of carrier (truck). Allowances have also been made for handling and discounts. If everything proceeds according to these expectations, the net cost of a kilogram of pewter would therefore be $8.80.

The **standard quantity per unit** for direct materials should reflect the amount of material going into each unit of finished product, as well as an allowance for unavoidable waste, spoilage, and other normal inefficiencies. After consulting with the production manager, Tom Kuchel, Terry Sherman prepared the following documentation for the standard quantity of pewter in a pair of bookends:

Material requirements as specified in the bill of materials for a pair of bookends, in kilograms	1.05
Allowance for waste and spoilage, in kilograms	0.05
Allowance for rejects, in kilograms	0.15
Standard quantity per pair of bookends, in kilograms	1.25

A **bill of materials** is a listing that shows the quantity of each type of material required to manufacture a unit of product. It is a handy source for determining the basic material input per unit, but it should be adjusted for waste and other factors, as shown above, when determining the standard quantity per unit of product. *Waste and spoilage* in the preceding table refers to materials that are wasted as a normal part of the production process or that spoil before they are used. *Rejects* refers to the direct material contained in units that are defective and must be scrapped.

Although it is common to recognize allowances for waste, spoilage, and rejects when setting standard costs, this practice is now coming into question. Those involved in TQM (total quality management) and similar improvement programs argue that no amount of waste or defects should be tolerated. If allowances for waste, spoilage, and rejects are built into the standard cost, the levels of those allowances should be periodically reviewed and reduced over time to reflect improved processes, better training, and better equipment.

Once the price and quantity standards have been set, the standard cost of material per unit of finished product can be computed as follows:

$$1.25 \text{ kg per unit} \times \$8.80 \text{ per kg} = \$11 \text{ per unit}$$

What Happened to the Raisins?

Management at an unnamed breakfast cereal company became concerned about the apparent waste of raisins in one of its products. A box of the product was supposed to contain 10 ounces of cereal and 2 ounces of raisins. However, the production process had been using an average of 2.5 ounces of raisins per box. To correct the problem, a bonus was offered to employees if the consumption of raisins dropped to 2.1 ounces per box or less—which would allow for about 5% waste. Within a month, the target was hit and bonuses were distributed. However, another problem began to appear. Market studies indicated that customers had become dissatisfied with the amount of raisins in the product. Workers had hit the 2.1-ounce per box target by drastically reducing the amount of raisins in rush orders. Boxes of the completed product are ordinarily weighed and if the weight is less than 12 ounces, the box is rejected. However, rush orders aren't weighed since that would slow down the production process. Consequently, workers were reducing the raisins in rush orders so as to hit the overall target of 2.1 ounces of raisins per box. This resulted in substandard boxes of cereal in rush orders and customer complaints. Clearly, managers need to be very careful when they set targets and standards. They may not get what they bargained for. Subsequent investigation by an internal auditor revealed that, due to statistical fluctuations, an average of about 2.5 ounces of raisins must be used to ensure that every box contains at least 2 ounces of raisins.

Source: Harper A. Roehm and Joseph R. Castellano, "The Danger of Relying on Accounting Numbers Alone," *Management Accounting Quarterly*, Fall 1999, pp. 4–9.

Setting Direct Labour Standards

APPLY

CC4: Develop standard costs for direct labour.

Direct labour price and quantity standards are usually expressed in terms of a labour rate and labour-hours. The **standard rate per hour** for direct labour should include not only wages earned, but also fringe benefits and other labour costs. Using last month's wage records and in consultation with the production manager, Terry determined the standard rate per hour at the Colonial Pewter Company as follows:

Basic wage rate per hour.	$10
Employment taxes at 10% of the basic rate	1
Fringe benefits at 30% of the basic rate	3
Standard rate per direct labour-hour.	$14

Many companies prepare a single standard rate for all employees in a department. This standard rate reflects the expected "mix" of workers, even though the actual wage rates may vary somewhat from individual to individual due to differing skills or seniority. A single standard rate simplifies the use of standard costs and also permits the manager to monitor the use of employees within departments. More is said on this point a little later. According to the standard computed above, the direct labour rate for Colonial Pewter should average $14 per hour.

The standard direct labour time required to complete a unit of product (generally called the **standard hours per unit**) is perhaps the single most difficult standard to determine. One approach is to divide each operation performed on the product into elemental body movements (such as reaching, pushing, and turning over). Published tables of standard times for such movements are available. These times can be applied to the movements and then added together to determine the total standard time allowed per operation. Another approach is for an industrial engineer to do a time and motion study, actually clocking the time required for certain tasks. As stated previously, the standard time should include allowances for breaks, personal needs of employees, cleanup, and machine downtime. After consulting with the production manager, Terry prepared the following documentation for the standard hours per unit:

Basic labour time per unit, in hours	1.9
Allowance for breaks and personal needs.	0.1
Allowance for cleanup and machine downtime	0.3
Allowance for rejects	0.2
Standard labour-hours per unit of product	2.5

Once the rate and time standards have been set, the standard labour cost per unit of product can be computed as follows:

2.5 hours per unit × $14 per hour = $35 per unit

Note that if Colonial Pewter implements lean business practices, managers would strive to reduce the allowances included in computing the labour standards.

Setting Variable Manufacturing Overhead Standards

APPLY

CC5: Develop standard costs for variable overhead.

As with direct labour, the price and quantity standards for variable manufacturing overhead are generally expressed in terms of rate and hours. The rate represents *the variable portion of the predetermined overhead rate* discussed in Chapter 4; the hours represent whatever hours base is used to apply overhead to units of product (usually machine-hours or direct labour-hours, as we learned in Chapter 4). At Colonial Pewter, the variable portion of the predetermined overhead rate is $3 per direct labour-hour. Therefore, the standard variable manufacturing overhead cost per unit is computed as follows:

$$2.5 \text{ hours per unit} \times \$3 \text{ per hour} = \$7.50 \text{ per unit}$$

Preparing the Standard Cost Card

A **standard cost card** is a document (report) containing the standard costs of the input resources required to produce one unit of a product or to provide one unit of service. The information contained in the document will vary depending upon the nature of the organization. Exhibit 8-1 contains the standard variable costs to produce one pewter bookend, the only product of the Colonial Pewter Company.

● APPLY

CC6: Prepare a standard cost card.

Inputs	(1) Standard Quantity or Hours	(2) Standard Price or Rate	(3) Standard Cost (1) × (2)
Direct materials..................	1.25 kg	$ 8.80	$11.00
Direct labour....................	2.5 hours	14.00	35.00
Variable manufacturing overhead....	2.5 hours	3.00	7.50
Total standard cost per unit.........			$53.50

Exhibit 8–1
Standard Cost Card—Variable Production Cost

As can be seen, the standard cost card lists the standard quantity required of each *input* resource (i.e., direct materials, direct labour, and variable overhead), the price paid to acquire one unit of that resource, and the cost per unit of the output. Observe that the **standard cost per unit** (of the output) is computed by multiplying the standard quantity and the standard price of all the input resources, and adding them up. The standard cost card informs the concerned manager that the standard variable production cost of one pewter bookend is $53.50.

Are Standards the Same as Budgets?

Standards and budgets are very similar. The major distinction between the two terms is that a standard is a *unit* amount, whereas a budget is a *total* amount. The standard cost for materials at Colonial Pewter is $11 per pair of bookends. If 1,000 pairs of bookends are to be manufactured during a budgeting period, then the budgeted cost of materials would be $11,000. In effect, *a standard can be viewed as the budgeted cost for one unit of product.*

Standard Costing and Process Re-engineering   IN BUSINESS TODAY

For Montreal-based Standard Life, tracking the time spent on projects was not easy until it started using the HMS TimeControl software to increase operations efficiency and streamline internal processes. The company uses the software to record time spent on each project, comparing the actual hours to budgeted hours to enable managers to make any future adjustments. As well, the software saves the company time in paying external contractors and consultants. Finally, the new software gave managers insights into the inconsistencies related to actual versus budgeted time.

Source: Gary Hilson, "Watching the Clock: Montreal's Standard Life Keeps a Close Eye on the Fourth Dimension When Managing Myriad Projects," *Computing Canada*, February 1, 2002, Volume 28(3), p. 23.

A General Model for Variance Analysis

Recall from Chapter 1 that planning and control are important tasks performed by managers; we mentioned that management accounting information is critical for performing these tasks effectively and efficiently. While standard cost information is useful for planning (budgets are prepared using standard cost data), it also provides the basis for evaluation and control. Most organizations prepare performance reports, which compare actual results at the end of a period with the budgeted performance for that period. Any deviation from the budget is called a **variance.** The performance report is a useful tool for managers to monitor activities on a periodic basis.

Although the performance report provides an overview of the actual performance during a period, the report merely *informs* managers of any deviations. Managers often need more details of the deviations (or variances) so that they can get more actionable information which they can then use to make changes, as necessary. The process of computing and interpreting variances is known as **variance analysis**. As a manager, you must identify the source(s) of the variances. Generally speaking, there are two sources of a variance: (1) the difference between the actual and budgeted (standard) price of inputs, and (2) the difference between the actual quantity (or volume) of inputs consumed and the standard quantity that was planned.

An important reason for separating standards into two categories—price and quantity—is that different managers are usually responsible for buying and for using inputs, and these two activities occur at different points in time. In the case of raw materials, for example, the purchasing manager is responsible for the price, and this responsibility is exercised at the time of purchase. In contrast, the production manager is responsible for the amount of the raw material used, and this responsibility is exercised when the materials are used in production, which may be days or weeks after the purchase date. It is important, therefore, that we cleanly separate discrepancies due to deviations from price standards from those due to deviations from quantity standards.

Price and Quantity Variances

A general model for computing standard cost variances for variable costs is presented in Exhibit 8–2. This model isolates price variances from quantity variances and shows how each of these variances is computed.[1] We will be using this model throughout the chapter to compute variances for direct materials, direct labour, and variable manufacturing overhead.

Exhibit 8–2

A General Model for Variance Analysis—Variable Production Costs

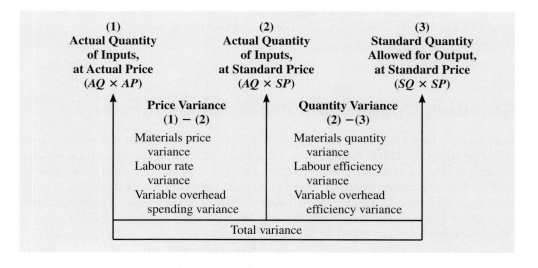

---

[1]Variance analysis of fixed costs is discussed in Chapter 9.

Three things should be observed from Exhibit 8–2. First, a price variance and a quantity variance can be computed for all three variable cost elements—direct materials, direct labour, and variable manufacturing overhead—even though the variance is not called by the same name in all cases. For example, a price variance is called a *materials price variance* in the case of direct materials, but a *labour rate variance* in the case of direct labour and an *overhead spending variance* in the case of variable manufacturing overhead.

Second, even though a price variance may be called by different names, it is computed in exactly the same way, regardless of whether you are dealing with direct materials, direct labour, or variable manufacturing overhead. The same is true with the quantity variance.

Third, variance analysis is actually a type of input–output analysis. The inputs represent the actual quantity of direct materials, direct labour, and variable manufacturing overhead used; the output represents the good production of the period, expressed in terms of the *standard quantity (or the standard hours) allowed for the actual output* (see column 3 in Exhibit 8–2). By **standard quantity allowed** or **standard hours allowed,** we mean the amount of direct materials, direct labour, or variable manufacturing overhead *that should have been used* to produce the actual output of the period. This could be more or could be less materials, labour, or overhead than was *actually* used, depending on the efficiency or inefficiency of operations. The standard quantity allowed is computed by multiplying the actual output in units by the standard input allowed per unit.

It is important to emphasize that a price variance occurs due to the difference between actual price and standard price—the quantity element is kept constant in the computation of this variance. Similarly, the quantity variance occurs due to the difference between actual and standard quantities of inputs used—the price element is kept constant in the computation of this variance. This is explained later in the chapter.

Although the general model for variance analysis is explained in the context of a manufacturing company, it is equally applicable to many service organizations. For example, Taco Time can use this model to compute the materials and labour-related variances pertaining to preparing a bean burrito. However, given that each customer order may be different, separately tracking the time for every burrito prepared may not be cost beneficial. In contrast, manufacturing companies usually produce in batches, and it is easier to track the quantity of input resources per batch.

With this general model as a foundation, we will now examine the price and quantity variances in more detail.

Using Standard Costs—Direct Materials Variances

After determining Colonial Pewter Company's standard costs for direct materials, direct labour, and variable manufacturing overhead, Terry Sherman's next step was to compute the company's variances for June, the most recent month. As discussed in the preceding section, variances are computed by comparing standard costs with actual costs. To facilitate this comparison, Terry referred to the standard cost data contained in Exhibit 8–1. This exhibit shows that the standard cost of direct materials per unit of product is as follows:

○ KNOW ○ APPLY

CC9: Explain and compute direct materials variances.

1.25 kilograms per unit × $8.80 per kilogram = $11 per unit

Colonial Pewter's purchasing records for June showed that 3,000 kg of pewter were purchased at a cost of $8.50 per kg. This cost figure included freight and handling, and was net of the quantity discount. All of the material purchased was used during June to manufacture 2,000 pairs of pewter bookends. Using these data and the standard costs from Exhibit 8–1, Terry computed the price and quantity variances shown in Exhibit 8–3.

The three arrows in Exhibit 8–3 point to three different total cost figures. The first, $25,500, refers to the actual total cost of 3,000 kilograms of pewter purchased during June at a price of $8.50 per kilogram. The second, $26,400, refers to what the pewter would have cost had the company bought it at the standard price of $8.80 per kilogram. The difference of $900 between these two figures is the *price variance*, which exists due to the difference between the actual and standard purchase prices ($0.30 × 3,000 kg = $900).

Exhibit 8–3
Variance Analysis—Direct
Materials

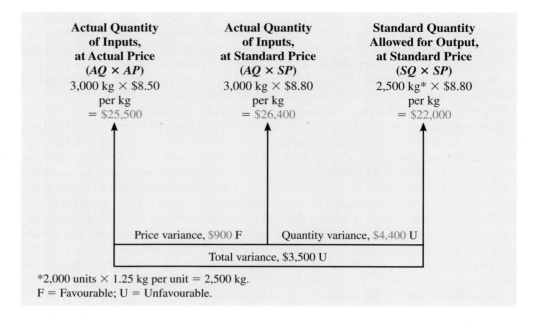

Actual Quantity of Inputs, at Actual Price (AQ × AP)	Actual Quantity of Inputs, at Standard Price (AQ × SP)	Standard Quantity Allowed for Output, at Standard Price (SQ × SP)
3,000 kg × $8.50 per kg = $25,500	3,000 kg × $8.80 per kg = $26,400	2,500 kg* × $8.80 per kg = $22,000

Price variance, $900 F   Quantity variance, $4,400 U

Total variance, $3,500 U

*2,000 units × 1.25 kg per unit = 2,500 kg.
F = Favourable; U = Unfavourable.

Also, observe that because the actual price is less than the standard price, this represents a favourable (F) situation because it contributes toward an *increase* in income compared with the budget. If the actual price had been higher than the standard price, this would represent an unfavourable (U) situation because it contributes toward a *decrease* in income compared with the budgeted income. You can see how variance analysis shows the effect on profitability of each individual variance.

The third cost figure in Exhibit 8–3, $22,000, is the standard cost of the pewter. According to the standard cost card in Exhibit 8–1, Colonial Pewter should have consumed a total of 2,500 kg of pewter to produce 2,000 bookends (1.25 kg × 2,000 = 2,500 kg) at a price of $8.80 per kilogram (the figure of 2,500 kilograms is known as the standard quantity of materials allowed for the actual output of 2,000 bookends). Alternatively, Exhibit 8–1 suggests that the standard cost of pewter for one bookend is $11. Therefore, the total standard cost of pewter for 2,000 bookends is $22,000 ($11 × 2,000). The difference of $4,400 between the second and third figures in Exhibit 8–3, ($26,400 − $22,000) is known as the *quantity (or usage) variance*. Note that this quantity variance arises because Colonial Pewter used 500 kilograms more pewter than planned ($8.80 × 500 = $4,400). Because the company used more materials than planned, the resulting variance is unfavourable (U).

The computations in Exhibit 8–3 reflect the fact that all of the material purchased during June was also used during June. How are the variances computed if the amount of material is purchased is different from what is used? To illustrate, assume that during June, the company purchased 3,000 kilos of materials, as before, but that it used only 2,100 kg of material during the month and produced only 1,600 units. In this case, the price variance and quantity variance would be as shown in Exhibit 8–4.

When should a price variance be computed and investigated? It is best if the materials price variance is computed when materials *are purchased*, rather than when they are placed into production. This permits earlier isolation of the variance, since materials may remain in storage some time before being used in production.

From Exhibit 8–4, observe that the price variance is computed on the entire amount of material purchased, as before, whereas the quantity variance is computed only on the portion of this material used in production during the month. A quantity variance on the 900 kilograms of material that was purchased during the month but *not* used in production will be computed in a future period when these materials are drawn out of inventory and used in production.

The situation illustrated in Exhibit 8–4 is common in companies that purchase materials well in advance of using them, storing the materials in warehouses while awaiting the production process. In companies that use a just-in-time purchasing policy, there would be no difference between the quantity purchased and the quantity used.

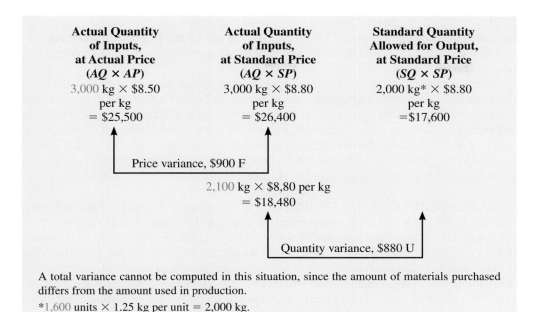

Exhibit 8–4
Variance Analysis—Direct Materials, When the Amount Purchased Differs from the Amount Used

Materials Price Variance—A Closer Look

A **materials price variance** measures the difference between the actual price paid for a given quantity of materials and what should have been paid according to the standard set by the managers. From Exhibit 8–3, this difference can be expressed by the following formula:

$$\text{Materials price variance} = (AQ \times AP) - (AQ \times SP)$$

Actual	Actual	Standard
Quantity	Price	Price

The formula can be factored into simpler form as follows:

$$\text{Materials price variance} = AQ(AP - SP)$$

Some managers prefer this simpler formula because it permits variance computations to be made very quickly. Using the data from Exhibit 8–3 in this formula, we have the following:

$$3{,}000 \text{ kg } (\$8.50 \text{ per kg} - \$8.80 \text{ per kg}) = \$900 \text{ F}$$

Notice that the answer is the same as that yielded in Exhibit 8–3. If the company wanted to put these data into a performance report, the data might appear as follows:

COLONIAL PEWTER COMPANY **Performance Report—Purchasing Department**						
	(1)	**(2)**	**(3)**	**(4)** **Difference in Price**	**(5)** **Total Price Variance**	
Item Purchased	**Quantity Purchased**	**Actual Price**	**Standard Price**	**(2) − (3)**	**(1) × (4)**	**Explanation**
Pewter	3,000 kg	$8.50	$8.80	$0.30	$900 F	Bargained for an especially favourable price

F = Favourable; U = Unfavourable.

ISOLATION OF VARIANCES   At what point should variances be isolated and brought to the attention of management? The answer is, the sooner the better. The sooner deviations from standard are brought to the attention of management, the sooner problems can be evaluated and corrected.

Once a performance report has been prepared, what does management do with the price variance data? The most significant variances should be viewed as "red flags," calling attention to the fact that an exception has occurred that will require some explanation and perhaps follow-up effort. Normally, the performance report itself will contain some explanation of the reason for the variance, as shown above. In the case of Colonial Pewter Company, the purchasing manager, Janet Warner, said that the favourable price variance resulted from bargaining for an especially favourable price.

RESPONSIBILITY FOR THE VARIANCE   Who is responsible for the materials price variance? Generally speaking, the purchasing manager has control over the price paid for goods and is therefore responsible for any price variances. Many factors influence the prices paid for goods, including how many units are ordered in a lot, how the order is delivered, whether the order is a rush order, and the quality of materials purchased. A deviation in any of these factors from what was assumed when the standards were set can result in a price variance. For example, purchase of second-grade materials, rather than top-grade materials, may result in a favourable price variance, since the lower-grade materials would generally be less costly (but perhaps less suitable for production). Although this may result in a favourable purchase price variance, it can lead to an unfavourable quantity variance, as explained later.

There may be times, however, when someone other than the purchasing manager is responsible for a materials price variance. Consider the situation where a sales representative, in order to please a customer (and meet her own personal sales targets), promises a shorter delivery schedule. What is the effect of this? The production department will be required to juggle its schedule to accommodate this request. The result? This will have a spiralling effect on all the input resources required for production—materials, labour, and overhead. Consequently, the purchasing manager might be required to order materials in a hurry and pay a significantly higher price than planned. Who should be held responsible for the resulting unfavourable materials price variance? Negative as this situation sounds, the potential bright side might be that this is a promising customer who will place large orders in the future if he is satisfied with how his first order is handled.

A word of caution is in order, however. Variance analysis should not be used as an excuse to conduct witch hunts or as a means of beating line managers and workers over the head. The emphasis must be on the control function in the sense of *supporting* the line managers and *assisting* them in meeting the goals that they have participated in setting for the company. In short, the emphasis should be positive, rather than negative. Dwelling excessively on the past, particularly in order to find someone to blame, can destroy morale and kill any cooperative spirit.

Materials Quantity Variance—A Closer Look

The **materials quantity variance** measures the difference between the actual quantity of materials used in production and the quantity that should have been used according to the standard set by managers. Although the variance is concerned with the physical usage of materials, it is generally stated in dollar terms, as shown in Exhibit 8–3. The formula for the materials quantity variance is as follows:

$$\text{Materials quantity variance} = (AQ \times SP) - (SQ \times SP)$$

Actual Quantity   Standard Price   Standard Quantity Allowed for Output

Again, the formula can be factored into simpler terms:

$$\text{Materials quantity variance} = SP(AQ - SQ)$$

Using the data from Exhibit 8–3 in the formula, we have the following:

$$\$8.80 \text{ per kg } (3,000 \text{ kg} - 2,500 \text{ kg*}) = \$4,400 \text{ U}$$

*2,000 units $\times$ 1.25 kg per unit = 2,500 kg.

The answer, of course, is the same as that yielded in Exhibit 8–3. The data might appear as follows if a formal performance report were prepared:

COLONIAL PEWTER COMPANY
Performance Report—Production Department

Type of Materials	(1) Standard Price	(2) Actual Quantity	(3) Standard Quantity Allowed	(4) Difference in Quantity (2) − (3)	(5) Total Quantity Variance (1) × (4)	Explanation
Pewter	$8.80	3,000 kg	2,500 kg	500 kg	$4,400 U	Second-grade materials unsuitable for production

F = Favourable; U = Unfavourable.

The materials quantity variance is best isolated at the time that materials are placed into production. Materials are drawn for the number of units to be produced, according to the standard bill of materials for each unit. Any additional materials are usually drawn with an excess materials requisition slip, which is different in colour from the normal requisition slips. This procedure calls attention to the excessive usage of materials *while production is still in process* and provides an opportunity for early control of any developing problem.

Excessive usage of materials can result from many factors, including faulty machines, inferior quality of materials, untrained workers, and poor supervision. Generally speaking, it is the responsibility of the production department to see that material usage is kept in line with standards. There may be times, however, when the *purchasing* department may be responsible for an unfavourable materials quantity variance. If the purchasing department obtains inferior quality materials in an effort to economize on price, the materials may be unsuitable for use and may result in excessive waste. Thus, purchasing, rather than production, would be responsible for the quantity variance. At Colonial Pewter, the production manager, Tom Kuchel, said that second-grade materials were the cause of the unfavourable materials quantity variance for June.

Rising Standard Costs or Just Large Variances?　　IN BUSINESS TODAY

Cost increases appear to have become the norm, and why not! According to a report in *Daily Commercial News*, rising oil prices pushed the average prices of raw materials in Canada up by 13.7% between July 2004 and July 2005. In contrast, the average price that manufacturers charged at the gate decreased by 0.3% over the same period. Is this a blip or should manufacturers revise the standard costs of their products? Moreover, the decreasing prices means that companies must accept lower profit margins. Any inefficiencies in production, leading to negative variances, must therefore be carefully scrutinized by management regardless of how small it is—the policy of management by exception may need revisiting!

Source: "Oil Costs Push Manufacturing Costs," *Daily Commercial News*, September 1, 2005, p.2.

Using Standard Costs—Direct Labour Variances

Terry's next step in determining Colonial Pewter's variances for June was to compute the direct labour variances for the month. Recall from Exhibit 8–1 that the standard direct labour cost per unit of product is $35, computed as follows:

$$2.5 \text{ hours per unit} \times \$14 \text{ per hour} = \$35 \text{ per unit}$$

During June, the company paid its direct labour workers $74,250, including employment taxes and fringe benefits, for 5,400 hours of work. This was an average of $13.75 per hour. Using these data and the standard costs from Exhibit 8–1, Terry computed the direct labour rate and efficiency variances that appear in Exhibit 8–5.

Note that the column headings in Exhibit 8–5 are the same as those used in the prior two exhibits, except that in Exhibit 8–5 the terms *hours* and *rate* are used in place of the terms *quantity* and *price*.

Exhibit 8–5

Variance Analysis—Direct Labour

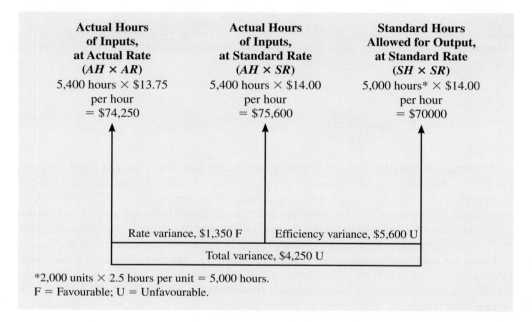

*2,000 units × 2.5 hours per unit = 5,000 hours.
F = Favourable; U = Unfavourable.

Labour Rate Variance—A Closer Look

As explained previously, the price variance for direct labour is commonly termed a **labour rate variance.** This variance measures any deviation from standard in the average hourly rate paid to direct labour workers. The formula for the labour rate variance is expressed as follows:

$$\text{Labour rate variance} = (AH \times AR) - (AH \times SR)$$

Actual Hours   Actual Rate   Standard Rate

The formula can be factored into simpler form as follows:

$$\text{Labour rate variance} = AH(AR - SR)$$

Using the data from Exhibit 8–5 in the formula, we see the following:

$$5,400 \text{ hours} (\$13.75 \text{ per hour} - \$14.00 \text{ per hour}) = \$1,350 \text{ F}$$

In most organizations, the rates paid to workers are quite predictable. Nevertheless, rate variances can arise through the way labour is used. Skilled workers with high hourly rates of pay may be given duties that require little skill and call for low hourly rates of pay. This will result in unfavourable labour rate variances, since the actual hourly rate of pay will exceed the standard rate specified for the particular task being performed. A reverse situation exists when unskilled or untrained workers are assigned to jobs that require some skill or training. The lower pay scale for these workers will result in favourable rate variances, although the workers may be inefficient. Finally, unfavourable rate variances can arise from overtime work at premium rates if any portion of the overtime premium is added to the direct labour account.

Who is responsible for controlling the labour rate variances? Assuming that the human resources (HR) department has done its homework in terms of accurately estimating the standard wage rates, keeping in mind the labour market conditions, competition and the economic conditions, and establishing reasonable HR resource policies and guidelines, it is unlikely that the HR department would be held responsible for any rate variances. However, a rate variance can occur due to the difference between the expected and actual labour mix used during the period. Since assigning labour to production is usually the production supervisor's responsibility, any variances resulting from a change in the mix of labour used should also be assigned to that individual.

Labour Efficiency Variance—A Closer Look

The quantity variance for direct labour, more commonly called the **labour efficiency variance,** measures the productivity of labour time. No variance is more closely watched by management, as it is widely believed that increasing the productivity of direct labour time is vital to reducing costs. This is particularly true in the case of labour-intensive operations, but may not be relevant in highly automated environments. The formula for the labour efficiency variance is expressed as follows:

$$\text{Labour efficiency variance} = (AH \times SR) - (SH \times SR)$$

Actual Hours   Standard Rate   Standard Hours Allowed for Output

Factored into simpler terms, the formula is as follows:

$$\text{Labour efficiency variance} = SR\,(AH - SH)$$

Using the data from Exhibit 8–5 in the formula, we have the following:

$$\$14.00 \text{ per hour } (5,400 \text{ hours} - 5,000 \text{ hours*}) = \$5,600 \text{ U}$$

*2,000 units × 2.5 hours per unit = 5,000 hours.

Possible causes of an unfavourable labour efficiency variance include poorly trained or motivated workers; poor quality materials, requiring more labour time in processing; faulty equipment, causing breakdowns and work interruptions; poor supervision of workers; and inaccurate standards. The managers in charge of production would generally be responsible for control of the labour efficiency variance. However, the variance might be chargeable to purchasing if the acquisition of poor materials resulted in excessive labour processing time.

When the labour force is essentially fixed in the short term, another important cause of an unfavourable labour efficiency variance is insufficient demand for the output of the factory. In some firms, the actual labour-hours worked are basically fixed—particularly in the short term. It is difficult, and perhaps even unwise, to constantly adjust the workforce in response to changes in the workload. Therefore, the only way a work centre manager can avoid an unfavourable labour efficiency variance in such firms is by keeping everyone busy all of the time. The option of reducing the number of workers on hand is not available.

Thus, if customer orders are insufficient to keep the workers busy, the work centre manager has two options—either accept an unfavourable labour efficiency variance or build inventory.[2] A central lesson of just-in-time (JIT) is that building inventory with no immediate prospect of sale is a bad idea. Inventory—particularly work-in-process inventory—can lead to high defect rates, obsolete goods, and generally inefficient operations. As a consequence, when the workforce is basically fixed in the short term, managers must be cautious about how labour efficiency variances are used. Some managers advocate dispensing with labour efficiency variances entirely in such situations—at least for the purposes of motivating and controlling workers on the shop floor.

DECISION MAKER   **Department Resources Manager**

You are the manager of the computer-generated special effects department for a company that produces special effects for high-profile films. You receive a copy of this month's performance report for your department and discover a large labour efficiency variance that is unfavourable. What factors might have contributed to this unfavourable variance?

Using Standard Costs—Variable Overhead Variances

⊜ KNOW   ⊜ APPLY

CC11: Explain and compute variable overhead variances.

The final step in Terry's analysis of Colonial Pewter's variances for June was to compute the variable manufacturing overhead variances. The variable portion of manufacturing overhead can be analyzed using the same basic formulas that are used to analyze direct materials and direct labour. Recall from Exhibit 8–1 that the standard variable manufacturing overhead is $7.50 per unit of product, computed as follows:

$$2.5 \text{ hours per unit} \times \$3 \text{ per hour} = \$7.50 \text{ per unit}$$

Colonial Pewter's cost records showed that the total actual variable manufacturing overhead cost for June was $15,390. Recall from our previous discussion of the direct labour variances that 5,400 hours of direct labour time were recorded during the month and that the company produced 2,000 pairs of bookends. Terry's analysis of this overhead data appears in Exhibit 8–6.

Exhibit 8–6

Variance Analysis—Variable Manufacturing Overhead

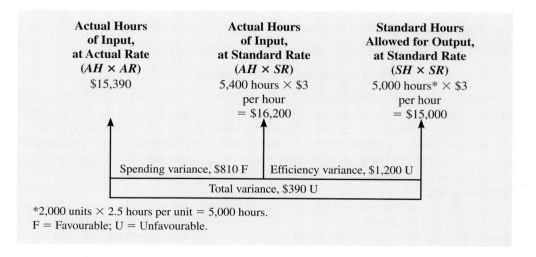

Actual Hours of Input, at Actual Rate (AH × AR)	Actual Hours of Input, at Standard Rate (AH × SR)	Standard Hours Allowed for Output, at Standard Rate (SH × SR)
$15,390	5,400 hours × $3 per hour = $16,200	5,000 hours* × $3 per hour = $15,000

Spending variance, $810 F   Efficiency variance, $1,200 U

Total variance, $390 U

*2,000 units × 2.5 hours per unit = 5,000 hours.
F = Favourable; U = Unfavourable.

---

[2]For further discussion, see Eliyahu M. Goldratt and Jeff Cox, *The Goal*, 2nd rev. ed. (Croton-on-Hudson, NY: North River Press, 1992).

Observe the similarities between Exhibits 8–5 and 8–6. These similarities arise from the fact that direct labour-hours are being used as a base for allocating overhead cost to units of product; thus, the same hourly figures appear in Exhibit 8–6 for variable manufacturing overhead as in Exhibit 8–5 for direct labour. The main difference between the two exhibits is in the standard hourly rate being used, which in this company is much lower for variable overhead.

Overhead Variances—A Closer Look

The formula for the **variable overhead spending variance** is expressed as follows:

Or, factored into simpler terms:

$$\text{Variable overhead spending variance} = AH(AR - SR)$$

Using the data from Exhibit 8–6 in the formula, we see the following:

$$5{,}400 \text{ hours } (\$2.85 \text{ per hour}^* - \$3 \text{ per hour}) = \$810 \text{ F}$$

*$15,390 ÷ 5,400 hours = $2.85 per hour.

The formula for the **variable overhead efficiency variance** is expressed as follows:

$$\text{Variable overhead efficiency variance} = (AH \times SR) - (SH \times SR)$$

Actual   Standard   Standard
Hours   Rate   Hours
    Allowed
    for Output

Or, factored into simpler terms:

$$\text{Variable overhead efficiency variance} = SR(AH - SH)$$

Again using the data from Exhibit 8–6, the computation of the variance would be as follows:

$$\$3.00 \text{ per hour } (5{,}400 \text{ hours} - 5{,}000 \text{ hours}^*) = \$1{,}200 \text{ U}$$

*2,000 units × 2.5 hours per unit = 5,000 hours.

We will reserve further discussion of the variable overhead spending and efficiency variances until the next chapter, where overhead analysis is discussed in depth.

Before proceeding further, it might be useful to summarize the standard and actual costs and the variances for Colonial Pewter Company; this is done in Exhibit 8–7. Comparing the total actual and standard costs for 2,000 units simply tells us that Colonial incurred an additional cost of $8,140 (>7.6% of standard cost). The numbers in Exhibit 8–7 clearly indicate that the cost increase was due to excess usage of the two inputs: direct materials and direct labour. Remember that variable overhead is allocated using direct labour as the base; therefore, the variable overhead efficiency variance is a result of the additional labour hours. Note also that managers at Colonial were able to acquire all three inputs at lower than the standard prices. It may be useful to examine the implications of variances in a little more detail.

Exhibit 8–7
Summary of Standard Costs and
Variances for Colonial Pewter
Company

	Direct Materials	Direct Labour	Variable Overhead	Total
Standard cost/unit	$11.00	$35.00	$7.50	$53.50
Standard cost/2,000 units	$22,000	$70,000	$15,000	$107,000
Actual cost/2,000 units	$25,500	$74,250	$15,390	$115,140
Price-related variance	$900 F	$1,350 F	$810 F	$3,060 F
Quantity-related variance	$4,400 U	$5,600 U	$1,200 U	$11,200 U
Total variance	$3,500 U	$4,250 U	$390 U	$8,140 U

IN BUSINESS TODAY   **Internal Standards or External Benchmarks?**

Some critics argue that standard costing systems have become obsolete in the modern business environment characterized by shortened product life cycles, rapid design, and process changes. However, a review of research pertaining to management accounting practices suggests that standard costing is very much alive. But, standards do not have to be internally developed. Many organizations (manufacturing and nonmanufacturing) use external standards (or *benchmarks*), rather than internal ones, to assess their performance along various dimensions. A recent survey of facilities management (FM) divisions within North American universities suggests that 54% benchmark their FM operations largely by comparing themselves to other universities on measures such as cleaning costs, maintenance costs, and energy expenditures. In addition, they may also use benchmarks established by the International Facilities Management Association (IFMA).

Sources: R. Faruquee, (2003), *Performance Measurement and Benchmarking in Facilities Management: A Survey of North American Universities*, MBA Thesis, University of Saskatchewan; A. Zoysa, and S. Herath, (2007), "Standard Costing in Japanese Firms: Re-examination of its Significance in the New Manufacturing Environment," *Industrial Management and Data Systems*, Vol. 107 (2), pp. 271–283.

**MANAGERIAL
ACCOUNTING
INACTION**

The Wrap-Up

In preparation for the scheduled meeting to discuss his analysis of Colonial Pewter's standard costs and variances, Terry distributed Exhibits 8–1 through 8–7, with supporting explanations, to the management group of Colonial Pewter. This included J. D. Wriston, the president of the company; Tom Kuchel, the production manager; and Janet Warner, the purchasing manager. J. D. Wriston opened the meeting with the following question:

J. D.: Terry, I think I understand the report you distributed, but just to make sure, would you mind summarizing the highlights of what you found?

Terry: As you can see, the biggest problems are the unfavourable materials quantity variance of $4,400 and the unfavourable labour efficiency variance of $5,600.

J. D.: Tom, you're the production boss. What do you think is responsible for the unfavourable labour efficiency variance?

Tom: It pretty much has to be the new production workers. Our experienced workers shouldn't have much problem meeting the standard of 2.5 hours per unit. We all knew that there would be some inefficiency for a while as we brought new people on board.

J. D.: No one is disputing that, Tom. However, $5,600 is a lot of money. Is this problem likely to go away very soon?

Tom: I hope so. If we were to contrast the last two weeks of June with the first two weeks, I'm sure we would see some improvement.

J. D.: I don't want to beat up on you, Tom, but this is a significant problem. Can you do something to accelerate the training process?

Tom: Sure. I could pair up each of the new guys with one of our old-timers and have them work together for a while. It would slow down our older guys a bit, but I'll bet the new workers would learn a lot.

J. D.: Let's try it. Now, what about that $4,400 unfavourable materials quantity variance?

Tom: Are you asking me?

J. D.: Well, I would like someone to explain it.

Tom: Don't look at me. It's that iron-contaminated pewter that Janet bought on her "special deal."

Janet: We got rid of that stuff months ago.

J. D.: Hold your horses. We're not trying to figure out who to blame here. I just want to understand what happened. If we can understand what happened, maybe we can fix it.

Terry: Tom, are the new workers generating a lot of scrap?

Tom: Yeah, I guess so.

J. D.: I think that could be part of the problem. Can you do anything about it?

Tom: I can watch the scrap real closely for a few days to see where it's being generated. If it is the new workers, I can have the old-timers work with them on the problem when I team them up.

J. D.: Good. Let's reconvene in a few weeks and see what has happened. Hopefully, we can get those unfavourable variances under control.

Standard Costing and Variance Analysis in an Activity-Based Costing Environment

Our example in this chapter uses direct labour-hours as the base to allocate overhead; we have used this simple method to compute the standard variable overhead cost and compute variable overhead variances. Using a single allocation base makes the computation much simpler. However, using a single allocation base may not provide accurate information to managers.

Standard costs can be developed using a more complex system such as activity-based costing, which we covered in Chapter 6. In fact, ABC and standard costing are not incompatible; however, moving to ABC is not a simple extension of the single overhead allocation base setting used in this chapter. Two main reasons underlie this complexity: (1) ABC uses multiple allocation bases, and (2) only the unit-level activities are directly proportional to production volume. The use of multiple allocation bases means that standards must be developed for costs pertaining to each activity (allocation base). Moreover, the existence of non-unit-level activities means that the costs pertaining to these activities may behave as step-fixed costs with respect to production volume. Consequently, developing standards for a single unit of production is conceptually more challenging in settings where ABC is used.

Variance Analysis and Management by Exception

The budgets and standard costs discussed in this and the preceding chapters reflect management's plans. If actual performance is close to the plans, there is little cause for immediate worry. What is important in such a context is to examine the standards (and budgets). Organizations that embrace lean business practices continuously look for ways to improve; a significant benefit of improvements is that they can result in reducing the level of input resources required by the organization (e.g., less materials, labour, and overhead). Any reduction in input requirements will directly impact standard costs; organizations must revise the standard costs to reflect such improvements.

What happens when actual results are different from the plan? More often than not, actual results *are* different from the plan, which means that management often ends up

 KNOW

CC12: Describe the principle of management by exception.

investigating the variances. However, are all variances worth investigating? The answer is no. Variances almost always occur because plans are prepared on the basis of certain assumptions that may not hold. Also, there are unforeseen events that one simply cannot consider during planning (economic downturns or upturns, natural or man-made disasters, exchange rate fluctuations, and so on).

How should managers decide which variances are worth investigating? One clue is the size of the variance either in absolute dollar figures or as percentage figures. For example, it is simply not worth management's time to spend time on a 0.5% variance from the standard. This is where the concept of *management by exception* is useful. Simply put, **management by exception** is a management philosophy where a manager directs attention toward those parts of the organization where the variances are significant as defined by the organization (e.g., 5% or more, or $5,000 or more). By focusing on the more significant variances, managers can hope to achieve significant gains from any improvements. Investigating a direct materials quantity variance of $500 is merely a waste of time when the total materials consumed cost over $1,000,000 during a given period. Time spent on investigating small variances often means that other (sometimes larger) variances may be neglected.

In addition to watching for large variances, managers must also pay attention to the pattern of variances. For example, if the labour efficiency variance is steadily increasing period after period, this should trigger an investigation, even though none of the variances is large enough by itself to warrant investigation. Timely attention to the pattern of variances can help in arresting the problem before it gets out of hand. For example, a rising trend of materials quantity and labour efficiency variances may suggest the existence of problems with the process or equipment used, which need to be looked into. In summary, variance analysis is a useful tool for managers and facilitates management by exception.

Evaluation of Controls Based on Standard Costs

KNOW

CC13: Describe the benefits and limitations of using standard costing for the purposes of control.

Advantages of Standard Costs

Standard cost systems have a number of advantages:

1. As stated previously, the use of standard costs is a key element in a management-by-exception approach. So long as costs remain within the standards, managers can focus on other issues. When costs fall significantly outside the standards, managers are alerted that there may be problems requiring attention. This approach helps managers focus on important issues.
2. As long as standards are viewed by employees as being reasonable, they can promote economy and efficiency. They provide benchmarks that individuals can use to judge their own performance.
3. Standard costs can greatly simplify bookkeeping. Instead of recording actual costs for each job, the standard costs for materials, labour, and overhead can be charged to jobs.
4. Standard costs fit naturally in an integrated system of "responsibility accounting." The standards establish what costs should be, who should be responsible for them, and whether actual costs are under control.

Potential Problems with the Use of Standard Costs

The use of standard costs can present a number of potential problems. Most of these problems result from improper use of standard costs and the management-by-exception principle, or from using standard costs in situations where they are not appropriate.

1. Standard cost variance reports are usually prepared on a monthly basis and often are released days or even weeks after the end of the month. As a consequence, the infor-

mation in the reports may be so stale that it is almost useless. Timely, frequent reports that are approximately correct are better than infrequent reports that are very precise but out of date by the time they are released. Some companies are now reporting variances and other key operating data daily or even more frequently.

2. If managers are insensitive and use variance reports as a club, morale may suffer. Employees should receive positive reinforcement for work well done. Management by exception, by its nature, tends to focus on the negative. If variances are used as a club, subordinates may be tempted to cover up unfavourable variances or take actions that are not in the best interests of the company to make sure the variances are favourable. For example, workers may put on a crash effort to increase output at the end of the month to avoid an unfavourable labour efficiency variance. In the rush to produce output, quality may suffer.

3. Labour quantity standards and efficiency variances make two important assumptions. First, they assume that the production process is labour-paced; if labour works faster, output will go up. However, output in many companies is no longer determined by how fast labour works; rather, it is determined by the processing speed of machines. Second, the computations assume that labour is a variable cost. However, direct labour may be essentially fixed. If labour is fixed, then an undue emphasis on labour efficiency variances creates pressure to build excess work-in-process and finished goods inventories.

4. In some cases, a "favourable" variance can be as bad as (or worse than) an "unfavourable" variance. For example, McDonald's has a standard for the amount of hamburger meat that should be in a Big Mac. A "favourable" variance means that less meat was used than the standard specifies. The result is a substandard Big Mac and possibly a dissatisfied customer.

5. There may be a tendency with standard cost reporting systems to emphasize meeting the standards to the exclusion of other important objectives, such as maintaining and improving quality, on-time delivery, and customer satisfaction. This tendency can be reduced by using supplemental performance measures that focus on these other objectives. (This is discussed in Chapter 10.)

6. Just meeting standards may not be sufficient; continual improvement may be necessary to survive in the current competitive environment. For this reason, some companies focus on the trends in the standard cost variances—aiming for continual improvement, rather than just meeting the standards. In other companies, engineered standards are being replaced either by a rolling average of actual costs, which is expected to decline, or by very challenging target costs.

In conclusion, managers should exercise considerable care in their use of a standard cost system. It is particularly important that managers go out of their way to focus on the positive, rather than just on the negative, and to be aware of possible unintended consequences.

Application Competency Summary

Application Competency	Deliverable	Source Documents and Key Information	Steps	Knowledge Competency
Develop standard costs for direct materials. ⦿ CC3	**Key Information** Ideal and practical quantity standards of direct materials per unit of output Standard price of direct materials per unit of output including other purchase-related costs Standard cost of direct materials per unit of output **Report/Document** No specific document	**Bill of Materials** Historical data of direct materials consumed per unit of output Historical records of direct materials cost **Purchase Orders** Price quotes from potential suppliers Purchase terms and conditions **Quality Records** Historical records of scrap, rejects, and other allowances	1. Determine the ideal quantity of DM required per unit of output based on historical data, and product and process design. 2. Add the normal waste allowed due to quality and other production considerations to determine the (practical) standard quantity of direct materials. 3. Determine the average price of the materials based on historical data and quotes from potential suppliers. 4. Add delivery and other purchase-related costs, deduct any discounts to determine the standard price of direct materials. 5. Multiply the standard quantity by the standard price to compute the standard cost of direct materials per unit of output.	Ideal and practical standards, price standards, quantity standards, and cost standards
Develop standard costs for direct labour. ⦿ CC4	**Key Information** Ideal and practical direct labour hours per unit of output Standard rate of direct labour per unit of output including benefits and taxes Standard cost of direct labour per unit of output **Report/Document** No specific document	**Annual Budget Documents** Direct labour required per unit of output Allowances for quality and other production considerations **Wage Agreement Documents** Direct labour wage rate	1. Determine the ideal direct labour hours required per unit of output based on historical data, and product and process design. 2. Add the normal allowance for rests and breaks, and additional time allowed due to normal quality and other production considerations to determine the (practical) standard quantity of direct materials. 3. Determine the average wage rate based on historical data and labour market conditions. 4. Add benefit expenses, taxes, and other expenses to determine the standard wage rate. 5. Multiply the standard labour hours by the standard rate to compute the standard cost of direct labour per unit of output.	

continued

Application Competency	Deliverable	Source Documents and Key Information	Steps	Knowledge Competency
Develop standard costs for variable overhead. ⊙ CC5	**Key Information** Ideal and practical quantity of overhead allocation base per unit of output Standard overhead allocation rate per unit of output Standard cost of variable overhead per unit of output **Report/Document** No specific document	**Annual Budget Documents** Variable overhead allocation base Estimated variable overhead for the period Estimated quantity of the allocation base for the period Quantity of allocation base required per unit of output	1. Identify the base used to allocate variable overhead. 2. Determine the standard quantity of the allocation base required per unit of output. 3. Compute the predetermined overhead allocation rate based on estimated overhead costs and the estimated quantity of the allocation base. 4. Multiply the standard quantity of the overhead allocation base by the predetermined overhead allocation rate to compute the standard cost of variable overhead per unit of output.	Ideal and practical standards, price standards, quantity standards and cost standards ⊙ CC1, 2
Prepare a standard cost card. ⊙ CC6	**Key Information** Standard costs of direct materials, direct labour, overhead, and total standard costs. **Report/Document** Standard cost card	**Annual Budget and Other Internal Documents** Standard price and quantity for direct materials, direct labour, and variable overhead	1. List the standard costs of direct materials, direct labour, and variable overhead per unit of output. 2. Add the three amounts to determine the total standard cost per unit of output.	Standard costs for direct materials, direct labour, and variable overhead ⊙ CC3, 4, 5
Compute direct materials variances. ⊙ CC9	**Key Information** Actual and standard price, quantity and cost of direct materials purchased/used Price and quantity variances **Report/Document** Performance report	**Production Reports** Actual output quantity **Bill of Materials** or **Direct Materials Account in the General Ledger** Quantity of direct materials used in production **Purchase Orders** Actual price of direct materials purchased **Standard Cost Card** Standard quantity of direct materials required for actual output, and standard price of direct materials	1. Determine the actual cost of direct materials purchased by multiplying the actual price by the actual quantity. 2. Compute the standard cost of the actual quantity purchased (used) by multiplying the standard price by the actual quantity. 3. The difference between the actual and standard costs of the actual quantity purchased is the price variance. 4. Compute the standard cost of the standard quantity required to produce the actual output by multiplying the standard price by the standard quantity. 5. The difference between the standard costs of the actual quantity used and the standard quantity that should have been used is the quantity variance.	Price and quantity variances, direct materials variances ⊙ CC8, 9

continued

Application Competency	Deliverable	Source Documents and Key Information	Steps	Knowledge Competency
Compute direct labour variances. ⬤ CC10	**Key Information** Actual and standard rate, quantity and cost of direct labour Rate and efficiency variances **Report/Document** Performance report	**Production Reports** Actual output quantity **Labour Time Tickets** or **Direct Labour Account in the General Ledger** Direct labour hours used in production **Payroll Records** Actual wage rate of direct labour used **Standard Cost Card** Standard direct hours required for actual output, and standard wage rate price of direct labour	1. Determine the actual cost of direct labour purchased by multiplying the actual rate by the actual hours used. 2. Compute the standard cost of the actual hours (used) by multiplying the standard rate by the actual hours. 3. The difference between the actual and standard costs of the actual hours used is the rate variance. 4. Compute the standard cost of the standard hours required to produce the actual output by multiplying the standard rate by the standard hours. 5. The difference between the standard costs of the actual hours used and the standard hours that should have been used is the efficiency variance.	Price and quantity variances, direct labour variances ⬤ CC8, 10
Compute variable overhead variances. ⬤ CC11	**Key Information** Actual and standard rate, quantity and cost of direct labour Rate and efficiency variances **Report/Document** Performance report	**Production Reports** Actual output quantity Actual quantity of the overhead allocation base used **Variable Overhead Account in the General Ledger** Actual variable overhead expenses Standard (allocated) variable overhead amount for actual output **Standard Cost Card** Standard quantity of the allocation base that should have been used to produce the actual output	1. Determine the actual cost of variable overhead from the overhead account ledgers. 2. Compute the standard cost of the actual quantity of the allocation base consumed by multiplying the standard rate by the actual quantity. 3. The difference between the actual and standard costs is the spending variance. 4. Compute the standard cost of the standard quantity of the allocation base required to produce the actual output by multiplying the standard rate by the standard quantity. 5. The difference between the standard costs of the actual quantity of the allocation base and the standard quantity that should have been used is the efficiency variance.	Price and quantity variances, variable overhead variances ⬤ CC8, 11

Guidance Answers to You Decide and Decision Maker

HOCKEY COACH (p. 317)

NHL records would be similar to ideal standards. They call for levels of effort and skill that have been attained only by professional hockey players under the best circumstances. Even though such standards might have a motivational value to professional hockey players, they would probably tend to discourage the players on your team if you told them that they needed to meet those expectations to receive recognition.

Practical standards are tight, but can be attained through reasonable, though highly efficient, efforts by the average worker. Practical standards might motivate your players to do their best on the ice rink and might help you identify problems requiring additional coaching or practice. Given the differing athletic abilities and skill levels among the players on your team, it might be best to start with each player's statistics from last season and then make adjustments to create benchmarks for each player.

After acknowledging your gratitude for the parent's interest in the team, you might remind the parents that the kids are playing on the team to have fun and develop their skills and self-confidence. Then, after explaining the pros and cons of each of the two types of standards, you can address how you set benchmarks for the players.

DEPARTMENT RESOURCES MANAGER (p. 330)

An unfavourable labour efficiency variance in the computer-generated special effects department might have been caused by inexperienced, poorly trained, or unmotivated employees; faulty hardware and/or software that may have caused work interruptions; and/or poor supervision of the employees in this department. In addition, it is possible that there was insufficient demand for the output of this department—resulting in idle time—or that the standard (or benchmark) for this department was inaccurate.

Review Problem: Standard Costs and Variance Analysis

Xavier Company manufactures a single product. The following information is available regarding the standards for the product.

- Each saleable finished unit consists of five grams of direct materials.
- As a result of the nature of the direct material used and the production process, 12.25% of the direct materials used in production is lost.
- The ideal direct labour time required to produce one saleable finished unit is 1.5 hours.
- Direct labour is paid for 8 hours, which includes an hour for breaks and clean-up.
- 5% of the units produced must be scrapped (at zero value) due to poor quality.
- Direct materials cost $400 per kilogram plus an additional 25% for customs and excise duties, and shipping costs.
- Direct labour is paid at $20 per hour.
- Variable overhead is allocated using direct labour-hours as a base, at a rate of $5 per hour.

During June, 2,000 units were produced. The costs associated with June's operations were as follows:

Materials purchased: 18 kilograms at $600 per kg	$10,800
Materials used in production: 14 kilograms	—
Direct labour: 4,000 hours at $19.50 per hour	$78,000
Variable manufacturing overhead costs incurred.	$20,800

Required:
1. Develop a standard cost card for the product produced by Xavier Company (use Exhibit 8-1 as a guide).
2. Compute the materials, labour, and variable manufacturing overhead variances for the month of June.

SOLUTION TO THE REVIEW PROBLEM

1. Standard Cost Card

Inputs	(1) Standard Quantity or Hours	(2) Standard Price or Rate	(3) Standard Cost (1) × (2)
Direct materials	6.0 grams	$ 0.50	$ 3.00
Direct labour	1.8 hours	20.00	36.00
Variable manufacturing overhead	1.8 hours	5.00	9.00
Total standard cost per unit			$48.00

Explanation of calculations:

Direct materials

Each unit of good (saleable) finished product consists of 5 grams; this is equivalent to 87.75% of the materials used (remember that 12.25% is lost).

Direct materials required to be used to produce one finished unit = 5 ÷ .8775 = 5.7 grams (rounded)

Also, remember that 5% of the finished units are scrapped due to poor quality. This means that to obtain 95 good (saleable) units, 100 must be produced. Therefore, additional direct materials must be used to account for quality problems.

Thus, the *standard quantity of direct materials* used to produce one *good* (saleable) finished unit is

$\quad$ 5.7 ÷ 0.95 = 6 grams

Standard price of direct materials = $400 + ($100 × 25%) = $500 per kg, or $0.50 per gram

Direct labour

Each unit of finished product requires 1.5 hours of direct labour.

Direct labour is paid for 8 hours per day, which includes 1 hour for breaks, clean-up, etc. This means labour is paid 8/7 times the amount of time actually worked to produce a product.

Paid labour hours required per unit = 1.5 × (8/7) = 1.714 hours.

Also, remember that 5% of the finished units are scrapped due to poor quality. This means that to obtain 95 good (saleable) units, 100 must be produced. Therefore, additional direct labour must be used to account for quality problems.

Thus, the *standard quantity of direct labour* required to produce one *good* (saleable) finished unit is

$\quad$ 1.714 ÷ 0.95 = 1.8 hours (rounded)

Variable overhead

Variable overhead is allocated using direct labour-hours (DLH) as the allocation base at $5 per DLH.

2. Variance Analysis

Materials Variances

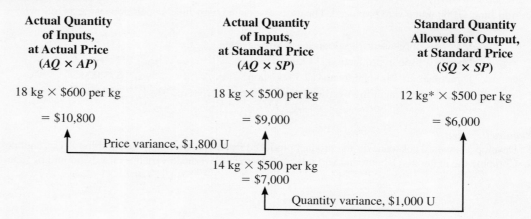

Actual Quantity of Inputs, at Actual Price (AQ × AP)	Actual Quantity of Inputs, at Standard Price (AQ × SP)	Standard Quantity Allowed for Output, at Standard Price (SQ × SP)
18 kg × $600 per kg	18 kg × $500 per kg	12 kg* × $500 per kg
= $10,800	= $9,000	= $6,000

Price variance, $1,800 U

14 kg × $500 per kg
= $7,000

Quantity variance, $1,000 U

A total variance cannot be computed in this situation, since the amount of materials purchased (18 kg) differs from the amount of materials used in production (14 kg).

*2,000 units $\times$ 6 grams per unit = 12 kg.

Using the formulas in the chapter, the same variances would be computed as:

$$\text{Materials price variance} = AQ(AP - SP)$$
$$18 \text{ kg } (\$600 \text{ per kg} - \$500 \text{ per kg}) = \$1,800 \text{ U}$$

$$\text{Materials quantity variance} = SP(AQ - SQ)$$
$$\$500 \text{ per kg } (14 \text{ kg} - 12 \text{ kg}) = \$1,000 \text{ U}$$

Labour Variances

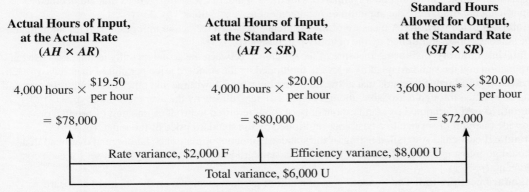

*2,000 units $\times$ 1.8 hours per unit = 3,600 hours.

Using the formulas in the chapter, the same variances would be computed as:

$$\text{Labour rate variance} = AH(AR - SR)$$
$$4,000 \text{ hours } (\$19.50 \text{ per hour} - \$20.00 \text{ per hour}) = \$2,000 \text{ F}$$

$$\text{Labour efficiency variance} = SR(AH - SH)$$
$$\$20.00 \text{ per hour } (4,000 \text{ hours} - 3,600 \text{ hours}) = \$8,000 \text{ U}$$

Variable Manufacturing Overhead Variances

*2,000 units $\times$ 1.8 hours per unit = 3,600 hours.

Using the formulas in the chapter, the same variances would be computed as:

$$\text{Variable overhead spending variance} = AH(AR - SR)$$
$$4,000 \text{ hours } (\$5.20 \text{ per hour*} - \$5.00 \text{ per hour}) = \$800 \text{ U}$$

*$20,800 $\div$ 4,000 hours = \$5.20 per hour.

$$\text{Variable overhead efficiency variance} = SR(AH - SH)$$
$$\$5.00 \text{ per hour } (4,000 \text{ hours} - 3,600 \text{ hours}) = \$2,000 \text{ U}$$

Glossary

Bill of materials A listing of the quantity of each type of material required to manufacture a unit of product. (p. 319)

Ideal standards Standards that allow for no machine breakdowns or other work interruptions and that require peak efficiency at all times. (p. 317)

Labour efficiency variance A measure of the difference between the actual hours taken to complete a task and the standard hours allowed, multiplied by the standard hourly labour rate. (p. 329)

Labour rate variance A measure of the difference between the actual hourly labour rate and the standard rate, multiplied by the number of hours worked during the period. (p. 328)

Management by exception A system of management in which standards are set for various operating activities, with actual results then compared with these standards. Any differences that are deemed significant are brought to the attention of management as "exceptions." (p. 334)

Materials price variance A measure of the difference between the actual unit price paid for an item and the standard price, multiplied by the quantity purchased. (p. 325)

Materials quantity variance A measure of the difference between the actual quantity of materials used in production and the standard quantity allowed, multiplied by the standard price per unit of materials. (p. 326)

Practical standards Standards that allow for normal machine downtime and other work interruptions, and can be attained through reasonable, though highly efficient, efforts by the average worker. (p. 317)

Standard cost Computed by standard quantity of input required to produce one unit of product or provide one unit of service to a customer multiplied by the standard price of the input. (p. 316)

Standard cost card A detailed listing of the standard amounts of materials, labour, and overhead that should go into a unit of product, multiplied by the standard price or rate that has been set for each cost element. (p. 321)

Standard cost per unit The standard cost of a unit of product as shown on the standard cost card; it is computed by multiplying the standard quantity or hours by the standard price or rate for each cost element. (p. 321)

Standard hours allowed The time that should have been taken to complete the period's output as computed by multiplying the actual number of units produced by the standard hours per unit. (p. 323)

Standard hours per unit The amount of labour time that should be required to complete a single unit of product, including allowances for breaks, machine downtime, cleanup, rejects, and other normal inefficiencies. (p. 320)

Standard price per unit The price that should be paid for a single unit of materials, including allowances for quality, quantity purchased, shipping, receiving, and other such costs, net of any discounts allowed. (p. 318)

Standard quantity allowed The amount of materials that should have been used to complete the period's output as computed by multiplying the actual number of units produced by the standard quantity per unit. (p. 323)

Standard quantity per unit The amount of materials that should be required to complete a single unit of product, including allowances for normal waste, spoilage, rejects, and similar inefficiencies. (p. 319)

Standard rate per hour The labour rate that should be incurred per hour of labour time, including employment taxes, fringe benefits, and other such labour costs. (p. 320)

Variable overhead efficiency variance The difference between the actual activity (direct labour-hours, machine-hours, or some other base) of a period and the standard activity allowed, multiplied by the variable part of the predetermined overhead rate. (p. 331)

Variable overhead spending variance The difference between the actual variable overhead cost incurred during a period and the standard cost that should have been incurred based on the actual activity of the period. (p. 331)

Variance The difference between standard prices and quantities on the one hand and actual prices and quantities on the other hand. (p. 322)

Variance analysis The process of computing and interpreting variances. (p. 322)

Questions

8–1 What is a quantity standard? What is a price standard?

8–2 Distinguish between ideal and practical standards.

8–3 What is meant by the term *variance*?

8–4 What is meant by the term *management by exception*?

8–5 Who is generally responsible for the materials price variance? The materials quantity variance? The labour efficiency variance?

8–6   The materials price variance can be computed at what two different points in time? Which point is better? Why?

8–7   What dangers lie in using standards as punitive tools?

8–8   What effect, if any, would you expect poor quality materials to have on direct labour variances?

8–9   If variable manufacturing overhead is applied to production on the basis of direct labour-hours and the direct labour efficiency variance is unfavourable, will the variable overhead efficiency variance be favourable or unfavourable, or could it be either? Explain.

8–10   Why can undue emphasis on labour efficiency variances lead to excess work-in-process inventories?

Brief Exercises

BRIEF EXERCISE 8–1   Setting Standards (CC1, 2, 3)

Victoria Chocolates, Ltd. makes premium handcrafted chocolate confections in London. The owner of the company is setting up a standard cost system and has collected the following data for one of the company's products, the Empire Truffle. This product is made with the finest white chocolate and various fillings. The following data pertain only to the white chocolate used in the product:

Material requirements, kilograms of white chocolate per dozen truffles . .	0.70 kilogram
Allowance for waste, kilograms of white chocolate per dozen truffles . . .	0.03 kilogram
Allowance for rejects, kilograms of white chocolate per dozen truffles. . .	0.02 kilogram
Purchase price, finest grade white chocolate	£7.50 per kilogram
Purchase discount	8% of purchase price
Shipping cost from the supplier in Belgium	£0.30 per kilogram
Receiving and handling cost	£0.04 per kilogram

Required:
1. Determine the standard price of one kilogram of white chocolate.
2. Determine the standard quantity of white chocolate for a dozen truffles.
3. Determine the standard cost of the white chocolate in a dozen truffles.

BRIEF EXERCISE 8–2   Materials Variance (CC3, 7, 8, 9)

Bandar Industries Berhad of Malaysia manufactures sporting equipment. One of the company's products, a football helmet for the North American market, requires a special plastic. During the quarter ending June 30, the company manufactured 70,000 helmets, using 45,000 kilograms of plastic in the process. The plastic cost the company RM 342,000. (The currency in Malaysia is the *ringgit*, which is denoted here by RM.)

According to the standard cost card, each helmet should require 0.6 kilograms of plastic, at a cost of RM 8 per kilogram.

Required:
1. What cost for plastic should have been incurred in the manufacture of the 70,000 helmets? How much does this cost vary from what was incurred?
2. Break down the difference computed in part (1) into a materials price variance and a materials quantity variance.

BRIEF EXERCISE 8–3   Direct Labour Variances (CC4, 7, 8, 10)

SkyChefs, Inc. prepares in-flight meals for a number of major airlines. One of the company's products is grilled salmon in dill sauce with new baby potatoes and spring vegetables. During the most recent week, the company prepared 4,000 of these meals using 960 direct labour-hours. The company paid these direct labour workers a total of $9,600 for this work, or $10 per hour.

According to the standard cost card for this meal, it should require 0.25 direct labour-hours at a cost of $9.75 per hour.

Required:
1. What direct labour cost should have been incurred to prepare the 4,000 meals? How much does this cost vary from what was incurred?
2. Break down the difference computed in part (1) into a labour rate variance and a labour efficiency variance.

BRIEF EXERCISE 8–4   Variable Overhead Variances (CC5, 7, 8, 11)

Logistics Solutions provides order fulfillment services for dot.com merchants. The company maintains warehouses that stock items carried by its dot.com clients. When a client receives an order from a customer, the order is forwarded to Logistics Solutions, which pulls the item from storage, packs it, and ships it to the customer. The company uses a predetermined variable overhead rate based on direct labour-hours.

In the most recent month, 120,000 items were shipped to customers using 2,300 direct labour-hours. The company incurred a total of $7,360 in variable overhead costs.

According to the company's standards, 0.02 direct labour-hour is required to fulfill an order for one item and the variable overhead rate is $3.25 per direct labour-hour.

Required:
1. What variable overhead cost should have been incurred to fill the orders for the 120,000 items? How much does this cost vary from what was incurred?
2. Break down the difference computed in part (1) into a variable overhead spending variance and a variable overhead efficiency variance.

BRIEF EXERCISE 8–5   Explanation of Direct Labour Variances (CC7, 8, 10)

A plant manager hired a large number of replacement production workers at the start of March because he was able to hire them for much less than the usual wage rate. As a result, the direct labour rate variance for March was favourable, but the direct labour efficiency variance for March was unfavourable. Explain what you would infer from the manager's short-term strategy and the success or failure of that strategy based on the two variances.

(Adapted © CGA-Canada)

Exercises

EXERCISE 8–1   Setting Standards; Preparing a Standard Cost Card (CC1, 2, 3, 6)

Martin Company manufactures a powerful cleaning solvent. The main ingredient in the solvent is a raw material called Echol. Information on the purchase and use of Echol follows:

Purchase of Echol   Echol is purchased in 30-litre containers at a cost of $130 per container. A discount of 3% is offered by the supplier for payment within 10 days, and Martin Company takes all discounts. Shipping costs, which Martin Company must pay, amount to $200 for an average shipment of 100 30-litre containers of Echol.

Use of Echol   The bill of materials calls for 15.2 litres of Echol per bottle of cleaning solvent. About 5% of all Echol used is lost through spillage or evaporation (the 15.2 litres above is the *actual* content per bottle). In addition, statistical analysis has shown that every 41st bottle is rejected at final inspection because of contamination.

Required:
1. Compute the standard purchase price for one litre of Echol.
2. Compute the standard quantity of Echol (in litres) per saleable bottle of cleaning solvent.
3. Using the data from parts (1) and (2), prepare a standard cost card showing the standard cost of Echol per bottle of cleaning solvent.

EXERCISE 8–2   Material and Labour Variances (CC7, 8, 9, 10)

Huron Company produces a commercial cleaning compound known as Zoom. The direct materials and direct labour standards for one unit of Zoom follow:

	Standard Quantity or Hours	Standard Price or Rate	Standard Cost
Direct materials...........	2.1 kilograms	$ 5.50 per kilogram	$11.55
Direct labour.............	0.2 hour	12.00 per hour	2.40

During the most recent month, the following activity was recorded:
a. 9,000 kilograms of material were purchased at a cost of $5.20 per kilogram.
b. All of the material purchased was used to produce 4,000 units of Zoom.
c. A total of 750 hours of direct labour time was recorded at a total labour cost of $10,425.

Required:
1. Compute the direct materials price and quantity variances for the month.
2. Compute the direct labour rate and efficiency variances for the month.

EXERCISE 8–3 Material Variances (CC7, 8, 9)
Refer to the data in Exercise 8–2. Assume that instead of producing 4,000 units during the month, the company produced only 3,000 units, using 6,700 kilograms of material in the production process. (The rest of the material purchased remained in inventory.)

Required:
Compute the direct materials price and quantity variances for the month.

EXERCISE 8–4 Labour and Variable Overhead Variances (CC7, 8, 10, 11)
Erie Company manufactures an MP3 player called the Jogging Mate. The company uses standards to control its costs. The labour standards that have been set for one Jogging Mate MP3 player are as follows:

Standard Hours	Standard Rate per Hour	Standard Cost
18 minutes	$12.00	$3.60

During August, 5,750 hours of direct labour time were recorded in the manufacture of 20,000 units of the Jogging Mate. The direct labour cost totalled $73,600 for the month.

Required:
1. What direct labour cost should have been incurred in the manufacture of the 20,000 units of the Jogging Mate? By how much does this differ from the cost that was incurred?
2. Break down the difference in cost from part (1) into a labour rate variance and a labour efficiency variance.
3. The budgeted variable manufacturing overhead rate is $4 per direct labour-hour. During August, the company incurred $21,850 in variable manufacturing overhead cost. Compute the variable overhead spending and efficiency variances for the month.

EXERCISE 8–5 Materials and Labour Variances (CC7, 8, 9, 10)
Dawson Toys, Ltd. produces a toy called the Maze. The company has recently established a standard cost system to help control costs with the following standards for the Maze toy:

> Direct materials: 8 microns per toy at $0.75 per micron
> Direct labour: 3 hours per toy at $12 per hour

During July, the company produced 4,200 Maze toys. Production data for the month on the toy follow:

Direct materials: 25,000 microns were purchased for use in production at a cost of $0.60 per micron. Some 5,000 of these microns were still in inventory at the end of the month.
Direct labour: 4,000 direct labour-hours were worked at a cost of $52,000.

Required:
1. Compute the following variances for July:
   a. Direct materials price and quantity variances.
   b. Direct labour rate and efficiency variances.
2. Prepare a brief explanation of the significance and possible causes of each variance.

EXERCISE 8–6 Material and Labour Efficiency (CC7, 8, 9, 10)
The following standard cost data are for Dixon Ltd. for January 2008:
Per unit:

> Direct material. . . . . . .   30 kilograms at $10 per kilogram
> Direct labour . . . .   8 hours at $24 per hour

During January, Dixon produced 720 units of output, 30 units less than expected. Direct materials purchased and used were 21,000 kg at $10.50 per kilogram. Direct labour used was 5,800 hours at $24.50 per hour.

Required:
1. What were the rate and efficiency variances for direct labour, respectively?
2. What were the price and quantity variances for direct material, respectively?

(Adapted © CGA-Canada)

Problems

PROBLEM 8–1 Variance Analysis in a Hospital (CC8, 9, 10, 11)

John Fleming, chief administrator for a district hospital, is concerned about costs for tests in the hospital's lab. Mr. Fleming has asked you to evaluate costs in the hospital's lab for the past month. The following information is available:

a. Basically, two types of tests are performed in the lab—blood tests and smears. During the past month, 1,800 blood tests and 2,400 smears were performed in the lab.

b. Small glass plates are used in both types of tests. During the past month, the hospital purchased 12,000 plates at a cost of $28,200. This cost is net of a 6% quantity discount. Some 1,500 of these plates were still on hand unused at the end of the month; there were no plates on hand at the beginning of the month.

c. During the past month, 1,150 hours of labour time were recorded in the lab. The cost of this labour time was $13,800.

d. Variable overhead cost last month in the lab for utilities and supplies totalled $7,820.

The hospital has never used standard costs. By searching industry literature, however, you have determined the following nationwide averages for hospital labs:

Plates: Two plates are required per lab test. These plates cost $2.50 each and are disposed of after the test is completed.

Labour: Each blood test should require 0.3 hour to complete, and each smear should require 0.15 hour to complete. The average cost of this lab time is $14 per hour.

Overhead: Overhead cost is based on direct labour-hours. The average rate for variable overhead is $6 per hour.

Mr. Fleming would like a complete analysis of the cost of plates, labour, and overhead in the lab for the last month so that he can get to the root of the lab's cost problem.

Required:

1. Compute a materials price variance for the plates purchased last month and a materials quantity variance for the plates used last month.

2. For labour cost in the lab:
   a. Compute a labour rate variance and a labour efficiency variance.
   b. In most hospitals, one-half of the workers in the lab are senior technicians and one-half are assistants. In an effort to reduce costs, the hospital employs only one-fourth senior technicians and three-fourths assistants. Would you recommend that this policy be continued? Explain.

3. Compute the variable overhead spending and efficiency variances. Is there any relationship between the variable overhead efficiency variance and the labour efficiency variance? Explain.

PROBLEM 8–2 Basic Variance Analysis (CC8, 9, 10, 11)

Becton Labs Inc. produces various chemical compounds for industrial use. One compound, called Fludex, is prepared by means of an elaborate distilling process. The company has developed standard costs for one unit of Fludex, as follows:

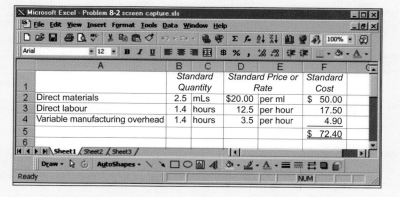

	Standard Quantity		Standard Price or Rate		Standard Cost
Direct materials	2.5	mLs	$20.00	per ml	$ 50.00
Direct labour	1.4	hours	12.5	per hour	17.50
Variable manufacturing overhead	1.4	hours	3.5	per hour	4.90
					$ 72.40

During November, the following activity was recorded by the company relative to production of Fludex:

a. Materials purchased, 12,000 ml at a cost of $225,000.

b. There was no beginning inventory of materials on hand to start the month; at the end of the month, 2,500 ml of material remained in the warehouse unused.

c. The company employs 35 lab technicians to work on the production of Fludex. During November, each worked an average of 160 hours at an average rate of $12 per hour.
d. Variable manufacturing overhead is assigned to Fludex on the basis of direct labour-hours. Variable manufacturing overhead costs during November totalled $18,200.
e. During November, 3,750 good units of Fludex were produced.

The company's management is anxious to determine the efficiency of the activities surrounding the production of Fludex.

Required:
1. For materials used in the production of Fludex:
   a. Compute the price and quantity variances.
   b. The materials were purchased from a new supplier who is anxious to enter into a long-term purchase contract. Would you recommend that the company sign the contract? Explain.
2. For direct labour employed in the production of Fludex:
   a. Compute the rate and efficiency variances.
   b. In the past, the 35 technicians employed in the production of Fludex consisted of 20 senior technicians and 15 assistants. During November, the company experimented with only 15 senior technicians and 20 assistants in order to save costs. Would you recommend that the new labour mix be continued? Explain.
3. Compute the variable overhead spending and efficiency variances. What relationship can you see between this efficiency variance and the labour efficiency variance?

PROBLEM 8–3   Comprehensive Variance Analysis (CC7, 8, 9, 10, 11)
Miller Toy Company manufactures a plastic swimming pool at its Westwood Plant. The plant has been experiencing problems for some time as shown by its June income statement:

CHECK FIGURE
(1a) Materials price
variance: $3,000 F
(2) Net variance: $16,290 U

	Budgeted	Actual
Sales (15,000 pools)................	$450,000	$450,000
Less: Variable expenses:		
Variable cost of goods sold*........	180,000	196,290
Variable selling expenses...........	20,000	20,000
Total variable expenses	200,000	216,290
Contribution margin.................	250,000	233,710
Less: Fixed expenses:		
Manufacturing overhead	130,000	130,000
Selling and administrative	84,000	84,000
Total fixed expenses................	214,000	214,000
Net income......................	$ 36,000	$ 19,710

*Contains direct materials, direct labour, and variable manufacturing overhead.

Janet Dunn, who has just been appointed general manager of the Westwood Plant, has been given instructions to "get things under control." Upon reviewing the plant's income statement, Ms. Dunn has concluded that the major problem lies in the variable cost of goods sold. She has been provided with the following standard cost per swimming pool:

	Standard Quantity or Hours	Standard Price or Rate	Standard Cost
Direct materials..........	1.5 kilograms	$4.00 per kilogram	$ 6.00
Direct labour	0.8 hours	6.00 per hour	4.80
Variable manufacturing overhead	0.4 hours*	3.00 per hour	1.20
Total standard cost			$12.00

*Based on machine-hours.

Ms. Dunn has determined that during June the plant produced 15,000 pools and incurred the following costs:

a. Purchased 30,000 kilograms of materials at a cost of $3.90 per kilogram.
b. Used 24,600 kilograms of materials in production. (Finished goods and work-in-process inventories are insignificant and can be ignored.)
c. Worked 11,800 direct labour-hours at a cost of $7.00 per hour.
d. Incurred variable manufacturing overhead cost totalling $18,290 for the month. A total of 5,900 machine-hours was recorded.

It is the company's policy to close all variances to cost of goods sold on a monthly basis.

Required:
1. Compute the following variances for June:
   a. Direct materials price and quantity variances.
   b. Direct labour rate and efficiency variances.
   c. Variable overhead spending and efficiency variances.
2. Summarize the variances that you computed in part (1) by showing the net overall favourable or unfavourable variance for the month. What impact did this figure have on the company's income statement? Show computations.
3. Pick out the two most significant variances that you computed in part (1). Explain to Ms. Dunn possible causes of these variances.

CHECK FIGURE
(2a) Labour rate variance: $3,200 U
(3) Variable overhead efficiency variance: $2,000 F

PROBLEM 8–4   Comprehensive Variance Analysis; Journal Entries (CC7, 8, 9, 10, 11, 14ᴬ, 15ᴬ)
Trueform Products Inc. produces a broad line of sports equipment and uses a standard cost system for control purposes. Last year, the company produced 8,000 of its varsity footballs. The standard costs associated with this football, along with the actual costs incurred last year, follow (per football):

	Standard Cost	Actual Cost
Direct materials:		
Standard: 3.7 feet at $5 per foot.............	$18.50	
Actual: 4.0 feet at $4.80 per foot.............		$19.20
Direct labour:		
Standard: 0.9 hour at $7.50 per hour.........	6.75	
Actual: 0.8 hour at $8 per hour		6.40
Variable manufacturing overhead:		
Standard: 0.9 hour at $2.50 per hour.........	2.25	
Actual: 0.8 hour at $2.75 per hour...........		2.20
Total cost per football	$27.50	$27.80

The president was elated when he saw that actual costs exceeded standard costs by only $0.30 per football. He stated, "I was afraid that our unit cost might get out of hand when we gave out those raises last year in order to stimulate output. But it's obvious our costs are well under control."

There was no inventory of materials on hand to start the year. During the year, 32,000 feet of materials were purchased and used in production.

Required:
1. For direct materials:
   a. Compute the price and quantity variances for the year.
   b. Prepare journal entries to record all activity relating to direct materials for the year.
2. For direct labour:
   a. Compute the rate and efficiency variances.
   b. Prepare a journal entry to record the incurrence of direct labour cost for the year.
3. Compute the variable overhead spending and efficiency variances.
4. Was the president correct in his statement that "our costs are well under control"? Explain.
5. State possible causes of each variance that you have computed.

PROBLEM 8–5 Setting Standards (CC1, 2, 3, 4, 5, 6)
Danson Company is a chemical manufacturer that supplies various products to industrial users. The company plans to introduce a new chemical solution, called Nysap, for which it needs to develop a standard product cost. The following information is available on the production of Nysap:

a. Nysap is made by combining a chemical compound (nyclyn) and a solution (salex), and boiling the mixture. A 20% loss in volume occurs for both the salex and the nyclyn during boiling. After boiling, the mixture consists of 9.6 litres of salex and 12 kilograms of nyclyn per 10-litre batch of Nysap.
b. After the boiling process is complete, the solution is cooled slightly before five kilograms of protet are added per 10-litre batch of Nysap. The addition of the protet does not affect the total liquid volume. The resulting solution is then bottled in 10-litre containers.
c. The finished product is highly unstable, and one 10-litre batch out of six is rejected at final inspection. Rejected batches have no commercial value and are thrown out.
d. It takes a worker 35 minutes to process one 10-litre batch of Nysap. Employees work an eight-hour day, including one hour per day for rest breaks and cleanup.

Required:
1. Determine the standard quantity for each of the raw materials needed to produce an acceptable 10-litre batch of Nysap.
2. Determine the standard labour time to produce an acceptable 10-litre batch of Nysap.
3. Assuming the following purchase prices and costs, prepare a standard cost card for materials and labour for one acceptable 10-litre batch of Nysap:

> Salex . . . .$1.50 per litre
> Nyclyn . . . . .2.80 per kilogram
> Protet .3.00 per kilogram
> Direct labour cost . . . . .9.00 per hour

(CMA adapted)

PROBLEM 8–6 Working Backwards from Labour Variances (CC4, 10)
The auto repair shop of Quality Motor Company uses standards to control the labour time and labour cost in the shop. The standard labour cost for a motor tune-up follows:

Job	Standard Hours	Standard Rate	Standard Cost
Motor tune-up	3	$9	$27.00

The record showing the time spent in the shop last week on motor tune-ups has been misplaced. However, the shop supervisor recalls that 50 tune-ups were completed during the week, and the controller recalls the following variance data relating to tune-ups:

> Labour rate variance . . . . $90 F
> Total labour variance . . . . 96 U

Required:
1. Determine the number of actual labour-hours spent on tune-ups during the week.
2. Determine the actual hourly rate of pay for tune-ups last week.

(Hint: A useful way to proceed would be to work from known to unknown data either by using the variance formulas or by using the columnar format shown in Exhibit 8–5.)

PROBLEM 8–7 Comprehensive Variance Problem (CC3, 4, 5, 6, 8, 9, 10, 11)
Highland Company produces a lightweight backpack that is popular with college students. Standard variable costs relating to a single backpack follow:

	Standard Quantity or Hours	Standard Price or Rate	Standard Cost
Direct materials.	?	$6 per metre	$?
Direct labour	?	?	?
Variable manufacturing overhead	?	$3 per hour	?
Total standard cost			$?

During March, 1,000 backpacks were manufactured and sold. Selected information relating to the month's production follows:

	Materials Used	Direct Labour	Variable Manufacturing Overhead
Total standard cost allowed*............	$16,800	$10,500	$4,200
Actual costs incurred	15,000	?	3,600
Materials price variance	?		
Materials quantity variance.............	1,200 U		
Labour rate variance		?	
Labour efficiency variance		?	
Variable overhead spending variance			?
Variable overhead efficiency variance			?

*For the month's production.

The following additional information is available for March's production:

Actual direct labour-hours	1,500
Standard overhead rate per hour...	$3.00
Standard price of one metre of materials	6.00
Difference between standard and actual cost per backpack produced during March.....	0.15 F

Overhead is applied to production on the basis of direct labour-hours.

Required:
1. What is the standard cost of a single backpack?
2. What was the actual cost per backpack produced during March?
3. How many metres of material are required at standard per backpack?
4. What was the materials price variance for March?
5. What is the standard direct labour rate per hour?
6. What was the labour rate variance for March? The labour efficiency variance?
7. What was the variable overhead spending variance for March? The variable overhead efficiency variance?
8. Prepare a standard cost card for one backpack.

CHECK FIGURE
(1a) Actual cost: $5.42/ft.
(2a) Standard labour
rate: $8.11

PROBLEM 8–8 Computations from Incomplete Data (CC3, 4, 8, 9, 10)
Sharp Company manufactures a product for which the following standards have been set:

	Standard Quantity or Hours	Standard Price or Rate	Standard Cost
Direct materials...........	3 feet	$7 per foot	$21
Direct labour.............	? hours	? per hour	?

During March, the company purchased direct materials at a cost of $55,650, all of which were used in the production of 3,200 units of product. In addition, 4,900 hours of direct labour time were worked on the product during the month. The cost of this labour time was $36,750. The following variances have been computed for the month:

Materials quantity variance	$4,500 U
Total labour variance	2,000 F
Labour efficiency variance	1,000 U

Required:

1. For direct materials:
   a. Compute the actual cost per foot for materials for March.
   b. Compute the materials price variance and a total variance for materials.
2. For direct labour:
   a. Compute the standard direct labour rate per hour.
   b. Compute the standard hours allowed for the month's production.
   c. Compute the standard hours allowed per unit of product.

(Hint: In completing the problem, it may be helpful to move from known to unknown data either by using the columnar format shown in Exhibits 8–3 and 8–5, or by using the variance formulas.)

PROBLEM 8–9   Variance Analysis with Multiple Lots (CC8, 9, 10)

Hillcrest Leisure Wear Inc. manufactures men's clothing. The company has a single line of slacks that is produced in lots, with each lot representing an order from a customer. As a lot is completed, the customer's store label is attached to the slacks before shipment.

Hillcrest has a standard cost system and has established the following standards for a dozen slacks:

CHECK FIGURE
(2b) Total quantity
variance: $216 U
(4b) Total labour efficiency
variance: $3,900 U

	Standard Quantity or Hours	Standard Price or Rate	Standard Cost
Direct materials...........	32 metres	2.40 per metre	$76.80
Direct labour.............	6 hours	7.50 per hour	45.00

During October, Hillcrest worked on three orders for slacks. The company's job cost records for the month reveal the following:

Lot	Units in Lot (dozens)	Materials Used (metres)	Hours Worked
48................	1,500	48,300	8,900
49................	950	30,140	6,130
50................	2,100	67,250	10,270

The following additional information is available:

a. Hillcrest purchased 180,000 metres of material during October at a cost of $424,800.
b. Direct labour cost incurred during the month for production of slacks amounted to $192,280.
c. There was no work-in-process inventory on October 1. During October, lots 48 and 49 were completed, and lot 50 was 100% complete as to materials and 80% complete as to labour.

Required:

1. Compute the materials price variance for the materials purchased during October.
2. Determine the materials quantity variance for October in both metres and dollars:
   a. For each lot worked on during the month.
   b. For the company as a whole.
3. Compute the labour rate variance for October.
4. Determine the labour efficiency variance for the month in both hours and dollars:
   a. For each lot worked on during the month.
   b. For the company as a whole.
5. In what situations might it be better to express variances in units (hours, metres, and so on), rather than in dollars? In dollars, rather than in units?

(CPA adapted)

PROBLEM 8–10 Comprehensive Variance Analysis with Incomplete Data; Journal Entries
(CC3, 4, 5, 6, 8, 9, 10, 11, 14ᴬ, 15ᴬ)

Maple Products Ltd. manufactures hockey sticks that are used worldwide. The standard cost of one hockey stick is as follows:

	Standard Quantity or Hours	Standard Price or Rate	Standard Cost
Direct materials...........	? feet	$3.00 per foot	$?
Direct labour.............	2 hours	? per hour	?
Variable manufacturing overhead..............	? hours	1.30 per hour	?
Total standard cost			$27.00

Last year, 8,000 hockey sticks were produced and sold. Selected cost data relating to last year's operations follow:

	Dr.	Cr.
Direct materials purchased (60,000 feet)	$174,000	
Wages payable (? hours).........................		$79,200*
Work in process—direct materials	115,200	
Direct labour rate variance		3,300
Variable overhead efficiency variance	650	

*Relates to the actual direct labour cost for the year.

The following additional information is available for last year's operations:

a. No materials were on hand at the start of last year. Some of the materials purchased during the year were still on hand in the warehouse at the end of the year.
b. The variable manufacturing overhead rate is based on direct labour-hours. Total actual variable manufacturing overhead cost for last year was $19,800.
c. Actual direct materials usage for last year exceeded the standard by 0.2 foot per stick.

Required:
1. For direct materials:
  a. Compute the price and quantity variances for last year.
  b. Prepare journal entries to record all activities relating to direct materials for last year.
2. For direct labour:
  a. Verify the rate variance given above and compute the efficiency variance for last year.
  b. Prepare a journal entry to record activity relating to direct labour for last year.
3. Compute the variable overhead spending variance for last year and verify the variable overhead efficiency variance given above.
4. State possible causes of each variance that you have computed.
5. Prepare a completed standard cost card for one hockey stick.

PROBLEM 8–11 Developing Standard Costs (CC2, 3, 4, 5, 6, 7, 8)

ColdKing Company is a small producer of fruit-flavoured frozen desserts. For many years, ColdKing's products have had strong regional sales on the basis of brand recognition; however, other companies have begun marketing similar products in the area, and price competition has become increasingly important. John Wakefield, the company's controller, is planning to implement a standard cost system for ColdKing and has gathered considerable information from his co-workers on production and material requirements for ColdKing's products. Wakefield believes that the use of standard costing will allow ColdKing to improve cost control and make better pricing decisions.

ColdKing's most popular product is raspberry sherbet. The sherbet is produced in 40-litre batches, and each batch requires 24 litres of good raspberries. The fresh raspberries are sorted by hand before they enter the production process. Because of imperfections in the raspberries and normal spoilage, one litre of berries is discarded for every four litres of acceptable berries. One minute is the standard direct labour time for the sorting that is required to obtain one litre of acceptable raspberries. The acceptable raspberries are then blended with the other ingredients; blending requires 12 minutes of direct labour time per batch. After blending, the sherbet is packaged in litre containers. Wakefield has gathered the following pricing information:

a. ColdKing purchases raspberries at a cost of $0.20 per litre. All other ingredients cost a total of $0.45 per four litres of sherbert.
b. Direct labour is paid at the rate of $9 per hour.
c. The total cost of material and labour required to package the sherbet is $0.38 per litre.

Required:
1. Develop the standard cost for the direct cost components (materials, labour, and packaging) of a 40-litre batch of raspberry sherbet. The standard cost should identify the standard quantity, standard rate, and standard cost per batch for each direct cost component of a batch of raspberry sherbet.
2. As part of the implementation of a standard cost system at ColdKing, John Wakefied plans to train those responsible for maintaining the standards on how to use variance analysis. Wakefield is particularly concerned with the causes of unfavourable variances.
   a. Discuss possible causes of unfavourable materials price variances and identify the individual(s) who should be held responsible for these variances.
   b. Discuss possible causes of unfavourable labour efficiency variances and identify the individual(s) who should be held responsible for these variances.

(CMA adapted)

PROBLEM 8–12   Comprehensive Variance Analysis (CC7, 8, 9, 10, 11)
You have been given the following list of variances for the Talonne Company:

CHECK FIGURE
(2) 13,000 hours

Direct materials price variance	$14,000 U
Direct materials quantity variance	10,000 U
Direct labour rate variance	8,320 F
Direct labour efficiency variance.	48,000 U
Variable overhead spending variance	1,920 U
Variable overhead efficiency variance.	4,000 U

You have also been given the following information:

Actual units produced	20,000
Budgeted units of production	16,000
Standard labour-hours for actual output	10,000
Standard material units for actual output	200,000
Actual direct labour costs	$ 199,680
Actual cost of direct materials	$ 264,000

Variable overhead is applied at the rate of $10.00 per direct labour-hour. The materials purchase price was $0.028 higher than the standard price of $0.50 per unit.

Required:
1. What was the actual number of units of direct materials purchased?
2. How many actual direct labour-hours were worked?
3. What was the standard cost per unit of output, assuming that variable costing was used?

(Adapted © CGA-Canada)

PROBLEM 8–13   Comprehensive Variance Analysis (CC7, 8, 9, 10)
Monterey Corporation has a union contract provision that guarantees a minimum wage of $1,250 per month to each direct labour employee. Currently, 125 employees are covered by this provision. All direct labour employees are paid $10.00 per hour. The direct labour budget for the current fiscal year was based on an annual rate of 250,000 direct labour-hours at $10 per hour, or a total of $2,500,000 per year. Because of the contract provision, $156,250 (125 × $1,250 per month) was treated as a fixed monthly cost. Each month's budget was calculated using the following formula: $156,250 + $7.00 per direct labour-hour.

CHECK FIGURE
(1) May: $36,250 F

Figures for the first three months of the fiscal year are as follows:

	April	May	June
Direct labour-hours worked.........	27,500	40,000	60,000
Direct labour costs budgeted........	?	?	?
Direct labour costs incurred	$ 275,000	$ 400,000	$ 600,000
Variance..........................	?	?	?

These figures are a source of concern because they show unfavourable variances when production is high, and favourable variances during slow months. The factory manager is certain that this trend does not reflect reality.

Required:
1. Calculate the variances for each of the months of April, May, and June. What is the explanation for the variances relative to the company's budget cost formula?
2. Explain the error in logic in this variance calculation and, using a formula for direct labour costs more appropriate to the actual cost behaviour, recalculate the variances for April, May, and June.

(Adapted © CGA-Canada)

CHECK FIGURE
(e) 1,050 kg

PROBLEM 8–14   Variance Analysis with Incomplete Data (CC8, 9, 10)
The following information concerns two manufacturing jobs:

Item	Job 321	Job 322
Units produced	210	170
Standards per unit		
Direct material quantity......	5 kg	6 kg
Material price	$2 per kg	$3 per kg
Direct labour hours	2 hours	3 hours
Labour rate	$15 per hour	$12 per hour
Actual consumption		
Direct material quantity......	1,000 kg	(e)
Material price	$3.00 per kg	(f)
Direct labour hours	400 hours	(g)
Labour rate	$16.00 per hour	(h)
Variances		
Material price	(a)	$ 600 F
Material quantity	(b)	$ 90 U
Labour rate	(c)	$ 200 F
Labour efficiency...........	(d)	$ 60 U

Required:
Determine the missing amounts for items (a) through (h). List the letters (a) to (h) in your answer and write your answers beside the corresponding letter. Show all calculations.

(Adapted © CGA-Canada)

CHECK FIGURE
(1) Total Direct Material
Cost Variance, $6,000 F

PROBLEM 8–15   Comprehensive Variance Analysis (CC7, 8, 9, 10, 11)
Gladiar Inc produces premium protective automotive covers. The direct materials and direct labour standards for one car cover are as follows:

	Standard Quantity or Hours	Standard Price or Rate	Standard Cost
Direct materials	6.0 metres of cloth	$9 per metre	$54
Direct labour	0.25 hours	$15 per hour	$ 3.75

In September, the following activity was recorded:
- 12,000 metres of cloth were purchased at a cost of $8.50 per metre.
- All of the material was used to produce 2,000 car covers.
- 525 direct labour-hours were recorded at a total labour cost of $7,875.

Required:
1. Compute the total direct material cost variance for September. Compute the direct materials price and quantity variances for the month.
2. Compute the total direct labour cost variance for September. Also identify the two types of variances included in this total and compute them.

(Adapted © CGA-Canada)

Building Your Skills

ANALYTICAL THINKING   (CC3, 4, 6, 8, 9, 10, 14ᴬ, 15ᴬ)

You are employed by Olster Company, which manufactures products for the senior citizen market. As a rising young executive in the company, you are scheduled to make a presentation in a few hours to your superior. This presentation relates to last week's production of Maxitol, a popular health tonic that is manufactured by Olster Company. Unfortunately, while studying ledger sheets and variance summaries by the poolside in the company's fitness area, you were bumped and dropped the papers into the pool. In desperation, you fished the papers from the water, but you have discovered that only the following fragments are readable:

CHECK FIGURE
(1) 120 batches
(2a) Actual cost: $7,700

Maxitol—Standard Cost Card

	Standard Quantity or Hours	Standard Price or Rate	Standard Cost
Material A.	24 litres	$2 per litr	$
Material B		per kilogr	
Direct labour		per ho	0
Standard cost per batc			$99.50

Maxitol—General Ledger Accounts

Raw Materials—A

Bal. 3/1	0		
Bal. 3/7	2,000		

Work in Process

Bal. 3/1	0		
Material A	5,760		
Bal. 3/7	0		

Material A—Price Variance

	300

Wages Payable

	4,100

Raw Materials—B

Bal. 3/1	70		2,500
Bal. 3/7	1,400		

Labour Rate Variance

500	

Material B—Quantity Variance

100	

Accounts Payable

	11,460

You remember that the accounts payable are for purchases of materials A and B. You also remember that only 10 direct-labour workers are involved in the production of Maxitol and that each worked 40 hours last week. The wages payable are for wages earned by these workers.

You realize that to be ready for your presentation, you must quickly reconstruct all data relating to Maxitol. As a start, you have called purchasing and found that 4,000 litres of material A and 400 kilograms of material B were purchased last week.

Required:
1. How many batches of Maxitol were produced last week? (This is a key figure; be sure it is right before going on.)
2. For material A:
   a. What was the cost of material A purchased last week?
   b. How many litres were used in production last week?
   c. What was the quantity variance?
   d. Prepare journal entries to record all activity relating to material A for last week.
3. For material B:
   a. What is the standard cost per pound for material B?
   b. How many kilograms of material B were used in production last week? How many kilograms should have been used at standard?
   c. What is the standard quantity of material B per batch?
   d. What was the price variance for material B last week?
   e. Prepare journal entries to record all activity relating to material B for last week.
4. For direct labour:
   a. What is the standard rate per direct labour-hour?
   b. What are the standard hours per batch?
   c. What were the standard hours allowed for last week's production?
   d. What was the labour efficiency variance for last week?
   e. Prepare a journal entry to record all activity relating to direct labour for last week.
5. Complete the standard cost card previously shown for one batch of Maxitol.

COMMUNICATING IN PRACTICE   (CC1, 2, 7, 13)

Make an appointment to meet with the manager of an auto repair shop that uses standards. In most cases, this would be an auto repair shop that is affiliated with a chain, such as PetroCanada or Canadian Tire, or the service department of a new-car dealer.

Required:
At the scheduled meeting, find out the answers to the following questions and write a memo to your instructor describing the information obtained during your meeting.
1. How are standards set?
2. Are standards practical or ideal?
3. Is the actual time taken to complete a task compared with the standard time?
4. What are the consequences of unfavourable variances? Of favourable variances?
5. Do the standards and variances create any potential problems?

ETHICS CHALLENGE   (CC1, 7, 13)

Stacy Cummins, the newly hired controller at Merced Home Products, Inc., was disturbed by what she had discovered about the standard costs at the Home Security Division. In looking over the past several years of quarterly earnings reports at the Home Security Division, she noticed that the first-quarter earnings were always poor, the second-quarter earnings were slightly better, the third-quarter earnings were again slightly better, and then the fourth quarter and the year always ended with a spectacular performance in which the Home Security Division always managed to meet or exceed its target profit for the year. She also was concerned to find letters from the company's external auditors to top management warning about an unusual use of standard costs at the Home Security Division.

When Ms. Cummins ran across these letters, she asked the assistant controller, Gary Farber, if he knew what was going on at the Home Security Division. Gary said that it was common knowledge in the company that the vice-president in charge of the Home Security Division, Preston Lansing, had rigged the standards at the Home Security Division in order to produce the same quarterly earnings pattern every year. According to company policy, variances are taken directly to the income statement as an adjustment to cost of goods sold.

Favourable variances have the effect of increasing net income, and unfavourable variances have the effect of decreasing net income. Lansing had rigged the standards so that there were always large favourable variances. Company policy was a little vague about when these variances have to be reported on the divisional income statements. While the intent was clearly to recognize variances on the income statement in the period in which they arise, nothing in the company's accounting manuals explicitly required this. So, for many years, Lansing had followed a practice of saving up the favourable variances and using them to create a nice smooth pattern of earnings growth in the first three quarters, followed by a big "Christmas present" of an extremely good fourth quarter. (Financial reporting regulations forbid carrying variances forward from one year to the next on the annual audited financial statements, and so all of the variances must appear on the divisional income statement by the end of the year.)

Ms. Cummins was concerned about these revelations and attempted to bring up the subject with the president of Merced Home Products but was told that "we all know what Lansing's doing, but as long as he continues to turn in such good reports, don't bother him." When Ms. Cummins asked if the board of directors was aware of the situation, the president somewhat testily replied, "Of course, they are aware."

Required:

1. How did Preston Lansing probably "rig" the standard costs—are the standards set too high or too low? Explain.
2. Should Preston Lansing be permitted to continue his practice of managing reported earnings?
3. What should Stacy Cummins do in this situation?

TEAMWORK IN ACTION   (CC1, 7, 13)

Terry Travers is the manufacturing supervisor of Aurora Manufacturing Company, which produces a variety of plastic products. Some of these products are standard items that are listed in the company's catalogue, while others are made to customer specifications. Each month, Travers receives a performance report showing the budget for the month, the actual activity, and the variance between budget and actual. Part of Travers' annual performance evaluation is based on his department's performance against budget. Aurora's purchasing manager, Sally Christensen, also receives monthly performance reports, and she, too, is evaluated partly on the basis of these reports.

The monthly reports for June had just been distributed when Travers met Christensen in the hallway outside their offices. Scowling, Travers began the conversation, "I see we have another set of monthly performance reports hand-delivered by that not very nice junior employee in the budget office. He seemed pleased to tell me that I'm in trouble with my performance again."

Christensen: I got the same treatment. All I ever hear about are the things I haven't done right. Now I'll have to spend a lot of time reviewing the report and preparing explanations. The worst part is that it's now the 21st of July so the information is almost a month old, and we have to spend all this time on history.

Travers: My biggest gripe is that our production activity varies a lot from month to month, but we're given an annual budget that's written in stone. Last month, we were shut down for three days when a strike delayed delivery of the basic ingredient used in our plastic formulation, and we had already exhausted our inventory. You know about that problem, though, because we asked you to call all over the country to find an alternative source of supply. When we got what we needed on a rush basis, we had to pay more than we normally do.

Christensen: I expect problems like that to pop up from time to time—that's part of my job—but now we'll both have to take a careful look at our reports to see where the charges are reflected for that rush order. Every month, I spend more time making sure I should be charged for each item reported than I do making plans for my department's daily work. It's really frustrating to see charges for things I have no control over.

Travers: The way we get information doesn't help, either. I don't get copies of the reports you get, and yet a lot of what I do is affected by your department and by most of the other departments we have. Why do the budget and accounting people assume that I should only be told about my operations, even though the president regularly gives us pep talks about how we all need to work together as a team?

Christensen: I seem to get more reports than I need, and I am never asked to comment on them until top management puts me on the carpet about my department's shortcomings. Do you ever hear comments when your department shines?

Travers: I guess they don't have time to review the good news. One of my problems is that all the reports are in dollars and cents. I work with people, machines, and materials. I need information to help me *this* month to solve *this* month's problems—not another report of the dollars expended *last* month or the month before.

Required:

Your team should discuss and then respond to the following questions. All team members should agree with and understand the answers and be prepared to report on those answers in class. (Each teammate can assume responsibility for a different part of the presentation.)

1. On the basis of the conversation between Terry Travers and Sally Christensen, describe the likely motivation and behaviour of these two employees as a result of the standard cost and variance reporting system that is used by Aurora Manufacturing Company.
2. List the recommendations that your team would make to Aurora Manufacturing Company to enhance employee motivation as it relates to the company's standard cost and variance reporting system.

(CMA adapted)

Don't forget to visit the Online Learning Centre for self-study quizzes, practice exams, and more! Visit www.mcgrawhill.ca/olc/brewer.

CHAPTER *Nine*

Flexible Budgets and Overhead Analysis

CHAPTER COMPETENCIES

After studying Chapter 9, you should be able to demonstrate the following competencies:

Competency	Know	Apply
Understand static and flexible budgets.		
CC1 Prepare a static budget performance report.		○
CC2 Explain flexible budgeting and prepare a flexible budget.	○	○
CC3 Prepare a flexible budget performance report.		○
Understand variable overhead variances.		
CC4 Prepare a variable overhead performance report.		○
CC5 Explain variable overhead spending variance.	○	
CC6 Explain variable overhead efficiency variance.	○	
Understand fixed overhead variances		
CC7 Prepare a flexible budget for fixed overhead costs.		○
CC8 Explain the concept of denominator activity.	○	
CC9 Compute a predetermined overhead rate.		○
CC10 Distinguish between overhead application in normal costing versus overhead application in standard costing.	○	
CC11 Explain and compute fixed overhead budget variance.	○	○
CC12 Explain and compute fixed overhead volume variance.	○	○
CC13 Explain overhead variance in terms of over-/under-applied overhead.	○	

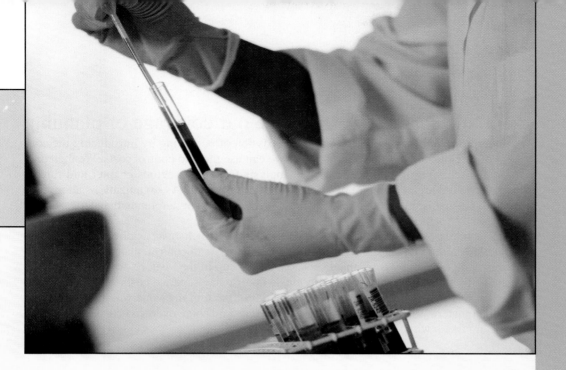

DECISION FEATURE
Overhead Costs: Burden or Opportunity?

It is not uncommon for many companies to use the term "burden" to refer to their overhead costs. But, are overhead costs really a burden? That depends. Overhead costs can easily become a burden if they are not properly managed. This can be very true in certain sectors of the economy, such as health care and manufacturing. Given the increasing share of overhead costs, most organizations are finding ways to get the "best bang for their buck."

Toronto Medical Laboratories (TML), an example of a strategic alliance consisting of three teaching hospitals and the medical services company MDS, Inc., has "invested" in overhead costs to reap big benefits. TML provides services that are of critical importance to hospitals: testing samples, such as blood, urine, sputum, and so on, and sending the results to the doctors. Accuracy and speed are extremely important variables that TML must always monitor. Therefore, the lab has invested in a highly automated and sophisticated lab testing system called ULTRA where robots do most of the repetitive work thereby eliminating any chance of human error. ULTRA also allows TML to be ahead on speed; it allows the lab to deliver results within just two hours!

Has TML cut costs? Well, not directly, but it has added 25% additional capacity without hiring an additional employee. This means it has the potential to increase revenues by 25% with the same level of overhead costs! Is overhead really a burden?

Source: "Vital Signs," www.canadianbusiness.com, 2002-12-09. Adaped with permission from *Canadian Business*.

A Look Back

In Chapter 7, we discussed budgeting—the process that is used by organizations to plan the financial aspects of their operations. We introduced management control and performance measures in Chapter 8 with a discussion of standard costs and variance analysis.

A Look at This Chapter

Chapter 9 continues our coverage of the budgeting process by presenting the flexible approach to budgeting. In addition to illustrating the use of a flexible budget to control overhead costs, we also expand the study of overhead variance analysis.

A Look Ahead

We continue the discussion of management control and performance measures in Chapter 10 by focusing on how decentralized organizations are managed.

I

n this chapter, we continue our coverage of planning and control. We begin by extending our discussion of budgeting by introducing the concept of flexible budgets and learning how we can use them to control costs. We then pick up our discussion of overhead variance analysis from the previous chapter and further expand on the topic. Why are overhead costs so important? As organizations adopt new initiatives (that is, implement lean business practices) and/or automate, they tend to incur additional expenses.

Controlling overhead costs poses special problems. Such costs as direct materials and direct labour are often easier to understand, and therefore to control, than overhead, which can include everything from the disposable coffee cup in the visitor's waiting area to the president's salary. Overhead is usually made up of many separate costs—many of which may be small. This makes it impractical to control them in the same way that such costs as direct materials and direct labour are controlled. And some overhead costs are variable, some are fixed, while others are a mixture of both.

Static and Flexible Budgets

Static Budget Performance Report

 APPLY

CC1: Prepare a static budget performance report.

The budgets we studied in Chapter 7 were *static budgets*. A **static budget** is prepared for a single planned level of activity. Consider the case of Rick's Hairstyling Salon, an upscale hair salon located in Victoria that is owned and managed by Rick Manzi. The salon has loyal customers—many of whom are wealthy retirees. Despite the glamour associated with his salon, Rick is a shrewd businessman. Recently, he has been attempting to get better control over his expenses, and at the urging of his accounting and business adviser, Victoria Kho, has begun to prepare monthly budgets.

At the end of February, Rick carefully prepared the March budget (see Exhibit 9–1); he believes that the number of customers served in a month is the best way to measure the overall level of activity in his salon. Rick refers to these visits as *client-visits*. A customer who comes into the salon and has his or her hair styled is counted as one client-visit. He was able to estimate direct labour costs (wages of stylists) rather easily; however, estimating overhead expenses was a slightly different story.

After some discussion with Victoria Kho, Rick identified three major categories of variable overhead costs—hairstyling supplies, client gratuities, and electricity—and four major categories of fixed costs—support staff salaries, rent, insurance, and utilities other than electricity (e.g., natural gas, water). Client gratuities consist of flowers, candies, and glasses of champagne that Rick offers to his customers while they are in the salon. Rick considers electricity to be a variable cost, since almost all of the electricity in the salon is consumed in running blow-dryers, curling irons, and other hairstyling equipment.

To develop the budget for variable overhead, Rick estimated that the average cost per client-visit should be $1.20 for hairstyling supplies, $4 for client gratuities, and $0.20 for electricity. On the basis of his estimate of 5,000 client-visits in March, Rick budgeted for $6,000 ($1.20 per client-visit × 5,000 client-visits) in hairstyling supplies, $20,000 ($4 per client-visit × 5,000 client-visits) in client gratuities, and $1,000 ($0.20 per client-visit × 5,000 client-visits) in electricity.

The budget for fixed overhead items was based on Rick's records of how much he had spent on these items in the past. The budget included $8,000 for support staff salaries, $12,000 for rent, $1,000 for insurance, and $500 for utilities other than electricity.

At the end of March, Rick prepared a report (which appears as Exhibit 9–1), comparing actual with budgeted costs. The simple report tells Rick that his salon had 200 additional client-visits during the month, which resulted in income of $23,070 compared to the budgeted level of $22,750. The problem with this report, as Rick immediately realized, is

Exhibit 9–1
Static Budget Performance
Report

RICK'S HAIRSTYLING SALON Static Budget Performance Report For the Month Ended March 31	Actual	Budgeted	Variance
Client-visits	5,200	5,000	200 F
Revenues	$114,400	$110,000	$4,400 F
Variable Expenses:			
Direct labour	40,040	38,750	1,290 U
Variable overhead:			
Hairstyling supplies.	6,400	6,000	400 U
Client gratuities	22,300	20,000	2,300 U
Electricity	1,020	1,000	20 U
Total variable expenses	69,760	65,750	4,010 U
Contribution margin	44,640	44,250	390 F
Less: Fixed Expenses:			
Support staff salaries	8,100	8,000	100 U
Rent	12,000	12,000	—
Insurance	1,000	1,000	—
Utilities other than electricity.	470	500	30 F
Total fixed expenses	21,570	21,500	70 U
Income from operations.	$ 23,070	$ 22,750	$ 320 F

that it compares costs and revenues at one level of activity (5,200 client-visits) with costs and revenues at a different level of activity (5,000 client-visits). Since Rick had 200 more client-visits than expected, his variable costs *should* be higher than budgeted. The static budget performance report confuses control over activity and control over costs. From Rick's standpoint, the increase in activity was good and should be counted as a favourable variance, but the increase in activity has an apparently negative impact on the costs in the report. Rick knew that something would have to be done to make the report more meaningful, but he was unsure of what to do. So, he made an appointment to meet with Victoria Kho to discuss the next step.

Victoria: How is the budgeting going?
Rick: Not bad. I didn't have any trouble putting together the overhead budget for March. I also made out a report comparing the actual costs for March with the budgeted costs, but that report isn't telling me what I really want to know.
Victoria: Because your actual level of activity didn't match your budgeted activity?
Rick: Right. I know that shouldn't affect my fixed costs, but we had a lot more client-visits than I had expected, and that had to affect my variable costs.
Victoria: So, you want to know whether the actual costs are justified by the actual level of activity you had in March?
Rick: Precisely.
Victoria: If you leave your reports and data with me, I can work on them later today, and by tomorrow I'll have a report to show to you. Actually, I have a styling appointment for later this week. Why don't I move my appointment up to tomorrow, and I will bring along the analysis so we can discuss it.
Rick: That's great.

**MANAGERIAL
ACCOUNTING
IN ACTION**

The Issue

RICK'S
hairstyling salon

The Flexible Budget

Unlike the static budget, a **flexible budget** contains estimates of costs at different levels of activity within a specified relevant range. Continuing with the case of Rick's Hairstyling Salon, flexible budgeting can be used to estimate the costs that Rick *should have* incurred for 5,200 client visits.

To illustrate how flexible budgets work, Victoria prepared a report as illustrated in Exhibit 9–2. It shows how overhead costs can be expected to change, depending on the monthly level of activity. Within the activity range of 4,900 to 5,200 client-visits, the fixed costs are expected to remain the same. For the variable costs, Victoria multiplied Rick's per-client costs ($7.75 for direct labour, $1.20 for hairstyling supplies, $4 for client gratuities, and $0.20 for electricity) by the appropriate number of client-visits in each column. For example, the $1.20 cost of hairstyling supplies was multiplied by 4,900 client-visits to give the total cost of $5,880 for hairstyling supplies at that level of activity. She also estimated revenues for the range of 4,900 to 5,200 client-visits using an average price of $22 per client-visit.

Exhibit 9–2

Flexible Budget

		RICK'S HAIRSTYLING SALON Flexible Budget For the Month Ended March 31			
Budgeted number of client-visits		5,000			
	Cost Formula (per client visit)	Activity (client visits)			
		4,900	5,000	5,100	5,200
Revenues	$ 22.00	$ 107,800	$ 110,000	$ 112,200	$ 114,400
Variable Expenses:					
Direct labour.	7.75	37,975	38,750	39,525	40,300
Variable overhead:		—	—	—	—
Hairstyling supplies.	1.20	5,880	6,000	6,120	6,240
Client gratuities	4.00	19,600	20,000	20,400	20,800
Electricity	0.20	980	1,000	1,020	1,040
Total variable expenses	$ 13.15	64,435	65,750	67,065	68,380
Contribution margin	$ 8.85	43,365	44,250	45,135	46,020
Less: Fixed Expenses:					
Support staff salaries		8,000	8,000	8,000	8,000
Rent		12,000	12,000	12,000	12,000
Insurance		1,000	1,000	1,000	1,000
Utilities other than electricity. . .		500	500	500	500
Total fixed expenses		21,500	21,500	21,500	21,500
Income from operations.		$ 21,865	$ 22,750	$ 23,635	$ 24,520

Flexible Budget Performance Report

Why is Rick asking these questions? The answer is simple: the differences in revenues, costs (and profits) presented in the static budget performance report (Exhibit 9-1) fail to separate the effect of a change in activity level from the effect of increased (or decreased) efficiency.

To answer Rick's questions, Victoria applied the flexible budgeting concept to create a new performance report. The flexible budget performance report, presented in Exhibit 9-3, compares the actual costs and revenues with budgeted amounts *for the activity level of 5,200 client visits*. In doing so, it focuses only on performance differences arising from operating efficiently (or inefficiently).

The flexible budget in Exhibit 9-2 shows an income of $24,520 at the activity level of 5,200 client-visits. However, the salon made only $23,070 during the month, i.e., $1,450 less than budgeted (see Exhibit 9-3). Observe that there is no difference in revenue, which means that the entire unfavourable variance of $1,450 arises from the cost side. Moreover, since we have eliminated any differences due to changes in activity level, the unfavourable variance is the result of operating inefficiently (that is, using more input resources than required and/or paying a higher price for the resources used). Because the flexible budget performance report uses a single activity level as the basis for comparison, it offers an "apples to apples" comparison unlike the static budget performance report, in Exhibit 9–1, which offers an "apples to oranges" comparison.

Exhibit 9–3
Flexible Budget Performance Report

RICK'S HAIRSTYLING SALON Flexible Budget Performance Report For the Month Ended March 31				
Budgeted number of client-visits	5,000			
Actual number of client-visits	5,200			
	Cost Formula (per client visit)	**Actual costs incurred for 5,200 client-visits**	**Budget based on 5,200 client-visits**	**Variance**
Revenues	$ 22.00	$ 114,400	$ 114,400	$ –
Variable Expenses:				
Direct labour.	7.75	40,040	40,300	260 F
Variable overhead:				
Hairstyling supplies.	1.20	6,400	6,240	160 U
Client gratuities	4.00	22,300	20,800	1,500 U
Electricity	0.20	1,020	1,040	20 F
Total variable expenses	$ 13.15	69,760	68,380	1,380 U
Contribution margin	$ 8.85	44,640	46,020	1,380 U
Less: Fixed Expenses:				
Support staff salaries		8,100	8,000	100 U
Rent		12,000	12,000	–
Insurance		1,000	1,000	–
Utilities other than electricity. . .		470	500	30 F
Total fixed expenses		21,570	21,500	70 U
Income from operations.		$ 23,070	$ 24,520	$ 1,450 U

The following discussion took place the next day at Rick's salon.

Victoria: Let me show you what I've got. [Victoria shows the report contained in Exhibit 9–3.] All I did was multiply the costs per client-visit by the number of client-visits you actually had in March for the variable costs. That allowed me to come up with a better benchmark for what the variable costs should have been.

Rick: That's what you labelled the "budget based on 5,200 client-visits"?

**MANAGERIAL
ACCOUNTING
IN ACTION**

The Wrap–up

Victoria: That's right. Your original budget was based on 5,000 client-visits, so it understated what the variable costs should be when you actually serve 5,200 customers.

Rick: That's clear enough. These variances aren't quite as shocking as the variances on my first report.

Victoria: Yes, but you still have an unfavourable variance of $1,500 for client gratuities.

Rick: I know how that happened. In March, there was a big fundraising dinner that I forgot about when I prepared the March budget. Many celebrities came here to attend the event. At any rate, to fit all of our regular clients in, we had to push them through here pretty fast. Everyone still got top-rate service, but I felt pretty bad about not being able to spend as much time as I usually do with each customer. So, I wanted to give my customers a little extra something to compensate them for the less personal service, and I ordered a lot of flowers, which I gave away by the bunch.

Victoria: Rick, I am sure the gesture was appreciated.

Rick: One thing bothers me about the report. Why are some of my actual fixed costs different from what I budgeted? Doesn't fixed mean that they are not supposed to change?

Victoria: We call these costs *fixed* because they shouldn't be affected by *changes in the level of activity.* However, that doesn't mean that they can't change for other reasons. For example, your utilities bill, which includes natural gas for heating, varies with the weather.

Rick: I can see that. March was warmer than normal, and so my utilities bill was lower than I had expected.

Victoria: The use of the term *fixed* seems to suggest that the cost can't be controlled, but that isn't true. It is often easier to control fixed costs than variable costs. For example, it would be fairly easy for you to change your insurance bill by adjusting the amount of insurance you carry. It would be much more difficult for you to have much of an impact on the variable electric bill, which is a necessary part of serving customers.

Rick: I think I understand, but it *is* confusing.

Victoria: Just remember that a cost is called *variable* if it is proportional to activity; it is called *fixed* if it does not depend on the level of activity. However, fixed costs can change for reasons having nothing to do with changes in the level of activity. And, controllability has little to do with whether a cost is variable or fixed. Fixed costs are often more controllable than variable costs.

The static budget performance report informs a manager about differences in activity levels (if any). It feeds back to the planning function; for example, Rick did not seem to spend much time on planning. He failed to include the possibility that the fundraising dinner to be attended by many celebrities could result in additional business. In other words, managers should consider internal and external factors when establishing a budget. A flexible budget performance report, on the other hand, is a good control tool.

Using the flexible budget approach, Rick Manzi now has a much better way of assessing whether costs are under control. The analysis is not so simple, however, in companies that provide a variety of products and services. The number of units produced or customers served may not be an adequate measure of overall activity. For example, does it make sense to count a Sony DVD, worth only a few dollars, as equivalent to a big-screen Sony TV? If the number of units produced is used as a measure of overall activity, then the DVD and the big-screen TV would be counted as equivalent. Clearly, the number of units produced (or customers served) may not be appropriate as an overall measure of activity when the organization has a variety of products or services; a common denominator may be needed.

The Measure of Activity—A Critical Choice

What should be used as the measure of activity when the company produces a variety of products and services? At least three factors are important in selecting an activity base to prepare a flexible budget:

1. There should be a causal relationship between the activity base and variable costs. Changes in the activity base should cause, or at least be highly correlated with, changes in the variable costs in the flexible budget, especially the variable overhead costs. Ideally, the variable overhead costs in the flexible budget should vary in direct proportion to changes in the activity base. For example, in a carpentry shop specializing in handmade wood furniture, the costs of miscellaneous supplies, such as glue, wooden dowels, and sandpaper, can be expected to vary with the number of direct labour-hours. Direct labour-hours would therefore be a good measure of activity to use in a flexible budget for the costs of such supplies. The use of activity-based costing can greatly help in identifying representative cost drivers (or activity bases).
2. The activity base should not be expressed in dollars or other currency. For example, direct labour cost is usually a poor choice for an activity base in flexible budgets. Changes in wage rates affect the activity base but do not usually result in a proportionate change in overhead. For example, we would not ordinarily expect to see a 5% increase in the consumption of glue in a carpentry shop if the workers receive a 5% increase in pay. Therefore, it is normally best to use physical, rather than financial, measures of activity in flexible budgets.
3. The activity base should be simple and easily understood. Using a base that is not easily understood will probably result in confusion and misunderstanding. It is difficult to control costs if people do not understand the reports or do not accept them as valid.

In the remainder of this chapter, we use the principles of flexible budgeting to analyze variable and fixed overhead variances.

Budgeting for Success   IN BUSINESS TODAY

What would you do if you wanted to really impress your boss? How does being under budget on more than 500 projects in one year sound? Eugene Roman, the Chief Information Officer of Bell Canada, has created his own success through a unique combination of budgeting skills and being able to bounce from idea to idea. Information technology departments have a habit of running projects over budget, but Roman has been able to gain credibility by generating reliable financial forecasts. Roman attributes his success to superior management control, proper cost management, and the ability to view costs from a different angle. "My groups have always delivered to the numbers. We work to the goal of a budget being met, but not overstepped. It starts with good planning and execution, and considers trade-offs and risk analysis. If there are problems, we find out how to recover and make it work. That's part and parcel of the package."

Source: John Cooper, "When in Rome . . . Renaissance man Eugene Roman sets the standard for excellence at Bell Canada," *CMA Management,* April, 2002, pp. 37–39. Adapted with permission from CMA Canada.

Variable Overhead Variances—A Closer Look

We will now revisit the variable overhead variances that we discussed in Chapter 8. Consider the case of MicroDrive Corporation, which uses machine-hours as the base to allocate variable overhead. Exhibit 9–4 presents the data pertaining to the year just completed.

Exhibit 9-4
MicroDrive Corporation Data

Budgeted production.	25,000 motors
Actual production	20,000 motors
Standard machine-hours per motor.	2 machine-hours per motor
Budgeted machine-hours (2 × 25,000)	50,000 machine-hours
Standard machine-hours allowed for the actual production (2 × 20,000).	40,000 machine-hours
Actual machine-hours.	42,000 machine-hours

Budgeted variable overhead costs per machine-hour:

Indirect labour.	$0.80 per machine-hour
Lubricants	0.30 per machine-hour
Power	0.40 per machine-hour

Actual total variable overhead costs:

Indiect labour	$36,000
Lubricants.	11,000
Power	2,000
Total actual variable overhead cost.	$71,000

Variable Overhead Performance

For the purposes of performance evaluation, two variable overhead flexible budgets can be prepared: one using the *actual* machine-hours worked during the year, (that is, 42,000) and another using the *standard* machine-hours allowed for actual production (that is, 40,000). We present the two flexible budgets in Exhibit 9–5—see columns (2) and (3). The numbers in column (2) are based on the actual machine-hours consumed during the year (42,000), whereas the numbers in column (3) are based on the standard machine-hours allowed for actual production (40,000). Managers may wonder which flexible budget to use to evaluate performance.

In reality, both flexible budgets provide information that is useful to assess performance. The difference between actual costs and flexible budget amounts based on the standard hours allowed for actual production amounts to $11,000 *unfavourable* as shown in column (4) of Exhibit 9–5.

What is the source of this variance? Broadly speaking, there are two sources:

- The company may have spent more than budgeted on the variable overhead resources, thereby resulting in a variable overhead spending variance.
- The company may not have used overhead resources efficiently, thereby resulting in a variable overhead efficiency variance.

Variable Overhead Spending Variance

Recall from Exhibit 8-6 (on page 330) that the variable overhead spending variance is computed as the difference between the actual variable overhead cost and the standard cost of the actual quantity of the variable overhead allocation base. Returning to our example, this *unfavourable* variance of $8,000 is shown in the second-to-last column of Exhibit 9–5. This is the difference between the actual cost and the flexible budget based on the actual machine-hours consumed during the year. If management is interested only in the spending variance, its performance report would be limited to reporting the actual costs, flexible budget based on the actual machine-hours, and the difference between the two.

The formula for the spending variance, introduced in Chapter 8, is:

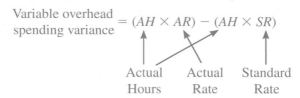

$$\text{Variable overhead spending variance} = (AH \times AR) - (AH \times SR)$$

Actual Hours   Actual Rate   Standard Rate

Exhibit 9–5

MicroDrive Corporation Variable Overhead Performance Report

MICRODRIVE CORPORATION
Variable Overhead Performance Report
For the Year Ended December 31

Budget allowances are based on 40,000 machine-hours—the time it *should have taken* to produce the year's output of 20,000 motors—as well as on the 42,000 *actual* machine-hours worked

This approach yields both a spending and an efficiency variance

Budgeted machine-hours	50,000
Actual machine-hours	42,000
Standard machine-hours allowed	40,000

Overhead Costs	Cost Formula (per machine-hour)	(1) Actual Costs Incurred 42,000 Machine-Hours (AH × AR)	(2) Budget Based on 42,000 Machine-Hours (AH × SR)	(3) Budget Based on 40,000 Machine-Hours (SH × SR)	(4) Total Variance (1) − (3)	Breakdown of the Total Variance	
						Spending Variance (1) − (2)	Efficiency Variance (2) − (3)
Variable overhead costs:							
Indirect labour	$0.80	$36,000	$33,600*	$32,000	$ 4,000 U	$2,400 U	$1,600 U
Lubricants	0.30	11,000	12,600	12,000	1,000 F	1,600 F	600 U
Power	0.40	24,000	16,800	16,000	8,000 U	7,200 U	800 U
Total variable overhead cost	$1.50	$71,000	$63,000	$60,000	$11,000 U	$8,000 U	$3,000 U

*42,000 machine-hours × $0.80 per machine-hour = $33,600. Other budget allowances are computed in the same way.
Note: Columns 1, 2, and 3 use the same calculations as shown in Exhibit 8–6 (numbers are different because the two examples are different).

Or, in factored form:

$$\text{Variable overhead spending variance} = AH\,(AR - SR)$$

INTERPRETING THE SPENDING VARIANCE   The variable overhead spending variance is useful only if the cost driver for variable overhead really is the actual hours worked. Then the flexible budget based on the actual hours worked is a valid benchmark that tells us how much *should* have been spent in total on variable overhead items during the period. The actual overhead costs would be larger than this benchmark, resulting in an unfavourable variance, if either: (1) the variable overhead items cost more to purchase than the standards allow, or (2) more variable overhead items were used than the standards allow. Consuming more variable overhead items than the standards allow will result in an increase in variable overhead costs. However, the cost increase has nothing to do with the actual price paid for acquiring individual overhead items (e.g., supplies). In reality, this is a usage issue—more resources have been consumed than planned. Nonetheless, it impacts the amount spent on variable overhead, thereby resulting in a spending variance. To avoid any confusion, it is important to note that variable overhead efficiency variance has nothing to do with how efficiently overhead resources are consumed; this is clarified following.

Variable Overhead Efficiency Variance

 KNOW

CC6: Explain variable overhead efficiency variance.

Often, management may be interested in knowing more than just the spending variance, and may turn its attention to the variable overhead efficiency variance. Recall once again from Exhibit 8–6 that variable overhead efficiency variance is computed as the difference between the standard cost of the *actual* quantity of the variable overhead allocation base and the standard cost of the *standard* quantity of the variable overhead allocation base. Returning to our example, this variance of $3,000 *unfavourable* is shown in the last column of Exhibit 9–5. It is the difference between the flexible budget based on the actual machine-hours consumed during the year and the flexible budget based on the standard machine-hours allowed for actual production during the year. Together, the spending and efficiency variances make up the total variable overhead variance of $11,000 *unfavourable* shown in column (4) of Exhibit 9–5.

INTERPRETING THE EFFICIENCY VARIANCE   From the previous chapters, we know that overhead costs are assigned or allocated to cost objects using one or more allocation bases (or activity bases). The variable overhead efficiency variance is a measure of the impact on variable overhead of how efficiently (or inefficiently) the activity (allocation) bases have been used. In a sense, the term *variable overhead efficiency variance* is a misnomer. It seems to suggest that it measures the efficiency with which variable overhead resources were used. It does not. It is an estimate of the indirect effect on variable overhead costs of efficiency in the use of the activity base.

Recall that the formula for efficiency variance, introduced in Chapter 8, is as follows:

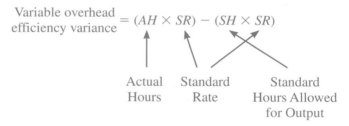

Or, in factored form:

$$\text{Variable overhead efficiency variance} = SR(AH - SH)$$

If more hours are worked than are allowed at standard, then the overhead efficiency variance will be unfavourable. However, as discussed previously, the inefficiency is not in the use of overhead *but, rather, in the use of the base itself.*

This point can be illustrated by looking again at Exhibit 9–5. Two thousand more machine-hours were used during the period than should have been used to produce the period's output. Each of these hours presumably required the incurrence of $1.50 of variable overhead cost, resulting in an unfavourable variance of $3,000 (2,000 hours × $1.50 = $3,000). Although this $3,000 variance is called an overhead efficiency variance, it could be better termed a machine-hours efficiency variance, since it results from using too many machine-hours, rather than from inefficient use of overhead resources. However, the term *overhead efficiency variance* is so firmly ingrained in day-to-day use that a change is unlikely. Even so, be careful to interpret the variance with a clear understanding of what it really measures.

CONTROL OF THE EFFICIENCY VARIANCE   Who is responsible for control of the overhead efficiency variance? Since the variance really reflects efficiency in the utilization of the base underlying the flexible budget, whoever is responsible for control of this base is responsible for control of the variance. If the base is direct labour-hours, then the supervisor responsible for the use of labour time will be responsible for any overhead efficiency variance.

Fixed Overhead Analysis

The analysis of fixed overhead costs differs from the analysis of variable overhead costs simply because of the fixed nature of the costs. We begin this section by discussing the preparation of a flexible budget for fixed overhead. Next, we review the need for and compute the predetermined overhead allocation rate. This review will be helpful because the predetermined overhead rate plays an important part in overhead analysis. Finally, we show how fixed overhead variances are computed, and make some observations about their usefulness to managers.

Fixed Overhead Flexible Budget

Recall from Chapters 2 and 3 that fixed costs remain constant, *in total*, within a relevant range of operations. This means that these costs will remain the same regardless of changes in planned activity levels within the relevant range. Returning to our MicroDrive example, let us assume that the relevant range of activity with respect to fixed overhead costs is between 40,000 and 60,000 machine-hours. This means that theoretically costs are not expected to fluctuate within this range of activity.

Exhibit 9–6 shows a flexible budget at various levels of activity (note that machine-hours is the base used to allocate overhead). The flexible budget shows both variable and fixed overhead costs. As can be seen, the total variable overhead costs increase as the level of machine-hours increases. However, the total fixed overhead costs stay constant at $300,000 within the relevant range regardless of the activity level.

APPLY

CC7: Prepare a flexible budget for fixed overhead costs.

	Cost Formula (per machine-hour)	Activity (in machine-hours)			
Overhead Costs		**40,000**	**45,000**	**50,000**	**55,000**
Variable overhead costs:					
Indirect labour........	$0.80	$ 32,000	$ 36,000	$ 40,000	$ 44,000
Lubricants...........	0.30	12,000	13,500	15,000	16,500
Power	0.40	16,000	18,000	20,000	22,000
Total variable overhead cost.........	$1.50	60,000	67,500	75,000	82,500
Fixed overhead costs:					
Amortization.........		100,000	100,000	100,000	100,000
Supervisory salaries ...		160,000	160,000	160,000	160,000
Insurance............		40,000	40,000	40,000	40,00
Total fixed overhead cost.........		300,000	300,000	300,000	300,000
Total overhead cost		$360,000	$367,500	$375,000	$382,500

MICRODRIVE CORPORATION
Flexible Budgets at Various Levels of Activity

Exhibit 9–6
MicroDrive Corporation Flexible Budgets

Flexible Budgets and Overhead Rates

Fixed costs come in large, indivisible pieces that by definition do not change with changes in the level of activity within a relevant range. This creates a problem in product costing, since a given level of fixed overhead cost spread over a small number of units will result in a higher cost per unit than if the same amount of cost is spread over a large number of units. Consider the data in the following table:

Month	(1) Fixed Overhead Cost	(2) Number of Units Produced	(3) Unit Cost (1) ÷ (2)
January	$6,000	1,000	$6.00
February	6,000	1,500	4.00
March	6,000	800	7.50

Notice that the large number of units produced in February results in a low unit cost ($4), whereas the small number of units produced in March results in a high unit cost ($7.50). This problem arises only in connection with the fixed portion of overhead, since by definition the variable portion of overhead remains constant on a per-unit basis, rising and falling in total proportionately with changes in the activity level. Most managers feel that the fixed portion of unit cost should be stabilized so that a single unit cost figure can be used throughout the year. As we learned in Chapter 4, this stability can be accomplished through use of the predetermined overhead rate.

● KNOW

CC8: Explain the concept of denominator activity.

DENOMINATOR ACTIVITY　　The formula that we used in Chapter 4 to compute the predetermined overhead rate is as follows:

$$\frac{\text{Predetermined}}{\text{overhead rate}} = \frac{\text{Estimated total manufacturing overhead cost}}{\text{Estimated total units in the allocation base (MH, DLH, etc.)}}$$

The estimated total units in the base in the formula for the predetermined overhead rate is called the **denominator activity.** Recall from our discussion in Chapter 4 that once an estimated activity level (denominator activity) has been chosen, it remains unchanged throughout the year, even if the actual activity turns out to be different from what was estimated. The reason for not changing the denominator is to maintain stability in the amount of overhead applied to each unit of product, regardless of when it is produced during the year. In the case of MicroDrive, the denominator activity level is 50,000 machine-hours (see Exhibit 9–4 on page 366).

● APPLY

CC9: Compute a predetermined overhead rate.

COMPUTING THE OVERHEAD RATE　　When we discussed predetermined overhead rates in Chapter 4, we did not explain how the estimated total manufacturing cost was determined. This figure can be derived from the flexible budget. Once the denominator level of activity has been chosen, the flexible budget can be used to determine the total amount of overhead cost that should be incurred at that level of activity. The predetermined overhead rate can then be computed using the following variation on the basic formula for the predetermined overhead rate:

$$\frac{\text{Predetermined}}{\text{overhead rate}} = \frac{\text{Overhead from the flexible budget at the denominator level of activity}}{\text{Denominator level of activity}}$$

To illustrate, the predetermined overhead rate for MicroDrive Corporation will be computed as follows:

$$\frac{\$375,000}{50,000 \text{ MHs}} = \$7.50 \text{ per MH}$$

Or, the company can break its predetermined overhead rate down into variable and fixed elements, rather than using a single combined figure:

$$\text{Variable element:} \frac{\$75,000}{50,000 \text{ MHs}} = \$1.50 \text{ per MH}$$

$$\text{Fixed element:} \frac{\$300,000}{50,000 \text{ MHs}} = \$6 \text{ per MH}$$

For every standard machine-hour of operation, work in process will be charged with $7.50 of overhead, of which $1.50 will be variable overhead and $6 will be fixed overhead. If a disk-drive motor takes two machine-hours to complete, then its cost will include $3 variable overhead and $12 fixed overhead, as shown on the following standard cost card:

Standard Cost Card—Per Motor	
Direct materials (assumed)	$14
Direct labour (assumed)	6
Variable overhead (2 MHs at $1.50 per MH)	3
Fixed overhead (2 MHs at $6 per MH)	12
Total standard cost per motor	$35

In summary, the flexible budget provides the estimated overhead cost needed to compute the predetermined overhead rate. Thus, the flexible budget plays a key role in determining the amount of fixed and variable overhead costs that will be charged to units of product.

Overhead Application in a Standard Cost System

To understand the fixed overhead variances, it is necessary first to understand how overhead is applied to work in process in a standard cost system. In Chapter 4, recall that we applied overhead to work in process on the basis of actual hours of activity (multiplied by the predetermined overhead rate). This procedure was correct, since at the time we were dealing with a normal cost system.[1] However, we are now dealing with a standard cost system. In such a system, overhead is applied to work in process on the basis of the *standard hours allowed for the output of the period,* rather than on the basis of the actual number of hours worked. This point is illustrated in Exhibit 9–7. In a standard cost system, every unit of product moving along the production line bears the same amount of overhead cost, regardless of any variations in efficiency that may have been involved in its production.

○ KNOW

CC10: Distinguish between overhead application in normal costing versus overhead application in standard costing.

Normal cost System Manufacturing Overhead		Standard Cost System Manufacturing Overhead	
Actual overhead costs incurred	Applied overhead costs: Actual hours × Predetermined overhead rate	Actual overhead costs incurred	Applied overhead costs: Standard hours allowed for actual output × Predetermined overhead rate
Under- or over-applied overhead		Under- or over-applied overhead	

Exhibit 9–7
Applied Overhead Costs: Normal Cost System versus Standard Cost System

[1]Normal cost systems are discussed in Chapter 4.

The Fixed Overhead Variances

To illustrate the computation of fixed overhead variances, we will again refer to the data for MicroDrive Corporation.

Denominator activity in machine-hours...........	50,000
Budgeted fixed overhead costs	$300,000
Fixed portion of the predetermined overhead rate (computed previously)...........	$6 per machine-hour

Let us assume that the following actual operating results were recorded for the year:

Actual machine-hours........................	42,000
Standard machine-hours allowed*	40,000
Actual fixed overhead costs:	
Amortization................................	$100,000
Supervisory salaries	172,000
Insurance...................................	36,000
Total actual cost	$308,000

*For the actual production during the year (20,000 units × 2 machine-hours per unit).

From these data, two variances can be computed for fixed overhead—a *budget variance* and a *volume variance*. The variances are shown in Exhibit 9–8.

Notice that overhead has been applied to work in process on the basis of 40,000 standard hours allowed for the output of the year, rather than on the basis of 42,000 actual hours worked. As stated previously, this keeps unit costs from being affected by any variations in efficiency.

The Budget Variance—A Closer Look

The **budget variance** is the difference between the actual fixed overhead costs incurred during the period and the budgeted fixed overhead costs as contained in the flexible budget. It can be computed as shown in Exhibit 9–8, or by using the following formula:

$$\text{Budget variance} = \text{Actual fixed overhead cost} - \text{Flexible budget fixed overhead cost}$$

Applying this formula to MicroDrive Corporation, the budget variance would be as follows:

$$\$308,000 - \$300,000 = \$8,000 \text{ U}$$

Exhibit 9–8
Computation of the Fixed Overhead Variances

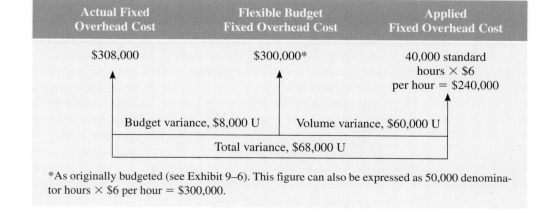

*As originally budgeted (see Exhibit 9–6). This figure can also be expressed as 50,000 denominator hours × $6 per hour = $300,000.

The variances computed for the fixed costs at Rick's Hairstyling Salon in Exhibit 9–3 are all budget variances, since they represent the difference between the actual fixed overhead cost and the budgeted fixed overhead cost from the flexible budget.

An expanded overhead performance report for MicroDrive Corporation appears in Exhibit 9–9. This report now includes the budget variances for fixed overhead, as well as the spending variances for variable overhead found in Exhibit 9–5.

Exhibit 9–9
Fixed Overhead Costs on the Overhead Performance Report

MICRODRIVE CORPORATION
Overhead Performance Report
For the Year Ended December 31

Budgeted machine-hours 50,000
Actual machine-hours............. 42,000
Standard machine-hours allowed 40,000

Overhead Costs	Cost Formula (per machine-hour)	Actual Costs 42,000 Machine-Hours	Budget Based on 42,000 Machine-Hours	Spending or Budget Variance
Variable overhead costs:				
Indirect labour.............	$0.80	$ 36,000	$ 33,600	$ 2,400 U
Lubricants	0.30	11,000	12,600	1,600 F
Power	0.40	24,000	16,800	7,200 U
Total variable overhead cost..............	$1.50	71,000	63,000	8,000 U
Fixed overhead costs:				
Amortization..............		100,000	100,000	—
Supervisory salaries		172,000	160,000	12,000
Insurance................		36,000	40,000	4,000 F
Total fixed overhead costs......		308,000	300,000	8,000 U
Total overhead cost...........		$379,000	$363,000	$16,000 U

The budget variances for fixed overhead can be very useful, since they represent the difference between how much *should* have been spent (according to the flexible budget) and how much was actually spent. For example, supervisory salaries has a $12,000 unfavourable variance. There should be some explanation for this large variance. Was it due to an increase in salaries? Was it due to overtime? Was another supervisor hired? If so, why was another supervisor hired?—this was not included in the budget when activity for the year was planned. Another factor causing increase in fixed overhead is investments in technology, such as the automated system implemented by TML (see opening decision feature). To the extent that the additional capacity created by the investment is not utilized, it will be seen as a burden despite some gains in efficiency.

The Volume Variance—A Closer Look

The **volume variance** is a measure of utilization of plant facilities. It can be computed as shown in Exhibit 9–8, or by using the following formula:

$$\text{Volume variance} = \text{Fixed portion of the predetermined overhead rate} \times \left(\text{Denominator hours} - \text{Standard hours allowed} \right)$$

Applying this formula to MicroDrive Corporation, the volume variance would be computed as follows:

$$\$6 \text{ per MH } (50,000 \text{ MH } - 40,000 \text{ MH}) = \$60,000 \text{ U}$$

Notice that this computation agrees with the volume variance as shown in Exhibit 9–8. As stated previously, the volume variance is a measure of utilization of available plant facilities. An unfavourable variance, as above, means that the company operated at an activity level *below* that planned for the period. A favourable variance would mean that the company operated at an activity level *greater* than that planned for the period.

It is important to note that the volume variance does not measure over- or underspending. The variance arises because 5,000 fewer units were produced during the budget period than planned (see Exhibit 9–4). This means that we spread the total fixed costs over a smaller number of units; each unit of product "absorbs" a greater portion of the overhead than planned. Managers must focus their attention on understanding why 5,000 fewer units were produced. The reasons could be many, such as a decline in orders (perhaps due to a downturn in the economy or due to lack of proper marketing), production problems, labour problems, or other factors. An effort must be made to ensure that planned production levels are achieved.

To summarize:

- If the planned and actual production levels are the *same*, then the denominator activity and standard hours allowed for the output of the period are the same, and there is no volume variance.
- If actual production is *less than* planned production, then the denominator activity is *greater than* the standard hours allowed for the output of the period, and the volume variance is unfavourable. This signals that the available facilities are under-utilized.
- If actual production is *greater than* planned production, then the denominator activity is *less than* the standard hours allowed for the output of the period, and the volume variance is favourable. This signals that utilization levels are higher than planned.

DECISION MAKER

Vice-President of Production

One of the company's factories produces a single product. The factory recently reported a significant unfavourable volume variance for the year. Sales for that product were less than anticipated. What should you do?

Cautions in Fixed Overhead Analysis

The reason we see a volume variance for fixed overhead is because the total fixed cost does not depend on activity; yet when applying the costs to work in process, we act *as if* the fixed costs were variable and depended on activity. This point can be illustrated graphically as in Exhibit 9–10. Observe that the fixed overhead costs are applied to work in process at a rate of $6 per hour *as if* they were variable. Treating these costs as if they were variable is necessary for product costing purposes, but there are some real dangers here. The manager can easily become misled, thinking that the fixed costs were, *in fact*, variable.

The manager must keep clearly in mind that fixed overhead costs come in large, indivisible pieces. Expressing fixed costs on a unit or per-hour basis, though necessary for product costing for external reports, is artificial. Increases or decreases in activity, in fact, have no effect on total fixed costs within the relevant range of activity. Even though fixed costs are expressed on a unit or per-hour basis, they are *not* proportional to activity. In a sense, the volume variance is the error that occurs as a result of treating fixed costs as variable costs in the costing system.

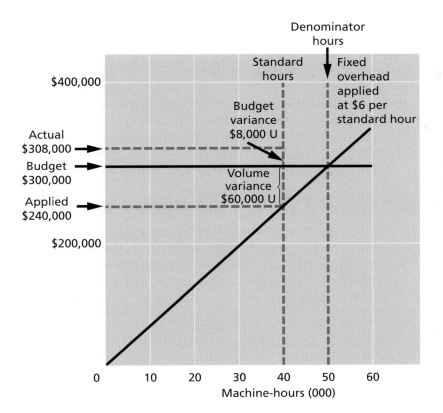

Exhibit 9–10
Graphic Analysis of Fixed
Overhead Variances

Because of the confusion that can arise concerning the interpretation of the volume variance, some companies present the volume variance in physical units (hours), rather than in dollars. These companies feel that stating the variance in physical units gives management a clearer signal concerning the cause of the variance.

Overhead Variances and Under- or Over-applied Overhead Cost

Four variances relating to overhead cost have been computed for MicroDrive Corporation in this chapter. These four variances are as follows:

Variable overhead spending variance (p. 366)	$ 8,000 U
Variable overhead efficiency variance (p. 368).	3,000 U
Fixed overhead budget variance (p. 372)	8,000 U
Fixed overhead volume variance (p. 372).	60,000 U
Total overhead variance	$79,000 U

Recall from Chapter 4 that under- or over-applied overhead is the difference between the amount of overhead applied to products and the actual overhead costs incurred during a period. Basically, the overhead variances we have computed in this chapter break down the under- or over-applied overhead into variances that can be used by managers for control purposes. Consequently, *the sum of the overhead variances equals the under- or over-applied overhead cost for a period.*

Furthermore, in a standard cost system, unfavourable variances are equivalent to under-applied overhead and favourable variances are equivalent to over-applied overhead. Unfavourable variances occur because more was spent on overhead than the standards allow. Under-applied overhead occurs when more was spent on overhead than was applied to products during the period. But in a standard costing system, the standard amount of overhead allowed is exactly the same amount of overhead applied to products. Therefore, in a standard costing system, unfavourable variances and under-applied overhead are the same thing, as are favourable variances and over-applied overhead.

For MicroDrive Corporation, the total overhead variance was $79,000 unfavourable. Therefore, its overhead cost was under-applied by $79,000 for the year. To solidify this point in your mind, *carefully study the review problem at the end of the chapter!* This review problem provides a comprehensive summary of overhead analysis, including the computation of under- or over-applied overhead cost in a standard cost system.

IN BUSINESS TODAY

Overhead Accounts: Fertile Ground for Fraud

Particularly in small companies, no one but the controller may understand concepts such as overhead variances and overapplied and underapplied overhead. Furthermore, a small company controller may be able to both authorize cash disbursements and account for them. Since small, closely held companies often do not hire external auditors, these circumstances create an ideal environment for fraud.

Such was the case in a small manufacturing company with 100 employees and $30 million in annual sales. The controller embezzled nearly $1 million from the company over three years by writing checks to himself. The consultant who uncovered the fraud was tipped off by the unusually high overhead variances that resulted from the controller recording fictitious expenses in the overhead accounts to offset the fraudulent cash disbursements. After the fraud was exposed, the company implemented various controls to reduce the risk of future problems, such as hiring an internal auditor and requiring periodic review of overhead variances to identify and explain significant discrepancies.

Source: John B. MacArthur, Bobby E. Waldrup, and Gary R. Fane, "Caution: Fraud Overhead," *Strategic Finance*, October 2004, pp. 28–32.

Is Variance Analysis a Timely Control Tool?

Given the importance of timely information for the purposes of decision making, should managers wait until the end of a period to find out about variances that occurred during that period? The answer really depends on why the flexible budgeting and variance analysis are used in an organization. In most cases, responsible managers will likely be aware of variances prior to the end of the budget period. Production managers can monitor the use of input resources on a daily basis and get an idea whether more or less quantities than planned will be used during the period. They can then take corrective actions even before the end of the budgeting period. In fact, such an action is desirable to avoid excessive deviations/cost over-runs.

However, without formally computing the variances in dollar amounts, they will not know the impact of the deviations on profitability. Organizations that use management by exception also find the variance reports useful for follow-up actions. Preparing variance reports is useful for financial accounting purposes in firms that use a standard cost accounting system. Any deviations can be appropriately closed to the proper accounts.

YOU DECIDE

Budget Analyst

Your company is in the process of implementing an ABC program and plans to use the flexible approach to budgeting. To aid in the analysis of the factory overhead once these plans are in place, how should the under- or over-applied overhead be analyzed? Who should be held responsible for each of the variances?

Application Competency Summary

Application Competency	Deliverable	Source Documents and Key Information	Steps	Knowledge Competency
Prepare a static budget performance report. ● CC1	**Key Information** Actual and budgeted revenues and costs, and variances **Report/Document** Static budget performance report	**Budgets** Budgeted volume of activity and the corresponding revenues and costs **Revenue and Expense Ledgers** Actual volume of activity and the corresponding revenues and costs	1. List the actual and budgeted activity volumes, revenues, and costs. 2. Deduct the budgeted revenues and costs from the corresponding actual amounts to compute variances. 3. For revenues, label positive differences as favourable (F); for costs label positive differences as unfavourable (U).	Role of budgeting ● CC1 (Ch. 7) Master budget ● CC3 (Ch. 7)
Prepare a flexible budget. ● CC2	**Key Information** Total variable and fixed costs at different levels of activity **Report/Document** Flexible budget	**Standard Cost Cards** Standard cost per unit of activity volume for variable costs **Annual Budget Documents** Expected fixed costs **Historical Activity and Cost Records** Relevant range of operations	1. Choose and list different activity levels within the relevant range. 2. Compute total variable costs for each activity level by multiplying the cost per unit of activity volume by the activity level. 3. List the estimated total fixed cost for each activity level (fixed amount).	Variable and fixed cost behaviour ● CC1 (Ch. 2) Relevant range of operations ● CC5 (Ch. 3)
Prepare a flexible budget performance report. ● CC3	**Key Information** Actual and flexible budget revenues and costs, and variances **Report/Document** Flexible budget performance report	**Flexible Budget** Budgeted revenues and costs corresponding to the actual activity level **Sales/Production Records** Actual sales/production volume **Revenue and Expense Ledgers** Actual revenues and costs	1. List the actual activity volumes, and the corresponding actual and flexible budget revenues and costs. 2. Deduct the flexible budget revenues and costs from the corresponding actual amounts to compute variances. 3. For revenues, label positive differences as favourable (F); for costs label positive differences as unfavourable (U).	Variances ● CC7 (Ch. 8)

continued

Application Competency	Deliverable	Source Documents and Key Information	Steps	Knowledge Competency
Prepare a variable overhead performance report. ○ CC4	*Key Information* Actual and flexible budget variable overhead costs corresponding to the actual activity volume Flexible budget variable overhead costs corresponding to the standard activity volume allowed for actual output Total variable overhead variance Variable overhead spending and efficiency variances *Report/Document* Variable overhead performance report	*Flexible Budget* Estimated variable overhead costs corresponding to the actual activity level and the standard activity level allowed for actual output *Sales/Production Records* Actual sales/production volume Actual consumption of overhead allocation base *Variable Overhead* Expense Ledger Actual overhead costs Applied overhead	1. List the actual variable overhead costs, and the flexible budget costs corresponding to the actual activity volume and the standard activity volume allowed for actual output. 2. Deduct the flexible budget amounts corresponding to the standard activity volume allowed from the actual costs to compute the total variable overhead variance. 3. Deduct the flexible budget amounts corresponding to the actual activity volume from the actual costs to compute the variable overhead spending variance. 4. Deduct the flexible budget amounts corresponding to the standard activity volume allowed from the flexible budget costs corresponding to the actual activity volume to compute the variable overhead efficiency variance.	Price and efficiency variances ○ CC8 (Ch. 8) Variable overhead variances ○ CC11 (Ch. 8) Flexible budgeting ○ CC2
Prepare a flexible budget for fixed overhead costs. ○ CC7	*Key Information* Estimated fixed overhead costs at different activity levels *Report/Document* Fixed overhead flexible budget	*Flexible Budget* Expected fixed overhead costs at different levels of activity *Historical Activity and Cost Records* Relevant range of operations	1. List the different activity levels within the relevant range of operations. 2. List the costs for the individual fixed overhead items under each activity level (same amounts under each activity level).	Variable and fixed cost behaviour ○ CC1 (Ch. 2) Relevant range of operations ○ CC5 (Ch. 3)
Compute a predetermined overhead rate. ○ CC9	*Key Information* Predetermined overhead rate *Report/Document* No specific report	*Annual Budget Documents* Denominator activity level and the corresponding fixed overhead cost	1. Divide the fixed overhead cost corresponding to the denominator activity level by the activity level to compute the predetermined overhead rate.	Overhead allocation ○ CC9 ○ CC2, 3 (Ch. 4)
Compute fixed overhead budget variance. ○ CC11	*Key Information* Fixed overhead budget variance *Report/Document* Overhead performance report	*Flexible Budget* Budgeted fixed overhead costs at actual activity level *Fixed Overhead Expense Ledger* Actual fixed overhead costs	1. List the actual and the flexible budget fixed overhead costs corresponding to the actual activity volume of the overhead allocation base. 2. Deduct the flexible budget amount from the actual amount to compute the fixed overhead budget variance.	Variances ○ CC7 (Ch. 8)

continued

Application Competency	Deliverable	Source Documents and Key Information	Steps	Knowledge Competency
Compute fixed overhead volume variance. CC12	*Key Information* Fixed overhead volume variance *Report/Document* No specific report	*Flexible Budget* Budgeted fixed overhead *Sales/Production Records* Actual sales/production volume Actual consumption of overhead allocation base *Fixed Overhead Expense Ledger* Applied fixed overhead	1. Compute the applied overhead amount by multiplying the standard quantity of the activity volume allowed for actual output by the predetermined overhead rate. 2. List the flexible budget fixed overhead costs corresponding to the actual activity volume of the overhead allocation base and the applied overhead amount. 3. Deduct the applied overhead from the flexible budget amount to compute the volume variance.	Variances CC7 (Ch. 8)

Guidance Answers to Decision Maker and You Decide

VICE-PRESIDENT OF PRODUCTION (p. 374)

An unfavourable fixed overhead volume variance means that the factory is operating at an activity level below the level that was planned for the year. You should meet with the vice-president of sales to determine why demand was less than planned. Was production part of the problem? Were orders delivered late? Were customers quoted lead times that were too long? Could production help increase demand by improving the quality of the product and the services provided to customers? If sales are declining and are not expected to rebound, you should consider how to make use of the excess capacity in this factory. You might consider whether the factory could be reconfigured to produce another product or if a section of the factory could be leased to another company.

BUDGET ANALYST (p. 376)

The under- or over-applied overhead should be broken into its four components: (1) the variable overhead spending variance, (2) the variable overhead efficiency variance, (3) the fixed overhead budget variance, and (4) the fixed overhead volume variance.

The person who purchases the variable overhead items (such as lubricants) and the supervisor(s) who direct(s) and/or control(s) the employees who are classified as indirect labour are responsible for the variable overhead spending variance. Whoever is responsible for the control of the activity base that is used to apply overhead should be responsible for the control of the variable overhead efficiency variance. The person(s) responsible for negotiating the purchase of the fixed overhead items (such as rent and insurance) and the supervisor(s) who directs and/or controls the support staff are responsible for the fixed overhead budget variance. The fixed overhead volume variance does not indicate that the company has overspent or underspent; it is a measure of utilization of available plant facilities. As such, the person responsible for determining the level of activity for the plant would be responsible for this variance.

Review Problem: Overhead Analysis

(This problem provides a comprehensive review of Chapter 9, including the computation of under- or over-applied overhead and its breakdown into the four overhead variances.)

Data for the manufacturing overhead of Aspen Company follow:

Overhead Costs	Cost Formula (per machine-hour)	Machine-Hours		
		5,000	6,000	7,000
Variable overhead costs:				
Supplies....................	$0.20	$ 1,000	$ 1,200	$ 1,400
Indirect labour...............	0.30	1,500	1,800	2,100
Total variable overhead cost........	$0.50	2,500	3,000	3,500
Fixed overhead costs:				
Amortization.................		4,000	4,000	4,000
Supervision..................		5,000	5,000	5,000
Total fixed overhead cost..........		9,000	9,000	9,000
Total overhead cost..............		$11,500	$12,000	$12,500

Five machine-hours are required per unit of product. The company has set denominator activity for the coming period at 6,000 machine-hours (or 1,200 units). The computation of the predetermined overhead rate would be as follows:

$$\text{Total:} \frac{\$12,000}{6,000 \text{ MH}} = \$2.00 \text{ per MH}$$

$$\text{Variable element:} \frac{\$3,000}{6,000 \text{ MH}} = \$0.50 \text{ per MH}$$

$$\text{Fixed element:} \frac{\$9,000}{6,000 \text{ MH}} = \$1.50 \text{ per MH}$$

Assume the following *actual* results for the period:

Number of units produced............	1,300 units
Actual machine-hours	6,800 machine-hours
Standard machine-hours allowed*......	6,500 machine-hours
Actual variable overhead cost	$4,200
Actual fixed overhead cost	9,400

*1,300 units × 5 machine-hours per unit.

Therefore, the company's manufacturing overhead account would appear as follows at the end of the period:

Manufacturing Overhead

Actual overhead costs	13,600*	13,000†	Applied overhead costs
Under-applied overhead	600		

*$4,200 variable + $9,400 fixed = $13,600.
†6,500 standard machine-hours × $2 per machine-hour = $13,000.
In a standard cost system, overhead is applied on the basis of standard hours, not actual hours.

Required:
Analyze the $600 under-applied overhead in terms of:
1. A variable overhead spending variance.
2. A variable overhead efficiency variance.
3. A fixed overhead budget variance.
4. A fixed overhead volume variance.

SOLUTION TO REVIEW PROBLEM

Variable Overhead Variances

Actual Hours of Input, at the Actual Rate (AH × AR)	Actual Hours of Input, at the Standard Rate (AH × SR)	Standard Hours Allowed for Output, at the Standard Rate (SH × SR)
$4,200	6,800 hours × $0.50 per hour = $3,400	6,500 hours × $0.50 per hour = $3,250

Variable overhead incurred

Variable overhead applied

Spending variance, $800 U   Efficiency variance, $150 U

These same variances in the alternative format would be as follows:

Variable overhead spending variance:

$$\text{Spending variance} = (AH \times AR) - (AH \times SR)$$
$$(\$4,200^*) - (6,800 \text{ hours} \times \$0.50 \text{ per hour}) = \$800 \text{ U}$$

*$AH \times AR$ equals the total actual cost for the period.

Variable overhead efficiency variance:

$$\text{Efficiency variance} = SR(AH - SH)$$
$$\$0.50 \text{ per hour } (6,800 \text{ hours} - 6,500 \text{ hours}) = \$150 \text{ U}$$

Fixed Overhead Variances

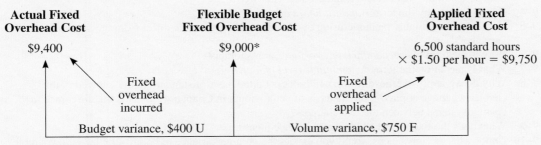

Actual Fixed Overhead Cost	Flexible Budget Fixed Overhead Cost	Applied Fixed Overhead Cost
$9,400	$9,000*	6,500 standard hours × $1.50 per hour = $9,750

Fixed overhead incurred

Fixed overhead applied

Budget variance, $400 U   Volume variance, $750 F

*Can be expressed as: 6,000 denominator hours × $1.50 per hour = $9,000.

These same variances in the alternative format would be as follows:

Fixed overhead budget variance:

$$\frac{\text{Budget}}{\text{variance}} = \frac{\text{Actual fixed}}{\text{overhead cost}} - \frac{\text{Flexible budget}}{\text{fixed overhead cost}}$$

$$\$9,400 - \$9,000 = \$400 \text{ U}$$

Fixed overhead volume variance:

$$\text{Volume variance} = \frac{\text{Fixed portion}}{\text{of the predetermined}} \times \left(\frac{\text{Denominator}}{\text{hours}} - \frac{\text{Standard}}{\text{hours}} \right)$$

$$\$1.50 \text{ per hour } (6,000 \text{ hours} - 6,500 \text{ hours}) = \$750 \text{ F}$$

Summary of Variances

A summary of the four overhead variances is given below:

Variable overhead:	
Spending variance	$800 U
Efficiency variance	150 U
Fixed overhead:	
Budget variance	400 U
Volume variance	750 F
Under-applied overhead	$600

Notice that the $600 summary variance figure agrees with the under-applied balance in the company's manufacturing overhead account. This agreement verifies the accuracy of our variance analysis.

Glossary

Budget variance A measure of the difference between the actual fixed overhead costs incurred during the period and budgeted fixed overhead costs as contained in the flexible budget. (p. 372)

Denominator activity The activity figure used to compute the predetermined overhead allocation rate. (p. 370)

Flexible budget A budget that is designed to cover a range of activity and that can be used to develop budgeted costs at any point within that range to compare with actual costs incurred. (p. 362)

Static budget A budget designed for only one level of activity. (p. 360)

Volume variance The variance that arises when actual output during a period is different from the planned output. It is a measure of how well the organization's facilities are utilized. (p. 373)

Questions

9–1 What is a static budget?

9–2 What is a flexible budget, and how does it differ from a static budget?

9–3 In comparing flexible budget data with actual data in a performance report for variable overhead, what variance(s) will be produced if the flexible budget data are based on actual hours worked? On both actual hours worked and standard hours allowed?

9–4 What is meant by the term *standard hours allowed?*

9–5 How does the variable manufacturing overhead spending variance differ from the materials price variance?

9–6 Why is the term *overhead efficiency variance* a misnomer?

9–7 What is meant by the term *denominator level of activity?*

9–8 Why do we apply overhead to work in process on the basis of standard hours allowed in this chapter when we applied it on the basis of actual hours in Chapter 4? What is the difference in costing systems between the two chapters?

9–9 What does the fixed overhead budget variance measure?

9–10 Under what circumstances would you expect the volume variance to be favourable? Unfavourable? Does the variance measure deviations in spending for fixed overhead items? Explain.

9–11 In Chapter 4, you became acquainted with the concept of under- or over-applied overhead. The under- or over-applied overhead can be broken down into what four variances?

9–12 If factory overhead is over-applied for August, would you expect the total of the overhead variances to be favourable or unfavourable?

Brief Exercises

BRIEF EXERCISE 9–1   Preparing a Flexible Budget (CC2)

An incomplete flexible budget is provided following for Lavage Rapide, a Swiss company that owns and operates a large automatic car wash facility near Geneva. The Swiss currency is the Swiss franc, which is denoted by SFr. The company charges 6 SFr per car wash.

| | Cost Formula (per car) | Activity (cars) | | |
| LAVAGE RAPIDE Flexible Budget For the Month Ended August 31 | | | | |
Overhead Costs		8,000	9,000	10,000
Variable overhead costs:				
Cleaning supplies	?	?	7,200 SFr	?
Electricity	?	?	2,700	?
Maintenance	?	?	1,800	?
Total variable overhead cost	?	?	?	?
Fixed overhead costs:				
Operator wages		?	9,000	?
Amortization		?	6,000	?
Rent		?	8,000	?
Total fixed overhead cost		?	?	?
Total overhead cost		?	?	?

Required:
Prepare flexible budgets for the three activity levels. (Use Exhibit 9–2 as your guide.)

BRIEF EXERCISE 9–2   Prepare a Static Budget (CC1)
Refer to the data in Brief Exercise 9–1. Lavage Rapide's owner-manager would like to prepare a budget for August assuming an activity level of 8,800 cars.

Required:
Prepare a static budget for August. (Use Exhibit 9–1 as your guide.)

BRIEF EXERCISE 9–3   Flexible Budget Performance Report (CC3)
Refer to the data in Brief Exercise 9–1. Lavage Rapide's actual level of activity during August was 8,900 cars, although the owner had constructed his static budget for the month assuming the level of activity would be 8,800 cars. The actual overhead costs incurred during August follow:

	Actual Costs Incurred for 8,900 Cars
Variable overhead costs:	
Cleaning supplies	7,080 SFr
Electricity	2,460
Maintenance	1,550
Fixed overhead costs:	
Operator wages	9,100
Amortization	7,000
Rent	8,000

On average, the company received 6.25 SFr per car wash.

Required:
Prepare a flexible budget performance report for August. (Use Exhibit 9–3 as your guide.)

BRIEF EXERCISE 9–4   Variable Overhead Performance Report (CC4)
Yung Corporation bases its variable overhead performance report on the actual direct labour-hours of the period. Data concerning the most recent year that ended on December 31 follow:

Budgeted DLHs	76,000
Actual DLHs	68,000
Standard DLHs allowed	70,000

Cost formula (per direct labour-hour):

Indirect labour	$0.60
Supplies	0.10
Electricity	0.05

Actual costs incurred:

Indirect labour	$42,400
Supplies	6,400
Electricity	3,200

Required:

Prepare a variable overhead performance report using the format in Exhibit 9–5. Compute both the variable overhead spending variances and the overhead efficiency variances.

BRIEF EXERCISE 9–5   Applying Overhead in a Standard Costing System (CC9, 10)

Privack Corporation has a standard cost system in which it applies overhead to products on the basis of the standard direct labour-hours allowed for the actual output of the period. Data concerning the most recent year appear below:

Variable overhead cost per DLH.	$2.00
Total fixed overhead cost per year	$250,000
Budgeted standard DLHs (denominator level of activity)	40,000
Actual DLHs.	39,000
Standard DLHs allowed for the actual output	38,000

Required:

1. Compute the predetermined overhead rate for the year.
2. Determine the amount of overhead that would be applied to the output of the period.

BRIEF EXERCISE 9–6   Fixed Overhead Variances (CC11, 12)

Primara Corporation has a standard cost system in which it applies overhead to products on the basis of the standard direct labour-hours allowed for the actual output of the period. Data concerning the most recent year appear below:

Total budgeted fixed overhead cost for the year.	$500,000
Actual fixed overhead cost for the year	$508,000
Budgeted standard direct labour-hours (denominator level of activity). . .	50,000
Actual direct labour-hours	54,000
Standard direct labour-hours allowed for the actual output	52,000

Required:

1. Compute the fixed portion of the predetermined overhead rate for the year.
2. Compute the fixed overhead budget variance and volume variance.

BRIEF EXERCISE 9–7   Flexible Budget Variance (CC3)

Capital Company budgeted production and sales of 63,000 units of Xeron in June, but produced and sold only 60,000 units. Variable manufacturing costs of $125,000 were incurred during this period. Variable manufacturing cost was budgeted at $2.25 per unit.

Required:

What is the flexible budget variance for the variable manufacturing cost?

(Adapted © CGA-Canada)

BRIEF EXERCISE 9–8   Flexible Budget Operating Income (CC2, 3)

The total static budget variance for KCC Ltd. for the month of December was $7,000 unfavourable. The total flexible budget variance was $3,000 U. The actual results for the month showed net operating income of $3,000.

Required:

What amount of operating income (loss) would the flexible budget have shown for December?

(Adapted © CGA-Canada)

BRIEF EXERCISE 9–9   Applying Overhead; Overhead Variances (CC10, 11, 12)

Medd Inc. has the following results for the current period:

	Budget	Actual
Fixed overhead	$156,000	$160,000
Units produced	6,500 units	6,000 units
Direct labour-hours (DLH)	13,000 hours	12,500 hours

Fixed overhead is applied at $12 per direct labour-hour. Variable overhead is applied at $27.50 per direct labour-hour. The standard per unit is 2 direct labour-hours. Actual variable overhead was $310,600.

Required:

1. Compute the fixed overhead budget variance.
2. Compute the total variable overhead variance.

(Adapted © CGA-Canada)

Exercises

EXERCISE 9–1   Prepare a Flexible Budget (CC2)

The cost formulas for Emory Company's manufacturing overhead costs are given below. These cost formulas cover a relevant range of 15,000 to 25,000 machine-hours each year.

Overhead Costs	Cost Formula
Utilities	$0.30 per MH
Indirect labour.	$52,000 plus $1.60 per MH
Supplies	$0.24 per MH
Maintenance	$20,000 plus $0.12 per MH
Amortization.	$100,000

Required:

Prepare a flexible budget in increments of 5,000 machine-hours. Include all costs in your budget.

EXERCISE 9–2   Variable Overhead Performance Report (CC4, 5, 6)

The variable portion of Murray Company's flexible budget for manufacturing overhead is given below:

Variable Overhead Costs	Cost Formula (per machine-hour)	Machine-Hours		
		10,000	12,000	14,000
Supplies.	$0.20	$ 2,000	$ 2,400	$ 2,800
Maintenance	0.70	7,000	8,400	9,800
Utilities	0.10	1,000	1,200	1,400
Rework time	0.40	4,000	4,800	5,600
Total variable overhead cost	$1.40	$14,000	$16,800	$19,600

During a recent period, the company recorded 11,500 machine-hours of activity. The variable overhead costs incurred were:

Supplies	$2,420
Maintenance	7,000
Utilities	1,070
Rework time	5,190

The budgeted activity for the period had been 12,000 machine-hours.

Required:
1. Prepare a variable overhead performance report for the period. Indicate whether variances are favourable (F) or unfavourable (U). Show only a spending variance on your report.
2. Discuss the significance of the variances. Might some variances be the result of others? Explain.

EXERCISE 9–3   Variable Overhead Variances with Performance Report (CC4)

The cheque-clearing office of your local credit union bank is responsible for processing all cheques that come to the bank for payment. Managers at the bank believe that variable overhead costs are essentially proportional to the number of labour-hours worked in the office, and so labour-hours is used as the activity base for budgeting and for performance reports for variable overhead costs in the department. Data for September, the most recent month, follow:

Budgeted labour-hours	3,050
Actual labour-hours	3,100
Standard labour-hours allowed for the actual number of cheques processed	3,250

	Cost Formula (per labour-hour)	Actual Costs Incurred in September
Variable overhead costs:		
Office supplies	$0.10	$ 365
Staff coffee lounge	0.20	520
Indirect labour	0.90	2,710
Total variable overhead cost	$1.20	$3,595

Required:
Prepare a variable overhead performance report for September for the cheque-clearing office that includes both spending and efficiency variances. (Use Exhibit 9–5 as a guide.)

EXERCISE 9–4   Predetermined Overhead Rates (CC9)

Operating at a normal level of 30,000 direct labour-hours, Lasser Company produces 10,000 units of product each period. The direct labour wage rate is $6 per hour. 7.5 metres of direct materials go into each unit of product; the material costs $3 per metre. The flexible budget used to plan and control manufacturing overhead costs is provided following (in condensed form):

Overhead Costs	Cost Formula (per direct labour-hour)	Direct Labour-Hours		
		20,000	30,000	40,000
Variable costs	$1.90	$ 38,000	$ 57,000	$ 76,000
Fixed costs		168,000	168,000	168,000
Total overhead cost		$206,000	$225,000	$244,000

Required:
1. Using 30,000 direct labour-hours as the denominator activity, compute the predetermined overhead rate and break it down into variable and fixed elements.
2. Complete the standard cost card below for one unit of product:

Direct materials, 7.5 metres at $3 per metre		$22.50
Direct labour,	?	?
Variable overhead,	?	?
Fixed overhead,	?	?
Total standard cost per unit		$?

EXERCISE 9–5 Predetermined Overhead Rates and Overhead Variances (CC9, 11, 12)

Norwall Company's flexible budget for manufacturing overhead (in condensed form) is given below:

Overhead Costs	Cost Formula (per machine-hour)	Machine-Hours 50,000	60,000	70,000
Variable costs	$4	$200,000	$240,000	$280,000
Fixed costs		300,000	300,000	300,000
Total overhead cost		$500,000	$540,000	$580,000

The following information is available for a recent period:
a. A denominator activity of 60,000 machine-hours is used to compute the predetermined overhead rate.
b. At the 60,000 standard machine-hours level of activity, the company should produce 40,000 units of product.
c. The company's actual operating results were as follows:

Number of units produced	41,000
Actual machine-hours	62,500
Actual variable overhead costs	$251,250
Actual fixed overhead costs	302,400

Required:
1. Compute the predetermined overhead rate and break it down into variable and fixed cost elements.
2. Compute the standard hours allowed for the actual production.
3. Compute the variable overhead spending and efficiency variances and the fixed overhead budget and volume variances.

EXERCISE 9–6 Fixed Overhead Variances (CC11, 12)

Selected operating information on three different companies for a recent year is shown following:

	Company A	B	C
Full-capacity MHs	15,000	27,000	30,000
Budgeted MHs*	12,500	25,000	30,000
Actual MHs.	12,500	26,000	28,000
Standard MHs allowed for actual production	13,000	23,000	30,000

*Denominator activity for computing the predetermined overhead rate.

Required:

For each company, state whether the company would have a favourable or unfavourable volume variance and why.

EXERCISE 9–7   Variable Overhead Performance Report (CC4)

The cost formulas for variable overhead costs in a machining operation follow:

Variable Overhead Costs	Cost Formula (per machine-hour)
Power..................................	$0.30
Setup time	0.20
Polishing wheels	0.16
Maintenance.............................	0.18
Total variable overhead cost	$0.84

During August, the machining operation was scheduled to work 11,250 machine-hours and to produce 4,500 units of product. The standard machine time per unit of product is 2.5 hours. A strike near the end of the month forced a cutback in production. Actual results for the month were as follows:

Actual MHs worked...............................	9,250
Actual number of units produced	3,600

Actual costs for the month were:

Variable Overhead Costs	Total Actual Costs	Per Machine-Hour
Power.......................	$2,405	$0.26
Setup time	2,035	0.22
Polishing wheels	1,110	0.12
Maintenance..................	925	0.10
Total variable overhead cost	$6,475	$0.70

Required:

Prepare an overhead performance report for the machining operation for August. Use the following column headings in your report:

Overhead Item	Cost Formula (per machine-hour)	Actual Costs Incurred 9,250 Machine-Hours	Budget Based on ? Machine-Hours	Budget Based on ? Machine-Hours	Breakdown of Total Variance		
					Total Variance	Spending Variance	Efficiency Variance

EXERCISE 9–8   Preparing Flexible Budgets (CC2)

MockToe Inc. (MTI) is a manufacturer of toaster ovens. To improve control over operations, the president of MTI wants to install a flexible budgeting system, rather than only the single master budget being used presently. The following data are available for MTI's expected costs for production levels of 90,000, 100,000, and 110,000 units.

Variable costs:

Manufacturing	$ 6.00/unit
Administrative	$ 3.00/unit
Selling.	$ 1.00/unit

Fixed costs:

Manufacturing	$ 150,000
Administrative	$ 80,000

Required:
1. Prepare a flexible budget for each of the three possible sales levels: 90,000, 100,000, and 110,000 units. Each toaster oven is expected to sell for $12.

(Adapted © CGA-Canada)

EXERCISE 9–9   Basic Variance Computation (CC1)

The following data were collected by Dakota Co. for the month of June:

Static budget data:

Sales	9,000 units @ $30/unit
Variable costs	$23 per unit
Total fixed costs.	$18,800

Actual results:

Sales.	9,600 units @ $29/unit
Variable costs.	$24 per unit
Total fixed costs.	$18,200

Required:
What was the June variance from the static budget operating income?

(Adapted © CGA-Canada)

EXERCISE 9–10   Fixed and Variable Overhead Variances (CC11, 12)

White River Inc. is a manufacturer of men's suits. Variable manufacturing overhead and fixed manufacturing overhead are allocated to each suit based on budgeted direct labour-hours. The following are the production data for White River. (There were no beginning or ending inventories.)

Budgeted variable overhead rate per DLH	$12
Budgeted DLHs per suit	4

Data for May 2008:	
Budgeted production volume	1,040 suits
Actual direct labour-hours	4,536 DLHs
Actual variable overhead costs	$52,164
Actual production volume.	1,080 suits
Budgeted fixed overhead costs	$62,400
Actual fixed overhead costs	$63,916

Required:
1. What was the variable overhead efficiency variance?
2. What was the fixed overhead production volume variance?

(Adapted © CGA-Canada)

Problems

PROBLEM 9–1   Preparing a Performance Report (CC4, 5, 6, 11, 12)

Several years ago, Westmont Company developed a comprehensive budgeting system for profit planning and control purposes. The line supervisors have been very happy with the system and with the reports being prepared on their performance, but both middle and upper management have expressed considerable dissatisfaction with the information being generated by the system. A typical manufacturing overhead performance report for a recent period is shown below:

WESTMONT COMPANY			
Overhead Performance Report—Assembly Department			
For the Quarter Ended March 31			
	Actual	**Budget**	**Variance**
Machine-hours	38,000	40,000	
Variable overhead costs:			
Indirect materials	$ 32,250	$ 34,000	$1,750 F
Rework time	8,560	9,200	640 F
Utilities	56,240	60,000	3,760 F
Machine setup	12,600	13,200	600 F
Total variable overhead cost	109,650	116,400	6,750 F
Fixed overhead costs:			
Maintenance	79,200	80,000	800 F
Inspection	60,000	60,000	—
Total fixed overhead cost	139,200	140,000	800 F
Total overhead cost	$248,850	$256,400	$7,550 F

After receiving a copy of this overhead performance report, the supervisor of the Assembly Department stated, "These reports are super. It makes me feel really good to see how well things are going in my department. I can't understand why those people upstairs complain so much."

The budget data above are for the original planned level of activity for the quarter.

Required:

1. The company's vice-president is uneasy about the performance reports being prepared and would like you to evaluate their usefulness to the company.
2. What changes, if any, would you recommend be made in the overhead performance report in order to give better insight into how well the supervisor is controlling costs?
3. Prepare a new overhead performance report for the quarter, incorporating any changes you suggested in part (2). (Include both the variable and the fixed costs in your report.)

PROBLEM 9–2   Preparing a Performance Report (CC1, 2, 3)

The St. Lucia Blood Bank, a private charity partly supported by government grants, is located on the Caribbean island of St. Lucia. The Blood Bank has just finished its operations for September, which was a particularly busy month due to a powerful hurricane that hit neighbouring islands causing many injuries. The hurricane largely bypassed St. Lucia, but residents of St. Lucia willingly donated their blood to help people on other islands. As a consequence, the Blood Bank collected and processed over 20% more blood than had been originally planned for the month.

A report prepared by a government official comparing actual costs to budgeted costs for the Blood Bank appears below. (The currency on St. Lucia is the East Caribbean dollar.) Continued support from the government depends on the Blood Bank's ability to demonstrate control over its costs.

ST. LUCIA BLOOD BANK Cost Control Report For the Month Ended September 30			
	Actual	**Budget**	**Variance**
Litres of blood collected	620	500	120 F
Variable costs:			
Medical supplies	$ 9,350	$ 7,500	$1,850 U
Lab tests	6,180	6,000	180 U
Refreshments for donors	1,340	1,000	340 U
Administrative supplies	400	250	150 U
Total variable cost	17,270	14,750	2,520 U
Fixed costs:			
Staff salaries	10,000	10,000	—
Equipment amortization	2,800	2,500	300 U
Rent	1,000	1,000	—
Utilities	570	500	70 U
Total fixed cost	14,370	14,000	370 U
Total cost	$31,640	$28,750	$2,890 U

The managing director of the Blood Bank was very unhappy with this report, claiming that his costs were higher than expected due to the emergency on the neighbouring islands. He also pointed out that the additional costs had been fully covered by payments from grateful recipients on the other islands. The government official who prepared the report countered that all of the figures had been submitted by the Blood Bank to the government; he was just pointing out that actual costs were a lot higher than promised in the budget.

Required:
1. Prepare a new performance report for September using the flexible budget approach. (Note: Even though some of these costs might be classified as direct costs, rather than as overhead, the flexible budget approach can still be used to prepare a flexible budget performance report.)
2. Do you think any of the variances in the report you prepared should be investigated? Why?

PROBLEM 9–3   Comprehensive Standard Cost Variances (CC8, 9, 10, 11, 12)
Flandro Company uses a standard cost system and sets predetermined overhead rates on the basis of direct labour-hours. The following data are taken from the company's budget for the current year:

Denominator activity (direct labour-hours)	20,000
Variable manufacturing overhead cost	$60,000
Fixed manufacturing overhead cost	136,000

The standard cost card for the company's only product is as follows:

Direct materials, 3 metres at $4.80	$14.40
Direct labour, 2 hours at $7	14.00
Manufacturing overhead, 140% of direct labour cost	19.60
Standard cost per unit	$48.00

CHECK FIGURE
(1) Standard cost: $48
(3) Volume variance:
$54,400 U

During the year, the company produced 6,000 units of product and incurred the following costs:

Materials purchased, 24,000 metres at $5.10	$122,400
Materials used in production (in metres)	18,500
Direct labour cost incurred, 11,600 hours at $7.50	$ 87,000
Variable manufacturing overhead cost incurred	34,580
Fixed manufacturing overhead cost incurred	69,400

Required:
1. Redo the standard cost card in a clearer, more usable format by detailing the variable and fixed overhead cost elements.
2. Prepare an analysis of the variances for materials and labour for the year.
3. Prepare an analysis of the variances for variable and fixed overhead for the year.
4. What effect, if any, does the choice of a denominator activity level have on unit standard costs? Is the volume variance a controllable variance from a spending point of view? Explain.

CHECK FIGURE
(3) Spending variance:
PZ6,000 U
Budget variance:
PZ1,200 F

PROBLEM 9–4   Applying Overhead; Overhead Variances (CC9, 10, 11, 12)
Chilczuk, S.A., of Gdansk, Poland, is a major producer of classic Polish sausage. The company uses a standard cost system to help in the control of costs. Overhead is applied to production on the basis of labour-hours. According to the company's flexible budget, the following manufacturing overhead costs should be incurred at an activity level of 70,000 labour-hours (the denominator activity level): (The currency in Poland is the *zloty*, which is denoted here by PZ.)

Variable overhead costs	PZ175,000
Fixed overhead costs.	420,000
Total overhead cost	PZ595,000

During the most recent year, the following operating results were recorded:

Activity:	
Actual labour-hours worked	60,000
Standard labour-hours allowed for output	64,000
Cost:	
Actual variable overhead cost incurred.	PZ156,000
Actual fixed overhead cost incurred	PZ418,800

At the end of the year, the company's manufacturing overhead account contained the following data:

Manufacturing Overhead

Actual	574,800	Applied	544,000
	30,800		

Management would like to determine the cause of the PZ30,800 under-applied overhead.
Required:
1. Compute the predetermined overhead rate. Break down the rate into variable and fixed cost elements.
2. Show how the PZ544,000 applied figure in the manufacturing overhead account was computed.
3. Analyze the PZ30,800 under-applied overhead figure in terms of the variable overhead spending and efficiency variances and the fixed overhead budget and volume variances.
4. Explain the meaning of each variance that you computed in part (3).

PROBLEM 9–5 Comprehensive Standard Cost Variances (CC9, 10, 11, 12)

"Wonderful! Not only did our salespeople do a good job in meeting the sales budget this year, but also our production people did a good job in controlling costs as well," said Kim Clark, president of Martell Company. "Our $18,000 overall manufacturing cost variance is only 1.5% of the $1,200,000 standard cost of products sold during the year. That's well within the 3% parameter set by management for acceptable variances. It looks like everyone will be in line for a bonus this year."

The company produces and sells a single product. A standard cost card for the product follows:

CHECK FIGURE
(3a) Efficiency variance:
     $7,500 U
(3b) Volume variance:
     $42,000 F

Standard Cost Card—Per Unit of Product	
Direct materials, 2 metres at $8.45 per metre	$16.90
Direct labour, 1.4 hours at $8 per hour	11.20
Variable overhead, 1.4 hours at $2.50 per hour	3.50
Fixed overhead, 1.4 hours at $6 per hour	8.40
Standard cost per unit	$40.00

The following additional information is available for the year just completed:

a. The company manufactured 30,000 units of product during the year.
b. A total of 64,000 metres of material was purchased during the year at a cost of $8.55 per metre. All of this material was used to manufacture the 30,000 units. There were no beginning or ending inventories for the year.
c. The company worked 45,000 direct labour-hours during the year at an average cost of $7.80 per hour.
d. Overhead is applied to products on the basis of direct labour-hours. Data relating to manufacturing overhead costs follow:

Denominator activity level (direct labour-hours)	35,000
Budgeted fixed overhead costs (from the overhead flexible budget)	$210,000
Actual variable overhead costs incurred	108,000
Actual fixed overhead costs incurred.	211,800

Required:

1. Compute the direct materials price and quantity variances for the year.
2. Compute the direct labour rate and efficiency variances for the year.
3. For manufacturing overhead, compute:
   a. The variable overhead spending and efficiency variances for the year.
   b. The fixed overhead budget and volume variances for the year.
4. Total the variances you have computed, and compare the net amount with the $18,000 mentioned by the president. Do you agree that bonuses should be given to everyone for good cost control during the year? Explain.

PROBLEM 9–6 Using Fixed Overhead Variances (CC9, 10, 11, 12)

The standard cost card for the single product manufactured by Cutter, Inc. is provided following:

CHECK FIGURE
(1) Standard hours allowed:
     28,500 hours

Standard Cost Card—Per Unit	
Direct materials, 3 metres at $7.50 per metre	$22.50
Direct labour, 3 hours at $7.75 per hour	23.25
Variable overhead, 3 hours at $1.50 per hour	4.50
Fixed overhead, 3 hours at $5 per hour	15.00
Total standard cost per unit	$65.25

Manufacturing overhead is applied to production on the basis of direct labour-hours. During the year, the company worked 27,000 hours and manufactured 9,500 units of product. Selected data relating to the company's fixed manufacturing overhead cost for the year are shown following:

Actual Fixed Overhead Cost	Flexible Budget Fixed Overhead Cost	Applied Fixed Overhead Cost
$148,700	?	? hrs. × $? = $?

Budget variance, $?   Volume variance, $7,500 U

Required:
1. What were the standard hours allowed for the year's production?
2. What was the amount of fixed overhead cost contained in the flexible budget for the year?
3. What was the fixed overhead budget variance for the year?
4. What denominator activity level did the company use in setting the predetermined overhead rate for the year?

CHECK FIGURE
(3) Volume variance: $54,000 U

PROBLEM 9–7   Relations among Fixed Overhead Variances (CC11, 12)
Selected information relating to Yost Company's operations for the most recent year is as follows:

Activity:
Denominator activity (machine-hours)   30,000
Standard hours allowed per unit   3
Number of units produced.   12,000

Costs:
Actual fixed overhead costs incurred. $267,000
Fixed overhead budget variance . . . .   3,000 F

The company applies overhead cost to products on the basis of machine-hours.

Required:
1. What were the standard hours allowed for the actual production?
2. What was the fixed portion of the predetermined overhead rate?
3. What was the volume variance?

CHECK FIGURE
(2) Total of spending and budget variances: $800 U

PROBLEM 9–8   Flexible Budget and Overhead Performance Report (CC2, 11, 12)
You have just been hired by FAB Company, the manufacturer of a revolutionary new garage door opening device. John Foster, the president, has asked that you review the company's costing system and "do what you can to help us get better control of our manufacturing overhead costs." You find that the company has never used a flexible budget, and you suggest that preparing such a budget would be an excellent first step in overhead planning and control.

After much effort and analysis, you are able to determine the following cost formulas for the company's normal operating range of 20,000 to 30,000 machine-hours each month:

Overhead Costs	Cost Formula
Utilities	$0.90 per machine-hour
Maintenance	$1.60 per machine-hour plus $40,000 per month
Machine setup.	$0.30 per machine-hour
Indirect labour.	$0.70 per machine-hour plus $130,000 per month
Amortization.	$70,000 per month

To show the president how the flexible budget concept works, you have gathered the following actual cost data for the most recent month, March, in which the company worked 26,000 machine-hours and produced 15,000 units:

Utilities	$ 24,200
Maintenance	78,100
Machine setup	8,400
Indirect labour	149,600
Amortization	71,500
Total cost	$331,800

The only variance in the fixed costs for the month was with amortization, which was increased as a result of a purchase of new equipment.

The company had originally planned to work 30,000 machine-hours during March.

Required:
1. Prepare a flexible budget for the company in increments of 5,000 hours.
2. Prepare an overhead performance report for the company for March. (Use the format illustrated in Exhibit 9–9.)
3. What additional information would you need to compute an overhead efficiency variance for the company?

PROBLEM 9–9 Overhead Performance Report (CC4, 5, 6, 11, 12)

CHECK FIGURE
(2) Total variance: $6,500 F

Frank Western, supervisor of the Machining Department for Freemont Company, was visibly upset after being reprimanded for his department's poor performance over the prior month. The department's performance report is given below:

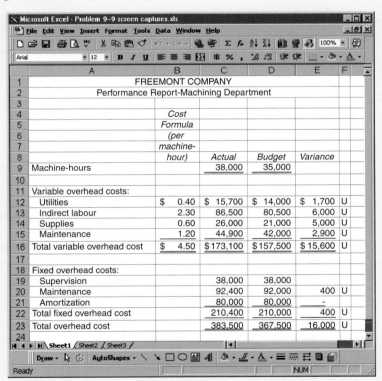

FREEMONT COMPANY
Performance Report-Machining Department

	Cost Formula (per machine-hour)	Actual	Budget	Variance	
Machine-hours		38,000	35,000		
Variable overhead costs:					
Utilities	$ 0.40	$ 15,700	$ 14,000	$ 1,700	U
Indirect labour	2.30	86,500	80,500	6,000	U
Supplies	0.60	26,000	21,000	5,000	U
Maintenance	1.20	44,900	42,000	2,900	U
Total variable overhead cost	$ 4.50	$173,100	$157,500	$ 15,600	U
Fixed overhead costs:					
Supervision		38,000	38,000		
Maintenance		92,400	92,000	400	U
Amortization		80,000	80,000	-	
Total fixed overhead cost		210,400	210,000	400	U
Total overhead cost		383,500	367,500	16,000	U

"I just can't understand all the red ink," said Western to Sarah Mason, supervisor of another department. "When the boss called me in, I thought he was going to give me a pat on the back because I know for a fact that my department worked more efficiently last month than it has ever worked before. Instead, he tore me apart. I thought for a minute that it might be over the supplies that were stolen out of our warehouse last month. But they only amounted to a couple of thousand dollars, and just look at this report. *Everything* is unfavourable, and I don't even know why."

The budget for the Machining Department had called for production of 14,000 units last month, which is equal to a budgeted activity level of 35,000 machine-hours (at a standard time of 2.5 hours per unit). Actual production in the Machining Department for the month was 16,000 units.

Required:
1. Evaluate the overhead performance report given above, and explain why the variances are all unfavourable.
2. Prepare a new overhead performance report that will help Mr. Western's superiors assess efficiency and cost control in the Machining Department. (Hint: Exhibit 9–5 may be helpful in structuring your report; however, the report you prepare should include both variable and fixed costs.)
3. Would the supplies stolen out of the warehouse be included as part of the variable overhead spending variance or as part of the variable overhead efficiency variance for the month? Explain.

CHECK FIGURE
(2) Standard cost: $46
(4) Volume variance:
      $24,000 F

PROBLEM 9–10   Applying Overhead; Overhead Variances (CC5, 6, 9, 10, 11, 12, 13)
Lane Company manufactures a single product that requires a great deal of hand labour. Overhead cost is applied on the basis of direct labour-hours. The company's condensed flexible budget for manufacturing overhead follows:

Overhead Costs	Cost Formula (per direct labour-hour)	Direct Labour-Hours		
		60,000	80,000	100,000
Variable costs	$2	$ 120,000	$160,000	$200,000
Fixed costs		480,000	480,000	480,000
Total overhead cost		$600,000	$640,000	$680,000

The company's product requires 1.5 kilograms of material that has a standard cost of $14 per kilogram and two hours of direct labour time that has a standard rate of $4.50 per hour.

The company planned to operate at a denominator activity level of 80,000 direct labour-hours and to produce 40,000 units of product during the most recent year. Actual activity and costs for the year were as follows:

Number of units produced	42,000
Actual direct labour-hours worked	85,000
Actual variable overhead cost incurred	$163,500
Actual fixed overhead cost incurred	483,000

Required:
1. Compute the predetermined overhead rate for the year. Break down the rate into variable and fixed elements.
2. Prepare a standard cost card for the company's product; show the details for all manufacturing costs on your standard cost card.
3. Do the following:
   a. Compute the standard hours allowed for the year's production.
   b. Complete the following Manufacturing Overhead T-account for the year:

Manufacturing Overhead

?	?
?	?

4. Determine the reason for any under- or over-applied overhead for the year by computing the variable overhead spending and efficiency variances and the fixed overhead budget and volume variances.
5. Suppose the company had chosen 85,000 direct labour-hours as the denominator activity, rather than 80,000 hours. State which, if any, of the variances computed in part (4) would have changed, and explain how the variance(s) would have changed. No computations are necessary.

CHECK FIGURE
(3) $768F

PROBLEM 9–11   Comprehensive Variance Analysis (CC5, 6, 11, 12)
Omega Ltd. manufactures digital compasses for navigation. The company's total overhead budget for April for the manufacture of 4,000 units was $99,200. Overhead is applied on the basis of direct labour-hours.

On the last day of the month, just as the 4,000th unit was completed after a total of 1,504 actual direct labour-hours, the hard drive crashed on the computer that contained the month's detailed cost information. With the computer out of commission, the cost accountant has had difficulty completing the variance analysis report. She has managed to put together the following incomplete information for April:

> *Variable overhead:*
> 0.4 DLH @ $8.00 per hour (from the standard cost card)
> Actual cost $16,800
> *Fixed overhead:*
> Budget variance . . . . $ 4,000 favourable

Required:
Compute the following for April:
1. Flexible budget variable overhead amount for the manufacture of the 4,000 units.
2. Variable overhead spending variance.
3. Variable overhead efficiency variance.
4. Budgeted fixed overhead.
5. Actual fixed overhead.

(Adapted © CGA-Canada)

PROBLEM 9–12   Overhead Variances (CC5, 6, 11, 12)
Sultan Company has developed the following standard overhead costs based on a capacity of 360,000 direct labour-hours.

> Variable overhead costs: 2 hours at $3 . . . . $ 6
> Fixed overhead costs: 2 hours at $5. . . . .   <u>10</u>
> $16

During May, 170,000 units were scheduled for production; however, only 160,000 units were actually produced. The following information relates to May's production:
a. Actual direct labour cost incurred was $1,288,000 for 330,000 actual hours of work.
b. Actual overhead costs incurred totalled $2,756,000 ($1,036,000 variable and $1,720,000 fixed).
c. All inventories are carried at standard cost.

Required:
1. Compute the variable overhead variances for May.
2. Compute the fixed overhead variances for May.
3. Explain the reasons for the variable overhead efficiency and production volume variances.

(Adapted © CGA-Canada)

CHECK FIGURE
(1) Variable overhead
spending variance
$46,000 U

PROBLEM 9–13   Flexible Budget Preparation (CC1, 3, 5, 6, 7)
K9 Groomers is in the dog grooming business. Its costs of operation are described by the following formulas:

> Grooming supplies (variable) . . . . . .   y = $0 + $4.00X
> Direct labour (variable) . . . .   y = $0 + $12.00X
> Overhead (mixed) . . . .   y = $8,000 + $1.00X

CHECK FIGURE
(1) Total cost for 550
DLHs = $17,350

Dani, the owner, has determined that direct labour-hours is the cost driver for all three cost categories. The groomers at K9 normally work a total of 650 direct labour-hours during each month. Each grooming job normally takes a groomer 1¼ hours. K9 charges its customers at the rate of $35 per hour.

Required:
1. Prepare a flexible budget for activity levels of 550, 600, and 700 direct labour-hours.
2. Explain why the variances calculated between actual and a flexible budget are more informative than the variances calculated between actual and a fixed budget.
3. Calculate the total cost per direct labour-hour at each of the activity levels specified in part (1).

(Adapted © CGA-Canada)

PROBLEM 9–14   Applying Overhead; Overhead Variances (CC5, 6, 11, 12)

KCI, Inc. uses a traditional standard costing system and variance analysis for the usual manufacturing categories—direct materials, direct labour, variable overhead, and fixed overhead. Both variable and fixed overhead are applied on the basis of direct labour-hours. At the normal level of 80,000 DLHs for March, budgeted direct manufacturing labour is $1,600,000, budgeted variable manufacturing overhead is $960,000, and budgeted fixed manufacturing overhead is $1,280,000.

The following actual results are reported for March:

Direct manufacturing labour costs incurred	$1,045,500
Total variable manufacturing overhead variance.	20,700 U
Variable manufacturing overhead efficiency variance.	36,000 U
Fixed manufacturing overhead incurred	1,194,920
Fixed manufacturing budget (or spending) variance.	85,080 F

In February, a labour dispute caused a major slowdown in production, resulting in an unfavourable direct labour efficiency variance. There was no direct labour rate variance. The labour dispute continued into March. Some workers quit in March. Their replacements had to be paid at higher rates that then had to be extended to all workers. The actual average wage rate in March exceeded the standard average wage rate by $0.50 per hour.

Required:
Compute the following for March:
1. Variable manufacturing overhead spending variance.
2. Total number of actual direct manufacturing labour-hours used.
3. Total number of standard direct manufacturing labour-hours allowed for the units produced.
4. Production volume variance.

(Adapted © CGA-Canada)

PROBLEM 9–15   Overall Variance Computation (CC5, 6)

Winter Inc., a manufacturing company, has the following standard costs for one unit of production:

Direct materials	(5 kg at $6.00)	$ 30
Direct labour	(3 hr at $15.00)	45
Factory overhead:		
Variable	(3 DLHs at $6.00)	18
Fixed	(3 DLHs at $12.00)	36
Total standard cost		$129

Actual results for the last quarter were as follows:

Production volume.		6,000 units
Direct materials	(36,000 kg at $6.30)	$226,800
Direct labour	(17,800 hr at $15.60)	277,680
Factory overhead:		
Variable		102,000
Fixed		186,000

Required:
Calculate the following for the last quarter for Winter Inc.:
1. Direct materials—price, efficiency and total variances.
2. Direct labour—rate, efficiency and total variances.
3. Variable overhead—spending, efficiency and total variances.

(Adapted © CGA-Canada)

Building Your Skills

ANALYTICAL THINKING   (CC4, 5, 6, 9, 11, 12)

A company that uses a standard cost system has provided the following data. The company's flexible budget for manufacturing overhead is based on standard machine-hours.

1.	Denominator activity in hours	?
2.	Standard hours allowed for units produced	32,000
3.	Actual hours worked................................	30,000
4.	Flexible budget variable overhead per machine-hour.......	$?
5.	Flexible budget fixed overhead (total)	?
6.	Actual variable overhead cost incurred	54,000
7.	Actual fixed overhead cost incurred...................	209,400
8.	Variable overhead cost applied to production*...........	?
9.	Fixed overhead cost applied to production*..............	192,000
10.	Variable overhead spending variance	?
11.	Variable overhead efficiency variance	3,500 F
12.	Fixed overhead budget variance.......................	?
13.	Fixed overhead volume variance	18,000 U
14.	Variable portion of the predetermined overhead rate.......	?
15.	Fixed portion of the predetermined overhead rate	?
16.	Under-applied (or over-applied) overhead	?

*Based on standard hours allowed for units produced.

Required:

Compute the unknown amounts. (Hint: One way to proceed would be to use the format for variance analysis found in Exhibit 8–6 for variable overhead and in Exhibit 9–8 for fixed overhead.)

COMMUNICATING IN PRACTICE   (CC1, 2, 3)

Use an online yellow pages directory, such as www.superpages.ca, or www.411.ca, to find a manufacturer in your area that has a website. Make an appointment with the controller or chief financial officer of the company. Before your meeting, find out as much as you can about the organization's operations from its website.

Required:

After asking the following questions, write a brief memorandum to your instructor that summarizes the information obtained from the company's website and addresses what you found out during your interview.

1. Are actual overhead costs compared with a static budget, a flexible budget, or something else?
2. Does the organization distinguish between variable and fixed overhead costs in its performance reports?
3. What are the consequences of unfavourable variances? Of favourable variances?

ETHICS CHALLENGE   (CC3)

Tom Kemper is the controller of the Brandon manufacturing facility of Kingston Enterprises, Incorporated. Among the many reports that must be filed with corporate headquarters is the annual overhead performance report. The report covers an entire fiscal year, which ends on December 31, and is due at corporate headquarters shortly after the beginning of the New Year. Kemper does not like putting work off to the last minute, and so just before Christmas he put together a preliminary draft of the overhead performance report. Some adjustments would be required for transactions that occur between Christmas and New Year's Day, but there are generally very few of these. A copy of the preliminary draft report, which Kemper completed on December 21, follows:

BRANDON MANUFACTURING FACILITY
Overhead Performance Report
December 21 Preliminary Draft

Budgeted machine-hours   200,000
Actual machine-hours   180,000

	Cost Formula (per machine-hour)	Actual Costs 180,000 Machine-Hours	Budget Based on 180,000 Machine-Hours	Spending or Budget Variance
Variable overhead costs:				
Power..................	$0.10	$ 19,750	$ 18,000	$ 1,750 U
Supplies...............	0.25	47,000	45,000	2,000 U
Abrasives.............	0.30	58,000	54,000	4,000 U
Total variable overhead cost .	$0.65	124,750	117,000	7,750 U
Fixed overhead costs:				
Amortization		345,000	332,000	13,000 U
Supervisory salaries......		273,000	275,000	2,000 F
Insurance..............		37,000	37,000	—
Industrial engineering		189,000	210,000	21,000 F
Factory building lease		60,000	60,000	—
Total fixed overhead cost....		904,000	914,000	10,000 F
Total overhead cost		$1,028,750	$1,031,000	$ 2,250 F

Melissa Ilianovitch, the general manager at the Brandon facility, asked to see a copy of the preliminary draft report at 4:45 p.m. on December 23. Kemper carried a copy of the report to her office where the following discussion took place:

Ilianovitch: Ouch! Almost all of the variances on the report are unfavourable. The only thing that looks good at all are the favourable variances for supervisory salaries and for industrial engineering. How did we have an unfavourable variance for amortization?

Kemper: Do you remember that milling machine that broke down because the wrong lubricant was used by the machine operator?

Ilianovitch: Only vaguely.

Kemper: It turned out we couldn't fix it. We had to scrap the machine and buy a new one.

Ilianovitch: This report doesn't look good. I was raked over the coals last year when we had just a few unfavourable variances.

Kemper: I'm afraid the final report is going to look even worse.

Ilianovitch: Oh?

Kemper: The line item for industrial engineering on the report is for work we hired Ferguson Engineering to do for us on a contract basis. The original contract was for $210,000, but we asked them to do some additional work that was not in the contract. Under the terms of the contract, we have to reimburse Ferguson Engineering for the costs of the additional work. The $189,000 in actual costs that appear on the preliminary draft report reflects only their billings up through December 21. The last bill they had sent us was on November 28, and they completed the project just last week. Yesterday, I got a call from Laura Sunder over at Ferguson and she said they would be sending us a final bill for the project before the end of the year. The total bill, including the reimbursements for the additional work, is going to be . . .

Ilianovitch: I am not sure I want to hear this.

Kemper: $225,000.

Ilianovitch: Ouch! Ouch! Ouch!

Kemper: The additional work we asked them to do added $15,000 to the cost of the project.

Ilianovitch: No way can I turn in a performance report with an overall unfavourable variance! They'll kill me at corporate headquarters. Call up Laura at Ferguson and ask her not to send the bill until after the first of the year. We have to have that $21,000 favourable variance for industrial engineering on the performance report.

Required:
What should Tom Kemper do? Explain.

TEAMWORK IN ACTION (C1, 2, 3, 4, 9)

Boyne University offers an extensive continuing education program in many cities throughout the state. For the convenience of its faculty and administrative staff and to save costs, the university employs a supervisor to operate a motor pool. The motor pool operated with 20 vehicles until February, when an additional automobile was acquired. The motor pool furnishes gasoline, oil, and other supplies for its automobiles. A mechanic does routine maintenance and minor repairs. Major repairs are done at a nearby commercial garage.

Each year, the supervisor prepares an operating budget that informs the university administration of the funds needed for operating the motor pool. Amortization (straight line) on the automobiles is recorded in the budget in order to determine the cost per kilometre of operating the vehicles.

The following performance report was prepared by a budget analyst who was recently hired by the university. It presents the operating budget for the current year, which was approved by the university. The performance report also shows actual operating costs for March of the current year compared with one-twelfth of the annual operating budget.

UNIVERSITY MOTOR POOL Performance Report for March				
	Annual Operating Budget	Monthly Budget*	March Actual	(Over) Under Budget
Gasoline	$ 70,000	$ 5,833	$ 6,633	$(800)
Oil, minor repairs, parts	3,000	250	380	(130)
Outside repairs	2,700	225	50	175
Insurance.................	6,000	500	525	(25)
Salaries and benefits	30,000	2,500	2,500	—
Amortization of vehicles.....	26,400	2,200	2,310	(110)
Total costs	$138,100	$11,508	$12,398	$(890)
Total kilometres	1,000,000	83,333	102,000	
Cost per kilometre..........	$0.1381	$0.1381	$0.1215	
Number of automobiles in use .	20	20	21	

*Annual operating budget ÷ 12 months.

The annual operating budget was constructed based on the following assumptions:

a. 20 automobiles in the motor pool.
b. 50,000 kilometres driven per year per automobile.
c. 10 kilometres per litre per automobile.
d. $0.70 per litre of gasoline.
e. $0.003 cost per kilometre for oil, minor repairs, and parts.
f. $135 cost per automobile per year for outside repairs.
g. $300 cost per automobile per year for insurance.

The supervisor of the motor pool is unhappy with the monthly performance report comparing budget and actual costs for March, claiming it presents an unfair picture of performance.

Required:

1. Using a flexible budgeting approach, prepare a new performance report for March showing budgeted costs, actual costs, and variances. All team members should understand how the revised performance report was prepared.
2. The team should discuss and then write up brief answers to the questions listed below. All team members should agree with and understand the answers.
   a. What are the deficiencies in the performance report that was prepared by the budget analyst?
   b. How does the revised performance report, which was prepared using a flexible budget approach, overcome these deficiencies?

(CMA adapted)

Don't forget to visit the Online Learning Centre for self-study quizzes, practice exams, and more! Visit www.mcgrawhill.ca/olc/brewer.

CHAPTER *Ten*

Organizational Structure and Performance Measurement

CHAPTER COMPETENCIES

After studying Chapter 10, you should be able to demonstrate the following competencies:

Competency	Know	Apply
Understand decentralization and reporting in a decentralized organization.		
CC1 Explain the role, strengths, and weaknesses of decentralization in organizations.	○	
CC2 Explain cost, revenue, profit, and investment centres.	○	
CC3 Explain segmented reporting and prepare a segmented performance report.	○	○
Explain key financial performance metrics reported in a decentralized organization.		
CC4 Define and compute the return on investment (ROI) measure.	○	○
CC5 Explain how changes in sales, expenses, and operating assets can influence the ROI.	○	
CC6 Define and compute the residual income (RI) measure.	○	○
CC7 Explain the economic value added (EVA) measure and compare it with residual income.	○	
CC8 Explain the concept of transfer pricing.	○	
Understand multi-dimensional performance reporting.		
CC9 Explain the concept of multi-dimensional performance reporting.	○	
CC10 Describe the balanced scorecard, outlining its strengths and weaknesses.	○	

10

DECISION FEATURE
Decentralization Gone Wrong

Great Canadian Bagel was once one of the fastest growing franchises in Canada. At the pinnacle of the franchise's success, there were more than 150 locations across Canada. In the summer of 2003, there were just 95 stores left, leaving many wondering what went wrong.

Great Canadian Bagel was founded in 1993. By 1996, the chain was named Entrepreneur of the Year by a Canadian hospitality and restaurant magazine, and another US trade magazine dubbed 1996 the "Year of the Bagel."

Each store was considered an independent investment centre because it was the responsibility of the franchise owner to control revenues and costs and budget for future investments. However, decision making was not fully decentralized; each store still relied on head office for numerous decisions, such as national marketing, new store locations, and the choice of suppliers. Indeed, strategy formulation was centralized, but not implementation. However, this level of independence did not work well when selling to large national chains, such as Loblaws and Costco; there was wide variation in quality and service among the franchises. Due to the inconsistency, Loblaws eventually terminated all deals with the company which cost some stores dearly.

"The people at head office now are going in the right direction," says one store owner. "But there's a lot of mistrust between the franchisees and the company." Former franchise owners still get together to lick their wounds, trade horror stories, and swap tales about the latest shutdowns.

Source: John Gray, "Sour Dough," *Canadian Business*, June 23, 2003, pp. 36–41. Reprinted with permission from *Canadian Business*.

A Look Back

We first discussed the budgeting process in Chapter 7. We then introduced management control and performance measures in Chapter 8 with a discussion of standard costs and variance analysis. Chapter 9 extended that discussion to overhead costs.

A Look at This Chapter

Chapter 10 continues our coverage of performance measurement by introducing return on investment and residual income measures to motivate managers and monitor progress toward achieving the company's goals.

A Look Ahead

In the next section, we begin our coverage of decision making and the management accounting tools available for that purpose. Chapter 11 describes the basics of cost-volume-profit (CVP) analysis, an essential tool for decision making.

Performance management is an important task for managers as it helps them in ensuring that the organization's overall objectives are met (or even exceeded). The previous two chapters introduced variance analysis, which is one tool that can be used by managers for the purposes of performance management. In a broader context, performance management includes specifying how individual units within an organization will be evaluated, what measures will be used to evaluate these units, and what actions will be taken to ensure continuous progress. We will discuss these issues in this chapter.

Decentralization in Organizations

⬤ **KNOW**

CC1: Explain the role, strengths, and weaknesses of decentralization in organizations.

In small organizations, a single manager or a small management team can usually make most decisions, including strategic and day-to-day operating decisions (this is known as a **centralized organization**). However, as organizations grow larger, it often becomes impossible for the top manager (or management team) to make decisions regarding all aspects of business. For example, it would be impossible for the top management team of the Real Canadian Superstore to make hiring decisions for a store in British Columbia or Saskatchewan. Such decisions are best left to individual store managers who know their personnel needs best. Top management would, however, likely be involved in establishing hiring policies and establishing the overall strategic direction for the retailer.

In the preceding example, the Superstore is considered a **decentralized organization,** which is one where decision making is not confined to a few top executives, but rather is spread throughout the organization, with managers at various levels making decisions that pertain to their area of responsibility. Most organizations fall between the two extremes of being fully decentralized or fully centralized. While certain functions/decisions can be carried out efficiently in a centralized setting, others work better in a decentralized setting. Organizational size, in terms of number of employees, is an important determinant of whether an organization should or should not be decentralized.

The decision to decentralize results in an organization being classified into different *segments*. For example, in a university, the first line of segmentation would be the different colleges or faculties (such as Business, Nursing, Education, and so on), and the second line of segmentation may be the individual departments within each college (e.g., Accounting, Marketing, and so on within the School of Business). In business organizations, individual segments may represent the different divisions, product lines, market territories, or even individual departments (e.g., Marketing, Purchasing, Accounting, Legal, Production, and so on).

It is important to remember that individual segments within an organization are not usually independent of one another. They must often work closely to achieve the objectives of the organization. Consequently, coordination and communication among the individual segments are important and sometimes challenging issues for top management.

Advantages and Disadvantages of Decentralization

Decentralization has many benefits, including:

- Top management is relieved of much day-to-day problem solving and is left free to concentrate on strategy, higher-level decision making, and coordinating activities.
- Decentralization provides lower-level managers with vital experience in making decisions. Without such experience, they would be ill-prepared to make decisions when they are promoted to higher-level positions.

- Added responsibility and decision-making authority often result in increased job satisfaction. It makes the job more interesting and provides greater incentives for people to put out their best efforts.
- Lower-level managers generally have more detailed and up-to-date information about conditions in their own area of responsibility than top managers. Therefore, the decisions of lower-level managers are often based on better information.
- It is difficult to evaluate a manager's performance if the manager is not given much latitude in what he or she can do.

Decentralization has four major disadvantages:

- Lower-level managers may make decisions without fully understanding the "big picture." While top-level managers typically have less detailed information about operations than the lower-level managers, they usually have more information about the company as a whole and may have a better understanding of the company's strategy.
- In a truly decentralized organization, there may be a lack of coordination among autonomous managers. This problem can be reduced by clearly defining the company's strategy and communicating it effectively throughout the organization.
- Lower-level managers may have objectives that are different from the objectives of the entire organization. For example, some managers may be more interested in increasing the sizes of their departments than in increasing the profits of the company.[1] To some degree, this problem can be overcome by designing performance evaluation systems that motivate managers to make decisions that are in the company's best interests of the company.
- In a strongly decentralized organization, it may be more difficult to effectively spread innovative ideas. Someone in one part of the organization may have a terrific idea that would benefit other parts of the organization, but without strong central direction the idea may not be shared with, and adopted by, other parts of the organization.

A Friend

DECISION MAKER

One of your friends from college started a business that designs Web sites, which has become a wildly successful startup. On the way to meet your friend for lunch, you think how great it would be to be your own boss—to be able to come and go as you please. At lunch, you hardly recognize her. She is tired and stressed, complains a lot about the hours she has been putting in to supervise various projects, and is puzzled by the high turnover that she has experienced at the managerial level. After all, as she notes, she keeps her hand in all of the major projects. What advice do you have for her?

Responsibility Centres

From a performance management perspective, there are two key issues relating to decentralization: (1) clarifying the decentralized segment manager's scope of responsibilities,

 KNOW

CC2: Explain cost, revenue, profit, and investment centres.

---

[1]There is a similar problem with top-level managers as well. The shareholders of the company have, in effect, decentralized by delegating their decision-making authority to the top managers. Unfortunately, top managers may abuse that trust by spending too much company money on palatial offices, rewarding themselves and their friends too generously, and so on. The issue of how to ensure that top managers act in the best interests of the owners of the company continues to puzzle experts. To a large extent, the owners rely on performance evaluation using return on investment and residual income measures, as discussed later in the chapter, and on bonuses and stock options. The stock market is also an important disciplining mechanism. If top managers squander the company's resources, the price of the company's shares will almost surely fall—resulting in a loss of prestige, bonuses, and possibly jobs.

and (2) deciding how the manager's performance will be evaluated. In order to resolve these issues, top management categorizes the individual segments into **responsibility centres,** which are segments of an organization whose manager is responsible and accountable for costs, revenues, profits, or investments. We will now discuss the four types of responsibility centres.

COST CENTRE   A **cost centre** is an organizational unit (or segment) whose manager is responsible for costs but not revenues, profits, or investments. Service departments, such as accounting, finance, general administration, human resources, and so on are usually classified as cost centres. In addition, production departments (or manufacturing facilities) may also be considered as cost centres. Managers of cost centres are expected to minimize costs, while ensuring that the outputs they provide to other segments within the organization meet the needs of these "consumer" segments (e.g., quality). Given the scope of responsibility of cost centre managers, standard cost information and annual budgets, discussed in the previous chapters, can be used as the base against which they can be measured. Moreover, the performance reports and variance reports previously explained will likely be useful in evaluating the periodic performance of cost centre managers. In a nutshell, any report that provides information on how well costs have been managed will provide useful information.

REVENUE CENTRE   A **revenue centre** is an organizational unit (or segment) whose manager is responsible for meeting revenue targets and is considered to have the authority to strongly influence (if not control) revenues. A typical example of a revenue centre is a sales office. Given the scope of a revenue centre manager's responsibility, a report detailing the revenue centre's revenue-related performance would be most useful. For example, information on revenue/sales variances would be useful. (Note: We do not discuss sales variances in this text.)

PROFIT CENTRE   In contrast to a cost or revenue centre, a **profit centre** is an organizational unit (or segment) whose manager is responsible for the unit's profitability and has the authority to strongly influence both costs and revenues. This means the manager does not need top management's approval for decisions affecting costs, revenues, or both. Managers of individual stores of a major retail chain would usually be responsible for profits and would likely be evaluated on the basis of profitability. Consequently, a report such as the income statement would be useful for the purposes of management control.

However, a key question might be how income is measured. A common measure of income is the net income presented in annual reports of organizations (e.g., see Exhibit 2–5)—also called *absorption costing income* as introduced in Chapter 4. Another measure of income is the *gross margin*, which is computed as sales revenues less the cost of goods sold. A third measure of income is the *contribution margin*, which is computed as sales revenues less variable costs.[2] A final measure of income is the *segment margin*, which is computed as contribution margin less the *directly traceable* fixed expenses for an individual segment. We will discuss segment margin a little later in this chapter.

INVESTMENT CENTRE   An **investment centre** is similar to a profit centre. In addition to profitability, the manager of an investment centre is also responsible for investing in operating assets. An individual division of a large corporation, such as Honeywell International Inc., would have responsibility for initiating investment proposals to fund research and development, modernize production equipment, and for improvement in other areas of the division. Once the proposal is approved, it is the investment centre manager's responsibility to ensure that the assets are utilized in such a manner that they provide the targeted returns. Investment centre managers are usually evaluated using such measures as return on investment or residual income.

---

[2]Refer to Chapter 3.

Borden Ladner Gervais (BLG) proves just how beneficial a decentralized management style can be. In March 2000, five regional law firms—Ladner Downs in Vancouver, Howard & Mackie in Calgary, Borden & Elliot in Toronto, Scott & Aylen in Ottawa, and McMaster Gervais in Montreal—merged to become a national firm, BLG.

Prior to the merger, the senior partners examined possibilities for a postmerger management structure. They wanted a system that would allow all five firms to maintain their unique culture while reaping the benefits of a national firm. It was decided that all day-to-day decisions would be controlled by the individual firms, while corporate/strategic decisions would be made by a national council. BLG's national council comprises members from all five firms and gives each firm an equal voice, despite differences in firm size. This new decentralized structure has worked wonders. In the aftermath of the merger, the new company boasts increased profits and a larger customer base.

Source: John Gray, "The Brothers in Law," *Canadian Business.* September 29, 2003, pp. 75–76.

An Example of Responsibility Centres

A partial organization chart for Universal Foods Corporation, a company in the snack food and beverage industry, appears in Exhibit 10–1. This partial organization chart indicates how the various business segments of the company are classified in terms of responsibility. Notice that the cost centres are the departments and work centres that do not generate significant revenues by themselves. These are staff departments, such as finance, legal, and human resources, and operating units, such as the bottling plant, warehouse, and beverage distribution centre. The profit centres are business segments that generate revenues and include the beverage, salty snacks, and confections product segments. The vice-president of operations oversees allocation of investment funds across the product segments and is responsible for revenues and costs, and thus is treated as an investment centre. Finally, corporate headquarters is an investment centre, since it is responsible for all revenues, costs, and investments.

Traceable and Common Fixed Costs

Performance reports are often compiled for a part of the organization, or segment, such as an investment centre. In such segment reports, a distinction should be drawn between *traceable fixed costs* and *common fixed costs*. A **traceable fixed cost** of a segment is a fixed cost that is incurred because of the existence of the segment and if the segment were eliminated, the fixed cost would disappear. Examples of traceable fixed costs include the following:

- The salary of the Phosphate business manager at IMC Global is a traceable fixed cost of the Phosphate business segment of IMC Global.
- The maintenance cost for the building in which Global Express XRS business jets are assembled is a traceable fixed cost of the aerospace segment of Bombardier.
- The liability insurance at Disney World is a traceable fixed cost of the Disney World business segment of the Disney Corporation.

A **common fixed cost** is a fixed cost that supports the operations of more than one segment, but is not traceable in whole or in part to any one segment. Even if the segment were entirely eliminated, there would be no change in a common fixed cost. Examples of common fixed costs include the following:

- The salary of the CEO of Nissan Canada is a common fixed cost of the various divisions of Nissan Canada.

Exhibit 10–1
Business Segments Classified as Cost, Profit, and Investment Centres

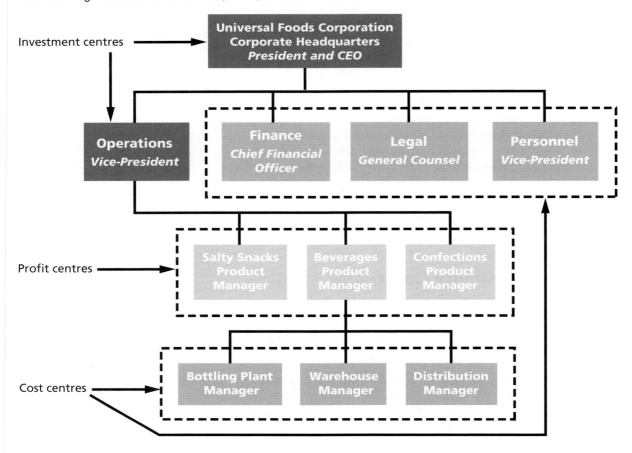

- The cost of the checkout equipment at a Safeway or Extra Foods grocery store is a common fixed cost of the various department within the store, such as groceries, produce, and bakery.
- The cost of the clinic's receptionist's salary is shared by a number of doctors and is a common fixed cost of the clinic. The cost is traceable to the clinic, but not to any one of the doctors.

Segmented Reporting

The performance of decentralized segments is often reported using segment reports. A **segment** is an individual unit within an organization whose manager has the responsibility to carry out its activities. A company's operations can be segmented in many ways. For example, Universal Foods can be segmented by its individual plants, geographic sales territory, or by its product lines. Exhibit 10–2 illustrates the different forms of segmenting a company.

Individual segment managers are responsible for their segments and are interested in knowing the performance of their segment. Similarly, senior management responsible for all three segments will be interested in the performance of the individual segments, as well as the operations in total. Exhibit 10–3A presents a report containing the performance of the three product segments, as well as the total of the three. The exhibit reports the sales revenues, variable expenses, and directly traceable expenses for each of the three segments and the combined total.

Exhibit 10–2
Segmenting a Company

Universal Foods Corporation

Corporate Headquarters

Halifax Plant   Edmonton Plant

Brandon Plant   Hamilton Plant

Segmenting by Plant

Segmenting by Geographic Territory

Beverages   Confections

Salty snacks

Segmenting by Product Line

According to the exhibit, the overall segment margin percentage of the company is just under 21% (that is, segment margin divided by sales). Although the Beverages segment reports the highest margin in terms of dollars ($500,000), the Confections segment provides a higher margin in terms of percentage (30%). The Salty Snacks segment generates the lowest margin both in terms of dollars and percentage.

Note, however, that the overall segment margin of $1.22 million is *not* the profit generated by the company. This is because the company incurs additional expenses of $900,000, which are not directly traceable to either of the three product segments—these are called *common expenses*. The net income of the company is $320,000.

One question we should ask is whether the common fixed expenses must be allocated among the individual segments. The argument in favour of allocating is that by doing so management will get a better picture of the proportion of the company's income generated by each segment. The argument against is that any allocation will be at best arbitrary and will unfairly penalize individual segment managers. For instance, assume that senior management decides to allocate common fixed expenses equally among the three segments. As shown in Exhibit 10–3B, this results in the Salty Snacks segment showing a loss of $30,000, which can result in negative consequences for the segment. A proper understanding of the alternative measures of income, and careful selection of the income measure to be used for the purposes of performance evaluation, are important in ensuring that management does not take undesirable actions.

Exhibit 10–3A
Profit Centre Segmented Report: Universal Foods Corporation

	Profit Centres			
	Salty Snacks	Beverages	Confections	Total Company
Sales	$2,320,000	$2,000,000	$1,500,000	$5,820,000
Less: Variable expenses:				
Direct materials.............	400,000	360,000	240,000	1,000,000
Direct labour...............	250,000	200,000	140,000	590,000
Manufacturing overhead......	150,000	140,000	120,000	410,000
Selling and other...........	250,000	200,000	150,000	600,000
Total variable expenses......	$1,050,000	$ 900,000	$ 650,000	$2,600,000
Contribution margin	$1,270,000	$1,100,000	$ 850,000	$3,220,000
Less: Traceable fixed expenses:				
Salaries and benefits	400,000	210,000	130,000	740,000
Office equipment............	190,000	120,000	80,000	390,000
Building rent...............	120,000	80,000	50,000	250,000
Selling and administrative.....	160,000	120,000	90,000	370,000
Other	130,000	70,000	50,000	250,000
Total fixed expenses........	$1,000,000	$ 600,000	$ 400,000	$2,000,000
Segment Margin	$ 270,000	$ 500,000	$ 450,000	$1,220,000
Less: Common fixed expenses:				
Senior management salaries ...				$500,000
Corporate office building				140,000
Legal and accounting				210,000
Other....................				50,000
Total common fixed expenses				900,000
Net income				$ 320,000
Segment margin %	11.64%	25.00%	30.00%	20.96%

Exhibit 10–3B
Revised Profit Centre Segmented Report: Universal Foods Corporation

	Profit Centres			
	Salty Snacks	Beverages	Confections	Total Company
Segment margin	$ 270,000	$500,000	$450,000	$1,220,000
Less: Common fixed expenses				
Allocated portion	300,000	300,000	300,000	900,000
Net income	$(30,000)	$200,000	$150,000	$ 320,000

In general, traceable costs should be assigned to segments, but common fixed costs should not be assigned to segments—to do so would overstate the costs that are actually caused by the segments and that could be avoided by eliminating the segments.

Decentralized Operations at the Bank

The Royal Bank Financial Group (RBFG) started reorganizing its management team and business structure in 1995 in an attempt to decentralize its operations. The flat, market-focused organization enabled each business unit manager to be held accountable for his own performance. When valuing loans and deposits and distributing costs of shared services, transfer pricing was used to ensure that the company still controlled its centralized processes (corporate services are centralized) and gained economies of scale. Transfer pricing is based on the principles of activity-based costing.

The RBFG established priorities, allocated resources, and measured performance on the basis of a "financial standard." Being successful in the market entails understanding the interests of many stakeholders—customers, employees, and shareholders. For example, the company used shareholder value growth as the governing objective, and the "value-added" metric for making strategic decisions, acquisitions, and so on.

Source: Paul A Sharman and John Shaw, "Royal Bank of Canada—Ahead of the Rest: Deploying Value-Based Management," *Focus Magazine* Web site: http://www.focusmag.com/back_issues/issue_05/pages/royalbank.htm, 2003. Adapted with permission from Focused Management, Inc.

Measuring Investment Centre Performance

We discussed the performance measurement of cost, revenue, and profit centres; let us now turn to the measurement of investment centre performance. In a truly decentralized organization, individual segments are usually classified as investment centres when they are run like independent businesses. In other words, they are responsible for all aspects of running the segment, including investing in assets.

Competition between investment centres is particularly keen for investment funds. How do top managers in corporate headquarters go about deciding who gets new investment funds as they become available, and how do these managers decide which investment centres are most profitably using the funds that have already been entrusted to their care? One of the most popular ways of making these judgments is to measure the rate of return that investment centre managers are able to generate on their assets. This rate of return is called the *return on investment*.

The Return on Investment (ROI) Formula

The **return on investment (ROI)** is defined as net operating income divided by average operating assets:

$$\text{ROI} = \frac{\text{Net operating income}}{\text{Average operating assets}}$$

> ○ KNOW   ○ APPLY
>
> CC4: Define and compute the return on investment (ROI) measure.

There are some issues about how to measure net operating income and average operating assets, but this formula seems clear enough. The higher the ROI of a business segment, the greater the profit generated per dollar invested in the segment's operating assets.

Net Operating Income and Operating Assets Defined

Notice that *net operating income,* rather than net income, is used in the ROI formula. **Net operating income** is income before interest and taxes and is sometimes referred to as *EBIT* (*earnings before interest and taxes*). The reason for using net operating income in the formula is that the income figure used should be consistent with the base to which it is applied. Note that the base (i.e., denominator) consists of *operating assets*. Thus, to be consistent we use net operating income in the numerator.

Operating assets include cash, accounts receivable, inventory, plant and equipment, and all other assets held for productive use in the organization. Examples of assets that would not be included in the operating assets category, (i.e., examples of nonoperating assets) would include land held for future use, an investment in another company, or a factory building rented to someone else. The operating assets base used in the formula is typically computed as the average of the operating assets between the beginning and the end of the year.

Plant and Equipment: Net Book Value or Gross Cost?

A major issue in ROI computations is the dollar amount of plant and equipment that should be included in the operating assets base. To illustrate the problem involved, assume that a company reports the following amounts for plant and equipment on its balance sheet:

Plant and equipment	$3,000,000
Less: Accumulated amortization	900,000
Net book value.	$2,100,000

What dollar amount of plant and equipment should the company include with its operating assets in computing ROI? One widely used approach is to include only the plant and equipment's *net book value*—that is, the plant's original cost less accumulated amortization ($2,100,000 in the preceding example). A second approach is to ignore amortization, including the plant's entire *gross cost* in the operating assets base ($3,000,000 in the example). Both these approaches are used in actual practice, even though they will obviously yield very different operating asset and ROI figures.

The following arguments can be raised for using net book value to measure operating assets and for using gross cost to measure operating assets in ROI computations:

Arguments for Using Net Book Value to Measure Operating Assets in ROI Computations:

- The net book value method is consistent with how plant and equipment are reported on the balance sheet (i.e., cost less accumulated amortization to date).
- The net book value method is consistent with the computation of operating income, which includes amortization as an operating expense.

Arguments for Using Gross Cost to Measure Operating Assets in ROI Computations:

- The gross cost method eliminates both the age of equipment and the method of amortization as factors in ROI computations. (Under the net book value method, ROI will tend to increase over time as net book value declines due to amortization.)
- The gross cost method does not discourage replacement of old, worn-out equipment. (Under the net book value method, replacing fully amortized equipment with new equipment can have a dramatic, adverse effect on ROI.)

Managers generally view consistency as the most important of the considerations above. As a result, a majority of companies use the net book value approach in ROI computations. *In this text, we will also use the net book value approach unless a specific exercise or problem directs otherwise.*

Controlling the Rate of Return

When we first defined the return on investment, we used the following formula:

$$\text{ROI} = \frac{\text{Net operating income}}{\text{Average operating assets}}$$

KNOW

CC5: Explain how changes in sales, expenses, and operating assets can influence the ROI.

We can modify this formula slightly by introducing sales as follows:

$$\text{ROI} = \frac{\text{Net operating income}}{\text{Sales}} \times \frac{\text{Sales}}{\text{Average operating assets}}$$

The first term on the right-hand side of the equation is the *margin*, which is defined as follows:

$$\text{Margin} = \frac{\text{Net operating income}}{\text{Sales}}$$

The **margin** is a measure of management's ability to control operating expenses in relation to sales. The lower the operating expenses per dollar of sales, the higher the margin earned. This, in itself, can be a useful measure even for a profit centre manager.

The second term on the right-hand side of the preceding equation is *turnover*, which is defined as follows:

$$\text{Turnover} = \frac{\text{Sales}}{\text{Average operating assets}}$$

Turnover is a measure of the sales that are generated for each dollar invested in operating assets.

The following alternative form of the ROI formula, which we will use most frequently, combines margin and turnover:

$$\text{ROI} = \text{Margin} \times \text{Turnover}$$

Which formula for ROI should be used—the original one stated in terms of net operating income and average operating assets or this one stated in terms of margin and turnover? Either can be used—they will always give the same answer. However, the margin and turnover formulation provides some additional insights.

Some managers tend to focus too much on margin and ignore turnover. To some degree at least, the margin can be a valuable indicator of a manager's performance. Standing alone, however, it overlooks one crucial area of a manager's responsibility—the investment in operating assets. Excessive funds tied up in operating assets, which depresses turnover, can be just as much of a drag on profitability as excessive operating expenses, which depress margin. One of the advantages of ROI as a performance measure is that it forces the manager to control the investment in operating assets, as well as to control expenses and the margin.

Du Pont pioneered the ROI concept and recognized the importance of looking at both margin and turnover in assessing the performance of a manager. The ROI formula is now widely used as the key measure of the performance of an investment centre. The ROI formula blends together many aspects of the manager's responsibilities into a single figure that can be compared with the returns of competing investment centres, with the returns of other firms in the industry, and with the past returns of the investment centre itself.

Du Pont also developed the diagram that appears in Exhibit 10–4. This exhibit helps managers understand how they can control ROI. An investment centre manager can increase ROI in basically three ways:

- Increase sales.
- Reduce expenses.
- Reduce assets.

Exhibit 10-4

Elements of Return on Investment

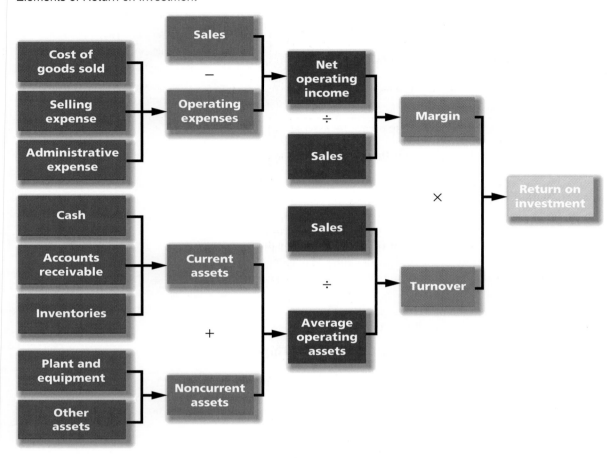

To illustrate how the rate of return can be improved by each of these three actions, consider how the manager of the Monthaven Burger Grill is evaluated. Burger Grill is a small chain of upscale casual restaurants that has been rapidly adding outlets via franchising. The Monthaven franchise is owned by a group of local surgeons who have little time to devote to management and little expertise in business matters. Therefore, they delegate operating decisions—including decisions concerning investment in operating assets, such as inventories—to a professional manager they have hired. The manager is evaluated largely on the basis of the ROI the franchise generates.

The following data represent the results of operations for the most recent month:

Net operating income.	$10,000
Sales.	100,000
Average operating assets	50,000

The rate of return generated by the Monthaven Burger Grill investment centre is as follows:

$$\text{ROI} = \text{Margin} \times \text{Turnover}$$

$$= \frac{\text{Net operating income}}{\text{Sales}} \times \frac{\text{Sales}}{\text{Average operating assets}}$$

$$= \frac{\$10,000}{\$100,000} \times \frac{\$100,000}{50,000}$$

$$= 10\% \times 2 = 20\%$$

As stated previously, to improve the ROI figure, the manager can (1) increase sales, (2) reduce expenses, or (3) reduce the operating assets.

APPROACH 1: INCREASE SALES Assume that the manager of the Monthaven Burger Grill is able to increase sales from $100,000 to $110,000. Given that some expenses are fixed, the increase in sales is likely to result in an increase in net operating income. Assume that the net operating income increases to $12,000. Assume that the operating assets remain constant. Then the new ROI would be:

$$\text{ROI} = \frac{\$12,000}{\$110,000} \times \frac{\$110,000}{\$50,000}$$

$$10.91\% \quad \times \quad 2.2 \quad = 24\% \text{ (as compared with 20\% above)}$$

However, an increase in sales may be due to additional marketing efforts (which may be costly). This may result in the income decreasing or staying the same. In such situations, the ROI will not increase. This is because the margin will decrease despite an increase in the turnover.

APPROACH 2: REDUCE EXPENSES Assume that the manager of the Monthaven Burger Grill is able to reduce expenses by $1,000 so that net operating income increases from $10,000 to $11,000. Assume that both sales and operating assets remain constant. Then the new ROI would be:

$$\text{ROI} = \frac{\$11,000}{\$100,000} \times \frac{\$100,000}{\$50,000}$$

$$11\% \quad \times \quad 2 \quad = 22\% \text{ (as compared with 20\% above)}$$

APPROACH 3: REDUCE ASSETS Assume that the manager of the Monthaven Burger Grill is able to reduce operating assets from $50,000 to $40,000, but that sales and net operating income remain unchanged. Then the new ROI would be:

$$\text{ROI} = \frac{\$10,000}{\$100,000} \times \frac{\$100,000}{\$40,000}$$

$$10\% \quad \times \quad 2.5 \quad = 25\% \text{ (as compared with 20\% above)}$$

A clear understanding of these three approaches to improving the ROI figure is critical to the effective management of an investment centre. We will now look at each approach in more detail.

Increase Sales

When first looking at the ROI formula, one is inclined to think that the sales figure is neutral, since it appears as the denominator in the margin computation and as the numerator in the turnover computation. We *could* cancel out the sales figure, but we do not do so for two reasons. First, this would tend to draw attention away from the fact that the rate of return is a function of *two* variables, margin and turnover. And second, it would tend to conceal the fact that a change in sales can affect both the margin and the turnover in an organization. A change in sales can affect the *margin* if expenses increase or decrease at a different rate from sales. For example, a company may be able to keep a tight control on its costs as its sales go up, with the result that net operating income increases more rapidly than sales and increases the margin. Or a company may have fixed expenses that remain constant as sales go up, resulting in an increase in the net operating income and in the margin. Either (or both) of these factors might have been responsible for the increase in the margin percentage from 10% to 10.91% illustrated in approach 1.

Further, a change in sales can affect the *turnover* if sales either increase or decrease without a proportionate increase or decrease in the operating assets. In the first approach above, for example, sales increased from $100,000 to $110,000, but the operating assets remained unchanged. As a result, the turnover increased from 2 to 2.2 for the period.

Reduce Expenses

Often, the easiest route to increased profitability and to a stronger ROI figure is to simply cut the "fat" out of an organization through a concerted effort to control expenses. When margins begin to be squeezed, this is generally the first line of attack by a manager. Discretionary fixed costs (that is, fixed costs that arise from annual decisions by management to spend in certain fixed cost areas) usually come under scrutiny first, and various programs are either curtailed or eliminated in an effort to cut costs. Managers must be careful, however, not to cut out muscle and bone along with the fat. Also, they must remember that frequent cost-cutting binges can destroy morale. Most managers now agree that it is best to stay "lean and mean" all of the time.

Reduce Assets

Managers have always been sensitive to the need to control sales, operating expenses, and operating margins. However, they have not always been equally sensitive to the need to control investment in operating assets. Firms that have adopted the ROI approach to measuring managerial performance report that one of the first reactions of investment centre managers is to trim their investment in operating assets. Managers soon realize that an excessive investment in operating assets reduces turnover and hurts the ROI. As these managers reduce their investment in operating assets, funds are released that can be used elsewhere in the organization.

How can an investment centre manager control the investment in operating assets? One approach is to eliminate unneeded inventory. Just-in-time (JIT) purchasing and JIT manufacturing have been extremely helpful in reducing inventories of all types, with the result that ROI figures have improved dramatically in some companies. Another approach is to devise various methods of speeding up the collection of receivables. For example, many firms now employ the lockbox technique, which enables customers in distant states to send their payments directly to post office boxes in their area. The funds are received and deposited by a local bank on behalf of the payee firm. This speeds up the collection process, since the payments are not delayed in the postal system. As a result of the expedited collection, the accounts receivable balance is reduced and the asset turnover is increased.

Criticisms of ROI

Although ROI is widely used in evaluating performance, it is not a perfect tool. The method is subject to the following criticisms:

- Just telling managers to increase ROI may not be enough. Managers may not know how to increase ROI; they may increase ROI in a way that is inconsistent with the company's strategy; or they may take actions that increase ROI in the short run but harm the company in the long run (such as cutting back on research and development).
- A manager who takes over a business segment typically inherits many committed costs over which the manager has no control. These committed costs make it difficult to fairly assess the performance of the manager relative to other managers.
- As discussed in the next section, a manager who is evaluated on the basis of ROI may reject investment opportunities that are profitable for the company as a whole.

Residual Income—Another Measure of Performance

Another approach to measuring an investment centre's performance focuses on a concept known as *residual income*. **Residual income (RI)** is the net operating income that an investment centre earns above the minimum required return on its operating assets. Residual income is computed as follows:

⬤ KNOW   ⬤ APPLY

CC6: Explain and compute the residual income (RI) measure.

Net operating income − (Required rate of return × Average operating assets)

For purposes of illustration, consider the following data for an investment centre—the Lethbridge Division of Western Canada Services Corporation.

WESTERN CANADA SERVICES CORPORATION Lethbridge Division Basic Data for Performance Evaluation	
Average operating assets..	$100,000
Net operating income	$ 20,000
Minimum required rate of return	15%

Western Canada Services Corporation has long had a policy of evaluating investment centre managers on the basis of ROI, but is considering a switch to residual income. The controller of the company, who is in favour of the change to residual income, has provided the following table that shows how the performance of the division would be evaluated under each of the two methods:

WESTERN CANADA SERVICES CORPORATION Lethbridge Division	Alternative Performance Measures	
	ROI	Residual Income
Average operating assets (a)	$100,000	$100,000
Net operating income (b)	$ 20,000	$ 20,000
ROI, (b) ÷ (a)...................................	20%	
Minimum required return (15% × $100,000)		15,000
Residual income		$ 5,000

The reasoning underlying the residual income calculation is straightforward. The company is able to earn a rate of return of at least 15% on its investments. Since the company has invested $100,000 in the Lethbridge Division in the form of operating assets, the company should be able to earn at least $15,000 (15% × $100,000) on this investment. Since the

Lethbridge Division's net operating income is $20,000, the residual income above and beyond the minimum required return is $5,000. If residual income is adopted as the performance measure to replace ROI, the manager of the Lethbridge Division would be evaluated on the basis of the growth from year to year in residual income.

Economic Value Added

Another measure that resembles the residual income is **economic value added** or simply **EVA**, which has recently been trademarked and popularized by the consulting firm Stern Stewart & Co. Like residual income, EVA is computed as follows:

$$EVA = NOPAT - (C \times TC)$$

where, NOPAT is the net operating profit after tax, C% is the cost of capital (measured in % terms), and TC is total capital. Observe that NOPAT, C, and TC are different from the measures used to compute residual income.

The essence of EVA is that accounting-based measures of both income and assets (capital) used to compute residual income are adjusted to potentially remove the inappropriate treatment of certain kinds of transactions. For example, while shareholders and managers typically consider outlays on research and development (R&D) as investments that have a potential future benefit, generally accepted accounting principles (GAAP) require organizations to immediately expense these outlays. The consulting firm recommends an adjustment to potentially *correct* GAAP's treatment of R&D outlays. In fact, Stern Stewart has identified over 160 potential adjustments although no more than twelve are commonly used.[3]

When RI or EVA is used to measure performance, the objective is to maximize the total amount of RI or EVA, not to maximize overall ROI. Organizations as diverse as Coca-Cola, Alcan, Domtar, and Grand & Toy have embraced some version of EVA/RI in recent years.

IN BUSINESS TODAY **Meeting Targets the Wrong Way**

Putting too much emphasis on meeting financial targets can lead to undesirable behavior. Michael C. Jensen reports, "I once watched the management of a manufacturing company struggle to reach their year-end targets. In late fall, they announced a price increase of 10% effective January 2. Now it may be that a price increase was needed, but it was not in line with the competition, nor was it likely that January 2, of all dates, was the best time for the increase. A price increase on January 2, would, however, cause customers to order before year-end and thereby help managers reach their targets." The short-term boost in sales comes at the cost of lost future sales and possible customer ill will.

Source: Michael C. Jensen, "Why Pay People to Lie?" *The Wall Street Journal*, January 8, 2001, p. A32.

---

[3]Other examples of areas where adjustments are to be made include deferred taxes, LIFO reserves, provisions for future liabilities, mergers and acquisitions, gains or losses due to changes in accounting rules, operating leases, expense recognition, amortization, taxes and balance sheet adjustments. For further details, see O'Hanlon and Peasnell, "Wall Street's Contribution to Management Accounting: The Stern Stewart EVA® Financial Management System," *Management Accounting Research*, 9, 1998, pp. 421–444, and Ehrbar, *EVA: The Real Key to Creating Wealth*, John Wiley & Sons, 1998, pp. 161–181.

Motivation and Residual Income

One of the primary reasons why the controller of Western Canada Services Corporation would like to switch from ROI to RI has to do with how managers view new investments under the two performance measurement schemes. The residual income approach encourages managers to make investments that are profitable for the entire company, but that would be rejected by managers who are evaluated by the ROI formula.

To illustrate this problem, suppose that the manager of the Lethbridge Division is considering purchasing a computerized diagnostic machine to aid in servicing marine diesel engines. The machine would cost $25,000 and is expected to generate additional operating income of $4,500 a year. From the company's standpoint, this would be a good investment, since it promises a rate of return of 18% ($4,500/$25,000), which is in excess of the company's minimum required rate of return of 15%.

If the manager of the Lethbridge Division is evaluated on the basis of residual income, she would be in favour of the investment in the diagnostic machine as shown following:

WESTERN CANADA SERVICES CORPORATION Lethbridge Division Performance Evaluated Using RI			
	Present	New Project	Overall
Average operating assets.......	$100,000	$25,000	$125,000
Net operating income	$ 20,000	$ 4,500	$ 24,500
Minimum required return	15,000	3,750*	18,750
Residual income	$ 5,000	$ 750	$ 5,750

*$25,000 × 15% = $3,750.

Since the project would increase the residual income of the Lethbridge Division, the manager would want to invest in the new diagnostic machine.

Now suppose that the manager of the Lethbridge Division is evaluated on the basis of ROI. The effect of the diagnostic machine on the division's ROI is computed as follows:

WESTERN CANADA SERVICES CORPORATION Lethbridge Division Performance Evaluated Using ROI			
	Present	New Project	Overall
Average operating assets (a)	$100,000	$25,000	$125,000
Net operating income (b)	$20,000	$4,500	$24,500
ROI, (b) ÷ (a)...............	20%	18%	19.6%

The new project reduces the division's ROI from 20% to 19.6%. This happens because the 18% rate of return on the new diagnostic machine, while above the company's 15% minimum rate of return, is below the division's present ROI of 20%. Therefore, the new diagnostic machine would drag the division's ROI down, even though it would be a good investment from the standpoint of the company as a whole. If the manager of the division is evaluated on the basis of ROI, she will be reluctant to even propose such an investment.

Basically, a manager who is evaluated on the basis of ROI will reject any project whose rate of return is below the division's current ROI, even if the rate of return on the project is above the minimum required rate of return for the entire company. In contrast, any project whose rate of return is above the minimum required rate of return for the company will result in an increase in residual income. Since it is in the best interests of the company as a whole to accept any project whose rate of return is above the minimum required rate of return, managers who are evaluated on the basis of residual income will tend to make better decisions concerning investment projects than managers who are evaluated on the basis of ROI.

Heads I Win, Tails You Lose

A number of companies, including AT&T, Armstrong Holdings, and Baldwin Technology, have stopped using residual income measures of performance after trying them. Why? Reasons differ, but "bonus evaporation is often seen as the Achilles' heel of value-based metrics [like residual income and EVA]—and a major cause of plans being dropped." Managers tend to love residual income and EVA when their bonuses are big, but clamor for changes in performance measures when bonuses shrink.

Source: Bill Richard and Alix Nyberg, "Do EVA and Other Value Metrics Still Offer a Good Mirror of Company Performance?" *CFO*, March 2001, pp. 56–64.

Divisional Comparison and Residual Income

The residual income approach has one major disadvantage: it cannot be used to compare the performance of divisions of different sizes. You would expect larger divisions to have a greater residual income than smaller divisions, not necessarily because they are better managed, but simply because of the bigger numbers involved.

As an example, consider the following residual income computations for Division X and Division Y:

	Division	
	X	**Y**
Average operating assets (a)	$1,000,000	$250,000
Net operating income	$ 120,000	$ 40,000
Minimum required return: 10% × (a)	100,000	25,000
Residual income	$ 20,000	$ 15,000

Observe that Division X has slightly more residual income than Division Y, but that Division X has $1,000,000 in operating assets as compared with only $250,000 in operating assets for Division Y. Thus, Division X's greater residual income is probably more a result of its size than the quality of its management. In fact, it appears that the smaller division is better managed, since it has been able to generate nearly as much residual income with only one-fourth as much in operating assets to work with. This problem can be reduced to some degree by focusing on the percentage change in residual income from year to year, rather than on the absolute amount of the residual income. In contrast, ROI is a standardized measure and lends itself to comparisons regardless of size.

Computing Profitability of Non-Revenue-Generating Segments

⬤ KNOW

CC8: Explain the concept of transfer pricing.

In fully decentralized organizations, individual segments are treated as profit or investment centres, regardless of whether they generate revenues from sales to external customers. Consider the information technology (IT) department of a large organization, which services other segments in the organization. Given its classification as a profit centre, it must show revenues so that its profitability can be computed. In such a setting, the IT department must *sell* its services to other segments within the organization in order to *generate* revenues. The term used for such an internal sale is *transfer*; all transfers occur at a pre-determined price known as the **transfer price**. A transfer pricing system is also used by large multinational corporations when they transfer products from a segment in one location to a segment in another. In some companies, transfers take place because the output of one segment may be the input of another (i.e., the two segments are interrelated).

How should the transfer price be determined? It is easy to see that on the one hand, the *buying* segment would like a low transfer price because it is a cost for the segment; on the other hand, the *selling* segment would prefer a high transfer price because the price determines the segment's revenue. This creates a real tension that organizations must deal with to ensure that there are no dysfunctional consequences resulting from the transfer-pricing policy established by senior management. Generally speaking, there are three methods that can be used to establish transfer prices: (1) market-based price, (2) cost-based price, and (3) negotiated price. All three approaches have their benefits and limitations, which are discussed in more advanced texts.

While it may sound simple, there are many complications in arriving at an acceptable transfer price. For example, should costs include just the variable costs or will they include fixed costs as well? What about common costs? Most organizations establish guidelines that govern the determination of transfer prices including what costs should be considered in determining a transfer price (in the case of cost-based pricing). Regardless of the methods used, the objective of management must be to motivate the segment managers to do what is in the best interest of both the overall organization and the individual segment. Senior management often employs other mechanisms to motivate segment managers to make decisions that are in the best interests of the organization. These may include evaluating and rewarding managers based on measures other than just profitability (we will discuss this in the next section).

The CRA Is Watching

Adopting a proactive approach to transfer pricing has never been more important. Companies are increasingly expanding their geographical boundaries resulting in the need for transfer pricing. The Canada Revenue Agency (CRA) has taken steps to ensure that it gets its piece of the pie. In the past year, the federal government hired over 300 auditors to examine transfer pricing practices adopted by these businesses. Transfer prices can no longer be a whimsical number created to "beat the tax man." A company must now be able to validate its chosen transfer prices.

Source: Hendrik Swaneveld and Martin Przysuski, "Transfer pricing now a Canadian priority," *CMA Management,* April, 2002, pp. 42–44. Adapted with permission from CMA Canada.

Multi-Dimensional Performance Measurement

Thus far, we have discussed financial measures of performance such as return on investment, variances, and profits. However, simply using financial measures can be myopic because (1) financial measures are typically *outcome* measures that provide *after-the-fact* information, and (2) financial measures are only one dimension of performance. Critics note that it is at least equally important, if not more important, to know *how* to achieve the desired financial results. They state that an important objective of performance measurement is that it must aid in the implementation of an organization's strategies, and reporting along multiple dimensions is critical in achieving this objective. Managers must know what factors influence financial performance and must establish measures that inform the organization on how well it is doing with those factors that influence the financial results.

> ◡ **KNOW**
>
> CC9: Explain the concept of multi-dimensional performance reporting.

Therefore, a multi-dimensional performance measurement system that includes *nonfinancial* performance measures can be useful.

One such multi-dimensional performance measurement system is the **balanced scorecard**, which contains measures along at least four dimensions: (1) financial, (2) customer, (3) internal business process, and (4) learning and growth. Measures pertaining to the learning and growth dimension are supposed to inform managers about the likely performance along the internal business process dimension. Similarly, measures along the internal business process dimension are supposed to inform about potential performance along the customer dimension and ultimately the financial dimension. Thus, a key feature of the scorecard is that measures along the different dimensions are linked to one another or integrated. In this sense, the balanced scorecard is an integrated performance measurement system.

The balanced scorecard provides a way of communicating a company's strategy to managers throughout the organization. A properly designed scorecard should allow managers to answer such questions as: Which customers should be targeted, and how can they be attracted and retained at a profit? Which internal business process must be improved to meet customer requirements? In short, a well-constructed balanced scorecard should provide managers with a road map that indicates how the company will achieve its financial objectives. Achieving the financial objectives is important to ensure the long-term viability of the business.

IN BUSINESS TODAY   **A Banker's Scorecard**

Is the balanced scorecard just for the use of some companies? Not at all! Over the past decade, many different types of organizations have adopted the balanced scorecard (or some variation of it)—private businesses, government corporations, hospitals, and educational institutions, to name a few. CIBC, one of Canada's large banks uses a balanced scorecard approach in reporting performance. As reported in its 2006 *Annual Accountability Report*, CIBC's scorecard consists of six dimensions: Financial, Clients, Employees, Community, Environment, and Governance.

Source: *CIBC Annual Accountability Report 2006*, available online at www.cibc.ca.

As an example, think of a car dealership that wants to increase its profitability and growth. A balanced scorecard for this dealership would include measures pertaining to the two objectives, and measures that influence the two objectives. Given that the generic profitability equation consists of two variables—sales revenues and costs—the scorecard should measure these two variables. Sales revenue and other sales-related measures, such as customer service, number of referrals, and customer satisfaction, will appear in the customer dimension of the scorecard. Cost and other operational measures that will lead to improvements in the customer and financial measures will appear along the internal business process dimension. These may include costs, quality, and delivery/service time—factors that are important to customers, thereby leading to an improvement in the customer measures. Finally, management of the dealership may believe that learning is very important in improving the other measures. Therefore, they may decide to track training hours within the learning and growth perspective. The key aspect in identifying the right performance measures is that the measures must be linked in a cause–effect relationship. Otherwise, the scorecard is simply a collection of *ad hoc* measures that may result in more confusion, rather than provide any direction to management.

A multi-dimensional performance measurement system, such as the balanced scorecard, can provide a more complete picture of an organization's performance. Although the concept is appealing and has been embraced by many types of organizations, including hospitals, universities, government departments and businesses, there are some key issues that managers must keep in mind when implementing a balanced scorecard within their organizations. First and foremost, top managers must fully support its implementation. Second, individual measures within the different dimensions must be well defined and should flow from the goals and objectives established by senior management. Third, the individual measures must be mutually reinforcing to ensure that employees are not pulled in different directions. Finally, the performance measurement system and the employee evaluation and compensation system must be linked. A system that emphasizes A and rewards B is a classic recipe for disaster.

Measuring Up to the Environment

IN BUSINESS TODAY

After decades of focusing exclusively on reporting financial performance, organizations have realized the need to widen their performance reporting horizon. Many have adopted multi-dimensional performance measurement systems such as the balanced scorecard. More recently, increased pressure from certain stakeholder groups has resulted in organizations considering performance with respect to environmental and social responsibility issues.

Dow Canada, a subsidiary of The Dow Chemical Company (USA), with plants in Alberta, Ontario, Quebec and Saskatchewan, is big on environmental stewardship. To reflect its progress against Dow's Global Environment, Health & Safety Goals, Dow Canada annually publishes a report for public consumption, which contains performance indicators such as process safety incidents, waste reduction, wastewater reduction, energy use, chemical emissions, and fines and penalties. An outcome of its commitment to environmental stewardship is that in July 2005 its Quebec site achieved five years without a loss of primary containment incident.

Source: D. Crawford and T. Scaletta, "The Balanced Scorecard and Corporate Social Responsibility: Aligning Values for Profit," *CMA Management*, October 2005, pp. 20-27; Dow Canada's 2005 Public Report available at: http://www.dow.com.

Application Competency Summary

Application Competency	Deliverable	Source Documents and Key Information	Steps	Knowledge Competency
Prepare a segmented performance report. CC3	*Key Information* Profit margin generated by each segment Net income for the whole organization *Report/Document* Segmented performance report	*Sales and Expense Ledgers* Sales revenue, variable costs, and directly traceable fixed costs by segment Common costs for the organization	1. Record the sales revenue, variable costs, and directly traceable fixed expenses for each segment. 2. Deduct variable costs from the sales revenues to compute segment contribution margin; deduct directly traceable fixed expenses from the contribution margin to compute segment margin.	Variable and fixed costs CC1 (Ch. 2) Direct and indirect costs CC3 (Ch. 2) Segment margin CC3

continued

Application Competency	Deliverable	Source Documents and Key Information	Steps	Knowledge Competency
Compute return on investment (ROI). ◯ CC4	*Key Information* Sales margin Asset turnover ROI *Report/Document* No specific document	*Sales Ledger* Sales revenue *Income Statement* Operating income *Operating Assets Ledgers or Balance Sheet* Operating assets	1. Divide operating income by sales revenue to compute sales margin. 2. Divide sales revenue by average operating assets to compute asset turnover. 3. Multiply sales margin by asset turnover to compute return on investment. 4. Alternatively, divide operating income by average operating assets to compute ROI.	Operating income ◯ CC13 (Ch. 2) ROI ◯ CC4
Compute residual income (RI). ◯ CC6	*Key Information* Residual income *Report/Document* No specific document	*Income Statement* Operating income *Operating Assets Ledgers or Balance Sheet* Operating assets *Management Documents* Required rate of return	1. Multiply the required rate of return by the average operating assets and deduct this amount from the operating income to compute residual income.	Operating income ◯ CC13 (Ch. 2) Residual income ◯ CC6

Guidance Answers to Decision Maker and You Decide

A FRIEND (p. 405)

It sounds like your friend's business is strongly centralized; that is, she makes all of the major decisions and takes responsibility for all of the major projects. Not only is your friend spreading herself too thin and burning out as a result, her managers seem to have little, if any, freedom. You might propose that she consider decentralizing the organization.

A strongly decentralized organization in which even the lowest-level managers and employees are free to make decisions may not be the answer, but some degree of decentralization would help the current situation. She would be relieved of much of the daily problem solving and could use the time to concentrate on strategy, higher-level decision making, and coordinating the activities of her managers. Not only would her managers become more skilled at making effective decisions, they would also probably enjoy their jobs more and should be more willing to remain with the company. If your friend is reluctant to make changes, you might suggest that she interview the managers who have left the company. Their comments may help point your friend in the right direction.

STORE MANAGER (p. 417)

Three approaches can be used to increase ROI:

- Increase sales—An increase in sales will positively impact the margin if expenses increase less than sales. An increase in sales will also affect turnover if there is not a proportionate increase in operating assets.
- Reduce expenses—This approach is often the first path selected by managers to increase profitability and ROI. You should start by reviewing the stores' discretionary fixed costs (such as advertising). It may be possible to cut some discretionary fixed costs with minimal damage to the long-term goals of the organization. You should also investigate whether there are adequate physical controls over the inventory of jewellery items. Thefts result in an increase in cost of goods sold without a corresponding increase in sales!

• Reduce assets—An excessive investment in operating assets (such as inventory) reduces turnover and hurts ROI. Given the nature of the operations of retail jewellery stores, inventory must be in sufficient quantities at specific times during the year (such as Christmas, Valentine's Day, and Mother's Day) or sales will suffer. However, those levels do not need to be maintained throughout the year.

Review Problem: Return on Investment and Residual Income

The Magnetic Imaging Division of Medical Diagnostics, Inc. has reported the following results for last year's operations:

Sales.	$25 million
Net operating income	3 million
Average operating assets	10 million

Required:
1. Compute the margin, turnover, and ROI for the Magnetic Imaging Division.
2. Top management of Medical Diagnostics, Inc. has set a minimum required rate of return on average operating assets of 25%. What is the Magnetic Imaging Division's residual income for the year?

SOLUTION TO REVIEW PROBLEM
1. The required calculations are as follows:

$$\text{Margin} = \frac{\text{Net operating income, \$3,000,000}}{\text{Sales, \$25,000,000}}$$

$$= 12\%$$

$$\text{Turnover} = \frac{\text{Sales, \$25,000,000}}{\text{Average operating assets, \$10,000,000}}$$

$$= 2.5$$

$$\text{ROI} = \text{Margin} \times \text{Turnover}$$

$$= 12\% \times 2.5$$

$$= 30\%$$

2. The residual income for the Magnetic Imaging Division is computed as follows:

Average operating assets	$10,000,000
Net operating income.	$ 3,000,000
Minimum required return (25% × $10,000,000)	2,500,000
Residual income.	$ 500,000

Glossary

Balanced scorecard A multi-dimensional performance measurement system, which contains measures along at least four dimensions: (1) financial, (2) customer, (3) internal business process, and (4) learning and growth. (p. 422)

Centralized organization An organization in which decision making is made by a single manager or a small management team. (p. 404)

Common fixed cost A fixed cost that supports more than one business segment, but is not traceable in whole or in part to any one of the business segments. (p. 407)

Cost centre An organizational segment whose manager is responsible for costs, but not revenues, profits, or investments. (p. 406)

Decentralized organization An organization in which decision making is not confined to a few top executives but, rather, is spread throughout the organization. (p. 404)

Economic value added (EVA) The net operating profit after tax that an investment centre earns above the cost of capital, similar to residual income. (p. 418)

Investment centre A business segment similar to a profit centre; in addition to profitability, the manager of an investment centre is also responsible for investments in operating assets. (p. 406)

Margin Measure of management's ability to control operating expenses in relation to sales. It is measured as net operating income divided by sales. (p. 413)

Net operating income Income before interest and income taxes have been deducted. (p. 411)

Operating assets Cash, accounts receivable, inventory, plant and equipment, and all other assets held for productive use in an organization. (p. 412)

Profit centre An organizational segment whose manager is responsible for the segment's profitability and has the authority to strongly influence both costs and revenues. (p. 406)

Residual income The net operating income that an investment centre earns above the required return on its operating assets. (p. 417)

Responsibility centre A segment of an organization whose manager is responsible and accountable for costs, revenues, profits, or investments. (p. 406)

Return on investment (ROI) Net operating income divided by average operating assets. It also equals margin multiplied by turnover. (p. 411)

Revenue centre An organizational segment whose manager is responsible for meeting revenue targets and is considered to have the authority to strongly influence (if not control) revenues. (p. 406)

Segment An individual unit within an organization whose manager has the responsibility to carry out its activities. (p. 408)

Traceable fixed cost A fixed cost that is incurred because of the existence of a particular business segment. (p. 407)

Transfer price The price charged when one segment of an organization provides goods or services to another. (p. 421)

Turnover The measure of the sales generated for each dollar invested in operating assets. It is computed by dividing sales by the average operating assets figure. (p. 413)

Questions

10–1 What is meant by the term *decentralization?*
10–2 What benefits result from decentralization?
10–3 Distinguish between a cost centre, a revenue centre, a profit centre, and an investment centre.
10–4 Define a segment of an organization. Give several examples of segments.
10–5 What is meant by the terms *margin* and *turnover?*
10–6 What are the three basic approaches to improving return on investment (ROI)?
10–7 What is meant by residual income?
10–8 In what way can the use of ROI as a performance measure for investment centres lead to bad decisions? How does the residual income approach overcome this problem?
10–9 What is meant by the term *transfer price*, and why are transfer prices needed?
10–10 Explain the balanced scorecard.

Brief Exercises

BRIEF EXERCISE 10–1   Principles of Decentralization (CC1)
Following are a number of terms associated with decentralization in organizations:

Cost centre	Profit centre
Segment	Investment centre
Responsibility centre	Transfer price
Job satisfaction	

Required:
Fill in the blanks with the appropriate terms from the list provided.
1. A(n) _____ is a part or activity of an organization about which managers would like cost, revenue, or profit data.
2. Added responsibility and decision-making authority often result in increased _____.
3. A(n) _____ is a business segment whose manager is responsible for both cost and revenue, but not over investment funds.

4. When one segment, such as a division of a company, provides goods or services to another segment of the company, the _____ will determine how much revenue the segment recognizes on the transaction.

5. A(n) _____ is a business segment whose manager is responsible for costs, but not over revenue or investment funds.

6. A(n) _____ is any segment of an organization whose manager is responsible and accountable for cost, revenue, or investment funds.

7. A(n) _____ is a business segment whose manager is responsible for cost, revenue, and investments in operating assets.

BRIEF EXERCISE 10–2   Segment Performance Report (CC3)

Klinker Corporation consists of three segments: North America, Europe, and Asia. Revenues during 2008 for the three segments were $1,200,000, $3,800,000, and $800,000 respectively. Variable costs amounted to 30% of sales for all three segments, whereas the fixed expenses for each segment were $270,000, $900,000, and $600,000 respectively. The common fixed expenses for the company amounted to $1,590,000 for the year.

Required:

Prepare a segmented performance report for Klinker Corporation.

BRIEF EXERCISE 10–3   Compute the ROI (CC4)

Alyeska Services Company, a division of a major oil company, provides various services to the operators of the North Slope oil field in Alaska. Data concerning the most recent year are as follows:

Sales............................	$5,625,000
Net operating income	450,000
Average operating assets	3,750,000

Required:

1. Compute the margin for Alyeska Services Company.
2. Compute the turnover for Alyeska Services Company.
3. Compute the ROI for Alyeska Services Company.

BRIEF EXERCISE 10–4   Effects of Changes in Sales, Expenses, and Assets on ROI (CC4, 5)

CommercialServices.com Corporation provides business-to-business services on the Internet. Data concerning the most recent year follow:

Sales............................	$6,000,000
Net operating income	300,000
Average operating assets	1,500,000

Required:

Consider each question below independently. Carry out all computations to two decimal places.

1. Compute the company's ROI.
2. The entrepreneur who founded the company is convinced that sales will increase next year by 50% and that net operating income would increase as a result by 200%, with no increase in average operating assets. What would be the company's ROI?
3. The chief financial officer of the company believes a more realistic scenario would be a $1,000,000 increase in sales, requiring a $250,000 increase in average operating assets, with a resulting $200,000 increase in net operating income. What would be the company's ROI in this scenario?

BRIEF EXERCISE 10–5   Residual Income (CC6)

Juniper Design Ltd. of Manchester, England, is a company specializing in providing design services to residential developers. Last year, the company had net operating income of £600,000 on sales of £3,000,000. The company's average operating assets for the year were £2,800,000 and its minimum required rate of return was 18%. (The currency used in England is the pound sterling, denoted by £.)

Required:

Compute the company's residual income for the year.

BRIEF EXERCISE 10–6   Calculating ROI (CC4)

The following information relates to Daniel Manufacturing Company for 2008:

Original cost of assets as of January 1, 2007	$200,000
Useful life of assets	10 years
Years of amortization taken as of January 1, 2008 (straight-line).	1 year
Operating income before 1 year of amortization for 2008	$ 40,000
Estimated salvage value.	$ 0

Required:

What is the ROI for 2008, using the beginning-of-year book value of the assets?

(Adapted © CGA-Canada)

BRIEF EXERCISE 10–7   Calculating RI (CC6)

Zhao Co. reported the following statistics and results for 2008:

ROI	14%
Invested capital (average operating assets)	$200,000
Return on sales	8%
Cost of capital	10%

Required:

What was Zhao's residual income for 2008?

(Adapted © CGA-Canada)

BRIEF EXERCISE 10–8   Calculating Net Investment (CC4, 5, 6)

Taj Ltd. reported the following statistics and results for 2008:

Net operating income	$45,000
Return on sales	7.5%
Asset turnover	2.4
Residual income	$10,000

Required:

What was the value of Taj's average operating assets in 2008?

(Adapted © CGA-Canada)

Exercises

EXERCISE 10–1   Preparing a Segment Performance Report (CC3)

Indi Services Corporation, headquartered in Bangalore, India, provides specialized information technology (IT) services and consists of three divisions: (1) Financial Services, (2) Health Services, and (3) Transportation Services. For 2008, it recorded the following data:

	Financial Services	Health Services	Transportation Services	Total
Sales revenues	$3,956,000	$5,594,000	$1,970,000	$11,520,000
Variable costs (% of sales)	28%	40%	45%	
Traceable costs	2,145,320	2,768,450	730,560	5,644,330
Common costs				1,590,000

Required:

1. Prepare a segment performance report showing the segment margin in dollars and percentages for all three divisions. Use Exhibit 10-3A as a guide.
2. Which segment is most profitable? Why?

EXERCISE 10–2   Computing and Interpreting ROI (CC4)

Selected operating data for two divisions of Outback Brewing, Ltd., of Australia, are as follows:

	Division	
	Queensland	New South Wales
Sales	$4,000,000	$7,000,000
Average operating assets.................	2,000,000	2,000,000
Net operating income	360,000	420,000
Property, plant, and equipment (net).........	950,000	800,000

Required:
1. Compute the rate of return for each division using the ROI formula stated in terms of margin and turnover.
2. Using the data, which divisional manager seems to be doing the better job? Why?

EXERCISE 10–3   Contrasting ROI and RI (CC4, 6)

Meiji Isetan Corp. of Japan has two regional divisions with headquarters in Osaka and Yokohama. Selected data on the two divisions follow (in millions of yen, denoted by ¥):

	Division	
	Osaka	Yokohama
Sales	¥4,500,000	¥13,500,000
Net operating income	315,000	1,080,000
Average operating assets.................	1,500,000	6,000,000

Required:
1. For each division, compute the ROI in terms of margin and turnover. Where necessary, carry computations to two decimal places.
2. Assume that the company evaluates performance by use of RI and that the minimum required return for any division is 15%. Compute the RI for each division.
3. Is Yokohama's greater amount of RI an indication that it is better managed than Osaka? Explain.

EXERCISE 10–4   Evaluating New Investments with ROI and RI (CC4, 6)

Selected sales and operating data for three divisions of a multinational structural engineering firm are provided following:

	Division		
	Asia	Europe	North America
Sales	$12,000,000	$14,000,000	$25,000,000
Average operating assets..........	3,000,000	7,000,000	5,000,000
Net operating income	600,000	560,000	800,000
Minimum required rate of return ...	14%	10%	16%

Required:
1. Compute the ROI for each division using the formula stated in terms of margin and turnover.
2. Compute the RI for each division.
3. Assume that each division is presented with an investment opportunity that would yield a 15% rate of return.
   a. If performance is being measured by ROI, which division or divisions will probably accept the opportunity? Reject? Why?
   b. If performance is being measured by RI, which division or divisions will probably accept the opportunity? Reject? Why?

EXERCISE 10–5   Effects of Changes in Profits and Assets on ROI (CC4, 5)

Pecs Alley is a regional chain of health clubs. The managers of the clubs, who have authority to make investments as needed, are evaluated based largely on ROI. The Springfield Club reported the following results for the past year:

Sales.............................	$4,200,000
Net operating income	210,000
Average operating assets	1,050,000

Required:

The following questions are to be considered independently. Carry out all computations to two decimal places.

1. Compute the club's ROI.
2. Assume that the manager of the club is able to increase sales by $210,000 and, as a result, net operating income increases by $54,600. Further assume that this is possible without any increase in operating assets. What would be the club's ROI?
3. Assume that the manager of the club is able to reduce expenses by $42,000 without any change in sales or operating assets. What would be the club's ROI?
4. Assume that the manager of the club is able to reduce operating assets by $210,000 without any change in sales or net operating income. What would be the club's ROI?

EXERCISE 10–6   ROI Relations (CC4)

Selected information is presented following concerning the four divisions of Scarf Ltd. for the past fiscal year:

	Arnen	Bodel	Curnor	Dertan
Net income	**(a)**	$500,000	**(e)**	$ 300,000
Average operating assets ..	$ 1,500,000	**(c)**	$2,000,000	$ 3,000,000
ROI	**(b)**	20%	12.5%	**(g)**
Required return	6%	18%	**(f)**	**(h)**
RI...................	$ 15,000	**(d)**	$ (50,000)	$ 0

Required:

For each missing amount represented by letters (a) through (h), calculate the correct amount.

(Adapted © CGA-Canada)

EXERCISE 10–7   Evaluation of Performance using ROI and RI (CC4, 6)

One division of a company has reported the following operating results for the year just ended:

Sales......................	$ 750,000
Operating income	90,000
Average operating assets	300,000

Required:

1. Compute the margin percentage, turnover, and ROI for this division.
2. If management sets a minimum required rate of return on average operating assets of 20%, what is the RI for this division for the year?
3. Explain the meaning of RI, and identify one strength and one weakness of measuring performance using RI.

(Adapted © CGA-Canada)

Problems

CHECK FIGURE
(2) Segment margin
   percentage, Personal
   computers, 5.1%

PROBLEM 10–1   Segmented Performance Report (CC2, 3)

Prairie Electronics, located in Regina, manufactures three product lines: (1) high-end speakers, (2) personal computers, and (3) hand-held devices. For 2009, it compiled the following budgeted data:

	High-end speakers	Personal computers	Hand-held devices	Total
Sales (in units)...........	340,000	550,000	440,000	
Price (per unit)...........	$1,500	$1,250	$375	
Variable costs per unit:				
Direct materials	$ 426	$ 384	$ 40	
Direct labour..........	120	210	48	
Overhead	80	110	37	
Shipping	30	30	4	
Sales commissions	20	20	2	
Direct fixed costs:				
Salaries..............	$61,560,000	70,250,000	40,330,000	
Utilities.............	41,250,000	55,005,000	12,500,600	
Amortization.........	59,000,250	112,600,000	30,250,000	
Common fixed costs:				
Corporate salaries......				$33,460,000
Building amortization...				27,900,800
Legal & Accounting				41,380,640
Other................				11,340,760

Required:
1. Prepare a segmented performance report; use Exhibit 10–3A as your guide.
2. Compute the contribution margin percentage (contribution margin divided by sales) and segment margin percentage. Based on the dollar amounts and percentages, how would you assess the performance of the three segments (i.e., the three product lines)?
3. Allocate the common fixed expenses equally to the three segments and prepare a performance report similar to the one in Exhibit 10–3B. As a manager overseeing all three segments, how would you react to the report?

PROBLEM 10–2   ROI Relations (CC4)

Provide the missing data in the following tabulation:

CHECK FIGURE
Bravo: 2.4 Turnover

	Division		
	Alpha	Bravo	Charlie
Sales	$?	$12,000,000	$?
Net operating income	?	1,200,000	210,000
Average operating assets...........	1,600,000	?	?
Margin........................	8%	?	7%
Turnover	6	?	?
ROI	?	24%	14%

PROBLEM 10–3   ROI and RI Relations (CC4, 6)

A family friend has asked your help in analyzing the operations of three anonymous companies. Supply the missing data in the tabulation below:

CHECK FIGURE
Company B residual
income: ($40,000)

	Company		
	A	B	C
Sales	$9,000,000	$7,000,000	$4,500,000
Net operating income	?	280,000	?
Average operating assets.............	3,000,000	?	1,800,000
Return on investment	18%	14%	?
Minimum required rate of return:			
Percentage.....................	16%	?	15%
Dollar amount..................	?	320,000	?
Residual income	?	?	90,000

PROBLEM 10–4   Comparison of Performance Using ROI (CC4, 5)

Comparative data on three companies in the same industry are provided as follows:

	Company		
	A	B	C
Sales	$1,650,000	$1,375,000	$?
Net operating income	231,000	192,500	?
Average operating assets.............	825,000	?	2,750,000
Margin............................	?	?	3.5%
Turnover	?	?	2
ROI	?	7%	?

Required:

1. What advantages can you see in breaking down the ROI computation into two separate elements, margin and turnover?
2. Fill in the missing information in the preceding table, and comment on the relative performance of the three companies in as much detail as the data permit. Make *specific recommendations* on steps to be taken to improve the ROI, where needed.

(Adapted from National Association of Accountants, *Research Report No. 35,* p. 34)

PROBLEM 10–5   ROI and RI (CC4, 6)

Financial data for Joel de Paris Inc. for last year follow:

JOEL DE PARIS INC.
Balance Sheet

	Ending Balance	Beginning Balance
Assets		
Cash	$ 120,000	$ 140,000
Accounts receivable	530,000	450,000
Inventory...................................	380,000	320,000
Plant and equipment, net......................	620,000	680,000
Investment in Buisson, S.A.	280,000	250,000
Land (undeveloped)	170,000	180,000
Total assets	$2,100,000	$2,020,000
Liabilities and Shareholders' Equity		
Accounts payable	$ 310,000	$ 360,000
Long-term debt	1,500,000	1,500,000
Shareholders' equity	290,000	160,000
Total liabilities and shareholders' equity	$2,100,000	$2,020,000

JOEL DE PARIS INC.
Income Statement

Sales		$4,050,000
Less: Operating expenses		3,645,000
Net operating income		405,000
Less: Interest and taxes:		
Interest expense............................	$ 150,000	
Tax expense................................	110,000	260,000
Net income		$ 145,000

The company paid dividends of $15,000 last year. The "Investment in Buisson, S.A.," on the balance sheet represents an investment in the shares of another company.

Required:
1. Compute the company's margin, turnover, and ROI for last year.
2. The board of directors of Joel de Paris Inc. has set a minimum required return of 15%. What was the company's residual income last year?

PROBLEM 10–6 ROI and RI (CC4, 5, 6)

"I know headquarters wants us to add on that new product line," said Dell Havasi, manager of Billings Company's Office Products Division. "But I want to see the numbers before I make any move. Our division has led the company for three years, and I don't want any letdown."

Billings Company is a decentralized organization with five autonomous divisions. The divisions are evaluated on the basis of the return that they are able to generate on invested assets, with year-end bonuses given to the divisional managers who have the highest ROI figures. Operating results for the company's Office Products Division for the most recent year are as follows:

Sales.	$10,000,000
Less: Variable expenses.	6,000,000
Contribution margin	4,000,000
Less: Fixed expenses.	3,200,000
Net operating income	$ 800,000
Divisional operating assets	$ 4,000,000

The company had an overall ROI of 15% last year (considering all divisions). The Office Products Division has an opportunity to add a new product line that would require an additional investment in operating assets of $1,000,000. The cost and revenue characteristics of the new product line per year would be:

Sales.	$2,000,000
Variable expenses	60% of sales
Fixed expenses.	$640,000

Required:
1. Compute the Office Products Division's ROI for the most recent year; also compute the ROI if the new product line were added.
2. If you were in Dell Havasi's position, would you be inclined to accept or reject the new product line? Explain.
3. Why do you suppose headquarters is anxious for the Office Products Division to add the new product line?
4. Suppose that the company views a return of 12% on invested assets as being the minimum that any division should earn and that performance is evaluated by the RI approach.
   a. Compute the Office Products Division's RI for the most recent year; also compute the RI as it would appear if the new product line were added.
   b. Under these circumstances, if you were in Dell Havasi's position, would you accept or reject the new product line? Explain.

PROBLEM 10–7 ROI Analysis (CC4, 5)

The income statement for Huerra Company for last year is provided:

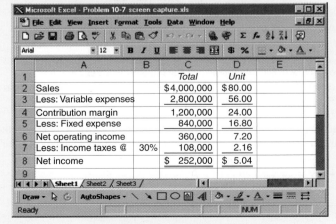

		Total	Unit
2	Sales	$4,000,000	$80.00
3	Less: Variable expenses	2,800,000	56.00
4	Contribution margin	1,200,000	24.00
5	Less: Fixed expense	840,000	16.80
6	Net operating income	360,000	7.20
7	Less: Income taxes @ 30%	108,000	2.16
8	Net income	$ 252,000	$ 5.04

The company had average operating assets of $2,000,000 during the year.

Required:

1. Compute the company's ROI for the period using the ROI formula stated in terms of margin and turnover.

For each of the following questions, indicate whether the margin and turnover will increase, decrease, or remain unchanged as a result of the events described, and then compute the new ROI figure. Consider each question separately, starting in each case from the data used to compute the original ROI in part (1).

2. By using JIT, the company is able to reduce the average level of inventory by $400,000. (The released funds are used to pay off short-term creditors.)
3. The company achieves a cost savings of $32,000 per year by using cheaper materials.
4. The company issues bonds and uses the proceeds to purchase machinery and equipment, thus increasing the average assets by $500,000. Interest on the bonds is $60,000 per year. Sales remain unchanged. The new more efficient equipment reduces production costs by $20,000 per year.
5. As a result of a more intense effort by the sales staff, sales are increased by 20%; operating assets remain unchanged.
6. Obsolete items of inventory carried on the records at a cost of $40,000 are scrapped and written off as a loss since they are unsaleable.
7. The company uses $200,000 of cash (received on accounts receivable) to repurchase and retire some of its common shares.

PROBLEM 10–8   ROI; RI; Decentralization (CC2, 3, 4, 5, 6)

Raddington Industries produces tool and die machinery for manufacturers. The company expanded vertically several years ago by acquiring Reigis Steel Company, one of its suppliers of alloy steel plates. Raddington decided to maintain Reigis' separate identity and therefore established the Reigis Steel Division as one of its investment centres.

Raddington evaluates its divisions on the basis of ROI. Management bonuses are also based on ROI. All investments in operating assets are expected to earn a minimum rate of return of 11%.

Reigis' ROI has ranged from 14% to 17% since it was acquired by Raddington. During the past year, Reigis had an investment opportunity that would yield an estimated rate of return of 13%. Reigis' management decided against the investment because it believed the investment would decrease the division's overall ROI.

Last year's income statement for Reigis Steel Division is given below. The division's operating assets employed were $19,440,000 at the end of the year, which represents an 8% increase over the previous year-end balance.

REIGIS STEEL DIVISION		
Divisional Income Statement		
For the Year Ended December 31		
Sales		$46,800,000
Cost of goods sold.		24,750,000
Gross margin.		22,050,000
Less: Operating expenses:		
Selling expenses	$ 8,430,000	
Administrative expenses	10,812,000	19,242,000
Net operating income		$ 2,808,000

Required:

1. Compute the following performance measures for the Reigis Steel Division:
   a. ROI. (Remember, ROI is based on the *average* operating assets, computed from the beginning-of-year and end-of-year balances.) State ROI in terms of margin and turnover.
   b. Residual income.
2. Would the management of Reigis Steel Division have been more likely to accept the investment opportunity it had last year if residual income were used as a performance measure instead of ROI? Explain.
3. The Reigis Steel Division is a separate investment centre within Raddington Industries. Identify the items Reigis must be free to control if it is to be evaluated fairly by either the ROI or RI performance measures.

(CMA adapted)

CHECK FIGURE
(3) $132,000

PROBLEM 10–9   Operating Income, ROI, and RI (CC2, 4, 5, 6)

AutoParts is a division of MPI International, located in Wadena, Saskatchewan. Auto Parts manufactures various automobile parts, such as bumpers, fenders, and axles, and sells them to major auto manufacturers. The division and its management are evaluated by senior corporate management on the basis of investment centre concepts. The following information pertains to operations of the Auto Parts division for 2007:

Total revenues	$ 21,250,000
Direct variable costs	8,750,000
Direct fixed costs	7,500,000
Allocated corporate costs	3,938,000

	Book Values		Market Values	
	Dec. 31, 2006	Dec. 31, 2007	Dec. 31, 2006	Dec. 31, 2007
Current assets	$ 1,250,000	$ 1,800,000		
Fixed assets	10,250,000	11,700,000		
Accumulated amortization	(1,250,000)	(1,750,000)		
Total operating assets	$ 10,250,000	$11,750,000	$9,500,000	$10,500,000
Liabilities	$ 3,000,000	$ 3,500,000		

Required:
1. Compute the margin, turnover, and ROI using operating income and the book value of average total operating assets.
2. Compute ROI using segment margin and average market value of operating assets.
3. Compute RI using operating income and book value of average net assets. Assume the required rate of return is 12%.

(Adapted © CGA-Canada)

CHECK FIGURE
(1) a) Project 4: ROI, 16%

PROBLEM 10–10   ROI and RI Relationships (CC4, 6)

Sushi Heavy Industries manufactures primarily heavy machinery and drilling installations for mining, oil wells, and other similar industries. The vice-president of the transport division, newly created for bulk transportation of raw materials, is preparing a capital budget for the coming year for inclusion in the company-wide capital budget. The managers of the six subdivisions of the transport division have each submitted a capital investment proposal to the vice-president, who must decide which project or projects to include in the submission to corporate head office. The proposals are listed following. All are considered equally risky.

Project	Investment Required	Expected Return
1	$4,800,000	$1,200,000
2	1,900,000	627,000
3	1,400,000	182,000
4	950,000	152,000
5	650,000	136,000
6	300,000	90,000

The vice-president must decide which of the proposed projects to include in the transport division's submission. Sushi has a cost of capital of 15%. The transport division has been allocated $7 million for capital investment purposes.

Required:
1. What will be the total investment, total return, ROI, and total RI under each of the following two conditions:
   a. The company has a rule that all projects with an expected return of 20% or more should be taken if funds are available.
   b. The vice-president is expected to maximize RI as computed using the 15% cost of capital.

2. Explain, and use a simple numerical example to illustrate, the benefit of ROI versus profitability (that is, net income) as a performance measure for comparing two divisions of different sizes.

(Adapted © CGA-Canada)

PROBLEM 10–11   Segment Performance Reporting, ROI, and RI (CC2, 3, 4, 5, 6)

Tasty Treats produces a variety of treats. For control purposes, the company is organized into three segments: (1) Baked Treats, (2) Fried Treats, and (3) Roasted Treats. The following data are available for the most recent year:

	Baked Treats	Fried Treats	Roasted Treats	Total
Sales (kg)...............	650,000	320,000	550,000	
Price per kg..............	$26.50	$18.75	$30.00	
Variable costs.............	60% of sales	35% of sales	$12.70 per unit	
Average operating assets....	$25 million	$20 million	$45 million	$100 million*

*Includes an additional $10 million of corporate-level operating assets.

Additional information follows:
1. Total fixed costs amounted to $14.5 million, of which $5.7 are common costs and are allocated equally to the three segments.
2. Of the remaining fixed costs, 28% is directly traceable to Baked Treats, 22% to Fried Treats, and the remainder to Roasted Treats.
3. The minimum required return is 9% at the segment level, and 7% for the overall corporation.

Required:
1. Prepare a segment performance report; include the allocated common costs in your report. Your report should show the contribution margin, segment margin and operating income for each segment and for the corporation.
2. Compute the ROI and RI for each segment using the segment margin and the operating income, and for the corporation using the operating income.
3. How will you evaluate the performance of each segment based on the different financial metrics that you computed in parts (1) and (2)?

Building Your Skills

ANALYTICAL THINKING   (CC1, 2, 4, 5, 6)

The Valve Division of Bendix Inc. produces a small valve that is used by various companies as a component part in their products. Bendix Inc. operates its divisions as autonomous units, giving its divisional managers great discretion in pricing and other decisions. Each division is expected to generate a rate of return of at least 14% on its operating assets. The Valve Division has average operating assets of $700,000. The valves are sold for $5 each. Variable costs are $3 per valve, and fixed costs total $462,000 per year. The division has a capacity of 300,000 valves each year.

Required:
1. How many valves must the Valve Division sell each year to generate the desired rate of return on its assets?
   a. What is the margin earned at this level of sales?
   b. What is the turnover at this level of sales?
2. Assume that the Valve Division's current ROI is just equal to the minimum required 14%. In order to increase the division's ROI, the divisional manager wants to increase the selling price per valve by 4%. Market studies indicate that an increase in the selling price would cause sales to drop by 20,000 units each year. However, operating assets could be reduced by $50,000 due to decreased needs for accounts receivable and inventory. Compute the margin, turnover, and ROI if these changes are made.
3. Refer to the original data. Assume again that the Valve Division's current ROI is just equal to the minimum required 14%. Rather than increase the selling price, the sales manager wants to reduce the selling price per valve by 4%. Market studies indicate that this would fill the plant to capacity. In order to carry the greater level of sales, however, operating assets would increase by $50,000. Compute the margin, turnover, and ROI if these changes are made.

4. Refer to the original data. Assume that the normal volume of sales is 280,000 valves each year at a price of $5 per valve. Another division of the company is currently purchasing 20,000 valves each year from an overseas supplier, at a price of $4.25 per valve. The manager of the Valve Division has adamantly refused to meet this price, pointing out that it would result in a loss for his division:

Selling price per valve		$4.25
Cost per valve:		
Variable	$3.00	
Fixed ($462,000 ÷ 300,000 valves)	1.54	4.54
Net loss per valve.		$(0.29)

The manager of the Valve Division also points out that the normal $5 selling price barely allows his division the required 14% rate of return. "If we take on some business at only $4.25 per unit, then our ROI is obviously going to suffer," he reasons, "and maintaining that ROI figure is the key to my future. Besides, taking on these extra units would require us to increase our operating assets by at least $50,000 due to the larger inventories and receivables we would be carrying." If the manager of the Valve Division accepts the transfer price of $4.25 for 20,000 units, how would that decision impact the Valve Division's ROI? Should the manager of the Valve Division accept the price of $4.25 per valve? Why, or why not?

COMMUNICATING IN PRACTICE (CC1, 2, 6)

How do the performance measurement and compensation systems of service firms compare with those of manufacturers? To study one well-run service-oriented business, ask the manager of your local Tim Horton's if he or she would spend some time with you discussing the performance measures that the company uses to evaluate store managers and how the performance measures tie in with their compensation.

Required:

After asking the following questions, write a brief memorandum to your instructor that summarizes what you discovered during your interview with the manager of the franchise.
1. What are Tim Horton's goals, that is, the broad, long-range plans of the company (e.g., to increase market share)?
2. What performance measures are used to help motivate the store managers and monitor progress toward achieving the corporation's goals?
3. Are the performance measures consistent with the store manager's compensation plan?

TEAMWORK IN ACTION (CC9)

The balanced scorecard is becoming an increasingly popular performance measurement system. Why?

Required:

Form teams and discuss the primary reason why companies might adopt a balanced scorecard type performance measurement system. List the primary advantages that companies have derived from adopting the scorecard. Ensure that all members of the team understand and agree with the team's consensus. Each member of the team should be prepared to present the team's conclusions in a class discussion.

(Hint: Look up articles in *CMA Management* and *Harvard Business Review* to guide your thinking.)

Don't forget to visit the Online Learning Centre for self-study quizzes, practice exams, and more! Visit www.mcgrawhill.ca/olc/brewer.

CHAPTER *Eleven*

Cost-Volume-Profit Relationships

CHAPTER COMPETENCIES

After studying Chapter 11, you should be able to demonstrate the following competencies:

Competency	Know	Apply
Understand the cost-volume-profit analysis framework.		
CC1 Explain the basics of cost-volume-profit (CVP) analysis.	○	
CC2 Explain and compute the concept of contribution margin ratio.	○	○
CC3 Explain how changes in activity affect contribution margin, contribution margin ratio, and net income.	○	
CC4 Explain, prepare, and interpret a CVP graph.	○	○
CC5 Outline the assumptions used in CVP analysis.	○	
Apply the CVP analysis framework.		
CC6 Apply the CVP framework to different managerial decisions.		○
CC7 Compute break-even sales using the equation method.		○
CC8 Compute break-even sales using the contribution margin approach.		○
CC9 Compute the sales needed to achieve a target profit.		○
CC10 Explain the effect of income tax on target profit analysis and compute the sales needed to achieve a target after-tax profit.	○	○
CC11 Explain and compute the margin of safety.	○	○
CC12 Explain the effect of cost structure on a company's profitability.	○	
CC13 Compute the degree of operating leverage and explain its usefulness.	○	○
CC14[A] Explain the concept of sales mix.	○	
CC15[A] Compute break-even sales in a multi-product environment.		○
Compare and contrast two important costing approaches.		
CC16[B] Differentiate between absorption and variable product costing.	○	
CC17[B] Prepare absorption and variable costing income statements.		○

Note: A and B refer to Appendix 11A and Appendix 11B respectively; both appendices are available online (see www.mcgrawhill.ca/olc/brewer).

DECISION FEATURE
Profit Comes in Different Packages

Starting out as a manufacturer of egg cartons, Cascades Inc., a $3.4 billion manufacturer of paper and packaging products, has added a number of products during its 40 long years of existence. The journey has been challenging to say the least. According to chairman Bernard Lemaire, the company "... has survived some volatile times," and continues to do so. The most critical component of improving profitability in 2006 was mitigating the negative effects of cost increases. Being able to do so requires a good understanding of the relationships between cost (both fixed and variable), price, volume, and profits (*cost-volume-profit analysis* as it is referred to in this chapter).

Lemaire noted that Cascades proved its ability to adapt to fast-changing conditions in 2006 and was confident of repeating the feat once again in the current year. Although the price factor proved favourable, the cost side did not largely due to the effects of the strong Canadian dollar. How did Cascades achieve this? One key method was through continuous improvement efforts to cut the level of costs and improve the efficiency of fixed assets, thereby increasing capacity utilization resulting in higher production volumes.

Performance in the first quarter of 2007 was good and the second quarter looks promising. Has Cascades survived the challenging times? It has survived for over 40 years; is this not enough?

Sources: Cascades Inc.'s 2006 Annual Report available online (www.cascades.com) R. Gibbens, "Cascades Boosts Profit in Challenging Climate," *CanWest News*. Don Mills, Ont.: May 11, 2007. p. 1.

A Look Back

In the last chapter we concluded our discussion of planning and control. We introduced the concept of decentralization and performance measures to evaluate different types of responsibility centres (profitability, return on investment and residual income).

A Look at This Chapter

This chapter begins our discussion on decision making. Here we describe the basics of cost-volume-profit (CVP) analysis, an essential management accounting tool for decision making.

A Look Ahead

In the next chapter, we discuss the core of decision making by introducing the concept of relevant costs and their application to various managerial decisions.

Cost-volume-profit (CVP) analysis is one of the

most powerful tools that managers have at their command. It helps them understand the interrelationships between cost, volume, and profit in an organization in order to determine, for example, the products to manufacture or sell, the pricing policy to follow, the marketing strategy to employ, and the type of production facilities to acquire. To help understand the role of CVP analysis in business decisions, consider the case of Acoustic Concepts, Inc., a company founded by Prem Narayan.

MANAGERIAL ACCOUNTING IN ACTION

The Issue

Accoustic Concepts, Inc.

Prem, an engineer, started Acoustic Concepts to market a radically new speaker he had designed for automobile sound systems. The speaker, called the Sonic Blaster, uses an advanced microprocessor chip to boost amplification to awesome levels. Prem contracted with a Taiwanese electronics manufacturer to produce the speaker. With seed money provided by his family, Prem placed an order with the manufacturer and ran advertisements in auto magazines.

The Sonic Blaster was a success. Sales grew to the point that Prem moved the company's headquarters out of his apartment and into rented quarters in a neighbouring industrial park. He also hired a receptionist, an accountant, a sales manager, and a small sales staff to sell the speakers to retail stores. The accountant, Bob Luchinni, had worked for several small companies where he had acted as a business advisor, as well as an accountant and bookkeeper. The following discussion occurred soon after Bob was hired:

Prem: Bob, I've got a lot of questions about the company's finances that I hope you can help answer.

Bob: We're in great shape. The loan from your family will be paid off within a few months.

Prem: I know, but I am worried about the risks I've assumed by expanding operations. What would happen if a competitor entered the market and our sales slipped? How far could sales drop before we start to lose money? Another question I've been trying to resolve is how much our sales would have to increase in order to justify the big marketing campaign the sales staff is pushing for.

Bob: Marketing always wants more money for advertising.

Prem: And they are always pushing me to drop the selling price on the speaker. I agree with them that a lower price will boost our volume, but I'm not sure the increased volume will offset the loss in revenue from the lower price.

Bob: It sounds like these questions are all related in some way to the relationships between our selling prices, our costs, and our volume. We shouldn't have a problem coming up with some answers. I'll need a day or two, though, to gather some data.

Prem: Why don't we set up a meeting for three days from now? That would be Thursday.

Bob: That'll be fine. I'll have some preliminary answers for you, as well as a model you can use for answering similar questions in the future.

Prem: Good. I'll be looking forward to seeing what you come up with.

The Basics of Cost-Volume-Profit Analysis

◗ KNOW

CC1: Explain the basics of CVP analysis.

Bob Luchinni's preparation for Thursday takes us back to the contribution margin income statement first presented in Chapter 3. A contribution margin approach to presenting the income statement is useful for the purposes of management decision making because it allows the manager to obtain a better understanding of costs under different situations. Bob will base his analysis on the following contribution margin income statement he prepared last month:

ACOUSTIC CONCEPTS, INC. Contribution Margin Income Statement For the Month of June			
	Total	Per Unit	Percentage
Sales (400 speakers)	$100,000	$250	100
Less: Variable expenses . . .	60,000	150	60
Contribution margin.	40,000	$100	40
Less: Fixed expenses	35,000		
Net income.	$ 5,000		

Note that sales, variable expenses, and contribution margin are expressed in total, on a per-unit basis and as a percentage. This is a good idea on income statements prepared for management's own use because it facilitates profitability analysis.

It emphasizes the behaviour of costs and therefore is extremely helpful to a manager in judging the impact on profits of changes in selling price, cost, or volume—such an analysis is known as the **cost-volume-profit analysis** or simply **CVP analysis**. Bob, a strong believer in going back to the basics, decided to capture the preceding income statement using the generic profit (income) equation, which also forms the basic principle that underlies CVP analysis:

$$\text{Profit} = \text{Sales} - (\text{Variable expenses} + \text{Fixed expenses})$$

We can transform this formula as follows:

$$\text{Profit} = \text{Sales} - \text{Variable expenses} - \text{Fixed expenses}$$
$$= \text{Contribution margin} - \text{Fixed expenses}$$

These formulas underlie the basics of CVP analysis, which we will use in the rest of this chapter.

Contribution Margin and Contribution Margin Ratio

Contribution margin is the amount remaining from sales revenue after variable expenses have been deducted. In addition to being expressed on a per-unit basis, contribution margin can also be expressed as a percentage of sales—40% as shown in the previous contribution margin income statement. This measure is known as the **contribution margin (CM) ratio**, and is computed as follows:

$$\text{CM ratio} = \frac{\text{Contribution margin}}{\text{Sales}}$$

For Acoustic Concepts, the computations are as follows:

$$\frac{\text{Total contribution margin, \$40,000}}{\text{Total sales, \$100,000}} = 40\%$$

In a company such as Acoustic Concepts that has only one product, the CM ratio can also be computed as follows:

$$\frac{\text{Per-unit contribution margin, \$100}}{\text{Per-unit sales, \$250}} = 40\%$$

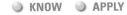
 KNOW   APPLY

CC2: Explain and compute the concept of contribution margin ratio.

● KNOW

CC3: Explain how changes in activity affect contribution margin, contribution margin ratio, and net income.

Contribution Margin, CM Ratio, and CVP Analysis

Contribution margin is the amount available to cover fixed expenses and then to provide profits for the period. Note the sequence here—contribution margin is used *first* to cover the fixed expenses, and then whatever remains goes toward profits. If the contribution margin is not sufficient to cover the fixed expenses, a loss occurs for the period. To illustrate with an extreme example, assume that Acoustic Concepts sells only one speaker during a particular month. The company's income statement will then appear as follows:

	Total	Per Unit	Percentage
Sales (1 speaker)	$ 250	$250	100
Less: Variable expenses . . .	150	150	60
Contribution margin.	100	$100	40
Less: Fixed expenses	35,000		
Net loss	$ (34,900)		

For each additional speaker that the company is able to sell during the month, $100 more in contribution margin will become available to help cover the fixed expenses. If a second speaker is sold, for example, then the total contribution margin will increase by $100 (to a total of $200) and the company's loss will decrease by $100, to $34,800:

	Total	Per Unit	Percentage
Sales (2 speakers)	$ 500	$250	100
Less: Variable expenses . . .	300	150	60
Contribution margin.	200	$100	40
Less: Fixed expenses	35,000		
Net loss	$ (34,800)		

If enough speakers can be sold to generate $35,000 in contribution margin, then all of the fixed costs will be covered and the company will have managed to at least *break even* for the month—that is, to show neither profit nor loss, simply covering all of its costs. This is the *concept* of "breaking even." In order to break even, the company will have to sell 350 speakers in a month, since each speaker sold yields $100 in contribution margin:

	Total	Per Unit	Percentage
Sales (350 speakers)	$ 87,500	$250	100
Less: Variable expenses . . .	52,500	150	60
Contribution margin.	35,000	$100	40
Less: Fixed expenses	35,000		
Net income.	$ –0–		

The quantity, 350, is the company's **break-even point.** That is, it is the level of sales at which profit (net income) is zero. Computation of the break-even point is discussed in detail later in the chapter. Note that at the break-even point, total contribution equals the total fixed expenses—both are $35,000.

Once the break-even point has been reached, net income will increase by the amount of the unit contribution margin for each additional unit sold. For example, if 351 speakers are sold in a month, then we can expect that the net income for the month will be

$100, since the company will have sold one speaker more than the number needed to break even:

	Total	Per Unit	Percentage
Sales (351 speakers)	$ 87,750	$250	100
Less: Variable expenses . . .	52,650	150	60
Contribution margin.	35,100	$100	40
Less: Fixed expenses	35,000		
Net income.	$ 100		

If 352 speakers are sold (two speakers above the break-even point), then we can expect that the net income for the month will be $200, and so on. To know what the profits will be at various levels of activity, therefore, it is not necessary to prepare a whole series of income statements. The manager can, instead, simply take the number of units to be sold over the break-even point and multiply that number by the unit contribution margin ($100 in our example). The result represents the anticipated profits for the period. Or, to estimate the effect of a planned increase in sales on profits, the manager can simply multiply the increase in units sold by the unit contribution margin. The result will be the expected increase in profits. To illustrate, if Acoustic Concepts is currently selling 400 speakers per month and plans to increase sales to 425 speakers per month, the anticipated impact on profits can be computed as follows:

Increased number of speakers to be sold	25
Contribution margin per speaker	× $100
Increase in net income	$2,500

These calculations can be verified as follows:

	Sales Volume			
	400 Speakers	425 Speakers	Difference 25 Speakers	Per Unit
Sales	$100,000	$106,250	$6,250	$250
Less: Variable expenses .	60,000	63,750	3,750	150
Contribution margin	40,000	42,500	2,500	$100
Less: Fixed expenses . . .	35,000	35,000	—0—	
Net income	$ 5,000	$ 7,500	$2,500	

To summarize these examples, if there were no sales, the company's loss would equal its fixed expenses. Each unit that is sold reduces the loss by the amount of the unit contribution margin. Once the break-even point has been reached, each additional unit sold increases the company's profit by the amount of the unit contribution margin.

The effect of changes in sales can also be measured using the CM ratio. To illustrate, notice that Acoustic Concepts has a CM ratio of 40%. This means that for each dollar increase in sales, total contribution margin will increase by 40 cents ($1 sales × CM ratio of 40%). As this example suggests, *the impact on contribution margin of any given dollar change in total sales can be computed in seconds by simply applying the CM ratio to the dollar change.* If, for example, Acoustic Concepts plans a $30,000 increase in sales during the coming month, management can expect the contribution margin to increase by $12,000 ($30,000 increased sales × CM ratio of 40%).

If fixed costs do not change, the change in the contribution margin will flow through to change net income. Each dollar increase in sales will increase net income by 40 cents ($1 sales × CM ratio of 40%). And a $30,000 increase in sales will increase net income by $12,000.

This is verified by the following table:

	Sales Volume			Percentage of Sales
	Current	Expected	Increase	
Sales	$100,000	$130,000	$30,000	100
Less: Variable expenses. . . .	60,000	78,000*	18,000	60
Contribution margin	40,000	52,000	12,000	40
Less: Fixed expenses.	35,000	35,000	—0—	
Net income	$ 5,000	$ 17,000	$12,000	

*$130,000 expected sales ÷ $250 per unit = 520 units. 520 units × $150 per unit = $78,000.

The CM ratio is particularly valuable in those situations where the manager must make trade-offs between more dollar sales of one product versus more dollar sales of another. Generally speaking, when trying to increase sales, products that yield the greatest amount of contribution margin per dollar of sales should be emphasized.

CVP Relationships in Graphical Form

○ KNOW   ○ APPLY

CC4: Explain, prepare, and interpret a CVP graph.

The relationships among revenue, cost, profit, and volume can be expressed graphically by preparing a **CVP graph.** A CVP graph highlights CVP relationships over wide ranges of activity, giving managers a perspective that can be obtained in no other way. To help explain his analysis to Prem Narayan, Bob Luchinni decided to prepare a CVP graph for Acoustic Concepts.

PREPARING THE CVP GRAPH In a CVP graph (sometimes called a *break-even chart*), unit volume is commonly represented on the horizontal (X) axis and dollars on the vertical (Y) axis. Preparing a CVP graph involves three steps. These steps are keyed to the graph in Exhibit 11–1:

1. Draw a line parallel to the volume axis to represent total fixed expenses. For Acoustic Concepts, total fixed expenses are $35,000.
2. Choose some volume of sales and plot the point representing total expenses (fixed and variable) at the activity level you have selected. In Exhibit 11–1, Bob chose a volume of 600 speakers. Total expenses at that activity level would be as follows:

Fixed expenses.	$ 35,000
Variable expenses (600 speakers × $150 per speaker) . . .	90,000
Total expenses	$125,000

After the point has been plotted, draw a line through it back to the point where the fixed expenses line intersects the dollar axis.
3. Again, choose a volume of sales and plot the point representing total sales dollars at the activity level you have selected. In Exhibit 11–1, Bob again chose a volume of 600 speakers. Sales at that activity level total $150,000 (600 speakers × $250 per speaker). Draw a line through this point back to the origin.

The interpretation of the completed CVP graph is given in Exhibit 11–2. The anticipated profit or loss at any given level of sales is measured by the vertical distance between the total revenue line (sales) and the total expenses line (variable expenses plus fixed expenses).

Exhibit 11–1
Preparing the CVP Graph

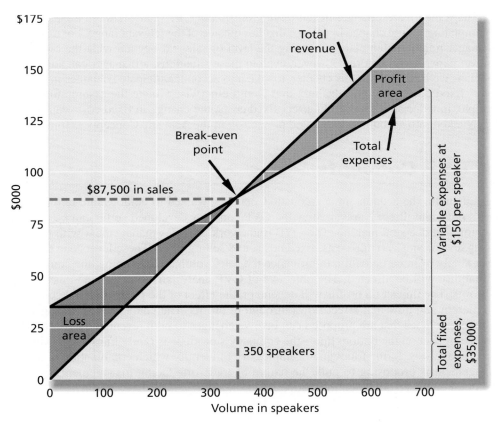

Exhibit 11–2
The Completed CVP Graph

The break-even point is the point at which the total revenue and total expenses lines intersect. Thus, the break-even point of 350 speakers in Exhibit 11–2 agrees with the break-even point computed earlier.

As discussed previously, when sales are below the break-even point—in this case, 350 units—the company suffers a loss. Notice that the loss (represented by the vertical distance between the total expense and total revenue lines) worsens as sales decline. When sales are above the break-even point, the company earns a profit and the size of the profit (represented by the vertical distance between the total revenue and total expense lines) increases as sales increase.

Assumptions of CVP Analysis

● KNOW

CC5: Outline the assumptions used in CVP analysis.

A number of assumptions underlie CVP analysis:

- Selling price is constant. The price of a product or service will not change as volume changes.
- Costs are linear and can be accurately divided into variable and fixed elements. The variable element is constant per unit, and the fixed element is constant in total over the entire relevant range.
- In multi-product companies, the sales mix is constant.
- In manufacturing companies, inventories do not change. The number of units produced equals the number of units sold.

While some of these assumptions may be violated in practice, the violations are usually not serious enough to call into question the basic validity of CVP analysis. For example, in most multi-product companies, the sales mix is constant enough so that the results of CVP analysis are reasonably valid.

Perhaps the greatest danger lies in relying on simple CVP analysis when a manager is contemplating a large change in volume that lies outside of the relevant range. For example, a manager might contemplate increasing the level of sales far beyond what the company has ever experienced before. However, even in these situations, a manager can adjust the model, as we have done in this chapter, to take into account anticipated changes in selling prices, fixed costs, and the sales mix that would otherwise violate the assumptions. For example, in a decision that would affect fixed costs, the change in fixed costs can be explicitly taken into account as illustrated previously in the Acoustic Concepts example.

Some Applications of CVP Concepts

● APPLY

CC6: Apply the CVP framework to managerial decisions.

Bob Luchinni, the accountant at Acoustic Concepts, wanted to demonstrate to the company's president, Prem Narayan, how the CVP concepts developed so far can be used in planning and decision making. The CVP framework provides management with the following *levers*: unit variable costs, fixed costs, and selling price. These levers can be used either singly or in combination to influence the sales volume. In so doing, the company's profitability will be affected. The objective of CVP analysis is to determine this impact on profits. The impact on profits will depend on the effect of the policy on total contribution margin and how that effect flows through to profits. The challenge for managers is that many policies that are proposed can involve changes to both revenues and costs. The ultimate impact on the bottom line—the company's profits—is rarely transparent without a careful analysis. In the following examples, try to identify which combination of levers management is proposing to pull, the nature of trade-offs facing management, and the effect of a proposed policy on the company's profits.

The following approach will be followed. First, the impact of a proposed policy on the *total* contribution margin will be determined. Second, the impact of a proposed policy on fixed costs will be determined, if necessary. By comparing these two impacts, it will be possible to determine the impact on the company's profits, that is, net income.

Example 1: Increase in Fixed Cost Leading to an Increase in Sales Volume

Acoustic Concepts is currently selling 400 speakers per month at a price of $250 per speaker. Variable costs are presently $150 per speaker. The sales manager feels that a

$10,000 increase in the monthly advertising budget will increase monthly sales by 30% to 520 speakers, thus increasing sales revenues by $30,000 from $100,000 to $130,000. Should the advertising budget be increased?

The policy proposes to pull the fixed cost lever—increase in the advertising budget. Volume is predicted to increase as a result. Before a decision can be taken to pull the lever, the impact on net income must be determined. The following table shows the effect of the proposed change in monthly advertising budget on net income:

	Current Sales	Sales with Additional Advertising Budget	Difference	Percentage of Sales
Sales	$100,000	$130,000	$30,000	100
Less: Variable expenses. .	60,000	78,000*	18,000	60
Contribution margin	40,000	52,000	12,000	40
Less: Fixed expenses. . . .	35,000	45,000†	10,000	
Net income	$ 5,000	$ 7,000	$ 2,000	

*520 units × $150 per unit = $78,000.

†$35,000 plus additional $10,000 monthly advertising budget = $45,000.

The increase in the advertising budget should be approved, since it would lead to an increase in net income of $2,000. There are two shorter ways to present this solution. The first alternative solution follows:

ALTERNATIVE SOLUTION 1

Expected total contribution margin:	
$130,000 × 40% CM ratio	$52,000
Present total contribution margin:	
$100,000 × 40% CM ratio	40,000
Incremental contribution margin	12,000
Change in fixed costs:	
Less: Incremental advertising expense	10,000
Increased net income	$ 2,000

Since in this case only the fixed costs and the sales volume change, the solution can be presented in an even shorter format, as follows:

ALTERNATIVE SOLUTION 2

Incremental contribution margin:	
$30,000 × 40% CM ratio	$12,000
Less: Incremental advertising expense	10,000
Increased net income	$ 2,000

Note that this approach does not depend on a knowledge of previous sales. Also, observe that it is unnecessary under either alternative to prepare an income statement. Both of the preceding solutions involve an **incremental analysis**, considering only those items of revenue, cost, and volume that will change if the new program is implemented. Although in each case a new income statement could have been prepared, most managers would prefer the incremental approach. It is simpler and more direct, focusing attention on the specific items involved in the decision. Finally, note that the expected impact on volume from the change in the advertising budget must be provided before you can decide to implement the proposed change to the advertising budget.

Example 2: Increase in Unit Variable Costs Leading to an Increase in Sales Volume

Acoustic Concepts is currently selling 400 speakers per month at a unit price of $250. Management is contemplating the use of higher-quality components, which would increase variable costs per unit from $150 to $160 (and thereby reducing the unit contribution by $10 per speaker). The sales manager predicts that the higher quality would increase sales by 20% to 480 speakers per month. Should the higher-quality components be used?

In this example, the proposal is to pull the variable cost per unit lever. The predicted impact on sales is an increase of 80 units. Now management must determine the impact on net income of the proposed policy. The way to do this is to determine the impact on total contribution and then the impact on fixed costs and then compare the two impacts.

The $10 increase in the unit variable costs will cause the unit contribution margin to drop from $100 to $90. The total contribution margin is expected to change as follows:

Expected total contribution margin with higher-quality components:	
480 speakers × $90 contribution margin per speaker	$43,200
Present total contribution margin:	
400 speakers × $100 contribution margin per speaker	40,000
Increase in total contribution margin	$ 3,200

Since fixed costs will not change, net income should increase by the $3,200 increase in total contribution shown previously. The higher-quality components should be used.

Example 3: Increase in Fixed Cost, Decrease in Selling Price, Leading to an Increase in Sales Volume

Acoustic Concepts is currently selling 400 speakers per month at a price of $250 per speaker. The variable costs are $150 per speaker. The sales manager would like to cut the selling price by $20 per speaker to $230 and increase the advertising budget by $15,000 per month. The sales manager argues that if these two steps are taken, unit sales will increase by 50% to 600 speakers per month. Should the changes be made?

Management is proposing to pull two levers—sales price and fixed costs—together to increase sales. A decrease of $20 per speaker in the selling price will reduce the unit contribution margin from $100 to $80. The increase in the advertising budget by $15,000 will cause fixed cost to increase by this amount. To determine the impact of these changes on net income, the effect on total contribution margin must be compared with the effect on fixed cost. This is shown in the following table:

Expected total contribution margin with higher volume due to a lower selling price and increase in the advertising budget:	
600 speakers × $80 contribution margin per speaker	$48,000
Present total contribution margin:	
400 speakers × $100 contribution margin per speaker	40,000
Incremental contribution margin (1)	8,000
Change in fixed costs:	
Increase in advertising budget (2)	15,000
Increase (reduction) in net income (1) – (2)	($7,000)

On the basis of the information above, the changes should not be made.

Example 4: Increase in Variable Cost per Unit and Decrease in Fixed Cost Leading to an Increase in Sales Volume

Acoustic Concepts is currently selling 400 speakers at a price of $250 per speaker. The variable costs are $150 per speaker. Fixed cost is $35,000. The sales manager would like to pay sales staff a commission of $15 per speaker sold, rather than pay them flat salaries that now total $6,000 per month. The sales manager is confident that the change will increase monthly sales by 15% to 460 speakers. Should the change be made?

In this example, management proposes to pull the variable cost and fixed cost levers, which is predicted to lead to an increase in sales. Paying a commission for each speaker sold instead of a flat salary will increase variable cost per speaker by $15 to $165 per speaker and reduce fixed cost by $6,000. Unit contribution margin will decrease by $15 to $85 per speaker. The impact of the these changes on total contribution margin and fixed cost is shown in the following table:

Expected total contribution margin with higher volume due to
  a higher variable cost per unit and decrease in fixed cost:
    460 speakers × $85 contribution margin per speaker $39,100
Present total contribution margin:
    400 speakers × $100 contribution margin per speaker 40,000
Incremental contribution margin (1) .... (900)
Change in fixed costs:
    Decrease in fixed cost from salaries avoided (2) .... (6,000)
Increase (reduction) in net income (1) – (2) .... $ 5,100

On the basis of the preceding analysis, the changes should be made. The company stands to increase net income by $5,100 by switching to a commission-based compensation system from the present policy of paying flat salaries.

The same conclusion can be obtained by preparing comparative income statements. This approach is shown in the following table:

	Present 400 Speakers per Month		Expected 460 Speakers per Month		Difference: Increase or (Decrease) in Net Income
	Total	Per Unit	Total	Per Unit	
Sales	$100,000	$250	$115,000	$250	$15,000
Less: Variable expenses.	60,000	150	75,900	165	(15,900)
Contribution margin ...	40,000	$100	39,100	$ 85	(900)
Less: Fixed expenses...	35,000		29,000		6,000
Net income	$ 5,000		$ 10,100		$ 5,100

Example 5: Calculation of Selling Price to Meet Profit Target

Acoustics Concepts has an opportunity to make a special-order bulk sale of 150 speakers to a wholesaler if an acceptable price can be worked out. This sale will not affect the company's regular sales or its fixed cost. Variable cost is $150 per speaker. Acoustic Concepts would like to make a profit of $3,000 from this sale. What price per speaker should be quoted?

Since the special sale will not affect fixed costs, the company's profits from the sale will be $3,000 if the total contribution margin from the sale is also $3,000. Since the sale is for 150 speakers, the contribution margin per speaker has to be $3,000 ÷ 150 = $20. Given a variable cost of $150 per speaker, the desired selling price per speaker will be the variable cost per speaker plus the contribution margin per speaker, that is, $150 + $20 = $170. The company should quote a price of $170 per speaker. The calculation is summarized as follows:

Variable cost per speaker	$150
Desired profit per speaker:	
$3,000 ÷ 150 speakers	20
Quoted price per speaker	$170

This example is different from the previous examples because it does not involve tracing the impact of pulling a combination of levers on profits. Instead, it illustrates the use of the CVP framework to determine a pricing policy for a special sales order, given costs and a profit target. The CVP framework is a flexible framework that can aid management in planning and decision making.

Importance of the Contribution Margin

CVP analysis seeks the most profitable combination of variable cost per unit, fixed cost, and selling price. These are levers available for management to pull to influence first volume and ultimately the company's profits. The examples we presented show that without a framework to analyze the effect of pulling the levers, management cannot determine if a proposed policy to improve profits should be adopted.

The challenge is that using a combination of levers involves trade-offs: you have to spend money to make money. Whether you come out ahead at the end will depend on whether the incremental total contribution compares favourably with the incremental fixed cost. Exhibit 11–3, a summary of the examples, illustrates this point.

In Example 1, management predicts an increase in volume from increasing the fixed cost. The increase in volume causes the total contribution margin to increase. Profits increased because this increase is greater that the increase in the fixed cost. In this example, management spends money (increases fixed cost) to make money (increase profits).

In Example 2, a volume increase is obtained because of an increase in variable cost per unit. Although the unit contribution margin decreased, the *total* contribution margin increased because of the increase in volume. The increase in the total contribution margin flows through to the bottom line because the fixed costs are unchanged.

Exhibit 11–3

Summary of CVP Examples Illustrating the Use of the CVP Framework for Decision Making

	Example 1	Example 2	Example 3	Example 4
Revenue lever: Selling price	Unchanged	Unchanged	Decrease by $20 per speaker	Unchanged
Cost lever: Variable cost per unit	Unchanged	Increase by $10 per speaker	Unchanged	Increase by $15 per speaker
Cost lever: Fixed cost	Increase by $10,000	Unchanged	Increase by $15,000	Decrease by $6,000
Predicted impact on volume	Increase by 120 speakers	Increase by 80 speakers	Increase by 200 speakers	Increase by 60 speakers
Calculated impact on total contribution margin	Increase by $12,000	Increase by $3,200	Increase by $8,000	Decrease by $900
Calculated impact on net income	Increase by $2,000	Increase by $3,200	Decrease by $7,000	Increase by $5,100

In Example 3, management decreases unit price and increases fixed cost. The increase in volume from taking these steps does not increase the total contribution margin sufficiently to cover the increase in fixed costs. Profits are reduced. Therefore, the proposed policy is rejected. Note here that simply looking at the total contribution margin alone is not enough if fixed costs are also changed. The correct conclusion can only be reached if a comparison is made of the impact on the total contribution margin with the impact on fixed cost.

In Example 4, management decreases fixed expenses and simultaneously increases variable cost per unit. The unit contribution margin is reduced. Management predicts an increase in volume from the steps taken. But the total contribution margin *decreases* from its current level because the increase in volume cannot offset the effect of the reduction in the unit contribution margin. Nonetheless, profits increase because fixed expense is reduced by more than the decrease in the total contribution margin. This example illustrates that a decline in contribution margin need not cause too much distress, provided fixed costs are reduced by even more.

In general, these examples illustrate that it is important to carefully analyze a policy using the CVP framework to determine the impact on profits, especially when there are increases (or decreases) to both costs and revenue. The key is that the effect of a policy on the total contribution margin must be compared with the effect of the policy on fixed cost. This is clear from Exhibit 11–3, where you can see that the impact on the bottom line follows from subtracting the impact on the total contribution margin from the impact on the fixed cost.

Finally, note that the size of the unit contribution margin (or the size of the CM ratio) will heavily influence the steps a company is willing to take to improve profits. For example, the greater the unit contribution margin for a product, the greater is the amount that a company will spend in order to increase sales volume by a given percentage (look at Example 1 again). This explains why companies with high-unit contribution margins (like car makers) advertise so heavily, while companies with low-unit contribution margins (such as appliance makers) tend to spend much less on advertising.

Break-Even Analysis

CVP analysis is sometimes referred to simply as *break-even analysis*. This is unfortunate because break-even analysis is just a special case of CVP analysis. Break-even analysis is designed to answer such questions as those asked by Prem Narayan, the president of Acoustic Concepts, concerning how far sales could drop before the company begins to lose money.

> ⊙ APPLY
>
> CC7: Compute break-even sales using the equation method.

Break-Even Computations

Previously in the chapter, we defined the break-even point to be the level of sales at which the company's profit is zero. The break-even point can be computed using either the *equation method* or the *contribution margin method*–the two methods are equivalent.

THE EQUATION METHOD The **equation method** centres on the contribution approach to the income statement illustrated previously. Recall that the format of this income statement can be expressed in equation form as follows:

$$\text{Profits} = \text{Sales} - (\text{Variable expenses} + \text{Fixed expenses})$$

Rearranging this equation slightly yields the following equation, which is widely used in CVP analysis:

$$\text{Sales} = \text{Variable expenses} + \text{Fixed expenses} + \text{Profits}$$

At the break-even point, profits are zero. Therefore, the break-even point can be computed by finding that point where sales equal the total of variable expenses plus the fixed expenses. For Acoustic Concepts, the break-even point in unit sales, Q, can be computed as follows:

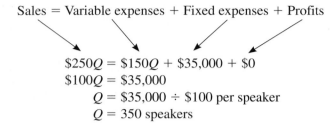

$$Sales = Variable\ expenses + Fixed\ expenses + Profits$$

$$\$250Q = \$150Q + \$35,000 + \$0$$
$$\$100Q = \$35,000$$
$$Q = \$35,000 \div \$100\ per\ speaker$$
$$Q = 350\ speakers$$

where:

Q = Number (quantity) of speakers sold

$\$250$ = Unit sales price

$\$150$ = Unit variable expenses

$\$35,000$ = Total fixed expenses

The break-even point in sales dollars can be computed by multiplying the break-even level of unit sales by the selling price per unit:

$$350\ speakers \times \$250\ per\ speaker = \$87,500$$

The break-even in total sales dollars, X, can also be directly computed as follows:

$$Sales = Variable\ expenses + Fixed\ expenses + Profits$$
$$X = 0.60X + \$35,000 + \$0$$
$$0.40X = \$35,000$$
$$X = \$35,000 \div 0.40$$
$$X = \$87,500$$

where:

X = Total sales dollars

0.60 = Variable expense ratio (Variable expenses $\div$ Sales)

$\$35,000$ = Total fixed expenses

Firms often have data available only in percentage or ratio form, and the approach we have just illustrated must then be used to find the break-even point. Note that use of ratios in the equation yields a break-even point in sales dollars, rather than in units sold. The break-even point in units sold is the following:

$$\$87,500 \div \$250\ per\ speaker = 350\ speakers$$

YOU DECIDE　　Recruit

Assume that you are being recruited by Connexus Corp. and have an interview scheduled later this week. You are interested in working for this company for a variety of reasons. In preparation for the interview, you did some research at your local library and gathered the following information about the company. Connexus is a company set up by two young engineers, George Searle and Humphrey Chen, to allow consumers to order music CDs on their cellphones. Suppose you hear on the radio a cut from a CD that you would like to own. If you subscribe to their service, you would pick up your

continued

YOU DECIDE

cellphone, punch "*CD," and enter the radio station's frequency and the time you heard the song, and the CD would be on its way to you.

Connexus charges about $17 for a CD, including shipping. The company pays its supplier about $13, leaving a contribution margin of $4 per CD. Because of the fixed costs of running the service (about $1,850,000 a year), Searle expects the company to lose about $1.5 million in its first year of operations on sales of 88,000 CDs.

What are your initial impressions of this company based on the information you gathered? What other information would you want to obtain during the job interview?

Adapted from: Peter Kafka, "Play It Again," *Forbes*, July 26, 1999, p. 94.

THE CONTRIBUTION MARGIN METHOD The **contribution margin method** is actually just a shortcut version of the equation method already described. The approach centres on the idea that each unit sold provides a certain amount of contribution margin that goes toward covering fixed costs. To find how many units must be sold to break even, divide the total fixed expenses by the unit contribution margin:

> APPLY
>
> CC8: Compute break-even sales using the contribution margin approach.

$$\text{Break-even point in units sold} = \frac{\text{Fixed expenses}}{\text{Unit contribution margin}}$$

Each speaker generates a contribution margin of $100 ($250 selling price, less $150 variable expenses). Since the total fixed expenses are $35,000, the break-even point is computed as follows:

$$\frac{\text{Fixed expenses}}{\text{Unit contribution margin}} = \frac{\$35,000}{\$100 \text{ per speaker}} = 350 \text{ speakers}$$

A variation of this method uses the CM ratio instead of the unit contribution margin. The result is the break-even in total sales dollars, rather than in total units sold.

$$\text{Break-even point in total sales dollars} = \frac{\text{Fixed expenses}}{\text{CM ratio}}$$

In the Acoustic Concepts example, the calculations are as follows:

$$\frac{\text{Fixed expenses}}{\text{CM ratio}} = \frac{\$35,000}{0.40} = \$87,500$$

This approach, based on the CM ratio, is particularly useful in those situations where a company has multiple product lines and wishes to compute a single break-even point for the company as a whole. More is said on this point in Appendix 11A.

Lean Manufacturing Helps Break Even

IN BUSINESS TODAY

What does lean manufacturing have to do with breaking even? Recall from Chapter 1 that implementing lean business principles can help companies reduce costs, which means less sales revenues are required to break even. This is exactly what 60-year-old Groupe Bocenor Inc. did. The company, with three plants in Quebec and employing over 500 people, is a leading manufacturer of doors and windows with customers in Canada and the United States. The company used a number of different strategies to improve its earnings, including implementing elements of a lean manufacturing program, which helped substantially lower the break-even point of its manufacturing operation. However, due to other reasons the company posted negative earnings before interest, income taxes, depreciation, and amortization (EBITDA) in 2007.

Sources: www.bocenor.com; "Fiscal 2006-2007: Groupe Bocenor Completes its Restructuring and Intensifies its Product and Market Development," *Canada NewsWire*, Ottawa: May 17, 2007. p.1.

Target Profit Analysis

○ APPLY

CC9: Compute the sales needed to achieve a target profit.

CVP formulas can be used to determine the sales volume needed to achieve a target profit. Suppose that Prem Narayan of Acoustic Concepts would like to earn a target profit of $40,000 per month. How many speakers would have to be sold?

THE CVP EQUATION One approach is to use the equation method. Instead of solving for the unit sales where profits are zero, you solve for the unit sales where profits are $40,000.

$$\text{Sales} = \text{Variable expenses} + \text{Fixed expenses} + \text{Profits}$$
$$\$250Q = \$150Q + \$35,000 + \$40,000$$
$$\$100Q = \$75,000$$
$$Q = \$75,000 \div \$100 \text{ per speaker}$$
$$Q = 750 \text{ speakers}$$

where:

Q = Number of speakers sold
250 = Unit sales price
150 = Unit variable expenses
$35,000$ = Total fixed expenses
$40,000$ = Target profit

Thus, the target profit can be achieved by selling 750 speakers per month, which represents $187,500 in total sales ($250 per speaker × 750 speakers).

THE CONTRIBUTION MARGIN APPROACH A second approach involves expanding the contribution margin formula to include the target profit:

$$\text{Unit sales to attain the target profit} = \frac{\text{Fixed expenses} + \text{Target profit}}{\text{Unit contribution margin}}$$
$$= \frac{\$35,000 + \$40,000}{\$100 \text{ per speaker}}$$
$$= 750 \text{ speakers}$$

This approach gives the same answer as the equation method, since it is simply a shortcut version of the equation method. Similarly, the dollar sales needed to attain the target profit can be computed as follows:

$$\text{Dollar sales to attain target profit} = \frac{\text{Fixed expenses} + \text{Target profit}}{\text{CM ratio}}$$
$$= \frac{\$35,000 + \$40,000}{0.40}$$
$$= \$187,500$$

Likewise, this approach gives the same answer as the equation method, since it is simply a shortcut version of the equation method.

Often, companies will state their desired target profit level as a percentage of sales rather than in dollars. For example, assume that Acoustics Concepts wishes to earn a profit equivalent to 20% of its sales. What should the sales be?

THE CVP EQUATION We can use the following equation to compute the required sales:

$$
\begin{aligned}
\text{Sales} &= \text{Variable expenses} + \text{Fixed expenses} + \text{Profits} \\
X &= 0.60\,X + \$35,000 + 0.20X \\
X &= 0.80\,X + \$35,000 \\
0.20X &= \$35,000 \\
X &= \$35,000 \div 0.20 = \$175,000
\end{aligned}
$$

At this level of sales, variable expenses will be $105,000 (60% of $175,000), which means that total expenses will be $140,000 ($105,000 + $35,000). The resulting profit will amount to $35,000 (the required 20% of $175,000).

The Effect of Income Tax

We did not include taxes in the our discussion of target profit analysis; however, most organizations (definitely for-profit businesses) are required to pay income tax.

Assume a 40% income tax rate; how will this change the analysis? In order to conduct the analysis, we must first convert the target after-tax income into before-tax income, then compute the required sales level exactly as we did before (in the no-tax situation). Why should we convert the target profit into before-tax numbers? We do this because our first measure of income on an income statement is a before-tax measure. Sales less costs results in a before-tax measure of income, which then attracts income tax.

How do we convert after-tax income into its before-tax equivalent? The formula is simple and is shown below.

$$
\begin{aligned}
\text{After-tax income (ATI)} &= (1 - t) \times \text{Before-tax income (BTI)} \\
\text{BTI} &= \text{ATI} \div (1 - t)
\end{aligned}
$$

Recall our example where the unit selling price was $250, unit variable cost was $150, and the annual fixed expenses were $35,000. We will use this basic data in illustrating the effect of income taxes on target profit analysis, that is, computing the sales level required to achieve a certain target profit. For the purposes of this analysis, we will use an income tax rate of 40%.

CASE 1 Assume that the company's target ATI is $40,000; we convert this amount into the target BTI as follows:

$$
\begin{aligned}
\text{BTI} &= \$40,000 \div (1 - 0.40) \\
&= \$66,667
\end{aligned}
$$

The unit sales required to achieve the target profit can now be computed as follows:

$$
\begin{aligned}
&(\text{Fixed expenses} + \text{BTI}) \div \text{Unit contribution margin} \\
&= (\$35,000 + \$66,667) \div \$100 \\
&\approx 1,017 \text{ units}
\end{aligned}
$$

We can compute the sales in dollars by multiplying 1,017 units by the sales price of $250, which will result in $254,250.

 KNOW APPLY

CC10: Explain the effect of income tax on target profit analysis and compute the sales needed to achieve a target after-tax profit.

CASE 2 Assume that the company's ATI is 20% of sales revenue (X); we convert this into the target BTI as follows:

$$BTI = 0.20X \div (1 - 0.40)$$
$$= 0.333X$$

The sales revenue (X) required to achieve the target profit can now be computed as follows:

$$X = 0.60 X + \$35,000 + 0.333X$$
$$0.067X = \$35,000$$
$$X = \$35,000 \div 0.067$$
$$\approx \$522,388$$

We can compute the sales in units by dividing $522,388 by the sales price of $250, which will result in approximately 2,090 units.

Notice that when we consider taxes, the sales required to achieve the target profit increases significantly compared to the previous *tax-free* situation. Tax is a real expense for organizations that they must consider in their planning and decision making.

The Margin of Safety

● APPLY   ● KNOW

CC11: Explain and compute the margin of safety.

The **margin of safety** is the excess of budgeted (or actual) sales over the break-even volume of sales. It states the amount by which sales can drop before losses begin to be incurred. The higher the margin of safety, the lower is the risk of not breaking even. The formula for its calculation is as follows:

Margin of safety = Total budgeted (or actual) sales − Break-even sales

The margin of safety can also be expressed in percentage form. This percentage is obtained by dividing the margin of safety in dollar terms by total sales:

$$\text{Margin of safety percentage} = \frac{\text{Margin of safety in dollars}}{\text{Total budgeted (or actual) sales}}$$

The calculations for the margin of safety for Acoustic Concepts are as follows:

Sales (at the current volume of 400 speakers) (a)	$100,000
Break-even sales (at 350 speakers)	87,500
Margin of safety (in dollars) (b)	$ 12,500
Margin of safety as a percentage of sales, (b) ÷ (a)	12.5%

This margin of safety means that at the current level of sales and with the company's current prices and cost structure, a reduction in sales of $12,500, or 12.5%, would result in just breaking even.

In a single-product firm like Acoustic Concepts, the margin of safety can also be expressed in terms of the number of units sold by dividing the margin of safety in dollars by the selling price per unit. In this case, the margin of safety is 50 speakers ($12,500 ÷ $250 per speaker = 50 speakers).

DECISION MAKER   **Loan Officer**

Ketan Trivedi and Bharat Shah, former oil merchants from Ahmedabad, India, opened a fast-food restaurant in Calgary, in the hopes of establishing a chain in Canada. They called their restaurant Chai and Snacks. For $6 per serving, Chai and Snacks offers 12 homemade snacks each day. Trivedi and Shah report that in their first year of operation,

continued

they netted $210,000 on sales of $700,000. They report that it costs about $2 per serving to make the snacks.

Assume that Trivedi and Shah have approached your bank for a loan. As the loan officer, you should consider a variety of factors, including the company's margin of safety. Assuming that other information about the company is favourable, would you consider Chai and Snacks' margin of safety to be comfortable enough to extend the loan?

It is Thursday morning, and Prem Narayan and Bob Luchinni are discussing the results of Bob's analysis.

Prem: Bob, everything you have shown me is pretty clear. I can see what impact some of the sales manager's suggestions would have on our profits. Some of those suggestions are quite good, and some are not so good. I also understand that our break-even is 350 speakers, and so we have to make sure we don't slip below that level of sales. What really bothers me is that we are only selling 400 speakers a month now. What did you call the 50-speaker cushion?
Bob: That's the margin of safety.
Prem: Such a small cushion makes me very nervous. What can we do to increase the margin of safety?
Bob: We have to increase total sales or decrease the break-even point or both.
Prem: And to decrease the break-even point, we have to either decrease our fixed expenses or increase our unit contribution margin?
Bob: Exactly.
Prem: And to increase our unit contribution margin, we must either increase our selling price or decrease the variable cost per unit?
Bob: Correct.
Prem: So, what do you suggest?
Bob: Well, the analysis doesn't tell us which of these to do, but it does indicate we have a potential problem here.
Prem: If you don't have any immediate suggestions, I would like to call a general meeting next week to discuss ways we can work on increasing the margin of safety. I think everyone will be concerned about how vulnerable we are to even small downturns in sales.
Bob: I agree. This is something everyone will want to work on.

MANAGERIAL ACCOUNTING IN ACTION

The Wrap Up

Acoustic Concepts, Inc.

CVP Considerations in Choosing a Cost Structure

As stated in Chapter 3, cost structure refers to the relative proportion of fixed and variable costs in an organization. An organization often has some latitude in trading off between these two types of costs. For example, fixed investments in automated equipment can reduce variable labour costs. In this section, we discuss the choice of a cost structure. We focus on the impact of cost structure on profit stability, in which *operating leverage* pays a key role.

Cost Structure and Profit Stability

When a manager has some latitude in trading off between fixed and variable costs, which cost structure is better–high variable costs and low fixed costs, or the opposite? No single answer to this question is possible; there may be advantages either way, depending on

KNOW

CC12: Explain the effect of cost structure on a company's profitability.

the specific circumstances. To show what we mean by this statement, refer to the income statements given below for two blueberry farms. Flat Farm depends on migrant workers to pick its berries by hand, whereas Balloon Farm has invested in expensive berry-picking machines. Consequently, Flat Farm has higher variable costs, but Balloon Farm has higher fixed costs:

	Flat Farm		Balloon Farm	
	Amount	Percent	Amount	Percentage
Sales	$100,000	100%	$100,000	100
Less: Variable expenses.	60,000	60	30,000	30
Contribution margin	40,000	40%	70,000	70
Less: Fixed expenses.	30,000		60,000	
Net income	$ 10,000		$ 10,000	

The question as to which farm has the better cost structure depends on many factors, including the long-term trend in sales, year-to-year fluctuations in the level of sales, and the attitude of the owners toward risk. If sales are expected to be above $100,000 in the future, then Balloon Farm probably has the better cost structure. The reason is that its CM ratio is higher, and its profits will therefore increase more rapidly as sales increase. To illustrate, assume that each farm experiences a 10% increase in sales without any increase in fixed costs. The new income statements would be as follows:

	Flat Farm		Balloon Farm	
	Amount	Percent	Amount	Percentage
Sales	$110,000	100%	$110,000	100
Less: Variable expenses. . .	66,000	60	33,000	30
Contribution margin	44,000	40%	77,000	70
Less: Fixed expenses.	30,000		60,000	
Net income	$ 14,000		$ 17,000	

Balloon Farm has experienced a greater increase in net income due to its higher CM ratio even though the increase in sales was the same for both farms.

What if sales drop below $100,000 from time to time? What are the break-even points of the two farms? What are their margins of safety? The computations needed to answer these questions are carried out following using the contribution margin method:

	Flat Farm	Balloon Farm
Fixed expenses	$ 30,000	$ 60,000
Contribution margin ratio	÷ 40%	÷ 70%
Break-even in total sales dollars	$ 75,000	$ 85,714
Total current sales (a)	$100,000	$100,000
Break-even sales	75,000	85,714
Margin of safety in sales dollars (b)	$ 25,000	$ 14,286
Margin of safety as a percentage of sales, (b) ÷ (a).	25.0%	14.3%

This analysis makes it clear that Flat Farm is less vulnerable to downturns than Balloon Farm. We can identify two reasons why it is less vulnerable. First, due to its lower fixed expenses, Flat Farm has a lower break-even point and a higher margin of safety, as shown by the preceding computations. Therefore, it will not incur losses as quickly as Balloon Farm in periods of sharply declining sales. Second, due to its lower CM ratio, Flat Farm will not lose contribution margin as rapidly as Balloon Farm when sales fall off. Thus, Flat Farm's income will be less volatile. We saw previously that this is a drawback when sales increase, but it provides more protection when sales drop.

   To summarize, without knowing the future, it is not obvious which cost structure is better. Both have advantages and disadvantages. Balloon Farm, with its higher fixed costs and lower variable costs, will experience wider swings in net income as changes take place in sales, with greater profits in good years and greater losses in bad years. Flat Farm, with its lower fixed costs and higher variable costs, will enjoy greater stability in net income and will be more protected from losses during bad years, but at the cost of lower net income in good years.

A Losing Cost Structure   IN BUSINESS TODAY

Both JetBlue and United Airlines use an Airbus 235 to fly from Dulles International Airport near Washington, DC, to Oakland, California. Both planes have a pilot, copilot, and four flight attendants. That is where the similarity ends. Based on 2002 data, the pilot on the United flight earned $16,350 to $18,000 a month compared to $6,800 per month for the JetBlue pilot. United's senior flight attendants on the plane earned more than $41,000 per year; whereas the JetBlue attendants were paid $16,800 to $27,000 per year. Largely because of the higher labour costs at United, its costs of operating the flight were more than 60% higher than JetBlue's costs. Due to intense fare competition from JetBlue and other low-cost carriers, United was unable to cover its higher operating costs on this and many other flights. Consequently, United went into bankruptcy at the end of 2002.

Source: Susan Carey, "Costly Race in the Sky," *The Wall Street Journal*, September 9, 2002, pp. B1 and B3.

Operating Leverage

A **lever** is a tool for multiplying force. By using a lever, you can move a massive object with only a modest amount of force. In business, *operating leverage* serves a similar purpose. **Operating leverage** is a measure of how sensitive net income is to percentage changes in sales. Operating leverage acts as a multiplier. If operating leverage is high, a small percentage increase in sales can produce a much larger percentage increase in net income.

   Operating leverage can be illustrated by returning to the data for the two blueberry farms. We previously showed that a 10% increase in sales (from $100,000 to $110,000 in each farm) results in a 70% increase in the net income of Balloon Farm (from $10,000 to $17,000) and only a 40% increase in the net income of Flat Farm (from $10,000 to $14,000). Thus, for a 10% increase in sales, Balloon Farm experiences a much greater percentage increase in profits than does Flat Farm. Therefore, Balloon Farm has greater operating leverage than Flat Farm.

   The **degree of operating leverage** at a given level of sales is computed by the following formula:

$$\text{Degree of operating leverage} = \frac{\text{Contribution margin}}{\text{Net income}}$$

The degree of operating leverage is a measure, at a given level of sales, of how a percentage change in sales volume will affect profits. To illustrate, the degree of operating leverage for the two farms at a $100,000 sales level would be computed as follows:

APPLY   KNOW

CC13: Compute the degree of operating leverage and explain its usefulness.

$$\text{Flat Farm: } \frac{\$40{,}000}{\$10{,}000} = 4$$

$$\text{Balloon Farm: } \frac{\$70{,}000}{\$10{,}000} = 7$$

Since the degree of operating leverage for Flat Farm is 4, the farm's net income grows four times as fast as its sales. Similarly, Balloon Farm's net income grows seven times as fast as its sales. Thus, if sales increase by 10%, then we can expect the net income of Flat Farm to increase by four times this amount, or by 40%, and the net income of Balloon Farm to increase by seven times this amount, or by 70%.

	(1) Percent Increase in Sales	(2) Degree of Operating Leverage	(3) Percentage Increase in Net Income (1) × (2)
Flat Farm.	10%	4	40
Balloon Farm	10%	7	70

What is responsible for the higher operating leverage at Balloon Farm? The only difference between the two farms is their cost structure. If two companies have the same total revenue and same total expense but different cost structures, then the company with the higher proportion of fixed costs in its cost structure will have higher operating leverage. Referring to our original example on page 458, when both farms have sales of $100,000 and total expenses of $90,000, one-third of Flat Farm's costs are fixed but two-thirds of Balloon Farm's costs are fixed. As a consequence, Balloon's degree of operating leverage is higher than Flat's.

The degree of operating leverage is not constant; it is greatest at sales levels near the break-even point and decreases as sales and profits rise. This can be seen from the following tabulation, which shows the degree of operating leverage for Flat Farm at various sales levels. (Data used earlier for Flat Farm are shown in colour.)

Sales	$75,000	$80,000	$100,000	$150,000	$225,000
Less: Variable expenses.	45,000	48,000	60,000	90,000	135,000
Contribution margin (a)	30,000	32,000	40,000	60,000	90,000
Less: Fixed expenses.	30,000	30,000	30,000	30,000	30,000
Net income (b)	$ -0-	$ 2,000	$ 10,000	$ 30,000	$ 60,000
Degree of operating leverage, (a) ÷ (b)	∞	16	4	2	1.5

Thus, a 10% increase in sales would increase profits by only 15% (10% × 1.5) if the company were operating at a $225,000 sales level, as compared with the 40% increase we computed earlier at the $100,000 sales level. The degree of operating leverage will continue to decrease the farther the company moves from its break-even point. At the break-even point, the degree of operating leverage will be infinitely large ($30,000 contribution margin ÷ $0 net income = ∞).

A manager can use the degree of operating leverage to quickly estimate what impact various percentage changes in sales will have on profits, without the necessity of preparing detailed income statements. As shown by our examples, the effects of operating leverage can be dramatic. If a company is near its break-even point, then even small percentage increases in sales can yield large percentage increases in profits. *This explains why management will often work very hard for only a small increase in sales volume.* If the degree of operating leverage is 5, then a 6% increase in sales would translate into a 30% increase in profits.

Application Competency Summary

Application Competency	Deliverable	Source Documents and Key Information	Steps	Knowledge Competency
Compute the contribution margin ratio. ○ CC2	*Key Information* Contribution margin to sales ratio *Report/Document* No specific report	*Sales, Cost/Expense Accounts in the General Ledger* Actual sales, variable and fixed costs *Master Budget* Budgeted sales, variable and fixed costs	1. Divide contribution margin by sales revenue (either in total or per unit) to compute the contribution margin ratio.	Contribution margin ○ CC16 (Ch. 3)
Prepare and intersect a CVP graph. ○ CC4	*Key Information* Cost and sales patterns Break-even point Profit and loss areas *Report/Document* CVP graph	*Sales, Cost/Expense Accounts in the General Ledger* Actual sales, variable and fixed costs *Master Budget* Budgeted sales, variable and fixed costs	1. Using number of units sold as the X-axis and total cost/sales (in dollars) as the Y-axis, draw three lines. 2. Draw a horizontal line representing the fixed cost line—this will intersect the Y-axis at the fixed cost point. 3. Draw a total cost line originating from the fixed cost point on the Y-axis—this upward-sloping straight line will increase correspondingly with the number of units sold. 4. Draw an upward-sloping sales revenue line from the origin. 5. Label the point where the total cost and sales revenue lines meet as the break-even point, and the area between the two lines above (below) the break-even point as the profit (loss) area.	Variable and fixed cost behaviour ○ CC1, 3 (Ch. 3)
Apply the CVP framework to different managerial decisions. ○ CC6	*Key Information* Impact of decision on sales, costs, and profitability *Report/Document* No specific report	*Sales, Cost/Expense Accounts in the General Ledger* Actual sales, variable and fixed costs *Master Budget* Budgeted sales, variable and fixed costs	1. Set up the basic profit equation using the base data, then alter the equation by plugging the revised numbers to assess the impact of different decisions on profitability.	Basic profit equation ○ CC1
Compute break-even sales using the equation method. ○ CC7	*Key Information* Sales required to incur no profit and no loss *Report/Document* No specific report	*Sales, Cost/Expense Accounts in the General Ledger* Actual sales, variable and fixed costs *Master Budget* Budgeted sales, variable and fixed costs	1. Set up the basic profit equation, equate profit to zero, and compute break-even sales units by manipulating the two sides of the equation: divide fixed expenses by the contribution margin per unit to compute break-even sales units.	

continued

Application Competency	Deliverable	Source Documents and Key Information	Steps	Knowledge Competency
Compute break-even sales using the contribution margin approach. ○ CC8	*Key Information* Sales required to incur no profit and no loss *Report/Document* No specific report	*Sales, Cost/Expense Accounts in the General Ledger* Actual sales, variable and fixed costs *Master Budget* Budgeted sales, variable and fixed costs	1. Compute contribution margin ratio. 2. Divide fixed expenses by the contribution margin ratio to compute the break-even sales dollars.	Basic profit equation ○ CC1 Contribution margin ratio ○ CC2
Compute the sales needed to achieve a target profit. ○ CC9	*Key Information* Sales required to achieve a specified before-tax target profit *Report/Document* No specific report	*Sales, Cost/Expense Accounts in the General Ledger* Actual sales, variable and fixed costs *Master Budget* Budgeted sales, variable and fixed costs	1. Set up the basic profit equation and compute the sales units by manipulating the two sides of the equation: divide fixed expenses plus target profit by the contribution margin per unit to compute the sales units.	Basic profit equation ○ CC1
Compute the sales needed to achieve a target after-tax profit. ○ CC10	*Key Information* Sales required to achieve a specified after-tax target profit *Report/Document* No specific report	*Sales, Cost/Expense Accounts in the General Ledger* Actual sales, variable and fixed costs *Master Budget* Budgeted sales, variable and fixed costs	1. Convert the after-tax profit to its equivalent before-tax amount. 2. Set up the basic profit equation and compute sales units by manipulating the two sides of the equation: divide fixed expenses plus target before-tax profit by the contribution margin per unit to compute the sales units.	
Compute the margin of safety. ○ CC11	*Key Information* Sales above break-even point *Report/Document* No specific report	*Sales, Cost/Expense Accounts in the General Ledger* Actual sales, variable and fixed costs *Master Budget* Budgeted sales, variable and fixed costs	1. Deduct the break-even sales from the actual or budgeted sales to compute the margin of safety in dollars.	Break-even point ○ CC7
Compute the degree of operating leverage. ○ CC13	*Key Information* Ratio of contribution margin to net income *Report/Document* No specific report	*Contribution Margin Income Statement* Contribution margin Net income	1. Divide contribution margin by net income to compute the degree of operating leverage.	Contribution margin ○ CC2 Cost structure ○ CC12

Guidance Answers to You Decide and Decision Maker

RECRUIT (p. 452)

You can get a feel for the challenges that this company will face by determining its break-even point. Start by estimating the company's variable expense ratio:

Variable cost per unit ÷ Selling price per unit = Variable expense ratio

$$\$13 \div \$17 = 76.5\%$$

Then, estimate the company's variable expenses:

$$\text{Sales} \times \text{Variable expense ratio} = \text{Estimated amount of variable expenses}$$
$$\$1,500,000 \times 0.765 = \$1,147,500$$

Next, put the contribution format income statement into an equation format to estimate the company's current level of fixed expenses:

$$\text{Sales} = \text{Variable expenses} + \text{Fixed expenses} + \text{Net income (loss)}$$
$$\$1,500,000 = \$1,147,500 + X + (\$1,500,000)$$
$$X = \$1,500,000 - \$1,147,500 + \$1,500,000$$
$$X = \$1,852,500$$

Finally, use the equation approach to estimate the company's break-even point:

$$\text{Sales} = \text{Variable expenses} + \text{Fixed expenses} + \text{Profits}$$
$$\$17Q = \$13Q + \$1,852,500 + \$0$$
$$\$4Q = \$1,852,500$$
$$Q = 463,125$$

Assuming that its cost structure stays the same, ConneXus needs to increase its sales by 527%—from 88,000 to 463,125 CDs—just to break even. After it reaches that break-even point, net income will increase by $4 (the contribution margin) for each additional CD that it sells. Joining the company would be a risky proposition; you should be prepared with some probing questions when you arrive for your interview. (For example, what steps does the company plan to take to increase sales? How might the company reduce its fixed and/or variable expenses so as to lower its break-even point?)

LOAN OFFICER (p. 456)

To determine the company's margin of safety, you need to determine its break-even point. Start by estimating the company's variable expense ratio:

$$\text{Variable cost per unit} \div \text{Selling price per unit} = \text{Variable expense ratio}$$
$$\$2 \div \$6 = 33.3\% \text{ or } \frac{1}{3}$$

Then, estimate the company's variable expenses:

$$\text{Sales} \times \text{Variable expense ratio} = \text{Estimated amount of variable expenses}$$
$$\$700,000 \times \frac{1}{3} = \$233,333$$

Next, put the contribution format income statement into an equation format to estimate the company's current level of fixed expenses:

$$\text{Sales} = \text{Variable expenses} + \text{Fixed expenses} + \text{Net income}$$
$$\$700,000 = \$233,333 + X + \$210,000$$
$$X = \$700,000 - \$233,333 - \$210,000$$
$$X = \$256,667$$

Use the equation approach to estimate the company's break-even point:

$$\text{Sales} = \text{Variable expenses} + \text{Fixed expenses} + \text{Profits}$$
$$X = \frac{1}{3}X + \$256,667 + \$0$$
$$\frac{2}{3}X = \$256,667$$
$$X = \$385,000$$

Finally, compute the company's margin of safety:

$$\text{Margin of safety} = (\text{Sales} - \text{Break-even sales}) \div \text{Sales}$$
$$= (\$700,000 - \$385,000) \div \$700,000$$
$$= 45\%$$

The margin of safety appears to be adequate; so, if the other information about the company is favourable, a loan would seem to be justified.

Review Problem: CVP Relationships

Voltar Company manufactures and sells a telephone answering machine. The company's contribution margin income statement for the most recent year is given below:

	Total	Per Unit	Percentage of Sales
Sales (20,000 units).........	$1,200,000	$60	100
Less: Variable expenses......	900,000	45	?
Contribution margin	300,000	$15	?
Less: Fixed expenses........	240,000		
Net operating income	$ 60,000		

Management is anxious to improve the company's profit performance and has asked for an analysis of a number of items.

Required:
1. Compute the company's CM ratio and variable expense ratio.
2. Compute the company's break-even point in both units and sales dollars. Use the equation method.
3. Assume that sales increase by $400,000 next year. If cost behaviour patterns remain unchanged, by how much will the company's net operating income increase? Use the CM ratio to determine your answer.
4. Refer to the original data. Assume that next year management wants the company to earn a minimum profit of $90,000. How many units will have to be sold to meet this target profit figure?
5. Refer to the original data. Compute the company's margin of safety in both dollar and percentage forms.
6. a. Compute the company's degree of operating leverage at the present level of sales.
   b. Assume that through a more intense effort by the sales staff the company's sales increase by 8% next year. By what percentage would you expect net income to increase? Use the operating leverage concept to obtain your answer.
   c. Verify your answer to part (b) by preparing a new income statement showing an 8% increase in sales.
7. In an effort to increase sales and profits, management is considering the use of a higher-quality speaker. The higher-quality speaker would increase variable costs by $3 per unit, but management could eliminate one quality inspector who is paid a salary of $30,000 per year. The sales manager estimates that the higher-quality speaker would increase annual sales by at least 20%.
   a. Assuming that changes are made as described above, prepare a projected income statement for next year. Show data on total, per-unit, and percentage bases.
   b. Compute the company's new break-even point in both units and dollars of sales. Use the contribution margin method.
   c. Would you recommend that the changes be made?

SOLUTION TO REVIEW PROBLEM

1.
$$\text{CM ratio} = \frac{\text{Contribution margin}}{\text{Selling price}} = \frac{\$15}{\$60} = 25\%$$

$$\text{Variable expense ratio} = \frac{\text{Variable expense}}{\text{Selling price}} = \frac{\$45}{\$60} = 75\%$$

2. Sales = Variable expenses + Fixed expenses + Profits

$\$60Q = \$45Q + \$240,000 + \$0$

$\$15Q = \$240,000$

$Q = \$240,000 \div \$15$ per unit

$Q = 16,000$ units; or at $60 per unit, $960,000

Alternative solution:

$X = 0.75X + \$240,000 + \$0$

$$0.25X = \$240,000$$
$$X = \$240,000 \div 0.25$$
$$X = \$960,000; \text{ or at } \$60 \text{ per unit, } 16,000 \text{ units}$$

3.
Increase in sales	$400,000
Multiply by the CM ratio	× 25%
Expected increase in contribution margin.	$100,000

Since the fixed expenses are not expected to change, net operating income will increase by the entire $100,000 increase in contribution margin computed above.

4. Equation method:

$$\text{Sales} = \text{Variable expenses} + \text{Fixed expenses} + \text{Profits}$$
$$\$60Q = \$45Q + \$240,000 + \$90,000$$
$$\$15Q = \$330,000$$
$$Q = \$330,000 \div \$15 \text{ per unit}$$
$$Q = 22,000 \text{ units}$$

Contribution margin method:

$$\frac{\text{Fixed expenses} + \text{Target profit}}{\text{Contribution margin per unit}} = \frac{\$240,000 + \$90,000}{\$15 \text{ per unit}} = 22,000 \text{ units}$$

5. Margin of safety in dollars = Total sales − Break-even sales

$$= \$1,200,000 - \$960,000 = \$240,000$$

$$\text{Margin of safety percentage} = \frac{\text{Margin of safety in dollars}}{\text{Total sales}} = \frac{\$240,000}{\$1,200,000} = 20\%$$

6. a. Degree of operating leverage $= \dfrac{\text{Contribution margin}}{\text{Net operating income}} = \dfrac{\$300,000}{\$60,000} = 5$

   b.
Expected increase in sales	8%
Degree of operating leverage	× 5
Expected increase in net operating income . . .	40%

   c. If sales increase by 8%, then 21,600 units (20,000 × 1.08 = 21,600) will be sold next year. The new income statement will be as follows:

	Total	Per Unit	Percentage of Sales
Sales (21,600 units)	$1,296,000	$60	100
Less: Variable expenses	972,000	45	75
Contribution margin.	324,000	$15	25
Less: Fixed expenses	240,000		
Net operating income.	$ 84,000		

Thus, the $84,000 expected net operating income for next year represents a 40% increase over the $60,000 net operating income earned during the current year:

$$\frac{\$84,000 - \$60,000}{\$60,000} = \frac{\$24,000}{\$60,000} = 40\% \text{ increase}$$

Notice from the income statement that the increase in sales from 20,000 to 21,600 units has resulted in increases in *both* total sales and total variable expenses. It is a common error to overlook the increase in variable expenses when preparing a projected income statement.

7. a. A 20% increase in sales would result in 24,000 units being sold next year: 20,000 units × 1.20 = 24,000 units.

	Total	Per Unit	Percentage of Sales
Sales (24,000 units)........	$1,440,000	$60	100
Less: Variable expenses.....	1,152,000	48*	80
Contribution margin	288,000	$12	20
Less: Fixed expenses.......	210,000†		
Net operating income	$ 78,000		

*$45 + $3 = $48; $48 ÷ $60 = 80%.
†$240,000 − $30,000 = $210,000.

Note that the change in per-unit variable expenses results in a change in both the per-unit contribution margin and the CM ratio.

b. $$\text{Break-even point in unit sales} = \frac{\text{Fixed expenses}}{\text{Contribution margin per unit}}$$

$$= \frac{\$210,000}{\$12 \text{ per unit}} = 17,500 \text{ units}$$

$$\text{Break-even point in dollar sales} = \frac{\text{Fixed expenses}}{\text{CM ratio}}$$

$$= \frac{\$210,000}{0.20} = \$1,050,000$$

c. Yes, on the basis of these data, the changes should be made. The changes will increase the company's net operating income from the present $60,000 to $78,000 per year. Although the changes will also result in a higher break-even point (17,500 units as compared with the present 16,000 units), the company's margin of safety will actually be wider than before:

$$\text{Margin of safety in dollars} = \text{Total sales} - \text{Break-even sales}$$
$$= \$1,440,000 - \$1,050,000 = \$390,000$$

As shown in part (5), the company's present margin of safety is only $240,000. Thus, several benefits will result from the proposed changes.

Glossary

Break-even point The level of sales at which profit is zero. The break-even point can also be defined as the point where total sales equals total expenses or as the point where total contribution margin equals total fixed expenses. (p. 442)

Contribution margin The amount available to cover fixed expenses and then provide profits for the period. (p. 442)

Contribution margin method A method of computing the break-even point in which the fixed expenses are divided by the contribution margin per unit. (p. 453)

Contribution margin ratio (CM ratio) The contribution margin as a percentage of total sales. (p. 441)

CVP analysis A tool that helps managers understand the interrelationships between cost, volume, and profit. (p. 441)

CVP graph A graph that highlights CVP relationships over wide ranges of activity. (p. 444)

Degree of operating leverage A measure, at a given level of sales, of how a percentage change in sales volume will affect profits. The degree of operating leverage is computed by dividing contribution margin by net income. (p. 459)

Equation method A method of computing the break-even point that relies on the equation, Sales = Variable expenses + Fixed expenses + Profits. (p. 451)

Incremental analysis An analytical approach that focuses only on those items of revenue, cost, and volume that will change as a result of a decision. (p. 447)

Lever A tool for multiplying force. (p. 459)

Margin of safety The excess of budgeted (or actual) sales over the break-even volume of sales. (p. 456)

Operating leverage A measure of how sensitive net income is to a given percentage change in sales. It is computed by dividing the contribution margin by net income. (p. 459)

Questions

11–1 What is meant by a product's CM ratio? How is this ratio useful in planning business operations?

11–2 Often, the most direct route to a business decision is to make an incremental analysis on the basis of the information available. What is meant by an *incremental analysis?*

11–3 Company A's cost structure includes costs that are mostly variable, whereas Company B's cost structure includes costs that are mostly fixed. In a time of increasing sales, which company will tend to realize the most rapid increase in profits? Explain.

11–4 What is meant by the term *operating leverage?*

11–5 A 10% decrease in the selling price of a product will have the same impact on net income as a 10% increase in the variable expenses. Do you agree? Why, or why not?

11–6 Define *break-even point.*

11–7 Name three approaches to break-even analysis. Briefly explain how each approach works.

11–8 In response to a request from your immediate supervisor, you have prepared a CVP graph portraying the cost and revenue characteristics of your company's product and operations. Explain how the lines on the graph and the break-even point would change if (a) the selling price per unit decreased, (b) fixed costs increased throughout the entire range of activity portrayed on the graph, and (c) variable costs per unit increased.

11–9 Al's Auto Wash charges $4 to wash a car. The variable costs of washing a car are 15% of sales. Fixed expenses total $1,700 monthly. How many cars must be washed each month for Al to break even?

11–10 What is meant by the term *margin of safety?*

Brief Exercises

BRIEF EXERCISE 11–1 Preparing a Contribution Margin Income Statement (CC1)

Whirly Corporation's most recent income statement is shown following:

	Total	Per Unit
Sales (15,000 units).......	$450,000	$30.00
Less: Variable expenses....	225,000	15.00
Contribution margin	225,000	$15.00
Less: Fixed expenses......	185,000	
Net income	$ 40,000	

Required:

Prepare a new income statement under each of the following conditions (consider each case independently):

1. The sales volume increases by 500 units.
2. The sales volume decreases by 500 units.
3. The sales volume is 12,335 units.

BRIEF EXERCISE 11–2 Computing and Using the CM Ratio (CC2, 3)

Last month when Holiday Creations, Inc. sold 50,000 units, total sales were $200,000, total variable expenses were $120,000, and total fixed expenses were $65,000.

Required:

1. What is the company's CM ratio?
2. Estimate the change in the company's net income if it were to increase its total sales by $1,000.

BRIEF EXERCISE 11–3 Changes in Variable Costs, Fixed Costs, Selling Price, and Volume (CC6)
Data for Hermann Corporation are shown following:

	Per Unit	Percentage of Sales
Sales price	$90	100
Less: Variable expenses	63	70
Contribution margin.	$27	30

Fixed expenses are $30,000 per month and the company is selling 2,000 units per month.

Required:
1. The marketing manager argues that a $5,000 increase in the monthly advertising budget would increase monthly sales by $9,000. Should the advertising budget be increased?
2. Refer to the original data. Management is considering using higher-quality components that would increase the variable cost by $2 per unit. The marketing manager believes the higher-quality product would increase sales by 10% per month. Should the higher-quality components be used?

BRIEF EXERCISE 11–4 Compute the Break-Even Point (CC7, 8)
Mauro Products has a single product, a woven basket whose selling price is $45 and variable cost is $36 per unit. The company's monthly fixed expenses are $12,600.

Required:
1. Compute company's break-even point in unit sales using the equation method.
2. Compute company's break-even point in sales dollars using the equation method and the CM ratio.
3. Compute company's break-even point in unit sales using the contribution margin method.
4. Compute company's break-even point in sales dollars using the contribution margin method and the CM ratio.

BRIEF EXERCISE 11–5 Prepare a CVP Graph (CC4)
Karlik Enterprises has a single product, whose selling price is $24 and variable cost is $18 per unit. The company's monthly fixed expense is $24,000.

Required:
1. Prepare a CVP graph for the company up to a sales level of 8,000 units.
2. Estimate the company's break-even point in unit sales using your CVP graph.

BRIEF EXERCISE 11–6 Compute the Level of Sales Required to Attain a Target Profit (CC9)
Lin Corporation has a single product whose selling price is $120 and whose variable cost is $80 per unit. The company's monthly fixed expense is $50,000.

Required:
1. Using the equation method, compute the unit sales that are required to earn a target profit of $10,000.
2. Using the contribution margin approach, compute the dollar sales that are required to earn a target profit of $15,000.

BRIEF EXERCISE 11–7 Brief Exercise 11–6 Revisited (CC10)
Refer to data in Brief Exercise 11–6. Assume a 40% tax rate and assume that the profit in the figures shown in parts (1) and (2) are after-tax amounts. Then, redo the Required again from Brief Exercise 11–6.

BRIEF EXERCISE 11–8 Compute the Margin of Safety (CC11)
Molander Corporation sells a sun umbrella used at resort hotels. Data concerning the next month's budget appear below:

Selling price	$30 per unit
Variable expense	$20 per unit
Fixed expense	$15,000 per month
Unit sales.	2,000 units per month

Required:
1. Compute the company's margin of safety.
2. Compute the company's margin of safety as a percentage of its sales.

BRIEF EXERCISE 11–9 Compute and Use the Degree of Operating Leverage (CC13)

Engberg Company's most recent monthly income statement appears following:

	Amount	Percentage of Sales
Sales....................	$80,000	100
Less: Variable expenses......	32,000	40
Contribution margin.........	48,000	60
Less: Fixed expenses........	38,000	
Net income...............	$10,000	

Required:
1. Compute the company's degree of operating leverage.
2. Using the degree of operating leverage, estimate the impact on net income of a 5% increase in sales.
3. Verify your estimate from part (2) by constructing a new income statement for the company assuming a 5% increase in sales.

BRIEF EXERCISE 11–10 Calculating Contribution Margin (CC1, 7, 8)

Dolly Inc. has a break-even point of 8,000 units. At that break-even point, variable costs are $8,000 and fixed costs are $4,000.

Required:
What is the contribution margin of the 401st unit sold?

(Adapted © CGA-Canada)

BRIEF EXERCISE 11–11 Break-Even Analysis; Calculation of Fixed costs (CC1, 7, 8)

Arctic Ltd. produces gloves.

Required:
If the sales price per glove is $8.50, the unit variable cost is $6.75, and the break-even point is at sales of 39,000 gloves, what are the total fixed costs?

(Adapted © CGA-Canada)

Exercises

EXERCISE 11–1 Using a Contribution Margin Format Income Statement (CC1, 3, 4, 5)

Miller Company's most recent income statement follows:

	Total	Per Unit
Sales (20,000 units)........	$300,000	$15.00
Less: Variable expenses.....	180,000	9.00
Contribution margin	120,000	$ 6.00
Less: Fixed expenses.......	70,000	
Net income	$ 50,000	

Required:
Prepare a new income statement under each of the following conditions (consider each case independently):
1. The sales volume increases by 15%.
2. The selling price decreases by $1.50 per unit, and the sales volume increases by 25%.
3. The selling price increases by $1.50 per unit, fixed expenses increase by $20,000, and the sales volume decreases by 5%.
4. The selling price increases by 12%, variable expenses increase by 60 cents per unit, and the sales volume decreases by 10%.

EXERCISE 11–2 Break-Even and Target Profit Analysis (CC1, 8, 9)

Lindon Company is the exclusive distributor for an automotive product. The product sells for $40 per unit and has a CM ratio of 30%. The company's fixed expenses are $240,000 per year.

Required:
1. What are the variable expenses per unit?
2. Using the equation method:
    a. What is the break-even point in units and sales dollars?
    b. What sales level in units and in sales dollars is required to earn an annual profit of $80,000?
    c. Assume that by using a more efficient shipper, the company is able to reduce its variable expenses by $4 per unit. What is the company's new break-even point in units and sales dollars?
3. Repeat part (2) using the unit contribution method.

EXERCISE 11–3 Operating Leverage (CC1, 13)

Magic Realm, Inc. has developed a new fantasy board game. The company sold 15,000 games last year at a selling price of $20 per game. Fixed costs associated with the game total $182,000 per year, and variable costs are $6 per game. Production of the game is entrusted to a printing contractor. Variable costs consist mostly of payments to this contractor.

Required:
1. Prepare an income statement for the game last year and compute the degree of operating leverage.
2. Management is confident that the company can sell 18,000 games next year (an increase of 3,000 games, or 20%, over last year). Compute:
    a. The expected percentage increase in net income for next year.
    b. The expected total dollar net income for next year. (Do not prepare an income statement; use the degree of operating leverage to compute your answer.)

EXERCISE 11–4 Break-Even Analysis and CVP Graphing (CC6, 7, 8)

The Hartford Symphony Guild is planning its annual dinner dance. The dinner dance committee has assembled the following expected costs for the event:

Dinner (per person)............................	$ 18
Favours and program (per person)	2
Band	2,800
Rental of ballroom	900
Professional entertainment during intermission ...	1,000
Tickets and advertising.......................	1,300

The committee members would like to charge $35 per person for the evening's activities.

Required:
1. Compute the break-even point for the dinner dance (in terms of the number of persons that must attend).
2. Assume that last year only 300 persons attended the dinner dance. If the same number attend this year, what price per ticket must be charged in order to break even?
3. Refer to the original data ($35 ticket price per person). Prepare a CVP graph for the dinner dance from a zero level of activity up to 700 tickets sold. Number of persons should be placed on the horizontal (X) axis, and dollars should be placed on the vertical (Y) axis.

EXERCISE 11–5 Break-Even Analysis, Target Profit Analysis, Margin of Safety, CM Ratio (CC2, 3, 7, 8, 9, 11)

Menlo Company manufactures and sells a single product. The company's sales and expenses for last quarter follow:

	Total	Per Unit
Sales.....................	$450,000	$30
Less: Variable expenses	180,000	12
Contribution margin..........	270,000	$18
Less: Fixed expenses	216,000	
Net income...............	$ 54,000	

Required:
1. What is the quarterly break-even point in units sold and in sales dollars?
2. Without resorting to computations, what is the total contribution margin at the break-even point?
3. How many units would have to be sold each quarter to earn a target profit of $90,000? Use the unit contribution method. Verify your answer by preparing a contribution income statement at the target level of sales.
4. Refer to the original data. Compute the company's margin of safety in both dollar and percentage terms.
5. What is the company's CM ratio? If sales increase by $50,000 per quarter and there is no change in fixed expenses, by how much would you expect quarterly net income to increase? (Do not prepare an income statement; use the CM ratio to compute your answer.)

EXERCISE 11–6 Break-Even and Target Profit Analysis (CC6, 7, 8, 9)

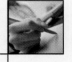

Outback Outfitters manufactures and sells recreational equipment. One of the company's products, a small camp stove, sells for $50 per unit. Variable expenses are $32 per stove, and fixed expenses associated with the stove total $108,000 per month.

Required:
1. Compute the break-even point in number of stoves and in total sales dollars.
2. If the variable expenses per stove increase as a percentage of the selling price, will it result in a higher or a lower break-even point? Why? (Assume that the fixed expenses remain unchanged.)
3. At present, the company is selling 8,000 stoves per month. The sales manager is convinced that a 10% reduction in the selling price would result in a 25% increase in monthly sales of stoves. Prepare two contribution margin income statements, one under present operating conditions, and one as operations would appear after the proposed changes. Show both total and per-unit data on your statements.
4. Refer to the data in part (3). How many stoves would have to be sold at the new selling price to yield a minimum net income of $35,000 per month?

EXERCISE 11–7 Interpretation of the CVP Graph (CC4)

A CVP graph, such as the one shown below, is a useful technique for showing relationships among costs, volume, and profits in an organization.

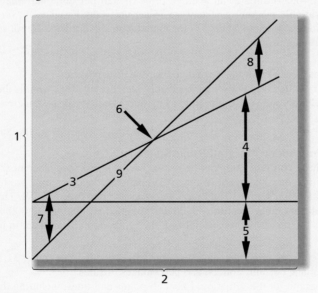

Required:
1. Identify the numbered components in the CVP graph.
2. State the effect of each of the following actions on line 3, line 9, and the break-even point. For line 3 and line 9, state whether the action will cause the line to:

- Remain unchanged.
- Shift upward.
- Shift downward.
- Have a steeper slope (i.e., rotate upward).
- Have a flatter slope (i.e., rotate downward).

- Shift upward *and* have a steeper slope.
- Shift upward *and* have a flatter slope.
- Shift downward *and* have a steeper slope.
- Shift downward *and* have a flatter slope.

In the case of the break-even point, state whether the action will cause the break-even point to:

- Remain unchanged.
- Increase.
- Decrease.
- Probably change, but the direction is uncertain.

Treat each case independently.

> x. *Example.* Fixed costs are reduced by $5,000 per period.
> *Answer* (see choices above): Line 3: Shift downward.
>   Line 9: Remain unchanged.
>   Break-even point: Decrease.

a. The unit selling price is increased from $18 to $20.
b. Unit variable costs are decreased from $12 to $10.
c. Fixed costs are increased by $3,000 per period.
d. 2,000 more units are sold during the period than were budgeted.
e. Due to paying salespersons a commission, rather than a flat salary, fixed costs are reduced by $8,000 per period and unit variable costs are increased by $3.
f. Due to an increase in the cost of materials, both unit variable costs and the selling price are increased by $2.
g. Advertising costs are increased by $10,000 per period, resulting in a 10% increase in the number of units sold.
h. Due to automating an operation previously done by workers, fixed costs are increased by $12,000 per period and unit variable costs are reduced by $4.

EXERCISE 11–8 Break-Even Analysis (CC6, 7)

Feltan Company operated at normal capacity during the current year, producing 50,000 units of its single product. Sales totalled 40,000 units at an average price of $20 per unit. Variable manufacturing costs were $8 per unit, and variable marketing costs were $4 per unit sold. Fixed costs were incurred uniformly throughout the year and amounted to $188,000 for manufacturing and $64,000 for marketing. There was no year-end work-in-process inventory.

Required:
1. What is Feltan's break-even point in sales dollars for the current year?
2. If Feltan's variable manufacturing costs unexpectedly increase by 10%, what is the new unit selling price that would yield the same contribution margin ratio as before the cost increase (rounded to the nearest cent)?

(Adapted © CGA-Canada)

EXERCISE 11–9 Contribution Margin Income Statement (CC1, 4)

Wancan Company wishes to present its operating results for the year ended December 31, 2008 in the form of a contribution margin income statement. Wancan Company produces a single product and has a relevant range between 20,000 and 80,000 units. Total production costs range from $321,875 to $966,875 at the low and high ends of the relevant range, respectively. Sales volume in 2008 was 32,000 units, and net income was $45,125. Wancan's product is highly specialized; therefore, no units are kept in inventory.

Required:
1. Prepare a contribution margin income statement for the year ended December 31, 2008. Include columns for total dollars, per-unit dollars, and percentages of sales.
2. Draw a rough CVP graph for this situation. Label all points and lines, including the break-even point.

(Adapted © CGA-Canada)

EXERCISE 11–10 Break-Even Analysis; Tax Calculation (CC6, 7, 10)

The following data is for the Biro Liu Company, a manufacturer of ballpoint pens:

Income tax rate	40 %
Selling price per unit	$2.75
Variable cost per unit	$2.20
Total fixed costs	$115,000

Required:
1. How many units must Biro Liu Company sell to earn an after-tax income of $30,000?
2. If total fixed costs doubled and contribution margin per unit was cut in half, what would happen to the break-even point?

(Adapted © CGA-Canada)

EXERCISE 11–11 Calculating the CM Ratio (CC3)

Following are the selling and cost information data concerning Realm Co.'s only product:

Selling price per unit	$100
Costs per unit:	
Direct material	20
Direct labour	30
Variable overhead	15
Fixed overhead	5
Commission	10% of sales

Required:
What is the CM ratio?

(Adapted © CGA-Canada)

EXERCISE 11–12 Break-Even and Target Profit Analysis (CC6, 7, 8, 9)

Walton Ltd. is considering replacing an existing machine with a new and faster machine that will produce a more reliable product (that is, better tolerances). The switch to a new machine resulting in a superior product is expected to allow Walton to increase its sale price for the product. The switch will increase fixed costs, but not the variable costs. The cost and revenue estimates are as follows:

Cost Item	Old Machine	New Machine
Monthly fixed costs	$240,000	$500,000
Variable cost per unit	28	28
Sales price per unit	36	40

Required:
1. Determine the break-even point in units for the two machines.
2. Determine the sales level in units at which the new machine will achieve a 10% target profit-to-sales ratio (ignore taxes).
3. Determine the sales level at which profits will be the same for either the old or new machine.
4. Which machine represents a lower risk if demand is uncertain? Explain.

(Adapted © CGA-Canada)

Problems

PROBLEM 11–1 Basic CVP Analysis (CC5, 7, 9, 13)

Feather Friends, Inc. makes a high-quality wooden birdhouse that sells for $20 per unit. Variable costs are $8 per unit, and fixed costs total $180,000 per year.

CHECK FIGURE
(2) Break-even: $300,000

Required:
Answer the following independent questions:
1. What is the product's CM ratio?
2. Use the CM ratio to determine the break-even point in sales dollars.
3. Due to an increase in demand, the company estimates that sales will increase by $75,000 during the next year. By how much should net income increase (or net loss decrease) assuming that fixed costs do not change?

4. Assume that the operating results for last year were as follows:

Sales	$400,000
Less: Variable expenses	160,000
Contribution margin	240,000
Less: Fixed expenses	180,000
Net income	$ 60,000

a. Compute the degree of operating leverage at the current level of sales.
b. The president expects sales to increase by 20% next year. By what percentage should net income increase?

5. Refer to the original data. Assume that the company sold 18,000 units last year. The sales manager is convinced that a 10% reduction in the selling price, combined with a $30,000 increase in advertising, would cause annual sales in units to increase by one-third. Prepare two contribution income statements, one showing the results of last year's operations and one showing the results of operations if these changes are made. Would you recommend that the company follow the sales manager's suggestion?

6. Refer to the original data. Assume again that the company sold 18,000 units last year. The president does not want to change the selling price. Instead, he wants to increase the sales commission by $1 per unit. He thinks that this move, combined with an increase in advertising, would increase annual sales by 25%. By how much could advertising be increased with profits remaining unchanged? Do not prepare an income statement; use the incremental analysis approach.

PROBLEM 11–2 Basic CVP Analysis; Cost Structure (CC3, 6, 7, 8, 9, 12)

Due to erratic sales of its sole product–a high-capacity battery for laptop computers–PEM, Inc. has been experiencing difficulty for some time. The company's income statement for the most recent month follows:

Sales (39,000 units × $30 per unit)	$1,170,000
Less: Variable expenses	819,000
Contribution margin	351,000
Less: Fixed expenses	360,000
Net loss	$ (9,000)

Required:
1. Compute the company's CM ratio and its break-even point in both units and dollars.
2. The president believes that a $16,000 increase in the monthly advertising budget, combined with an intensified effort by the sales staff, will result in an $80,000 increase in monthly sales. If the president is right, what will be the effect on the company's monthly net income or loss? (Use the incremental approach in preparing your answer.)
3. Refer to the original data. The sales manager is convinced that a 10% reduction in the selling price, combined with an increase of $120,000 in the monthly advertising budget, will cause unit sales to double. What will the new income statement look like if these changes are adopted?
4. Refer to the original data. The Marketing Department thinks that a fancy new package for the laptop computer battery would help sales. The new package would increase packaging costs by 75 cents per unit. Assuming no other changes, how many units would have to be sold each month to earn a profit of $9,750?
5. Refer to the original data. By automating certain operations, the company could reduce variable costs by $3 per unit. However, fixed costs would increase by $144,000 each month.
    a. Compute the new CM ratio and the new break-even point in both units and dollars.
    b. Assume that the company expects to sell 52,000 units next month. Prepare two income statements, one assuming that operations are not automated and one assuming that they are. (Show data on per-unit and percentage bases, as well as in total, for each alternative.)
    c. Would you recommend that the company automate its operations? Explain.

PROBLEM 11–3 Basic CVP Analysis and Graphing (CC4, 5, 7, 8)

The Fashion Shoe Company operates a chain of women's shoe shops around the country. The shops carry many styles of shoes that are all sold at the same price. Sales personnel in the shops are paid a substantial commission on each pair of shoes sold (in addition to a small basic salary) in order to encourage them to be aggressive in their sales efforts.

The following cost and revenue data relate to Shop 48 and are typical of one of the company's many outlets:

	A	B	C	D	E
1		*Per Pair*			
2		*of Shoes*			
3	Sales price	$ 30.00			
4					
5	Variable expenses:				
6	Invoice cost	$ 13.50			
7	Sales commission	4.50			
8	Total variable expenses	$ 18.00			
9					
10		*Annual*			
11	Fixed expenses:				
12	Advertising	$ 30,000			
13	Rent	20,000			
14	Salaries	100,000			
15	Total fixed expenses	$ 150,000			
16					

Microsoft Excel - Problem 11-3 screen capture.xls

Required:
1. Calculate the annual break-even point in dollar sales and in unit sales for Shop 48.
2. Prepare a CVP graph showing cost and revenue data for Shop 48 from a zero level of activity up to 20,000 pairs of shoes sold each year. Clearly indicate the break-even point on the graph.
3. If 12,000 pairs of shoes are sold in a year, what would be Shop 48's net income or loss?
4. The company is considering paying the store manager of Shop 48 an incentive commission of 75 cents per pair of shoes (in addition to the salesperson's commission). If this change is made, what will be the new break-even point in dollar sales and in unit sales?
5. Refer to the original data. As an alternative to part (4), the company is considering paying the store manager 50 cents commission on each pair of shoes sold in excess of the break-even point. If this change is made, what will be the shop's net income or loss if 15,000 pairs of shoes are sold?
6. Refer to the original data. The company is considering eliminating sales commissions entirely in its shops and increasing fixed salaries by $31,500 annually. If this change is made, what will be the new break-even point in dollar sales and unit sales for Shop 48? Would you recommend that the change be made? Explain.

PROBLEM 11–4 Break-Even and Target Profit Analysis (CC9)

CHECK FIGURE
(1) 300 sweatshirts

The Shirt Works sells a large variety of T-shirts and sweatshirts. Steve Hooper, the owner, is thinking of expanding his sales by hiring local high school students, on a commission basis, to sell sweatshirts bearing the name and mascot of the local high school.

These sweatshirts would have to be ordered from the manufacturer six weeks in advance, and they could not be returned because of the unique printing required. The sweatshirts would cost Mr. Hooper $8 each with a minimum order of 75 sweatshirts. Any additional sweatshirts would have to be ordered in increments of 75.

Since Mr. Hooper's plan would not require any additional facilities, the only costs associated with the project would be the costs of the sweatshirts and the costs of the sales commissions. The selling price of the sweatshirts would be $13.50 each. Mr. Hooper would pay the students a commission of $1.50 for each shirt sold.

Required:
1. To make the project worthwhile, Mr. Hooper would require a $1,200 profit for the first three months of the venture. What level of sales in units and in dollars would be required to reach this target net income? Show all computations.
2. Assume that the venture is undertaken and an order is placed for 75 sweatshirts. What would be Mr. Hooper's break-even point in units and in sales dollars? Show computations and explain the reasoning behind your answer.

PROBLEM 11–5 Changes in Fixed and Variable Costs; Break-Even and Target Profit Analysis (CC6, 7, 8, 9, 12)

Neptune Company produces toys and other items for use in beach and resort areas. A small, inflatable toy has come on the market that the company is anxious to produce and sell. Enough capacity exists in the company's plant to produce 16,000 units of the toy each month. Variable costs to manufacture and sell one unit would be $1.25, and fixed costs associated with the toy would total $35,000 per month.

The company's Marketing Department predicts that demand for the new toy will exceed the 16,000 units that the company is able to produce. Additional manufacturing space can be rented from another company at a fixed cost of $1,000 per month. Variable costs in the rented facility would total $1.40 per unit, due to somewhat less efficient operations than in the main plant. The new toy will sell for $3 per unit.

Required:
1. Compute the monthly break-even point for the new toy in units and in total dollar sales. Show all computations in good form.
2. How many units must be sold each month to make a monthly profit of $12,000?
3. If the sales manager receives a bonus of 10 cents for each unit sold in excess of the break-even point, how many units must be sold each month to earn a return of 25% on the monthly investment in fixed costs?

PROBLEM 11–6 CVP Graphing; Incremental Analysis; Operating Leverage (CC4, 6, 7, 8, 9, 13)

Angie Silva has recently opened The Sandal Shop in Brisbane, Australia, a store that specializes in fashionable sandals. Angie has just received a degree in business, and she is anxious to apply the principles she has learned to her business. In time, she hopes to open a chain of sandal shops. As a first step, she has prepared the following analysis for her new store:

Sales price per pair of sandals...........	$40
Variable expenses per pair of sandals	16
Contribution margin per pair of sandals ...	$24
Fixed expenses per year:	
Building rental......................	$15,000
Equipment amortization	7,000
Selling	20,000
Administrative......................	18,000
Total fixed expenses..................	$60,000

Required:
1. How many pairs of sandals must be sold each year to break even? What does this represent in total dollar sales?
2. Prepare a CVP graph for the store from a zero level of activity up to 5,000 pairs of sandals sold each year. Indicate the break-even point on your graph.
3. Angie has decided that she must earn at least $18,000 the first year to justify her time and effort. How many pairs of sandals must be sold to reach this target profit?
4. Angie now has two salespersons working in the store—one full time and one part time. It will cost her an additional $8,000 per year to convert the part-time position to a full-time position. Angie believes that the change would bring in an additional $25,000 in sales each year. Should she convert the position? Use the incremental approach (do not prepare an income statement).
5. Refer to the original data. During the first year, the store sold only 3,000 pairs of sandals and reported the following operating results:

Sales (3,000 pairs).........	$120,000
Less: Variable expenses.....	48,000
Contribution margin	72,000
Less: Fixed expenses.......	60,000
Net income	$ 12,000

a. What is the store's degree of operating leverage?
b. Angie is confident that with a more intense sales effort and with a more creative advertising program she can increase sales by 50% next year. What would be the expected percentage increase in net income? Use the degree of operating leverage to compute your answer.

CHECK FIGURE
(3) 2,052 haircuts

PROBLEM 11–7 Break-Even and Target Profit Analysis (CC7, 8, 9)

Janice owns the Cute Cut Salon. She employs five stylists and pays each a base salary of $1,500 per month. One of the stylists serves as the manager, receiving an extra $500 per month. In addition to the base salary, each stylist receives a commission of $6 per haircut. Each stylist can do as many as 20 haircuts a day, but the average is 14 haircuts each per day. The Cute Cut Salon is open an average of 24 days per month. Other costs are incurred as follows:

Advertising	$500 per month
Rent	$1,000 per month
Supplies	$1.50 per haircut
Utilities	$300 per month plus $0.50 per haircut
Magazines	$50 per month
Cleaning supplies	$0.25 per haircut
Price per haircut.	$15.00

Required:
1. Compute the monthly break-even point for the following:
   a. Number of haircuts.
   b. Total sales dollars.
   c. As a percentage of maximum capacity.
2. In February, 1,500 haircuts were given. Compute net income for February.
3. If John would like a $4,000 monthly profit, compute the number of haircuts that must be given per month to achieve this profit.
4. In March, 1,600 haircuts were given. Assuming demand is sufficient, would it be possible for stylists to give enough haircuts in April to achieve a monthly average profit equal to the target profit of $4,000? Consider only the two-month period of March and April.

(Adapted © CGA-Canada)

CHECK FIGURE
(1) Part (b); $8,186,700

PROBLEM 11–8 Comprehensive CVP Analysis (CC6, 7, 8)

Deng Corp. produces hydraulic lifts that are used by hospitals to move bedridden patients. The costs of manufacturing and marketing the hydraulic lifts at the company's standard normal volume of 3,000 units per month are as follows:

Costs per unit for hydraulic lifts:

Unit manufacturing costs	
Variable materials	$ 550
Variable labour	825
Variable overhead	420
Fixed overhead	660
Total unit manufacturing costs	$ 2,455

Unit marketing costs	
Variable	$ 275
Fixed	770
Total unit marketing costs	1,045
Total unit costs.	$ 3,500

Required:
1. At a sales price of $4,350 per unit, what is (a) the break-even volume in units and (b) the break-even sales in dollars?
2. Market research indicates that if the unit sale price were reduced from $4,350 to $3,850, the monthly sales volume would increase to 3,500 units, which is well within production capacity limitations.

Assuming the same cost patterns as shown above, what would be the dollar impact on monthly sales, costs, and income? Should the price be reduced?

3. Deng is considering implementing a quality inspection system, which will increase the fixed manufacturing overhead costs per unit to $705. However, this will reduce the average materials, labour, and variable overhead costs by $15, $17, and $13 per unit respectively. Compute the new break-even sales in units and dollars. At a sales level of 3,000 units, will the implementation of the quality inspection system result in a higher profit? Compute the profit impact of this change at a sales level of 3,500 units. Comment on the results.

(Adapted © CGA-Canada)

CHECK FIGURE
(3) 1,011 units, $909,900

PROBLEM 11–9 Contribution Margin; Break-Even Analysis; Target Profit Analysis
(CC2, 7, 8, 10, 11, 13)

Smoky Corporation produces barbecues, selling each unit for $900. Current annual production and sales volume is 2,400 barbecues. This is the activity level used by the company to determine its fixed manufacturing overhead rate. The company has a 25% tax rate. Other cost information is as follows:

Direct material cost per unit	$ 200
Direct labour cost per unit.	100
Variable manufacturing overhead per unit.	50
Variable selling expenses per unit	10
Total variable costs per unit.	360
Total fixed manufacturing costs.	$ 750,000

Required:

1. Compute the contribution margin and CM ratio for the company.
2. Compute the break-even point in units and in sales dollars for the company.
3. Compute Smoky's margin of safety in units and in dollars.
4. Compute Smoky's degree of operating leverage (DOL). If sales increase by 40%, by how much will before-tax profit increase?
5. If the company wants to earn $410,000 after taxes, how many units will it have to sell?

(Adapted © CGA-Canada)

CHECK FIGURE
(a) Case 2 Variable
    expenses: $60,000
(b) Case 4 Fixed
    expenses: $185,000

PROBLEM 11–10 Break-Even Analysis (CC1, 3, 7, 8, 15ᴬ)

Fill in the missing amounts in each of the eight case situations following. *Treat each case independently.* (Hint: One way to find the missing amounts would be to prepare a contribution margin income statement for each case, enter the known data, and then compute the missing items.)

a. Assume that only one product is being sold in each of the four following case situations:

Case	Units Sold	Sales	Variable Expenses	Contribution Margin per Unit	Fixed Expenses	Net Income (Loss)
1. . . .	15,000	$180,000	$120,000	$?	$ 50,000	$?
2. . . .	?	100,000	?	10	32,000	8,000
3. . . .	10,000	?	70,000	13	?	12,000
4. . . .	6,000	300,000	?	?	100,000	(10,000)

b. Assume that more than one product is being sold in each of the four following case situations:

Case	Sales	Variable Expenses	Average Contribution Margin (percent)	Fixed Expenses	Net Income (Loss)
1.	$500,000	$?	20	$?	$ 7,000
2.	400,000	260,000	?	100,000	?
3.	?	?	60	130,000	20,000
4.	600,000	420,000	?	?	(5,000)

ANALYTICAL THINKING (CC2, 6, 7, 12, 13)

CHECK FIGURE
(1) Operating leverage: 2.725

The marketing manager, Raj Mehta, picked up the phone to call Susan Ahmed, the company's cost accounting assistant and Raj's personal friend.

Raj: "Hi Susan. Can you help me understand something that came up at a meeting earlier today? It was about break-even and we discussed cost structure and operating leverage."

Susan: "What's the problem?"

Raj: "The president was talking about automating certain parts of the operations and was throwing out different alternatives."

Susan: "What's new about that?"

Raj: "Well, he was saying something about the changes to the cost structure as a result of that, and that our break-even points might change. As the marketing guy, I would like to better understand the implications of all these proposals for me. How will these potential changes affect my function in the company? Can we meet tomorrow afternoon about this? In the meantime, I will ask my assistant to provide you with enough details to compute some numbers for me."

Susan: "Sounds good, Raj. Now you owe me one!"

Susan worked with the following documents to conduct her analysis:

- The contribution margin income statement for the most recent year.
- Rough notes regarding three new proposals being considered.

Contribution Margin Income Statement	
Sales revenues (300,000 units)	$78,000,000
Less: Variable costs	
Variable cost of goods sold	35,100,000
Variable selling and administrative expenses	23,400,000
Contribution margin.	$19,500,000
Less: Fixed costs	
Manufacturing.	9,560,000
Selling and administrative.	2,783,000
Net income.	$ 7,157,000

Notes regarding the new proposals:

- Invest in automation in three areas of sales and marketing: (1) order entry, (2) sales administration, and (3) sales distribution. As a result of this proposal, the contribution margin ratio is expected to increase by 8% and simultaneously increase annual fixed costs by $9,570,500.
- Invest in automation in three areas of the organization: (1) sales administration, (2) human resources and corporate office, and (3) manufacturing operations. This move is expected to increase the contribution margin ratio by 11% and simultaneously increase annual fixed costs by $11,280,000. The total cost savings will be divided equally between the manufacturing and nonmanufacturing functions.
- Invest in an ABC system and a new performance measurement system, which will increase the annual fixed costs by $1,800,000. This move will eliminate the need for a total of 33 accounting and administrative clerical staff at an average cost of $32,000 per year and streamline operations.

Required:

Assume the role of Susan Ahmed and answer the following questions for Raj Mehta:

1. Recreate the preceding contribution margin income statement with additional columns for per-unit amounts and cost percentages (except for fixed costs). Also, compute the break-even point and operating leverage for the year.

2. Prepare three new contribution margin income statements to reflect the three proposals (assuming there is no effect on sales). Ensure that your statements contain columns for per-unit amounts and percentages.

3. How will the three proposals affect the break-even sales for the company? Which proposal will result in the highest increase in income from increases in sales (within the relevant range of operations)? Support your answer with computations.

CHECK FIGURE
(1a) Break-even:
$12,000,000

COMMUNICATING IN PRACTICE (CC6, 7, 8, 13)

Pittman Company is a small but growing manufacturer of telecommunications equipment. The company has no sales force of its own; rather, it relies completely on independent sales agents to market its products. These agents are paid a commission of 15% of selling price for all items sold.

Barbara Cheney, Pittman's controller, has just prepared the following budgeted income statement for next year:

PITTMAN COMPANY
Budgeted Income Statement
For the Year Ended December 31

Sales..............................		$16,000,000
Manufacturing costs:		
Variable	$7,200,000	
Fixed overhead.....................	2,340,000	9,540,000
Gross margin		6,460,000
Selling and administrative costs:		
Commissions to agents	2,400,000	
Fixed marketing costs	120,000*	
Fixed administrative costs	1,800,000	4,320,000
Net operating income.................		2,140,000
Less: Fixed interest cost..............		540,000
Income before income taxes		1,600,000
Less: Income taxes (30%)		480,000
Net income........................		$ 1,120,000

*Primarily amortization on storage facilities.

As Barbara handed the statement to Karl Vecci, Pittman's president, she commented, "I went ahead and used the agents' 15% commission rate in completing these statements, but we've just learned that they refuse to handle our products next year unless we increase the commission rate to 20%."

"That's the last straw," Karl replied angrily. "Those agents have been demanding more and more, and this time they've gone too far. How can they possibly defend a 20% commission rate?"

"They claim that after paying for advertising, travel, and the other costs of promotion, there's nothing left over for profit," replied Barbara.

"I say it's just plain robbery," retorted Karl. "And I also say it's time we dumped those guys and got our own sales force. Can you get your people to work up some cost figures for us to look at?"

"We've already worked them up," said Barbara. "Several companies we know about pay a 7.5% commission to their own salespeople, along with a small salary. Of course, we would have to handle all promotion costs, too. We figure our fixed costs would increase by $2,400,000 per year, but that would be more than offset by the $3,200,000 (20% × $16,000,000) that we would avoid on agents' commissions."

The breakdown of the $2,400,000 cost figure follows:

Salaries:		
Sales manager...............	$ 100,000	
Salespersons	600,000	
Travel and entertainment	400,000	
Advertising	1,300,000	
Total	$2,400,000	

"Super," replied Karl. "And I note that the $2,400,000 is just what we're paying the agents under the old 15% commission rate."

"It's even better than that," explained Barbara. "We can actually save $75,000 a year because that's what we're having to pay the auditing firm now to check out the agents' reports. So, our overall administrative costs would be less."

"Pull all of these numbers together, and we'll show them to the executive committee tomorrow," said Karl. "With the approval of the committee, we can move on the matter immediately."

Required:
1. Compute Pittman Company's break-even point in sales dollars for next year assuming:
   a. That the agents' commission rate remains unchanged at 15%.
   b. That the agents' commission rate is increased to 20%.
   c. That the company employs its own sales force.
2. Assume that Pittman Company decides to continue selling through agents and pays the 20% commission rate. Determine the volume of sales that would be required to generate the same net income as contained in the budgeted income statement for next year.
3. Determine the volume of sales at which net income would be equal, regardless of whether Pittman Company sells through agents (at a 20% commission rate) or employs its own sales force.
4. Compute the degree of operating leverage that the company would expect to have on December 31 at the end of next year assuming:
   a. That the agents' commission rate remains unchanged at 15%.
   b. That the agents' commission rate is increased to 20%.
   c. That the company employs its own sales force.
   Use income *before* income taxes in your operating leverage computation.
5. On the basis of the data in parts (1) through (4), draft a memorandum to Barbara Cheney that sets forth your recommendation as to whether the company should continue to use sales agents (at a 20% commission rate) or employ its own sales force. Give reasons for your recommendation.

(CMA adapted)

SKILLS CHALLENGER (CC1, 6, 7, 8)

CHECK FIGURE
(2) 16,349 patient-days

Wymont Hospital operates a general hospital with separate departments, such as Pediatrics, Maternity, and Surgery. Wymont Hospital charges each department for services to its patients, such as meals and laundry, and for administrative services, such as billing and collections. Space and bed charges are fixed for the year.

Last year, the Pediatrics Department at Wymont Hospital charged its patients an average of $145 per day, had a capacity of 80 beds, operated 24 hours per day for 365 days, and had total revenue of $3,504,000.

Expenses charged by the hospital to the Pediatrics Department for the year were as follows:

	Basis for Allocation	
	Patient-Days (variable)	Bed Capacity (fixed)
Dietary	$ 107,380	
Janitorial		$ 26,000
Laundry	70,000	
Laboratory	119,500	
Pharmacy	84,500	
Repairs and maintenance	13,000	14,280
General administrative services		263,500
Rent		550,600
Billings and collections	217,500	
Other	45,120	57,620
	$657,000	$912,000

The only personnel directly employed by the Pediatrics Department are supervising nurses, nurses, and aides. The hospital has minimum personnel requirements for Pediatrics based on total annual patient-days in Pediatrics. Hospital requirements, beginning at the minimum expected level of operation, follow:

Annual Patient-Days	Aides	Nurses	Supervising Nurses
10,000–14,000	21	11	4
14,001–17,000	22	12	4
17,001–23,725	22	13	4
23,726–25,550	25	14	5
25,551–27,375	26	14	5
27,376–29,200	29	16	6

These staffing levels represent full-time equivalents, and it should be assumed that the Pediatrics Department always employs only the minimum number of required full-time equivalent personnel.

Annual salaries for each class of employee are: supervising nurses, $54,000; nurses, $39,000; and aides, $15,000. Salary expense for last year was $216,000, $507,000, and $330,000 for supervising nurses, nurses, and aides, respectively.

Required:
1. Compute the following:
   a. The number of patient-days in the Pediatrics Department for last year. (Each day a patient is in the hospital is known as a *patient-day.*)
   b. The variable cost per patient-day for last year.
   c. The total fixed costs, including both allocated fixed costs and personnel costs, in the Pediatrics Department for each level of operation shown above (i.e., total fixed costs at the 10,000–14,000 patient-day level of operation, total fixed costs at the 14,001–17,000 patient-day level of operation, and so on).
2. Using the data computed in part (1) and any other data as needed, compute the *minimum* number of patient-days required for the Pediatrics Department to break even. You may assume that variable and fixed cost behaviour and that revenue per patient-day will remain unchanged in the future.
3. Determine the minimum number of patient-days required for the Pediatrics Department to earn an annual "profit" of $200,000.

(CPA adapted)

TEAMWORK IN ACTION (CC1, 12)

The cost structure of the airline industry can serve as the basis for a discussion of a number of different cost concepts. Airlines also provide an excellent illustration of the concept of operating leverage, the sensitivity of a firm's operating profits to changes in demand, and the opportunities and risks presented by such a cost structure. Airline profits and share prices are among some of the most volatile on Wall Street. A study of the U.S. airline industry disclosed the following operating cost categories and their percentage of total operating cost:[*]

Uniform System of Accounts Required by the Department of Transportation	Mean Percentage of Operating Cost, 1981–85
Fuel and oil	24.3%
Flying operations labour (flight crews—pilots, co-pilots, navigators, and flight engineers)	8.6
Passenger service labour (flight attendants)	4.6
Aircraft traffic and servicing labour (personnel servicing aircraft and handling passengers at gates, baggage, and cargo)	8.9
Promotions and sales labour (reservations and sales agents, advertising and publicity)	9.0
Maintenance labour (maintenance of flight equipment and ground property and equipment)	7.0
Maintenance materials and overhead	2.1
Ground property and equipment (landing fees, and rental expenses and amortization for ground property and equipment)	12.5
Flight equipment (rental expenses and amortization on aircraft frames and engines)	8.4
General overhead (administrative personnel, utilities, insurance, communications, etc.)	14.6
Total	100.0%

---

[*]R. D. Banker and H. H. Johnson, "An Empirical Study of Cost Drivers in the U.S. Airline Industry," *The Accounting Review*, July 1993, pp. 576–601.

Required:

1. Your team should discuss and then write a brief description of the objectives of airline cost accounting systems. All team members should agree with and understand the description.
2. Each member of the team should present an answer to one of the following questions to the other team members, who should confirm or correct the answer.
    a. For each of the accounts listed above, indicate whether the costs in the account are mainly fixed or variable with respect to the number of flights flown—regardless of how many passengers are carried on the flights. Assume that all flights always fly nearly full and the airline already operates out of the airport. On the basis of this analysis, estimate the percentage of costs that are fixed with respect to the number of flights flown.
    b. For each of the accounts listed above, indicate whether the costs in the account are mainly fixed or variable with respect to the number of passengers carried on a particular scheduled flight. On the basis of this analysis, estimate the percentage of costs that are fixed with respect to the number of passengers carried on a particular scheduled flight.
3. The team should discuss and then write brief answers to the following questions. All team members should agree with and understand the answers.
    a. What conclusions do you draw about the nature of fixed and variable costs on the basis of your analysis to part (2)?
    b. Why are profits more sensitive (more variable) to changes in demand when the cost structure contains a high proportion of fixed costs? What is probably a more effective way to improve the profitability of an airline–increase the number of flights or increase the average number of passengers on flights the airline already flies?

Don't forget to visit the Online Learning Centre for self-study quizzes, practice exams, and more! Visit www.mcgrawhill.ca/olc/brewer.

CHAPTER *Twelve*

Relevant Costs for Decision Making

CHAPTER COMPETENCIES

After studying Chapter 12, you should be able to demonstrate the following competencies:

Competency	Know	Apply
Understand and apply the relevant costing approach to decision making.		
CC1 Explain the relevant cost analysis framework as it applies to managerial decision making.	○	
CC2 Distinguish between relevant and irrelevant costs for decision making.	○	
CC3 Apply the relevant cost analysis framework to an equipment replacement decision.		○
CC4 Apply the relevant cost analysis framework to a business addition/deletion decision.		○
CC5 Apply the relevant cost analysis framework to a make-or-buy (outsourcing) decision.		○
CC6 Apply the relevant cost analysis framework to a special order decision.		○
CC7 Explain target costing.	○	
Understand decision making in a constrained setting.		
CC8 Explain decision making in a constrained resource environment.	○	
CC9 Compute the contribution margin per unit of a constrained resource.		○
CC10 Explain how constraints are managed.	○	

Fiction

12

DECISION FEATURE
Getting the Customer Involved

Special orders are one-time orders. Generally, managers accept special orders that generate additional (or incremental) profits and reject those that do not. However, managers sometimes accept a special order if they believe doing so can lead to additional future sales; this is often the case with book sellers.

Processing a special book order is costly—the bookseller must locate and order the book from a publisher, and call the customer when it arrives. Moreover, they incur additional shipping costs and the usual quantity discounts are not available. Finally, this can be risky because the customer may not return to pick up the book and pay for it. Canada's leading bookseller, Chapters (now part of Indigo Books and Music Inc.) took a different approach. It installed e-commerce kiosks in each of its superstores in cooperation with Chapters Online (which it owns).

Chapters' customers are able to check the availability of a book using the in-store kiosks, which access a real-time database. If the title is in the store, the customer is directed to the appropriate shelf; if not, the customer can order the book at the kiosk. The kiosks overcome two of the major problems of special ordering books. First, the process is no longer labour-intensive because customers special order their own books, which are shipped directly to them. Second, rather than being risky, special orders immediately generate cash for the company (payment is due when the order is placed). The decision to accept or reject special orders is no longer the issue it once was for the managers of the superstores.

The in-store kiosks are working well for the company and are useful for much more than just special ordering books. In 2005, using the in-store kiosks, Harry Potter fans were able to pre-order their copy of "Harry Potter and the Half Blood Prince," which they could pick up at the store's 'Get It First' event or have it delivered to their home at no extra charge.

Sources: Indigo Books and Music Inc.'s Web site (www.chapter.indigo.ca); J. Berry, "Kiosks Take Special Orders," *Internetweek*, May 8, 2000 (3 pages); "Get It First! Harry Potter Fans Can Get the Book the Minute It's Released with Chapters and Indigo," *Canada NewsWire*, Ottawa: Apr 5, 2005, p. 1.

A Look Back

We began our discussion on decision making in Chapter 11 by introducing CVP analysis.

A Look at This Chapter

We continue our coverage of the decision-making process in Chapter 12 by focusing on the use of relevant cost data when analyzing alternatives. In general, only those costs and benefits that differ between alternatives are relevant when making a decision. This basic idea is applied in a wide variety of situations in this chapter.

A Look Ahead

The common approaches to making major investment decisions, which can have significant long-term implications for any organization, are discussed in Chapter 13.

Making decisions is one of the basic functions of a

manager. Managers are constantly faced with making decisions about what products or services to sell, what production methods to use, whether to make or buy component parts, what prices to charge, what channels of distribution to use, whether to accept special orders at special prices, and so forth. Decision making is often a difficult task that is complicated by the existence of numerous alternatives and massive amounts of data, only some of which may be relevant.

Every decision involves choosing from between at least two alternatives. In making a decision, the costs and benefits of one alternative must be compared with the costs and benefits of other(s). Once the costs and benefits are identified, managers must identify the alternative that offers the highest net incremental benefit. However, before rushing to make a decision based solely on financial considerations, managers must identify and evaluate any qualitative criteria that may be relevant to the decision. Generic steps in the decision-making process are illustrated in Exhibit 12–1.

⚬ **KNOW**

CC1: Explain the relevant cost analysis framework as it applies to managerial decision making.

Exhibit 12–1

The Decision-Making Process

Note: Steps 2 and 3 may be replaced by a single step, in which only the incremental/differential costs are considered. The manager must be careful to include all the relevant costs in the analysis.

Costs that differ between alternatives are called **relevant costs.** Distinguishing between relevant and irrelevant cost and benefit data is critical for two reasons. First, irrelevant data can be ignored and need not be analyzed. This can save decision makers tremendous amounts of time and effort. Second, bad decisions can easily result from erroneously including irrelevant cost and benefit data when analyzing alternatives. To be successful in decision making, managers must be able to tell the difference between relevant and irrelevant data, and must be able to correctly use the relevant data in analyzing alternatives.

The purpose of this chapter is to develop these skills by illustrating their use in a wide range of decision-making situations. We hasten to add that these decision-making skills are as important in your personal life as they are to managers in the business world. After completing your study of this chapter, you should be able to think more clearly about decisions in all facets of your life. You may find it helpful to turn back to Chapter 2 and refresh your memory concerning different cost concepts before reading on.

Cost Concepts for Decision Making

Identifying Relevant Costs and Benefits

Only those costs and benefits that differ in total between alternatives are relevant in a decision. This, of course, means that whether a particular cost is relevant is usually specific to the decision under consideration. For example, if the decision pertains to family entertainment and the alternatives are renting a movie versus going to the theatre, the relevant costs are those that differ between the two alternatives. A cost that must be incurred regardless of which alternative is chosen is not relevant to the decision. Examples of relevant costs include: (1) the cost of renting a movie, (2) the ticket prices at the theatre, and (3) the cost of popcorn and drinks at the theatre. The difference in costs between the two alternatives is known as the **differential cost** (or *incremental* cost). Moreover, when one alternative is chosen, costs associated with the other alternative are not incurred, which means that they are avoidable. An **avoidable cost** is one that can be eliminated in whole or in part by choosing one alternative over the other. In contrast, the monthly rent (or mortgage) for the family's home is irrelevant to the decision—it must be incurred regardless of which alternative is chosen—and therefore is an unavoidable cost.

Let us add a slight twist to the decision. Assume that the family made a decision to go to the theatre and bought tickets online for $7 each. You just found out that instead of going to the theatre, you could instead mow your neighbour's lawn and potentially earn $15 to $20. By choosing to be entertained, you must forego the *opportunity* to earn some money. This amount of $15 (to be conservative) is an opportunity cost on the one hand and is relevant to the decision. An **opportunity cost** is the potential benefit that is given up when one alternative is selected over another. On the other hand, given that the ticket has already been purchased, and assuming it cannot be returned for a refund, the ticket cost is considered as a sunk cost. A **sunk cost** is a cost that has already been incurred and one that cannot be avoided.

As a general rule, there are two important characteristics of relevant costs: (1) they differ among alternatives, and (2) they are costs that are incurred in the future. Consequently, sunk costs and costs that do not differ among alternatives are not considered relevant. In contrast, avoidable, incremental, or differential costs are always relevant,[1] as are opportunity costs.

To identify the costs that are avoidable (differential) in a particular decision situation and are therefore relevant, you should follow these steps:

1. Eliminate costs and benefits that do not differ between alternatives. These irrelevant costs consist of (a) sunk costs, and (b) future costs that do not differ between alternatives.
2. Use the remaining costs and benefits that do differ between alternatives in making the decision. The costs that remain are the differential, or avoidable, costs.

The Sunk Cost Trap   IN BUSINESS TODAY

Hal Arkes, a psychologist at Ohio University, asked 61 college students to assume they had mistakenly purchased tickets for both a $50- and a $100-ski trip for the same weekend. They could go on only one of the ski trips and would have to throw away the unused ticket. He further asked them to assume that they would actually have more fun on the $50 trip. Most of the students reported that they would go on the less enjoyable $100 trip. The larger cost mattered more to the students than having more fun. However, the sunk costs of the tickets should have been totally irrelevant in this decision. No matter which trip was selected, the actual total cost was $150—the cost of both tickets. And since this cost does not differ between the alternatives, it should be ignored. Like these students, most people have a great deal of difficulty ignoring sunk costs when making decisions.

Source: John Gourville and Dilip Soman, "Pricing and the Psychology of Consumption," *Harvard Business Review*, September 2002, pp. 92–93.

---

[1]The terms *avoidable cost*, *incremental cost*, *differential cost*, and *relevant cost* are often used interchangeably.

Different Costs for Different Purposes

It is important to recognize that costs relevant in one decision situation are not necessarily relevant in another. For example, suppose you have plans to go out for a late evening dinner. The choice between a movie and renting a DVD is not relevant to your choice of restaurant. The cost of dining out will depend on the choice of the restaurant; therefore, the dining costs at alternative restaurants will be relevant to your choice of the restaurant. However, the cost of the movie ticket and the rental cost of the DVD are not relevant in this situation. Simply put, you require *different costs for different purposes*. The costs you require to decide between a movie and renting a DVD are different from those that you require for deciding which restaurant to go to for a late evening dinner. In *each* decision situation, you must examine the data and isolate the relevant costs. Otherwise, you can easily become misled by irrelevant data.

The concept of "different costs for different purposes" is basic to managerial accounting; we shall see its application frequently in the pages that follow.

Sunk Costs Are Not Relevant Costs

One of the most difficult conceptual lessons that managers must learn is that sunk costs are never relevant in decision making.

MANAGERIAL ACCOUNTING IN ACTION

The Issue

SOARING
W I N G S , I N C .

⚪ **APPLY**

CC3: Apply the relevant cost analysis framework to an equipment replacement decision.

SoaringWings Inc. is a small manufacturer of high-quality hang-gliders. The most critical component of a hang-glider is its metal frame, which must be very strong, yet very light. The frames are made by brazing together tubes of high-strength, but lightweight, metal alloys. Most of the brazing must be done by hand, but some can be done in an automated process by machine. Pete Kronski, the production manager of SoaringWings Inc., has been trying to convince J. J. Marker, the company's president, to purchase a new brazing machine from Furimoro Industries. This machine would replace an old brazing machine from Bryston Inc. that generates a large amount of scrap and waste.

On a recent blustery morning, Pete and J. J. happened to drive into the company's parking lot at the same time. The following conversation occurred as they walked together into the building.

Pete: Morning, J. J. Have you had a chance to look at the specifications on the new brazing machine from Furimoro Industries that I gave you last week?
J. J.: Are you still bugging me about the brazing machine?
Pete: You know it's almost impossible to keep that old Bryston brazing machine working within tolerances.
J. J.: I know, I know. But we're carrying the Bryston machine on the books for $140,000.
Pete: That's right. But I've done some investigating, and we could sell it for $90,000 to a plumbing company in town that doesn't require as tight tolerances as we do.
J. J.: Pete, that's just brilliant! You want me to sell a $140,000 machine for $90,000 and take a loss of $50,000. Do you have any other great ideas this morning?
Pete: J. J., I know it sounds far-fetched, but we would actually save money buying the new machine.
J. J.: I'm skeptical. However, if you can show me the hard facts, I'll listen.
Pete: Fair enough. I'll do it.

Book Value of Old Equipment

Pete first gathered the following data concerning the old machine and the proposed new machine:

Old Machine		Proposed New Machine	
Original cost	$175,000	List price new	$200,000
Remaining book value	140,000	Expected life	4 years
Remaining life.	4 years	Disposal value in four years . .	$ –0–
Disposal value now	$ 90,000	. . . . . Annual variable expenses	
Disposal value in four years . .	–0–	to operate.	300,000
Annual variable expenses		Annual revenue from sales . . .	500,000
to operate.	345,000		
Annual revenue from sales . . .	500,000		

Should the old machine be disposed of and the new machine purchased? The first reaction of SoaringWings' president was to say no, since disposal of the old machine would result in a *loss* of $50,000:

Old Machine	
Remaining book value.	$140,000
Disposal value now	90,000
Loss if disposed of now.	$ 50,000

However, this analysis is wrong. The investment that has been made in the old machine is a sunk cost. The portion of this investment that remains on the company's books (the book value of $140,000) should not be considered in a decision about whether to buy the new machine. It is *not* a cost of any kind. The firm has not incurred it. It is merely an artifact of an accounting policy, which apportions the original (sunk) cost of $175,000 to future periods. Pete Kronski verified the irrelevance of the book value of the old machine by the following analysis:[2]

	Total Cost and Revenues—Four Years		
	Keep Old Machine	Purchase New Machine	Differential Costs and Benefits
Sales	$ 2,000,000	$ 2,000,000	$ –0–
Variable expenses	(1,380,000)	(1,200,000)	180,000
Cost of the new machine.	—	(200,000)	(200,000)
Amortization of the old machine or book value write-off	(140,000)	(140,000)*	–0–
Disposal value of the old machine . . .	—	90,000*	90,000
Total net operating income over the four years	$ 480,000	$ 550,000	$ 70,000

*For external reporting purposes, the $140,000 remaining book value of the old machine and the $90,000 disposal value would be netted together and deducted as a single $50,000 loss.

Looking at all four years together, notice that the firm will be $70,000 better off by purchasing the new machine. The $140,000 book value of the old machine had *no effect* on the

---

[2]The analysis of the machine replacement decision makes the following simplifying assumptions: (1) we assume that the amortization treatment for both machines is identical; 2) there are no taxes; 3) both machines are assumed to last for the same length of time; and 4) there is no time value of money. The relevance of time value of money concept for decision making is considered in Chapter 13. A separate procedure exists for situations where the useful lives of equipment are different. This text does not consider such situations.

outcome of the analysis. If the old machine is kept and used, then the $140,000 book value is deducted in the form of amortization. If the old machine is sold, the $140,000 book value is deducted in the form of a lump-sum write-off. Either way, the differential cost is zero.

FOCUSING ON RELEVANT COSTS What costs in the previous example are relevant in the decision concerning whether to buy the new machine? Looking at the original cost data, we should eliminate (1) the sunk costs, and (2) the future costs and benefits that do not differ between the alternatives at hand.

1. The sunk costs:
   a. The original investment, $175,000. The remaining book value of the old machine ($140,000) is also irrelevant because it is not a cost as such.
2. The future costs and benefits that do not differ:
   a. The sales revenue ($500,000 per year).
   b. The variable expenses (to the extent of $300,000 per year).

The costs and benefits that remain will form the basis for a decision. The analysis is as follows:

	Differential Costs and Benefits—Four Years
Reduction in variable expense promised by the new machine ($45,000* per year × 4 years)	$ 180,000
Cost of the new machine	(200,000)
Disposal value of the old machine	90,000
Net advantage of the new machine	$ 70,000

*$345,000 − $300,000 = $45,000.

Note that the items above are the same as those in the last column of the previous analysis and represent those costs and benefits that differ between the two alternatives. Also, observe that all of these figures represent *cash flows*. The company pays out or receives these amounts. Armed with this analysis, Pete feels confident that he would be able to explain the financial advantages of the new machine to the president of the company.

MANAGERIAL ACCOUNTING IN ACTION

The Wrap-Up

SOARING
WINGS, INC.

Pete Kronski took his analysis to the office of J. J. Marker, the president of SoaringWings, where the following conversation took place.

Pete: J. J., do you remember that discussion we had about the proposed new brazing machine?
J. J.: Sure I remember. Did you find out that I'm right?
Pete: Not exactly. Here's the analysis where I compare the profit with the old machine over the next four years to the profit with the new machine.
J. J.: I see you're claiming the profit is $70,000 higher with the new machine. Are you assuming higher sales with the new machine?
Pete: No, I have assumed total sales of $2,000,000 over the four years in either situation. The real advantage comes with the reduction in variable expenses of $180,000.
J. J.: Where are those reductions going to come from?
Pete: The new brazing machine should cut our scrap and rework rate at least in half. That results in substantial savings in materials and labour costs.
J. J.: What about the $50,000 loss on the old machine?
Pete: What really matters is the $200,000 cost of the new machine and the $90,000 salvage value of the old machine. The book value of the old machine is irrelevant. No matter what we do, it will eventually flow through the income statement as a charge in one form or another.
J. J.: I find that hard to accept, but it is difficult to argue with your analysis.

Pete: The analysis actually understates the advantages of the new machine. We don't catch all of the defects caused by the old machine, and defective products are sometimes sold to customers. With the new machine, I expect our warranty costs to decrease and our repeat sales to increase. And, I would hate to be held responsible for any accidents caused by defective brazing by our old machine.

J. J.: Okay, I'm convinced. Put together a formal proposal, and we'll present it at the next meeting of the board of directors.

Future Costs That Do Not Differ Are Not Relevant Costs

We stated previously that people often have difficulty accepting the idea that sunk costs are never relevant in a decision. Some people also have difficulty accepting the principle that future costs that do not differ between alternatives are never relevant in a decision. An example will help illustrate how future costs *should* be handled in a decision.

An Example of Irrelevant Future Costs

A company is contemplating the purchase of a new labour-saving machine that will cost $30,000 and have a 10-year useful life. Data concerning the company's annual sales and costs with and without the new machine follow:

	Current Situation	Situation with the New Machine
Units produced and sold	5,000	5,000
Selling price per unit.	$ 40	$ 40
Direct materials cost per unit	14	14
Direct labour cost per unit	8	5
Variable overhead cost per unit.	2	2
Fixed costs, other	62,000	62,000
Fixed costs, new machine	—	3,000

The new machine promises a saving of $3 per unit in direct labour costs ($8 − $5 = $3), but it will increase fixed costs by $3,000 per year. All other costs, as well as the total number of units produced and sold, will remain the same. Following the steps outlined previously, our analysis is as follows:

1. Eliminate the sunk costs. (No sunk costs are included in this example.)
2. Eliminate the future costs and benefits that do not differ between the alternatives.
   a. The selling price per unit and the number of units sold do not differ between the alternatives. (Therefore, total future sales revenues will not differ.)
   b. The direct materials cost per unit, the variable overhead cost per unit, and the number of units produced do not differ between the alternatives. (Therefore, total future direct materials costs and variable overhead costs will not differ.)
   c. The "Fixed costs, other" do not differ between the alternatives.

The remaining costs—direct labour costs and the fixed costs associated with the new machine—are the only relevant costs.

Savings in direct labour costs ($5,000 units at a cost saving of $3 per unit)	$15,000
Less: Increase in fixed costs	3,000
Net annual cost savings promised by the new machine	$12,000

This solution can be verified by looking at *all* of the cost data (both those that are relevant and those that are not) under the two alternatives. This is done in Exhibit 12–2.

Exhibit 12–2
Differential Cost Analysis

	5,000 Units Produced and Sold		
	Current Situation	Situation with New Machine	Differential Costs and Benefits (New – Old)
Sales	$200,000	$200,000	$ –0–
Variable expenses:			
Direct materials............	70,000	70,000	–0–
Direct labour..............	40,000	25,000	15,000
Variable overhead	10,000	10,000	–0–
Total variable expenses.......	120,000	105,000	
Contribution margin	80,000	95,000	
Less: Fixed expenses:			
Other	62,000	62,000	–0–
New machine	–0–	3,000	(3,000)
Total fixed expenses	62,000	65,000	
Net operating income	$ 18,000	$ 30,000	$12,000

Note from the exhibit that the net advantage in favour of buying the machine is $12,000–the same answer we obtained by focusing on just the relevant costs. Thus, we can see that future costs that do not differ between alternatives are, indeed, irrelevant in the decision-making process and can be safely eliminated from the analysis.

Why Isolate Relevant Costs?

Isolating relevant costs is desirable for at least two reasons. First, only rarely will enough information be available to prepare a detailed income statement for both alternatives. Assume, for example, that you are called on to make a decision relating to a *single operation* of a multidepartmental, multiproduct firm. Under these circumstances, it would be virtually impossible to prepare an income statement of any type. You would have to rely on your ability to recognize which costs are relevant and which are not in order to assemble those data necessary to make a decision.

Second, mingling irrelevant costs with relevant costs may cause confusion and distract attention from the matters that are really critical. Furthermore, the danger always exists that an irrelevant piece of information may be used improperly, resulting in an incorrect decision. The best approach is to ignore irrelevant data, basing the decision entirely on the relevant data.

Relevant cost analysis, combined with the *contribution approach* to the income statement, provides a powerful tool for making decisions.[3] We will investigate various uses of this tool in the remaining sections of this chapter.

---

[3]Using the contribution margin approach (see Chapter 3), the unit contribution margin (unit price less unit variable cost) improves by $3 thereby increasing the total contribution margin for a sales volume of 5,000 units by $15,000. Since fixed costs increase by only $3,000, net income will increase by $15,000 − $3,000 = $12,000.

Costs and Decision Making at Rogers and Lantic Ltd.

Rogers and Lantic Sugar Ltd. has secured contracts with many candy makers, food companies, and other industrial customers. However, the company has faced the choice of becoming a value-added manufacturer by expanding beyond their existing packaging and refining duties.

A lucrative contract proposed from Kraft Foods Inc. has attracted Rogers and Lantic's attention. Basically, Kraft has moved its entire LifeSavers production line to a Montreal plant in an effort to reduce substantial production costs, and a supplier was needed. Since LifeSavers are composed of 99% sugar, the sugar-laden company can anticipate an additional 25,000 tonnes of sugar sales per year. Instead of just supplying sugar to Kraft, Rogers and Lantic has the option to operate and manage the LifeSavers production line from mixing to packaging the candy. The company would have to acquire new facilities in order to carry out this plan. As well, to move up in the value chain, Rogers and Lantic would have to expand their operations.

For Kraft, the decision to allow Rogers and Lantic to take over the LifeSavers manufacturing and packaging is a make-or-buy decision. For Rogers and Lantic, this is an opportunity to add a new line of business. The disadvantage to Rogers and Lantic is the risk of competing against its own customers in an effort to procure higher profit margins. Furthermore, observers believe that many companies that have gone beyond their core business in hopes of more rewards end up in ruins. If Rogers and Lantic is not careful, it can end up being flattened by its customers-turned-competitors. However, if Rogers and Lantic can find a winning strategy to add value to its products and become a multibillion dollar company, it may have a leading edge in the industry.

Source: Brian Banks, "How Sweet It Is," *Canadian Business*, April 1, 2002, pp. 54–57. Reprinted with permission of Brian Banks.

Adding and Dropping Product Lines and Other Segments

Decisions relating to whether old product lines or other segments of a company should be dropped and new ones added are among the most difficult that a manager has to make. In such decisions, many qualitative and quantitative factors must be considered. Ultimately, however, any final decision to drop an old segment or to add a new one is going to hinge primarily on the impact the decision will have on net operating income. To assess this impact, you must make a careful analysis of the costs involved.

 APPLY

CC4: Apply the relevant cost analysis framework to a business addition/deletion decision.

WestJet Expands Routes

WestJet was founded in 1996 by Clive Beddoe, Mark Hill, Tim Morgan, and Donald Bell, four Calgary entrepreneurs who saw an opportunity to provide low-fare air travel across Western Canada. Through researching other successful airlines in North America—and in particular low-cost carriers from throughout the continent—the team followed the primary examples of Southwest Airlines and Morris Air, and determined that a similar concept could be successful in Western Canada.

On February 29, 1996, the airline started flight operations with 220 employees and three aircraft to the cities of Vancouver, Kelowna, Calgary, Edmonton, and Winnipeg. Since that time, the company has continued to expand, bringing more western cities into

WestJet's world. In 1996, WestJet added Victoria, Regina, and Saskatoon to its route network. Today, WestJet serves markets all across Canada, connecting Canadians from the Maritimes, Quebec, Ontario, and Western Canada.

In 2000, WestJet's four founders were honoured as "The Ernst & Young Entrepreneur of the Year" for Canada, in recognition of the contributions they have made to Canadian travellers and the lives of all of WestJet's people and shareholders. In 2003, WestJet celebrated its 27th quarter of profitability with its third quarter 2003 results.

Source: www.westjet.com.

An Illustration of Cost Analysis

Consider the three major product lines—drugs, cosmetics, and housewares—of the Discount Drug Company. Sales and cost information for the preceding month for each separate product line and for the store in total are given in Exhibit 12–3.

What can be done to improve the company's overall performance? One product line–housewares–shows a net operating loss for the month. Perhaps dropping this line would cause profits in the company as a whole to improve. In deciding whether the line should be dropped, management should reason as follows:

If the housewares line is dropped, then the company will lose $20,000 per month in contribution margin. By dropping the line, however, it may be possible to avoid some fixed costs. For example, it may be possible to discharge certain employees or to reduce advertising costs. If by dropping the housewares line the company is able to avoid more in fixed costs than it loses in contribution margin, then it would be better off if the line were eliminated, since overall net income should improve. However, if the company is not able to avoid as much in fixed costs as it loses in contribution margin, then the housewares line should be retained. In short, the manager should ask, "What costs can I avoid if I drop this product line?"

As we have seen from our previous discussion, not all costs are avoidable. For example, some of the costs associated with a product line may be sunk costs. Other costs may be allocated fixed costs that will not differ in total, regardless of whether the product line is dropped or retained.

Exhibit 12–3
Discount Drug Company
Product Lines

	Product Line			
	Drugs	**Cosmetics**	**Housewares**	**Total**
Sales	$125,000	$75,000	$50,000	$250,000
Less: Variable expenses.......	50,000	25,000	30,000	105,000
Contribution margin	75,000	50,000	20,000	145,000
Less: Fixed expenses:				
Salaries	29,500	12,500	8,000	50,000
Advertising	1,000	7,500	6,500	15,000
Utilities	500	500	1,000	2,000
Amortization—fixtures......	1,000	2,000	2,000	5,000
Rent.....................	10,000	6,000	4,000	20,000
Insurance................	2,000	500	500	3,000
General administrative	15,000	9,000	6,000	30,000
Total fixed expenses	59,000	38,000	28,000	125,000
Net operating income (loss) ...	$ 16,000	$12,000	$ (8,000)	$ 20,000

To show how the manager should proceed in a product-line analysis, suppose that the management of the Discount Drug Company has analyzed the costs being charged to the three product lines and determined the following:

1. The salaries expense represents salaries paid to employees working directly in each product-line area. All of the employees working in housewares would be discharged if the line is dropped.
2. The advertising expense represents direct advertising of each product line and is avoidable if the line is dropped.
3. The utilities expense represents utilities costs for the entire company. The amount charged to each product line is an allocation based on space occupied and is not avoidable if the product line is dropped.
4. The amortization expense represents amortization on fixtures used for display of the various product lines. Although the fixtures are nearly new, they are custom-built and will have little resale value if the housewares line is dropped.
5. The rent expense represents rent on the entire building housing the company; it is allocated to the product lines on the basis of sales dollars. The monthly rent of $20,000 is fixed under a long-term lease agreement.
6. The insurance expense represents insurance carried on inventories within each of the three product-line areas.
7. The general administrative expense represents the costs of accounting, purchasing, and general management, which are allocated to the product lines on the basis of sales dollars. Total administrative costs will not change if the housewares line is dropped.

With this information, management can identify costs that can and cannot be avoided if the product line is dropped:

	Not Avoidable*	Avoidable	Total Cost
Salaries		$ 8,000	$ 8,000
Advertising		6,500	6,500
Utilities	$ 1,000		1,000
Amortization—fixtures	2,000		2,000
Rent	4,000		4,000
Insurance		500	500
General administrative	6,000		6,000
Total fixed expenses	$13,000	$15,000	$28,000

*These costs represent either (1) sunk costs or (2) future costs that will not change whether the housewares line is retained or discontinued.

To determine how dropping the line will affect the overall profits of the company, we can compare the contribution margin that will be lost with the costs that can be avoided if the line is dropped:

Contribution margin lost if the housewares line is discontinued (see Exhibit 12–3)	$(20,000)
Less: Fixed costs that can be avoided if the housewares line is discontinued (see above)	15,000
Decrease in overall company net operating income	$ (5,000)

In this case, the fixed costs that can be avoided by dropping the product line are less than the contribution margin that will be lost. Therefore, based on the data provided, the housewares line should be retained unless a more profitable use can be found for the floor and counter space that it is occupying. (The issue of opportunity cost of floor space is considered later in the chapter.)

A Comparative Format

Some managers prefer to approach decisions of this type by preparing comparative income statements showing the effects on the company as a whole of either keeping or dropping the product line in question. A comparative analysis of this type for the Discount Drug Company is shown in Exhibit 12–4.

As shown in the right-most column, overall company net operating income will decrease by $5,000 each period if the housewares line is dropped. This is the same answer, of course, as we obtained in our previous analysis.

Exhibit 12–4
A comparative Format for Product-Line Analysis

	Keep Housewares	Drop Housewares	Difference: (Drop – Keep) Net Income Increase or (Decrease)
Sales.	$50,000	$ –0–	$(50,000)
Less: Variable expenses	30,000	–0–	30,000
Contribution margin	20,000	–0–	(20,000)
Less: Fixed expenses:			
Salaries.	8,000	–0–	8,000
Advertising	6,500	–0–	6,500
Utilities	1,000	1,000	–0–
Amortization—fixtures	2,000	2,000	–0–
Rent	4,000	4,000	–0–
Insurance	500	–0–	500
General administrative.	6,000	6,000	–0–
Total fixed expenses	28,000	13,000	15,000
Net operating income (loss)	$ (8,000)	$(13,000)	$ (5,000)

Beware of Allocated Fixed Costs

Our conclusion that the housewares line should not be dropped seems to conflict with the data shown previously in Exhibit 12–3. Recall from that exhibit that the housewares line is showing a loss, rather than a profit. Why keep a line that is showing a loss? The explanation for this apparent inconsistency lies, at least in part, with the *common fixed costs* that are being allocated to the product lines. A **common fixed cost** is a fixed cost that supports the operations of more than one segment of an organization and is not avoidable in whole or in part by eliminating any one segment. For example, the salary of the CEO of a company ordinarily would not be cut if any one product line were dropped, and so it is a common fixed cost of the product lines. In fact, if dropping a product line is a good idea that results in higher profits for the company, the compensation of the CEO is likely to increase, rather than decrease, as a result of dropping the product line. One of the great dangers in allocating common fixed costs is that such allocations can make a product line (or other segment of a business) *look* less profitable than it really is. By allocating the common fixed costs among all product lines, the housewares line has been made to *look* as if it were unprofitable, whereas, in fact, dropping the line would result in a decrease in overall company net operating income. This point can be seen clearly if we recast the data in Exhibit 12–3 and eliminate the allocation of the common fixed costs. This recasting of data is shown in Exhibit 12–5 (which is similar to Exhibit 10–2A).

Notice that the common fixed expenses have not been allocated to the product lines in Exhibit 12–5. Only the fixed expenses that are traceable to the product lines and that could be avoided by dropping the product lines are assigned to them. For example, the fixed expenses of advertising the housewares product line can be traced to that product line and can be eliminated if that product line is dropped. However, the general administrative expenses, such as the CEO's salary, cannot be traced to the individual product lines and would not be eliminated if any one product line were dropped. Consequently, these common fixed expenses are not allocated to the product lines in Exhibit 12–5 as they were in Exhibit 12–3. The allocations in Exhibit 12–3 provide a misleading picture that suggests that portions of the fixed common expenses can be eliminated by dropping individual product lines—this is not the case.

Exhibit 12–5

Discount Drug Company Product Lines—Recast in Contribution Format (from Exhibit 12–3)

	Product Line			
	Drugs	Cosmetics	Housewares	Total
Sales	$125,000	$75,000	$50,000	$250,000
Less: Variable expenses.........	50,000	25,000	30,000	105,000
Contribution margin	75,000	50,000	20,000	145,000
Less: Traceable fixed expenses:				
Salaries..................	29,500	12,500	8,000	50,000
Advertising..............	1,000	7,500	6,500	15,000
Amortization—fixtures	1,000	2,000	2,000	5,000
Insurance	2,000	500	500	3,000
Total traceable fixed expenses....	33,500	22,500	17,000	73,000
Product-line segment margin	$ 41,500	$27,500	$ 3,000*	72,000
Less: Common fixed expenses:				
Utilities.................				2,000
Rent				20,000
General administrative.......				30,000
Total common fixed expenses....				52,000
Net operating income				$ 20,000

*The impact of dropping the housewares line will be the $3,000 segment margin plus $2,000 representing amortization expense. The amortization expense must be added back to obtain the impact on profits because it represents a noncash charge. In other words, the company does not actually *incur* this expense. Thus, it can be seen that if the housewares line is dropped, the company will *lose* $5,000.

Exhibit 12–5 gives us a much different perspective of the housewares line than does Exhibit 12–3. As shown in Exhibit 12–5, the housewares line is covering all of its own traceable fixed costs and is generating a $3,000 *segment margin* toward covering the common fixed costs of the company. The **segment margin** is the difference between the revenue generated by a segment and its own traceable costs. Unless another product line can be found that will generate more than a $3,000 segment margin, the company would be better off keeping the housewares line. By keeping the line, the company's overall net operating income would be higher than if the product line were dropped.

Additionally, we should note that managers may choose to retain an unprofitable product line (when considered *by itself*) if the line is necessary to the sale of other products or if it serves as a *magnet* to attract customers. Bread, for example, is not an especially profitable line in food stores, but customers expect it to be available, and many would undoubtedly shift their buying elsewhere if a particular store decided to stop carrying it. In other words, bread may be profitable if its impact on sales of other items is included in the analysis.

Finally, note that this issue of common fixed cost and the distortions introduced by allocating such costs lie at the heart of the rationale for an ABC management system. This was covered in Chapter 6. You can see that the analysis in Exhibit 12–5 could not have been done if it was not possible to *trace* the fixed expenses to the various segments. The ability to carry out this type of tracing is clearly the key.

IN BUSINESS TODAY

The Trap Laid by Fully Allocated Costs

A bakery distributed its products through route salespersons, each of whom loaded a truck with an assortment of products in the morning and spent the day calling on customers in an assigned territory. Believing that some items were more profitable than others, management asked for an analysis of product costs and sales. The accountants to whom the task was assigned allocated all manufacturing and marketing costs to products to obtain a net profit for each product. The resulting figures indicated that some of the products were being sold at a loss, and management discontinued these products. However, when this change was put into effect, the company's overall profit declined. It was then seen that by dropping some products, sales revenues had been reduced without commensurate reduction in costs because the common manufacturing costs and route sales costs had to be continued in order to make and sell the remaining products.

The Make-or-Buy Decision

● APPLY

CC5: Apply the relevant cost analysis framework to a make-or-buy (outsourcing) decision.

A decision about whether to produce a fabricated part internally, rather than to buy the part externally from a supplier, is called a **make-or-buy decision.** This is also known as an *outsourcing* or *subcontracting decision*. To provide an illustration of a make-or-buy decision, consider Mountain Goat Cycles. The company is now producing the heavy-duty gear shifters used in its most popular line of mountain bikes. The company's accounting department reports the following costs of producing the shifter internally:

	Per Unit	8,000 Units
Direct materials	$ 6	$ 48,000
Direct labour	4	32,000
Variable overhead	1	8,000
Supervisor's salary.	3	24,000
Amortization of special equipment	2	16,000
Allocated general overhead	5	40,000
Total cost	$21	$168,000

An outside supplier has offered to sell Mountain Goat Cycles 8,000 shifters a year at a price of only $19 each. Should the company stop producing the shifters internally and start purchasing them from the outside supplier? To approach the decision from a financial point of view, the manager should again focus on the differential costs. As we have seen, the differential costs can be obtained by eliminating those costs that are not avoidable–that is, by eliminating (1) the sunk costs, and (2) the future costs that will continue regardless of whether the shifters are produced internally or purchased outside. The costs that remain after making these eliminations are the costs that are avoidable to the company by purchasing outside. If these avoidable costs are less than the outside purchase price, then the company should continue to manufacture its own shifters and reject the outside supplier's offer. That is, the company should purchase outside only if the outside purchase price is less than the costs that can be avoided internally as a result of stopping production of the shifters.

Looking at the cost data for producing the shifter internally, note first that amortization of special equipment is listed as one of the costs of producing the shifters internally. Since the equipment has already been purchased, this amortization is a sunk cost and is therefore irrelevant. If the equipment could be sold, its salvage value would be relevant. Or if the machine could be used to make other products, this could be relevant as well. However, we will assume that the equipment has no salvage value and that it has no other use than making the heavy-duty gear shifters.

Also, notice that the company is allocating a portion of its general overhead costs to the shifters. Any portion of this general overhead cost that would actually be eliminated if the gear shifters were purchased, rather than made, would be relevant in the analysis. However, it is likely that the general overhead costs allocated to the gear shifters are, in fact, common to all items produced in the factory and would continue unchanged even if the shifters are purchased from the outside. Such allocated common costs are not differential costs (since they do not differ between the make-or-buy alternatives) and should be eliminated from the analysis along with the sunk costs.

The variable costs of producing the shifters (materials, labour, and variable overhead) are differential costs, since they can be avoided by buying the shifters from the outside supplier. If the supervisor can be discharged and his or her salary avoided by buying the shifters, then it too will be a differential cost and relevant to the decision. Assuming that both the variable costs and the supervisor's salary can be avoided by buying from the outside supplier, then the analysis takes the form shown in Exhibit 12–6.

Exhibit 12–6
Mountain Goat Cycles
Make-or-Buy Analysis

	Production Cost per Unit	Per-Unit Differential Costs		Total Differential Costs—8,000 Units	
		Make	Buy	Make	Buy
Direct materials	$ 6	$ 6		$ 48,000	
Direct labour	4	4		32,000	
Variable overhead	1	1		8,000	
Supervisor's salary	3	3		24,000	
Amortization of special equipment.	2	—		—	
Allocated general overhead	5	—		—	
Outside purchase price			$19		$152,000
Total cost	$21	$14	$19	$112,000	$152,000
Difference in favour of continuing to make.			$5		$40,000

Since it costs $5 less per unit to continue to make the shifters, Mountain Goat Cycles should reject the outside supplier's offer. However, there is one additional factor that the company may wish to consider before coming to a final decision. This factor is the opportunity cost of the space now being used to produce the shifters.

The Changing Trends of Human Resource Management   IN BUSINESS TODAY

Change seems to be the only constant in today's business world! A significant change both in Canada and the United States is the replacement of full-time employees with part-timers. Employers do not have to provide benefits to the part-time employees, which results in cost savings. Another trend is the outsourcing of manufacturing and other processing activities to countries like Mexico, India, China, etc. Yet another trend is that many businesses are outsourcing specific functions, such as payroll management, to companies such as ADP Canada Employer Services, which employs over 1,800 employees and operates from five locations: Calgary, Montreal, Toronto, Vancouver, and Winnipeg. The company has over 50,000 clients. While outsourcing can provide cost savings, it can also lead to negative consequences such as job losses!

Sources: E. Finn, "When Greed Has No Limits: Outsourcing and Job 'Restructuring' Swell Corporate Profits," *CCPA Monitor*, Feb. 2007, Vol.13, Issue 8, p. 4; "92 Percent of Canadians Pass the Buck: ADP Outsource It! Index," *Canada NewsWire*, Ottawa: May 23, 2007, p.1; www.adp.ca.

The Matter of Opportunity Cost

If the space now being used to produce the shifters *would otherwise be idle*, then Mountain Goat Cycles should continue to produce its own shifters and the supplier's offer should be rejected, as stated previously. Idle space that has no alternative use has an opportunity cost of zero.

But what if the space now being used to produce shifters could be used for some other purpose? In that case, the space would have an opportunity cost that would have to be considered in assessing the desirability of the supplier's offer. What would this opportunity cost be? It would be the segment margin that could be derived from the best alternative use of the space.

To illustrate, assume that the space now being used to produce shifters could be used to produce a new cross-country bike that would generate a segment margin of $60,000 per year. Under these conditions, Mountain Goat Cycles would be better off to accept the supplier's offer and to use the available space to produce the new product line:

	Make	Buy
Differential cost per unit (see prior example)...........	$ 14	$ 19
Number of units needed annually....................	× 8,000	× 8,000
Total annual cost.................................	112,000	152,000
Opportunity cost–segment margin forgone on a potential new product line	60,000	
Total cost......................................	$172,000	$152,000
Difference in favour of purchasing from the outside supplier................................		$ 20,000

Opportunity costs are not recorded in accounts of an organization. They do not represent actual dollar outlays. Rather, they represent economic benefits that are *foregone* as a result of pursuing some course of action. The opportunity costs of Mountain Goat Cycles are sufficiently large in this case to make continued production of the shifters very costly from an economic point of view.

DECISION MAKER ## Vice-President of Production

You are faced with a make-or-buy decision. The company currently makes a component for one of its products but is considering whether it should instead purchase the component. If the offer from an outside supplier were accepted, the company would no longer need to rent the machinery that is currently being used to manufacture the component. You realize that the annual rental cost is a fixed cost, but recall some sort of warning about fixed costs. Is the annual rental cost relevant to this make-or-buy decision?

Special Orders

 APPLY

CC6: Apply the relevant cost analysis framework to a special order decision.

Managers often must evaluate whether a *special order* should be accepted, and if the order is accepted, the price that should be charged. A **special order** is a one-time order that is not considered part of the company's normal ongoing business. To illustrate, Mountain Goat Cycles has just received a request from the Charlottetown Police Department to produce 100 specially modified mountain bikes at a price of $740 each. The bikes would be used to patrol some of the more densely populated residential sections of the city. Mountain Goat Cycles can easily modify its City Cruiser model to fit the specifications of the

Charlottetown Police. The normal selling price of the City Cruiser bike is $930, and its unit product cost is $750 as shown below:

Direct materials	$ 400
Direct labour	225
Manufacturing overhead	125
Unit product cost	$750

The variable portion of the manufacturing overhead is $25 per unit. The order would have no effect on the company's total fixed manufacturing overhead costs.

The modifications to the bikes consist of welded brackets to hold radios, nightsticks, and other gear. These modifications would require $50 in incremental variable costs. In addition, the company would have to pay a graphics design studio $2,000 to design and cut stencils that would be used for spray painting the Charlottetown Police Department's logo and other identifying marks on the bikes.

This order should have no effect on the company's other sales. The production manager says that she can handle the special order without disrupting any of the regular scheduled production.

What effect would accepting this order have on the company's net operating income?

Only the incremental costs and benefits are relevant. Since the existing fixed manufacturing overhead costs would not be affected by the order, they are not incremental costs and are therefore not relevant. The incremental net operating income can be computed as follows:

	Per Unit	Total 100 Bikes
Incremental revenue	$740	$74,000
Incremental costs:		
Variable costs:		
Direct materials.	400	40,000
Direct labour.	225	22,500
Variable manufacturing overhead	25	2,500
Special modifications	50	5,000
Total variable cost.	$700	70,000
Fixed cost:		
Purchase of stencils.		2,000
Total incremental cost.		72,000
Incremental net operating income.		$ 2,000

Therefore, even though the price on the special order ($740) is below the normal unit product cost ($750) and the order would require incurring additional costs, the order would result in an increase in net operating income. In general, a special order is profitable as long as the incremental revenue from the special order exceeds the incremental costs of the order. We must note, however, that it is important to make sure that there is, indeed, idle capacity and that the special order does not cut into normal sales. For example, if the company was operating at capacity, opportunity costs would have to be taken into account as well as the incremental costs that have already been detailed previously.

Pricing New Products: Target Costing

When offering a new product or service for the first time, a company must decide on its selling price. A cost-based approach has often been followed in practice. In this approach, the product is first designed and produced, then its cost is determined and its price is com-

 KNOW

CC7: Explain target costing.

puted by adding a markup to the cost. This *cost-plus* approach to pricing suffers from a number of drawbacks–the most obvious being that customers may not be willing to pay the price set by the company. If the price is too high, customers may decide to purchase a similar product from a competitor or, if no similar competing product exists, they may decide not to buy the product at all.

Target costing provides an alternative, market-based approach to pricing new products. In the **target costing** approach, management estimates how much the market will be willing to pay for the new product even before the new product has been designed. The company's required profit margin is subtracted from the estimated selling price to determine the target cost for the new product. A cross-functional team consisting of designers, engineers, cost accountants, marketing personnel, and production personnel is charged with the responsibility of ensuring that the cost of the product is ultimately less than the target cost. If at some point in the product development process it becomes clear that it will not be possible to meet the target cost, the new product is abandoned.

The target costing approach to pricing has a number of advantages over the cost-plus approach. First, the target costing approach is focused on the market and the customer. A product is not made unless the company is reasonably confident that customers will be willing to buy the product at a price that provides the company with an adequate profit. Second, the target costing approach instills a much higher level of cost-consciousness than the cost-plus approach and probably results in less expensive products that are more attractive to customers. The target cost lid creates relentless pressure to drive out unnecessary costs. In the cost-plus approach, there is little pressure to control costs, since whatever the costs turn out to be, the price will be higher. This allows designers and engineers to create products with expensive features that customers may not actually be willing to pay for. Because of these advantages, more and more companies are abandoning the cost-plus approach to new product pricing in favour of the target costing approach.

YOU DECIDE

Tutor

Your financial accounting instructor has suggested that you should consider working with selected students in her class as a tutor. Should you adopt a cost-plus or target costing approach to setting your hourly fee?

Utilization of a Constrained Resource

 KNOW

CC8: Explain decision making in a constrained resource environment.

Managers are routinely faced with the problem of deciding how constrained resources are going to be utilized. A department store, for example, has a limited amount of floor space and therefore cannot stock every product that may be available. A manufacturing firm has a limited number of machine-hours and a limited number of direct labour-hours at its disposal. When a limited resource of some type restricts the company's ability to satisfy demand, the company is said to have a **constraint.** Because of the constrained resource, the company cannot fully satisfy demand, and so the manager must decide how the constrained resource should be used. Fixed costs are usually unaffected by such choices, and so the manager should select the course of action that will maximize the firm's *total* contribution margin.

APPLY

CC9: Compute the contribution margin per unit of a constrained resource.

Contribution in Relation to a Constrained Resource

To maximize total contribution margin, a firm should promote those products or accept those orders that provide the highest unit contribution margin *per unit of the constrained resource.* To illustrate, Mountain Goat Cycles makes a line of panniers—saddlebags for bicycles. There are two models offered—a touring model and a mountain model. Cost and revenue data for each pannier model are provided following:

	Model	
	Mountain Pannier	Touring Pannier
Selling price per unit.	$25	$30
Variable cost per unit	10	18
Contribution margin per unit	$15	$12
Contribution margin (CM) ratio	60%	40%

The mountain pannier appears to be much more profitable than the touring pannier. It has a $15 per unit contribution margin as compared with only $12 per unit for the touring model, and it has a 60% CM ratio as compared with only 40% for the touring model.

But now let us add one more piece of information—the plant that makes the panniers is operating at capacity. At Mountain Goat Cycles, the machine or process that is limiting overall output is called the **bottleneck**—it is the constraint. The bottleneck is a particular stitching machine. The mountain pannier requires two minutes of stitching time, while the touring pannier requires one minute of stitching time. In this situation, if additional time becomes available on the stitching machine, which product is more profitable to produce? To answer this question, the manager should look at the *contribution margin per unit of the constrained resource.* This figure is computed by dividing the contribution margin by the amount of the constrained resource a unit of product requires. These calculations are carried out below for the mountain and touring panniers.

	Model	
	Mountain Pannier	Touring Pannier
Contribution margin per unit (above) (a)	$15	$12
Time on the stitching machine required to produce one unit (b)	2 min.	1 min.
Contribution margin per unit of the constrained resource, (a) ÷ (b).	$7.50/min.	$12/min.

Each minute of processing time on the stitching machine devoted to the touring pannier results in an increase of $12 in contribution margin and profits. The comparable figure for the mountain pannier is only $7.50 per minute. Therefore, more units of the touring model should be made using the additional time. Even though the mountain model has the larger per-unit contribution margin and the larger CM ratio, the touring model provides the larger contribution margin in relation to the constrained resource.

To verify that the touring model is, indeed, the more profitable product, suppose an hour of additional stitching time is available and that there are unfilled orders for both products. Total contribution margin will increase by $7.50/min. × 60 min. = $450, if the mountain pannier is made; and total contribution margin will increase by $12/min. × 60 min. = $720 if the touring pannier is made.

This example clearly shows that looking at unit contribution margins alone is not enough; the contribution margin must be viewed in relation to the amount of the constrained resource each product requires.

Theory of Constraints Software

Indalex Aluminum Solutions Group is the largest producer of soft alloy extrusions in North America. The company has installed a new generation of business intelligence software created by pVelocity, Inc., of Toronto, Ontario. The software "provides decision makers across our entire manufacturing enterprise with time-based financial metrics using TOC concepts to identify bottlenecks." And, it "shifts the focus of a manufacturing company from traditional cost accounting measurements to measuring the generation of dollars per unit of time." For example, instead of emphasizing products with the largest gross margins or contribution margins, the software helps managers to identify and emphasize the products that maximize the contribution margin per unit of the constrained resource.

Source: Mike Alger, "Managing a Business as a Portfolio of Customers," *Strategic Finance*, June 2003, pp. 54–57.

Managing Constraints

☞ KNOW

CC10: Explain how constraints are managed.

Profits can be increased by effectively managing the organization's constraints. One aspect of managing constraints is to decide how to utilize them best. As discussed previously, if the constraint is a bottleneck in the production process, the manager should select the product mix that maximizes the total contribution margin. In addition, the manager should take an active role in managing the constraint itself. Management should focus efforts on increasing the efficiency of the bottleneck operation and on increasing its capacity. Such efforts directly increase the output of finished goods and will often pay off in an almost immediate increase in profits.

It is often possible for a manager to effectively increase the capacity of the bottleneck, which is called **relaxing** (or **elevating**) **the constraint.** For example, the stitching machine operator could be asked to work overtime. This would result in more available stitching time and hence more finished goods that can be sold. The benefits from relaxing the constraint in such a manner are often enormous and can be easily quantified. The manager should first ask, "What would I do with additional capacity at the bottleneck if it were available?" In the example, if there are unfilled orders for both the touring and mountain panniers, the additional capacity would be used to process more touring panniers, since that would be a better use of the additional capacity. In that situation, the additional capacity would be worth $720 per hour. Since overtime pay for the operator is likely to be much less than $720 per hour, running the stitching machine on overtime would be an excellent way to increase the profits of the company while satisfying customers as well.

To reinforce this concept, suppose that making touring panniers has already been given top priority and consequently there are only unfilled orders for the mountain pannier. How much would it be worth to the company to run the stitching machine overtime in this situation? Since the additional capacity would be used to make the mountain pannier, the value of that additional capacity would drop to $7.50 per minute or $450 per hour. Nevertheless, the value of relaxing the constraint would still be quite high.

These calculations indicate that managers should pay great attention to bottleneck operations. If a bottleneck machine breaks down or is ineffectively utilized, the losses to the company can be quite large. In our example, for every minute the stitching machine is down due to breakdowns or setups, the company loses between $7.50 and $12. The losses on an hourly basis are between $450 and $720! In contrast, there is no such loss of contribution margin if time is lost on a machine that is not a bottleneck–such machines have excess capacity anyway.

The implications are clear. Managers should focus much of their attention on managing bottlenecks. As we have discussed, managers should emphasize products that most profitably utilize the constrained resource. They should also make sure that products are processed smoothly through the bottlenecks, with minimal lost time due to breakdowns and setups. And, they should try to find ways to increase the capacity at the bottlenecks.

The capacity of a bottleneck can be effectively increased in a number of ways, including:

- working overtime on the bottleneck
- subcontracting some of the processing that would be done at the bottleneck
- investing in additional machines at the bottleneck
- shifting workers from processes that are not bottlenecks to the process that is a bottleneck
- focusing business process improvement efforts, such as TQM and business process re-engineering on the bottleneck
- reducing defective units (Each defective unit that is processed through the bottleneck and subsequently scrapped takes the place of a good unit that could be sold.)

The last three methods of increasing the capacity of the bottleneck are particularly attractive, since they are essentially free and may even yield additional cost savings.

Finally, note that the analysis considered a single constraint. When there are multiple bottlenecks, the method of analysis is more complicated. The basic idea, however, is still the same.

Application Competency Summary

Application Competency	Deliverable	Source Documents and Key Information	Steps	Knowledge Competency
Apply the relevant cost analysis framework to an equipment replacement decision. CC3	*Key Information* The different alternatives Avoidable costs and benefits Net incremental benefit	*Asset/Cost/Expense Accounts in the General Ledger* Operating costs of existing equipment Salvage value of existing equipment *Quotes from Potential Suppliers of Equipment* Estimated purchase price of new equipment Estimated operating costs of new equipment *Sales/Production Reports* Production and sales quantities	1. List the costs and benefits associated with keeping the existing equipment and purchasing new equipment. 2. Eliminate sunk costs and future costs that are identical between alternatives (e.g., book value of old equipment, allocated common costs). 3. Compute the net incremental benefit of replacing existing equipment.	Variable and fixed costs CC1 (Ch. 2) Direct and indirect costs CC3 (Ch. 2)
Apply the relevant cost analysis framework to a business addition/deletion decision. CC4	*Report/Document* No specific document (report structure may vary from company to company)	*Various Accounts in the General Ledger* Current revenues and costs associated with the operations of existing segments *Planning Documents* Estimated revenues and costs associated with a proposed new segment	1. List the costs associated with existing segments/product lines. 2. Identify (and list) the benefits and costs associated with adding a new segment. 3. In the decision to drop a segment, identify the costs that can be avoided by dropping the segment. 4. Compute the net incremental benefit to the company of adding or dropping a segment.	Differential, opportunity and sunk costs CC6 (Ch. 2) Relevant and irrelevant costs CC2

continued

Application Competency	Deliverable	Source Documents and Key Information	Steps	Knowledge Competency
Apply the relevant cost analysis framework to a make-or-buy (outsourcing) decision. ◎ CC5	*Key Information* The different alternatives Avoidable costs and benefits Net incremental benefit *Report/Document* No specific document (report structure may vary from company to company)	*Cost/Expense/Inventory Accounts in the General Ledger* Existing production-related costs *Master Budget* Estimated price, quantity and costs *Planning Documents* Estimated additional costs of receiving, inspection, storage and handling, and other supplier-related administrative costs	1. Compute the total purchasing-related costs (including the purchase costs, incremental, receiving, inspection, storage and handling, and supplier-related administrative costs). 2. List the avoidable production costs (or the estimated directly traceable incremental production costs). 3. Compute the net incremental benefit of make versus buy (or vice-versa).	Variable and fixed costs ◎ CC1 (Ch. 2) Direct and indirect costs ◎ CC3 (Ch. 2) Differential, opportunity and sunk costs ◎ CC6 (Ch. 2) Relevant and irrelevant costs ◎ CC2
Apply the relevant cost analysis framework to a special order decision. ◎ CC6		*Schedule of COGM* Existing production costs *Master Budget* Estimated production costs (including a breakdown of the variable and fixed components) *Customer Enquiry Documents (Request for Quotes, Orders)* Order quantity and price per unit	1. Compute the revenues associated with the special order. 2. Compute the total variable costs and the total incremental (new) fixed costs associated with the order. 3. Compute the net incremental benefit from the order.	
Compute the contribution margin of a constrained resource. ◎ CC9	*Key Information* Contribution margin per unit of product/service Contribution margin per unit of the constrained resource *Report/Document* No specific document (report structure may vary from company to company)	*Resource Capacity Documents (e.g., Budgets)* Capacity of constrained resource *Production Reports, Standard Cost Card* Estimated or actual consumption of constrained resource per unit of a product/service *Variable Cost Report, Budget* Contribution margin per unit of individual product/service	1. Compute the contribution margin per unit for each product/service. 2. Divide the contribution margin by the quantity of the constrained resource consumed per unit by each product/service.	Decision making in a constrained resource environment ◎ CC8 Unit contribution margin ◎ CC16 (Ch. 3) Contribution margin ratio ◎ CC4 (Ch. 11)

Guidance Answers to Decision Maker and You Decide

VICE-PRESIDENT OF PRODUCTION (p. 500)

The warning that you recall about fixed costs in decisions relates to *allocated* fixed costs. Allocated fixed costs often make a product line or other segment of a business appear less profitable than it really is. However, in this situation, the annual rental cost for the machinery is an *avoidable* fixed cost, rather than an allocated fixed cost. An avoidable fixed cost is a cost that can be eliminated in whole or in part by choosing one alternative over another. Because the annual rental cost of the machinery can be avoided if the company purchases the components from an outside supplier, it is relevant to this decision.

TUTOR (p. 502)

Individuals who provide services to others often struggle to decide how to charge for their services. As a tutor, you probably will not incur any significant costs, unless you agree to provide the supplies (such as paper, pencils, calculators, or study guides) or software that might be required to assist the students you will be tutoring. As such, a cost-plus approach may not be a practical way to set the hourly fee (or price) for your services. On the other hand, if you use a target costing approach, you would estimate how much the market (that is, other students who require tutoring services) would be willing to pay for the tutoring services. How would you obtain this information? You probably should ask your instructor. If your institution offers tutoring services to its students, you should inquire about the fee that is charged by that office or department. You should check the student newspaper (or local newspapers) to determine the going rate for tutors. If you plan to tutor instead of working at a part-time job, you should consider the opportunity cost (that is, the hourly rate that you will be forgoing).

Review Problem: Relevant Costs

Charter Sports Equipment manufactures round, rectangular, and octagonal trampolines. Data on sales expenses for the past month follow:

| | Total | Trampoline | | |
		Round	Rectangular	Octagonal
Sales..........................	$1,000,000	$140,000	$500,000	$360,000
Less: Variable expenses............	410,000	60,000	200,000	150,000
Contribution margin	590,000	80,000	300,000	210,000
Less: Fixed expenses:				
Advertising—traceable	216,000	41,000	110,000	65,000
Amortization of special equipment ..	95,000	20,000	40,000	35,000
Line supervisors' salaries...........	19,000	6,000	7,000	6,000
General factory overhead*.........	200,000	28,000	100,000	72,000
Total fixed expenses	530,000	95,000	257,000	178,000
Net operating income (loss)..........	$ 60,000	$ (15,000)	$ 43,000	$ 32,000

*A common cost that is allocated on the basis of sales dollars.

Management is concerned about the continued losses shown by the round trampolines and wants a recommendation as to whether the line should be discontinued. The special equipment used to produce the trampolines has no resale value. If the round trampoline model is dropped, the two line supervisors assigned to the model would be discharged.

Required:

1. Should production and sale of the round trampolines be discontinued? You may assume that the company has no other use for the capacity now being used to produce the round trampolines. Show computations to support your answer.
2. Recast the preceding data in a format that would be more usable to management in assessing the long-term profitability of the various product lines.

SOLUTION TO REVIEW PROBLEM

1. No, production and sale of the round trampolines should not be discontinued. Computations to support this answer follow:

Contribution margin lost if the round trampolines are discontinued ...		$(80,000)
Less: Fixed costs that can be avoided:		
Advertising—traceable......................................	$41,000	
Line supervisors' salaries	6,000	47,000
Decrease in net operating income for the company as a whole		$(33,000)

The amortization of the special equipment represents a sunk cost; therefore, it is not relevant to the decision. The general factory overhead is allocated and will presumably continue regardless of whether the round trampolines are discontinued; thus, it also is not relevant to the decision.

ALTERNATIVE SOLUTION TO REVIEW PROBLEM

	Keep Round Trampolines	Drop Round Trampolines	Difference: Net Income Increase or (Decrease)
Sales	$140,000	$ –0–	$(140,000)
Less: Variable expenses	60,000	–0–	60,000
Contribution margin	80,000	–0–	(80,000)
Less: Fixed expenses:			
Advertising–traceable	41,000	–0–	41,000
Amortization of special equipment	20,000	20,000	–0–
Line supervisors' salaries	6,000	–0–	6,000
General factory overhead	28,000	28,000	–0–
Total fixed expenses	95,000	48,000	47,000
Net operating income (loss)	$ (15,000)	$(48,000)	$ (33,000)

2. If management wants a clear picture of the profitability of the segments, the general factory overhead should not be allocated. It is a common cost and therefore should be deducted from the total product-line segment margin, as shown in Exhibit 12–5. A more useful income statement format would be as follows:

	Trampoline			
	Round	Rectangular	Octagonal	Total
Sales	$140,000	$500,000	$360,000	$1,000,000
Less: Variable expenses	60,000	200,000	150,000	410,000
Contribution margin	80,000	300,000	210,000	590,000
Less: Traceable fixed expenses:				
Advertising—traceable	41,000	110,000	65,000	216,000
Amortization of special equipment	20,000	40,000	35,000	95,000
Line supervisors' salaries	6,000	7,000	6,000	19,000
Total traceable fixed expenses	67,000	157,000	106,000	330,000
Product-line segment margin	$ 13,000	$143,000	$104,000	260,000
Less: Common fixed expenses				200,000
Net operating income (loss)				$ 60,000

Glossary

Avoidable cost Any cost that can be eliminated (in whole or in part) by choosing one alternative over another in a decision-making situation. In managerial accounting, this term is synonymous with *relevant cost* and *differential cost*. (p. 487)

Bottleneck A machine or process that limits total output because it is operating at capacity. (p. 503)

Common fixed cost A fixed cost that supports the operations of more than one segment of an organization and is not avoidable in whole or in part by eliminating any one segment. (p. 496)

Constraint A limitation under which a company must operate, such as limited machine time available or limited raw materials available that restricts the company's ability to satisfy demand. (p. 502)

Differential cost Any cost that differs between alternatives in a decision-making situation. In managerial accounting, this term is synonymous with *avoidable cost, incremental cost,* and *relevant cost.* (p. 487)

Make-or-buy decision A decision as to whether an item should be produced internally or purchased from an outside supplier. (p. 498)

Opportunity cost The potential benefit given up when one alternative is selected over another. (p. 487)

Relaxing (or **elevating**) **the constraint** An action that increases the capacity of a bottleneck. (p. 504)

Relevant cost A cost that differs between alternatives in a particular decision. In managerial accounting, this term is synonymous with *avoidable cost* and *differential cost.* (p. 486)

Segment margin The difference between the revenue generated by a segment and its own traceable cost. (p. 497)

Special order A one-time order that is not considered part of the company's normal ongoing business. (p. 500)

Sunk cost Any cost that has already been incurred and cannot be changed by any decision made now or in the future. (p. 487)

Target costing Before launching a new product, management estimates how much the market will be willing to pay for the product and then takes steps to ensure that the cost of the product will be low enough to provide an adequate profit margin. (p. 502)

Questions

12–1   What is a *relevant cost?*

12–2   Define the following terms: *incremental cost, opportunity cost,* and *sunk cost.*

12–3   Are variable costs always relevant costs? Explain.

12–4   The original cost of a machine the company already owns is irrelevant in decision making. Explain why this is so.

12–5   "Sunk costs are easy to spot–they're simply the fixed costs associated with a decision." Do you agree? Explain.

12–6   "Variable costs and differential costs mean the same thing." Do you agree? Explain.

12–7   "All future costs are relevant in decision making." Do you agree? Why?

12–8   Prentice Company is considering dropping one of its product lines. What costs of the product line would be relevant to this decision? Irrelevant?

12–9   "If a product line is generating a loss, then that's pretty good evidence that the product line should be discontinued." Do you agree? Explain.

12–10 What is the danger in allocating common fixed costs among product lines or other segments of an organization?

12–11 How does opportunity cost enter into the make-or-buy decision?

12–12 Give four examples of possible constraints.

12–13 How will relating product contribution margins to the constrained resource they require help a company ensure that profits will be maximized?

12–14 Airlines sometimes offer reduced rates during certain times of the week to members of a businessperson's family if they accompany him or her on trips. How does the concept of relevant costs enter into the decision to offer reduced rates of this type?

Brief Exercises

BRIEF EXERCISE 12–1 Identifying Relevant Costs (CC2)

Following are a number of costs that may be relevant in decisions faced by the management of Svahn, AB, a Swedish manufacturer of sailing yachts:

Item	Case 1 Relevant	Case 1 Not Relevant	Case 2 Relevant	Case 2 Not Relevant
a. Sales revenue				
b. Direct materials.......................				
c. Direct labour........................				
d. Variable manufacturing overhead.........				
e. Amortization—Model B100 machine				
f. Book value—Model B100 machine				

continued

g. Disposal value—Model B100 machine . . . .

h. Market value—Model B300
   machine (cost). . . . .

i. Amortization—Model B300 machine . . . . .

j. Fixed manufacturing overhead (general) . . .

k. Variable selling expense . . . .

l. Fixed selling expense . . . .

m. General administrative overhead . . . .

Required:

Copy the preceding costs onto your answer sheet and place an X in the appropriate column to indicate whether each cost is relevant or not relevant in the following situations (part (1) relates to Case 1, and part (2) relates to Case 2):

1. Management is considering purchasing a Model B300 machine to use in addition to the company's present Model B100 machine. This will increase the company's production and sales. The increase in volume will be large enough to require increases in fixed selling expenses and in general administrative overhead, but not in the fixed manufacturing overhead.

2. Management is instead considering replacing its present Model B100 machine with a new Model B300 machine. The Model B100 machine would be sold. This change will have no effect on production or sales, other than some savings in direct materials costs due to less waste.

BRIEF EXERCISE 12–2 Equipment Replacement Decision (CC3)

Waukee Railroad is considering the purchase of a powerful, high-speed wheel grinder to replace a standard wheel grinder that is now in use. Selected information on the two machines follows:

	Standard Wheel Grinder	High-Speed Wheel Grinder
Original cost new	$35,000	$52,500
Accumulated amortization to date	10,500	—
Current salvage value	15,750	—
Estimated cost per year to operate	26,250	12,250
Remaining years of useful life	5 years	5 years

Required:

Prepare a computation covering the five-year period that will show the net advantage or disadvantage of purchasing the high-speed wheel grinder. Use only relevant costs in your analysis.

BRIEF EXERCISE 12–3 Dropping or Retaining a Segment (CC4)

Bed & Bath, a retailing company, has two departments, Hardware and Linens. A recent monthly income statement for the company follows:

	Department		
	Hardware	Linens	Total
Sales	$3,000,000	$1,000,000	$4,000,000
Less: Variable expenses.	900,000	400,000	1,300,000
Contribution margin	2,100,000	600,000	2,700,000
Less: Fixed expenses.	1,400,000	800,000	2,200,000
Net operating income (loss)	$ 700,000	$ (200,000)	$ 500,000

A study indicates that $340,000 of the fixed expenses being charged to Linens are sunk costs or allocated costs that will continue even if the Linens Department is dropped. In addition, the elimination of the Linens Department will result in a 10% decrease in the sales of the Hardware Department. If the Linens Department is dropped, what will be the effect on the net operating income of the company as a whole?

BRIEF EXERCISE 12–4 Make-or-Buy Decision (CC5)

For many years Futura Company has purchased the starters that it installs in its standard line of farm tractors. Due to a reduction in output of some of its products, the company has idle capacity that could be used to produce the starters. The chief engineer has recommended against this move, however, pointing out that the cost to produce the starters would be greater than the current $12.60 per unit purchase price:

	Per Unit	Total
Direct materials.	$ 4.65	
Direct labour	4.05	
Supervision	2.25	$90,000
Amortization	1.50	60,000
Variable manufacturing overhead	0.90	
Rent	0.45	18,000
Total production cost	$13.80	

A supervisor would have to be hired to oversee production of the starters. However, the company has sufficient idle tools and machinery that no new equipment would have to be purchased. The rent charge above is based on space utilized in the plant. The total rent on the plant is $148,000 per period. Amortization is due to obsolescence, rather than wear and tear. Prepare computations to show the dollar advantage or disadvantage per period of making the starters.

BRIEF EXERCISE 12–5 Special Order (CC6)

Delta Company produces a single product. The cost of producing and selling a single unit of this product at the company's normal activity level of 60,000 units per year is:

Direct materials	$5.10
Direct labour	3.80
Variable manufacturing overhead	1.00
Fixed manufacturing overhead	4.20
Variable selling and administrative expense	1.50
Fixed selling and administrative expense	2.40

The normal selling price is $21 per unit. The company's capacity is 75,000 units per year. An order has been received from a mail-order house for 15,000 units at a special price of $14 per unit. This order would not affect regular sales.

Required:

1. If the order is accepted, by how much will annual profits be increased or decreased? (The order will not change the company's total fixed costs.)
2. Assume the company has 1,000 units of this product left over from last year that are vastly inferior to the current model. The units must be sold through regular channels at reduced prices. What unit cost figure is relevant for establishing a minimum selling price for these units? Explain.

BRIEF EXERCISE 12–6 Utilization of a Constrained Resource (CC8, 9)

Benoit Company produces three products, A, B, and C. Data concerning the three products follow (per unit):

	Product		
	A	B	C
Selling price	$132.00	$92.40	$115.50
Less: Variable expenses:			
Direct materials	39.60	24.75	14.85
Other variable expenses	39.60	44.55	66.00
Total variable expenses	79.20	69.30	80.85
Contribution margin	$52.80	$23.10	$34.65
CM ratio	40%	25%	30%

Demand for the company's products is very strong, with far more orders each month than the company has raw materials available to produce. The same material is used in each product. The material costs $4.95 per kilogram with a maximum of 8,230 kilograms available each month.

Required:
Which orders would you advise the company to accept first, those for A, for B, or for C? Which orders second? Third?

BRIEF EXERCISE 12–7 Accept or Reject Special Order (CC6)
Brown Corp.'s weekly production output is 800 units of a product that sells for $20 per unit and has variable costs of $16 per unit. Maximum capacity is 1,000 units per month. Total fixed costs per month are $7,800. A special order is received for 100 units at a price of $18 per unit.

Required:
What should be considered in deciding whether to accept or reject the order at this price?

(Adapted © CGA-Canada)

BRIEF EXERCISE 12–8 Identification of Relevant Costs (CC2)
Veggie Inc. has approached Homestead Co. with a proposal to build a greenhouse supply warehouse. Homestead would provide a building to store supplies and would handle all recordkeeping. Homestead has a storage barn that is not currently in use. Shelving would be required for stacking the product and a special concrete pad would be added for delivery truck access. The existing Homestead accountant would assume the additional accounting duties and would receive an additional $5,000 per annum. Homestead would be paid a fee based on the volume of product stored.

Required:
Which of the following items is not a relevant consideration in deciding whether to establish a greenhouse supply warehouse?

1) Book value of the storage barn.   3) Farmers' supply accountant's raise.
2) Cost of a special concrete pad.   4) Projected volume of product for storage.

(Adapted © CGA-Canada)

Exercises

EXERCISE 12–1 Identifying Relevant Costs (CC2)
Bill has just returned from a duck hunting trip. He has brought home eight ducks. Bill's friend John disapproves of duck hunting, and to discourage Bill from further hunting, John has presented him with the following cost estimate per trip:

Camper and equipment:	
Cost, $12,000; usable for 8 seasons; 10 hunting trips per season.	$150
Travel expense (pickup truck):	
100 kilometres at $0.12 per kilometre (gas, oil, and tires–$0.07 per kilometre:	
amortization and insurance—$0.05 per kilometre)	12
Shotgun shells (two boxes).	20
Boat:	
Cost, $2,320, usable for 8 seasons; 10 hunting trips per season.	29
Hunting license:	
Cost, $30 for the season; 10 hunting trips per season.	3
Money lost playing poker:	
Loss, $18 (Bill plays poker every weekend).	18
A fifth of Old Grandad:	
Cost, $8 (used to ward off the cold)	8
Total cost.	$240
Cost per duck ($240 ÷ 8 ducks).	$ 30

Required:
1. Assuming that the duck hunting trip Bill has just completed is typical, what costs are relevant to a decision as to whether Bill should go duck hunting again this season?
2. Suppose that Bill gets lucky on his next hunting trip and shoots 10 ducks in the amount of time it took him to shoot eight ducks on his last trip. How much would it have cost him to shoot the last two ducks?
3. Which costs are relevant in a decision of whether Bill should give up hunting? Explain.

EXERCISE 12–2 Identification of Relevant Costs; Equipment Replacement (CC1, 2)

Hollings Company sells office furniture in the Rocky Mountain area. As part of its service, Hollings delivers furniture to customers.

The costs associated with the acquisition and annual operation of a delivery truck are given below:

Insurance	$2,320
Licences	362.50
Taxes (vehicle)	217.50
Garage rent for parking (per truck)	1,740
Amortization ($13,050 ÷ 5 years)	2,610*
Gasoline, oil, tires, and repairs	0.10 per km

*Based on obsolescence, rather than on wear and tear.

Required:

1. Assume that Hollings Company has purchased one truck and that the truck has been driven 72,500 kilometres during the first year. Compute the average cost per kilometre of owning and operating the truck.
2. At the beginning of the second year, Hollings Company is unsure whether to use the truck or leave it parked in the garage and have all hauling done commercially. (The state requires the payment of vehicle taxes even if the vehicle is not used.) What costs from the previous list are relevant to this decision? Explain.
3. Assume that the company decides to use the truck during the second year. Near year end, an order is received from a customer over 1,450 kilometres away. What costs from the previous list are relevant in a decision between using the truck to make the delivery or having the delivery done commercially? Explain.
4. Occasionally, the company could use two trucks at the same time. For this reason, some thought is being given to purchasing a second truck. The total kilometres driven would be the same as if only one truck were owned. What costs from the previous list are relevant to a decision over whether to purchase the second truck? Explain.

EXERCISE 12–3 Dropping or Retaining a Segment (CC4)

Thalassines Kataskeves, S.A., of Greece makes marine equipment. The company has been experiencing losses on its bilge pump product line for several years. The most recent quarterly income statement for the bilge pump product line follows:

THALASSINES KATASKEVES, S.A.
Income Statement–Bilge Pump
For the Quarter Ended March 31

Sales		€850,000
Less: Variable expenses:		
Variable manufacturing expenses	€330,000	
Sales commissions	42,000	
Shipping	18,000	
Total variable expenses		390,000
Contribution margin		460,000
Less: Fixed expenses:		
Advertising	270,000	
Amortization of equipment (no resale value)	80,000	
General factory overhead	105,000*	
Salary of product-line manager	32,000	
Insurance on inventories	8,000	
Purchasing department expenses	45,000†	
Total fixed expenses		540,000
Net operating loss		€(80,000)

*Common costs allocated on the basis of machine-hours.
†Common costs allocated on the basis of sales dollars.

The currency in Greece is the euro, denoted by €. The discontinuance of the bilge pump product line would not affect sales of other product lines and would have no noticeable effect on the company's total general factory overhead or total Purchasing Department expenses.

Required:
Would you recommend that the bilge pump product line be discontinued? Support your answer with appropriate computations.

EXERCISE 12–4 Make-or-Buy Decision (CC5)

Han Products manufactures 55,500 units of part S-6 each year for use on its production line. At this level of activity, the cost per unit for part S-6 is as follows:

Direct materials	$ 6.66
Direct labour	18.50
Variable overhead	4.44
Fixed overhead.	16.65
Total cost per part	$46.25

An outside supplier has offered to sell 55,500 units of part S-6 each year to Han Products for $38.85 per part. If Han Products accepts this offer, the facilities now being used to manufacture part S-6 could be rented to another company at an annual rental of $148,000. However, Han Products has determined that two-thirds of the fixed overhead being applied to part S-6 would continue even if part S-6 were purchased from the outside supplier.

Required:
Prepare computations to show the net dollar advantage or disadvantage of accepting the outside supplier's offer.

EXERCISE 12–5 Evaluating a Special Order (CC6)

Imperial Jewellers is considering a special order for 20 handcrafted gold bracelets for a major upscale wedding. The gold bracelets are to be given as gifts to members of the wedding party. The normal selling price of a gold bracelet is $189.95 and its unit product cost is $149 as shown following:

Materials	$ 84.00
Direct labour	45.00
Manufacturing overhead	20.00
Unit product cost	$149.00

The manufacturing overhead is largely fixed and unaffected by variations in how much jewellery is produced in any given period. However, $4 of the overhead is variable with respect to the number of bracelets produced. The customer who is interested in the special bracelet order would like special filigree applied to the bracelets. This filigree would require additional materials costing $2 per bracelet and would also require acquisition of a special tool costing $250 that would have no other use once the special order is completed. This order would have no effect on the company's regular sales and the order could be fulfilled using the company's existing capacity without affecting any other order.

Required:
What effect would accepting this order have on the company's net operating income if a special price of $169.95 is offered per bracelet for this order? Should the special order be accepted at this price?

EXERCISE 12–6 Utilization of a Constrained Resource (CC8, 9)

Barlow Company manufactures three products: A, B, and C. The selling price, variable costs, and contribution margin for one unit of each product follow:

	Product		
	A	B	C
Selling price	$ 90	$135	$120
Less: Variable expenses:			
Direct materials.	12	36	16
Other variable expenses	51	45	74
Total variable expenses.	63	81	90
Contribution margin	$ 27	$ 54	$ 30
Contribution margin ratio	30%	40%	25%

The same raw material is used in all three products. Barlow Company has only 5,000 kilograms of material on hand and will not be able to obtain any more material for several weeks due to a strike in its supplier's plant. Management is trying to decide which product(s) to concentrate on next week in filling its backlog of orders. The material costs $4 per kilogram.

Required:

1. Compute the amount of contribution margin that will be obtained per kilogram of material used in each product.
2. Which orders would you recommend that the company work on next week–the orders for product A, product B, or product C? Show computations.
3. A foreign supplier could furnish Barlow with additional stocks of the raw material at a substantial premium over the usual price. If there is unfilled demand for all three products, what is the highest price that Barlow Company should be willing to pay for an additional kilogram of materials?

EXERCISE 12–7 Make-or-Buy Decision (CC5)

TBI Ltd. makes tennis balls and other tennis-related items. This year's expected production of tennis balls is 10,000 tins (each consisting of three tennis balls). Cost data are as follows:

	Per Tin	10,000 Tins
Product costs directly traceable to balls:		
Direct materials	$2.00	$20,000
Direct labour	1.00	10,000
Variable manufacturing overhead	0.75	7,500
Fixed manufacturing overhead		2,500
Common costs allocated to this product line.		15,000
		55,000

The full cost of one tin of tennis balls is $5.50 per unit. TBI has received an offer from an outside supplier to supply any desired quantity of balls at a price of $4.10 per tin of three tennis balls. The cost accounting department has provided the following information:

a. Costs of direct materials, direct labour, and variable overhead will be saved if the balls are purchased from outside.
b. The direct fixed manufacturing overhead is the cost of leasing the die machine that stamps out the balls. The machine can produce a maximum of 60,000 balls per year. If the balls are bought, the machine will no longer be needed.
c. No other costs would be affected.

Required:

1. Prepare an analysis showing whether TBI would be better off making or buying the balls at a projected volume of 10,000 tins (30,000 tennis balls).
2. At what volume would TBI be indifferent between making and buying? What does the indifference point indicate?
3. State *two* other factors, either quantitative or qualitative, that TBI should consider before making the final decision.

(Adapted © CGA-Canada)

EXERCISE 12–8 Dropping or Retaining a Segment (CC4)

Emily has gathered the following income statement for the ladies shoe department of a large department store:

Sales		$ 1,500,000
Less: Variable expenses........		700,000
Contribution margin		800,000
Less: Fixed expenses:		
Wages	$ 550,000	
Insurance on inventory	20,000	
Advertising	200,000	770,000
Net operating income		$ 30,000

Compared to other departments, the ladies shoe department has poor profitability. Management is considering dropping the department entirely. If the department is dropped, a job must be created elsewhere for one employee who has been with the firm for many years. This employee has an annual salary of $40,000 and many years until retirement.

Required:
Prepare an analysis to determine whether the shoe department should be dropped, and make a recommendation to management about this decision.

(Adapted © CGA-Canada)

EXERCISE 12–9 Make-or-Buy Decision (CC5)

Bullitt Corp is evaluating its make-or-buy decision for several of its products. For one product, the costs per part are as follows:

Direct materials	$ 7.50
Direct labour (all variable cost)....................	5.00
Variable manufacturing overhead	1.00
Fixed, traceable, manufacturing overhead............	2.00
Fixed, allocated common manufacturing overhead.....	2.50
Unit product cost	$18.00

The current level of production of this part is 1,000 units. Of the traceable manufacturing overhead, 50% consists of amortization of special equipment that has no salvage value and 50% consists of salaries that could be avoided if the production of the part is discontinued. For this part, an outside supplier will sell parts to Bullitt at a price of $15 per unit if the company purchases 1,000 units.

Required:
Assess whether Bullitt should continue to produce this part internally or whether it should purchase it from the outside supplier.

(Adapted © CGA-Canada)

Problems

CHECK FIGURE
(2) Net advantage: $30,000

PROBLEM 12–1 Equipment Replacement Decision (CC3)

Murl Plastics Inc. purchased a new machine one year ago at a cost of $30,000. Although the machine operates well, the president of Murl Plastics is wondering if the company should replace it with a new electronic machine that has just come on the market. The new machine would slash annual operating costs by two-thirds, as shown in the comparative data following:

	Present Machine	Proposed New Machine
Purchase cost new..................	$30,000	$45,000
Estimated useful life new	6 years	5 years
Annual operating costs	$21,000	$7,000
Annual straight-line amortization......	5,000	9,000
Remaining book value	25,000	—
Salvage value now	5,000	—
Salvage value in 5 years	–0–	–0–

In trying to decide whether to purchase the new machine, the president has prepared the following analysis:

Book value of the old machine	$25,000
Less: Salvage value	5,000
Net loss from disposal	$20,000

"Even though the new machine looks good," said the president, "we can't get rid of that old machine if it means taking a huge loss on it. We'll have to use the old machine for at least a few more years."

Sales are expected to be $100,000 per year, and selling and administrative expenses are expected to be $63,000 per year, regardless of which machine is used.

Required:
1. Prepare a summary income statement covering the next five years, assuming:
   a. That the new machine is not purchased.
   b. That the new machine is purchased.
2. Determine the desirability of purchasing the new machine using only relevant costs in your analysis.

PROBLEM 12–2 Dropping or Retaining a Product (CC4)

The Regal Cycle Company manufactures three types of bicycles—a dirt bike, a mountain bike, and a racing bike. Data on sales and expenses for the past quarter follow:

CHECK FIGURE
(1) Decrease in net operating income: $11,000

	Dirt Bikes	Mountain Bikes	Racing Bikes	Total
Sales	$90,000	$150,000	$60,000	$300,000
Less: Variable manufacturing and selling expenses	27,000	60,000	33,000	120,000
Contribution margin	63,000	90,000	27,000	180,000
Less: Fixed expenses:				
Advertising, traceable	10,000	14,000	6,000	30,000
Amortization of special equipment . . .	6,000	9,000	8,000	23,000
Salaries of product-line managers. . . .	12,000	13,000	10,000	35,000
Common allocated costs*	18,000	30,000	12,000	60,000
Total fixed expenses	46,000	66,000	36,000	148,000
Net operating income (loss)	$17,000	$ 24,000	$ (9,000)	$ 32,000

*Allocated on the basis of sales dollars.

Management is concerned about the continued losses shown by the racing bikes and wants a recommendation as to whether the line should be discontinued. The special equipment used to produce racing bikes has no resale value and does not wear out.

Required:
1. Should production and sale of the racing bikes be discontinued? Show computations to support your answer.
2. Recast the preceding data in a format that would be more useful to management in assessing the long-term profitability of the various product lines.

PROBLEM 12–3 Discontinuing a Flight (CC4)

Profits have been decreasing for several years at Pegasus Airlines. In an effort to improve the company's performance, consideration is being given to dropping several flights that appear to be unprofitable.

A typical income statement for one such flight (flight 482) follows:

CHECK FIGURE
(1) Decrease in profits: $6,400

Ticket revenue (175 seats × 40% occupancy × $200 ticket price)	$28,000	100.0%
Less: Variable expenses ($15 per person)	2,100	7.5
Contribution margin	25,900	92.5%

continued

Less: Flight expenses:	
Salaries, flight crew	3,600
Flight promotion	1,500
Amortization of aircraft	3,100
Fuel for aircraft	13,600
Liability insurance	8,400
Salaries, flight assistants	1,000
Baggage loading and flight preparation	3,400
Overnight costs for flight crew and	
assistants at destination	600
Total flight expenses	35,200
Net operating loss	$ (9,300)

The following additional information is available about flight 482:

a. Members of the flight crew are paid fixed annual salaries, whereas the flight assistants are paid by the flight.
b. One-third of the liability insurance is a special charge assessed against flight 482 because in the opinion of the insurance company, the destination of the flight is in a "high-risk" area. The remaining two-thirds would be unaffected by a decision to drop flight 482.
c. The baggage loading and flight preparation expense is an allocation of ground crews' salaries and amortization of ground equipment. Dropping flight 482 would have no effect on the company's total baggage loading and flight preparation expenses.
d. If flight 482 is dropped, Pegasus Airlines has no authorization at present to replace it with another flight.
e. Amortization of aircraft is due entirely to obsolescence. Amortization due to wear and tear is negligible.
f. Dropping flight 482 would not allow Pegasus Airlines to reduce the number of aircraft in its fleet or the number of flight crew on its payroll.

Required:
1. Prepare an analysis showing what impact dropping flight 482 would have on the airline's profits.
2. The airline's scheduling officer has been criticized because only about 50% of the seats on Pegasus' flights are being filled compared with an average of 60% for the industry. The scheduling officer has explained that Pegasus' average seat occupancy could be improved considerably by eliminating about 10% of the flights but that doing so would reduce profits. Explain how this could happen.

CHECK FIGURE
(1) The part can be made inside the company for $6 less per unit

PROBLEM 12–4 Make-or-Buy Decision (CC5)
Troy Engines Ltd. manufactures a variety of engines for use in heavy equipment. The company has always produced all of the necessary parts for its engines, including all of the carburetors. An outside supplier has offered to produce and sell one type of carburetor to Troy Engines Ltd. for a cost of $35 per unit. To evaluate this offer, Troy Engines Ltd. has gathered the following information relating to its own cost of producing the carburetor internally:

	Per Unit	15,000 Units per Year
Direct materials	$14	$210,000
Direct labour	10	150,000
Variable manufacturing overhead	3	45,000
Fixed manufacturing overhead, traceable	6*	90,000
Fixed manufacturing overhead, allocated	9	135,000
Total cost	$42	$630,000

*One-third supervisory salaries; two-thirds amortization of special equipment (no resale value).

Required:
1. Assuming that the company has no alternative use for the facilities that are now being used to produce the carburetors, should the outside supplier's offer be accepted? Show all computations.
2. Suppose that if the carburetors were purchased, Troy Engines Ltd. could use the freed capacity to launch a new product. The segment margin of the new product would be $150,000 per year. Should Troy Engines Ltd. accept the offer to buy the carburetors for $35 per unit? Show all computations.

PROBLEM 12–5 Accept or Reject a Special Order (CC6)

Polaski Company manufactures and sells a single product called a Ret. Operating at capacity, the company can produce and sell 30,000 Rets per year. Costs associated with this level of production and sales are as follows:

CHECK FIGURE
(1) Net increase in profits: $65,000

e**X**cel

	Unit	Total
Direct materials.	$15	$ 450,000
Direct labour	8	240,000
Variable manufacturing overhead	3	90,000
Fixed manufacturing overhead	9	270,000
Variable selling expense	4	120,000
Fixed selling expense	6	180,000
Total cost.	$45	$1,350,000

The Rets normally sell for $50 each. Fixed manufacturing overhead is constant at $270,000 per year within the range of 25,000 through 30,000 Rets per year.

Required:

1. Assume that due to a recession, Polaski Company expects to sell only 25,000 Rets through regular channels next year. A large retail chain has offered to purchase 5,000 Rets if Polaski is willing to accept a 16% discount off the regular price. There would be no sales commissions on this order; thus, variable selling expenses would be slashed by 75%. However, Polaski Company would have to purchase a special machine to engrave the retail chain's name on the 5,000 units. This machine would cost $10,000. Polaski Company has no assurance that the retail chain will purchase additional units any time in the future. Determine the impact on profits next year if this special order is accepted.

2. Refer to the original data. Assume again that Polaski Company expects to sell only 25,000 Rets through regular channels next year. The Canadian Army would like to make a one-time-only purchase of 5,000 Rets. The Army would pay a fixed fee of $1.80 per Ret, and in addition it would reimburse Polaski Company for all costs of production (variable and fixed) associated with the units. Since the Army would pick up the Rets with its own trucks, there would be no variable selling expenses of any type associated with this order. If Polaski Company accepts this order, by how much will profits be increased or decreased for the year?

3. Assume the same situation as that described in part (2), except that the company expects to sell 30,000 Rets through regular channels next year. Thus, accepting the Canadian Army's order would require giving up regular sales of 5,000 Rets. If the Army's order is accepted, by how much will profits be increased or decreased from what they would be if the 5,000 Rets were sold through regular channels?

PROBLEM 12–6 Utilization of a Constrained Resource (CC8, 9)

The Walton Toy Company manufactures a line of dolls and a doll dress sewing kit. Demand for the dolls is increasing, and management requests assistance from you in determining an economical sales and production mix for the coming year. The company has provided the following information:

CHECK FIGURE
(2) Total direct labour hours: 140,000

e**X**cel

X Microsoft Excel - Problem 12-6 screen capture.xls

File Edit View Insert Format Tools Data Window Help

	A	B	C	D	E	
1	Product	Estimated Demand Next Year (Units)	Selling Price per Unit	Direct Materials	Direct Labour	
2	Debbie	50,000	$ 13.50	$ 4.30	$ 3.20	
3	Trish	42,000	5.50	1.10	2.00	
4	Sarah	35,000	21.00	6.44	5.60	
5	Mike	40,000	10.00	2.00	4.00	
6	Sewing kit	325,000	8.00	3.20	1.60	
7						

The following additional information is available:

a. The company's plant has a capacity of 130,000 direct labour-hours per year on a single-shift basis. The company's present employees and equipment can produce all five products.
b. The direct labour rate is $8 per hour; this rate is expected to remain unchanged during the coming year.
c. Fixed costs total $520,000 per year. Variable overhead costs are $2 per direct labour-hour.
d. All of the company's nonmanufacturing costs are fixed.
e. The company's present inventory of finished products is negligible and can be ignored.

Required:
1. Determine the contribution margin per direct labour-hour expended on each product.
2. Prepare a schedule showing the total direct labour-hours that will be required to produce the units estimated to be sold during the coming year.
3. Examine the data you have computed in parts (1) and (2). Indicate how much of each product should be made so that total production time is equal to the 130,000 hours available.
4. What is the highest price, in terms of a rate per hour, that Walton Toy Company would be willing to pay for additional capacity (that is, for added direct labour time)?
5. Assume again that the company does not want to reduce sales of any product. Identify ways in which the company could obtain the additional output.

(CPA heavily adapted)

CHECK FIGURE
(1) Advantage to buy:
Afl 126,000

PROBLEM 12–7 Make-or-Buy Analysis; Equipment Replacement Decision (CC3, 4)
"In my opinion, we ought to stop making our own drums and accept that outside supplier's offer," said Wim Niewindt, managing director of Antilles Refining, N.V., of Aruba. "At a price of 36 florins per drum, we would be paying 10 florins less than it costs us to manufacture the drums in our own plant. (The currency in Aruba is the florin, denoted by Afl.) Since we use 120,000 drums a year, that would be an annual cost savings of 600,000 florins." Antilles Refining's present cost to manufacture one drum follows (based on 120,000 drums per year):

Direct material	Afl 20.70
Direct labour.............................	12.00
Variable overhead.........................	3.00
Fixed overhead (Afl 5.60 general company overhead, Afl 3.20 amortization and, Afl 1.50 supervision)	10.30
Total cost per drum........................	Afl 46.00

A decision about whether to make or buy the drums is especially important at this time, since the equipment being used to make the drums is completely worn out and must be replaced. The choices facing the company are as follows:

Alternative 1: Purchase new equipment and continue to make the drums. The equipment would cost Afl 1,620,000; it would have a six-year useful life and no salvage value. The company uses straight-line amortization.
Alternative 2: Purchase the drums from an outside supplier at Afl 36 per drum under a six-year contract.

The new equipment would be more efficient than the equipment that Antilles Refining has been using and, according to the manufacturer, would reduce direct labour and variable overhead costs by 30%. The old equipment has no resale value. Supervision cost (Afl 180,000 per year) and direct materials cost per drum would not be affected by the new equipment. The new equipment's capacity would be 180,000 drums per year. The company has no other use for the space being used to produce the drums.
The company's total general company overhead would be unaffected by this decision.

Required:
1. To assist the managing director in making a decision, prepare an analysis showing the total cost and the cost per drum under each of the two alternatives stated previously. Assume that 120,000 drums are needed each year. Which course of action would you recommend to the managing director?
2. Would your recommendation in part (1) be the same if the company's needs were: (a) 150,000 drums per year or (b) 180,000 drums per year? Show computations to support your answer, with costs presented on both a total and a per-unit basis.
3. What other factors would you recommend that the company consider before making a decision?

PROBLEM 12–8 Shutting Down or Continuing to Operate a Plant (CC4)

(*Note: This type of decision is similar to that of dropping a product line.*)

Birch Company normally produces and sells 30,000 units of RG-6 each month. RG-6 is a small electrical relay used in the automotive industry as a component part in various products. The selling price is $22 per unit, variable costs are $14 per unit, fixed manufacturing overhead costs total $150,000 per month, and fixed selling costs total $30,000 per month.

Employment contract strikes in the companies that purchase the bulk of the RG-6 units have caused Birch Company's sales to temporarily drop to only 8,000 units per month. Birch Company estimates that the strikes will last for about two months, after which time sales of RG-6 should return to normal. Due to the current low level of sales, however, Birch Company is thinking about closing its own plant during the two months that the strikes are on. If Birch Company does close its plant, it is estimated that fixed manufacturing overhead costs can be reduced to $105,000 per month and that fixed selling costs can be reduced by 10%. Start-up costs at the end of the shutdown period would total $8,000. Since Birch Company uses JIT production methods, no inventories are on hand.

Required:

1. Assuming that the strikes continue for two months, as estimated, would you recommend that Birch Company close its own plant? Show computations in good form.
2. At what level of sales (in units) for the two-month period should Birch Company be indifferent between closing the plant or keeping it open? Show computations. (*Hint: This is a type of break-even analysis, except that the fixed cost portion of your break-even computation should include only those fixed costs that are relevant [i.e., avoidable] over the two-month period.*)

PROBLEM 12–9 Relevant Cost Analysis in a Variety of Situations (CC1, 2, 5, 6)

Andretti Company has a single product called a Dak. The company normally produces and sells 60,000 Daks each year at a selling price of $32 per unit. The company's unit costs at this level of activity follow:

Direct materials.	$10.00	
Direct labour.	4.50	
Variable manufacturing overhead. . . .	2.30	
Fixed manufacturing overhead.	5.00	($300,000 total)
Variable selling expenses	1.20	
Fixed selling expenses	3.50	($210,000 total)
Total cost per unit	$26.50	

A number of questions relating to the production and sale of Daks follow. *Treat each question independently*.

Required:

1. Assume that Andretti Company has sufficient capacity to produce 90,000 Daks each year without any increase in fixed manufacturing overhead costs. The company could increase its sales by 25% above the present 60,000 units each year if it were willing to increase the fixed selling expenses by $80,000. Would the increased fixed expenses be justified?
2. Assume again that Andretti Company has sufficient capacity to produce 90,000 Daks each year. A customer in a foreign market wants to purchase 20,000 Daks. Import duties on the Daks would be $1.70 per unit, and costs for permits and licences would be $9,000. The only selling costs that would be associated with the order would be $3.20 per unit shipping cost. You have been asked by the president to compute the per-unit break-even price on this order.
3. The company has 1,000 Daks on hand that have some irregularities and are therefore considered to be *seconds*. Due to the irregularities, it will be impossible to sell these units at the normal price through regular distribution channels. What unit cost figure is relevant for setting a minimum selling price?
4. Due to a strike in its supplier's plant, Andretti Company is unable to purchase more material for the production of Daks. The strike is expected to last for two months. Andretti Company has enough material on hand to continue to operate at 30% of normal levels for the two-month period. As an alternative, Andretti could close its plant down entirely for the two months. If the plant were closed, fixed overhead costs would continue at 60% of their normal level during the two-month period; the fixed selling costs would be reduced by 20% while the plant was closed. What would be the dollar advantage or disadvantage of closing the plant for the two-month period?
5. An outside manufacturer has offered to produce Daks for Andretti Company and to ship them directly to Andretti's customers. If Andretti Company accepts this offer, the facilities that it uses to produce Daks would be idle; however, fixed overhead costs would be reduced by 75% of their present level.

Since the outside manufacturer would pay for all the costs of shipping, the variable selling costs would be only two-thirds of their present amount. Compute the unit cost figure that is relevant for comparison to whatever quoted price is received from the outside manufacturer.

PROBLEM 12–10 Make-or-Buy Decision (CC5)

Orman Co purchases sails and produces sailboats. It currently produces 1,200 sailboats per year, operating at normal capacity, which is about 80% of full capacity. Orman purchases sails at $260 each, but the company is considering using the excess capacity to manufacture the sails instead. The manufacturing cost per sail would be $100 for materials, $80 for direct labour, and $100 for overhead. The $100 overhead is based on $72,000 annual fixed overhead that is allocated using normal capacity. The president of Orman has come to you for advice. "It would cost me $280 to make the sails," she says, "but only $260 to buy them. Should I continue buying them or have I missed something?"

Required:
1. Prepare a per-unit analysis of differential costs. Briefly explain whether Orman should make or buy the sails.
2. If Orman suddenly finds an opportunity to rent out the unused capacity of its factory for $80,000 per year, would your answer to part (1) change? Briefly explain.
3. Identify *three* qualitative factors that should be considered by Orman in this make-or-buy decision.

(Adapted © CGA-Canada)

PROBLEM 12–11 Relevant Cost Analysis (CC1, 2, 3)

Alpha Corporation Ltd. makes specialized metal engine stampings for one of the major automobile manufacturers. Alpha is considering replacing one of the stamping machines presently used in the production of this product. The new machine would have a useful life equal to the remaining useful life of the current machine. However, the controller is hesitant because the stamping machine is a specialized piece of equipment and, due to the limited second-hand market for such a machine, the current one could only be sold for $150,000, resulting in a loss on disposal of $250,000.

The following data are available on all aspects of the two alternatives:

	Current Machine	New Machine
Original cost	$750,000	$ 500,000
Useful life remaining in years	7	7
Current age in years	8	0
Book value	$400,000	—
Salvage value at end of useful life	0	0
Disposal value now	150,000	—
Disposal value in 7 years	0	0
Annual cash operating costs	36,000	20,000

Required:
Ignoring income taxes and time value of money, prepare a quantitative analysis of the best course of action for Alpha Corporation, in respect of the two alternatives.

(Adapted © CGA-Canada)

PROBLEM 12–12 Accept or Reject Order (CC6)

Melissa has created a successful business manufacturing and selling "Sparkles," a high-end soft, stuffed unicorn for young children. She sells them to department stores for $50 each. Current manufacturing capacity is 20,000 unicorns per year. Costs to manufacture and sell each stuffed animal are as follows:

Direct materials	$ 5.50
Direct labour	7.00
Variable overhead	10.00
Fixed overhead	12.00
Variable selling expenses	3.00

Melissa is currently manufacturing and selling 20,000 unicorns per year. A British department store has contacted Melissa with a one-time offer to buy 2,000 units. The store wants its own label attached to each stuffed animal, which will add $0.50 per unit to the costs of manufacturing. No selling expenses need be incurred on this transaction.

Required:
1. Determine the per-unit opportunity cost of selling to the British department store.
2. Determine the minimum selling price that Melissa should set.
3. Discuss briefly two of the qualitative factors Melissa should consider in making the decision to accept or reject this offer.

(Adapted © CGA-Canada)

PROBLEM 12–13 Equipment Replacement Decision (CC3)

For two years, Lexon Corporation has operated a successful business making miniature fibreglass boats. The moulds that it uses for the boat hull forms have deteriorated. The production manager of Lexon can either refurbish the moulds or replace them. The moulds were originally purchased two years ago for $600,000. They have an expected useful life of three more years, a terminal disposal value of $0 at the end of that time, a current disposal value of $90,000, and a book value of $360,000. Following are expected costs under the two alternatives.

CHECK FIGURE
1. Differential savings over three years from replacing; $180,000

	Refurbish	Replace
Capital cost	$300,000	$750,000
Variable manufacturing cost per hull	$ 12	$ 9
Expected production and sales of boats per year	60,000 units	60,000 units
Selling price per boat	$ 25	$ 25

The expected useful life of the old moulds after refurbishing is three years. Refurbishing would not affect the terminal disposal value. The expected useful life of the replacement moulds is three years with $0 disposal value at the end of that time. If the old mould is refurbished, the additional $300,000 would be amortized over the remaining three years of life. The new equipment would be amortized on a straight-line basis.

Required:
1. Should Lexon refurbish or replace the moulds? Show all calculations and explain.
2. The capital expenditure to replace the moulds is $750,000, but the demand is not known for certain. For what annual sales/production quantity would Lexon prefer to (a) replace the moulds or (b) refurbish the moulds? Briefly explain.

(Adapted © CGA-Canada)

Building Your Skills

ANALYTICAL THINKING (CC4)

Tracey Douglas is the owner and managing director of Heritage Garden Furniture Ltd., a South African company that makes museum-quality reproductions of antique outdoor furniture. Tracey would like advice concerning the advisability of eliminating the model C3 lawnchair. These lawnchairs have been among the company's best-selling products, but they seem to be unprofitable.

A condensed statement of operating income for the company and for the model C3 lawnchair for the quarter ended June 30 follows: (The currency in South Africa is the rand, denoted here by R.)

CHECK FIGURE
(2) Minimum sales: R60,000

	Model C3 Lawnchair	All Products
Sales	R300,000	R2,900,000
Cost of sales:		
Direct materials	122,000	759,000
Direct labour	72,000	680,000
Fringe benefits (20% of direct labour)	14,400	136,000
Variable manufacturing overhead	3,600	28,000
Building rent and maintenance	4,000	30,000
Amortization	19,100	75,000
Total cost of sales	235,100	1,708,000
Gross margin	64,900	1,192,000

continued

Selling and administrative expenses:		
Product manager's salaries	10,000	75,000
Sales commissions (5% of sales)	15,000	145,000
Fringe benefits (20% of salaries and commissions)	5,000	44,000
Shipping	10,000	120,000
General administrative expenses.	48,000	464,000
Total selling and administrative expenses.	88,000	848,000
Net operating income (loss)	R(23,100)	R344,000

The following additional data have been supplied by the company:

a. Direct labour is a variable cost at Heritage Garden Furniture.
b. All of the company's products are manufactured in the same facility and use the same equipment. Building rent, maintenance, and amortization are allocated to products using various bases. The equipment does not wear out through use; it eventually becomes obsolete.
c. There is ample capacity to fill all orders.
d. Dropping the model C3 lawnchair would have no effect on sales of other product lines.
e. Inventories of work in process or finished goods are insignificant.
f. Shipping costs are traced directly to products.
g. General administrative expenses are allocated to products on the basis of sales dollars. There would be no effect on the total general administrative expenses if the model C3 lawnchair were dropped.
h. If the model C3 lawnchair were dropped, the product manager would be laid off.

Required:
1. Given the current level of sales, would you recommend that the model C3 lawnchair be dropped? Prepare appropriate computations to support your answer.
2. What would sales of the model C3 lawnchair have to be, at minimum, in order to justify retaining the product? (*Hint: Set this up as a break-even problem, but include only the relevant costs from part (1)*.)

CHECK FIGURE
(1) Savings per box to make: $0.20

COMMUNICATING IN PRACTICE (CC5)

Silven Industries, which manufactures and sells a highly successful line of summer lotions and insect repellents, has decided to diversify in order to stabilize sales throughout the year. A natural area for the company to consider is the production of winter lotions and creams to prevent dry and chapped skin.

After considerable research, a winter products line has been developed. However, Bob Murdock, Silven's president, has decided to introduce only one of the new products for this coming winter. If the product is a success, further expansion in future years will be initiated.

The product selected (called Chap-Off) is a lip balm that will be sold in a lipstick-type tube. The product will be sold to wholesalers in boxes of 24 tubes for $8 per box. Because of excess capacity, no additional fixed overhead costs will be incurred to produce the product. However, a $90,000 charge for fixed overhead will be absorbed by the product under the company's absorption costing system.

Using the production and sales estimates of 100,000 boxes of Chap-Off, the Accounting Department has developed the following costs per box:

Direct material	$3.60
Direct labour	2.00
Manufacturing overhead	1.40
Total cost	$7.00

The preceding costs include costs for producing both the lip balm and the tube into which the lip balm is to be placed. As an alternative to making the tubes, Silven has approached a supplier to discuss the possibility of purchasing the tubes for Chap-Off. The purchase price of the empty tubes from the supplier would be $1.35 per box of 24 tubes. If Silven Industries accepts the purchase proposal, it is predicted that direct labour and variable manufacturing overhead costs per box of Chap-Off would be reduced by 10% and that direct materials costs would be reduced by 25%.

Required:
Write a memorandum to the president that answers the following questions. Use headings to organize the information presented in the memorandum. Include computations to support your answers, where appropriate.

1. Should Silven Industries make the tubes for the lip balm or buy them from the supplier? How much would be saved by making this decision?

2. What is the maximum purchase price that would be acceptable to Silven Industries if the tubes for the lip balm were bought from a supplier?

3. As noted previously, the Accounting Department assumed that 100,000 boxes of Chap-Off would be produced and sold. However, the vice-president of sales estimates that 120,000 boxes of Chap-Off can be sold. This higher volume would require additional equipment at an annual rental of $40,000. Assuming the company buys the tubes from the supplier at $1.35 per box of 24 tubes and that the supplier will not accept an order for less than 100,000 boxes of tubes, should Silven Industries make the tubes for the lip balm or buy them from the supplier? What are the total costs of producing 120,000 boxes of Chap-Off assuming that the company makes the tubes? What are the total costs assuming that the company buys the tubes? How much would be saved by buying the tubes, rather than making them internally?

4. Refer to the information in part (3). Assume that a different supplier will accept an order of any size for the tubes at $1.35 per box of 24 tubes. Should Silven Industries make the tubes for the lip balm or buy them from the supplier?

5. What qualitative factors should be considered in this make-or-buy decision?

(CMA heavily adapted)

ETHICS CHALLENGE (CC4)

Haley Romeros had just been appointed vice-president of the Rocky Mountain Region of the Bank Services Corporation (BSC). The company provides cheque-processing services to small banks. The banks send cheques presented for deposit or payment to BSC, which records the data on each cheque in a computerized database. BSC then sends the data electronically to a Canadian Payments Association cheque-clearing centre where the appropriate transfers of funds are made between banks. The Great Lakes Region has three cheque-processing centres, which are located in Burlington, Kingston, and Owen Sound, Ontario. Prior to her promotion to vice-president, Haley Romeros had been the manager of a cheque-processing centre in Nova Scotia.

Immediately upon assuming her new position, Haley requested a complete financial report for the just-ended fiscal year from the region's controller, John Littlebear. Haley Romeros specified that the financial report should follow the standardized format required by corporate headquarters for all regional performance reports. That report follows:

BANK SERVICES CORPORATION (BSC)
Great Lakes Region
Financial Performance

	Cheque-Processing Centres			
	Kingston	Burlington	Owen Sound	Total
Sales	$20,000,000	$18,000,000	$12,000,000	$50,000,000
Operating expenses:				
Direct labour............	12,500,000	11,000,000	8,500,000	32,000,000
Variable overhead	350,000	310,000	190,000	850,000
Equipment amortization ...	1,300,000	1,400,000	1,200,000	3,900,000
Facility expense..........	900,000	800,000	1,100,000	2,800,000
Local administrative expense*	140,000	160,000	150,000	450,000
Regional administrative expense†	600,000	540,000	360,000	1,500,000
Corporate administrative expense‡	1,900,000	1,710,000	1,140,000	4,750,000
Total operating expense	17,690,000	15,920,000	12,640,000	46,250,000
Net operating income	$ 2,310,000	$ 2,080,000	$ (640,000)	$ 3,750,000

*Local administrative expenses are the administrative expenses incurred at the cheque-processing centres.
†Regional administrative expenses are allocated to the cheque-processing centres on the basis of sales.
‡Corporate administrative expenses are charged to segments of the company, such as the Rocky Mountain Region and the cheque-processing centres at the rate of 9.5% of their sales.

Upon seeing this report, Haley Romeros summoned John Littlebear for an explanation.

Romeros: What's the story on Owen Sound? It didn't have a loss the previous year did it?

Littlebear: No, the Owen Sound facility has had a nice profit every year since it opened six years ago, but Owen Sound lost a big contract this year.

Romeros: Why?

Littlebear: One of our national competitors entered the local market and bid very aggressively on the contract. We couldn't afford to meet the bid. Owen Sound's costs–particularly their facility expenses–are just too high. When Owen Sound lost the contract, we had to lay off a lot of employees, but we could not reduce the fixed costs of the Owen Sound facility.

Romeros: Why is Owen Sound's facility expense so high? It's a smaller facility than either Kingston or Burlington, yet its facility expense is higher.

Littlebear: The problem is that we are able to rent suitable facilities very cheaply at Kingston and Burlington. No such facilities were available at Owen Sound; we had them built. Unfortunately, there were big cost overruns. The contractor we hired was inexperienced at this kind of work and, in fact, went bankrupt before the project was completed. After hiring another contractor to finish the work, we were way over budget. The large amortization charges on the facility didn't matter at first because we didn't have much competition at the time and could charge premium prices.

Romeros: Well, we can't do that anymore. The Owen Sound facility will obviously have to be shut down. Its business can be shifted to the other two cheque-processing centres in the region.

Littlebear: I would advise against that. The $1,200,000 in amortization at the Owen Sound facility is misleading. That facility should last indefinitely with proper maintenance. And, it has no resale value; there is no other commercial activity around Owen Sound.

Romeros: What about the other costs at Owen Sound?

Littlebear: If we shifted Owen Sound's business over to the other two processing centres in the region, we wouldn't save anything on direct labour or variable overhead costs. We might save $90,000 or so in local administrative expense, but we would not save any regional administrative expense and corporate headquarters would still charge us 9.5% of our sales as corporate administrative expense.

In addition, we would have to rent more space in Kingston and Burlington in order to handle the work transferred from Owen Sound; that would probably cost us at least $600,000 a year. And don't forget that it will cost us something to move the equipment from Owen Sound to Kingston and Burlington. And the move will disrupt service to customers.

Romeros: I understand all of that, but a money-losing processing centre on my performance report is completely unacceptable.

Littlebear: But if you shut down Owen Sound, you are going to throw some loyal employees out of work.

Romeros: That's unfortunate, but we have to face hard business realities.

Littlebear: And you would have to write off the investment in the facilities at Owen Sound.

Romeros: I can explain a write-off to corporate headquarters; hiring an inexperienced contractor to build the Owen Sound facility was my predecessor's mistake. But they'll have my head at headquarters if I show operating losses every year at one of my processing centres. Owen Sound has to go. At the next corporate board meeting, I am going to recommend that the Owen Sound facility be closed.

Required:

1. From the standpoint of the company as a whole, should the Owen Sound processing centre be shut down and its work redistributed to other processing centres in the region? Explain.
2. Do you think Haley Romeros's decision to shut down the Owen Sound facility is ethical? Explain.
3. What influence should the amortization on the facilities at Owen Sound have on prices charged by Owen Sound for its services?

TEAMWORK IN ACTION (CC5, 8, 9)

Sportway Inc. is a wholesale distributor supplying a wide range of moderately priced sporting equipment to large chain stores. About 60% of Sportway's products are purchased from other companies, while the remainder of the products are manufactured by Sportway. The company has a Plastics Department that is currently manufacturing moulded fishing tackle boxes. Sportway is able to manufacture and sell 8,000 tackle boxes annually, making full use of its direct labour capacity at available workstations. Following are the selling price and costs associated with Sportway's tackle boxes.

Selling price per box..................		$86.00
Cost per box:		
Moulded plastic	$ 8.00	
Hinges, latches, handle...............	9.00	
Direct labour ($15 per hour)..........	18.75	
Manufacturing overhead..............	12.50	
Selling and administrative cost.........	17.00	65.25
Net operating income per box...........		$20.75

Because Sportway believes it could sell 12,000 tackle boxes if it had sufficient manufacturing capacity, the company has looked into the possibility of purchasing the tackle boxes for distribution. Maple Products, a steady supplier of quality products, would be able to provide up to 9,000 tackle boxes per year at a price of $68 per box delivered to Sportway's facility.

Traci Kader, Sportway's production manager, has suggested that the company could make better use of its Plastics Department by manufacturing skateboards. To support her position, Traci has a market study that indicates an expanding market for skateboards. Traci believes that Sportway could expect to sell 17,500 skateboards annually at a price of $45 per skateboard. Traci's estimate of the costs to manufacture the skateboards is presented below.

Selling price per skateboard		$45.00
Cost per skateboard:		
Moulded plastic	$5.50	
Wheels, hardware	7.00	
Direct labour ($15 per hour).	7.50	
Manufacturing overhead.	5.00	
Selling and administrative cost.	9.00	34.00
Net operating income per skateboard		$11.00

In the Plastics Department, Sportway uses direct labour-hours as the application base for manufacturing overhead. Included in the manufacturing overhead for the current year is $50,000 of fixed overhead costs, of which 40% is traceable to the Plastics Department and 60% is allocated factorywide manufacturing overhead cost. The remaining manufacturing overhead cost is variable with respect to direct labour-hours. The skateboards could be produced with existing equipment and personnel in the Plastics Department.

For each unit of product that Sportway sells, regardless of whether the product has been purchased or is manufactured by Sportway, there is an allocated $6 fixed cost per unit for distribution. This $6 per unit is included in the selling and administrative cost for all products. The remaining amount of selling and administrative cost for all products—purchased or manufactured—is variable. The total selling and administrative cost figure for the purchased tackle boxes would be $10 per unit.

Required:

Your team should discuss and then respond to the following questions. All team members should agree with and understand the answers (including the calculations supporting the answers) and be prepared to report to the class. (Each teammate can assume responsibility for a different part of the presentation.)

1. Determine the number of direct labour-hours per year being used to manufacture tackle boxes.
2. Compute the contribution margin per unit for:
   a. Purchased tackle boxes.
   b. Manufactured tackle boxes.
   c. Manufactured skateboards.
3. Determine the number of tackle boxes (if any) that Sportway should purchase and the number of tackle boxes and/or skateboards that it should manufacture, and compute the improvement in net income that would result from this product mix over current operations.

(CMA adapted)

Don't forget to visit the Online Learning Centre for self-study quizzes, practice exams, and more! Visit www.mcgrawhill.ca/olc/brewer.

CHAPTER *Thirteen*

Capital Budgeting Decisions

CHAPTER COMPETENCIES

After studying Chapter 13, you should be able to demonstrate the following competencies:

Competency	Know	Apply
Understand the basics of capital budgeting analysis.		
CC1 Describe some business decisions that rely on capital budgeting analysis.	○	
CC2 Explain the distinction between screening decisions and preference decisions.	○	
CC3 Determine the acceptability of an investment project using the net present value (NPV) method.	○	
CC4 Describe the typical cash flows in a capital budgeting analysis without taxes.	○	
CC5 Outline the simplifying assumptions made in a capital budgeting analysis.	○	
CC6 Explain the logic of ignoring financing-related cash flows and the choice of the appropriate discount rate in capital budgeting analysis.	○	
Perform a basic capital budgeting analysis using the NPV method.		
CC7 Prepare an NPV analysis of two competing projects using either the total-cost approach or the incremental-cost approach.		○
CC8 Compute the NPV of a project when no revenues are involved.		○
Apply the profitability index to rank projects.		
CC9 Rank projects in order of preference using the profitability index.		○
Understand and apply the internal rate of return method.		
CC10 Compute the internal rate of return (IRR) of a project, interpret it, and explain its use for project selection.	○	○
CC11 Contrast the IRR and NPV methods in project selection.	○	
Understand and apply the payback period and the simple rate of return methods.		
CC12 Calculate the payback period of an investment project.		○
CC13 Explain the payback method and its potential to mislead a manager.	○	
CC14 Calculate the simple rate of return (SRR) of a project.		○
CC15 Explain the disadvantages of the SRR method for project selection.	○	
Understand and apply the mechanics of time value of money calculations.		
CC16[A] Compute the present value of a series of cash flows.		○
Understand the concept of inflation and incorporate its effect on cash flows in capital budgeting.		
CC17[C] Explain the distinction between real and nominal cash flows.	○	
CC18[C] Compute the price index number for a future year given the annual rate of inflation.		○
CC19[C] Explain the distinction between real and nominal rates of return.	○	
Understand and incorporate the impact of taxes on cash flows in capital budgeting analysis.		
CC20[D] Explain the impact of tax deductibility of amortization (i.e., capital cost allowance (CCA)).	○	
CC21[D] Compute the present value of CCA tax shields.		○
CC22[D] Compute the NPV of a project when cash flows related to the ownership and disposal of depreciable property are included in the analysis.		○

Note: A, B, C, and D refer to Appendices 13A, 13B, 13C, and 13D respectively; all are available online at www.mcgrawhill.ca/olc/brewer.

DECISION FEATURE
Invest Less, Make More

Steven Burd became the CEO of Safeway, one of the largest food and drug retailers in North America, in 1992. At the time, Safeway was operating approximately 1,100 stores, which occupied approximately 39 million square feet of retail space. Burd immediately slashed annual capital spending from $550 million to $290 million. He justified the decision as follows: "We had projects that were not returning the cost of money. So we cut spending back, which made the very best projects come to the surface."

Safeway set a minimum 22.5% pretax return on investment in all new store and remodeling projects. In addition to opening new stores, Burd felt that the company could increase sales by expanding existing stores that are in excellent locations. With its new approach to capital budgeting firmly in place, Safeway started to steadily increase its capital spending on both new stores and remodeling projects. Ten years after implementing the new decision-making process, Safeway's 1,782 stores occupied 78.8 million square feet of retail space.

Sources: Safeway, Inc. Web site; and Robert Berner, "Safeway's Resurgence Is Built on Attention to Detail," *The Wall Street Journal*, October 2, 1998, p. B4.

A Look Back

A basic framework for the decision-making process centred on the notion of relevant costs and benefits was used in a wide variety of situations in Chapter 12.

A Look at This Chapter

Chapter 13 expands the coverage of the decision-making process by focusing on decisions about significant outlays on long-term projects. A variety of techniques used by managers faced with these decisions are reviewed and illustrated.

A Look Ahead

Financial statement analysis is covered in Chapter 14 on the Online Learning Centre. This analysis uses financial statements to assess the financial health of a company. The focus in Chapter 14 is on analysis of trends and the use of financial ratios. Chapter 15, also on the Online Learning Centre, discusses the statement of cash flows.

T he term **capital budgeting** is used to describe how managers plan significant outlays on projects that have long-term implications, such as the purchase of new equipment and the introduction of new products. Most companies have many more potential projects than can actually be funded. Hence, managers must carefully select those projects that promise the greatest future return. How well managers make these capital budgeting decisions is a critical factor in the long-term profitability of the company.

Capital budgeting involves *investment*—a company must commit funds now in order to receive a return in the future. Investments are not limited to shares and bonds. Purchase of inventory or equipment is also an investment. For example, Tri-Con Global Restaurants Inc. makes an investment when it opens a new Pizza Hut restaurant. Mountain Equipment Co-op makes an investment when it installs a new computer to handle customer billing. DaimlerChrysler makes an investment when it redesigns a product, such as the Jeep Eagle, and must retool its production lines. Merck & Co. invests in medical research. Amazon. com makes an investment when it redesigns its website. All of these investments are characterized by a commitment of funds today in the expectation of receiving a return in the future in the form of additional cash inflows or reduced cash outflows.

Capital Budgeting—Planning Investments

Typical Capital Budgeting Decisions

KNOW

CC1: Describe some business decisions that rely on capital budgeting analysis.

The types of business decisions that require capital budgeting analysis are virtually any decisions that involve an outlay now in order to obtain some return (increase in revenue or reduction in costs) in the future. Typical capital budgeting decisions include:

- Cost reduction decisions: Should new equipment be purchased to reduce costs?
- Expansion decisions: Should a new plant, warehouse, or other facility be acquired to increase capacity and sales?
- Equipment selection decisions: Which of several available machines would be the most cost effective to purchase?
- Lease-or-buy decisions: Should new equipment be leased or purchased?
- Equipment replacement decisions: Should old equipment be replaced now or later?

KNOW

CC2: Explain the distinction between screening decisions and preference decisions.

Capital budgeting decisions tend to fall into two broad categories—*screening decisions* and *preference decisions*. **Screening decisions** are those relating to whether a proposed project meets some preset standard of acceptance. For example, a firm may have a policy of accepting projects only if they promise a return of, say, 20% on the investment. The required rate of return is the minimum rate of return a project must yield to be acceptable.

Preference decisions, by contrast, are those in which you select from among several *competing* courses of action. To illustrate, a firm may be considering several different machines to replace an existing machine on the assembly line. The choice of which machine to purchase is a *preference* decision.

In this chapter, we initially discuss ways of making screening decisions. Preference decisions are discussed toward the end of the chapter.

The Time Value of Money

As stated previously, business investments commonly involve returns that extend over fairly long periods. Therefore, in approaching capital budgeting decisions, you must employ techniques that recognize the *time value of money*. In other words, a dollar today is worth more than a dollar a year from now. The same concept applies in choosing between investment projects. Those projects that promise returns earlier in time are preferable to those that promise returns later in time.

The capital budgeting techniques that recognize the preceding two characteristics of business investments most fully are those that involve *discounted cash flows.* We will spend most of this chapter illustrating the use of discounted cash flow methods in making capital budgeting decisions. If you are not already familiar with discounting and the use of present value tables, you should read Appendix 13A on the Online Learning Centre before proceeding any further.

Several approaches can be used to evaluate investments using discounted cash flows. The easiest method to use is the *net present value method,* which is the subject of the next several sections.

The Net Present Value Method

Under the net present value method, the present value of a project's cash inflows is compared with the present value of the project's cash outflows. The difference between the present value of these cash flows, called the **net present value (NPV),** determines whether the project is an acceptable investment. To illustrate, let us assume the following data:

KNOW

CC3: Determine the acceptability of an investment project using the NPV method.

EXAMPLE A

Harper Company is contemplating the purchase of a machine capable of performing certain operations that are now performed manually. The machine will cost $5,000, and it will last for five years. At the end of the five-year period, the machine will have a zero scrap value. Use of the machine will reduce labour costs by $1,800 per year. Harper Company requires a minimum return of 20% before taxes on all investment projects.[1]

Should the machine be purchased? Harper Company must determine whether a cash investment now of $5,000 can be justified if it will result in an $1,800 reduction in cost each year over the next five years. It may appear that the answer is obvious, since the total cost savings is $9,000 (5 × $1,800). However, the company can earn a 20% return by investing its money elsewhere. It is not enough that the cost reductions cover just the original cost of the machine; they must also yield at least a 20% return, or the company would be better off investing the money elsewhere.

To determine whether the investment is desirable, management must discount the stream of annual $1,800 cost savings to its present value and then compare it with the cost of the new machine. Since Harper Company requires a minimum return of 20% on all investment projects, this rate is used in the discounting process. Exhibit 13–1 shows how this analysis is done.

Initial cost	$5,000
Life of the project (years)	5
Annual cost savings	$1,800
Salvage value	–0–
Required rate of return	20%

Item	Year(s)	Amount of Cash Flow	20% Factor	Present Value of Cash Flows
Annual cost savings	1–5	$ 1,800	2.991*	$5,384
Initial investment	Now	(5,000)	1.000	(5,000)
Net present value				$ 384

*From Exhibit 13B–4 in Appendix 13B on the Online Learning Centre.

Exhibit 13–1
NPV Analysis of a Proposed Project

---

[1]For simplicity, we ignore taxes and inflation.

According to the analysis, Harper Company should purchase the new machine. The present value of the cost savings is $5,384, as compared with a present value of only $5,000 for the investment required (cost of the machine). Deducting the present value of the investment required from the present value of the cost savings gives a *net present value* of $384. Whenever the net present value is zero or greater, as in our example, an investment project is acceptable. Whenever the net present value is negative (the present value of the cash outflows exceeds the present value of the cash inflows), an investment project is not acceptable. In summary:

If the Net Present Value Is . . .	Then the Project Is . . .
Positive	Acceptable, since it promises a return greater than the required rate of return.
Zero	Acceptable, since it promises a return equal to the required rate of return.
Negative.	Not acceptable, since it promises a return less than the required rate of return.

A full interpretation of the solution would be as follows: The new machine promises more than the required 20% rate of return. This is evident from the positive net present value of $384. Harper Company could spend up to $5,384 for the new machine and still obtain the minimum required 20% rate of return. The net present value of $384, therefore, shows the amount of *cushion* or *margin of error*. One way to look at this is that the company could underestimate the cost of the new machine by up to $384 or overestimate the net present value of the future cash savings by up to $384, and the project would still be financially attractive.

Emphasis on Cash Flows

 KNOW

CC4: Describe the typical cash flows in a capital budgeting analysis without taxes.

In capital budgeting decisions, the focus is on cash flows, not on accounting net income. The reason for this is that accounting net income is based on accrual concepts that ignore the timing of cash flows into and out of an organization. From a capital budgeting standpoint, the timing of cash flows is important, since a dollar received today is more valuable than a dollar received in the future. Therefore, even though the accounting net income figure is useful for many things, it is not ordinarily used in discounted cash flow analysis.[2] However, accounting net income can, in some situations, be the starting point for determining the cash flows of a project. In these cases, the manager must make appropriate adjustments to net income (like adding back amortization) to arrive at the project's cash flows. We will not consider this approach further in this chapter.

What kinds of cash flows should the manager look for? Although they will vary from project to project, certain types of cash flows tend to recur, as explained in the following paragraphs.

TYPICAL CASH OUTFLOWS   Most projects will have an immediate cash outflow in the form of an initial investment in equipment or other assets. In addition, some projects require that a company expand its working capital. **Working capital** is current assets (cash, accounts receivable, and inventory) less current liabilities. When a company takes on a new project, the balances in the current asset accounts will often increase. For example, opening a new Ikea store would require additional cash in sales registers, increased accounts receivable for new customers, and more inventory to stock the shelves. These

---

[2]Under certain conditions, capital budgeting decisions can be correctly made by discounting appropriately defined accounting net income. However, this approach requires advanced techniques that are beyond the scope of this text.

additional working capital needs should be treated as part of the initial investment in a project. Also, many projects require periodic outlays for repairs and maintenance and for additional operating costs. These should all be treated as cash outflows for capital budgeting purposes.

TYPICAL CASH INFLOWS   On the cash inflow side, a project will normally either increase revenues or reduce costs. Either way, the amount involved should be treated as a cash inflow for capital budgeting purposes. *A reduction in costs is equivalent to an increase in revenues.* Cash inflows are also frequently realized from salvage of equipment. This can occur at the start of a project when old equipment is replaced and at the end of a project when equipment is sold. In addition, any working capital that was tied up in the project can be released for use elsewhere at the end of the project and should be treated as a cash inflow. Working capital is released, for example, when a company sells off its inventory or collects its receivables.

In summary, the following types of cash flows are common in business investment projects:

Cash outflows:
   Initial investment (including installation costs).
   Increased working capital needs.
   Repairs and maintenance.
   Incremental operating costs.
Cash inflows:
   Incremental revenues.
   Reduction in costs.
   Salvage value.
   Release of working capital.

Simplifying Assumptions

There are a number of assumptions that underlie our treatment of the NPV method.

TIMING OF CASH FLOWS   The first assumption is that at all cash flows occur at the end of the period. Typically cash flows will occur throughout a period, but our assumption will make calculations easier.

REINVESTMENT OF CASH INFLOWS   The second assumption is that all surplus cash inflows generated by the project are immediately reinvested at a rate of return equal to the discount rate, until the end of the project. Without this assumption, (say, if the cash flows from a project are simply kept locked up in a safe until the project ends) the net present value will not be accurate.

PROJECTS ARE CARBON COPIES OF THE FIRM   The third assumption is that the risk of investing in a project is identical to the risk you would face if you bought the company outright—that is, if you purchased all of the outstanding securities of the company. This means that projects are basically clones of the company in so far as risk is concerned. This assumption is very important to the choice of the discount rate in NPV analysis and to the procedure for handling financing-related cash flows. This is explained following.

TREATMENT OF INFLATION   Although somewhat unrealistic, we will assume that there is no inflation. When inflation exists, we will need to adjust either the cash flows or the discount rate. A brief discussion of these adjustments is provided in Appendix 13C on the Online Learning Centre.

 KNOW

CC5: Outline the simplifying assumptions made in a capital budgeting analysis.

INCOME TAXES   The NPV method usually considers cash flows only on an *after-tax* basis. This, in turn, requires that we use an after-tax discount rate and that we focus on after-tax cash flows. The effect of income taxes on revenues and costs should be fully reflected in the analysis. This includes taking into account the tax deductibility of amortization. Amortization in itself is not a cash flow, but is treated as an expense when calculating income taxes and hence results in tax savings. These tax savings—called *tax shields*—are cash inflows and must be treated as such in any NPV analysis involving depreciable property. In Canada, a complex set of rules governs the calculation of amortization for tax purposes. The amount allowed as a deduction is called the **capital cost allowance (CCA)**. These rules, as well as the techniques for calculating CCA, after-tax discount rates, and after-tax cash flows, are discussed briefly in Appendix 13D on the Online Learning Centre. A more complete treatment can be found in advanced texts on corporate finance.

IN BUSINESS TODAY   A Return on Investment of 100%

During negotiations to build a replacement for the old Fenway Park in Boston, the Red Sox offered the city approximately $2 million per year over 30 years in exchange for an investment of $150 million by the city for land acquisition and cleanup. In May 2000, after denying his lack of support for the project, Boston Mayor Thomas M. Menino stated that his goal is a 100% rate of return on any investment that is made by the city. Some doubt that the Red Sox would be able to pay players' salaries if the team were required to meet the mayor's goal. The mayor has countered with a list of suggestions for raising private funds (such as selling shares to the public, as the Celtics did in 1986). Private funds would reduce the investment that would need to be made by the city and, as a result, reduce the future payments made to the city by the Red Sox.

Source: Meg Vaillancourt, "Boston Mayor Wants High Return on Investment in New Ballpark," *Knight-Ridder/Tribune Business News*, May 11, 2000, pITEM00133018. Reprinted with permission of Knight Ridder/Tribune Information Services.

Choosing a Discount Rate

The discount rate should be the company's minimum required rate of return. A positive net present value means that the project's return exceeds the minimum required rate of return. A negative net present value means that the project's return is less than the minimum required rate of return.

What is a company's minimum required rate of return? The company's *cost of capital* is usually regarded as the minimum required rate of return. The **cost of capital** is the average rate of return the company must pay to its long-term creditors and to shareholders for the use of their funds. The cost of capital is the minimum required rate of return because if a project's rate of return is less than the cost of capital, the company does not earn enough of a return to compensate its creditors and shareholders. Therefore, any project with a rate of return less than the cost of capital should not be accepted.

The cost of capital serves as a *screening device* in net present value analysis. When the cost of capital is used as the discount rate, any project with a negative net present value does not cover the company's cost of capital and therefore should be discarded as unacceptable.

Financing-Related Cash Flows

A common source of confusion for students is how to handle cash inflows from borrowing and cash outflows for making interest payments and principal repayments. Given our simplifying assumptions and our choice of the company's cost of capital for the discount rate,

◔ KNOW

CC6: Explain the logic of ignoring financing-related cash flows and the choice of an appropriate discount rate in capital budgeting analysis.

the rule is very simple: *ignore all financing-related cash flows.* The impact on the project of the financing decisions made to fund the project is captured in the company's cost of capital—the discount rate. More advanced discussions of this topic will consider specific cases where our simple rule requires modification. For our purposes, this rule will suffice.

Negotiator for the Red Sox

DECISION MAKER

As stated previously, Boston Mayor Thomas M. Menino's goal is a 100% rate of return on any investment that is made by the city to build a new park for the Red Sox. How would you respond to the mayor?

An Extended Example of the Net Present Value Method

To conclude our discussion of the net present value method, we present the following extended example of how it is used to analyze an investment proposal. This example will also help tie together (and to reinforce) many of the ideas developed thus far.

EXAMPLE B

Under a special licensing arrangement, Swinyard Company has an opportunity to market a new product in the western Canada for a five-year period. The product would be purchased from the manufacturer, with Swinyard Company responsible for all costs of promotion and distribution. The licensing arrangement could be renewed at the end of the five-year period at the option of the manufacturer. After careful study, Swinyard Company has estimated the following costs and revenues for the new product:

Cost of equipment needed.	$ 60,000
Working capital needed	100,000
Overhaul of the equipment in four years	5,000
Salvage value of the equipment in five years	10,000
Annual revenues and costs:	
Sales revenues.	200,000
Cost of goods sold (cash)	125,000
Out-of-pocket operating costs (for salaries,	
advertising, and other direct costs) 35,000	

At the end of the five-year period, the working capital would be released for investment elsewhere if the manufacturer decided not to renew the licensing arrangement. Swinyard Company's discount rate and cost of capital is 20%. Would you recommend that the new product be introduced?

This example involves a variety of cash inflows and cash outflows. The solution is given in Exhibit 13–2.

Exhibit 13–2

The NPV Method—An Extended Example

Sales revenues (cash)	$200,000
Less: Cost of goods sold (cash)	125,000
Less: Out-of-pocket costs for salaries, advertising, etc.	35,000
Annual net cash inflows	$ 40,000

continued

Item	Year(s)	Amount of Cash Flows	20% Factor	Present Value of Cash Flows
Purchase of equipment	Now	$ (60,000)	1.000	$ (60,000)
Working capital needed.	Now	(100,000)	1.000	(100,000)
Overhaul of equipment	4	(5,000)	0.482*	(2,410)
Annual net cash inflows from sales of the product line	1–5	40,000	2.991†	119,640
Salvage value of the equipment	5	10,000	0.402*	4,020
Working capital released.	5	100,000	0.402*	40,200
Net present value.				$ 1,450

*From Exhibit 13B–3 in Appendix 13B on the Online Learning Centre.
†From Exhibit 13B–4 in Appendix 13B on the Online Learning Centre.

Notice particularly how the working capital is handled in this exhibit. It is counted as a cash outflow at the beginning of the project and as a cash inflow when it is released at the end of the project. Also, notice how the sales revenues, cost of goods sold, and out-of-pocket costs are handled. **Out-of-pocket costs** are actual cash outlays for salaries, advertising, and other operating expenses. Cost of goods sold are also assumed to be cash costs. Amortization involves no current cash outlay and hence is not considered here.

Since the overall net present value is positive, the new product should be added, assuming the company has no better use for the investment funds.

Expanding the Net Present Value Method

  APPLY

CC7: Prepare an NPV analysis of two competing projects using either the total-cost approach or the incremental-cost approach.

So far, our examples have involved only a single investment alternative. We will now expand the NPV method to include two alternatives. Note that if all projects have a negative net present value *none* should be accepted. In addition, we will integrate the concept of relevant costs into the discounted cash flow analysis.

The NPV method can be used to compare competing investment projects in two ways. One is the *total-cost approach*, and the other is the *incremental-cost approach*. Each approach is illustrated following.

The Total-Cost Approach

The total-cost approach is the most flexible method for comparing projects. To illustrate the mechanics of this approach, let us assume the following data:

EXAMPLE C
Don Ferry Company provides a ferry service across the Don River. One of its ferries is in poor condition. This ferry can be renovated at an immediate cost of $20,000. Further repairs and an overhaul of the motor will be needed five years from now at a cost of $8,000. In all, the ferry will be usable for 10 years if this work is done. At the end of 10 years, the ferry will have to be scrapped at a salvage value of approximately $6,000. The scrap value of the ferry right now is $7,000. It will cost $30,000 each year to operate the ferry, and revenues will total $40,000 annually.

As an alternative, Don Ferry Company can purchase a new ferry at a cost of $36,000. The new ferry will have a life of 10 years, but it will require some repairs at the end of 5 years. It is estimated that these repairs will amount to $3,000. At the end of 10 years, it is estimated that the ferry will have a scrap value of $6,000. It will cost $21,000 each year to operate the ferry, and revenues will total $40,000 annually.

Don Ferry Company requires a return of at least 18% before taxes on all investment projects.

Should the company purchase the new ferry or renovate the old ferry? Exhibit 13–3 gives the solution using the total-cost approach.

Two points should be noted from the exhibit. First, observe that *all* cash inflows and *all* cash outflows are included in the solution under each alternative. No effort has been made to isolate those cash flows that are relevant to the decision and those that are not relevant. The inclusion of all cash flows associated with each alternative gives the approach its name—the *total-cost* approach.

Second, note that a net present value figure is computed for each of the two alternatives. This is a distinct advantage of the total-cost approach in that an unlimited number of alternatives can be compared side by side to determine the best action. For example, another alternative for Don Ferry Company would be to get out of the ferry business entirely. If management desired, the net present value of this alternative could be computed to compare with the alternatives shown in Exhibit 13–3. Still other alternatives might be open to the company. Once management has determined the net present value of each alternative, it can select the course of action that promises to be the most profitable. In the case at hand, given only the two alternatives, the best alternative is to purchase the new ferry.[3]

Exhibit 13–3

The Total-Cost Approach to Project Selection

			New Ferry	Old Ferry	
Annual revenues			$40,000	$40,000	
Annual cash operating costs			21,000	30,00	
Net annual cash inflows			$19,000	$10,00	

Item	Year(s)	Amount of Cash Flows	18% Factor*	Present Value of Cash Flows
Buy the new ferry:				
Initial investment.	Now	$(36,000)	1.000	$(36,000)
Repairs in five years	5	(3,000)	0.437	(1,311)
Net annual cash inflows	1–10	19,000	4.494	85,386
Salvage of the old ferry.	Now	7,000	1.000	7,000
Salvage of the new ferry	10	6,000	0.191	1,146
Net present value.				56,221
Keep the old ferry:				
Initial repairs.	Now	(20,000)	1.000	(20,000)
Repairs in five years	5	(8,000)	0.437	(3,496)
Net annual cash inflows	1–10	10,000	4.494	44,940
Salvage of the old ferry.	10	6,000	0.191	1,146
Net present value.				22,590
Net present value in favour of buying the new ferry				$ 33,631

*All factors are from Exhibits 13B–3 and 13B–4 in Appendix 13B on the Online Learning Centre.

---

[3]The alternative with the highest NPV is not always the best choice, although it is the best choice in this case. For further discussion, see the upcoming section, *Preference Decisions—The Ranking of Investment Projects.*

The Incremental-Cost Approach

When only two alternatives are being considered, the incremental-cost approach offers a simpler and more direct route to a decision. Unlike the total-cost approach, it focuses only on differential costs.[4] The procedure is to include in the discounted cash flow analysis only those costs and revenues that *differ* between the two alternatives being considered. To illustrate, refer again to the data in Example C relating to Don Ferry Company. The solution using only differential costs is presented in Exhibit 13–4.

Two things should be noted from the data in this exhibit. First, note that the net present value in favour of buying the new ferry of $33,631 shown in Exhibit 13–4 agrees with the net present value shown under the total-cost approach in Exhibit 13–3. This agreement should be expected, since the two approaches are just different roads to the same destination.

Second, notice that the costs used in Exhibit 13–4 are just the differences between the costs shown for the two alternatives in the prior exhibit. For example, the $16,000 incremental investment required to purchase the new ferry in Exhibit 13–4 is the difference between the $36,000 cost of the new ferry and the $20,000 cost required to renovate the old ferry from Exhibit 13–3. The other figures in Exhibit 13–4 have been computed in the same way.

Exhibit 13–4
The Incremental-Cost Approach to Project Selection

Item	Year(s)	Amount of Cash Flows	18% Factor*	Present Value of Cash Flows
Incremental investment required to purchase the new ferry	Now	$(16,000)	1.000	$(16,000)
Repairs in five years avoided	5	5,000	0.437	2,185
Increased net annual cash inflows.	1–10	9,000	4.494	40,446
Salvage of the old ferry.	Now	7,000	1.000	7,000
Difference in salvage value in 10 years . . .	10	–0–	—	–0–
Net present value in favour of buying the new ferry				$ 33,631

*All factors are from Exhibits 13B–3 and 13B–4 in Appendix 13B on the Online Learning Centre.

Least-Cost Decisions

○ APPLY

CC8: Compute the NPV of a project when no revenues are involved.

Revenues are not directly involved in some decisions. For example, a company that does not charge for delivery service may need to replace an old delivery truck, or a company may be trying to decide whether to lease or to buy its fleet of executive cars. In such situations, where no revenues are involved, the most desirable alternative will be the one that promises the *least total cost* from the present value perspective. Hence, these are known as *least-cost decisions*. To illustrate a least-cost decision, assume the following data:

EXAMPLE D
Val-Tek Company is considering the replacement of an old threading machine. A new threading machine is available that could substantially reduce annual operating costs. Selected data relating to the old and the new machines are presented following:

---

[4]Technically, the incremental-cost approach is misnamed, since it focuses on differential costs (that is, on both cost increases and decreases), rather than just on incremental costs. As used here, the term *incremental costs* should be interpreted broadly to include both cost increases and cost decreases.

	Old Machine	New Machine
Purchase cost when new	$20,000	$25,000
Salvage value now	3,000	—
Annual cash operating costs	15,000	9,000
Overhaul needed immediately	4,000	—
Salvage value in six years	–0–	5,000
Remaining life	6 years	6 years

Val-Tek Company's cost of capital is 10%.

Exhibit 13–5 provides an analysis of the alternatives using the total-cost approach.

As shown in the exhibit, the new machine has the lowest total cost when the present value of the net cash outflows is considered. An analysis of the two alternatives using the incremental-cost approach is presented in Exhibit 13–6. As before, the data in this exhibit represent the differences between the alternatives as shown under the total-cost approach.

Exhibit 13–5

The Total-Cost Approach (Least-Cost Decision)

Item	Year(s)	Amount of Cash Flows	10% Factor*	Present Value of Cash Flows
Buy the new machine:				
Initial investment.	Now	$(25,000)	1.000	$(25,000)†
Salvage of the old machine.	Now	3,000	1.000	3,000†
Annual cash operating costs	1–6	(9,000)	4.355	(39,195)
Salvage of the new machine	6	5,000	0.564	2,820
Present value of net cash outflows				(58,375)
Keep the old machine:				
Overhaul needed now	Now	(4,000)	1.000	(4,000)
Annual cash operating costs	1–6	(15,000)	4355	(65,325)
Present value of net cash outflows				(69,325)
Net present value in favour of				
buying the new machine				$ 10,950

*All factors are from Exhibits 13B–3 and 13B–4 in Appendix 13B on the Online Learning Centre.
†These two items could be netted into a single $22,000 incremental-cost figure ($25,000 − $3,000 = $22,000).

Exhibit 13–6

The Incremental-Cost Approach (Least-Cost Decision)

Item	Year(s)	Amount of Cash Flows	10% Factor*	Present Value of Cash Flows
Incremental investment required to				
purchase the new machine	Now	$(21,000)	1.000	$(21,000)†
Salvage of the old machine.	Now	3,000	1.000	3,000†
Savings in annual cash operating costs. . . .	1–6	6,000	4.355	26,130
Difference in salvage value in six years . . .	6	5,000	0.564	2,820
Net present value in favour of buying				
the new machine				$ 10,950

*All factors are from Exhibits 13B–3 and 13B–4 in Appendix 13B on the Online Learning Centre.
†These two items could be netted into a single $18,000 incremental-cost figure ($21,000 − $3,000 = $18,000).

Preference Decisions—The Ranking of Investment Projects

◗ APPLY

CC9: Rank projects in order of preference using the profitability index.

Recall that when considering investment opportunities, managers must make two types of decisions—screening decisions and preference decisions. Screening decisions pertain to whether some proposed investment is acceptable. Preference decisions come *after* screening decisions and attempt to answer the following question: How do the remaining investment proposals, all of which have been screened and provide an acceptable rate of return, rank in terms of preference? That is, which one(s) would be *best* for the firm to accept?

Preference decisions are more difficult to make than screening decisions because investment funds are usually limited. This often requires that some (perhaps many) otherwise very profitable investment opportunities must be passed up.

Sometimes, preference decisions are called rationing decisions or ranking decisions because they ration limited investment funds among many competing alternatives, or there may be many alternatives that must be ranked.

If the NPV method is used to rank projects, the net present value of one project cannot be compared directly with the net present value of another project unless the investments in the projects are of equal size. For example, assume that a company is considering two competing investments, as shown following:

	Investment	
	A	B
Investment required	$(80,000)	$(5,000)
Present value of cash inflows	81,000	6,000
Net present value	$ 1,000	$ 1,000

Each project has a net present value of $1,000, but the projects are not equally desirable. The project requiring an investment of only $5,000 is much more desirable when funds are limited than the project requiring an investment of $80,000. To compare the two projects on a valid basis, the present value of the cash inflows should be divided by the investment required. The result is called the **profitability index.** The formula for the profitability index follows:

$$\text{Profitability index} = \frac{\text{Present value of cash inflows}}{\text{Investment required}} \qquad (1)$$

The profitability indexes for the two preceding investments would be computed as follows:

	Investment	
	A	B
Present value of cash inflows (a).......	$81,000	$6,000
Investment required (b)	$80,000	$5,000
Profitability index, (a) ÷ (b)	1.01	1.20

When using the profitability index to rank competing investment projects, the preference rule is as follows: *The higher the profitability index, the more desirable is the project.* Applying this rule to the two preceding investments, investment B should be chosen over investment A.

The profitability index is an application of the techniques for utilizing scarce resources. In this case, the scarce resource is the limited funds available for investment, and the profitability index is similar to the contribution margin per unit of the scarce resource.

A few details should be clarified with respect to the computation of the profitability index. The "Investment required" refers to any cash outflows that occur at the beginning of the project, reduced by any salvage value recovered from the sale of old equipment. The "Investment required" also includes any investment in working capital that the project may need. Finally, we should note that the "Present value of cash inflows" is net of all *out*flows that occur after the project starts.

Choosing a Cat

Sometimes a long-term decision does not have to involve present value calculations or any other sophisticated analytical technique. White Grizzly Adventures of Meadow Creek, British Columbia, needs two snowcats for its powder skiing operations—one for shuttling guests to the top of the mountain and one to be held in reserve in case of mechanical problems with the first. Bombardier of Canada sells new snowcats for $250,000 and used, reconditioned snowcats for $150,000. In either case, the snowcats are good for about 5,000 hours of operation before they need to be reconditioned. From White Grizzly's perspective, the choice is clear. Since both new and reconditioned snowcats last about 5,000 hours, but the reconditioned snowcats cost $100,000 less, the reconditioned snowcats are the obvious choice. They may not have all of the latest bells and whistles, but they get the job done at a price a small operation can afford.

Bombardier snowcats do not have passenger cabs as standard equipment. To save money, White Grizzly builds its own custom-designed passenger cab for about $15,000, using recycled Ford Escort seats and industrial-strength aluminum for the frame and siding. If purchased retail, a passenger cab would cost about twice as much and would not be as well-suited for snowcat skiing.

Source: Brad and Carole Karafil, owners and operators of White Grizzly Adventures, www.whitegrizzly.com.

The Internal Rate of Return Method

The **internal rate of return (IRR)** of a project is defined as the discount rate that makes the net present value of the project equal zero. The internal rate of return is sometimes referred to as the *yield* of the project. It is interpreted as the rate of return promised by the project over the project's useful life. We will consider three aspects of the internal rate of return: (1) its calculation, (2) its interpretation, and (3) its usefulness for decision-making about projects as compared with the net present value rule.

○ KNOW ○ APPLY

CC10: Compute the IRR of a project, interpret it, and explain its use for project selection.

Calculating the Internal Rate of Return of a Project

To illustrate the calculation of the internal rate of return assume the following data:

EXAMPLE E

Chantal Enterprises is planning to add a new line of clothes for sale through its retail outlets during the summer. The cost of the clothing will be $142,514. The net cash inflow from the sale of these clothes at the end of one year following the purchase is forecast at $149,700. Determine the internal rate of return of this project.

The internal rate of return is the discount rate which will make the project's net present value equal 0. To calculate it, we use the following steps:

(A) Set up the net present value calculation using the internal rate of return as the discount rate.
(B) Set the net present value equal to 0.
(C) Solve for the internal rate of return.

Step A:

$$NPV = -\$142,514 + \frac{\$149,700}{(1 + IRR)}$$

Step B:

$$0 = -\$142,514 + \frac{\$149,700}{(1 + IRR)}$$

Step C:

$$0 = -\$142,514 + \frac{\$149,700}{(1 + IRR)}$$

$$\$142,514 = \frac{\$149,700}{(1 + IRR)}$$

$$\$142,514 \times (1 + IRR) = \$149,700$$

$$1 + IRR = \frac{\$149,700}{\$142,514}$$

$$IRR = 1.0504 - 1 = 0.0504$$

It was simple to solve for the internal rate of return here because the project had a single cash flow occurring in the first year. You can also estimate the internal rate of return using the present value tables in Appendix 13B as follows: Calculate the present value factor $1/(1 + IRR)$, and use the present value table in Exhibit 13B–3 (on the Online Learning Centre) to determine the rate of return it represents. The present value factor is as follows:

$$PV \ factor = \frac{1}{(1 + IRR)} = \frac{\$142,514}{\$149,700} = 0.952 \ (rounded)$$

Use the 1-period line in the table in Exhibit 13B–3 because the cash flow occurs in period 1. Locate 0.952 (or the number closest to it). In our example, 0.952 occurs in the 1-period line under the 5% column. Therefore, we can conclude that the internal rate of return is approximately 5%.

This was a very simple example to illustrate the principle underlying the calculation of the internal rate of return. The table method will provide a rough estimate, within 1%, of the internal rate of return, but will work for only single cash flows or annuities.[5] In practice, a project can last for several years, and have nonconstant cash flows. This makes the *mathematics* (step C) of the calculation complex, but steps A and B will stay the same. Practitioners use computer programs or spreadsheets to complete step C. To illustrate this, consider the next example.

EXAMPLE F

Rivers Company is considering a project to upgrade its wharves. The project cost is estimated at $2.1 million. The annual savings in maintenance costs and revenue from increased barge traffic is projected as follows:

Year	1	2	3	4	5
Cash Flow	$490,000	$445,000	$476,000	$510,000	$435,000

The wharves will require further upgrading after five years; therefore, management is interested in determining if the projected cash flows during the upcoming five-year period are sufficient to warrant proceeding with the proposed upgrade. Determine the internal rate of return of the project.

---

[5]If the single cash flow occurs in year n, the present value factor is written as $1/(1 + IRR)^n$. Locate the present value factor in the n-period line of Exhibit 13B–3 (on the Online Learning Centre) to find the rate of return. When cash flows are an annuity, calculate the annuity factor as follows:

Annuity factor = Investment required ÷ Net annual cash inflow

Then, you would consult Exhibit 13B–4 (on the Online Learning Centre). If the number of periods is 5, you would look in the 5-period line for the annuity factor you calculated to see what rate of return it represents.

Step A:

$$NPV = -\$2,100,000 + \frac{\$490,000}{(1 + IRR)} + \frac{\$445,000}{(1 + IRR)^2} + \frac{\$476,000}{(1 + IRR)^3} + \frac{\$510,000}{(1 + IRR)^4} + \frac{\$435,000}{(1 + IRR)^5}$$

Step B:

$$0 = -\$2,100,000 + \frac{\$490,000}{(1 + IRR)} + \frac{\$445,000}{(1 + IRR)^2} + \frac{\$476,000}{(1 + IRR)^3} + \frac{\$510,000}{(1 + IRR)^4} + \frac{\$435,000}{(1 + IRR)^5}$$

Step C:
Use a spreadsheet program, such as Microsoft Excel. The following screenshot shows the answer.

	A	B	C	D	E	F	G
1				Rivers Company			
2			IRR Calculation for the Wharf Upgrading Project				
3							
4	Year	0	1	2	3	4	5
5	Cash flow	-2,100,000	$490,000	$445,000	$476,000	$510,000	$435,000
6							
7	IRR	3.9869%					
8							

We used the formula = IRR(B5:G5, 0) in cell B7 to compute the internal rate of return. The syntax of the formula is

$$= IRR \text{ (}cell\ range\ for\ the\ cash\ flows,\ initial\ guess\ value\ for\ IRR\text{)}$$

We used a value of 0 for the initial guess. The default is 0.1. The internal rate of return is 3.9869%.

Interpretation and Use of the IRR

The project's internal rate of return is the rate of return *promised* by the cash flows of the project. If the wharf project at Rivers Company provides the cash flows that have been forecast for each year *and*, if each cash flow is immediately reinvested at the rate of 3.9869% per year, then the net present value of the project at a discount rate of 3.9869% will be equal to 0.

This, however, does not tell you how the internal rate of return can be used to decide if a project is worthwhile. For example, should Rivers Company go ahead with the wharf upgrade? To decide whether to accept a project, the internal rate of return must be compared with the company's cost of capital. The cost of capital will play the role of a *hurdle rate*. The logic behind this is that if the project cannot yield at least the cost of the funds tied up in it, it will not be profitable. The decision rule using the internal rate of return can be stated as follows: *If the internal rate of return is equal to or greater than the cost of capital, the project should be accepted. If the internal rate of return is less than the cost of capital, the project should be rejected.*

Suppose the cost of the capital for the wharf project is 5%. Since the internal rate of return of 3.9869% is *less* than the hurdle rate of 5%, Rivers Company will reject the project.

The idea that a project should earn a rate of return greater than the cost of capital to be acceptable is very appealing. This is the basic principle of the internal rate of return method. But the complexity behind the calculation of the internal rate of return can make it appear mysterious. Note that the cost of capital in the internal rate of return method is the hurdle rate. In the net present value method, the cost of capital is the *discount rate*.

Comparison of the IRR and the NPV Methods

There are two issues to consider when comparing the IRR and the NPV methods. The IRR method assumes that the cash flows of the project are reinvested, when received, *at a rate equal to the internal rate of return*. This is a difficult assumption to satisfy, in practice, especially when the internal rate of return is large. The reason is that when cash flows are received, it is unlikely that the firm has other investment opportunities that can provide a rate of return as high as the internal rate of return. It is more reasonable to expect that the firm will have access to projects that will provide a rate of return equalling the opportunity cost of capital. For example, the cash flows can be used to pay off creditors or redeem shares. Such a move will yield a return equal to the opportunity cost of capital. In the net present value method, this is precisely the assumption made, namely, that the cash flows are reinvested at the firm's cost of capital. This makes the NPV method more attractive.

The second issue has to do with the question that many managers ask about the two methods: "Will the two methods provide an identical signal about whether projects should be accepted or rejected?" The answer here is that the net present value will always provide the correct signal regarding acceptance or rejection of project. The IRR method can, in certain situations, provide the wrong signal. A complete explanation of this point cannot be given here, but the bottom line can be stated simply as, *you can always trust the signal provided by the project's NPV*. For this reason, if you are going to use only one method, you should stick with the NPV method.

Other Approaches to Capital Budgeting Decisions

The NPV and IRR methods have gained widespread acceptance as decision-making tools. Other methods of making capital budgeting decisions are also used, however, and are preferred by some managers. In this section, we discuss two such methods known as *payback* and *simple rate of return*. Both methods have been in use for many years, but have been declining in popularity as primary tools for project evaluation.

The Payback Method

The payback method focuses on the *payback period*. The **payback period** is the length of time that it takes for a project to recoup its initial cost out of the cash receipts that it generates. This period is sometimes referred to as the time that it takes for an investment to pay for itself. The basic premise of the payback method is as follows: the more quickly the cost of an investment can be recovered, the more desirable is the investment.

The payback period is expressed in years. *When the net annual cash inflow is the same every year*, the following formula can be used to compute the payback period:

$$\text{Payback period} = \frac{\text{Investment required}}{\text{Net annual cash inflow*}} \qquad (2)$$

*If new equipment is replacing old equipment, this becomes incremental net annual cash inflow.

To illustrate the payback method, assume the following data:

EXAMPLE G
York Company needs a new milling machine. The company is considering two machines: machine A and machine B. Machine A costs $15,000 and will reduce operating costs by $5,000 per year. Machine B costs only $12,000, but will also reduce operating costs by $5,000 per year.

Required:
Which machine should be purchased according to the payback method?

$$\text{Machine A payback period} = \frac{\$15,000}{\$5,000} = 3.0 \text{ years}$$

$$\text{Machine B payback period} = \frac{\$12,000}{\$5,000} = 2.4 \text{ years}$$

According to the payback calculations, York Company should purchase machine B, since it has a shorter payback period than machine A.

Payback and Uneven Cash Flows

When the cash flows associated with an investment project change from year to year, the simple payback formula that we just outlined is no longer usable, and the computations involved in deriving the payback period can be fairly complex. Consider the following data:

Year	Investment	Cash Inflow
1	$4,000	$1,000
2		–0–
3		2,000
4	2,000	1,000
5		500
6		3,000
7		2,000
8		2,000

What is the payback period on this investment? The answer is 5.5 years, but to obtain this figure, you must track the unrecovered investment year by year. The steps involved in this process are shown in Exhibit 13–7. By the middle of the sixth year, sufficient cash inflows will have been realized to recover the entire investment of $6,000 ($4,000 + $2,000).

Year	(1) Beginning Unrecovered Investment	(2) Investment	(3) Cash Inflow	(4) Ending Unrecovered Investment (1) + (2) − (3)
1	$ 0	$4,000	$1,000	$3,000
2	3,000		–0–	3,000
3	3,000		2,000	1,000
4	1,000	2,000	1,000	2,000
5	2,000		500	1,500
6	1,500		3,000	–0–
7	–0–		2,000	–0–
8	–0–		2,000	–0–

Exhibit 13–7
Payback and Uneven Cash Flows

An Extended Example of Payback

As shown by formula (2) on the preceding page, the payback period is computed by dividing the investment in a project by the net annual cash inflows that the project will generate. If new equipment is replacing old equipment, then any salvage to be received on disposal of the old equipment should be deducted from the cost of the new equipment, and only the *incremental* investment should be used in the payback computation. In addition, any amortization deducted in arriving at the project's net income must be added back to obtain the project's expected net annual cash inflow. To illustrate, assume the following data:

EXAMPLE H

Goodtime Fun Centres Inc. operates many outlets in the eastern provinces. Some of the vending machines in one of its outlets provide little revenue, and so the company is considering removing the machines and installing equipment to dispense soft ice cream. The equipment would cost $80,000 and have an eight-year useful life. Incremental annual revenues and costs associated with the sale of ice cream would be as follows:

Sales	$150,000
Less: Cost of ingredients	90,000
Contribution margin	60,000
Less: Fixed expenses:	
Salaries	27,000
Maintenance	3,000
Amortization	10,000
Total fixed expenses	40,000
Net income	$ 20,000

The vending machines can be sold for a $5,000 scrap value. What is the payback period of the proposed project?

An analysis of the payback period of the proposed equipment is given in Exhibit 13–8. Several things should be noted from the data in this exhibit. First, note that amortization is added back to net income to obtain the net annual cash inflow from the new equipment. As stated previously in the chapter, amortization is not a cash outlay; thus, it must be added back to net income to adjust net income to a cash basis. Second, note in the payback computation that the salvage value from the old machines has been deducted from the cost of the new equipment and that only the incremental investment has been used in computing the payback period.

The proposed equipment has a payback period of 2.5 years.

Exhibit 13–8

Computation of the Payback Period

Step 1: *Compute the net annual cash inflow.* Since the net annual cash inflow is not given, it must be computed before the payback period can be determined:

Net income (given above)	$20,000
Add: Noncash deduction for amortization.	10,000
Net annual cash inflow	$30,000

Step 2: *Compute the payback period.* Using the net annual cash inflow figure from step (1), the payback period can be determined as follows:

Cost of the new equipment	$80,000
Less: Salvage value of old equipment	5,000
Investment required	$75,000

$$\text{Payback period} = \frac{\text{Investment required}}{\text{Net annual cash inflow}}$$

$$= \frac{\$75,000}{\$30,000} = 2.5 \text{ years}$$

Investing in an MBA

IN BUSINESS TODAY

The financial benefit of earning an MBA degree is enhanced earning power; the costs include both tuition and the opportunity cost of lost salary for two years. Forbes magazine computed both the net present value and the payback period for 80 full-time MBA programs. Forbes looked at the first five years of enhanced earnings after the degree is granted and the costs of getting the degree. The net present value of an MBA varies a great deal—ranging from over $100,000 at Harvard to $1,000 or less at some institutions. The payback periods show less variation. The quickest paybacks are at Harvard and Ohio State—3.3 years. The slowest payback is about five years. Earnings that extend beyond the five-year horizon are ignored in the Forbes analysis. If these earnings had been included, the net present values of degrees at even the lowest-ranked schools would have increased substantially.

Source: Kurt Brandenhausen, "The Bottom Line on B-Schools," *Forbes*, February 7, 2000, pp. 100–104.

Evaluation of the Payback Method

The payback period only tells a manager how long it will take for a project to recover its investment. It *does not say anything about a project's profitability*. It is possible for a project to have a shorter payback in comparison with another project *and* not be as profitable. There are three reasons for the payback method to potentially mislead a manager.

 KNOW

CC13: Explain the payback method and its potential to mislead a manager.

DIFFERENT USEFUL LIVES   Consider Example G on page 544. Machine B has a shorter payback period than machine A. This suggests that machine B is preferable. However, the example did not provide any data on the useful lives of the machines. Suppose that machine A has a 10-year useful life, whereas machine B has a 5-year useful life. Note that when the useful lives of alternative projects are different, simple comparisons of their net present value or payback period should not be made. Why? It will take two purchases of machine B to provide the same service as machine A. If, on the one hand, a manager is going to use a machine for only five years, then the analysis should include the disposal value of machine A. On the other hand, if the manager intends to operate the machine for 10 years, then the analysis of machine B should include the cash flow from the second purchase of machine B in year 5. Clearly, an analysis that relies only on the payback period will miss these points.

TIME VALUE OF MONEY   The payback period weighs all cash flows equally, regardless of when the cash flows occur. However, we know that cash flows received in a previous period are more valuable than those received in a later period. This flaw in the payback period method can cause a manager to make a wrong decision. Consider the following simple example. Two alternative projects cost $8,000 each. The cash flows from these projects are shown following.

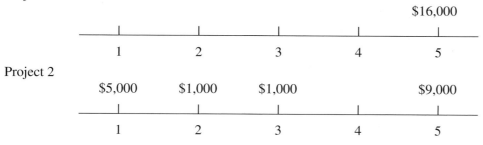

Both projects have a payback period of five years, but project 2 will return most of its cash flows earlier and is, thus, more desirable—a point that will be missed if you rely only on the payback period.

CASH FLOWS BEYOND THE PAYBACK CUTOFF DATE   Sometimes, managers specify that projects must meet a *cutoff* date criterion for the payback period for the project to be acceptable. Such a policy will discard any project that fails to return its cost by the cutoff date. This can be dangerous, since the cash flows that occur beyond the cutoff date are never considered. Consider the following data:

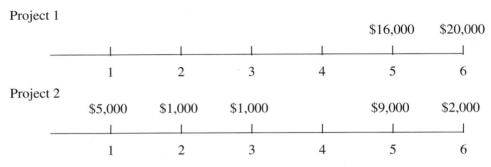

Project 1

| | | | | | $16,000 | $20,000 |

| 1 | 2 | 3 | 4 | 5 | 6 |

Project 2

| $5,000 | $1,000 | $1,000 | | $9,000 | $2,000 |

| 1 | 2 | 3 | 4 | 5 | 6 |

Now, suppose that project 1 and 2 both have a cost of $7,000 and that management wants a payback period of four years or less. Project 2, which has a payback of three years, will pass this test, but project 1 will fail the test and will be rejected. But a net present value analysis will take into consideration all of the cash flows of both projects. Such an analysis will show that project 1 is more profitable than project 2.

In a rapidly changing marketplace, it is not uncommon for managers to demand that projects have small payback periods because if the cash flows do not materialize in the first two years, they are highly unlikely to surface later. Textbook publishing is a good illustration of this concept. Publishers often tell authors that if a textbook is not adopted for use in its first two years after publishing, it is unlikely to find a market thereafter. This also explains why textbooks undergo revision once every three or four years. Be careful. These instances do *not* justify the unquestioning use of the payback method. Note that when rapid payback is suggested, an assumption is made that cash flows beyond the cutoff date are unlikely to be obtained. Therefore, we hope that it is clear to you that the payback method will not always provide the proper signal for project acceptance or rejection and must be used carefully.

The Simple Rate of Return Method

APPLY

CC14: Calculate the SRR of an investment project.

The **simple rate of return (SRR)** method is another capital budgeting technique that does not involve discounted cash flows. The method is also known as the *accounting rate of return*, the *unadjusted rate of return*, and the *financial statement method*.

Unlike the other capital budgeting methods that we have discussed, the simple rate of return method does not focus on cash flows. Rather, it focuses on accounting net income. The approach is to estimate the revenues that will be generated by a proposed investment and then to deduct from these revenues all of the projected operating expenses associated with the project. This net income figure is then related to the initial investment in the project, as shown in the following formula:

$$\text{Simple rate of return} = \frac{\overbrace{\text{Incremental revenues}} - \overbrace{\begin{array}{c}\text{Incremental expenses,}\\\text{including amortization}\end{array}} = \overbrace{\begin{array}{c}\text{Incremental}\\\text{net income}\end{array}}}{\text{Initial investment*}} \tag{3}$$

*The investment should be reduced by any salvage from the sale of old equipment.

Or, if a cost reduction project is involved, formula (3) becomes:

$$\text{Simple rate of return} = \frac{\text{Cost savings} - \text{Amortization on new equipment}}{\text{Initial investment*}} \qquad (4)$$

*The investment should be reduced by any salvage from the sale of old equipment.

EXAMPLE I

Brigham Tea Inc. is a processor of a low-acid tea. The company is contemplating purchasing equipment for an additional processing line. The additional processing line would increase revenues by $90,000 per year. Incremental cash operating expenses would be $40,000 per year. The equipment would cost $180,000 and have a nine-year life. No salvage value is projected.

Required:
Compute the simple rate of return.

SOLUTION:
By applying the formula for the simple rate of return found in formula (3), we can compute the following simple rate of return:

$$\text{Simple rate of return} = \frac{\left[\begin{array}{c} \$90,000 \\ \text{Incremental} \\ \text{revenues} \end{array} \right] - \left[\begin{array}{c} \$40,000 \text{ Cash operating expenses} \\ + \$20,000 \text{ Amortization} \end{array} \right]}{\$180,000 \text{ Initial investment}}$$

$$= \frac{\$30,000}{\$180,000}$$

$$= 16.7\%$$

EXAMPLE J

Midwest Farms Inc. hires people on a part-time basis to sort eggs using an old egg-sorting machine. The cost of this process is $30,000 per year. The company is investigating the purchase of a new egg-sorting machine that would cost $90,000 and have a 15-year useful life. The machine would have negligible salvage value, and it would cost $10,000 per year to operate and maintain. The egg-sorting equipment currently being used could be sold now for a scrap value of $2,500.

Required:
Compute the simple rate of return on the new egg-sorting machine.

SOLUTION:
A cost reduction project is involved in this situation. By applying the formula for the simple rate of return found in formula (4), we can compute the simple rate of return as follows:

$$\text{Simple rate of return} = \frac{\$20,000* \text{ Cost savings} - \$6,000\dagger \text{ Amortization on new equipment}}{\$90,000 - \$2,500}$$

$$= 16.0\%$$

*$30,000 − $10,000 = $20,000 cost savings.
†$90,000 ÷ 15 years = $6,000 amortization.

Criticisms of the SRR Method

The most damaging criticism of the SRR method is that it does not consider the time value of money. A dollar received 10 years from now is viewed as being just as valuable as a dollar received today. Thus, the manager can be misled if the alternatives being considered have different cash flow patterns.

Additionally, many projects do not have uniform cash flows and incremental revenues and expenses over their useful lives. As a result, the simple rate of return will fluctuate from year to year, with the possibility that a project may appear to be desirable in some

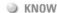 **KNOW**

CC15: Explain the disadvantages of the SRR method for project selection.

years and undesirable in others. In contrast, the NPV method provides a single figure that summarizes all of the cash flows over the entire useful life of the project.

IN BUSINESS TODAY **Social Responsibility Issues in Ecuador**

The stagnant economy of Ecuador has provided an opportunity for Calgary-based oil company EnCana Corp. to dip into the abundant oil reserves of the South American country. Although the company insisted that a win-win situation would be realized for the Ecuadorian stakeholders, citizens have had to live in disarray due to a 500-kilometre Oleoducto de Crudos Pesados (OCP) (Spanish for "heavy crude oil pipeline.") The pipeline currently pumps approximately 50,000 barrels of oil per day. When the pipeline is complete, EnCana anticipates shipping as much as 90,000 barrels per day. This had led many people to protest against the "corporate greed and environmental irresponsibility" which has forced them to live in less than desirable conditions despite the fact the Ecuadorian government, concerned with carrying heavy international debt, has declared OCP a national priority. In mid-2001, the initial investment of US$900 million for OCP was financed by a range of international banks in the face of skepticism expressed by many observers. EnCana, aware of the criticisms of engaging in Third World projects, defended itself by referring to the opportunity provided by the project to boost the Ecuadorian industry. The company believes that whether it operates in Ecuador or Canada, "the objective should be to create wealth for society, including our shareholders, while leaving a legacy which absolutely minimizes negative impacts" (quoted in *World Energy Magazine* in March 2000). Delays, mounting costs, protests, and other uncertainties surrounding the project have led Moody's Investors Service to downgrade OCP's debt rating to almost junk status. EnCana, however, has not wavered in its commitment to the project. With the pipeline at the 85% completion stage, EnCana aims to stick with the project.

Source: Matthew McClearn, "Down the Tube," *Canadian Business*, February 17, 2003, pp. 33–40. Reprinted with permission from *Canadian Business*.

Postaudit of Investment Projects

A **postaudit** of an investment project involves a follow-up after the project has been approved to see whether expected results are actually realized. This is a key part of the capital budgeting process that provides an opportunity to see if realistic data are being submitted to support capital budgeting proposals. It also provides an opportunity to reinforce successful projects as needed, to strengthen or perhaps salvage projects that are encountering difficulty, to terminate unsuccessful projects before losses become too great, and to improve the overall quality of future investment proposals.

In performing a postaudit, the same technique should be used as was used in the original approval process. That is, if a project was approved on the basis of a net present value analysis, then the same procedure should be used in performing the postaudit. However, the data used in the postaudit analysis should be *actual observed data*, rather than estimated data. This affords management an opportunity to make a side-by-side comparison to see how well the project has worked out. It also helps assure that estimated data received on future proposals will be carefully prepared, since the persons submitting the data will know that their estimates will be given careful scrutiny in the postaudit process. Actual results that are far out of line with original estimates should be carefully reviewed by management. Those managers responsible for the original estimates should be required to provide a full explanation of any major differences between estimated and actual results.[6]

---

[6]For further discussion, see Lawrence A. Gordon and Mary D. Myers, "Postauditing Capital Projects," *Management Accounting* 72, no. 7 (January 1991), pp. 39–42. This study of 282 large U.S. companies states that "an increasing number of firms are recognizing the importance of the postaudit stage" (p. 41).

Investor

Each of the following situations is independent. Work out your own solution to each situation, and then check it against the solution provided.

1. John has just reached age 58. In 12 years, he plans to retire. Upon retiring, he would like to take an extended vacation, which he expects will cost at least $4,000. What lump-sum amount must he invest now to have the needed $4,000 at the end of 12 years if the rate of return is:
   a. 8%?
   b. 12%?

2. The Morgans would like to send their daughter to an expensive music camp at the end of each of the next five years. The camp costs $1,000 a year. What lump-sum amount would have to be invested now to have the $1,000 at the end of each year if the rate of return is:
   a. 8%?
   b. 12%?

3. You have just received an inheritance from a relative. You can invest the money and either receive a $20,000 lump-sum amount at the end of 10 years or receive $1,400 at the end of each year for the next 10 years. If your minimum desired rate of return is 12%, which alternative should you select?

Application Competency Summary

Application Competency	Deliverable	Source Documents and Key Information	Steps	Knowledge Competency
Prepare an NPV analysis of two competing projects using either the total-cost approach or the incremental-cost approach. ◷ CC7	*Key Information:* **Total cost approach** The net present value of each of the alternatives being considered **Incremental cost approach** The net present value of the differential cash flows (go versus status quo) –applies only if there are exactly two alternatives *Report/Document* No specific document; report should contain details of the project's NPV analysis	*Source Documents* Various documents that provide information about the cash flows for each alternative and the company's cost of capital *Required Information* Cash flows of the alternatives including working capital requirements and recovery; cost of capital	1. Total cost approach: a) Determine the cash flows of each alternative considered separately. b) Calculate the NPV of each alternative. c) Choose the alternative with highest NPV. 2. Incremental cost approach: a) Determine the differential cash flows (alternative less status quo). b) Calculate the NPV of the differential cash flows. c) Choose the alternative if the NPV is positive; otherwise, choose the status quo.	Identifying the type and amount of cash flows pertaining to an alternative. ◷ CC4 Cost of capital or the opportunity cost of capital appropriate for the risk of the alternative. ◷ CC6 The mechanics of present value calculations. ◷ CC15

continued

Application Competency	Deliverable	Source Documents and Key Information	Steps	Knowledge Competency
Compute the NPV of a project when no revenues are involved. ⚪ CC8	*Key Information:* The alternative with the lowest cost on a present value basis *Report/Document* No specific document/report	*Source Documents* Various documents with information on expenditures and cost savings pertaining to the alternative *Required Information* Cash flows detailing the expenditures and savings in costs relating to an alternative	1. Use either a total cost or a differential cost approach. (The cost savings of an alternative relative to the alternative of status quo can be used.) See above. 2. Remember the relevant cash flows are cost flows; the best decision is the one with the lower present value of costs.	Cost savings are also benefits and certain decision situations will not involve revenues directly; Cost of capital ⚪ CC6 Present value calculation mechanics ⚪ CC15
Rank projects in order of preference using the profitability index. ⚪ CC9	*Key Information:* Project rankings using the profitability index *Report/Document* No specific document	*Source Documents* NPV analysis of each project being ranked *Required Information* Present value of cash flows of each project and the corresponding investment required	Profitability index is the ratio of the present value of the cash flows to the investment required. Calculate as follows: 1. Determine the present value of the cash flows. 2. Compute the ratio of the present value of the cash flows to the investment required.	Present value of relevant cash flows and the value of the investment required
Compute the IRR of an alternative, interpret it, and explain its use for project selection. ⚪ CC10	*Key Information:* The IRR of an alternative, its interpretation and its use in recommending a decision to management *Report/Document* No specific document	As above	1. **Algebraic method:** a) Set up an equation for the NPV calculation using the relevant cash flows and IRR as a discount rate; i.e., write out the expression for the NPV using the cash flows and using the equation $(1 + IRR)$ for the discount factor. b) Set the NPV equal to 0. c) Solve the resulting equation for the IRR. 2. **Spreadsheet method:** This is applied when the project life is two or more periods. a) and b) As above. c) Enter the cash flows on a spreadsheet. Assume that the cell range is B5:G5. Choose a target cell, e.g. B7. In the target cell, enter the formula =IRR(B5:G5, 0). The result in cell B7 will be the IRR.	Identify and determine the relevant cash flows ⚪ CC4 Cost of capital as a hurdle rate and its role in project selection decisions ⚪ CC10

continued

Application Competency	Deliverable	Source Documents and Key Information	Steps	Knowledge Competency
			3. Interpretation and use: The IRR is the number, which, if used as the discount rate, will result in an NPV of 0. This means that if the value of the IRR was also the cost of capital, then the NPV of the project will be 0. The use of a higher opportunity cost of capital logically will lead to a negative NPV; and a lower cost of capital than the IRR will yield a positive NPV. Thus, managers should accept projects if the opportunity cost of capital is less than the IRR.	
Calculate the payback period of an investment project. ◯ CC12	*Key Information:* The payback period of a project *Report/Document* No specific document	*Source Documents* Various documents detailing the timing and the amount of cash flows *Required Information* Timing and amount of the project's cash flows including the investment required	1. **When net annual cash flow is the same for each period:** Apply the formula: Payback period = Investment required ÷ Net annual cash flow. 2. *Uneven cash flows:* a) Proceeding period by period, calculate the ending unrecovered investment as follows: beginning unrecovered investment plus any investment made in the period less the cash inflow during the period. b) The payback period is the period at which the unrecovered investment is zero.	Identification and calculation of the amount and timing of relevant cash flows of a project ◯ CC4
Calculate the SRR of a project. ◯ CC14	*Key Information:* The simple rate of return of a project *Report/Document* No specific document	*Source Documents* Various documents detailing cash flows (timing and amount) *Required Information* Project's cash flows	The method is applied using the incremental cash flow approach. 1) Subtract from the cash flows of a particular alternative to the status quo the cash flow of the status quo, proceeding period by period. and obtain the differential cash flows. 2) Calculate the simple rate of return as follows: Incremental revenues less incremental expenses including amortization expense) ÷ Initial investment net of any cash inflows from closing down the status quo.	Accounting net income versus economic profit

continued

Application Competency	Deliverable	Source Documents and Key Information	Steps	Knowledge Competency
Compute the price index number for a future year given the annual rate of inflation. CC18	*Key Information:* The price index number reflecting the purchasing power of money in a given year relative to that of a base year *Report/Document*	*Source Documents* Documents detailing forecasts of financial variables including the forecasts of the price level *Required Information* Anticipated rate of inflation per period	If year 0 is the base year and the annual rate of inflation is denoted as i, the price index number for a given year n is $(1 + i)^n$. The *price* in the future year (n) relative to the price in the base year will be the base year price multiplied by the price index number.	Concept of compounding and discounting
Compute the NPV of a project when cash flows related to the ownership and disposal of depreciable property are included in the analysis. CC21 and 22	*Key Information:* Project NPV *Report/Document* Report detailing the capital budgeting analysis of the project	*Source Documents* Documents detailing the relevant cash flows such as information about the applicable CCA rates *Required Information* Relevant cash flows including initial investment, investment and recovery of working capital, net annual operating cash flows after taxes, proceeds of salvage, tax rate, CCA rates, discount rate, the tax shields related to the use and disposal of depreciable equipment	Project NPV is calculated as follows: (Capital outlay) + (Investment in working capital) + Present value of net operating cash flow after tax + Present value of the recovery of working capital + Present value of salvage + Present value of the CCA tax shields of equipment.* * Use the formula on page 571 in Appendix 13D (on the Online Learning Centre).	Cash flows identification (amount and timing) CC4 Present value mechanics CC16 Nominal versus real rates of return and cash flows CC17 and 19 Tax-related cash flow impact of depreciable capital property: ownership and use in project CC20

Guidance Answers to Decision Maker and You Decide

NEGOTIATOR FOR THE RED SOX (p. 535)

Apparently, the mayor is suggesting that 100% is the appropriate rate of return for discounting the cash flows that would be received by the city to their net present value. You might respond by pointing out that an organization's cost of capital is usually regarded as the minimum required rate of return. Because the City of Boston does not have shareholders, its cost of capital might be considered the average rate of return that must be paid to its long-term creditors. It is highly unlikely that the city pays interest of 100% on its long-term debt.

Note that it is very possible that the term return on investment is being misused either by the mayor, the media, or both in this situation. The mayor's goal might actually be a 100% recovery of the city's investment from the Red Sox. Rather than expecting a 100% return *on* investment, the mayor may simply want a 100% return *of* investment. Taking the time to clarify the mayor's intent might change the course of negotiations.

INVESTOR (p. 551)

The solutions to the three questions are presented following. If you did not know how to approach these problems or did not arrive at the correct answers, you should study Appendix 13A on the Online Learning Centre.

1. a. The amount that must be invested now would be the present value of the $4,000, using a discount rate of 8%. From Exhibit 13B–3 in Appendix 13B (on the Online Learning Centre), the factor for a

discount rate of 8% for 12 periods is 0.397. Multiplying this discount factor by the $4,000 needed in 12 years will give the amount of the present investment required: $4,000 × 0.397 = $1,588.

  b. We will proceed as we did in part (a), but this time we will use a discount rate of 12%. From Exhibit 13B–3 in Appendix 13B, the factor for a discount rate of 12% for 12 periods is 0.257. Multiplying this discount factor by the $4,000 needed in 12 years will give the amount of the present investment required: $4,000 × 0.257 = $1,028.

  Note that as the discount rate (desired rate of return) increases, the present value decreases.

2. This part differs from part (1) in that we are now dealing with an annuity, rather than with a single future sum. The amount that must be invested now will be the present value of the $1,000 needed at the end of each year for five years. Since we are dealing with an annuity, or a series of annual cash flows, we must refer to Exhibit 13B–4 in Appendix 13B for the appropriate discount factor.

  a. From Exhibit 13B–4 in Appendix 13B, the discount factor for 8% for five periods is 3.993. Therefore, the amount that must be invested now to have $1,000 available at the end of each year for five years is $1,000 × 3.993 = $3,993.

  b. From Exhibit 13B–4 in Appendix 13B, the discount factor for 12% for five periods is 3.605. Therefore, the amount that must be invested now to have $1,000 available at the end of each year for five years is $1,000 × 3.605 = $3,605.

  Again, note that as the discount rate (desired rate of return) increases, the present value decreases. At a higher rate of return, we can invest less than would have been needed if a lower rate of return were being earned.

3. For this part, we will need to refer to both Exhibits 13B–3 and 13B–4 in Appendix 13B. From Exhibit 13B–3, we will need to find the discount factor for 12% for 10 periods, then apply it to the $20,000 lump sum to be received in 10 years. From Exhibit 13B–4, we will need to find the discount factor for 12% for 10 periods, then apply it to the series of $1,400 payments to be received over the 10-year period. Whichever alternative has the higher present value is the one that should be selected.

$$\$20,000 \times 0.322 = \$6,440$$
$$\$1,400 \times 5.650 = \$7,910$$

Thus, you would prefer to receive the $1,400 per year for 10 years, rather than the $20,000 lump sum.

Review Problem: Comparison of Capital Budgeting Methods

Lamar Company is studying a project that would have an eight-year life and require a $1,600,000 investment in equipment. At the end of eight years, the project would terminate and the equipment would have no salvage value. The project would provide net income each year as follows:

Sales..................................		$3,000,000
Less: Variable expenses................		1,800,000
Contribution margin....................		1,200,000
Less: Fixed expenses:		
Advertising, salaries, and other		
fixed out-of-pocket costs............	$700,000	
Amortization	200,000	
Total fixed expenses...................		900,000
Net income...........................		$ 300,000

The company's discount rate is 18%.

Required:
1. Compute the net annual cash inflow from the project.
2. Compute the project's net present value. Is the project acceptable?
3. Compute the project's payback period. If the company requires a maximum payback of three years, is the project acceptable?
4. Compute the project's simple rate of return.

SOLUTION TO REVIEW PROBLEM

1. The net annual cash inflow can be computed by deducting the cash expenses from sales:

Sales...	$3,000,000
Less: Variable expenses.................................	1,800,000
Contribution margin......................................	1,200,000
Less: Advertising, salaries, and other fixed out-of-pocket costs.....................................	700,000
Net annual cash inflow	$ 500,000

Or it can be computed by adding back amortization to net income:

Net income...	$300,000
Add: Noncash deduction for amortization............	200,000
Net annual cash inflow	$500,000

2. The net present value can be computed as follows:

Item	Year(s)	Amount of Cash Flows	18% Factor	Present Value of Cash Flows
Cost of new equipment.....	Now	$(1,600,000)	1.000	$(1,600,000)
Net annual cash inflow.....	1–8	500,000	4.078	2,039,000
Net present value..........				$ 439,000

Yes, the project is acceptable, because it has a positive net present value.

3. The formula for the payback period is as follows:

$$\text{Payback period} = \frac{\text{Investment required}}{\text{Net annual cash inflow}}$$

$$= \frac{\$1,600,000}{\$500,000}$$

$$= 3.2 \text{ years}$$

No, the project is not acceptable when measured by the payback method. The 3.2 years payback period is greater than the maximum three years set by the company.

4. The formula for the simple rate of return is as follows:

$$\text{Simple rate of return} = \frac{\overset{\text{Incremental}}{\text{revenues}} - \overset{\text{Incremental expenses,}}{\text{including amortization}} = \overset{\text{Net}}{\text{income}}}{\text{Initial investment}}$$

$$= \frac{\$300,000}{\$1,600,000}$$

$$= 18.75\%$$

Glossary

Capital budgeting The process of planning significant outlays on projects that have long-term implications, such as the purchase of new equipment or the introduction of a new product. (p. 530)
Capital cost allowance (CCA) The amount allowed as a tax deduction for the calculation of amortization. (p. 534)
Cost of capital The average rate of return the company must pay to its long-term creditors and to shareholders for the use of their funds. (p. 534)

Internal rate of return (IRR) The discount rate at which the net present value of an investment project is zero; thus, the internal rate of return represents the return promised by a project over its useful life. (p. 541)

Net present value (NPV) The difference between the present value of the cash inflows and the present value of the cash outflows of an investment project. (p. 531)

Out-of-pocket costs Actual cash outlays for salaries, advertising, repairs, and similar costs. (p. 536)

Payback period The length of time that it takes for a project to recover its initial cost out of the cash receipts that it generates. (p. 544)

Postaudit The follow-up after a project has been approved and implemented to determine whether expected results are actually realized. (p. 550)

Preference decision A decision as to which of several competing acceptable investment proposals is best. (p. 530)

Profitability index The ratio of the present value of a project's cash inflows to the investment required. (p. 540)

Screening decision A decision as to whether a proposed investment meets some preset standard of acceptance. (p. 530)

Simple rate of return (SRR) The rate of return computed by dividing a project's annual accounting net income by the initial investment required. (p. 548)

Working capital The excess of current assets over current liabilities. (p. 532)

Questions

13–1   What is the difference between capital budgeting screening decisions and capital budgeting preference decisions?

13–2   What is meant by the term *time value of money?*

13–3   What is meant by the term *discounting?*

13–4   Why is the NPV method of making capital budgeting decisions superior to other methods, such as the payback and SRR methods?

13–5   What is NPV? Can it ever be negative? Explain.

13–6   If a firm has to pay interest of 14% on long-term debt, then its cost of capital is 14%. Do you agree? Explain.

13–7   What is meant by an investment project's internal rate of return? How is the internal rate of return computed?

13–8   Explain how the cost of capital serves as a screening tool when dealing with the NPV method.

13–9   As the discount rate increases, the present value of a given future cash flow also increases. Do you agree? Explain.

13–10 Refer to Exhibit 13–2. Is the return on this investment proposal exactly 20%, slightly more than 20%, or slightly less than 20%? Explain.

13–11 Why are preference decisions sometimes called *rationing* decisions?

13–12 How is the profitability index computed, and what does it measure?

13–13 What is the preference rule for ranking investment projects under the net present value method?

13–14 Can an investment with a profitability index of less than 1.00 be an acceptable investment? Explain.

13–15 What is meant by the term *payback period?* How is the payback period determined?

13–16 How can the payback method be useful to the manager?

13–17 What is the major criticism of the payback and SRR methods of making capital budgeting decisions?

Brief Exercises

BRIEF EXERCISE 13–1   NPV Method (CC3)
The management of Kunkel Company is considering the purchase of a machine that would reduce operating costs. The machine will cost $40,000, and it will last for eight years. At the end of the eight-year period, the machine will have zero scrap value. Use of the machine will reduce operating costs by $7,000 per year. The company requires a minimum return of 12% before taxes on all investment projects.

Required:
1. Determine the net present value of the investment in the machine.
2. What is the difference between the total, undiscounted cash inflows and cash outflows over the entire life of the machine?

BRIEF EXERCISE 13–2   NPV Analysis of Competing Projects (CC7)

Labeau Products Ltd., of Perth, Australia, has $122,500 to invest. The company is trying to decide between two alternative uses for the funds. The alternatives follow:

	Invest in Project X	Invest in Project Y
Investment required	$122,500	$122,500
Annual cash inflows	31,500	—
Single cash inflow at the end of 10 years	—	525,000
Life of the project	10 years	10 years

The company's discount rate is 18%.

Required:
Which alternative would you recommend that the company accept? Show all computations using the NPV approach. Prepare a separate computation for each project.

BRIEF EXERCISE 13–3   Profitability Index (CC9)

Information on four investment proposals is provided following:

	Investment Proposal			
	A	B	C	D
Investment required.	$(45,000)	$(50,000)	$(35,000)	$(60,000)
Present value of cash inflows ..	63,000	45,000	52,500	80,000
Net present value.	$ 18,000	$ (5,000)	$ 17,500	$ 20,000
Life of the project	5 years	7 years	6 years	6 years

Required:
1. Compute the profitability index for each investment proposal.
2. Rank the proposals in terms of preference.

BRIEF EXERCISE 13–4   Payback Method (CC10)

The management of Unter Corporation is considering an investment with the following characteristics:

Year	Investment	Cash Inflow
1.	$15,000	$1,000
2.	8,000	2,000
3.	—	2,500
4.	—	4,000
5.	—	5,000
6.	—	6,000
7.	—	5,000
8.	—	4,000
9.	—	3,000
10.	—	2,000

Required:
1. Determine the payback period of the investment.
2. Would the payback period be affected if the cash inflow in the last year were several times as large?

BRIEF EXERCISE 13–5   SRR Method (CC14)

The management of Ballard MicroBrew is considering the purchase of an automated bottling machine for $120,000. The machine would replace an old piece of equipment that costs $30,000 per year to operate. The new machine would have a useful life of 10 years with no salvage value. The new machine would cost $12,000 per year to operate. The old machine currently in use could be sold now for a scrap value of $40,000.

Required:
Compute the SRR on the new automated bottling machine.

BRIEF EXERCISE 13–6   Payback Period (CC10)

Puerto Airlines is considering an investment of $330,000 in loading equipment. Management anticipates net cash savings of $100,000 in year 1. The savings will increase by 50% in year 2 and then increase by another 40% in year 3. The minimum desired rate of return is 15%.

Required:
What is the payback period for this investment?

(Adapted © CGA-Canada)

BRIEF EXERCISE 13–7   Varied Capital Budgeting Decisions (CC10, 12)

Treat each part independently.

Required:
1. How many years, approximately, would it take for your money to double with a 12% interest rate?
2. A $100,000 investment is expected to generate $27,750 in cash savings at the end of five years. What is the approximate internal rate of return?

(Adapted © CGA-Canada)

BRIEF EXERCISE 13–8   Payback Period (CC10)

The following data relate to a new machine purchased by a company to increase its production:

Cost	$ 45,000
Salvage value at the end of the 5th year	18,000
Estimated annual cost savings from the new machine	6,500
Life	5 years
Amortization method.	Straight-line
Average tax rate.	30%

Required:
What is the payback period?

(Adapted © CGA-Canada)

Exercises

EXERCISE 13–1   NPV Analysis (CC3, 7)

Windhoek Mines Ltd. of Namibia is contemplating the purchase of equipment to exploit a mineral deposit that is located on land to which the company has mineral rights. An engineering and cost analysis has been made, and it is expected that the following cash flows would be associated with opening and operating a mine in the area:

Cost of new equipment and timbers	R206,250
Working capital required	75,000
Net annual cash receipts	90,000*
Cost to construct new roads in three years	30,000
Salvage value of equipment in four years	48,750

*Receipts from sales of ore, less out-of-pocket costs for salaries, utilities, insurance, and so forth.

(The currency in Namibia is the rand, here denoted by R.)

It is estimated that the mineral deposit would be exhausted after four years of mining. At that point, the working capital would be released for reinvestment elsewhere. The company's discount rate is 20%.

Required:
Determine the NPV of the proposed mining project. Should the project be accepted? Explain.

EXERCISE 13–2   NPV Analysis of Competing Projects (CC7)
Perrot Industries has $265,000 to invest. The company is trying to decide between two alternative uses of the funds. The alternatives follow:

	Project	
	A	**B**
Cost of equipment required	$265,000	—
Working capital investment required	—	$265,000
Annual cash inflows.	55,650	42,400
Salvage value of equipment in six years	21,200	—
Life of the project	6 years	6 years

The working capital needed for project B will be released at the end of six years for investment elsewhere. Perrot Industries' discount rate is 14%.

Required:
Which investment alternative (if either) would you recommend that the company accept? Show all computations using the NPV method. Prepare a separate computation for each project.

EXERCISE 13–3   Profitability Index (CC9)
The management of Revco Products is exploring five different investment opportunities. Information on the five projects under study follows:

	Project Number				
	1	**2**	**3**	**4**	**5**
Investment required.	$(270,000)	$(450,000)	$(400,000)	$(360,000)	$(480,000)
Present value of cash inflows at a 10% discount rate	336,140	522,970	379,760	433,400	567,270
Net present value.	$ 66,140	$ 72,970	$ (20,240)	$ 73,400	$ 87,270
Life of the project	6 years	3 years	5 years	12 years	6 years

The company's required rate of return is 10%; thus, a 10% discount rate has been used in the preceding present value computations. Limited funds are available for investment, and so the company cannot accept all of the available projects.

Required:
1. Compute the profitability index for each investment project.
2. Rank the five projects according to preference, in terms of:
   a. Net present value.
   b. Profitability index.
3. Which ranking do you prefer? Why?

EXERCISE 13–4   Payback and SRR Methods (CC10, 14)
A piece of labour-saving equipment has just come onto the market that Mitsui Electronics Ltd. could use to reduce costs in one of its plants in Japan. Relevant data relating to the equipment follow (currency is in thousands of yen, denoted by ¥):

Purchase cost of the equipment	¥216,000
Annual cost savings that will be provided by the equipment	¥45,000
Life of the equipment.	12 years

Required:
1. Compute the payback period for the equipment. If the company requires a payback period of four years or less, would the equipment be purchased?
2. Compute the simple rate of return on the equipment. Use straight-line amortization based on the equipment's useful life. Would the equipment be purchased if the company requires a rate of return of at least 14%?

EXERCISE 13–5   Basic Present Value Concepts (CC7)

Kathy Myers frequently purchases shares and bonds, but she is uncertain how to determine the rate of return that she is earning. For example, three years ago she paid $13,000 for 200 common shares of Malti Company. She received a $420 cash dividend on the shares at the end of each year for three years. At the end of three years, she sold the shares for $16,000. Kathy would like to earn a return of at least 14% on all of her investments. She is not sure whether the Malti Company shares provided a 14% return and would like some help with the necessary computations.

Required:
Using the NPV method, determine whether the Malti Company shares provided a 14% return. Round all computations to the nearest whole dollar.

EXERCISE 13–6 IRR and NPV (CC7, 12)

Scalia's Cleaning Service is investigating the purchase of an ultrasound machine for cleaning window blinds. The machine would cost $136,700, including invoice cost, freight, and training of employees to operate it. Scalia's has estimated that the new machine would increase the company's cash flows, net of expenses, by $25,000 per year. The machine would have a 14-year useful life with no expected salvage value.

Required:
(Ignore income taxes.)
1. Compute the machine's internal rate of return to the nearest whole percent.
2. Compute the machine's net present value. Use a discount rate of 16%, and use the format shown in Exhibit 13–5. Why do you have a zero net present value?
3. Suppose that the new machine would increase the company's annual cash flows, net of expenses, by only $20,000 per year. Under these conditions, compute the internal rate of return to the nearest whole percent.

EXERCISE 13–7   IRR (CC12)

NutCo Inc.'s sales forecasts for the next four years are 500,000 nut bars a year. The president estimates that he can save $800 per year in fixed cash operating costs plus $0.05/bar during the next four years if he buys a machine to automate the process at a cost of $90,000. A salvage value of $6,000 is expected at the end of the four-year period. The company's minimum desired rate of return is 10%.

Required:
What is the internal rate of return for the investment of the machine?

(Adapted © CGA-Canada)

Problems

PROBLEM 13–1   Basic NPV Analysis (CC7)

The Sweetwater Candy Company would like to buy a new machine that would automatically dip chocolates. The dipping operation is currently done largely by hand. The machine the company is considering costs $120,000. The manufacturer estimates that the machine would be usable for 12 years, but would require the replacement of several key parts at the end of the sixth year. These parts would cost $9,000, including installation. After 12 years, the machine could be sold for about $7,500.

The company estimates that the cost to operate the machine will be only $7,000 per year. The present method of dipping chocolates costs $30,000 per year. In addition to reducing costs, the new machine will increase production by 6,000 boxes of chocolates per year. The company realizes a contribution margin of $1.50 per box. A 20% rate of return is required on all investments.

Required:
1. What are the net annual cash inflows that will be provided by the new dipping machine?
2. Compute the new machine's net present value. Use the incremental cost approach and round all dollar amounts to the nearest whole dollar.

CHECK FIGURE
(1) Annual cash flows: $32,000

CHECK FIGURE
(1) Annual cash receipts:
$66,108

PROBLEM 13–2   NPV Analysis (CC7)

In eight years, Kent Duncan will retire. He has $300,000 to invest, and he is exploring the possibility of opening a self-service car wash. The car wash could be managed in the free time he has available from his regular occupation, and it could be closed easily when he retires. After careful study, Kent has determined the following:

a. A building, in which a car wash could be installed, is available under an eight-year lease at a cost of $3,400 per month.
b. Purchase and installation costs of equipment would total $300,000. In eight years, the equipment could be sold for about 10% of its original cost.
c. An investment of an additional $4,000 would be required to cover working capital needs for cleaning supplies, change funds, and so forth. After eight years, this working capital would be released for investment elsewhere.
d. Both a car wash and a vacuum service would be offered with a wash costing $3.00 and the vacuum costing 50 cents per use.
e. The only variable costs associated with the operation would be 46 cents per wash for water and 20 cents per use of the vacuum for electricity.
f. In addition to rent, monthly costs of operation would be: cleaning, $900; insurance, $150; and maintenance, $1,000.
g. Gross receipts from the car wash would be about $2,700 per week. According to the experience of other car washes, 70% of the customers using the wash would also use the vacuum.

Kent will not open the car wash unless it provides at least a 10% return, since this is the amount that could be earned by simply placing the $300,000 in high-grade securities.

Required:
1. Assuming that the car wash will be open 52 weeks a year, compute the expected net annual cash receipts (gross cash receipts less cash disbursements) from its operation. (Do not include the cost of the equipment, the working capital, or the salvage value in these computations.)
2. Would you advise Kent to open the car wash? Show computations using the NPV method of investment analysis. Round all dollar figures to the nearest whole dollar.

CHECK FIGURE
(1) NPV: $2,119 in favour
of new truck

PROBLEM 13–3   Total-Cost and Incremental-Cost Approaches (CC7)

Bilboa Freightlines, S.A., of Panama, has a small truck that it uses for intracity deliveries. The truck is in bad repair and must be either overhauled or replaced with a new truck. The company has assembled the following information. (Panama uses the U.S. dollar as its currency):

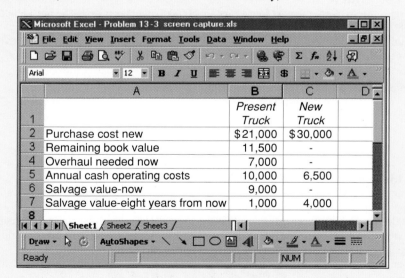

A	B	C
	Present Truck	*New Truck*
Purchase cost new	$21,000	$30,000
Remaining book value	11,500	-
Overhaul needed now	7,000	-
Annual cash operating costs	10,000	6,500
Salvage value-now	9,000	-
Salvage value-eight years from now	1,000	4,000

If the company keeps and overhauls its present delivery truck, then the truck will be usable for eight more years. If a new truck is purchased, it will be used for eight years, after which it will be traded in on another truck. The new truck would be diesel-operated, resulting in a substantial reduction in annual operating costs, as shown above.

The company computes depreciation on a straight-line basis. All investment projects are evaluated using a 16% discount rate.

Required:
1. Should Bilboa Freightlines keep the old truck or purchase the new one? Use the total-cost approach to net present value in making your decision. Round to the nearest whole dollar.
2. Redo part (1), this time using the incremental-cost approach.

PROBLEM 13–4   Keep or Sell Property (CC7)

Raul Martinas, professor of languages at Eastern University, owns a small office building adjacent to the university campus. He acquired the property 10 years ago at a total cost of $530,000—$50,000 for the land and $480,000 for the building. He has just received an offer from a realty company that wants to purchase the property; however, the property has been a good source of income over the years, and so Professor Martinas is unsure whether he should keep it or sell it. His alternatives are as follows:

a. **Keep the property.** Professor Martinas' accountant has kept careful records of the income realized from the property over the past 10 years. These records indicate the following annual revenues and expenses:

Rental receipts		$140,000
Less: Building expenses:		
Utilities	$25,000	
Amortization of building	16,000	
Property taxes and insurance	18,000	
Repairs and maintenance	9,000	
Custodial help and supplies	40,000	108,000
Net operating income		$ 32,000

Professor Martinas makes a $12,000 mortgage payment each year on the property. The mortgage will be paid off in eight more years. He has been amortizing the building by the straight-line method, assuming a salvage value of $80,000 for the building, which he still thinks is an appropriate figure. He feels sure that the building can be rented for another 15 years. He also feels sure that 15 years from now the land will be worth three times what he paid for it.

b. **Sell the property.** A realty company has offered to purchase the property by paying $175,000 immediately and $26,500 per year for the next 15 years. Control of the property would go to the realty company immediately. To sell the property, Professor Martinas would need to pay the mortgage off, which could be done by making a lump-sum payment of $90,000.

Required:

Assume that Professor Martinas requires a 12% rate of return. Would you recommend he keep or sell the property? Show computations using the total-cost approach to net present value.

PROBLEM 13–5   Ranking of Projects (CC7, 9)

Oxford Company has limited funds available for investment and must ration the funds among five competing projects. Selected information on the five projects follows:

Project	Investment Required	Net Present Value	Life of the Project (years)
A	$480,000	$132,969	7
B	405,000	126,000	12
C	300,000	105,105	7
D	525,000	114,408	3
E	450,000	(26,088)	6

The net present values above have been computed using a 10% discount rate. The company wants your assistance in determining which project to accept first, which to accept second, and so on.

CHECK FIGURE
Keep the property alternative: $309,402 PV of cash flows

CHECK FIGURE
(1) Project B profitability index: 1.31

Required:

1. Compute the profitability index for each project.
2. In order of preference, rank the five projects in terms of:
   a. Net present value.
   b. Profitability index.
3. Which ranking do you prefer? Why?

CHECK FIGURE
(2) Return: 15.0%

PROBLEM 13–6   SRR and Payback Methods (CC10, 14)

Sharkey's Fun Centre contains a number of electronic games, as well as a miniature golf course and various rides located outside the building. Paul Sharkey, the owner, would like to construct a water slide on one portion of his property. Paul has gathered the following information about the slide:

a. Water slide equipment could be purchased and installed at a cost of $330,000. According to the manufacturer, the slide would be usable for 12 years, after which it would have no salvage value.
b. Paul would use straight-line amortization on the slide equipment.
c. To make room for the water slide, several rides would be dismantled and sold. These rides are fully amortized, but they could be sold for $60,000 to an amusement park in a nearby city.
d. Paul has concluded that about 50,000 more people would use the water slide each year than have been using the rides. The admission price would be $3.60 per person (the same price that the Fun Centre has been charging for the rides).
e. On the basis of experience at other water slides, Paul estimates that incremental operating expenses each year for the slide would be as follows: salaries, $85,000; insurance, $4,200; utilities, $13,000; and maintenance, $9,800.

Required:

1. Prepare an income statement showing the expected incremental net income each year from the water slide.
2. Compute the SRR expected from the water slide. On the basis of this computation, would the water slide be constructed if Paul requires an SRR of at least 14% on all investments?
3. Compute the payback period for the water slide. If Paul requires a payback period of five years or less, should the water slide be constructed?

CHECK FIGURE
(1b) Return: 13.1%

PROBLEM 13–7   SRR and Payback Analyses of Two Machines (CC10, 14)

Westwood Furniture Company is considering the purchase of two different machines, as described following:

Machine A. A compacting machine has just come onto the market that would permit Westwood Furniture Company to compress sawdust into various shelving products. At present the sawdust is disposed of as a waste product. The following information is available on the machine:

  a. The machine would cost $420,000 and would have a 10% salvage value at the end of its 13-year useful life. The company uses straight-line amortization and considers salvage value in computing amortization deductions.
  b. The shelving products manufactured from use of the machine would generate revenues of $300,000 per year. Variable manufacturing costs would be 20% of sales.
  c. Fixed expenses associated with the new shelving products would be as follows (per year): advertising, $40,000: salaries, $110,000; utilities, $5,200; and insurance, $800.

Machine B. A second machine has come onto the market that would allow Westwood Furniture Company to automate a sanding process that is now done largely by hand. The following information is available:

  a. The new sanding machine would cost $234,000 and would have no salvage value at the end of its 13-year useful life. The company would use straight-line amortization on the new machine.
  b. Several old pieces of sanding equipment that are fully amortized would be disposed of at a scrap value of $9,000.
  c. The new sanding machine would provide substantial annual savings in cash operating costs. It would require an operator at an annual salary of $16,350 and $5,400 in annual maintenance costs. The current, hand-operated sanding procedure costs the company $78,000 per year in total.

Westwood Furniture Company requires a simple rate of return of 15% on all equipment purchases. Also, the company will not purchase equipment unless the equipment has a payback period of four years or less.

Required:
1. For machine A:
   a. Prepare an income statement showing the expected net income each year from the new shelving products. Use the contribution format.
   b. Compute the simple rate of return.
   c. Compute the payback period.
2. For machine B:
   a. Compute the simple rate of return.
   b. Compute the payback period.
3. According to the company's criteria, which machine, if either, should the company purchase?

PROBLEM 13–8   NPV Analysis of Securities (CC7)

Linda Clark received $175,000 from her mother's estate. She placed the funds into the hands of a broker, who purchased the following securities on Linda's behalf:

a. Common shares were purchased at a cost of $95,000. The shares paid no dividends, but they were sold for $160,000 at the end of three years.
b. Preferred shares were purchased at their par value of $30,000. The shares paid a 6% dividend (based on par value) each year for three years. At the end of three years, the shares were sold for $27,000.
c. Bonds were purchased at a cost of $50,000. The bonds paid $3,000 in interest every six months. After three years, the bonds were sold for $52,700. (Note: In discounting a cash flow that occurs semiannually, the procedure is to halve the discount rate and double the number of periods. Use the same procedure in discounting the proceeds from the sale.)

The securities were all sold at the end of three years so that Linda would have funds available to open a new business venture. The broker stated that the investments had earned more than a 16% return, and he gave Linda the following computation to support his statement:

Common shares:	
Gain on sale ($160,000 − $95,000)	$65,000
Preferred shares:	
Dividends paid (6% × $30,000 × 3 years).	5,400
Loss on sale ($27,000 − $30,000)	(3,000)
Bonds:	
Interest paid ($3,000 × 6 periods).	18,000
Gain on sale ($52,700 − $50,000)	2,700
Net gain on all investments	$88,100

$$\frac{\$88{,}100 \div 3 \text{ years}}{\$175{,}000} = 16.8\%$$

Required:
1. Using a 16% discount rate, compute the net present value of *each* of the three investments. On which investment(s) did Linda earn a 16% rate of return? (Round computations to the nearest whole dollar.)
2. Considering all three investments together, did Linda earn a 16% rate of return? Explain.
3. Linda wants to use the $239,700 proceeds ($160,000 + $27,000 + $52,700 = $239,700) from sale of the securities to open a retail store under a 12-year franchise contract. What net annual cash inflow must the store generate for Linda to earn a 14% return over the 12-year period? Round computations to the nearest whole dollar.

PROBLEM 13–9   IRR; Sensitivity Analysis (CC12)

Dr. Heidi Floss is the managing partner of the Crestwood Dental Clinic. Floss is trying to determine whether the clinic should move patient files and other items out of a spare room in the clinic and use the room for dental work. She has determined that it would require an investment of $142,950 for equipment and related costs to prepare the room for use. On the basis of receipts being generated from other rooms in the clinic, Black estimates that the new room would generate a net cash inflow of $37,500 per year. The equipment purchased for the room would have a seven-year estimated useful life.

Required:
(Ignore income taxes.)

1. Compute the IRR on the equipment for the new room to the nearest whole percent. Verify your answer by computing the NPV of the equipment using the IRR you have computed as the discount rate.
2. Although seven years is the average life for dental equipment, Floss knows that due to changing technology, this life can vary substantially. Compute the IRR to the nearest whole percent if the life of the equipment was (*a*) five years and (*b*) nine years, rather than seven years. Is there any information provided by these computations that you would be particularly anxious to show Floss?
3. Refer to the original data. Assume that the equipment is purchased and that the room is opened for dental use. However, due to an increasing number of dentists in the area, the clinic is able to generate only $30,000 per year in net cash receipts from the new room. At the end of five years, the clinic closes the room and sells the equipment to a newly licensed dentist for a cash price of $61,375. Compute the IRR (to the nearest whole percent) that the clinic earned on its investment over the five-year period. Round all dollar amounts to the nearest whole dollar. (Hint: A useful way to proceed is to find the discount rate that will cause the net present value of the investment to be equal to, or near, zero).

CHECK FIGURE
(1) SRR = 14.2%
    (rounded)

PROBLEM 13–10   SRR; Payback; IRR (CC10, 12, 14)

Château Beaune is a family-owned winery located in the Burgundy region of France, headed by Gerard Despinoy. The harvesting season in early fall is the busiest time of the year for the winery, and many part-time workers are hired to help pick and process grapes. Despinoy is investigating the purchase of a harvesting machine that would significantly reduce the amount of labour required in the picking process. The harvesting machine is built to straddle grapevines, which are laid out in low-lying rows. Two workers are carried on the machine just above ground level, one on each side of the vine. As the machine slowly crawls through the vineyard, the workers cut bunches of grapes from the vines, and the grapes fall into a hopper. The machine separates the grapes from the stems and other woody debris. The debris is then pulverized and spread behind the machine as a rich ground mulch. Despinoy has gathered the following information relating to the decision of whether to purchase the machine (the French currency is the euro, which is denoted by the symbol €):

a. The winery would save €190,000 per year in labour costs with the new harvesting machine. In addition, the company would no longer have to purchase and spread ground mulch—at an annual savings of €10,000.
b. The harvesting machine would cost €480,000. It would have an estimated 12-year useful life and zero salvage value. The winery uses straight-line amortization.
c. Annual out-of-pocket costs associated with the harvesting machine would be insurance, €1,000; fuel, €9,000; and a maintenance contract, €12,000. In addition, two operators would be hired and trained for the machine, and they would be paid a total of €70,000 per year, including all benefits.
d. Despinoy feels that the investment in the harvesting machine should earn at least a 16% rate of return.

Required:
(Ignore income taxes.)

1. Determine the annual net savings in cash operating costs that would be realized if the harvesting machine was purchased.
2. Compute the SRR expected from the harvesting machine. (Hint: This is a cost-reduction project.)
3. Compute the payback period on the harvesting machine. Despinoy will not purchase equipment unless it has a payback period of five years or less. Under this criterion, should the harvesting machine be purchased?
4. Compute (to the nearest whole percent) the IRR promised by the harvesting machine. On the basis of this computation, does it appear that the SRR is an accurate guide in investment decisions?

Building Your Skills

CHECK FIGURE
(1) NPV: $78,001 in
    favour of leasing

ANALYTICAL THINKING   (CC7)

Top-Quality Stores Inc. owns a nationwide chain of supermarkets. The company is going to open another store soon, and a suitable building site has been located in an attractive and rapidly growing area. In discussing how the company can acquire the desired building and other facilities needed to open the new store, Sam Watkins, the company's vice-president in charge of sales, stated, "I know most of our competitors are starting to lease facilities, rather than buy, but I just can't see the economics of it. Our development people tell me that we can buy the building site, put a building on it, and get all the store fixtures we need for just $850,000. They also say that property taxes, insurance, and repairs would run $20,000 a year."

When you figure that we plan to keep a site for 18 years, that's a total cost of $1,210,000. But then when you realize that the property will be worth at least a half million in 18 years, that's a net cost to us of only $710,000. What would it cost to lease the property?"

"I understand that Beneficial Insurance Company is willing to purchase the building site, construct a building and install fixtures to our specifications, and then lease the facility to us for 18 years at an annual lease payment of $120,000," replied Lisa Coleman, the company's executive vice-president.

"That's just my point," said Sam. "At $120,000 a year, it would cost us a cool $2,160,000 over the 18 years. That's three times what it would cost to buy, and what would we have left at the end? Nothing! The building would belong to the insurance company!"

"You're overlooking a few things," replied Lisa. "For one thing, the treasurer's office says that we could only afford to put $350,000 down if we buy the property, and then we would have to pay the other $500,000 off over four years at $175,000 a year. So, there would be some interest involved on the purchase side that you haven't figured in."

"But that little bit of interest is nothing compared with over 2 million bucks for leasing," said Sam. "Also, if we lease, I understand we would have to put up an $8,000 security deposit that we wouldn't get back until the end. And besides that, we would still have to pay all the yearly repairs and maintenance costs just like we owned the property. No wonder those insurance companies are so rich if they can swing deals like this."

"Well, I'll admit that I don't have all the figures sorted out yet," replied Lisa. "But I do have the operating cost breakdown for the building, which includes $7,500 annually for property taxes, $8,000 for insurance, and $4,500 for repairs and maintenance. If we lease, Beneficial will handle its own insurance costs and, of course, the owner will have to pay the property taxes. I'll put all this together and see if leasing makes any sense with our required rate of return of 16%. The president wants a presentation and recommendation in the executive committee meeting tomorrow. Let's see, Development said the first lease payment would be due now and the remaining ones due in years 1–17. Development also said that this store should generate a net cash inflow that's well above the average for our stores."

Required:

1. Using the NPV approach, determine whether Top-Quality Stores Inc. should lease or buy the new facility. Assume that you will be making your presentation before the company's executive committee, and remember that the president detests sloppy, disorganized reports.
2. What reply will you make in the meeting if Sam Watkins brings up the issue of the building's future sales value?

COMMUNICATING IN PRACTICE   (CC3, 12, 14)

Use an online yellow pages directory, such as www.superpages.ca, or www.411.ca, to find a manufacturer in your area that has a website. Make an appointment with the controller or chief financial officer of the company. Before your meeting, find out as much as you can about the organization's operations from its website.

Required:

After asking the following questions about a capital budgeting decision that was made by the management of the company, write a brief memorandum to your instructor that summarizes the information obtained from the company's website and addresses what you found out during your interview.

1. What was the nature of the capital project?
2. What was the total cost of the capital project?
3. Did the project costs stay within budget (or estimate)?
4. What financial criteria were used to evaluate the project?

TEAMWORK IN ACTION   (CC3, 7, 9)

Kingsley Products Ltd. is using a model 400 shaping machine to make one of its products. The company is expecting to have a large increase in demand for the product and is anxious to expand its production capacity. Two possibilities are under consideration:

CHECK FIGURE
(1) NPV: $30,046 in favour of the model 400 machine

Alternative 1. Purchase another model 400 shaping machine to operate along with the currently owned model 400 machine.

Alternative 2. Purchase a model 800 shaping machine and use the currently owned model 400 machine as standby equipment. The model 800 machine is a high-speed unit with double the capacity of the model 400 machine.

The following additional information is available on the two alternatives:

a. Both the model 400 machine and the model 800 machine have a 10-year life from the time they are first used in production. The scrap value of both machines is negligible and can be ignored. Straight-line amortization is used.

b. The cost of a new model 800 machine is $300,000.

c. The model 400 machine now in use cost $160,000 three years ago. Its present book value is $112,000, and its present market value is $90,000.

d. A new model 400 machine costs $170,000 now. If the company decides not to buy the model 800 machine, then the currently owned model 400 machine will have to be replaced in seven years at a cost of $200,000. The replacement machine will be sold at the end of the tenth year for $140,000.

e. Production over the next 10 years is expected to be as follows:

Year	Production in Units
1	40,000
2	60,000
3	80,000
4–10	90,000

f. The two models of machines are not equally efficient. Comparative variable costs per unit are as follows:

	Model	
	400	800
Materials per unit	$0.25	$0.40
Direct labour per unit	0.49	0.16
Supplies and lubricants per unit	0.06	0.04
Total variable cost per unit	$0.80	$0.60

g. The model 400 machine is less costly to maintain than the model 800 machine. Annual repairs and maintenance costs on a model 400 machine are $2,500.

h. Repairs and maintenance costs on a model 800 machine, with a model 400 machine used as standby, would total $3,800 per year.

i. No other factory costs will change as a result of the decision between the two machines.

j. Kingsley Products requires a 20% rate of return on all investments.

Required:

The team should discuss and then respond to the following. All team members should agree with and understand the answers (including the calculations supporting the answers) and be prepared to report the information developed in class. (Each teammate can assume responsibility for a different part of the presentation.)

1. Which alternative should the company choose? Use the NPV approach.

2. Suppose that the cost of labour increases by 10%. Would this make the model 800 machine more or less desirable? Explain. No computations are needed.

3. Suppose that the cost of materials doubles. Would this make the model 800 machine more or less desirable? Explain. No computations are needed.

Don't forget to visit the Online Learning Centre for self-study quizzes, practice exams, and more! Visit www.mcgrawhill.ca/olc/brewer.

Online LearningCentre

Photo Credits

Index